W9-BQS-356

Core Questions in Philosophy
A Text with Readings

Third Edition

Elliott Sober

University of Wisconsin–Madison

Prentice Hall

Upper Saddle River, New Jersey 07458

Library of Congress Cataloging-in-Publication Data

Sober, Elliott.
   Core questions in philosophy : a text with readings / Elliott Sober.—3rd ed.
     p. cm.
   Includes bibliographical references and index.
   ISBN 0-13-083537-4
    1. Philosophy—Introductions.   I. Title.
  BD21.S615   2001
  100 21′05 12-02—dc99

                                              99-059137

Editorial-in-Chief: Charlyce Jones Owen
Acquisitions Editor: Ross Miller
Assistant Editor: Katie Janssen
Production Liaison: Fran Russello
Editorial/Production Supervision and Interior Design: Joseph Barron/P.M. Gordon
   Associates, Inc.
Prepress and Manufacturing Buyer: Tricia Kenney
Art Director: Jayne Conte
Cover Illustration: Corbis Digital Stock
Copy Editor: Steven-Michael Patterson

This book was set in 10/12 Baskerville by Pub-Set, Inc.
and was printed and bound by RR Donnelly & Sons Company.
The cover was printed by Phoenix Color Corp.

 ©2001, 1995 by Prentice Hall, Inc.
A Division of Pearson Education
Upper Saddle River, New Jersey 07458

All rights reserved. No part of this book may be reproduced, in any form or by any means, without permission in writing from the publisher.

Printed in the United States of America
10 9 8 7 6 5 4 3 2

ISBN 0-13-083537-4

Prentice-Hall International (UK) Limited, *London*
Prentice-Hall of Australia Pty. Limited, *Sydney*
Prentice-Hall of Canada Inc., *Toronto*
Prentice-Hall Hispanoamericana, S.A., *Mexico*
Prentice-Hall of India Private Limited, *New Delhi*
Prentice-Hall of Japan, Inc., *Tokyo*
Pearson Education Asia Pte. Ltd., *Singapore*
Editora Prentice-Hall do Brasil, Ltda., *Rio de Janeiro*

For Aaron

Contents

PART III   Theory of Knowledge

Lectures

Readings

PART IV   Philosophy of Mind

Lectures

Readings

PART V Ethics

Lectures

Readings

Boxes

Preface

The philosophical problems investigated in this book concern fundamental facts about our place in the universe. Many of us were brought up to believe that God exists, that there is a real difference between right and wrong, that we can freely choose what sort of lives to lead, and that it is possible for us to gain knowledge of the world we inhabit. A major goal of philosophy is to discover whether these opinions can be rationally defended or are just comfortable illusions.

Core Questions in Philosophy emphasizes the idea that philosophy is a subject devoted to *evaluating arguments* and *constructing theories*. This is not the same as describing the history of what various philosophers have thought. Although I discuss historical texts, I do so because they are rich sources of ideas pertinent to answering philosophical questions. The point is not to say solemn and respectful words about worthy figures now dead, but to engage them in dialogue—to grapple with the theories they have proposed, to criticize these theories, even to improve upon them.

Besides proposing answers to philosophical questions, I also try to make clear which questions I have *not* answered. I hope that the reader will approach what I say the way I have approached the philosophical texts I discuss. This is a book to argue with, to dissect. It isn't my goal to have the reader accept without question the conclusions I reach.

This work is a combination *textbook with readings*. The text part (which I call "Lectures") is followed by a group of related readings (drawn from Plato, Aristotle, Aquinas, Anselm, Descartes, Hume, Kant, Mill, and others). The lectures flow together, so that the main areas covered—philosophy of religion, epistemology, philosophy of mind, and ethics—are connected to each other to make a coherent whole.

The lectures are intended to be *launching pads* from which readers can pursue issues on their own. I believe students are best able to think about philosophy if they first are provided with some basic tools and concepts. It is the purpose of the lectures to provide these *core ideas*.

Following the lectures in Parts II through V, there are a number of readings; these are drawn mainly from historical texts, although a few are by contemporary philosophers. The lectures often discuss these readings, but the area of overlap is far from total. Many lectures contain material that isn't touched on in any reading; and the readings raise a wealth of issues that the lectures don't address. The lectures are intended to stand on their own as well as to provide points of entry into the readings.

Each lecture is followed by review questions and by problems for further thought. These should help readers to consolidate their understanding of what I have said and to think creatively about related problems. The lectures often contain material in "boxes"; these boxes provide a nutshell restatement of a main idea or a brief discussion of a related matter that may interest the reader. A list of the boxes immediately follows the table of contents. Each main part of the text includes suggestions for further reading. And there is a glossary at the end of the book that provides simple definitions of the main concepts used.

Besides covering a number of traditional topics, this book also takes up some contemporary theories and problems, both from philosophy and from other disciplines. Creationism and evolutionary theory are hotly debated now. The issues they raise are continuous with a tradition of argument in philosophy of religion that goes back (at least) to Aquinas, Hume, and Paley. The relation of mind and body is as old a problem as philosophy engages, but the ideas of Freud and Skinner get a hearing along with those of Descartes. In ethics there has long been a debate as to whether ethical truths are discovered or created. Plato and Sartre are separated by more than 2,000 years, but both speak to this issue. The problem of free will raises the question of whether every event is caused. Here the contribution of modern physics must be brought into contact with a perennial problem of philosophy. Philosophy isn't the same as biology, psychology, or physics, but the problems of philosophy cannot be isolated from the sciences. One aim of this book is to connect philosophical problems with ideas derived from a wider culture.

The etymology of the word *philosopher* is *lover of wisdom*. This doesn't guarantee that all philosophers are wise, nor even that each individual philosopher is devoted to the attainment of wisdom. Philosophers *should* strive for wisdom; whether they do so, and whether they attain it, are separate questions.

Wisdom involves understanding—seeing how things fit together. When the pieces of a puzzle are fitted together, one attains a sense of wholeness. Current philosophy is embedded in a historical tradition of philosophical discourse. It also is connected with problems in the sciences, the other humanities, and the arts. This book aims to give the reader a sense of these multiple connections.

Acknowledgments

My debts to my colleagues in philosophy here in Madison are enormous. A fixed point in my work week has been discussions of the ideas and techniques that go into presenting central problems of philosophy to new students. My philosophical outlook, as well as the view I have of teaching, have been shaped by these conversations.

It is a pleasure to thank Michael Byrd, Claudia Card, Fred Dretske, Ellery Eells, Berent Enç, Malcolm Forster, Martha Gibson, Paula Gottlieb, Andy Levine, Steve Nadler, Terry Penner, Mark Singer, Dennis Stampe, Daniel Wikler, and Keith Yandell. They were generous enough to suffer my trespasses onto philosophical terrain that belonged more to them than to me. Some read parts of this book and gave me comments; others listened patiently while I tried out what I thought was a new angle.

The first two editions of *Core Questions in Philosophy* elicited a steady stream of correspondence and phone calls from teachers of philosophy and their students. These took a variety of forms; there was praise and blame, suggestions on how to do better, and even a few not-so-gentle suggestions that I should turn my attention to other projects. On the whole, though, I was happy with what I heard, though this didn't mean that I felt that I should leave the book unchanged. I thank everyone who took the trouble to let me know what they thought. Usually (but not always), they will find evidence that I listened to what they said in the way this edition differs from the ones before.

Deserving of special mention are Richard Behling, Keith Butler, Paul Christopher, Phil Gasper, Ronald Glass, Richard Hanley, John Hines, Burton Hurdle, Charles Kielkopf, Bradley Monton, Howard Pospesel, Roy Sorensen, and (especially) Stephen Wykstra. Their suggestions for changing the book were extremely valuable.

Writing an introduction to philosophy is a challenge. The challenge is to reconstruct what a problem or idea would sound like to someone who hasn't studied the subject before. The project requires that one return to the beginning—to the fundamentals of the subject. I hope that what I found by beginning again will be useful to those who are beginning for the first time.

PART I
INTRODUCTION

LECTURE 1

What Is Philosophy?

Do you have a philosophy? Most people answer this question by saying "yes." What do people mean when they talk about their "philosophies?" They usually have in mind a set of beliefs that they admit are difficult to prove are true, but which none-theless are important to the way they think of themselves and the world they inhabit. Sometimes people describe their philosophies by saying what they think makes an action right or wrong. The statement "it's part of my philosophy that people should help each other" might be an example. Thus, a person's philosophy might include the fundamental ethical principles they believe. But people often have more than *ethics* in mind when they talk about their philosophies. A religious person might say that it is part of his or her philosophy that God exists; an atheist might say that it is part of his or her philosophy that there is no God and that there is no life after death. These propositions are important to the people who believe them. They describe what exists; philosophers would say that they are part of *metaphysics,* not ethics. Meta-physics is the part of philosophy that attempts to describe, in very general terms, what there is.

If everyday people think of their philosophies as the beliefs they have that are dif-ficult to prove but important, how does this idea of philosophy relate to how philoso-phers understand their own subject? Sometimes a term is used in ordinary talk in a way that differs dramatically from the way it is used by specialists. People sometimes say that tomatoes are vegetables, but a botanist will tell you that tomatoes are a fruit. Everyday people say they are concerned about "ecology," but biologists understand "ecology" in a very different way. Perhaps philosophers use the term "philosophy" in a way that departs fundamentally from what ordinary people mean when they say that they have a philosophy.

To gain a better purchase on what philosophy is, I'm going to discuss the question of what is distinctive about philosophy from two angles. First, I'll sketch some of the main philosophical problems that I'll examine in this book. That is, I'll describe some *examples* of philosophy. But giving examples doesn't really answer the question "What is philosophy?" If you asked "What is a mammal?" and I showed you a human being, a hippo, and a cat, these examples might give you a *hint* about what a mammal is. However, citing examples isn't the same as saying what it is to be a mammal.

That is why there will be a second stage to my discussion of what philosophy is. After giving some examples of philosophical problems, I'll present some theories about what philosophy is. I believe these theories have merit, though, I admit, none is entirely adequate.

EXAMPLES

The first philosophical problem we'll consider is whether God exists. Some philosophers have constructed arguments that attempt to establish that God exists; others have tried to show there is no God. I'll evaluate some of the more influential arguments and try to see whether they work.

The second problem we will consider concerns knowledge. It is pretty clear that belief and knowledge are different. Some people long ago thought the earth is flat. They *believed* this, but they didn't know it, since it isn't true. Of course, they *thought* they knew it, but that is different. It also is pretty clear that true belief isn't the same as knowledge. If you believe something for no reason at all, but happen to be right by accident, you have true belief but not knowledge. For example, think of a gullible gambler at a race track who believes for no good reason that the first horse in every race will win. Occasionally, this person will be right—he will have a true belief. But it isn't plausible to say that he knew, on those races about which he turned out to be right, that the first horse would win. So having knowledge involves something more than having a true belief.

The philosophical problem about knowledge will split into two parts. First, there are the questions: What is knowledge? What makes knowledge different from true belief? Second, there is the question: Given some clarification of what knowledge is, do human beings ever have it? One philosophical position we will consider says that we human beings don't know anything. Sure, we have beliefs. And granted, some of our beliefs are true. Knowledge, however, we never have. We don't even know those things we take to be most obvious. This position is called *philosophical skepticism.* We will consider arguments for skepticism and arguments that attempt to refute it.

The third philosophical subject that will be addressed in this book consists of a collection of topics from the philosophy of mind. The first of these is the so-called mind/body problem. You have a mind; you also have a brain. What is the relationship between these items? One possible answer is that they are identical. Although "mind" and "brain" are two words, they name the same thing, just like the names "Superman" and "Clark Kent." An alternative position in this area is called *dualism;* it says that the mind and the brain are different things. We will consider other theories that have been advanced about the mind/body problem as well.

Another topic from the philosophy of mind that we'll address concerns human freedom. Each of us has the personalities we have because we inherited a set of genes from our parents and then grew up in a sequence of environments. Genes plus environments make us the sorts of people we are. We didn't choose the genes we have, nor did we choose the environments we experienced in early life. These were thrust upon us from the outside. Each of us performs certain actions and abstains from performing others. This pattern of what we do and don't do results from the personalities we have. Can we be said to perform actions freely? Is it really in our control to perform some actions and abstain from others? Perhaps our actions aren't freely chosen because they are the results of factors that were totally outside of our control—namely, our genes and environment.

Of course, we talk in everyday life about people doing things "of their own free will." We also think of ourselves as facing real choices, as exercising control over what we do. However, the philosophical problem of freedom asks whether this common way of thinking is really defensible. Maybe freedom is just an illusion. Perhaps we tell ourselves a fairy tale about our own freedom because we can't face the fact that we aren't free. The philosophical problem will be to see whether we can be free if our personalities are the results of factors outside our control.

The last problem area I'll address is ethics. In everyday life, we frequently think that some actions are right and others are wrong. The philosophical problem about this familiar attitude divides into two parts. First, we'll want to consider whether there really are such things as ethical facts. Maybe talk about ethics, like talk about freedom, is just an elaborate illusion. Consider a parallel question about science. In every science, there are questions that are controversial. For example, physicists have different opinions about how the solar system began. But most of us think that there is something else to physics besides opinions. There are facts about what the world is really like.

Clashes of opinion occur in what I'll call the *subjective realm*. Here we find one human mind disagreeing with another. But facts about physics exist in the *objective realm*. Those facts exist independently of anybody's thinking about them. They are out there, and science aims to discover what they are. In science, there are both subjective opinions and objective facts—people have beliefs, but there also exist, independently of what anyone believes, a set of facts concerning the way the world really is. The question about ethics is whether both these realms (subjective and objective) exist in ethics, or if only one of them does. We know that people have different ethical opinions. The question is whether, in addition to those opinions, there are ethical facts. In other words, does ethics parallel the description I've just given of science, or is there a fundamental difference here?

	Subjective realm	*Objective realm*
Science	scientific opinions	scientific facts
Ethics	ethical opinions	ethical facts

The idea that there are no ethical facts, only ethical opinions, I'll call *ethical subjectivism.* According to subjectivism, the claim that "murder is always wrong" and the claim that "murder is sometimes permissible" are *both* misguided—there are no facts about the ethics of murder for us to have opinions about. We'll consider arguments supporting and criticizing this position.

The second question that arises in ethics is this: If there are ethical facts, what are they? Here we assume a positive answer to the first question and then press on for more details. One theory we'll consider is *utilitarianism,* which says that the action you should perform in a given situation is the one that will produce the greatest happiness for the greatest number of individuals. This may sound like common sense, but in fact, I'll argue that there are some serious problems with this ethical theory.

THREE THEORIES ABOUT WHAT PHILOSOPHY IS

I've just described a menu of four central philosophical problems: God, knowledge, mind, and ethics. What makes them all *philosophical* problems? Instead of giving examples, can we say something more general and complete about what distinguishes philosophy from other areas of inquiry? I'll offer three theories about what is characteristic of at least some philosophical problems.

Several of the problems just described involve *fundamental questions of justification.* There are many things that we believe without hesitation or reflection. These beliefs that are second nature to us are sometimes called "common sense." Common sense says that the senses (sight, hearing, touch, taste, and smell) provide each of us with knowledge of the world we inhabit. Common sense also says that people often act "of their own free will." And common sense holds that some actions are right while others are wrong. Philosophy examines the fundamental assumptions we make about ourselves and the world we inhabit and tries to determine whether those assumptions are rationally defensible.

Another characteristic of many philosophical questions is that they are very *general;* often, they're more general than the questions investigated in specific sciences. Physicists have asked whether there are electrons. Biologists have investigated whether genes exist. And geologists have sought to find out if the continents rest on movable plates. However, none of these sciences really bothers with the question of why we should think there are physical objects. The various sciences simply *assume* there are things outside the mind; they then focus on more specific questions about what those things are like. In contrast, it is a characteristically philosophical question to ask why you should believe there is anything at all outside your mind. The idea that your mind is the only thing that exists is called *solipsism.* Philosophers have addressed the question of whether solipsism is true. This is a far more general question than the question of whether electrons, genes, or continental plates exist.

The third view of what philosophy is says that philosophy is the enterprise of *clarifying concepts.* Consider some characteristic philosophical questions: What is knowledge? What is freedom? What is justice? Each of these concepts applies to some things but not to others. What do the things falling under the concept have in common, and how do they differ from the things to which the concept does not apply?

We must be careful here, since many questions that aren't especially philosophical sound just like the examples just given. Consider some characteristic scientific questions: What is photosynthesis? What is acidity? What is an electron? How does the first batch of questions differ from these? One difference between these questions concerns the ways in which *reason* and *observation* help answer them. You probably are aware that philosophy courses don't include laboratory sections. Philosophers usually don't perform experiments as part of their inquiries. Yet, in many sciences (though not in all), laboratory observation is quite central.

This doesn't mean that observation plays no role in philosophy. Many of the philosophical arguments we will consider begin by making an observation. For example, in Lecture 5, I'll consider an argument for the existence of God that begins with the following assertion: Organisms are complicated things that are remarkably well-adapted to the environments they inhabit. The thing to notice here is that this fact is something we know by observation. So philosophers, as well as scientists, do rely on observations.

Nonetheless, there is something distinctive about how observations figure in a philosophical inquiry. Usually, the observations that are used in a philosophical theory are familiar and obvious to everyone. A philosopher will try to show by reasoning that those observations lead to some rather surprising conclusions. That is, although philosophy involves both observation and reasoning, it is the latter that in some sense does more of the work. As you will see in what follows, philosophical disputes often involve disagreements about reasoning; rarely are such disputes decidable by making an observation.

Each of these ways of understanding what philosophy is should be taken with a grain of salt (or perhaps with two). I think there is something to be said for each, even though each is somewhat simplified and distorting.

THE NATURE OF PHILOSOPHY HAS CHANGED HISTORICALLY

One thing that makes it difficult to say "what philosophy is" is that the subject has been around at least since the ancient Greeks and has changed a great deal. There are many problems that are just as central to philosophy now as they were to the ancient Greeks; but there are other problems that have broken away from philosophy and now are thought of as purely scientific.

For example, ancient Greek philosophers discussed what the basic constituents of physical things are. Thales (who lived around 580 B.C.) thought that everything is made of water; many other theories were discussed as well. Now such questions are thought to be part of physics, not philosophy. Similarly, until the end of the nineteenth century, universities put philosophy and psychology together in the same academic department. It is only recently that the two subjects have been thought of as separate. Scientists in the seventeenth century—for example, Isaac

Newton—used the term "natural philosophy" to refer to what we now think of as science. And the term "scientist" was invented in the nineteenth century by the British philosopher William Whewell. The idea that philosophy and science are separate subjects may seem clear now, but the separation we now find natural was not so obvious in the past. Many of the problems that we now regard as philosophical are problems that have not broken away from philosophy and found their way into the sciences. Perhaps there are problems now taken to be philosophical that future generations won't regard as such. The shifting historical nature of what counts as philosophy helps make it difficult to say anything very precise about what that subject is.

PHILOSOPHICAL METHOD

Having tried to say something about what philosophy is, I now want to say something about what philosophy is *not* (at least not in this book). You may have the impression that doing philosophy involves lying under a tree staring up at the sky, making deep and mysterious pronouncements off the top of your head that sound very important but which are hard to make sense of when you try to think about them clearly. I'll call this *the mystical guru model* of philosophy. Your experience reading this book won't correspond to this impression.

There is, however, another experience you've probably had that comes closer. If you took a high school geometry course, you'll remember proving theorems from axioms. If your geometry course was like the one I had, the axioms were given to you with very little explanation of why you should believe them. Maybe they looked pretty obvious to you, and so you didn't wonder very much about their plausibility. Anyhow, the main task was to use the axioms to prove theorems. You started with the axioms as assumptions and then showed that if they are true, other statements must be true as well.

Philosophers tend to talk about "arguments" rather than "proofs." The goal is to try to reach answers to important philosophical questions by reasoning correctly from assumptions that are plausible. For example, in Lecture 4, I'll examine some attempts to prove that God exists. The idea here is to start with assumptions that practically anybody would grant are true and then show that these assumptions lead to the conclusion that there is a God. This resembles what you may have done in geometry: Starting with simple and supposedly obvious assumptions, you were able to establish something less obvious and more complex—for example, that the sum of the angles of a triangle equals two right angles (180 degrees).

Sometimes the philosophical questions we'll consider will strike you as difficult, deep, even mysterious. I won't shy away from such questions. I'll try, however, to address them with clarity and precision. The goal is to take hard questions and deal with them clearly, which, I emphasize, should never involve trying to pull the wool over someone's eyes by making deep-sounding pronouncements that mean who-knows-what.

SUMMARY

I began this lecture by describing how everyday people use the term "philosophy." In fact, their usage is not so distant from what philosophers mean by the term. Philosophy *does* address the most fundamental beliefs we have about ourselves and the world we inhabit. Precisely because these assumptions are so central to the way we think and act, it is difficult to step back for a moment from these assumptions and examine them critically. The French have an expression, "the most difficult thing for a fish to see is water." Some assumptions are so natural and seemingly obvious that it is hard to see that we are making assumptions at all. Philosophy is the effort to help us identify these assumptions and evaluate them.

Each of us *does* have a philosophy. What divides some people from others is their willingness to ask probing questions about what they believe and why. This is what philosophy as a discipline tries to add to the philosophies that each of us carries with us through our lives.

Review Questions

1. What is the difference between objective and subjective?
2. If you want to say what philosophy is, why isn't it enough to list some examples of philosophical problems?

A Problem for Further Thought

Which of the ideas presented here about what philosophy is also apply to mathematics? Which do not?

LECTURE 2

Deductive Arguments

Philosophy involves constructing and evaluating arguments. In this respect, philosophy is no different from any other rational activity—mathematicians do this, as do economists, physicists, and people in everyday life. The distinctive thing about philosophy isn't that philosophers construct and evaluate arguments; what is distinctive is the kinds of questions those arguments aim to answer. In the previous lecture, I talked about what makes a question philosophical. The goal in this lecture is to develop some techniques that can be used to tell whether an argument is good or bad.

ARGUMENTS

An argument divides into two parts: the premisses and the conclusion. The premisses and the conclusion are statements; each is expressed by a declarative sentence. Each is either true or false. When people argue that a given statement is true, they will provide reasons for thinking this. The reasons are the premisses of their argument; premisses are assumptions. The statement to be established is the argument's conclusion.

In high school geometry, you talked about axioms and theorems. Axioms are assumptions (premisses); the theorem (the conclusion) is what is supposed to follow from those assumptions. In geometry you may have spent little or no time asking whether the axioms are true. Not so for the philosophical arguments I'll discuss in this book. We'll want to see whether the premisses are plausible. We'll also want to see whether the premisses, if they were true, would provide a reason for thinking the conclusion is true as well. I'll pose these two questions again and again.

GOOD ARGUMENTS

I want to talk about different kinds of "good arguments." What does "good" mean? A good argument is *rationally persuasive;* it gives you a good reason to think the conclusion is true. Advertisers and politicians sometimes use arguments that trick people into believing what they say. These arguments sometimes persuade people, but they don't always provide *good* reasons.

A good argument should have true premisses; if the premisses are false, how could they provide you a good reason to believe the conclusion? But more is required than this. In the following argument, the premiss is true, but it doesn't provide you a good reason to think that the conclusion is true:

Grass is green

Roses are red

What is wrong here is that the premisses are irrelevant to the conclusion. A good argument should contain true premisses, but it also should cite premisses that are related in the right way to the conclusion. The truth of the premisses should give you a reason to think that the conclusion is true. The three types of "good argument" that I'll now describe differ in what relationship their premisses and conclusions have to each other.

Good arguments can be divided into two categories, and one of those categories can be divided into two more:

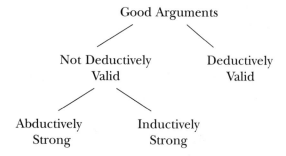

I'll treat the three categories (deductively valid, inductively strong, and abductively strong) as *mutually exclusive:* If an argument belongs to one category, it can't belong to any of the others. At the end of Lecture 3, I'll modify this classification slightly.

You may have heard some of this terminology before. Deduction is what you do in a mathematical proof. Induction involves sampling from a population to decide what its characteristics are. Abduction may be a less familiar term. It has nothing to do with kidnaping. The word was invented by the nineteenth-century American philosopher Charles Sanders Peirce. Philosophers sometimes use the longer label "inference to the best explanation" to describe what Peirce meant by abduction.

I'll consider deduction in this lecture, induction and abduction in the next. The goal in each case is to describe some of the considerations that are relevant to deciding whether an argument is good or bad.

DEDUCTIVE VALIDITY DEFINED

The first type of good argument consists of ones that are "deductively valid." Here are two examples of this type of argument:

All fish swim.	All particles have mass.
All sharks are fish.	All electrons are particles.
All sharks swim.	All electrons have mass.

In these arguments, the premisses are the statements above the horizontal line; the conclusion is the statement below. These arguments say that the premisses are true and that, therefore, the conclusion also is true.

Here is what deductive validity means:

> *A deductively valid argument* is an argument that has the following property: *IF* its premisses were true, its conclusion would have to be true.

I've capitalized the word *IF.* I'd print it in bright colors if I could, because it is important not to forget this two-letter word. *A valid argument doesn't have to have true premisses.* What is required is that the conclusion would have to be true, *IF* the premisses were true.

Take a minute to look at these two arguments. Convince yourself that they are deductively valid.

"VALIDITY" IS A TECHNICAL TERM

What philosophers and logicians mean by "valid" doesn't have much in common with what we mean by "valid" in ordinary English. In everyday life, we say that an idea is "valid" if it is plausible or true. The technical use of the term differs from ordinary usage in two ways. First, we never say that a *statement* or an *idea* is valid or invalid. Validity is a property of *arguments,* and of arguments only. Second, an argument can be valid even if the statements it contains are wildly implausible. A valid argument can have false premisses and a false conclusion.

Here is an example:

> All plants have minds.
>
> All ladders are plants.
> _____
>
> All ladders have minds.

LOGICAL FORM

What makes an argument deductively valid? The three example arguments described so far have different subject matters. The first is about fish, the second is about particles, and the third is about plants. Though they are about different things, they have the same structure. The structural property that they have in common is called their "logical form." Think of each argument as the result of substituting terms into the following skeleton:

> All Bs are Cs
>
> All As are Bs
> _____
>
> All As are Cs

This is the logical form of the three arguments given. You can think of A, B, and C as blanks into which terms may be substituted. Take a minute to see how the arguments just stated can be obtained from the above skeleton by substitution—by "filling in the blanks."

An argument is valid or invalid solely by virtue of the logical form it has. The subject matter of the argument is irrelevant. Since the three example arguments have the same logical form, they are all valid or all invalid. They have the same logical form, so they are in the same boat. As already mentioned, they are valid. Indeed, each and every of the millions of arguments you can construct by substitution into the above skeleton is valid as well.

INVALIDITY

The definition of validity tells you what a deductively *invalid* argument will be like. If there is even the smallest possibility that the conclusion could be false when the premisses are true, then the argument is deductively invalid.

The ladder argument is valid, though all the statements it contains are false. Is the reverse situation possible? Can an argument be *invalid,* even though all the statements it contains are true? The answer is *yes.* Here's an example:

> Emeralds are green.
> _____
> Lemons are yellow.

The premiss is true and so is the conclusion. So why isn't the argument deductively valid? The definition of validity says that the premisses in a valid argument must provide an *absolute* guarantee that the conclusion is true. But the fact that emeralds are green doesn't guarantee that lemons must be yellow. The color of lemons isn't entailed by the fact that emeralds are green. Validity concerns the *relationship* of premisses to conclusion, not the question of whether the premisses and the conclusion each happen to be true.

Sometimes it isn't so obvious that an argument is invalid. The above example is pretty blatant—the premiss has nothing to do with the conclusion. But what do you think of the following argument? Is it valid or not?

> If Jones stands in the heavy rain without an umbrella, then Jones will get wet.
> Jones is wet.
> _____
> Jones was standing in the heavy rain without an umbrella.

Imagine that all three of the statements in this argument are true. Imagine that Jones is now standing before you soaking wet and that Jones just came in from the rain.

Even though all the statements in this argument are true, this argument is invalid. It is just like the argument about emeralds and lemons. Though premisses and conclusion happen to be true, the premisses don't *guarantee* that the conclusion must be true.

How can we see this more clearly? I said before that all arguments that have the same logical form are in the same boat. This means that if the argument about Jones is invalid, so is each and every argument that has the same form. Let's begin by isolating the argument's logical form. Here it is:

> If P, then Q
> Q
> _____
> P

What do *P* and *Q* stand for in this argument skeleton? You can substitute any statement (declarative sentence) you please for these letters to obtain an argument with this logical form. Notice that the letters in this skeleton differ in their function from the letters in the previous skeleton. There, *A*, *B*, and *C* are blanks into which terms denoting kinds of things ("fish," "electrons," etc.) can be substituted.

Anyhow, we now have the logical form of the argument about Jones. If it is invalid, so are *all* arguments that have the same logical form. This means that if there is even one argument that has this logical form, in which the premises are true and the conclusion false, then the argument form is invalid. This will mean that the initial argument about Jones is invalid as well.

Here is an argument that has this logical form that settles the question:

> If Sam lives in Wisconsin, then Sam lives in the U.S.A.
>
> Sam lives in the U.S.A.
> _____
> Sam lives in Wisconsin.

The premises of this argument are true, but the conclusion, I assure you, is false. The Sam I'm talking about lives in California.

TESTING FOR INVALIDITY

So here's a strategy to use if you want to know whether an argument is invalid: First, ignore the content and isolate the logical form (the "skeleton") of the argument. Get rid of the distracting subject matter since that is irrelevant; what you want to focus on is the logical form. Second, see if you can invent an argument that has this logical form in which the premises are true and the conclusion is false. If you can find even one rotten apple of this type, you are finished. If there is even one argument with this property, then *every* argument of that form is invalid.

When an argument has true premises and a false conclusion, it is quite obvious that the truth of the premises doesn't *guarantee* that the conclusion must be true. The premises can't be guaranteeing this, since the conclusion is false. But this tells you something general. It tells you that each and every argument of this form will be such that the premises don't guarantee the truth of the conclusion.

So far, I've presented some examples of arguments. I've explained that a valid argument needn't have true statements in it and that an argument composed solely of true statements needn't be valid. This should make you wonder whether there is any connection at all between the question of whether an argument is valid and the question of whether the premises and conclusion are true.

There *is* a connection. It is illustrated by the following table. If an argument is valid, it can exhibit three of the four following combinations in which the premises are either all true or not all true and the conclusion is either true or false:

Premisses

		All true	Not all true
Conclusion	True	possible	possible
	False	impossible	possible

This table indicates that a valid argument can't have true premisses and a false conclusion. However, the fact that an argument is valid leaves open which of the other three cells the argument occupies.

What can be said of an *in*valid argument? If an argument is invalid, are any of the four combinations impossible? I leave this to you to figure out by consulting the definition of validity.

When you find an invalid argument, you may want to ask if the argument can be repaired. Is there anything that can be done to an invalid argument to make it valid? There is. By adding premisses, you can turn a deductively invalid argument into a valid one. Consider the following argument:

> Smith lives in the U.S.A.
> _____
> Smith lives in Wisconsin.

This is invalid, but it can be made valid by adding a premiss:

> Smith lives in the U.S.A.
> Everyone who lives in the U.S.A. lives in Wisconsin.
> _____
> Smith lives in Wisconsin.

Notice that the conclusion now follows from the premisses. The trouble is the second premiss is false.

In the preceding pair of arguments, fixing the defect of invalidity just substitutes one problem for another; instead of having to criticize an argument's invalidity, you have to criticize its premisses for not being true. The following argument pair is different. Here one can repair the defect of invalidity and obtain a perfectly fine argument.

Notice first that the following argument isn't deductively valid:

> Smith lives in Wisconsin.
> _____
> Smith lives in the U.S.A.

The argument can be repaired, however, by adding a premiss:

Smith lives in Wisconsin.

Everyone who lives in Wisconsin lives in the U.S.A.

———————————

Smith lives in the U.S.A.

This argument is valid and has true premisses as well.

You can see from these two pairs of arguments that invalidity is easy to fix. Just add premisses. What is harder is to add premisses that not only make the argument valid, but are true as well.

This idea will come up repeatedly when I discuss various philosophical arguments. I sometimes will claim an argument is invalid. When this happens, you should ask yourself whether the argument can be repaired. Often, the price of making the argument valid (by adding a premiss) is that you have to supply a new premiss you think is false. In making this addition, you are trading one defect (invalidity) for another (false premisses). If you can't repair the argument so that it is both valid and has all true premisses, then you should consider the possibility that there is something fundamentally flawed about the whole line of argument. On the other hand, sometimes an invalid argument can be replaced by a valid one merely by supplying a true premiss that maybe you neglected to mention because it is so obvious. In this case, the defect in the original argument isn't so fundamental.

So far I've emphasized two questions that we will want to ask about arguments:

Conditionals

If/then statements are called conditionals. Conditional statements have other statements as components. For example, the statement "If pigs fly, then grass is green" is a statement of the form "If P, then Q," where P and Q are themselves statements.

In the statement "If P, then Q," P is called the antecedent and Q is called the consequent. A conditional doesn't say that its antecedent is true; the statement "If Joe drinks arsenic, then Joe will die" doesn't say that Joe drinks arsenic. A conditional doesn't say that its consequent is true; "If there is a nuclear war, then Washington will be attacked" doesn't say that Washington will be attacked.

Conditionals can be rewritten without changing what they say. Consider the statement "If you live in Wisconsin, then you live in the U.S.A." This is equivalent in meaning to saying that "If you don't live in the U.S.A., then you don't live in Wisconsin." The conditional "If P, then Q" is equivalent to "If not-Q, then not-P," no matter what P and Q happen to be. Here's a piece of terminology: "If not-Q, then not-P" is the *contrapositive* of the conditional "If P, then Q." A conditional and its contrapositive are equivalent.

Consider the following two conditionals: "If P, then Q" and "If Q, then P." Are they equivalent? That is, do they mean the same thing? The answer is *no*. "If you live in Wisconsin, then you live in the U.S.A." is true, but "If you live in the U.S.A., then you live in Wisconsin" is false. These two if/then statements can't mean the same thing, since what the one says is true while what the other says is false. "If Q, then P" is termed the *converse* of the conditional "If P, then Q." A conditional and its converse aren't equivalent.

(1) Is the argument deductively valid?

(2) Are all the premisses true?

If the answer to both questions is *yes,* the conclusion of the argument must be true.

Arguments are tools. We use them to do things. When the goal is rational persuasion, a good argument will provide a good reason to think the conclusion is true. If an argument is deductively valid and has true premisses, is that sufficient to make it good? To see why validity and true premisses aren't enough, consider the following argument:

> Lemons are yellow.
> _____
> Lemons are yellow.

Here the conclusion merely repeats what the premiss asserts. This argument is valid and the premiss is true. But there is something defective about this argument. What is it?

CIRCULARITY, OR BEGGING THE QUESTION

This argument is *circular; it begs the question.* Suppose you didn't know whether to think that lemons are yellow. The above argument wouldn't help you resolve your uncertainty. The argument would be useless in this regard: *If you don't already know whether the conclusion is true, this argument won't help you answer the question.*

Good arguments are tools that help answer questions about whether their conclusions are true. A good argument should give you a reason to accept the conclusion if you don't already believe the conclusion is true. So besides checking to see if an argument is deductively valid and has true premisses, you also should see if the argument begs the question.

Begging the Question

To understand what makes an argument question-begging, it is useful to examine some examples.

Suppose you were trying to convince someone that God exists. The argument you give for thinking this is true is that the Bible says there is a God. Would this argument convince someone who didn't already believe that there is a God? Probably not. Anyone who doubts there is a God probably doesn't think that everything the Bible says is true.

Here's a second example. Someone is very suspicious about the reliability of consumer magazines. You try to convince him that *Consumer Reports* is reliable by pointing out that *Consumer Reports* ranks itself very highly in an article evaluating the reliability of consumer magazines. Probably your argument will fail to convince.

In these two examples, identify the premisses and conclusion in each argument. Then describe what it is about the argument that makes it question-begging.

TRUTH

One other idea needs clearing up before I leave the topic of deductive validity. You'll notice that the definition of validity makes use of the idea of truth. What is truth?

There are deep philosophical questions here, most of which I'll skirt. My goal is to describe the concept of truth I'll be using in this book. It is beyond the scope of this book to defend this choice or to fully develop its implications. To begin with, whether a statement is true is an entirely different question from whether you or anybody believes it. Whether someone believes the statement "The Rocky Mountains are in North America" is a psychological question. If beings with minds had never populated the earth, I suppose no one would have thought about the location of this mountain range. But this doesn't affect the question of whether the statement is true. There can be truths that no one believes. Symmetrically, there can be propositions that everyone thinks are true, but that aren't. There can be beliefs that aren't true.

When I say that a certain sentence has the property of being true, what am I saying? Consider the English sentence "The Rocky Mountains are in North America." When I say that this sentence is true, am I attributing some mysterious property to it? Not really. All I'm saying is that the world is the way the sentence says it is. When I say that the sentence is true, all I'm saying is that the Rocky Mountains are in North America. So in a way, the concept of truth is often "redundant." Sometimes when I use the concept of truth, I could say the same thing without using that concept.

In high school English, your teacher may have told you to avoid redundancy. If you hand in an essay containing the sentence "Oscar is an unmarried bachelor," the essay might come back with "unmarried" crossed out and the marginal comment "avoid redundancy." The word "unmarried" is redundant because "Oscar is an unmarried bachelor" means exactly the same thing as "Oscar is a bachelor." Adding the word "unmarried" is to spill useless ink.

The Redundancy Theory of Truth claims that the word "true" is redundant in just this sense. "It is true that the Rockies are in North America" says exactly what the sentence "The Rockies are in North America" asserts. This helps show why truth isn't a mysterious property. If you believe a statement P, you also believe that P is true. So, if you have any beliefs about the world at all, you should be quite comfortable applying the concept of truth to those beliefs.

"TRUE FOR ME"

You'll see from these remarks that the expression "It is true for me" can be dangerously misleading. Sometimes saying that something is true for you just means that you believe it. If that is what you want to say, just use the word "belief" and leave truth out of it. However, there is a more radical idea that might be involved here. Someone might use the expression "true for me" to express the idea that each of us makes our own reality and that the beliefs we have constitute that reality. I'll assume this is a mistake. My concept of truth assumes a fundamental division between the way things really are and the way they may seem to be to this or that individual mind. This is what I meant in Lecture 1 by distinguishing the objective realm and the subjective realm.

WISHFUL THINKING

Closely related to this distinction between objective and subjective is a piece of advice: *We should avoid wishful thinking*. Most of the things we believe aren't made true by our believing them. That the Rockies are in North America is a fact that is independent of our thought and language. We don't bring this geographical fact into being by thinking or talking in the way we do.

SELF-FULFILLING PROPHESIES

In saying this, I'm not denying that the thoughts we have often affect the world outside the mind. If I think to myself "I can't hit a baseball," this may have the effect that I do badly in the batter's box; here my believing something has the effect that the belief is made true. This is the idea of a "self-fulfilling prophesy." Notice how this causal chain works:

Thought	*Action*	*Truth*
I believe that I won't hit the baseball. $\longrightarrow$	I swing too high. $\longrightarrow$	I don't hit the baseball.

I have no problem with the idea that various statements may be caused to be true by individuals thinking thoughts to themselves. What I deny is that the mere act of thinking, unconnected with action or some other causal pathway, can make statements true. I'm rejecting the idea that the world is arranged so that it spontaneously conforms to the ideas we happen to entertain.

Later in this book, I'll investigate whether there are any exceptions to this principle that says to avoid wishful thinking. Maybe there are some statements that become true just because we think they are. Here are some philosophical claims we'll consider:

Mathematical statements and definitions are made true by our regarding them as such; for example, "2 + 3 = 5" is true just because we choose to define our terminology ("2," "+," etc.) in the way we do (Lecture 4).

Some statements about the contents of my own mind (for example, "I am in pain") are made true just by my believing they are true (Lecture 13).

Ethical statements are true just because God, society, or some individual agent thinks they are (Lecture 30).

I'm mentioning these philosophical claims here without tipping my hand as to whether I think any of them is plausible. If any of them were correct, they would count as exceptions to the pattern I've just described. For the moment, though, I'm merely noting that belief and truth are generally very separate questions.

Review Questions

1. When is a statement or idea valid? (a trick question)
2. Define what it means to say that an argument is deductively valid.
3. Invent an example of a valid argument that has false premises and a true conclusion. Invent an example of an invalid argument that has true premises and a true conclusion.
4. Can a statement be a premiss in one argument and a conclusion in another? If you think so, give an example.
5. Which of the following argument forms is valid? Which is invalid? For each of the invalid ones, construct an example of an argument with that form in which the premisses are true and the conclusion false:

(a)
$$\frac{\text{If } P, \text{ then } Q}{Q}$$
$$P$$

(b)
$$\frac{\text{If } P, \text{ then } Q}{P}$$
$$Q$$

(c)
$$\frac{\text{If } P, \text{ then } Q}{\text{Not-}Q}$$
$$\text{Not-}P$$

(d)
$$\frac{\text{If } P, \text{ then } Q}{\text{Not-}P}$$
$$\text{Not-}Q$$

6. A sign on a store says "No shoes, no service." Does this mean that if you wear shoes, then you will be served?
7. What does it mean to say that an argument is "circular," that it "begs the question"? Construct an example of an argument of this type different from the ones presented in this lecture.
8. What does it mean to say that truth is objective, not subjective?

Problems for Further Thought

1. The Redundancy Theory of Truth may seem plausible as an account of what the following sentence means:

It is true that the Rockies are in North America.

Does it work as well as an explanation of what the following sentence means?

Some statements that are true have not been formulated yet.

2. Consider the following argument:

> I release an otherwise unsupported apple from my hand
> a few feet from the earth's surface.
> _____
> The apple falls to earth.

Is this argument deductively valid? What is the logical form of this argument?

3. (Here is a problem that was drawn to my attention by Richard Behling.) In this lecture, I said that each argument has a *single* logical form. This is the skeleton into which terms can be substituted to obtain the argument. What I said is an oversimplification, however. A given argument can be obtained from *many* logical forms. For example, consider the following argument:

> Fred lives in California.
> If Fred lives in California, then Fred lives in the U.S.A.
> _____
> Fred lives in the U.S.A.

This argument can be obtained from *both* of the following skeletons by substitution:

$$
\text{(a)} \quad \frac{\begin{array}{l} X \\ \textit{If X, then Y} \end{array}}{Y} \qquad\qquad \text{(b)} \quad \frac{\begin{array}{l} R \\ S \end{array}}{T}
$$

Argument form (a) is valid, but (b) is *in*valid. The argument about Fred is valid.

Here's the problem: Use the concept of logical form to define when an argument is valid, and when it is invalid, without falling into the trap of thinking that each argument has *exactly one* logical form.

4. In this lecture, I claimed that there are "objective truths." Do you agree? Construct an argument in which you try to demonstrate that such things exist, or that they do not.

LECTURE 3

Inductive and Abductive Arguments

In Lecture 2, I explained the idea of deductive validity. In a deductively valid argument the premisses provide an *absolute guarantee* that the conclusion is true: If the premisses are true, there is no way in the world that the conclusion can be false. If the premisses are true, the conclusion can't be false.

DEDUCTIVE VALIDITY A LIMITATION

This feature of deductive arguments may sound like a virtue. It is a good thing when an argument provides this sort of strong guarantee. This virtue, however, can also represent a kind of limitation. Granted, a deductively valid argument that has true premisses can't have a false conclusion; but it also is a property of such arguments that the conclusion can't say anything that wasn't already contained in the premisses.

To see what this means, consider what you could validly deduce from the result of some opinion survey. Suppose you were interested in finding out what percentage of registered voters in a county are Democrats. You don't feel like contacting each of them and asking, so you open the phone book and make, let's say, 1,000 telephone calls.

Suppose the result of your survey is that 60 percent of the people called say they are Democrats. What you want to know is the percentage of Democrats in the whole county. Could you make a deductively valid argument here? Can you deduce that (about) 60 percent of the voters are Democrats from a premiss that describes the result of your survey?

The answer is *no*, for two reasons. The fact that 60 percent of the people called *said* they are Democrats doesn't deductively guarantee that any of them are. And even if 60 percent of the people called are Democrats, you can't validly deduce from this that (about) 60 percent of the voters in the county are Democrats. That is, neither of the following arguments is deductively valid:

> 60% of the people called said they are Democrats.
> ———————————————
> 60% of the people called are Democrats.

> 60% of the people called are Democrats.
> ———————————————
> About 60% of the voters in the county are Democrats.

Why can't you deduce these things validly? The reason is that in a deductively valid argument, it is impossible for the conclusion to be false if the premisses are true. But it *is* possible that everyone you called in your survey lied. And, in addition, it is possible that the percentage of Democrats in the whole county is only 25 percent, even if nobody lied in your phone survey.

In saying this, I'm not saying that the people you called actually lied. And I'm not saying that the real percentage in the whole county is only 25 percent. I'm just saying that these are possible, given the result of your phone calls. The result of your telephone survey doesn't absolutely rule out these possibilities; this means you can't *deduce* the percentage of Democrats in the whole county from what the 1,000 people said on the phone.

So the absolute guarantee that a deductively valid argument provides has this limitation: Insisting that an argument be deductively valid prohibits you from reaching conclusions that go beyond the information given in the premises.

It would make sense to insist that an argument be deductively valid if you wanted to avoid even the smallest risk of having a false conclusion with true premises. However, we often are willing to gamble. For example, we might think that the result of the phone survey does provide information about the composition of the county. We might think that the result of the survey gives us a pretty good reason for concluding that about 60 percent of the county voters are Democrats. In saying this, though, the "good reason" isn't a deductively valid one.

NONDEDUCTIVE INFERENCE—A WEAKER GUARANTEE

We have here a fundamental characteristic of nondeductive inference. Suppose we conclude that about 60 percent of the voters in the county are Democrats, based on the premiss that 60 percent of the people called said they were Democrats. In this case the premiss doesn't provide an absolute guarantee that the conclusion is true. However, there is a lesser kind of guarantee that this premiss may provide. If the argument is a strong one, the premiss makes the conclusion *probable;* it provides a *good reason* for thinking the conclusion is true; it makes the conclusion *plausible.* Instead of an absolute guarantee, we have here a weaker guarantee. You are running a risk of being wrong about your conclusion, even if your premiss is true. But this risk might be a reasonable one to take; the conclusion might be a good bet, given that the premiss is true.

TWO GAMBLING STRATEGIES

The language in the previous paragraph suggests that you can think about the difference between deductive and nondeductive arguments in terms of ideas about gambling. Consider two sorts of gamblers. The first I'll call the *extreme conservative.* This individual refuses to wager unless winning is a sure thing. The second individual I'll call the *thoughtful risk taker.* This individual at times enters into risky gambles hoping to win.

Each strategy has its virtue and its limitation. The virtue of the conservative strategy is that you'll never lose a gamble. Its limitation is that there are gambles you will decline that you could have won. The limitation of thoughtful risk taking is that you can lose money. Its virtue is that it can lead you to win wagers by taking risks.

Limiting yourself to deductive arguments is a conservative strategy. You avoid the risk of reaching false conclusions from true premises. The limitation is that you decline to say anything that goes beyond the evidence. Nondeductive arguments are riskier. The gain is that you can reach true conclusions that go beyond what the premisses say; the risk is that you may reach a false conclusion from true premises.

PREDICTIVE BELIEFS

In science as well as in everyday life, we make nondeductive inferences all the time. We often are prepared to take risks. Each of us has beliefs about the future. These, however, aren't deduced from observations we have made in the present and past.

UNIVERSAL LAWS

Science is a risky business in another way. Scientists often try to reach conclusions about *universal laws*. An example is Isaac Newton's (1642–1727) universal law of gravitation, which you may have studied in high school. This law says that the gravitational attraction between two bodies is proportional to the products of their masses and is inversely proportional to the square of the distance between them. This law was intended to describe how much gravitational attraction there would be between two objects, no matter where those objects are located and no matter when those objects exist. Newton's law is *universal* in scope—it describes what is true at any time and place. This isn't an isolated example. In lots of sciences, there are universal statements that scientists think are well supported by evidence.

Could Newton have deduced his law from the observations he made and the experiments he conducted? *No.* His law is universal in scope. His observations, however, were conducted in a rather narrowly limited range of places and times. Newton didn't go backward in time to check if his law held true in 3,000,000 B.C. Nor did he send a spaceship to a distant galaxy to do the required measurements. When scientists conclude that a universal law is true or probably true, based on premises that describe the observations they have made, they aren't making a deductively valid argument.

Science is a very ambitious enterprise. Science ventures beyond what is strictly observed in the here and now, just as the conclusion in a nondeductive argument ventures beyond the information strictly contained in the premises.

DETECTIVE WORK

I said before that nondeductive arguments are constantly used in both science and in everyday life. Newton was my scientific example. Let me describe the calculations of Sherlock Holmes as my everyday one.

Holmes was constantly telling Watson that he figures out detective problems by "deduction." Now there is no doubt that Holmes was a very good detective. The question, though, is whether he solved his puzzles by strictly deductive methods.

My view is that he didn't. Holmes didn't observe the crimes he was later called upon to investigate. What he observed were *clues*. For example, suppose Holmes is trying to solve a murder. He wonders whether Moriarty is the murderer. The clues Holmes gathers include a gun, a cigar butt, and a fresh footprint, all found at the scene of the crime. Suppose the gun has an "M" carved in the handle, the cigar is Moriarty's favorite brand, and the footprint is the size that would be produced by Moriarty's ample foot.

Could Holmes deduce from these clues that Moriarty is the murderer? No. Although the above information may make that conclusion plausible or probable, it doesn't absolutely rule out the possibility that someone else did the dirty deed.

I've been emphasizing that in a strong nondeductive inference, the premises make the conclusion plausible or probable; they don't absolutely guarantee that the conclusion must be true. I now want to talk about the difference between two sorts of nondeductive inference—inductive and abductive.

INDUCTION

I'll begin with some properties of induction. Inductive inference involves taking a description of some sample and extending that description to items outside the sample. The voter survey discussed before provides an example:

60% of the county voters called are Democrats.

———————————

About 60% of the county voters are Democrats.

Notice that in this example the vocabulary present in the argument's conclusion is already present in the premiss. Although the conclusion goes beyond what the premiss asserts (which is what makes the argument nondeductive), no new concepts are introduced in the conclusion.

TWO FACTORS INFLUENCE INDUCTIVE STRENGTH

In the case of deduction, I said that an inference is either deductively valid or it isn't. Validity is a yes/no affair. It is like pregnancy. Inductive strength, however, isn't a yes/no matter; arguments are either stronger or weaker. Inductive strength is a matter of degree.

Two factors affect how strong or weak an inductive argument is. The first is sample size. If you called 1,000 individuals in your phone survey, that would make the conclusion stronger than if you had called only 100.

The second factor is the representativeness or unbiasedness of the sample. If you called 1,000 individuals drawn at random from a list of voters, that would make the resulting inference stronger than if you had called 1,000 members of labor unions. The percentage of Democrats in labor unions is higher than that in the population as a whole. If so, you are biasing your sample by drawing it exclusively from a union membership list.

By making a telephone survey, you are failing to contact people who don't have phones. Is this a problem? That depends. If the percentage of Democrats with phones is approximately equal to the percentage of Democrats among registered voters, no bias is introduced. On the other hand, if people with phones are disproportionately Democrats or disproportionately Republicans, your phone survey will have introduced a bias.

How do you avoid having a biased sample? Sometimes this is done by "randomization." If you have a list of all the county voters, drawing names "at random" means that each name has the same chance of being selected. However, this process of selecting at random can fail to ensure an unbiased sample. For example, suppose you draw names at random, but all the people you contact happen to be women. If women are disproportionately Democrats or disproportionately Republicans, your sample is biased.

I don't say that random draws from the voter list will *probably* result in this sort of bias. My point is just that randomizing doesn't absolutely guarantee that your sample is unbiased.

I won't say more here about how you can avoid having a biased sample. This fine point aside, the basic idea is this: Inductive arguments are stronger or weaker according to (1) the sample size, and (2) the unbiasedness of the sample.

ABDUCTION

I now move to abduction—inference to the best explanation. I'll begin with an example of an abductive inference that was important in the history of science. After saying what is distinctive about this form of inference, I'll describe two principles that are relevant to deciding whether an abductive inference is strong or weak.

Gregor Mendel (1822–1884) was an experimental biologist who worked in a monastery in Moravia. He is credited with having discovered genes, the particles in living things that allow parents to transmit characteristics to offspring in reproduction.

INFERRING WHAT ISN'T OBSERVED

The first thing to note about Mendel's discovery is that he never actually saw a gene (or an "element," as Mendel called them). Although more powerful microscopes made this possible later, Mendel never saw even one of them. Rather, Mendel reasoned that the observations he made could be explained if genes existed and had the characteristics he specified.

Mendel ran breeding experiments in the monastery's garden. He crossed tall pea plants with short ones and noted the proportion of tall and short plants among the offspring. Similarly, he crossed plants that had wrinkled peas with plants that had smooth peas, and he noted the mix of wrinkled and smooth plants among the progeny. He then crossed some of those offspring with each other, and he saw the proportion of various characteristics found in the next generation.

Mendel observed that when plants of certain sorts are crossed, their offspring exhibit characteristics in very definite proportions. Mendel asked himself a question that never figured in my discussion of induction. He asked *why* the crosses produced offspring with characteristics distributed into such proportions.

This why-question led Mendel to invent a story. He said: Suppose each plant contains particles (genes) that control the observed characteristics of tall and short, wrinkled and smooth, in certain specific ways. He conjectured that each parent contributes half its genes to the offspring and that this process occurs in accordance with definite rules. The whole invented story had this property: If the story were true, that would explain why the breeding experiments had the results that Mendel observed them to have.

It should be quite clear that Mendel's theory of the gene went beyond the observations then available to him. He never saw a gene, but his theory postulates the existence of such things. I noted before that it is a general feature of nondeductive inference, whether inductive or abductive, that the conclusion goes beyond the premises. We see here, however, a respect in which abduction differs from induction.

ABDUCTION DIFFERS FROM INDUCTION

If Mendel had made an inductive inference, he simply would have claimed that the observed results of the experiments he ran in his garden would also occur anywhere the experiment was carried out. His experiment was made in Europe at the end of the nineteenth century. An inductive extension of the description true of his experiment might conclude that the same results would occur in twentieth-century North America as well.

Had Mendel limited himself to this suggestion, no one would remember him now as the father of genetics. His important inference was abductive, not inductive. He didn't simply claim the experiment could be replicated. Rather, he formulated a theoretical explanation of *why* the results occurred. Mendel's inference drew a conclusion concerning something he did *not* see (genes), based on premises that described what he *did* see (the results of the experimental crossings).

CAN YOU DEDUCE THE EXPLANATION FROM THE OBSERVATIONS?

Let's attend to Mendel's inference more carefully. The following is *not* a deductively valid argument:

Experimental crosses in the pea plants were observed to exhibit such-and-such results.

There are genes, and they obey laws *L*.

Remember: You can't validly deduce a theory from a set of observations.

Why can't you do this? Basically, the last argument attempts to infer a theory about the cause from the observation of its effects. There are, however, lots of possible causes that might have been responsible for the observed effects. The argument is deductively invalid for the same reason the following argument is also invalid:

A pistol with an "M" on the handle, an El Supremo cigar butt, and a size 12 footprint were found next to the murder victim's body.

Moriarty is the murderer.

Though Moriarty may be the most plausible suspect, the clues, in themselves, don't absolutely guarantee that he is the only possible one.

Mendel and Holmes were making an inference about what is *probably* true, given the observations. They weren't inferring what is *absolutely guaranteed* to be true by the observations.

DEDUCING OBSERVATIONAL PREDICTIONS FROM A THEORY

If a set of observations doesn't deductively imply a theory, then perhaps the reverse is true: Maybe a theory deductively implies some observations. This corresponds more closely to what Mendel did. He saw that his theory of the gene implies that certain experimental results ought to occur. He then saw that those predictions came true. He concluded that the truth of the predictions was evidence that the theory is true.

WHEN THE PREDICTION COMES TRUE

So a better representation of Mendel's inference might go like this. The theory entailed a prediction. The prediction came true. Hence, the theory is probably true. What we now need to see is that the following form of argument is not deductively valid:

If there are genes and they obey laws *L*, then experimental crosses in the pea plants should exhibit such-and-such results.

Experimental crosses in the pea plants were observed to exhibit such-and-such results.

There are genes and they obey laws *L*.

This is deductively invalid for the same reason that the following argument is too:

> If Jones lives in Wisconsin, then Jones lives in the U.S.A.
>
> Jones lives in the U.S.A.
> _____
>
> Jones lives in Wisconsin.

Note that these two arguments have the same logical form.

Scientists often test their theories by seeing whether the predictions made by the theories come true. There is nothing wrong with doing this. The point, however, is that the truth of the theory doesn't follow deductively from the truth of the prediction. Scientists are reasoning *non*deductively when they decide that a theory is plausible because its predictions have come true. We might summarize this point by saying that *successful prediction isn't absolutely conclusive proof that the theory is true.*

WHEN THE PREDICTION TURNS OUT TO BE FALSE

On the other hand, if the predictions entailed by Mendel's theory had come out false, that would have allowed him to deduce that the theory is mistaken. That is, the following argument *is* deductively valid:

> If there are genes and they obey laws *L,* then experimental crosses
> in the pea plants should exhibit such-and-such results.
>
> Experimental crosses in the pea plants didn't exhibit
> such-and-such results.
> _____
>
> It is false that there are genes and they obey laws *L.*

We might summarize this point by saying that *a failed prediction is conclusive proof that the theory implying the prediction is false.*

HOW TRUE PREDICTIONS AND FALSE PREDICTIONS ARE INTERPRETED

Let's generalize these points. Let *T* be a theory and *P* a prediction the theory makes. If the prediction comes out true, we can't deduce that the theory is true. If, however, the prediction comes out false, we can deduce the theory is false:

Invalid	*Valid*
If *T,* then *P*	If *T,* then *P*
P	Not *P*
_____	_____
T	Not *T*

Deducing That a Theory Is True

Recall from Lecture 2 that a deductively invalid argument can be turned into a valid one by adding premises. I now will exploit this fact to show how the truth of a theory can be deduced from the fact that it makes a successful prediction, *if you make certain further assumptions.*

Suppose we wish to design an experiment that tests two theories. Here the problem isn't one of evaluating a single theory, but of seeing which of two theories is more plausible. To test one theory (T_1) against another (T_2), we want to find a prediction over which they disagree. Suppose T_1 predicts that P will be true, while T_2 predicts that P will be false. If we assume that one or the other theory is true, we can find out whether P comes true, and then deduce which theory is true. For example, if P turns out to be true, we can reason as follows:

T_1 or T_2

If T_1, then P.

If T_2, then not-P.

P

———————

T_1

Notice that this argument is deductively valid. Also note that if P had turned out to be false, we could have deduced that T_2 is correct.

As an exercise, describe a situation in which an observation plus some further assumptions allow you to deduce which theory is true.

The difference between these two arguments—one deductively valid, the other not—suggests there is an important difference between the way scientists argue that theories are true and the way they argue that theories are false. It is possible to reject a theory just on the basis of the false predictions it makes, using a deductively valid argument; but it isn't possible to accept a theory just on the basis of the true predictions it makes, using a deductively valid argument. I'll discuss this difference again in Lecture 8.

So far I've explained how a deductively valid argument can lead a scientist to reject a suggested explanation. But how do scientists ever interpret observations as providing strong evidence in favor of the explanations they consider? This must involve a nondeductive inference. But what are the rules that govern such inferences? I now will present two ideas that are relevant to evaluating abductive arguments. These I call the *Surprise Principle* and the *Only Game in Town Fallacy.*

THE SURPRISE PRINCIPLE: WHEN DOES SUCCESSFUL PREDICTION PROVIDE STRONG EVIDENCE?

I've argued that you can't validly deduce that a theory is true just from the fact that some prediction it makes comes true. But maybe only a small modification of this idea is needed. Perhaps all we need to say is that a theory is made highly probable or plausible when a prediction it makes comes true. I now want to explain why this reformulation also won't do.

An unconscious patient is brought into the emergency room of a hospital. What is wrong? What would explain the fact that the patient is unconscious? The doctor on duty considers the hypothesis that the patient is having a heart attack. How should the doctor test whether this hypothesis true? Well, the hypothesis predicts that the patient will have a heart (after all, if someone is having a heart attack, he or she must have a heart). The doctor verifies that this prediction is correct—the patient, indeed, does have a heart. Has the doctor thereby obtained strong evidence that the patient is having a heart attack? Clearly not. This is an example in which you don't obtain serious support for a hypothesis just by showing that one of its predictions is correct.

You go to the gym and someone tells you he is an Olympic weight lifter. You reason that if he is an Olympic weight lifter, he should be able to pick up the hat you are wearing. You offer him your hat; he lifts it without difficulty. Have you thereby obtained strong evidence that he is an Olympic weight lifter? Clearly not. Once again, the hypothesis under test isn't strongly supported by the fact that one of its predictions turns out to be correct.

What has gone wrong in these two cases? In the first example, the presence of a heart isn't strong evidence that the patient is having a heart attack. The reason is that you would expect the individual to have a heart even if he weren't having a heart attack. In the second example, the man's lifting the hat isn't strong evidence that he is an Olympic weight lifter. The reason is that you would expect him to be able to do this even if he weren't an Olympic lifter.

What should you look for if you want to test the hypothesis that the patient has had a heart attack? What you want to find is a symptom that you would expect to find if the patient were having a heart attack, *but would expect not to find if the patient were not having a heart attack.* Suppose an erratic EKG (electrocardiogram) almost always occurs when there is a heart attack but rarely occurs when there is no heart attack. This means that the presence of an erratic EKG would be strong evidence that the patient is suffering a heart attack.

What sort of test should you use if you want to see if the man in the gym really is an Olympic weight lifter? Suppose Olympic weight lifters (of this man's weight) can almost always lift 400 pounds, but people who aren't Olympic lifters can rarely do this. This means that his managing to lift 400 pounds would be strong evidence that he is an Olympic weight lifter.

Think of the unconscious patient and the weight lifter as posing *discrimination problems.* The problem is to find evidence that strongly discriminates between two hypotheses. In the first example, the competing hypotheses are

H_1: The patient is having a heart attack.

H_2: The patient isn't having a heart attack.

An erratic EKG strongly favors H_1 over H_2; the mere fact that the patient has a heart doesn't strongly favor H_1 over H_2.

The same holds true for the second example. The problem is to find evidence that discriminates between the following two hypotheses:

H_1: This man is an Olympic weight lifter.

H_2: This man isn't an Olympic weight lifter.

The fact that the man can lift 400 pounds strongly favors H_1 over H_2; the fact that he can lift a hat doesn't.

The Surprise Principle describes what it takes for an observation to strongly favor one hypothesis over another:

> *The Surprise Principle:* An observation O strongly supports H_1 over H_2 if both the following conditions are satisfied, but not otherwise: (1) if H_1 were true, O is to be expected; and (2) if H_2 were true, O would have been unexpected.

Let's apply this principle to the first example. Consider the observation that the patient has an erratic EKG. If the patient were having a heart attack (H_1), we would expect him to have an erratic EKG. And if the patient weren't having a heart attack (H_2), we would expect him not to have an erratic EKG. This explains why the erratic EKG is strong evidence of a heart attack—the EKG strongly favors H_1 over H_2.

Now consider the observation that the patient has a heart. If the patient were having a heart attack, we would expect him to have a heart. But we would expect him to have a heart even if he weren't having a heart attack. This explains why the presence of a heart isn't strong evidence that the patient is having a heart attack—the observation doesn't strongly favor H_1 over H_2. We were looking for an explanation of why the erratic EKG provides telling evidence whereas the presence of a heart doesn't. The key is to be found in condition (2) of the Surprise Principle.

Take a few minutes and apply the Surprise Principle to the example of the weight lifter. Make sure you see how the principle explains why being able to lift a hat isn't strong evidence, whereas being able to lift 400 pounds is.

No Surprise/Surprise

The Surprise Principle involves two requirements. It would be more descriptive, though more verbose, to call the idea the No Surprise/Surprise Principle.

The Surprise Principle describes when an observation O strongly favors one hypothesis (H_1) over another (H_2). There are two requirements:

(1) If H_1 were true, you would expect O to be true.

(2) If H_2 were true, you would expect O to be false.

That is, (1) if H_1 were true, O would be unsurprising; (2) if H_2 were true, O would be surprising.

The question to focus on is *not* whether the hypotheses (H_1 or H_2) would be surprising. The Surprise Principle has nothing to do with this.

To apply the Surprise Principle, you must get clearly in mind what the hypotheses are and what the observation is.

EVIDENCE MAY DISCRIMINATE BETWEEN SOME HYPOTHESES, BUT NOT BETWEEN OTHERS

In the examples of the heart attack and the weight lifter, H_2 says only that H_1 is false. In other abductions, however, H_2 may say more than this. Suppose you see someone crossing campus carrying several philosophy books. You wonder whether the person is a philosophy major. Two hypotheses to consider are

H_1: The person is a philosophy major.

H_2: The person is an engineering major.

The observation you have made favors H_1 over H_2. But now consider the following third hypothesis:

H_3: The person isn't a student, but is in the business of buying and selling philosophy books.

Although your observation discriminates between H_1 and H_2, it doesn't discriminate between H_1 and H_3.

This brings out an important fact about how the Surprise Principle applies to abductive inferences. *If you want to know whether an observation strongly supports a hypothesis, ask yourself what the alternative hypotheses are.* For an observation to strongly support a hypothesis is for it to strongly favor that hypothesis over the others with which it competes.

TRUE PREDICTION ISN'T ENOUGH

The point of the examples about the unconscious patient and the weight lifter was to show why successful prediction doesn't necessarily provide strong evidence. If someone is having a heart attack, that predicts that he will have a heart; but the presence of a heart isn't strong evidence the person is having a heart attack. If someone is an Olympic weight lifter, that predicts that he will be able to lift a hat; but lifting a hat isn't strong evidence the person is an Olympic weight lifter.

There is a scene in the Monty Python movie *The Life of Brian* that illustrates this idea. The setting is a marketplace. Around the perimeter of the market are assorted prophets and soothsayers. The camera pans from one to the other. We see that in each case, the prophet holds a crowd of people in rapt attention. The first prophet predicts that tomorrow a purple monster will rise out of the desert and devour three villages. The crowd is amazed at these predictions and no doubt will conclude that the prophet has special powers to foresee the future if the predictions come true.

After showing us a few prophets of this sort, the camera comes to an individual who very calmly makes the following predictions: Tomorrow, many people will get up early. Others will sleep longer. Some people will decide to have breakfast, while others will postpone eating until later in the day. And so on. The joke is that the crowd in front of this guy is just as awestruck as the crowds were in front of the more out-landish prophets.

There is a lesson here. How would you test the hypothesis that someone has special powers to foresee the future? If he predicts events that people without special powers can easily predict, it isn't very impressive that his predictions come true. If, however, he predicts events that normal people aren't able to foresee, and then these predictions come true, we are more impressed. The Surprise Principle explains why the success of "safe" predictions provides less compelling evidence than the success of "daring" predictions.

Here's a related example of the Surprise Principle in action. Many people thought that the astrologer Jeanne Dixon had special powers to predict the future. After all, she predicted the JFK assassination and several other events that no one could have guessed were going to happen. If Jeanne Dixon played it safe and only predicted events that everybody knew were going to happen, we wouldn't be impressed. But aren't we being sensible in reasoning that she probably does have special powers, since this and other daring predictions have come true?

Although this reasoning may seem to conform to the Surprise Principle, it doesn't. The thing people sometimes forget is that Jeanne Dixon made thousands of predictions and most of them turned out false. It isn't surprising at all that some handful of these should have come out true. Although Jeanne Dixon predicted the Kennedy assassination, which surprised (practically) everyone when it happened, it isn't at all surprising that someone with no special powers should be lucky a few times every thousand tries. The Surprise Principle, properly understood, tells us why we shouldn't take Jeanne Dixon's few successes as strong evidence that she had special powers.

MODEST FAVORING

The Surprise Principle says when an observation *strongly* favors one hypothesis over another. However, sometimes our observations are not so resolute and unequivocal. Sometimes the observations (O) favor one hypothesis (H_1) over another (H_2), but only modestly. This will be true when H_1 confers on O a higher probability than H_2 does, but the difference is modest. What the Surprise Principle and this idea about O's modestly favoring H_1 over H_2 have in common is this: Both make use of the idea that an observation favors one hypothesis (H_1) over another (H_2). This will be true when the probability of O, according to H_1, exceeds the probability of O, according to H_2.

THE SURPRISE PRINCIPLE SUMMARIZED

In summary, the Surprise Principle gives advice on what a hypothesis must do if it is to be strongly supported by the predictions it makes. First, the hypothesis shouldn't make false predictions. Second, among the true predictions the hypothesis makes, there should be predictions we would expect not to come true if the hypothesis were false.

An Investment Swindle

Suppose you received a letter every month for a year from an investment firm. In each letter, a prediction is made as to whether "the stock of the month" will increase or decline in value during the next 30 days. You keep track of what happens to the stocks described each month. Each prediction comes true. Would you conclude from this that the investment firm has a method for reliably predicting stock market events?

Some years ago an "investment firm" sent out such letters, but the mailing was a swindle. The firm began with a list of 10,000 investors. In the first month, 5,000 investors received letters predicting that stock *A* would go up; the other 5,000 received letters saying that stock *A* would go down. The firm then waited to see which prediction came true. During the second month, the firm sent letters to the 5,000 people who had received a true prediction during the first month. In the second month, 2,500 investors received letters predicting that stock *B* would go up; the other 2,500 received letters saying that *B* would go down. The process was repeated, so that by the end of 10 months a small number of investors had received 10 letters, each containing a successful prediction.

The company then wrote to those people, asking each to invest a large sum of money. Many people did so. The company then absconded with the funds. (This story is from Daniel Dennett's *Brainstorms*, Cambridge, Mass., MIT Press, 1978.)

The investors who were swindled thought they were making a reasonable abductive inference on the basis of the company's track record. Describe the premiss, the conclusion, and the reasoning that led the investors to think the conclusion was highly plausible. Were the investors making a strong inference?

When we ask whether an observation O strongly supports some hypothesis H_1, the Surprise Principle requires that we specify what the alternative hypotheses are against which H_1 competes. It may turn out that O strongly favors H_1 over H_2, but that O doesn't strongly favor H_1 over H_3. The example of the person carrying philosophy books across campus was given to illustrate this point.

THE ONLY GAME IN TOWN FALLACY

I turn now to a second principle for evaluating abductive inferences. Suppose you and I are sitting in a cabin in the woods. We hear a strange rumbling sound in the attic. You ask, "I wonder what that could be?" To which I reply, "That is the sound of gremlins bowling in the attic."

You, being a sensible person, reply, "I really don't think there are gremlins in the attic." I then challenge you to produce a more plausible explanation of the noises. You reply "Gosh, I really don't have any idea why those noises occurred. I just think your story is implausible."

To this humble admission on your part, I give this rejoinder: "Look, my story, if true, would explain why we just heard those strange noises. If you don't want to accept my explanation, you must produce a more plausible explanation of your own. If you can't, you have to accept my explanation of the noises."

What I just did was commit an abductive fallacy (mistake in reasoning), which I'll call the *Only Game in Town Fallacy.* The fact that you can't think of a more plausible explanation of the noises doesn't oblige you to accept the story I constructed. There is an alternative, which is simply to admit that the noises are something you don't know how to explain.

Abduction is sometimes described loosely as follows: If a theory explains some observation, and if no rival account is available that can do a better job of explaining it, then you should accept the theory. Although this description of abduction is roughly correct, it makes the mistake of sanctioning the Only Game in Town Fallacy. The fact that no rival account is better than the explanation I construct doesn't show my explanation is even minimally plausible. My gremlin theory is pretty silly, although maybe there is nothing now available that is clearly superior to it.

I won't try to fine-tune the idea of abductive inference any further. Induction is less well understood than deduction, but abduction is even less well understood than induction. We now have before us the basic idea of inference to the best explanation. We've seen that it is an important part of the scientific method. And I've described two principles that are reasonable guides to evaluating whether an abductive inference is strong or weak.

Review Questions

1. What is the difference between deductive validity and inductive strength?
2. What is the difference between induction and abduction?
3. What factors affect how strong an inductive argument is?
4. Suppose a given observation discriminates between two hypotheses, but a second observation fails to do this. Construct an example, different from the ones presented in this lecture, illustrating the point. Show how the Surprise Principle applies to your example.
5. An observation can succeed in discriminating between some pairs of hypotheses but fail to discriminate between others. Construct an example that illustrates this point that is different from the ones presented in this lecture. Show how the Surprise Principle applies to your example.
6. What is the Only Game in Town Fallacy? What does it mean to call it a "fallacy?"

Problems for Further Thought

1. Suppose you wanted to find out what percentage of the adults in your county are vegetarians. You obtain a list of unmarried adults in the county and contact them to do a survey. Is this sample a biased one?
2. Although induction and abduction were described in this lecture as separate kinds of inference, they have a good deal in common. The Surprise Principle was

introduced as applying to abduction, but it applies to induction as well. Suppose an urn is filled with 1,000 balls, each of them either red or green. You reach into the urn, sampling at random, and bring out 100 balls. Your sample contains 51 red balls and 49 green ones. Here are some hypotheses to consider:

H_1: All the balls in the urn are green.

H_2: 75% of the balls are green.

H_3: 50% of the balls are green.

H_4: 25% of the balls are green.

Suppose you think that H_1 and H_2 are the only possibilities. Does the observation strongly support one over the other? Which? How does the Surprise Principle apply to this question? Suppose, instead, that you think that H_2 and H_3 are the only possibilities. Does the sample strongly support one over the other? If so, which? Suppose, finally, that you think that all four hypotheses are possible. Which is best supported? Why?

3. Why think that any of the beliefs you have about the world outside your own mind are true? For example, why are you now entitled to think there is a printed page in front of you? Presumably, you believe this on the basis of sense experience (sight, touch, etc.). Construct an abductive argument whose conclusion is that there is a printed page in front of you. Make sure your inference obeys the Surprise Principle. Does this abductive argument prove there is a printed page in front of you? Explain.

4. At the beginning of Lecture 2, I presented deductive validity, inductive strength, and abductive strength as mutually exclusive categories. This means that if an argument belongs to one category, it doesn't belong to any of the others. This is generally correct, but not always. Here is an inductive argument that isn't deductively valid:

I've observed 1,000 emeralds and all have been green.

———————————

All emeralds are green.

However, by adding a premiss, I can produce a deductively valid argument:

I've observed 1,000 emeralds and all have been green.

If there are over 500 emeralds in the universe, they will all have the same color.

———————————

All emeralds are green.

Both of these arguments are inductive in the sense that both involve drawing a sample from a population and reaching a conclusion about that population. If so, some inductively strong arguments are also deductively valid.

The same point holds for abductively strong arguments. Usually, they aren't deductively valid. But sometimes they are. Construct a strong abductive argument that obeys the Surprise Principle. Show how it can be made deductively valid by adding or modifying a premiss.

5. There is a difference between *not expecting O* and *expecting not-O*. A person who never considers whether O is true does not expect O, but it would be wrong to say that she expects not O. Of course, if someone expects not O, it will also be true that she does not expect O. Thus, "S expects not O" implies "S does not expect O," but the reverse is not true. With this logical point in mind, explain why condition 2 of the Surprise Principle is formulated by saying "H_2 leads you to expect not-O," rather than saying that "H_2 does not lead you to expect O."

Suggestions for Further Reading

ON THE NATURE OF PHILOSOPHY

The essays in Charles Bontempo and S. Jack Odell (eds.), *The Owl of Minerva: Philosophers on Philosophy*, New York, McGraw-Hill, 1975.

Bertrand Russell, "The Value of Philosophy," in *The Problems of Philosophy*, Oxford, Oxford University Press, 1950.

ON DIFFERENT FORMS OF ARGUMENT

Monroe Beardsley, *Thinking Straight*, Englewood Cliffs, New Jersey, Prentice Hall, 1975.

Irving Copi, *Informal Logic*, New York, Macmillan, 1986.

Robert Fogelin, *Understanding Arguments*, New York, Harcourt, Brace, Jovanovich, 1978.

Ronald Giere, *Understanding Scientific Reasoning*, New York, Holt, Rinehart, and Winston, 1984.

Merrilee Salmon, *Logic and Critical Thinking*, San Diego, Harcourt, Brace, Jovanovich, 1984.

PART II
PHILOSOPHY
OF RELIGION

Aquinas's First Four Ways

Saint Thomas Aquinas (c. 1224–1274) was an enormously accomplished theologian and philosopher. In his masterwork, the *Summa Theologiae,* he presents five proofs that God exists (Aquinas called them "the five ways"). I'll discuss the first four now and the fifth in the next lecture.

Each of Aquinas's arguments begins with some simple observation that is supposed to be obvious to everyone. For example, the first argument begins with the observation that physical objects are in motion. Each argument then proceeds through various other premises to the conclusion that the explanation of the initial observation is that there is a God. Aquinas intends each of his proofs to be deductively valid.

In Lecture 3, I stressed that most of the hypotheses that scientists are interested in testing can't be deduced from observations. For example, Mendel couldn't deduce the existence and characteristics of genes from the observations he made on his pea plants. The same is true in Aquinas's arguments, as he fully realizes: You can't deduce the existence and characteristics of God just from the sorts of simple observations with which his arguments begin. The existence of motion doesn't, all by itself, deductively imply the existence of God. Aquinas's arguments always include additional principles. It is these further principles that are supposed to link the starting observation with the conclusion that God exists.

THE CONCEPT OF GOD

Before describing Aquinas's arguments, I need to say something about what he means by "God" and how I'll use that term. Aquinas took God to be a person—one who is all-powerful (omnipotent), all-knowing (omniscient), and entirely good (omnibenevolent). This conception of God is a familiar one in the traditions of Judaism,

Christianity, and Islam. So when Aquinas tries to prove that there is a God, it is an entity of this kind that he wants to show exists.

I'll assume provisionally that God, if such a being exists, has the characteristics just mentioned. If we don't start with some preliminary picture of what God is, we won't know what we are talking about when we ask whether God exists. However, it is important to recognize that this conception of God is not the only one that is possible. Indeed, in Lecture 11, I'll consider an argument that suggests that God, if there is such a being, can't be all-powerful, all-knowing, and all-good. So we have to recognize that God might lack one or more of the traits I mentioned above. This is why the traditional definition I'll be using is simple: it's a useful place to begin discussion.

Another caveat I should mention is that my versions of Aquinas's arguments won't be accurate in all respects. It is often a subtle historical question what this or that philosopher had in mind in a given text. In this case and later in this book, when I discuss the ideas of other philosophers, I often will examine somewhat simplified versions of the arguments they constructed. You may well ask: Why is it worthwhile studying simplified versions of a great philosopher's arguments? Admittedly, there is a loss, but there also is a gain. The main point to be made here, at the beginning of an introductory text, is that it is useful to evaluate these simpler arguments before more subtle arguments are addressed. At any rate, there is ample philosophical material to think about in the arguments I'll describe, even if these arguments don't capture the thoughts of various great thinkers with total accuracy and completeness.

THE FIRST TWO ARGUMENTS: MOTION AND CAUSALITY

Aquinas's first argument for the existence of God is the argument from motion. Here it is, formulated as a deductive argument:

(I) (1) In the natural world, there are objects that are in motion.

      (2) In the natural world, objects that are in motion are always sent into motion by objects other than themselves.

      (3) In the natural world, causes must precede their effects.

      (4) In the natural world, there are no infinite cause/effect chains.

      ―――――――――

      (5) Hence there is an entity outside of the natural world (a *super*natural being), which causes the motion of the first moving object that exists in the natural world.

      ―――――――――

      (6) Hence, God exists.

Aquinas's second argument generalizes the ideas found in the first. Whereas the first argument is about motion in particular, the second argument is about causality in general:

(II) (1) The natural world includes events that occur.

      (2) In the natural world, every event has a cause, and no event causes itself.

(3) In the natural world, causes must precede their effects.

(4) In the natural world, there are no infinite cause/effect chains.
_____

(5) Hence there is an entity outside of nature (a supernatural being), which causes the first event that occurs in the natural world.
_____

(6) Hence, God exists.

In both these arguments, I've drawn two horizontal lines to indicate that (5) is supposed to follow from premisses (1)–(4) and that (6) is supposed to follow from (5).

What do premisses (2) and (3) mean in these two arguments? Let's begin with an object (O_1) that is in motion now. Since it is in motion, there must be an earlier object—call it O_2—that sent O_1 into motion. If O_2 was itself in motion, O_2 must trace back to a previous mover, O_3. And so on. In the second argument, the subject is causality, not motion, but the idea is basically the same.

Premiss (4) says that there can't be a chain that extends infinitely far back into the past. The idea is that cause/effect chains (or mover/movee chains) leading from the present back into the past have finitely many links. The arrow in the following diagram represents the relationship of causality:

$$\text{Past} \qquad \text{Present} \qquad \text{Future}$$
$$O_f \longrightarrow \ldots \longrightarrow O_3 \longrightarrow O_2 \longrightarrow O_1 \longrightarrow \ldots$$

Although Aquinas's argument focuses on chains that extend from present back into the past, his principle (4) also has implications about chains that extend from the present forward into the future. These also must have finitely many links. Cause/effect chains must be finite in both directions.

I'll begin with two specific criticisms—one aimed at argument I, the other aimed at argument II. After that, I'll lump the two arguments together and formulate some objections that apply to both.

AQUINAS ON THE CAUSE OF MOTION

Aquinas thinks (premiss 1-2) that if an object is in motion, it must be caused to move by something outside itself. Aquinas got this idea from Aristotle's physics. Aristotle (384–322 B.C.) held that if an object continues to move, its motion must be sustained by a force that keeps it in motion. If you remove the force, the object stops moving.

This idea didn't survive into modern physics. You may remember from high school physics that Newton, in the seventeenth century, held that an object remains in constant uniform motion unless acted on by a force. Recall that one of Newton's laws of motion is $F = ma$. This means that if an object of mass m is acted on by a force of value F, then it will accelerate to degree a. This Newtonian law says that an object that isn't acted on by a force won't accelerate, which means it will remain at rest *or in uniform motion*. Newton's laws say that an object can remain in motion forever without there being any force that sustains its motion.

Newton's laws do not exclude the following possibility: The universe contains exactly one physical object, which always moves in uniform motion without any forces ever acting on it. Of course, Newton's laws don't say that the universe we live in is like this. Our universe obviously contains more than one material object. My point, though, is that Newton's theory of motion was different from Aristotle's and so was different from Aquinas's. Aristotle and Aquinas thought that motion requires an outside force; Newton and more modern physical theories hold that it is acceleration, not simply change in position, that requires a force.

It is not difficult to rescue Aquinas's first argument from this Newtonian objection. Just replace his talk of motion with the concept of acceleration. If objects accelerate there must be a force that causes them to do so. Then we are led by the same line of reasoning to the conclusion that there must exist a supernatural entity that causes the first accelerating object in nature to accelerate.

GOD IS A PERSON, NOT JUST A CAUSE THAT EXISTS OUTSIDE OF NATURE

I turn now to some problems that the two arguments share. First, it is important to see that proposition (S)—that there is an entity outside of nature that causes the first moving object in nature to move, or that causes the first event in nature to occur—does not guarantee the existence of God, where this is understood to mean a person with something like the traditional properties of omnipotence, omniscience, and omnibenevolence. As Aquinas himself realized, conclusion (6) does not follow from proposition (5), in either argument.

THE BIRTHDAY FALLACY

Another problem arises when we ask whether the argument shows that there is *precisely one* first cause, or instead shows only that there is *at least one*. Suppose we grant that each causal chain in nature has a first member. According to Aquinas, each of these first members must be caused by some event outside of nature. However, it does not follow that there is exactly one such event outside of nature that set all causal chains in the natural world in motion. Here it is important to see the difference between the following two propositions; the first is different from and doesn't deductively imply the second:

Every event in the natural world traces back to an event that occurs outside nature.

There is a single event outside of the natural world to which each event in nature traces back.

The difference here parallels the logical difference between the following two propositions, the first of which is true and the second false:

Every person has a birthday—a day on which he or she was born.

There is a single day that is everybody's birthday.

I want to give a name to the mistaken idea that the second proposition follows from the first. I'll call it the *Birthday Fallacy*.

So one problem with arguments I and II is that they don't show there is exactly one first cause or unmoved mover; at best, they show that there is at least one. To think otherwise is to commit the Birthday Fallacy.

WHY CAN'T NATURE BE INFINITELY OLD?

Another objection to Aquinas's first two arguments is his claim that cause/effect chains cannot extend infinitely far into the past. Why is this impossible? If the natural world were infinitely old, each event could be caused by an earlier event. Every event that occurs in nature could have a cause that also existed in nature, so there would be no reason to infer that something outside of nature must exist as the cause of what occurs inside.

Aquinas thinks he has an answer to this question. He doesn't simply *assume* that causal chains extending into the past must be finite in length; he has an *argument* that he thinks shows why this is so. Here is his argument, which I'll reconstruct in terms of an example of a present event—your reading this page now:

You are reading this page now.

A causal chain that extends from this present event infinitely into the past, by definition, lacks a first member.

If a causal chain lacked a first member, then all subsequent events in the chain could not occur.

——————————

Hence, the causal chain leading up to your reading this page now must be finitely old.

The third premiss is where this argument goes wrong. Even if we assume that no event in nature can happen without its having a cause, it doesn't follow that there has to be a first natural event.

Many traditional theists will agree that the world could have an infinite future—that it could go on forever. However, if an infinite future is possible, why is an infinite past ruled out? If there doesn't have to be a last event in the history of the natural world, why must there be a first? There seems to be no reason to accept Aquinas's claim that causal chains can't extend infinitely into the past.

WHY MUST EVERY EVENT IN NATURE HAVE A CAUSE?

This brings me to my last objection to Aquinas's first two arguments for the existence of God. Even if the natural world is only finitely old, why must there be an explanation of the first event that occurs in that world? That is, why must *every* event that occurs in nature have a cause?

Do scientists assume that every event has a cause? Well, it is true that scientists often try to discover the causes of events that they observe. However, this activity of searching does not require that one actually *believe* that every event has a cause. Perhaps there are exceptions to this generalization. One tries to find causal explanations for the events one observes for this reason: if you don't look, you won't discover the cause if there is one. Better to look and fail to find than never to look at all.

THE THIRD ARGUMENT: CONTINGENCY

Aquinas's third argument for the existence of God, like the first two, begins with an observation that everybody would agree is true. The observation is put in language that may be unfamiliar, but once explained, it seems evident enough. The observation is that contingent things exist.

What does it mean to say that a thing is contingent? The opposite of contingency is necessity. What makes an object contingent or necessary?

NECESSARY AND CONTINGENT BEINGS

You, I, the Washington Monument, the human race, the Earth, the solar system, and the Milky Way are all examples of contingent things. Although all of us exist, we needn't have existed. The world could have failed to include any of us. If the particular sperm and egg that produced you hadn't encountered each other, you wouldn't have come into existence. Your parents would have had other kids or no children at all. Likewise for the human race; although the world obviously includes human beings, it needn't have.

Contingent things depend for their existence on something or other happening. In contrast, a necessary being is something that must exist no matter what. It doesn't depend for its existence on anything.

POSSIBLE WORLDS

I want to represent the concepts of necessity and contingency by introducing a new idea. Consider the totality of things that have existed, now exist, or will exist at any place in the universe. This totality comprises a giant object that I'll call "the actual world."

Imagine a census of the objects in the actual world. We might display this census on a very long time line, in which the durations of various objects are represented:

$$\vdash w \dashv$$
$$\vdash x \dashv \qquad \vdash y \dashv \qquad \vdash z \dashv$$

Past	Now	Future

Notice that the life spans, or durations, of objects w and x overlap. Objects w and x existed in the past and now are no more. Object y came into existence in the past, exists now, and will continue to exist until some future date, when it will cease to be. Object z hasn't yet come into being, but it will.

Of course, this is a dreadfully incomplete census of everything that was, is, or will be. Never mind. You get the idea: The actual world consists of everything that has existed, exists now, or will exist, anywhere in the universe.

We know the world needn't have had precisely the census it does. Some of the objects in this census might have failed to exist. Other objects, which don't actually exist, might have done so. Let's call each possible way the world might have been a "possible world." There are many of these.

We now may say that an object is contingent if it exists in some but not all possible worlds. And an object is necessary if it exists in all possible worlds. Suppose the following are the censuses found in several possible worlds. As before, the horizontal line represents time within a possible world:

w x	y	z	Actual world
a b	y	z	Possible world 1
a c	d	z	Possible world 2

Past	Present	Future

Notice that w exists in the actual world, but not in the two alternative possible worlds represented. On the other hand, y exists in the actual world and in the first possible world, but not in the second.

Object z is different—it exists in all of the possible worlds depicted. Of course, there are more than three possible worlds, since there are more than two alternative ways the actual world might have been (the actual world, of course, is one of the possible worlds). Would z continue to appear if we listed not just a few possible worlds, but all of them? That is the question of whether z is a necessary being.

I cited some examples of contingent things—you, the Washington Monument, the Earth, and a few others. These examples might strike you as typical of everything that exists. That is, you might find plausible the following philosophical conjecture: Everything that exists is contingent. Familiar objects clearly have this property. But is *everything* contingent? Aquinas argues in his third proof of the existence of God that not everything is contingent. There is at least one necessary being, namely God.

Here is how his proof goes:

III (1) Contingent things exist.

    (2) Each contingent thing has a time at which it fails to exist ("contingent things are not omnipresent").

------

    (3) So, if everything were contingent, there would be a time at which nothing exists (call this an "empty time").

    (4) That empty time would have been in the past.

    (5) If the world were empty at one time, it would be empty forever after (a conservation principle).

------

    (6) So, if everything were contingent, nothing would exist now.

    (7) But clearly, the world is not empty (see premiss 1).

------

    (8) So there exists a being who is not contingent.

    Hence, God exists.

Aquinas's argument has two stages. First, there is his defense of proposition (6), which is contained in premises (1)–(5). Second, there is his use of proposition (6) to establish the existence of God. Before considering why Aquinas thinks (6) is correct, I want to focus on his use of (6) and (7) to infer proposition (8).

REDUCTIO AD ABSURDUM

Aquinas's proof of (8) from (6) and (7) has a distinctive logical form. His proof is a *reductio ad absurdum* argument (a "reductio," for short).

When I talked about deductive validity in Lecture 2, I emphasized that the word "valid" in logic and philosophy doesn't mean what it means in everyday life. The same holds for the idea of reducing something to absurdity. In ordinary speech this means something like "making a mockery of an idea." In logic, however, reductio arguments are perfectly good arguments—they are deductively valid.

Here's how a reductio argument works. You want to prove a proposition P. To do this, you argue that if P were false, some proposition A would have to be true. But you construct the argument so that A is an obvious falsehood (an "absurdity"). From this, you may validly conclude that P is true. Reductio arguments, in other words, have the following valid logical form:

    If P is false, then A is true.

    A is false.

    P is true.

Aquinas tries to establish the existence of a necessary being by reductio. He argues that if only contingent beings existed, the world would now be empty. But it is obviously false that the world is now empty. Hence, not everything is contingent—there must exist at least one necessary being.

Let's now examine Aquinas's defense of proposition (6). Why should we think the world would now be empty if there were no necessary beings? Aquinas's reasons for thinking this are contained in premisses (1)–(5).

CONTINGENCY AND ETERNITY

I'll begin by registering an objection to premiss (2). Contrary to Aquinas, I submit that a contingent thing can be eternal; the fact that an object is contingent doesn't mean that there must be a time at which it fails to exist. I'll grant that familiar contingent objects aren't eternal. You are an example. You might have failed to exist; in addition, there was a time before you were born and there will be a time after you die. But this is just an example. We want to know whether *all* contingent beings must fail to be eternal.

Notice first that the considerations affecting contingency differ from those affecting the question of eternity. How can you tell whether an object is contingent in a diagram like the one given before showing the actual world and two possible worlds? You look *down* the list of possible worlds, checking to see if the object in question is present in each one. In that diagram, we might say that contingency is represented "vertically." Eternality is different. To see whether an object present in a given possible world is eternal, you look *across* the representation of that possible world, checking to see if it exists at all times in that world. So eternality is represented "horizontally."

Could an object exist in only some possible worlds and still exist at all times in the actual world? That is, could an object be both contingent and eternal? Aquinas says no. Here is a consideration that suggests he may be wrong.

The idea that material objects are made of very small indivisible particles has had a long history, going back at least to the ancient Greeks. Of course, we no longer think of atoms as indivisible particles—we have long since learned to talk about subatomic particles. Suppose for the moment, however, that the word "atom" names such indivisible particles. These particles are the basic building blocks of all material things.

One idea that has been put forward in atomistic theories is that atoms (fundamental particles) can't be created or destroyed. Large objects made of atoms can be created and destroyed by assembling and disassembling collections of atoms. But the basic particles themselves can't be destroyed, because you can't break them into pieces. Again, I'm not saying that this is true of the objects we now regard as the smallest material particles. I mention it only to describe a possible view of atoms.

Atoms, on the view I'm describing, are eternal. If a given atom exists now, it has always existed and it always will exist. Let's call one of the atoms that populates the actual world by the name "Charlie." Charlie is eternal.

Does it follow that Charlie is a necessary being—that the world couldn't have failed to include him? I would say not. The world could have contained more atoms than it does, or fewer. Indeed, it doesn't seem impossible that the world might have been entirely empty of matter. So Charlie, like all the atoms that happen to actually exist, is a contingent being.

If this is right, then Aquinas's premiss (2) is mistaken. Charlie, I've claimed, is a contingent being, but he is eternal. So contingent things needn't have a time at which they fail to exist.

The argument I've given against premiss (2) depends on a particular theory about the nature of atoms. If atoms really are indestructible, I can claim to have refuted Aquinas's premiss. But are they, in fact, indestructible? Again, remember I'm discussing the smallest units of matter here. This is how I'm using the word "atom."

CONSERVATION LAWS IN PHYSICS

Current physics doesn't support the view that atoms are indestructible. Before Einstein, physics upheld a principle that said that the quantity of mass in the universe is constant. But Einstein replaced this classical conservation law with another one. Mass isn't conserved; rather, a quantity that Einstein called "mass-energy" is conserved. This principle says that mass can be destroyed; it may be converted into energy. Modern physics, therefore, doesn't seem to allow me to tell my story about Charlie, the indestructible atom.

So matter *can* be destroyed, according to current theory. But this doesn't mean that every contingently existing particle WILL be destroyed, sooner or later. It is the latter claim that Aquinas advances in premiss (2). I don't know of any good reason to think this is so, although I'll leave the question open.

My conclusion thus far is that premiss (2) is mistaken; a contingent thing doesn't have to have a time at which it fails to exist. Let's move on.

THE BIRTHDAY FALLACY

The transition from premiss (2) to statement (3) involves a fallacy. Even if we grant that every contingent entity has a time at which it fails to exist, we can't conclude that there is an empty time. The fallacy here is the same one discussed concerning Aquinas's first two arguments. Recall the point about birthdays; "Everybody has a birthday" does not deductively imply that there is a day that is everyone's birthday.

To make this point graphic, consider the following possible world, in which no object is eternal, and yet there is no empty time:

$$\longleftarrow \quad {\vdash}1{-\!/} \quad {\vdash}3{-\!/} \quad {\vdash}5{-\!/} \quad \longrightarrow$$
$${\vdash}2{-\!/} \quad {\vdash}4{-\!/} \quad {\vdash}6{-\!/}$$

Past	Present	Future

The arrows at the beginning and end indicate the pattern should be repeated indefinitely into the past and into the future.

So the supposition that everything is contingent doesn't imply an empty time. But there is an additional unjustified step. Even if there does have to be an empty time, why must it have been in the past? I see no reason to assume this.

NECESSARY BEINGS OTHER THAN GOD

I've noted some problems in Aquinas's attempted reductio proof that not everything is contingent. Suppose, however, that Aquinas could show that there is at least one necessary being. Could he conclude from this that God exists? I want to argue that this, too, doesn't follow. In discussing Aquinas's first two arguments, I claimed that the existence of God doesn't follow from the existence of a first cause. I now want to suggest that the existence of God doesn't follow from the existence of a necessary being.

To explain why this is so, I have to develop an idea from the philosophy of mathematics. Until now, I've described necessity and contingency as properties of entities. You and I are contingent beings, for example. Now, however, I want to use the ideas of contingency and necessity as properties of propositions. Propositions, or statements, are true or false. They also have the properties of necessity and contingency.

NECESSARY AND CONTINGENT PROPOSITIONS

Necessity and contingency as properties of propositions are definable in a way that parallels the way this distinction applies to entities. A proposition is necessarily true if it is true in all possible worlds. A proposition is necessarily false if it is false in all possible worlds. Contingent propositions are true in some possible worlds and false in others. A true statement is contingent if it is true in the actual world, though false in some possible world.

It is easy to cite examples of contingent propositions. Consider the fact that the U.S.A. is, in the twentieth century, a nation in North America. This is true, though only contingently so. Consider the following contingent falsehood: The Rocky Mountains are no higher than 6,000 feet above sea level. This is false, but there are possible worlds in which it is true.

MATHEMATICAL TRUTHS

Are there any necessary truths? Many philosophers have held that mathematical truths are necessarily true. Consider the fact that $7 + 3 = 10$. It isn't just that this happens to be true in the actual world. There is no possible world in which it is false. The sum of 7 and 3 could not fail to equal 10.

To see why this is at least a plausible view of mathematical propositions, you've got to be clear on what the proposition says. The proposition doesn't say that if you put seven rabbits together with three others, there will be ten bunnies forever after. Rabbits reproduce, but this doesn't contradict any fact of arithmetic. Take another example: If you pour three cups of sugar into seven cups of water, you will not obtain ten cups of liquid. But, again, this doesn't contradict the fact that $7 + 3 = 10$. Arithmetic is unaffected by this result; it just so happens that liquids don't always combine additively.

NAMES DIFFER FROM THE THINGS NAMED

Here is a somewhat more subtle point to notice. The proposition that $7 + 3 = 10$ doesn't say anything about the language we may use in expressing that fact to ourselves. It is a contingent fact that human beings use the numeral "7" to refer to the number 7.

We might have called that number by another name—we might have used the numeral "2" to denote the number 7. Similarly, it is a contingent fact that we use the symbol "=" to represent the relation of equality. So it is a contingent fact that the sentence "$7 + 3 = 10$" expresses what it does; and it is a contingent fact that that sentence expresses a true proposition rather than a false one. But this doesn't show that $7 + 3$ might not have equaled 10. The fact couldn't have been otherwise, even though we might have used our terminology differently.

The distinction I'm drawing here is very obvious in some contexts, though it is easy to lose sight of in others. Few things are more different than a thing and its name. You are a person, but your name isn't. Your name contains a certain number of letters, but you don't. Your name is a linguistic entity, but you aren't.

We mark this difference by using quotation marks. If we want to talk about a thing, we use its name. If we want to talk about the name of a thing, we put the name in quotation marks. So if I want to talk about a big mountain in western North America, I might say that the Rocky Mountains are tall. But if I want to talk about the mountain range's name, I'd say that the phrase "the Rocky Mountains" contains 17 letters.

NUMBERS AREN'T NUMERALS

This is obvious, when you think about it. When it comes to mathematics, however, we tend to confuse these ideas. Numerals are names of numbers. But the number and its name are different, just as the phrase "the Rocky Mountains" differs from the mountains themselves. I grant that it is a contingent matter that the sentence "$7 + 3 = 10$" expresses a truth. I deny, however, that $7 + 3$ might have failed to equal 10. The idea is that the proposition is necessarily true, even though it is a contingent fact that the sentence expresses the proposition it does. Just as your name is part of a language, though you aren't, so the sentence "$7 + 3 = 10$" is a part of language, though the proposition it expresses isn't.

SETS

So what does the proposition that $7 + 3 = 10$ actually mean? It doesn't say anything about rabbit reproduction or about the way volumes combine when poured together. Nor does it say anything about the language we use. You can think of this statement as describing a basic property of mathematical objects called *sets*.

First, I need a bit of terminology. The *union* of two sets is the set that includes all the members of the first and all the members of the second, and no others. A set is any collection of objects. So the set {Groucho Marx, Napoleon, the Eiffel Tower} is a three-member set, and the set {Napoleon, the Rocky Mountains, the French Revolution} is also a three-member set. The items in a set needn't have anything special in common with each other. There are sets of similar things, but there also are sets of dissimilar things. The union of the two sets just mentioned is this set: {Groucho Marx, Napoleon, the Eiffel Tower, the Rocky Mountains, the French Revolution}.

The proposition that 7 + 3 = 10 can be understood to say the following: Consider any two sets such that the first contains exactly seven objects and the second contains exactly three. If these sets have no common members, then the union of these two sets will have precisely ten members.

Notice that the arithmetic proposition doesn't say that the Rocky Mountains exist, or that there are at least seven material things in the universe. The arithmetic fact doesn't rule out the possibility that the world contains no material objects at all. It simply describes a basic property of the operation of set-theoretic union.

NECESSITY AND CERTAINTY ARE DIFFERENT

I need to add a final clarification of the thesis that mathematical truths are necessary. In saying that it is a necessary truth that 7 + 3 = 10, I'm not saying that I know that the proposition is true with absolute certainty. Nor am I saying that I'll never change my mind on the question of whether 7 + 3 equals 10.

This is a rather subtle point, because we sometimes express our lack of certainty about a proposition by saying that maybe the proposition isn't so. If I think there will be rain tomorrow, but entertain some small doubt that this will be so, I may express this by saying, "Possibly it won't rain tomorrow." But my certainty or uncertainty is a fact about *me*. It is a fact in the *subjective* realm. I want to distinguish this question from the question of whether a given proposition has the property of necessity or contingency. The latter question doesn't have anything special to do with me. Necessity and contingency are *objective*.

Here is a nonmathematical example that may make this clearer. Could there be perpetual motion machines? A machine of this sort wouldn't require any energy input to keep running, but it would provide a constant output of energy. Scientists for many hundreds of years tried to design such a machine. They always failed. Finally, in the nineteenth century, physicists working in the area called thermodynamics proved that perpetual motion machines are impossible.

Consider the proposition that there are or will be perpetual motion machines. This is, we now believe, a falsehood. Is it a necessary falsehood? I would say yes. It isn't just that no one will bother to build one; the point is that it is impossible to build one. This, at least, is what science tells us.

Now I'll ask an entirely separate question: Am I absolutely certain that no such machine will ever exist? I guess I'm not absolutely certain. After all, science has been wrong before, and so maybe it now is wrong when it says that such machines are impossible. Opinion has changed through history on the question of whether such machines could be built. Before the nineteenth century, many serious scientists thought such machines are possible. Later, opinion changed. Maybe it will change again.

So the certainty that a single scientist or a community of scientists may have about the issue may change. But there is something that doesn't change. Either it is possible for such things to exist or it isn't. This should convince you that *certainty* and *necessity* are different. People may change their degree of certainty about a proposition; they may even think at one time that it is true, but later on think that it is false. But the proposition itself doesn't change from true to false. Nor does a proposition cease to be necessary just because people stop believing it.

So, to say that arithmetic truths are necessary isn't to say that people are certain about arithmetic. Nor is it to say that people have never changed their minds about arithmetic propositions. Again, these are questions about our attitudes toward the propositions. But whether a proposition is necessary or not has nothing to do with our attitudes. In this respect, necessity is like truth—both are objective issues, independent of what people happen to believe.

To sum up, I've described a prominent view in the philosophy of mathematics. It holds that arithmetic truths are necessary. I haven't provided that view with a complete defense, but I hope you can see what it asserts. I also hope it is at least somewhat plausible, if not entirely convincing.

What has this material about mathematics to do with the conclusion of Aquinas's third proof? Recall that Aquinas reasons that if there is a necessary being, then God must exist. Part of my point in talking about mathematical necessity here is that I want to describe a necessary being that no one would think is God.

NUMBERS ARE NECESSARY BEINGS

Consider the fact that arithmetic includes various existence statements. Besides asserting that $7 + 3 = 10$, arithmetic also asserts that there is a prime number immediately after 10. If, however, arithmetic truths are necessary, then it is a necessary truth that there exists a prime number immediately after 10. To put it bluntly, the philosophy of mathematics I've described holds that the number 11 is a necessary being. It exists in all possible worlds. This follows from the thesis that arithmetic truths are necessary and from the fact that arithmetic contains existence claims.

The conclusion that there is a God doesn't follow from the assertion that not everything is contingent. A philosopher of mathematics might claim that the number 11 is a necessary being, but this wouldn't entail that God exists. This is my last criticism of Aquinas's third argument.

AQUINAS'S FOURTH ARGUMENT: PROPERTIES THAT COME IN DEGREES

I won't spend much time on Aquinas's fourth proof of the existence of God. It is rooted in an Aristotelian view of causality that seems radically implausible now. Here's the argument:

(1) Objects have properties to greater or lesser extents.

(2) If an object has a property to a lesser extent, then there exists some other object that has that property to the maximum possible degree (call this a maximum exemplar of the property).

(3) So, there is an entity that has all properties to the maximum possible degree.
———————————————
Hence, God exists.

The argument begins with an observation that is obviously true: Some things are more powerful and some less; some are more intelligent and others less, and so on. The second premiss, however, seems entirely implausible. The fact that Charlie Chaplin is less than maximally funny doesn't mean that there must exist a maximally funny comedian. And the fact that we are somewhat intelligent, though not perfectly so, doesn't seem to require that there exists a perfectly intelligent being.

The Aristotelian idea that Aquinas is using here is roughly as follows. Aristotle thought that fire is the maximally hot substance. When other objects are hot to some lesser degree, this is because fire is mixed in them to some extent. The property of heat can occur to a less than maximal degree in human beings, for example, only because there exists this substance, fire, which is hot to the maximum possible degree. Fire is the maximum exemplar of heat, from which lesser degrees of heat derive.

There are other problems with the argument. If each property has a maximum exemplar, it doesn't follow that there is an entity that is a maximum exemplar of all properties. Recall the Birthday Fallacy: The fact that everyone has a birthday doesn't imply that there is a single day on which everyone was born. So even if there is a maximum exemplar of intelligence, a maximum exemplar of power, and a maximum exemplar of moral goodness, it doesn't follow that there is a single entity who is all-knowing, all-powerful, and all-good.

Finally, there is the problem of contradiction. If intelligence has its maximum exemplar, then stupidity would have to have its maximum exemplar as well. By Aquinas's argument, this leads us to say that there is a single being who is both maximally intelligent and maximally stupid. But this is impossible. That concludes what I want to say about Aquinas's fourth way.

CRITICIZING AN ARGUMENT VERSUS SHOWING THE ARGUMENT'S CONCLUSION IS FALSE

None of the four arguments I've discussed here is successful. Does this mean there is no God? It means no such thing. There may be other arguments for the existence of God that are convincing. That the four arguments discussed here don't work doesn't mean that no argument will work. Not one word has been said here that shows that atheism is true. All we have seen is that some arguments for theism are flawed. In the next lecture, I'll consider Aquinas's fifth argument for the existence of God. Maybe it will fare better.

Review Questions

1. What objections are there to the first cause argument?
2. What is the Birthday Fallacy? How does it figure in the discussion of Aquinas's arguments?
3. Explain what it means for an object to be necessary or contingent. What is a "possible world"
4. How are necessity and eternality related? How does this bear on Aquinas's third argument?
5. What is a reductio argument? Give an example.
6. What is the difference between necessity and certainty? What is meant by saying that necessity is "objective"?
7. What would it mean for something to be a first cause without being God? What would it mean for something to necessarily exist without being God?

Problems for Further Thought

1. I formulated Aquinas's proofs by having him talk about objects that exist in "nature" (in "the natural world"). What does "nature" include? Does it include just the things we can see or hear or touch or taste or smell? After all, the selection from Aquinas in the Readings translates Aquinas as talking about the "sensible" world. How would interpreting his argument in this way affect its plausibility? What other interpretations of "nature" make sense in this context?
2. In discussing Aquinas's third proof, I talked about Charlie the atom as an example of a thing that is both eternal and contingent. Could something exist that is both necessary and noneternal? It would exist at *some* time in each possible world, though it would not exist at *all* times in the actual world. Can you give an example of such a thing?

LECTURE 5

The Design Argument

Aquinas's fifth argument for the existence of God has come to be called the Argument from Design. It has a variety of forms, some of which I'll describe. To start things off, here is a formulation that is close to the one Aquinas uses:

(1) Among objects that act for an end, some have minds whereas others do not.

(2) An object that acts for an end, but does not itself have
    a mind, must have been designed by a being that has a mind.

(3) Hence, there exists a being with a mind who designed
    all mindless objects that act for an end.

———————————

Hence, God exists.

Note as a preliminary point that the transition from (2) to (3) commits the Birthday Fallacy described in Lecture 4. If each mindless object that acts for an end has a designer, it doesn't follow that there is a *single* designer of all the mindless objects that act for an end.

GOAL-DIRECTED SYSTEMS

What does Aquinas mean by "act for an end?" This phrase corresponds to the modern idea of a goal-directed system. Human beings act for an end because they have desires; these desires represent the ends or purposes or goals to which behavior is directed. Human beings are capable of goal-directed behavior because they have minds. Consider, however, a different example: a guided missile. It is a goal-directed system. Its goal or function is to reach and destroy its target. If the target veers off to the side, the missile can adjust its behavior so that it will achieve its purpose.

Guided missiles are goal-directed systems, but they don't have minds. How is this possible? The answer is consistent with what Aquinas says in premiss (2). Guided missiles are *artifacts*. They are devices built by creatures with minds—namely, human beings. This is how missiles obtained the machinery that allows them to engage in goal-directed behavior.

Are there other examples of goal-directed systems besides human beings and artifacts? Nonhuman organisms provide a third category. Even bacteria, which evidently don't have beliefs and desires, seek out nutrients and avoid poisonous chemicals. It seems plausible to describe them as having the goal of surviving and reproducing. They are able to modify their behavior to achieve these ends.

Does the list stop here with human beings, artifacts, and nonhuman organisms? Aquinas followed Aristotle in thinking that even inanimate objects like rocks and comets have goals. This idea pretty much went out of fashion with the Scientific Revolution in the seventeenth century. It now seems implausible to describe a rock as being hard "in order to resist destruction." It also seems strange to say that rocks fall toward the center of the Earth when they are released "in order to attain the location that it is in their nature to seek." But this is how Aristotle thought about rocks, and Aquinas followed him here. Both thought that everything, whether living or not, should be understood *teleologically*—that is, as a goal-directed system. (This will be discussed further in Lecture 33.)

I won't take issue with this general teleological picture, except to note that it is far more encompassing than the one provided by modern science. However, this point does not affect the design argument as I have formulated it. What is required is just that *some* mindless objects are goal-directed.

TWO KINDS OF DESIGN ARGUMENT

It will be useful to distinguish two kinds of design arguments. Aquinas would have been willing to endorse them both. David Hume (1711–1776), who examined various design arguments in his *Dialogues Concerning Natural Religion* (1779), discusses both sorts. I'll call these two sorts of arguments *global* design arguments and *local* design arguments.

A global design argument cites some general feature of the whole universe and argues that this feature should be explained by the hypothesis that it is the product of intelligent design. An example would be the argument that proposes to explain why the laws of nature are quite simple. Newton himself argued that the simplicity of natural laws is evidence that there exists an intelligent and perfect God who was their author.

A local design argument focuses on a more specific feature of the universe and claims that the hypothesis that God exists is the best or the only plausible explanation of that fact. The example I'll consider here concerns features of the organisms we observe on Earth. They are goal-directed systems; they are complex systems equipped with the ability to modify their behavior so that they can survive and reproduce.

In this lecture, I'll begin with the local argument just mentioned, in which it is special features of living things (including ourselves) that are said to require explanation. In Lecture 7, I'll return to design arguments that are global.

PALEY'S WATCH

In the eighteenth century and the early nineteenth century in Great Britain, design arguments were the rage. Numerous books were published arguing that the existence of God was required to explain this or that feature of the world we observe. One of the most influential works of this sort was produced by William Paley (1743–1805). Whereas Aquinas formulated his version of the design argument as a deductively valid argument, I'm going to interpret Paley's argument as an abductive argument, an inference to the best explanation.

Paley's striking formulation of the design argument goes like this: Suppose you were walking on a beach (actually, Paley talks about walking on a "heath") and found a watch lying on the sand. Opening it up, you see it is an intricate piece of machinery. You see the machinery is complex; the parts work together to allow the hands to measure out equal intervals of time with considerable precision. What could explain the existence and characteristics of this object?

H_1: The Random Hypothesis

One hypothesis to consider I will call the *Random Hypothesis*. By the random action of the waves on the sand, a watch was accidentally produced. You may be willing to concede that this explanation is possible. But surely it isn't very plausible. The idea that waves beating on sand could produce an object of such intricacy doesn't make a lot of sense. It is about as plausible as suggesting that a monkey randomly pounding on a typewriter will write out the complete works of Shakespeare.

H_2: The Design Hypothesis

A far more plausible explanation is the *Design Hypothesis*. The intricacy of the watch suggests that it is the product of intelligence. This hypothesis says that the watch exists because there was a watchmaker who produced it.

Why do we think the Design Hypothesis is more plausible than the Random Hypothesis? If there were a Designer at work, then it wouldn't be surprising that the watch is complex and well suited to the task of measuring temporal intervals. If, however, the only process at work were waves pounding on sand, then it would be enormously surprising that the watch have these characteristics. The observed features of the watch are possible, according to either hypothesis. But they are rather probable according to one, and vastly improbable according to the other. In preferring the Design Hypothesis, we prefer the hypothesis that strains our credulity less.

I hope you see that Paley's argument uses the Surprise Principle described in Lecture 3. You've made some observations (call them O) and are considering whether O strongly favors one hypothesis (H_2) over another (H_1). The Surprise Principle says that O strongly favors H_2 over H_1 if H_2 says that O is very probable while H_1 says that O is quite improbable. O would be unsurprising if H_2 were true, but O would be very surprising if H_1 were true.

Not only do we infer the existence of a watchmaker from the watch we found; we also can infer something about the watchmaker's characteristics. We can say that the designer must have been fairly intelligent to produce an object of such intricacy. Chimps are somewhat intelligent, but it is dubious that a chimp could have made the watch. Rather, what we naturally infer is that the watchmaker must have had an intelligence at least on the order of human intelligence, given the features of the watch we observe.

THE ANALOGY

So far in this argument, Paley is simply describing what common sense would say about the watch on the beach. Paley then suggests an analogy. Look around the living world. Notice that it is filled with organisms that are extremely intricate and adapted. In fact, organisms are far more complicated than watches. And as well suited as a watch is to the task of measuring time, organisms are even better suited to the tasks of surviving and reproducing.

How can we explain the fact that organisms are so amazingly intricate and adapted? One possibility is the Random Hypothesis—that by a process akin to waves pounding on sand, orchids, crocodiles, and people came into existence. The other alternative is the Design Hypothesis—that an organism maker of considerable intelligence made the impressive pieces of machinery we call living things.

Which explanation is more plausible? If the Random Hypothesis says that the existence of a watch is very improbable, then the Random Hypothesis also must say that the existence of intricate and adapted organisms is very improbable. So if inferring the existence of a watchmaker is plausible in the first case, then inferring the existence of a designer of all life is plausible in the second.

Finally, we may ask how intelligent this maker of organisms must be, given the intricacy and fineness of adaptation that organisms exhibit. From what watches are like, we can infer that watchmakers must be pretty smart. By the same reasoning, we infer that the maker of organisms must be very, very intelligent—far more intelligent than human beings are. Paley's design argument concludes that the intricacy and adaptedness of organisms are best explained by postulating the existence of an *extremely* intelligent designer.

ABDUCTIONS OFTEN POSTULATE UNOBSERVED ENTITIES

There is a point that pertains to all of Aquinas's arguments that should be emphasized here. The design argument claims there is something we observe—the complexity and adaptedness of living things—that is best explained by the hypothesis that there is a God. The conclusion of the argument concerns the existence of something we haven't observed directly. Although there may be defects in this argument, the fact that it reaches a conclusion about a being we haven't observed isn't one of them. Recall from Lecture 3 that abductive arguments frequently have this characteristic. It would cripple science to limit theorizing to a description of what scientists have actually observed.

So my view of Paley's argument is that it is an abductive argument:

> Organisms are intricate and well suited to the tasks of survival and reproduction.
> ═══════════════
> Hence, organisms were created by intelligent design.

I've drawn a double line here to indicate that the argument doesn't aim at being deductively valid.

To show this is a strong abductive argument, Paley argues that it is analogous to a second inference to the best explanation:

> The watch is intricate and well suited to the task of measuring time.
> ═══════════════
> Hence, the watch was created by intelligent design.

Paley claims that if you grant that the second abductive argument is convincing, you should grant that the first one is convincing as well.

HUME'S CRITICISMS OF THE DESIGN ARGUMENT

Hume's *Dialogues on Natural Religion* contain several criticisms of the design argument. Sometimes he is talking about global design arguments—ones that argue that the entire universe must be the product of intelligent design. At other times, Hume addresses local arguments—ones that focus on the adaptedness and intricacy of organisms.

I've claimed that design arguments are abductive. Hume paints a very different picture. He represents the arguments as being *inductive arguments* or *arguments from analogy*. This may not look like a very important difference, since all of these formulations involve a nondeductive inference. But you will see in what follows that two of Hume's criticisms of design arguments aren't very convincing if we think of the design argument as an inference to the best explanation.

IS THE DESIGN ARGUMENT A WEAK ARGUMENT FROM ANALOGY?

In this section, I'll discuss a criticism of the argument from design that Hume develops in Part II of his *Dialogues* (see the paragraph beginning "What I chiefly scruple . . .").

To see what Hume has in mind when he talks about arguments from analogy, consider the following example of an analogy argument:

> Human beings circulate their blood.
> ===========
> Dogs circulate their blood.

I've drawn a double line between the premiss and the conclusion, again to indicate that the argument isn't deductively valid. In this argument, let's call human beings the *analogs* and dogs the *targets*. I say that dogs are the targets here because they are the items about which the argument aims to reach a conclusion. Hume suggests, with some plausibility, that such arguments are stronger or weaker depending on how similar the analogs are to the targets. To see what he means here, compare the above argument with the following one:

> Human beings circulate their blood.
> ===========
> Plants circulate their blood.

This argument is quite weak, because human beings and plants aren't very similar.

We can formulate Hume's point by saying that an analogy argument has the following logical form:

Object *A* has property *P.*

Object *A* and object *T* are similar to degree *n.*

$$n\left[\rule{0pt}{0pt}\frac{}{}\right.$$

T has property *P.*

A is the analog and *T* is the target. The number *n* measures the degree of similarity between *A* and *T.* It goes from a minimum value of 0 (meaning that A and *T* aren't similar at all) to a maximum value of 1 (meaning that they share all their characteristics). This number also represents a probability—that is why "*n*" is next to the double line separating premises from conclusion. A high value of *n* means that *A* and *T* are very similar and that the premises make the conclusion very probable. This expresses Hume's idea that the more similar *A* and *T* are, the more probable it is that the target object *T* has the property found in the analog *A.*

Hume uses this idea about analogy arguments to criticize the design argument. He thinks the design argument has the following form:

Watches are the products of intelligent design.

$$n\left[\rule{0pt}{0pt}\frac{}{}\right.$$

The universe is the product of intelligent design.

This is a very weak argument, Hume says, since the analog is really not very similar to the target. Watches resemble the universe as a whole in some ways, but fail to do so in a great many others. So *n* has a low value.

Here Hume is criticizing what I've called a global design argument—an argument that focuses on some large-scale feature of the entire universe. Hume's point, however, also applies to local design arguments—to arguments that focus on organisms and their characteristics:

Watches are the products of intelligent design.

$$n\left[\rule{0pt}{0pt}\frac{}{}\right.$$

Organisms are the product of intelligent design.

Hume's criticism is that organisms are really not very similar to watches. Watches are made of metal, but organisms aren't. Kangaroos hop around, but watches don't. Organisms reproduce and obtain nutrition from their environment, but watches don't. And so on. Since analog and target are so dissimilar, the analogy argument is a very weak one; *n* is low here as well.

Hume's idea is that the strength or weakness of an analogy argument depends on the *overall similarity* of target and analog. You look at all the known characteristics of target and analog and try to say how similar they are overall. I grant that if you did this, you would conclude that watches and kangaroos aren't very similar.

My view, however, is that this doesn't undermine the design argument at all when that argument is taken to be an abductive one. It is entirely irrelevant whether watches and kangaroos both have fur, or whether both hop around, or whether both reproduce. The design argument focuses on *a single pair of features* of each of these and asks how it should be explained. A watch's intricacy, as well as its being well suited to measuring time, require that we think of it as the product of intelligent design. Paley's claim is that an organism's intricacy, as well as its being well suited to the tasks of survival and reproduction, ought to be explained in the same way. It doesn't matter that the one is made of metal while the other isn't. *Overall* similarity is irrelevant.

The fundamental idea of Paley's argument is that the Surprise Principle tells us that the Design Hypothesis is better supported than the Random Hypothesis, given the observations we have made about living things. This argument stands on its own. To use the Surprise Principle in this case, it doesn't matter whether organisms are similar to watches or to anything else. I conclude that Hume is mistaken to criticize the design argument as a weak argument from analogy.

IS THE DESIGN ARGUMENT A WEAK INDUCTION?

A second criticism that Hume levels at the design argument rests on thinking that the argument must be inductive if it is to make sense. (Here I have in mind the paragraph in Part II of the *Dialogues* that begins "And can you blame me . . ."; see especially the passage that begins "When two species of objects . . .")

Recall from Lecture 2 that inductive arguments involve observing a sample and extrapolating from it to some claim about one or more objects not in the sample. For example, suppose I call a large number of voters registered in a county and find that almost all are Democrats. This seems to license the inference that the next voter I call will probably be a Democrat. Hume observes, again with some plausibility, that the strength of an inductive inference is influenced by sample size. In particular, if my sample had included just one individual, I would be on rather shaky ground if I used this as my basis for predicting what the next voter called would be like. My inference would be on even shakier ground if I ventured a guess about the next telephone call having never sampled even a single voter. A sample size of zero is just plain silly; an inductive argument can't be weaker than that.

Hume claims that if we are to have a reason for thinking that the universe we inhabit is the product of intelligent design, we would have to base this conclusion on induction. What would this involve? We would have to examine a large number of other universes and see that most or all of them were the result of intelligent design. If our sample size were sufficiently large, that would justify a conclusion about the universe we inhabit.

But how big *is* our sample size? It is zero. The only universe we have ever experienced is the one we inhabit. And we can't claim to have observed that this universe contains a designer of living things. So no inductive argument can be constructed here.

My view is that this is true, but irrelevant. Small sample size does weaken an inductive argument. The design argument isn't an inductive argument, however. Hume assumed that the only sorts of inferences worth taking seriously are inductive and deductive. But this I deny. There is abduction as well. Mendel didn't have to observe that lots of different organisms have genes before he could conclude that his pea plants have genes. Mendel never saw a single gene, but this didn't prevent him from inferring their existence. His inference was abductive, not inductive.

I've reviewed two of Hume's criticisms of the design argument. They don't work. Of course, this doesn't mean that the argument has no flaws, only that we have yet to uncover one. The design argument that Paley formulated considers two competing hypotheses—the hypothesis of intelligent design and the hypothesis of random physical processes. In the mid-nineteenth century, a new hypothesis was formulated that we now need to consider as a third alternative—this is Darwin's theory of evolution by natural selection. In the next lecture, I'll describe what this hypothesis asserts and discuss how it compares to the hypothesis of intelligent design.

Review Questions

1. What does it mean to say that the design argument is an abductive argument?
2. What is the difference between a global design argument and a local design argument?
3. How does Paley's argument about the watch use the Surprise Principle?
4. Hume formulated a principle that states how the strength of an analogy argument may be measured. What is it?
5. What two criticisms did Hume make of the design argument? Are these good criticisms if the argument is understood to be abductive in character?

Problems for Further Thought

1. It might be suggested that one difference between Paley's argument about the watch and his argument about organisms is that we have seen watchmakers, but have never directly observed God. Does this point of difference undermine the force of Paley's design argument?
2. I mentioned in passing that modern science no longer takes seriously the idea that *all* things are goal-directed systems. Consider the following pair of propositions. Can you think of a reason that the first of them might be true, whereas the second might be rejected?

    The function of the heart is to pump blood.

    The function of rain is to provide farm crops with water.

    What does it mean to attribute a "function" to something?

LECTURE 6

Evolution and Creationism

In this lecture, I want to describe some of the main lines of evidence that lead biologists to think the hypothesis of evolution is correct. Whereas Aquinas, Paley, and others held that the intricacy and adaptedness of organisms can be explained only by viewing them as the product of intelligent design, the modern theory of evolution, stemming from Charles Darwin's (1809–1882) ideas, holds otherwise.

Because this is an introductory text, I won't be able to describe all the interlocking arguments biologists now offer for evolutionary theory. Nor will I be able to give all the details on even the ones I do touch on. I also won't take much time to address all the criticisms of evolutionary theory that creationists have advanced.

CREATIONISM

Creationists (sometimes calling themselves "scientific creationists") are present-day defenders of the design argument. Although they agree among themselves that intelligent design is needed to explain some features of the living world, they disagree with each other about various points of detail. Some hold that the earth is young (around 10,000 years old), whereas others concede that it is ancient—about 4.5 billion years old, according to current geology.

Some creationists maintain that each species was separately created by an intelligent designer, whereas others concede that biologists are right when they assert, as Darwin did, that all life on earth traces back to a common ancestor.

A further point of disagreement concerns which characteristics of organisms demand explanation by intelligent design. Some hold that every complex adaptation—the wings of birds, the temperature regulation system found in mammals, the eye—requires explanation in terms of intelligent design. Others disagree with modern science much less; they assert that only one or two features of life forms demand intelligent design explanations. These creationists agree with current biology, except when they consider the origin of life or the emergence of consciousness.

To further clarify what creationism involves, let's consider three possible relationships that might obtain among God (G), mindless evolutionary processes (E), and the observed features of organisms (O):

$$
\begin{array}{ll}
\text{(theistic evolutionism)} & G \longrightarrow E \longrightarrow O \\[4pt]
\text{(atheistic evolutionism)} & E \longrightarrow O \\[4pt]
\text{(creationism)} & G \longrightarrow E \longrightarrow O \\
& \underbrace{}
\end{array}
$$

Theistic evolutionism says that God set mindless evolutionary processes in motion; these processes, once underway, suffice to explain the observed features of organisms.

Atheistic evolutionism denies that there is a God, but otherwise agrees with theistic evolutionism that mindless evolutionary processes are responsible for what we see in organisms. Creationism, as I understand it, disagrees with both theistic evolutionism and atheistic evolutionism. Creationism maintains not just that God set mindless evolutionary processes in motion, but that he also periodically intervenes in these mindless processes, doing work that mindless natural processes are inherently incapable of doing.

You can see from these three options that belief in evolutionary theory is not the same as atheism. In my opinion, current evolutionary theory is neutral on the question of whether there is a God. Evolutionary theory can be supplemented with a claim, either *pro* or *con,* concerning whether God exists. Evolutionary theory, however, is not consistent with creationism. Evolutionary theory, as I understand it, holds that mindless evolutionary processes suffice to explain the features of living things. Creationism denies this.

SOME CREATIONIST ARGUMENTS

Some of the most frequently repeated creationist arguments contain mistakes and confusions. For example, creationists have argued that evolutionary theory is on shaky ground because hypotheses about the distant past can't be proven with absolute certainty. They are right that evolutionary theory isn't absolutely certain, but then nothing in science is absolutely certain. What one legitimately strives for in science is powerful evidence showing that one explanation is far more plausible than its competitors. Biologists now regard the hypotheses of evolution as about as certain as any hypothesis about the prehistoric past could be. Naturally, no scientist was on the scene some 3.8 billion years ago when life started to exist on Earth. It is nonetheless possible, however, to have strong evidence about matters that one can't directly observe, as I hope my previous discussion of abduction has made clear.

Another example of an error creationists make is their discussion of the Second Law of Thermodynamics. They claim this law makes it impossible for order to arise from disorder by natural processes. Natural processes can lead an automobile to disintegrate into a junk heap, but creationists think the law says that no natural process can cause a pile of junk to assemble itself into a functioning car. Here creationists are arguing that a physical law is inconsistent with the claim that life evolved from nonlife.

What the Second Law actually says is that a *closed system* will (with high probability) move from states of greater order to states of lesser order. But if the system isn't closed, the law says nothing about what will happen. So if the Earth were a closed system, its overall level of disorder would have to increase. But, of course, the Earth is no such thing—energy from the sun is a constant input.

If we think of the universe as a whole as a closed system, then thermodynamics does tell us that disorder will increase overall. But this overall trend doesn't prohibit "pockets" of order from arising and being maintained. The Second Law of Thermodynamics offers no basis whatever for thinking that life couldn't have evolved from nonlife.

A full treatment of the evolution versus creationism debate would require me to describe the positive explanations that creationists have advanced. If you want to compare evolutionary theory and creationism, you can't just focus on whatever difficulties there may be in evolutionary ideas. You've also got to look carefully at what the alternative is. Doing this produces lots of difficulties for creationism. The reason is that creationists have either been woefully silent on the details of the explanation they want to defend, or they have produced detailed stories that can't withstand scientific scrutiny. For example, "young earth creationists," as I mentioned, maintain that the earth is only a few thousand years old. This claim conflicts with a variety of very solid scientific findings, from geology and physics. It isn't just evolutionary theory that you have to reject if you buy into this version of creationism, but a good deal of the rest of science as well.

As I also indicated above, there are many different versions of creationism. Creationism is not a single theory, but a cluster of similar theories. In the present lecture, I won't attempt to cover all these versions, but will focus mainly on one of them. The one I'm going to start off with isn't Paley's, but it is worth considering nonetheless. According to the version of creationism I want to examine, God designed each organism to be perfectly adapted to its environment. In this lecture, I'll explain what Darwin's theory says and why I think it is vastly superior to this version of creationism. However, we can't conclude from this that Darwinism is superior to *all* forms of creationism. In fact, I'll conclude the lecture by describing a second version of creationism that is immune to the criticisms that undermine the "perfectionist" version. And I'll return, at the end, to the version of creationism that Paley actually defends.

DARWIN'S TWO-PART THEORY

In 1859 Darwin put forward his theory of evolution in his book *The Origin of Species.* Many of his ideas are still regarded as correct. Some have been refined or expanded. Others have been junked entirely. Although evolutionary theory has developed a long way since Darwin's time, I'll take his basic ideas as a point of departure.

Darwin's theory contains two main elements. First, there is the idea that all present-day life is related. The organisms we see didn't come into existence independently by separate creation. Rather, organisms are related to each other by a family tree. You and I are related. If we go back far enough in time, we'll find a human being who is an ancestor of both of us. The same is true of you and a chimp, though, of course, one must go back even further in time to reach a common ancestor. And so it is for any two present-day organisms. Life evolved from nonlife, and then descent with modification gave rise to the diversity we now observe.

Notice that this first hypothesis of Darwin's says nothing about why new characteristics arose in the course of evolution. If all life is related, we may ask why it is that we find the variety of organisms we do. Why aren't all living things identical? The second part of Darwin's theory is the idea of natural selection. This hypothesis tries to explain why new characteristics appear and become common and why some old characteristics disappear.

It is very important to keep these two elements in Darwin's theory separate. The idea that all present-day living things are related isn't at all controversial. The idea that natural selection is the principal cause of evolutionary change is *somewhat* controversial, although it is still by far the majority view among biologists.

Part of the reason it is important to keep these ideas separate is that some creationists have tried to score points by confusing them. Creationists sometimes suggest that the whole idea of evolution is something even biologists regard with great doubt and suspicion. But the idea that all life is related isn't at all controversial. What is controversial, at least to some degree, are ideas about natural selection.

I'll begin by describing the basic idea of natural selection. Then I'll say a little about what is still somewhat controversial about the idea. I'll then turn to the quite separate idea that all life is related and describe some of the lines of evidence that make biologists regard this idea as overwhelmingly plausible.

NATURAL SELECTION

Here's a simple example of how natural selection works. Imagine a population of zebras that all have the same top speed. They can't run faster than 38 mph. Now imagine that a novelty appears in the population. A mutation occurs—a change in the genes found in some zebra—that allows that newfangled zebra to run faster—at 42 mph, say. Suppose running faster is advantageous, because a fast zebra is less likely to be caught and eaten by a predator than a slow one is. Running fast enhances the organism's *fitness*—its ability to survive and reproduce.

If running speed is passed on from parent to offspring, what will happen? What will occur (probably) is that the fast zebra will have more offspring than the average slow zebra. As a result, the percentage of fast zebras increases. In the next generation, fast zebras enjoy the same advantage, and so the characteristic of being fast will again increase in frequency. After a number of generations, we expect all the zebras to have this new characteristic. Initially, all the zebras ran at 38 mph. After the selection process runs its course, all run at 42 mph.

So the process comes in two stages. First, a novel mutation occurs, creating the variation upon which natural selection operates. Then, natural selection goes to work changing the composition of the population:

Start	*Then*	$\longrightarrow$	*Finish*
100% run at 38 mph.	A novel mutant runs at 42 mph; the rest run at 38 mph.		100% run at 42 mph.

We may summarize how this process works by saying that natural selection occurs in a population of organisms when there is *inherited variation in fitness*. Let's analyze what this means. The organisms must *vary;* if all the organisms are the same, then there will be no variants to select among. What is more, the variations must be passed down from parents to offspring. This is the requirement of *inheritance*. Lastly, it must be true that the varying characteristics in a population affect an organisms's *fitness*—its chance of surviving and reproducing. If these three conditions are met, the population will evolve. By this, I mean that the frequency of characteristics will change.

The idea of natural selection is really quite simple. What Darwin did was to show how this simple idea has many implications and applications. Merely stating this simple idea wouldn't have convinced anyone that natural selection is the right explanation of life's diversity. The power of the idea comes from the numerous detailed applications.

Notice that the introduction of novel characteristics into a population is a precondition for natural selection to occur. Darwin didn't have a very accurate picture of how novel traits arise. He theorized about this, but didn't come up with anything of lasting importance. Rather, it was later in the nineteenth century that Mendel started to fill in this detail. Genetic mutations, we now understand, are the source of the variation on which natural selection depends.

Notice that the little story I've told describes a rather modest change that occurs *within* a species of zebras. A single species of zebras goes from one running speed to another. Yet, Darwin's 1859 book was called *The Origin of Species*. How does change within a species help explain the coming into existence of new species—of *speciation*?

SPECIATION

Darwin's hypothesis was that small changes in a population (like the one I just described) add up. Given enough little changes, the organisms will become very different. Modern evolutionists usually tell a story like the following one. Think of a single population of zebras. Imagine a small number of zebras are separated from the rest of the population for some reason; maybe they wander off or a river changes course and splits the old population in two. If the resulting populations live in different environments, selection will lead them to become increasingly different. Characteristics that are advantageous in one population will not be advantageous in the other. After a long time, the populations will have diverged. They will have become so different from each other that individuals from the one can't breed with individuals from the other. Because of this, they will be two species, not two populations belonging to the same species.

Pretty much everybody in Darwin's day, including those who thought that God created each species separately, would have agreed that the little story about zebras evolving a greater speed could be true. The real resistance to Darwin's theory focused on his thesis that the mechanism responsible for small-scale changes *within* species also gives rise to large-scale changes, namely, to the origin of *new* species. This was a daring hypothesis, one that is now the mainstream view in evolutionary theory, though it is still somewhat controversial.

In saying that it is still somewhat controversial, I mean that there are evolutionists today who doubt that natural selection had the importance Darwin thought it did. They hold that other mechanisms play an important role in evolution. They grant that natural selection is part of the story, but deny it is the whole story. Deciding how important natural selection has been is a subject of continuing investigation in evolutionary theory.

Another kind of open question exists about natural selection. Even biologists who hold that natural selection is the major cause of evolution are sometimes puzzled about how it applies in particular cases. For example, it is still rather unclear why sexual reproduction evolved. Some creatures reproduce sexually, others asexually. Why is this? Even biologists who expect that the answer will be in terms of natural selection are puzzled.

So there are two sorts of open questions pertaining to natural selection. First, there is the issue of how important natural selection has been in the evolution of life. Second, there is the question of how the idea of natural selection should be applied to account for this or that characteristic. What I want to emphasize about both these questions is that they aren't questions about whether we are related to chimps. This isn't controversial. The questions I've mentioned so far have to do with the mechanism that accounts for *why* life evolved as it did, not *whether* it evolved.

THE TREE OF LIFE

I turn now to this uncontroversial idea. Why do biologists think it is so clear that living things are related to each other—that there is a family tree of terrestrial life just like there is a family tree of your family? Two kinds of evidence have seemed persuasive. I won't give the details here; rather, I want to describe the *kinds* of arguments biologists deploy. As a philosopher, I'm more interested that you grasp the logic of the arguments; for the biological details, you'll have to consult a biology book.

To illustrate how one line of argument works, consider this simple problem. Suppose I assign a philosophy class the job of writing an essay on the meaning of life. As I read through the papers, I notice that two students have handed in papers that are word-for-word identical. How should I explain this striking similarity?

One possibility, of course, is that the students worked independently and by coincidence arrived at exactly the same result. The independent origin of the two papers isn't impossible. But I would regard this hypothesis as extremely implausible. Far more convincing is the idea that one student copied from the other or that each of them copied from a common source—a paper downloaded from the Internet, perhaps. This hypothesis is a more plausible explanation of the observed similarity of the two papers.

THE PRINCIPLE OF THE COMMON CAUSE

The plagiarism example illustrates an idea that the philosopher Hans Reichenbach (in *The Direction of Time,* University of California Press, 1956) called the *Principle of the Common Cause.* Let's analyze the example more carefully to understand the rationale of the principle.

Why, in the case just described, is it more plausible that the students copied from a common source than that they wrote their papers independently? Consider how probable the matching of the two papers is, according to each of the two hypotheses. If the two students copied from a common source, then it is rather probable that the papers should closely resemble each other. If, however, the students worked independently, then it is enormously improbable that the two papers should be so similar. Here we have an application of the Surprise Principle, described in Lecture 3: If one hypothesis says that the observations are very probable whereas the other hypothesis says that the observations are very improbable, then the observations strongly favor the first hypothesis over the second. The Principle of the Common Cause makes sense because it is a consequence of the Surprise Principle.

The example just described involves hypotheses that describe mental activity—when students plagiarize they use their minds, and the same is true when they write papers independently. However, it is important to see that the Principle of the Common Cause also makes excellent sense when the hypotheses considered do not describe mental processes.

I have a barometer at my house. I notice that when it says "high," there usually is a storm the next day; and when it says "low," there usually is no storm the next day. The barometer reading on one day and the weather on the next are *correlated*. It may be that this correlation is just a coincidence; perhaps the two events are entirely independent. However, a far more plausible hypothesis is that the reading on one day and the weather on the next trace back to a common cause—namely, the weather at the time the reading is taken:

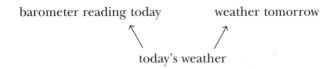

The common cause hypothesis is more plausible because it leads you to expect the correlation of the two observed effects. The separate cause hypothesis is less plausible because it says that the observed correlation is a very improbable coincidence. Notice that the hypotheses here considered do not describe the mental activities of agents.

ARBITRARY SIMILARITIES AMONG ORGANISMS

I'll now apply this principle to the evolutionary case. One reason biologists think all life is related is that all organisms (with some minor exceptions) use the same genetic code. To understand what this means, think of the genes in your body as a set of instructions for constructing more complex biological items—amino acids and then proteins, for example. The total sequence of genes in your body and the sequence in a frog's are different. The striking fact, however, is that the gene that codes for a given amino acid in a frog codes for that very same amino acid in people. As far as we now know, there is no reason why the genes that code for a given amino acid had to code for that acid rather than some other. The code is arbitrary; there is no functional reason why it has to be the way it is. [Don't be misled by my talk of codes here. This word may suggest intelligent design, but this isn't what biologists mean. Genes *cause* amino acids to form; for present purposes, this is a perfectly satisfactory way to understand what it means for genes to "code for" this or that amino acid.]

How are we to explain this intricate similarity among the genetic codes that different species use? If the species arose independently of each other, we would expect them to use different genetic codes. But if those species all trace back to a common ancestor, it is to be expected that they will share the same genetic code. The Principle of the Common Cause underlies the belief that evolutionary biologists have that all living things on earth have common ancestors.

IMPERFECT ADAPTATION

There is a second feature of life that lends plausibility to the hypothesis that different species have common ancestors. It is the fact that organisms are *not* perfectly adapted to their environments. When I described Paley's design argument in Lecture 5, I tried to convey the idea that Paley was very impressed by the perfection of nature. Paley thought this exquisite fittingness of organisms to the environments they inhabit can be explained only by the hypothesis of intelligent design. Since Darwin's time, however, biologists have looked more closely at this idea. What biology tells us is that organisms are *not* perfectly suited to their environments. They are suited in a passable, often makeshift, way. Adaptation is often imperfect; it is good enough so that species avoid extinction, at least in the short run.

Consider first an example that the biologist Stephen Jay Gould discusses in his book *The Panda's Thumb* (W.W. Norton, 1980). Pandas are vegetarians; bamboo shoots are pretty much the only thing they eat. A panda strips bamboo by running the branch between its paw and what seems to be a thumb. On closer examination, however, it is clear that this thumb isn't an opposable digit. Rather, the thumb is a spur of bone that sticks out from the panda's wrist.

This device for preparing bamboo is really quite clumsy. It would be no great challenge for a skillful engineer to design a better thumb for the panda to use. If God had made organisms perfectly adapted to their ways of life, it really would be quite puzzling why the panda is so ill-equipped. The hypothesis that pandas are closely related to carnivorous bears, however, allows us to understand why pandas have such an odd appliance attached to their wrists. There is a remarkable similarity between the paw structure of pandas and that of their nearest relatives. The panda's thumb is a modification of a structure that its ancestors possessed.

In short, the panda's thumb is puzzling if you subscribe to the hypothesis that God made each organism perfectly adapted to its environment. On the other hand, the hypothesis that pandas are descended from carnivorous bears makes it unsurprising that they have thumbs of the sort they do. The Surprise Principle says that the latter hypothesis is the more plausible one.

A creationist might concede that the panda's thumb is not an adaptation that exists to help individual pandas, but then suggest that the trait exists for the sake of maintaining the balance of nature. If pandas were more efficient at stripping bamboo, perhaps bamboo plants would go extinct and this would disrupt the stability of the whole ecosystem. Here the creationist is making a new suggestion, one that needs to be evaluated on its own terms. The suggestion is that an intelligent designer constructed ecosystems so that they would be stable.

To see how this idea runs into problems, we must shift to a new type of example. Biologists estimate that over 99% of the species that have ever existed are now extinct. Ecosystems are *not* terribly stable, in that there have been periodic mass extinctions that have wiped out wide swaths of the living world. Just as we find that individual organisms are not perfectly suited to the tasks of surviving and reproducing, we also find that ecosystems are far from perfectly suited to the tasks of remaining stable and persisting through time.

There is another pattern of argument that biologists use, one that resembles what they say about the panda's thumb. Biologists claim that *vestigial organs* are evidence that various species have a common ancestor. You may recall from high school biology that human embryos develop gill slits and then lose them. These gill slits, as far as scientists know, have no function; if each species were separately designed by a superintelligent designer who wanted organisms to be perfectly adapted, it would be very surprising to find gill slits in humans. However, if human beings are descended from ancestors who had gills as adults, the characteristic found in human embryos would be easier to understand. Natural selection modified the ancestral condition; human beings have gills only in the embryo stage, rather than in both the embryo and in the adult. A similar line of argument is used to explain why chicken embryos have teeth, which are resorbed into the gum before the chick is born.

I've mentioned two lines of evidence that lead biologists to think that all life is related. There is the fact of arbitrary similarity and the fact of imperfect adaptation. Both are evidence favoring the hypothesis that life evolved—that organisms alive today are descended from common ancestors and diverged from each other by the process of natural selection. These two types of evidence count against the idea that organisms originated independently as the result of a superintelligent designer's making each of them perfectly adapted.

NEARLY PERFECT ADAPTATION

I've emphasized the importance of *imperfect* adaptation as evidence for evolution. More nearly *perfect* adaptation provides evidence that is much less telling. For example, consider the fact that sharks and whales both have a streamlined body shape. Is this strong evidence that they have a common ancestor? I would say not. There is an obvious functional reason why creatures that spend their lives swimming through water should be shaped like this. If there is life in other galaxies and if some of that life is about as big as a whale or shark and also lives in water, we would probably expect it to have this sort of shape. Even if terrestrial life and life on other galaxies aren't descended from common ancestors, there are *some*

Humans from Nonhumans, Life from Nonlife

When people hear about the idea of evolution, there are two parts of the theory that sometimes strike them as puzzling. First, there is the idea that human beings are descended from apelike ancestors. Second, there is the idea that life evolved from nonliving materials.

Scientists believe the first of these statements because there are so many striking similarities between apes and human beings. This isn't to deny that there are differences. However, the similarities (of which a few examples are given in this lecture) would be expected if humans and apes have a common ancestor, but would be quite surprising if each species was separately created by a superintelligent designer.

There is a big difference between having evidence humans are descended from apelike ancestors and *having an explanation of precisely why this happened*. The evidence for there being a common ancestor is pretty overwhelming; but the details of why evolution proceeded in just the way it did are less certain. Students of human evolution continue to investigate why our species evolved as it did. In contrast, the claim that we did evolve isn't a matter of scientific debate.

What about the second idea—that life arose from nonlife? Why not maintain that God created the first living thing and then let evolution by natural selection produce the diversity we now observe? Notice that this is a very different idea from what creationists maintain. They hold that each species is the result of separate creation by God. They deny that present-day species are united by common descent from earlier life forms.

One main sort of evidence for thinking that life evolved from nonlife on Earth about four billion years ago comes from laboratory experiments. Scientists have created laboratory conditions that resemble the ones they believe were present shortly after the Earth came into existence about four and one-half billion years ago. They find that the nonliving ingredients present then can enter into chemical reactions, the products of which are simple organic materials.

For example, it is possible to run electricity (lightning) through a "soup" of inorganic molecules and produce amino acids. Why is this significant? Amino acids are an essential stage in the process whereby genes construct an organism. Similar experiments have generated a variety of promising results.

This subject in biology—*prebiotic evolution*—is very much open and incomplete. No one has yet been able to get inorganic materials to produce *DNA*. But the promising successes to date suggest that further work will further illuminate how life arose from nonlife.

Laboratory experiments don't aim to create a multicellular organism from inorganic materials. No one wants to make a chicken out of carbon, ammonia, and water. Evolution by natural selection proceeds by the accumulation of very small changes. So the transition from nonlife to life must involve the creation of a rather simple self-replicating molecule. Chickens came much later.

A self-replicating molecule is a molecule that makes copies of itself. A molecule of this sort is able to reproduce; with accurate replication, the offspring of a molecule will resemble its parent. Once a simple self-replicating molecule is in place, evolution by natural selection can begin.

It may sound strange to describe a simple self-replicating molecule as being "alive." Such a molecule will do few of the things that a chicken does. But from the biological point of view reproduction and heredity (that is, similarity between parents and offspring) are of the essence.

similarities we would expect to find nonetheless. I conclude that the streamlined shape of whales and sharks isn't strong evidence that they evolved from a common ancestor. The Surprise Principle explains why some similarities, but not others, are evidence for the hypothesis that there is a tree of life uniting all organisms on earth.

A NEW PROBLEM

My argument so far has focused on comparing the following two hypotheses:

H_1: Life evolved by the process of natural selection.

H_2: A superintelligent designer separately created each species and made each of them perfectly adapted to their environment.

My view is that the available observations favor the first hypothesis over the second.

There are, however, other hypotheses besides H_2 that might flesh out the idea that intelligent design is part of the explanation of some of the features that we observe in the living world. As mentioned earlier, creationism comes in many forms; H_2 is just one of them. Consider, for example, the following hypothesis:

H_3: God created each species separately, but endowed them with the very characteristics they would have had if they had evolved by natural selection.

H_3 is a wild card; although the observations I've mentioned strongly favor H_1 over H_2, they don't strongly favor H_1 over H_3. Nothing I have said shows that evolutionary theory is superior to the form of creationism just described.

PREDICTIVE EQUIVALENCE

Why is this? The reason is that H_1 and H_3 are *predictively equivalent*. If H_1 predicts that life will have a particular feature, so does H_3. Although arbitrary similarities and imperfect adaptations disconfirm H_2, they are perfectly consistent with H_3.

Does this mean the evolution hypothesis, H_1, isn't very well supported? I would say not. Consider the following pair of hypotheses:

J_1: You are now looking at a printed page.

J_2: You are now looking at a salami.

You have excellent evidence that J_1 is true and that J_2 is false. J_1 predicts that you are having particular sensory experiences; if J_1 is true, you should be having certain visual, tactile, and gustatory sensations (please take a bite of this page). J_2 makes quite different predictions about these matters. The sensory experiences you now are having strongly favor J_1 over J_2.

Now, however, let's introduce a wild card. What evidence do you have that J_1 *as opposed to J_3* is true:

J_3: There is no printed page in front of you, but someone is now systematically misleading you into thinking that there is a printed page in front of you.

J_1 and J_3 are predictively equivalent. The experiences you now are having tell you that J_1 is more plausible than J_2, but they don't strongly favor J_1 over J_3.

In the section of this book that focuses on Descartes's *Meditations* (Lecture 13), the problem of choosing between J_1 and J_3 will be examined in detail. For now, what I want you to see is this: When you ask whether some hypothesis (H_1 or J_1, for example) is strongly supported by the evidence, you must ask yourself what the alternatives are against which the hypothesis is to be compared. If you compare H_1 (or J_1) with H_2 (or J_2), you'll conclude that H_1 (or J_1) is extremely well supported. However, the problem takes on a quite different character if you compare H_1 with H_3 (or J_1 with J_3). This is a point that I discussed when the Surprise Principle was introduced in Lecture 3.

PALEY'S VERSION OF CREATIONISM

Where does Paley's version of the design hypothesis fit into our discussion of creationism? Well, Paley spends a lot of pages in his book *Natural Theology* celebrating what he thinks is the perfection of the adaptive contrivances found in nature. Paley describes what he takes to be nature's perfection in order to develop a more detailed picture of the characteristics that the intelligent designer possesses. For example, Paley thinks that organisms are by-and-large *happy;* he thinks this shows that God is *benevolent.* However, Paley's discussion of adaptive perfection comes *after* he presents his argument that an intelligent designer exists. Paley is very careful to separate his initial argument that God exists from his subsequent arguments that attempt to ascertain God's characteristics. And when we attend to Paley's argument for God's existence, we find that Paley says quite clearly that his argument does *not* depend on our observing that adaptations are perfect. Even if the watch we found on the beach kept time *im*perfectly, we'd still conclude that it was produced by intelligent design. Paley concludes, by the same reasoning, that the design hypothesis is overwhelmingly plausible even if we find that organisms are *not* perfectly adapted to their environments.

We therefore have to conclude that H_2 is not the best way to represent the version of creationism that Paley wanted to defend. The problem is not that H_2 misrepresents what Paley believed. Rather, the problem is that Paley's argument for the existence of an intelligent designer considers a version of creationism that does not predict whether organisms will be perfectly or imperfectly adapted. Thus, the fact that H_1 is better supported than H_2 does not settle whether H_1 is better supported than the bare hypothesis that life has properties that are due to intelligent design. Let us call this stripped-down and minimalistic hypothesis H_4.

The versions of creationism I have labeled H_2 and H_3 do make predictions about what we observe. This is why we were able to compare those predictions with the ones that are generated by evolutionary theory. However, what does H_4 predict about the characteristics of living things? The problem is that H_4 appears to be *untestable.* It cannot be said that evolutionary theory is better supported by the observations than H_4 is; the reason is that it is impossible to evaluate what H_4 tells us to expect when we look at organisms. We will return to the concept of testability in Lecture 9.

CONCLUDING REMARKS

Creationism comes in many forms. Some of them make very definite predictions about what we observe. The version that says that God made organisms so that they are perfectly adapted to their environments makes predictions that do not accord with what we observe. The version that says that God made organisms to look exactly as they would if they had evolved by the mindless process of natural selection makes the same predictions that evolutionary theory makes, and so our observations do not allow us to discriminate between evolutionary theory and this "mimicking" version of creationism. Finally, the bare, minimalistic version of creationism that says that God had some (unspecified) impact on the traits of living things is, I suggest, untestable. We have not found a version of creationism that makes definite predictions about what we observe *and* which is better supported by the observations than evolutionary theory is. Is there a version of creationism that has these two characteristics?

Review Questions

1. What are the two main elements of Darwin's theory?
2. Describe what the Principle of the Common Cause says. How is this principle related to the Surprise Principle? How is it used by biologists to decide whether different species have a common ancestor?
3. The geneticist François Jacob said (in "Evolution and Tinkering," *Science*, Vol. 196, 1977, pp. 1161–1166) that "natural selection does not work as an engineer works. It works like a tinkerer—a tinkerer who does not know exactly what he is going to produce but uses whatever he finds around him." What does Jacob mean here? How is this point relevant to evaluating whether the hypothesis of evolution or the hypothesis of intelligent design is a more plausible explanation of the characteristics of living things?
4. What does it mean to say that two theories are predictively equivalent? Can the Design Hypothesis be formulated so that the existence of imperfect adaptations isn't evidence against it?

Problems for Further Thought

1. Louis Pasteur (1822–1895) developed scientific evidence against the hypothesis of "spontaneous generation." For example, he argued that maggots developing on rotten meat aren't the result of life springing spontaneously from nonliving materials; the maggots were hatched from eggs laid there by their parents. Does Pasteur's discovery mean life couldn't have evolved from nonliving materials?

2. Suppose you are a crew member on the Star Ship Enterprise, bound for a new planet. You know there is intelligent life there; the question you want to answer is whether these life forms have ever had any contact with Earth. Which sorts of observations would be relevant and which irrelevant to this question? Defend your interpretation. How is this problem related to the Principle of the Common Cause?

LECTURE 7

Can Science Explain Everything?

In the previous lecture, we failed to identify a version of the design hypothesis that does a better job than evolutionary theory of accounting for the observed features of living things. It is a further question whether there are versions of creationism that do better than the versions I described. If there are not, then creationism should be discarded as an explanation of the characteristics that organisms possess. But this result would not show that the design hypothesis has no role to play at all. Perhaps there are other features of the universe, distinct from the ones discussed in biology, that we should explain by postulating the existence of an intelligent designer.

Here is another way to pose this problem: A naturalistic explanation seeks to explain features of the world by describing the natural processes that produced them. A supernaturalistic explanation, on the other hand, attempts to explain features of the world by describing the supernatural processes (the processes that occur outside of nature) that produced them. Is there reason to think that every feature of the

---

"But How Do You Explain God?"

Sometimes people object to the suggestion that the existence of God is the explanation of a fact by asking: "But how do you explain the existence of God?" The implications behind this question is that it isn't plausible to say that God explains something unless you are able to explain why God exists.

This criticism of abductive arguments for the existence of God isn't a good one. Mendel was quite right to think that the existence of genes explains something. However, Mendel had no idea how to explain the fact that genes exist. For hundreds of years before Newton's time, mariners had good evidence that the tides are correlated with the phases of the Moon, even though they had no very plausible explanation for why this should be so. And as noted in the previous lecture, evolutionists have excellent evidence that human beings are descended from apelike ancestors, even though the explanation of this evolutionary event is still somewhat unclear.

So if abductive arguments for the existence of God are defective, this isn't because no one knows how to explain why God exists.

world has a naturalistic explanation? If so, the hypothesis of a supernatural God isn't needed to explain anything.

The question I want to explore in this lecture is this: Should we expect that science will sooner or later do for every fact about the world what I think Darwin did for the intricacy and adaptedness of organisms? That is, will science sooner or later be able to explain everything and do this without postulating the existence of God?

SCIENTIFIC IGNORANCE

It is easy to find facts about the world that science can't explain now. Every scientific discipline has its open questions. These are the things that keep scientists busy. Scientists don't spend their time repeating to each other things everybody already knows; rather, they devote their energies to trying to puzzle out answers to heretofore unanswered questions.

Because there are plenty of facts about the world that science can't now explain, it is easy to construct a particular kind of abductive argument for the existence of God. I mentioned in the previous lecture that evolutionary theory is currently unable to explain why some species reproduce sexually while others don't.

Consider the following theological explanation for this puzzling fact: There is a God, and God decided to make organisms reproduce in precisely the way they do. Whereas evolutionists can't (now) explain patterns of reproduction, a theologian can do this just by saying, "It was God's will."

I doubt that any scientist would argue that patterns of reproduction will never be explained scientifically. To be sure, evolutionists cannot *now* explain certain facts about sex. But science isn't over yet; it is reasonable to suspect that this example of scientific ignorance is only temporary.

THE ONLY GAME IN TOWN FALLACY

What should we say *now*? Apparently, we can accept the theological explanation sketched above, or have no explanation at all for why some species, but not others, reproduce sexually. I think it is clear that we aren't obliged to accept the theological explanation. To think we are required to accept the theological explanation just because it is the only one on the table is to commit the Only Game in Town Fallacy.

Recall the anecdote from Lecture 3. If you and I are sitting in a cabin and hear noises in the attic, it is easy to formulate an explanation of those noises. I suggest the noises are due to gremlins bowling. This hypothesis has the property that if it were true, it would explain why we heard the noises. But this fact about the gremlin hypothesis doesn't mean that the hypothesis is plausible.

Instead of accepting a theological explanation of why organisms reproduce as they do, we should consider the option of simply admitting that we at present don't understand. If my prediction about the future of evolutionary theory is correct, we eventually will have a satisfactory scientific explanation. We just have to be patient.

I now want to consider a very different kind of scientific ignorance. Suppose there are facts about the world that science *in principle* can't explain. It isn't a temporary gap, but a permanent one, I'm now considering. If there are such facts, then the choice won't be between a theological explanation and a naturalistic explanation that science will eventually produce; the choice will be between a theological explanation and no explanation at all—not now or in the future.

THE TWO QUESTIONS

There are two questions I want to consider: (1) Are there any facts about the world that science is inherently incapable of explaining? (2) If there are, can we plausibly argue that the best explanation of why those facts are true is that God exists?

To answer the first of these questions, I'll sketch a picture of how scientific explanation works. I then will argue that this view of scientific explanation implies there are certain facts about the world that science can't explain. It isn't just that scientists haven't worked out the explanation *yet;* the point is that the nature of scientific explanation precludes their ever doing so.

WHAT IS A SCIENTIFIC EXPLANATION?

There are two kinds of things science aims to explain. It aims to explain particular *events* and it aims to explain *generalizations*. An example of the first type of problem would be the astronomer's question, "Why did the solar system come into existence?" An example of the second type would be the chemist's question, "Why does it take two atoms of hydrogen and one of oxygen for hydrogen and oxygen to combine to form a molecule of water?"

Don't confuse these two explanatory projects. Generalizations are true or false. Events aren't true or false; they happen or fail to happen. An event happens at a certain place and time. True generalizations, however, describe what is true of *all* places and times. I want to focus here on what scientists do when they explain *events*.

My thesis is that science explains an event by describing its causes. I'll assume further (although this isn't strictly necessary for what I want to conclude) that a cause has to precede its effects. So the causal explanation of an event E_1 that happens now is provided by citing one or more events in the past and showing how those events produced E_1.

Suppose we show that E_1 was caused by E_2. We then might be interested in explaining why E_2 occurred. This might lead us to describe a still earlier event, E_3. And so on. This project leads us to describe causal chains, which trace back into the past.

Aquinas (Lecture 4) believed causal chains extending back into the past can have only finitely many links. I'll make no assumption about this.

So far, I've described two relationships that can obtain between events: (1) some events precede others in time; (2) some events cause others. There is a third relationship. Some events are *parts* of other events. Consider the relationship between the storming of the Bastille and the French Revolution. The storming of the Bastille marked the beginning of the French Revolution. Both of these are events; the first is *part* of the second.

I want to focus on what science does when it tries to explain a spatiotemporal event. By "spatiotemporal," I simply mean that the event in question happened at some place and at some time. Of course, lots of events are "spread out." They don't occur in an instant, but take some length of time to occur. And they take place in a volume of space, not at a single spatial point. For example, the French Revolution lasted about 10 years and it took place in France.

A THESIS ABOUT EXPLANATION

My thesis is this: For science to be able to say why a spatiotemporal event E occurred, there must be events in space and time that aren't included in E. I assume that no event explains itself. So if science is to explain E, there must be some event outside of E (but still inside of space and time) that can be cited as the explanation.

It follows from this thesis that answerable why-questions about spatiotemporal events must focus on *part* of what happens in the history of the spatiotemporal universe. Why-questions can't be answered if they ask why the *whole history* of the spatio-temporal universe was as it was.

Consider an exhaustive description of the past, present, and future of what happens in space and time:

$$\ldots \longrightarrow E_3 \longrightarrow E_2 \longrightarrow E_1 \longrightarrow \ldots$$

Past   Present   Future

E_1 is explicable, because there is something besides E_1 in the world that can be cited to do the explaining. And if E_1 is part of some bigger event (the way the storming of the Bastille is part of the French Revolution), then that more inclusive event will be explicable only if there is something outside of it that we can cite by way of explanation.

Such answerable why-questions about events I'll call local why-questions. They focus on part of what has happened in the world's history. In contrast to them are *global* questions—questions that ask for an explanation of the totality of what has happened in the whole universe's history. I claim science can't answer global why-questions.

WHY IS THERE SOMETHING RATHER THAN NOTHING?

Here's an example of a global why-question: *Why is there something rather than nothing?* This question doesn't ask why there is something *now*. That, of course, is a local question, which can be answered by saying that the universe was nonempty in the past, and then perhaps citing a conservation law (as Aquinas did—see Lecture 4) that says that if the world is nonempty at one time, it is nonempty forever after. What I have in mind here is the question of why the universe *ever* contained anything. That is, why wasn't the universe entirely devoid of material objects throughout its history?

The spatiotemporal universe is the totality of everything that was, is, or will be, anywhere. There is nothing impossible about a universe that contains no material objects. Obviously, the actual world isn't this way. The actual world (the one we inhabit) corresponds to one total history. An empty universe corresponds to a different total history. Both of these totalities are possible, but only one is actual. The question of why there is something rather than nothing asks why the first of these possible worlds, rather than the second, is actual. My claim is that science can't answer this question.

CAN PHYSICS EXPLAIN THE ORIGIN OF THE UNIVERSE?

Don't be misled by the fact that physicists talk about explaining the "origin of the universe." This makes it sound like they are explaining why the universe is nonempty. My view is that they are doing no such thing. Rather, they are addressing a rather different question. The Big Bang Theory doesn't show why the universe, in my sense of the word, came into existence. The universe, according to the way I'm using the term, includes *everything* that there ever was, is, or will be. If the Big Bang produced the world we now inhabit, then the universe includes two stages: First, there was a Big Bang, and then there was the world we now inhabit. The Big Bang doesn't explain why the universe exists; the Big Bang is *part* of the universe. The scientific question addressed by physicists is local, not global.

So the question "Why this totality, rather than that one?" isn't scientifically answerable, because it is global. Can a theological answer be provided? Let's imagine that God isn't a material object; he (or she or it) is outside the totality I'm calling "the universe." Can we explain why the material universe is nonempty by saying that God decided to make one totality actual rather than another?

LEIBNIZ: GOD CHOOSES WHICH POSSIBLE WORLD TO ACTUALIZE

The seventeenth-century philosopher/scientist Gottfried Leibniz (1646–1716) thought this form of explanation is plausible. He said that God considered the set of all possible worlds and decided to make one of them actual. He did this by finding which world is best. This is why we live in the best of all possible worlds. If you think the world we inhabit is morally imperfect, you may doubt Leibniz's story. In Lecture 11, I'll consider this issue when I take up the problem of evil.

Leibniz had another kind of perfection in mind, in addition to moral perfection. Leibniz thought this is the best of all possible worlds in the sense that this world has the maximum diversity of phenomena and the maximum simplicity of laws. Scientific laws are simple, but the kinds of events that happen in our world are enormously rich. This joint property of our world is what makes it perfect in this nonmoral sense.

I won't discuss the details of Leibniz's theory. My point is that he proposed a theological explanation for why there is something rather than nothing in the world of space and time. This fact about the world, being global, can't be scientifically explained. The question I want to pose is this: If a fact can be explained by the hypothesis that there is a God, but can't be explained scientifically, is this a good enough reason to conclude there is a God?

CLARKE: GOD EXPLAINS WHY THE ACTUAL WORLD CONSISTS OF ONE TOTAL HISTORY RATHER THAN ANOTHER

Another anticipation of the argument for the existence of God we are considering is due to the British philosopher Samuel Clarke (1675–1729). Clarke thought he saw a way to improve an argument that Aquinas proposed. As noted in Lecture 4, Aquinas's second argument for the existence of God depends on the universe's being finitely old. Clarke's argument, presented in his 1705 book *A Demonstration of the Being and Attributes of God,* does not depend on that assumption. He asks us to consider the entire totality of events that occur in the world of space and time. Why did this history occur rather than some other? Clarke says that there are two possibilities: The entire history occurred for no reason at all, or it was brought into existence by a being who exists outside of space and time, namely God. Clarke rejected the first suggestion as patently absurd; there *must* be a reason why the world is comprised of one total history rather than another. That reason is God.

If science is incapable of explaining why the world of space and time includes one total history rather than another, should we accept the claim that God exists because this hypothesis, if true, would explain this global fact? In similar fashion, should we accept the claim that God exists because it is able to explain why there is something rather than nothing (a fact that science is unable to explain)?

THE ONLY GAME IN TOWN FALLACY, AGAIN

I think the answer to these questions is *no*. Once again, the Only Game in Town Fallacy needs to be considered. There is a second option besides accepting the only explanation available. This is to admit that there are things about the universe we don't understand *and never will*. Why there is something rather than nothing may be inherently inexplicable; the same may be true of the question of why the world contains one total set of events rather than another.

I grant that *if* (1) there were an all-powerful God who exists outside of space and time and *if* (2) a God outside of the material world could nonetheless create a material world and *if* (3) God wanted to make the world nonempty, then this would explain why there is something rather than nothing in the spatiotemporal universe. These suppositions would explain the fact in question. But that doesn't show that this explanatory story is at all plausible.

CAUSALITY

To see what is problematic about this suggested explanation, consider the causal relationship it says exists between God and the totality of the material universe. God is outside of space and time, but nonetheless manages to bring the whole material world into existence. This causal relationship is extremely hard to understand.

Think of the kinds of causal relationships we discuss in science and in everyday life. For example, we say that throwing the rock at the window caused the window to break. Here a causal relationship is said to obtain between two events, each of which occurred at a particular place and at a particular time. This is characteristic of well-understood claims about causality; *causation is a relationship that obtains between events that occur within space and time.* This is why it is so puzzling to say that a God outside of space and time causes the world of space and time to come into being.

I think it is misleading to use the statement "God did it" as a substitute for the statement "I really can't explain why this or that fact is true." The first statement advances an explanation, while the second admits to not having one. If the existence of God is to explain something, it must have more going for it than the fact that the observation under consideration is otherwise inexplicable.

I said before that evolutionary theory cannot now explain why some species reproduce sexually while others don't. This doesn't mean evolutionists can't make vague pronouncements like "The pattern is due to natural selection." This vague remark is available to anyone who wants to make it. No scientist, however, would regard this single sentence as a satisfying explanation. The question—the main question—would be *how* natural selection managed to produce the results it did. What made sexual reproduction advantageous in some species and asexual reproduction advantageous in others? It is this more detailed question that, to date, hasn't been answered satisfactorily.

There is an analogy here with the theological case. The theologian can say "God did it." The evolutionist can say "Natural selection did it." A scientist would regard the latter explanation as unsatisfying, because it is too short on details. Why should the theological explanation be taken any more seriously? Part of what is missing in the theological story is any indication of *how* or *why* God did what he did.

This may help explain why the theological explanation of patterns of reproduction shouldn't be embraced. A theological explanation so short on details leaves too many questions unanswered to be convincing. In this circumstance, perhaps it is more plausible to admit we don't understand than to pretend "God did it" gives us much by way of understanding.

A similar diagnosis can be offered of why the theological explanation of why there is something rather than nothing is so unsatisfying. To say "God did it" is to leave too much unexplained. How is it possible for something outside of space and time to cause the entire spatiotemporal universe to come into being? Why should God have preferred to actualize this possible world rather than any of the others? To the degree that we don't understand these matters, we should conclude that the theological explanation is really not much of an explanation at all.

My conclusion is that science may not be able to explain everything. There are facts now known to be true that science hasn't been able to account for. And even if science progresses, as I expect it to do, there will remain facts that are intrinsically resistant to scientific treatment. Not only has science not explained them yet; it never will, because it can't. Of course, we should be open to the possibility that explanations from outside of science may have some plausibility. My point here is that bringing in the existence of God is often to trade one mystery for another, with no net gain in our understanding.

Review Questions

1. What is the difference between a global why-question and a local why-question?
2. Can science answer global why-questions? Why or why not?
3. Is it possible to have evidence that something exists without having an explanation for why the thing exists?
4. Consider the following argument: "If science can't explain some fact, but a theological story, if true, would explain that fact, then the fact is strong abductive evidence that the theological story is true." How is the Only Game in Town Fallacy relevant to assessing this argument?
5. What does it mean to say that causation is a relationship that obtains between events in space and time? If this were a correct claim about causation, what implications would it have for the idea that God explains the sorts of global facts discussed in this lecture?

Problems for Further Thought

1. Philosophers sometimes use the term *brute fact* to describe a fact that is so simple and obvious that it can't be justified or explained by appeal to any other fact. Consider the relationship between x and y described in the statement "$x = y$." This is the relationship of *identity*. This is a relationship that everything bears to itself; "the Eiffel Tower = the Eiffel Tower" is true, but "the Eiffel Tower = the Statue of Liberty" is false. What explains the fact that everything is self-identical? Is this true because of the way we use the identity sign "="? Is it a brute fact?
2. In this lecture, I claimed that nothing explains itself. In everyday speech, however, we talk about something's being "self-explanatory." What does this mean? Is there a conflict between what I've said about explanation and the everyday idea? We also use the term "self-starter" to describe some people. Does this conflict with the idea that nothing causes itself?
3. Blaise Pascal, a seventeenth-century philosopher whom I'll discuss in Lecture 10, once said, "The truth of religion lies in its very obscurity." What does this mean, and is it true?

LECTURE 8

The Ontological Argument

The various arguments I've considered so far for the existence of God include premisses we know to be true by experience. By using our senses (of sight, hearing, touch, etc.), we know that objects are in motion and that organisms are intricate and adapted. What is more, there is no other way to know these things; sensory experience is indispensable. Such propositions are called *a posteriori*. Notice the prefix *post*, meaning "after." An a posteriori truth is one that requires experience to be known (or justified). Accordingly, the arguments for the existence of God considered thus far are called *a posteriori* arguments.

A POSTERIORI AND A PRIORI

Are all propositions a posteriori? Many philosophers have thought there are propositions that can be known to be true by reason alone. These propositions are termed *a priori*. Note the word "prior"; such propositions are knowable prior to, or independently of, experience. Standard examples are mathematical truths and definitions. We can know that $7 + 3 = 10$ and that bachelors are unmarried merely by thinking about the concepts involved. You don't have to do experiments or conduct surveys to find out whether such statements are true. Reason suffices.

Let's be clear on what it means to claim that a given proposition is a priori. To say that we know a priori that bachelors are unmarried doesn't mean we were born with the concepts of bachelorhood and marriage. For a proposition to be a priori, it isn't essential that the concepts contained in the proposition be *innate*. Maybe none of us is born with the concept of a bachelor; maybe we must have various experiences to acquire that concept. Even if the concepts were acquired through experience, however, that wouldn't show the proposition fails to be a priori. To say that a proposition is a priori true means that *IF* you understand the concepts involved, then reason will suffice for you to decide that the proposition is true. Don't forget the *IF* in this idea. The idea that there is a priori knowledge doesn't require that there be innate concepts.

The Ontological Argument for the existence of God is an a priori argument. It aims to establish the truth of theism without reliance on any a posteriori premiss. In particular, the idea is that we can prove that God must exist simply by examining the definition of the concept of God.

DEFINITIONS AND EXISTENCE

This should strike you as a very surprising thing to try to do. Consider other definitions. For example, a bachelor is by definition an adult unmarried male. The thing to notice about this definition is that it doesn't imply there are any bachelors. If you think about it, this seems to be true of most definitions. You can define what it is to be a unicorn or a golden mountain, but the definitions won't settle whether there are such things.

When we consider concepts like *bachelor, unicorn,* or *golden mountain,* the definitions specify what it would take to be an individual of the kind in question; the definitions don't say whether there are zero, one, or many things of that kind. The Ontological Argument claims the concept of God is different: From the definition of the concept of God, the existence of God is supposed to follow.

So the proposition that bachelors are unmarried is a priori, whereas the proposition that bachelors exist is a posteriori. The definition doesn't imply the existence claim. Are there any nontheistic examples of existence claims that can be known a priori? Perhaps existence claims in mathematics furnish examples. If mathematics is a priori, then mathematical existence claims are a priori. So it is an a priori truth that there exists a prime number between 12 and 14.

It is philosophically debatable whether there are any a priori truths at all. I won't discuss that issue here, however, but will go along with the idea that mathematical truths are a priori. This means that since mathematics contains existence claims, there are (I'll assume) at least some existence statements that are a priori true. It follows that if there is a mistake in the Ontological Argument for the existence of God, it isn't to be found in the fact that it says that some existence claims are a priori true.

ANSELM'S ARGUMENT

The Ontological Argument was formulated by Saint Anselm (1033–1109), who became archbishop of Canterbury. Aquinas, who lived in the thirteenth century, rejected this argument and recommended in its stead the five a posteriori arguments we examined in Lectures 4 and 5. Philosophers down to the present have discussed the Ontological Argument and have constructed different versions of it. Here I'll consider a simplified formulation of the argument:

(O) (1) God is by definition the greatest being possible.

   (2) A being who fails to exist in the actual world (while existing in other possible worlds) is less perfect than a being who exists in all possible worlds.

   ―――――――

   Hence, God exists, necessarily.

I label the argument "O" for future reference.

Premiss (1): Conceivability and Possibility

Premiss (1) is intended to capture what Anselm meant by saying that God is a being "than which none greater can be conceived." It isn't just that God is the most perfect being that happens to exist in the actual world. The actual world, after all, might contain only grossly imperfect beings, so that God's being the best of these wouldn't mean he is *all*-powerful, *all*-knowing, and *all*-good. The idea is that God is a being who is the best possible being. There is no more perfect being in any possible world. (If you're a bit vague on the idea of a "possible world," go back to Lecture 4 and review.)

Although I gloss Anselm's first premiss by saying that God is the best possible being, I want to note an important difference between possibility and conceivability. What is possible is an objective question; it doesn't depend on what people know or believe. Whether we can conceive of something, however, is a fact about us as knowing subjects. Hence, conceivability is a subjective notion. (This should remind you of the point made in Lecture 4 that necessity and certainty are different.)

What can be conceived of may vary from individual to individual. We can conceive of things that dogs can't conceive of; and perhaps there are superintelligent beings elsewhere in the universe who can conceive of things that are beyond our grasp. In contrast, there is a sense of the term *possible,* which I'm using here, according to which what is possible doesn't vary from one thinker to another.

It is impossible, according to Einstein's special theory of relativity, for an object that has positive mass to go faster than the speed of light. This simply can't be done, no matter how powerful a rocket ship you build. Yet, I think this is something we can conceive of; we can describe what it would mean to go faster than the speed of light.

Newton thought that travel faster than the speed of light was possible. He not only could conceive of what this would be, he thought it was possible. But we now view Newton as mistaken. It isn't possible to do this, and it never has been. For something to be possible, it isn't enough that you can conceive of its happening or that you can't see any reason why it couldn't happen.

If the human mind is limited in various ways, then maybe the most perfect being we can conceive of is still grossly imperfect in many ways. Maybe an ant can't conceive of a creature greater than an anteater, but that doesn't mean anteaters are the most perfect possible beings. Anselm, though he used the word "conceivable," really meant possible, I think. God isn't just the best being we frail human beings can conceptualize; God is supposed to be the best possible being.

Premiss (2): Necessary Existence Is a Perfection

If a being exists in all possible worlds, it is a necessary being, not a contingent one. Why does Anselm think God's perfection demands that God be a necessary being? A contingent thing depends for its existence on other things. You and I are contingent things; we exist only because certain other contingent beings acted as they did. But a truly perfect being, Anselm thinks, wouldn't depend for its existence on anything contingent. It would exist unconditionally. According to Anselm's second premiss, a necessary being is more perfect than a contingent one. So if God has all the perfections, he must be a necessary being, not a contingent one.

The Ontological Argument *looks* like it is deductively valid: If God has all the perfections and if necessary existence is a perfection, then God exists necessarily. But

A Priori/A Posteriori and Necessity/Contingency

In Lecture 4, the ideas of necessity and contingency were introduced. A possible world, roughly, is a way the world might be. A necessary truth is a proposition that is true in all possible worlds; a contingent truth is a proposition that is true in the actual world, but not in all possible worlds.

In this lecture, the ideas of *a priori* and *a posteriori* propositions were introduced. An a priori proposition can be known (or justified) independent of experience. How is the distinction between necessary and contingent propositions related to the distinction between a priori and a posteriori propositions?

This is a deep, controversial, and fundamental philosophical question. Some philosophers hold that the two distinctions divide up the propositions in exactly the same way. That is, they hold that all necessary propositions are a priori and that all contingent propositions are a posteriori. According to this theory, all the propositions that natural science discovers by observation are contingent.

Some of the discussion in previous lectures has assumed that this theory is false. I've suggested that empirical science (that is, science that relies on observation) is able to discover what is really possible. In Lecture 4, I mentioned some examples. I said that thermodynamics has discovered that perpetual motion machines are impossible (that is, it is a necessary truth that there are no perpetual motion machines); I also stated that Einstein's theories of relativity say that no particle (with positive rest mass) can go faster than the speed of light (that is, that objects with positive rest mass necessarily go slower than the speed of light).

In other words, I've suggested that some a posteriori propositions are necessary, even though other a posteriori propositions are contingent.

What about a priori propositions? The examples discussed so far of a priori propositions (like "bachelors are unmarried" and "2 + 3 = 5") are all cases of necessary truths. So the question remains: Are there any a priori propositions that are contingent?

The examples I'll give provide a preview of material that will be discussed in Lecture 13. Consider the proposition each of us formulates when we say to ourselves "I exist." You know this proposition to be true without using sight, hearing, taste, touch, or smell. Thought alone allows you to see that it is true. So it is a priori. The same seems to be true for the proposition you formulate by saying to yourself "I am thinking."

Yet, it isn't a necessary truth that you exist. You might have failed to do so. If this line of thinking is right, we may conclude that the proposition each of us considers when we say to ourselves "I exist" or "I am thinking" is a priori and contingent.

Fill in the following table with examples of the four types of propositions indicated:

	Necessary	Contingent
A priori		
A posteriori		

from Anselm's time down to the present, there have been doubters. Many philosophers (both theists and atheists) have thought that the Ontological Argument must involve a mistake.

GAUNILO'S CRITICISM

Anselm describes a criticism formulated by his contemporary, Gaunilo. Gaunilo says the argument must be defective, since if it weren't, you could prove the existence of a perfect island by a similar a priori argument. What did Gaunilo have in mind?

Let's start with the concept of an island. The first point is that the concept of islandhood resembles the concept of bachelorhood. Its definition doesn't deductively imply that there are any objects of the kind defined. So any attempt to provide an a priori proof that islands exist must fail.

Now let's define a new concept: Call it a *P*-island. A *P*-island is an island than which none greater can be conceived. *P*-islands are just like islands, except they are, by definition, maximally perfect. Gaunilo thought there can be no a priori demonstration that there are *P*-islands. Perhaps no such thing exists; and if there happen to be *P*-islands, this isn't something that could be discovered by reason alone.

Consider, however, the following argument, which mimics the structure of the Ontological Argument:

(I) (1) A *P*-island is by definition the greatest possible island.

(2) An island that fails to exist in the actual world (while existing in other possible worlds) is less perfect than an island that exists in all possible worlds.

Hence, a *P*-island exists necessarily.

I label this argument "I" for future reference.

Gaunilo's conclusion wasn't that there are *P*-islands (as well as *P*-bagels, *P*-comedians, and so on). Rather, he thought this argument about islands must be defective. It seems crazy to think the existence of a perfect island could be proved a priori. Gaunilo concluded that Anselm's argument must have a mistake in it as well.

What sort of mistake did Gaunilo think these two arguments commit? He believed that the two premises of the Island Argument are true. But Gaunilo holds that these premises don't deductively imply the conclusion; the existence of a perfect island doesn't follow from these a priori premises. Gaunilo concludes that the Island Argument (I) is invalid. He alleges that the same is true of the Ontological Argument (O).

How Are the Ontological Argument and the Island Argument Related?

Notice that Gaunilo's argument was obtained from Anselm's by substituting "*P*-island" for "God," and "island" for "being." We saw in Lecture 2 that the validity of an argument depends on its form, not on its subject matter. Gaunilo was suggesting that since his Island Argument is invalid, so too is Anselm's argument about God. Gaunilo thought the Island-Conclusion doesn't follow from the Island-Premisses. By parity of reasoning, he claims Anselm's conclusion doesn't follow from Anselm's premisses.

Gaunilo is making an argument about these two arguments. In particular, he attempts to show Anselm's argument is invalid by reductio (see Lecture 4 for this piece of terminology). Gaunilo argues as follows:

> If the Ontological Argument is deductively valid, then the Island Argument is deductively valid.
>
> The Island Argument is not deductively valid.
> _____
>
> The Ontological Argument is not deductively valid.

ANSELM'S REPLY

Anselm scornfully replies to this criticism. He says that his argument applies to God—the greatest possible being. It doesn't apply to a *P*-island—the greatest possible island.

Anselm's brief reply to Gaunilo is, to my mind, incomplete, at best. The same may be said of Gaunilo's criticism. Gaunilo's reductio argument, if it worked, would show that there has to be a mistake somewhere in Anselm's reasoning, but Gaunilo doesn't show exactly where the mistake occurs. As noted before, Anselm's argument *looks* valid; if it isn't, we would like to see exactly where it goes wrong. In the same way, Anselm's reply doesn't show where Gaunilo has gone wrong; Anselm just asserts the Island Argument is in some unspecified way not relevant.

Let's press Anselm for details. Could Anselm mean that the Ontological Argument is deductively valid, even though the Island Argument isn't? This seems implausible, since deductive validity doesn't depend on an argument's subject matter, only on its form, and the two arguments seem to have the same logical form.

Another possibility would be that Anselm is claiming the premisses of the Island Argument are implausible, though the premisses of the Ontological Argument are quite plausible. If Anselm were right about this, the arguments would be disanalogous. But the first premiss of the Ontological Argument and the first premiss of the Island Argument seem to be on a par. Anselm holds that his own definition of God is correct; it is hard to see how Gaunilo's definition of a *P*-island could be mistaken.

What about the second premisses of the two arguments? If necessary existence is a perfection for beings in general, why isn't it a perfection for islands in particular? I feel a little shaky about my ability to make such judgments about "perfection," but I don't see why the second premiss of the Ontological Argument should be accepted and the second premiss of the Island Argument rejected. I conclude that the two arguments are fully parallel, contrary to what Anselm says in reply to Gaunilo. Gaunilo, I think, is on to something.

KANT: "EXISTENCE IS NOT A PROPERTY OF EXISTING THINGS"

Centuries after the Ontological Argument was first presented, Immanuel Kant (1724–1804) suggested that the argument makes the mistake of assuming existence is a property. Anselm defines God as a being with all possible perfections. This means that for any property *C*, if *C* is a perfection, then God has *C*. Anselm then treats existence (or necessary existence) as a property and proceeds to conclude that God has that property. So Kant is right to say that Anselm treats existence as a property of existing things. But why should this be a mistake?

When we say that tigers are fierce, we are predicating a property of tigers—namely, the property of fierceness. But when we say that tigers exist, Kant thought we aren't attributing the property of existence to those things. Rather, we are saying something about the concept of tigerhood. To say that tigers exist is to say that the concept of tigerhood is instantiated (that is, that the concept is exemplified by one or more things in the actual world). The proposition that tigers are fierce is about tigers, which are flesh-and-blood felines. But the proposition that tigers exist is about a concept; it isn't about flesh-and-blood felines at all.

So Kant's claim is that Anselm made the mistake of treating existence as a property of existing things. I find this criticism inconclusive. I don't see why existence isn't a property of existing things. Granted, it may sound funny to talk about a property that everything under the sun possesses; most properties apply to some things but not to others. And maybe it is true that "Tigers exist" can be paraphrased as "The concept of tigerhood is exemplified." However, these facts don't show that existence isn't a property of existing things.

DISPENSING WITH PERFECTION

Anselm's argument (O) makes use of the idea that God is perfect. Gaunilo's parody of Anselm—Gaunilo's Island Argument (I)—also makes use of that concept. Gaunilo and Anselm shared a worldview according to which everything in the universe occupies a particular position on the Great Chain of Being. At the top is God, next come the angels, then human beings, then animals, and then plants. Anselm and Gaunilo believed it was an entirely objective question how perfect a given thing is.

I want to suggest that we can see a defect in the Ontological Argument by setting aside the concept of perfection. Let's not worry about inferring a being's existence from its perfection. Let's not worry about how perfect a particular thing is or about whether perfection is objective. Let's simply define a being as an existing thing and see what happens.

Unicorns don't exist. The concept of unicornhood isn't exemplified in the actual world. Consider, however, a new concept, which I call *E*-unicornhood. An *E*-unicorn is by definition something that is an existing unicorn. Does it follow from the definition of an *E*-unicorn that there are *E*-unicorns? Not at all. The concept includes the property of existence, but that doesn't imply anything about the concept's being exemplified. The definition simply describes what a thing must be like if it is to count as an *E*-unicorn. The definition tells us that if something is an *E*-unicorn, then that thing will have the property of existing.

Let's define the concept of an *E*-God. An *E*-God is a being who is all-powerful, all-knowing, and all-good and who actually exists. Does it follow from the definition of an *E*-God that there is an *E*-God? Not at all. The definition simply describes what a thing must be like if it is to count as an *E*-God. The definition tells us that if something is an *E*-God, then that thing will have the property of existing.

CONCLUSION

When we define God, we are saying what a being would have to be like to be God. Parallel remarks apply to defining unicorns or golden mountains.

Anselm argued that our concept of God has built into it the idea that God necessarily exists. Just as God is by definition omnipotent, it also is true that God, by definition, necessarily exists.

My criticism of the Ontological Argument comes to this: Let's grant that God is by definition the greatest possible being. And let us grant that necessary existence is a perfection. What follows from this is that necessary existence is part of the concept of God. Existence is built into the concept of God, just as omnipotence is. But the fact that existence is built into a concept doesn't imply there are things to which the concept applies.

If we concede that God is defined as an omnipotent being, all this means is that if God exists, then that being must be omnipotent. Likewise, if we concede that God is defined as a necessarily existent being, we are merely saying that if there is a God, then that being necessarily exists. The definitions don't entail the existence of anything that is omnipotent nor of anything that necessarily exists. It is for this reason that the Ontological Argument is invalid.

Review Questions

1. What is the difference between an a posteriori proposition and an a priori proposition? What is the difference between saying that a proposition is a priori and saying that it is innate? Give an example of an a posteriori existence claim and an example of an a priori existence claim.
2. What is the difference between saying that a proposition is possible and saying that it is conceivable?
3. How does Gaunilo's point about islands bear on Anselm's argument about God? What is a reductio argument? In what way is Gaunilo employing this form of argumentation?
4. Why did Kant think that "existence is not a property of existing things"? Does this provide a successful criticism of the Ontological Argument?
5. Suppose God is, by definition, a being that exists in all possible worlds. Does it follow that God exists?

Problems for Further Thought

1. Consult the original text of Anselm's argument and Gaunilo's reply. Give a formulation of the argument that is more true to the text than the one presented in this lecture.
2. I've argued that building the idea of existence into a concept doesn't ensure that anything actually exemplifies the concept. That is the point of considering *E*-unicorns. Now, however, consider the opposite problem. Is it possible to define a concept so that the definition ensures that *nothing* can exemplify it? Construct a definition that does this. How is it possible that definitions can have negative implications about existence, but not positive implications?
3. Do the following arguments have the same logical form? Explain your answer.

> God has every perfection.
>
> Existence is a perfection.
> _____
> God exists.

> Sam has every novel by Dickens.
>
> *David Copperfield* is a novel by Dickens.
> _____
> Sam has *David Copperfield*.

LECTURE 9

Is the Existence of God Testable?

Up to this point, I've taken the question of whether God exists to be perfectly meaningful. It may be difficult to answer, but I've assumed there *is* an answer. Theists, atheists, and agnostics agree on this. I've assumed the sentence "God exists" says something; the question is whether what it says is true, and whether we can know this.

LOGICAL POSITIVISM

Some philosophers—advocates of the position called *logical positivism*—have an altogether different view of this problem. They hold that the sentence "God exists" is meaningless. It isn't true and it isn't false either. They hold that it is misguided to argue about whether God exists. Their idea is that we have been misled by a superficial grammatical similarity between the sentence "God exists" and the sentence "Genes exist." The latter expresses a scientific statement that can be justified or rejected by appeal to evidence. In contrast, the former sentence expresses no proposition at all. Positivism maintains that we shouldn't try to answer the question of whether God exists, but should reject it as meaningless.

THE TESTABILITY THEORY OF MEANING

Positivists advanced a theory that is supposed to justify this philosophical thesis. This is the *Testability Theory of Meaning*. It holds that for a sentence to be meaningful, it must be either a priori or a posteriori. The Testability Theory of Meaning also includes specific proposals for how these two categories should be understood.

As explained in Lecture 8, a truth is a priori if it can be justified without appeal to sense experience—it can be justified by reason alone. And a truth is a posteriori if it must rely on sense experience for its justification.

This is what it means for a truth to be a priori or a posteriori. But falsehoods can fall into these categories as well. A mathematical truth like "2 + 3 = 5" can be justified by reason alone; but the mathematical falsehood "2 + 4 = 7" can be *disproved* by reason alone. And just as the statement "There is a book in front of you now" is an a posteriori truth, so the statement "There is no book in front of you now" is an a posteriori falsehood.

Some meaningful statements are true; others are false. In saying that each meaningful sentence is either a priori or a posteriori, positivists are saying that every meaningful sentence is *decidable in principle*. That is, they maintain that if *S* is a meaningful sentence, then it is possible to figure out whether *S* is true. If there is no way in principle to figure out whether *S* is true, positivists conclude that *S* is meaningless.

I now turn to the positivists' account of what makes a sentence a priori or a posteriori. Once each of these categories is clarified, they think the claim that God exists can be seen to fall into neither category. Positivists conclude the claim is meaningless.

ANALYTICITY

Positivists (and some other philosophers besides) hold that all a priori statements are *analytic*. An analytic truth (as opposed to a *synthetic* one) is a definition or a deductive consequence of a definition. The truth of "All bachelors are unmarried" follows from the definitions of the terms that occur in it. "Either it is raining or it is not raining" likewise follows from the definition of "or." Symmetrically, positivism maintains that all a posteriori statements are *synthetic*—if a sentence depends on sense experience for its justification, its truth doesn't follow from definitions alone.

Where does the sentence "God exists" fit into this classification? Positivists reject the whole strategy behind the Ontological Argument. They hold that "God exists" isn't decidable from definitions alone. So the sentence isn't a priori. This means that if "God exists" is meaningful, it must be a posteriori. We now must examine the account positivists give of what makes a sentence a posteriori.

FALSIFIABILITY

Positivists say that the sentence "God exists" is *untestable*. There is no way to use observations to decide whether it is true.

Defenders of the Testability Theory of Meaning have argued that sentences are tested by deducing predictions from them that can be checked by making observations. Mendel tested his genetic theory by deducing from it a prediction about the proportions of different characteristics that there should be in his pea plants. He then was able to check these predictions observationally. Positivists argue the sentence "God exists" makes no predictions whatever; so it is untestable.

Sometimes the idea of observational testability is developed with reference to the concept of *falsification*. If a theory makes a prediction that can be checked observationally, the theory runs the risk of being refuted by observations. This is what the influential philosopher of science Karl Popper (not a positivist himself) meant by saying that a scientific theory should be falsifiable. This doesn't mean a scientific theory should be false. *Falsifiable* doesn't mean *false*. What is crucial is that the theory rule out at least some possible observations.

In science, confirmation and disconfirmation are intimately connected. An experiment has different possible outcomes. If some outcomes would be evidence *in favor of* the hypothesis, then other outcomes would be evidence *against* it. If you propose an experiment for testing a hypothesis and you think that every possible result would indicate the hypothesis is true, there is no reason to run the experiment. The only way the experiment could offer you real evidence in favor of the hypothesis is if there were some possible results that would undermine the hypothesis. You then get evidence supporting the hypothesis if you run the experiment and find that those possible refuting outcomes don't come to pass. Getting evidence in favor of a hypothesis requires that the hypothesis rule out something. What does the sentence "God exists" rule out? Is there anything we can imagine observing that would be evidence against theism? For example, if we observed that there is moral evil in the world, would that count against the hypothesis that there is a God? In Lecture 11, I'll discuss this question in some detail. For now, I'll merely note that theists have usually not taken the existence of evil to count against theism. They say that if the world had been morally perfect, that would be consistent with the existence of God; and if the world happens to contain moral evil, that too can be reconciled with theism. It seems that theists usually can reconcile their belief in God with just about anything they see.

Consider the doomsday pronouncements that pop up from time to time in different religions. Every so often, some religious group gets the idea that God is about to bring the world to an end. Such predictions have yet to come true. What has been the result of these failed predictions? A few end-of-the-worlders have had their faith shaken. But, after some reflection, most theists have decided that the failed predictions of the end-of-the-worlders don't count against the hypothesis that there is a God. If the world had come to an end, theists would have taken this to support their belief that there is a God; but when the world fails to come to an end, these same people continue to believe that God exists.

I hope these remarks convey the flavor of what positivists are getting at when they claim that the hypothesis that God exists is untestable. I now want to be a little more precise about these ideas. I begin with two definitions:

A hypothesis *H* is *strongly falsifiable* if *H* implies at least one observation statement *O*.

An *observation statement* is a statement whose truth or falsehood can be determined by direct observation.

Notice that strong falsifiability allows a hypothesis to be refuted by a valid deductive argument if the observational prediction it makes turns out to be false:

If *H,* then *O.*

Not-*O*

_____

Not-*H*

AUXILIARY ASSUMPTIONS NEEDED

I agree that the hypothesis that God exists isn't strongly falsifiable. The same is true, however, of most of the hypotheses that science investigates. *Hypotheses rarely deductively imply predictions all by themselves.* Rather, you must conjoin auxiliary assumptions *A* to a hypothesis *H* to get *H* to deductively imply an observational prediction *O.* It isn't *H* that implies *O,* but *H & A* that does the trick.

I'll illustrate this idea with an example from outside science. Consider Sherlock Holmes again. Holmes wishes to test the hypothesis that Moriarty is the murderer. Does this hypothesis, all by itself, tell Holmes what he will observe at the scene of the crime? Not at all. Auxiliary assumptions are needed.

If Holmes knows Moriarty wears a size 12 shoe, smokes El Supremo cigars, and fires a gun of type X, these auxiliary assumptions may lead him to expect to find certain clues. If he discovers a size 12 footprint, and El Supremo butt on the carpet next to the victim, and a bullet from a type X gun, his auxiliary assumptions may lead him to think that Moriarty is probably the murderer. On the other hand, if Holmes were to make *other* auxiliary assumptions, then the hypothesis that Moriarty is the murderer would lead Holmes to make quite different predictions. If Holmes thought that Moriarty didn't smoke, that he has a size 8 shoe, and that he prefers to use a knife, then the hypothesis that Moriarty is the murderer would *not* predict the clues Holmes found. The clues found at the scene of the crime don't say anything one way or the other about whether Moriarty is the murderer until auxiliary assumptions are added.

So most of the hypotheses we test don't, all by themselves, deductively imply observationally checkable statements. They do so only when supplemented with auxiliary assumptions. Where does this leave the thesis that the hypothesis that God exists isn't testable?

The sentence "God exists" isn't strongly falsifiable. But that is uninteresting, since most scientific hypotheses aren't strongly falsifiable either. This brings us to the next question: Is the hypothesis that God exists testable when it is supplemented with auxiliary assumptions?

The answer is *yes*. Consider the following candidate:

A_1: If there is a God, there will be living things in the world and they will be perfectly adapted to their environments.

A_2: If there is a God, there will be no living things.

A_3: If there is a God, there will be living things in the world, but they will not be perfectly adapted to their environments.

The hypothesis that there is a God, when conjoined with A_1, predicts something we can check by making observations. The same would be true if we conjoined the theistic hypothesis with A_2 or with A_3.

So there is a twofold parallel between the hypothesis that God exists and a scientific hypothesis (or a detective's hypothesis): The hypothesis isn't strongly falsifiable, but it is testable when conjoined with auxiliary assumptions. Does this mean that the hypothesis that God exists is no less testable than the hypotheses of science?

There does seem to be a difference between these cases, although it isn't to be characterized in terms of the idea of strong falsifiability. In the case of Holmes's testing whether Moriarty is the murderer, I noted that different sets of auxiliary assumptions entail different predictions about what Holmes will find at the scene of the crime. If A_4 is true, we get one set of predictions; if A_5 is true, we get a quite different set:

A_4: Moriarty smokes El Supremo cigars, has a size 12 shoe, and uses a type X gun.

A_5: Moriarty does not smoke, has a size 8 shoe, and uses a knife as his preferred murder weapon.

If Holmes is to say whether the clues at the scene of the crime count for or against the hypothesis that Moriarty is the murderer, he must decide which of A_4 and A_5 is true.

AUXILIARY ASSUMPTIONS MUST BE INDEPENDENTLY ESTABLISHED

In the scientific case, as well as in the case of detective work, there is an important fact about auxiliary assumptions that goes beyond what I've said so far. Not only are auxiliary assumptions needed if the hypothesis is to make observational predictions; in addition, *those auxiliary assumptions must be checkable independent of the hypothesis under test*. For example, Holmes can interpret the clues found at the scene of the crime once he decides whether A_4 or A_5 is true. And in addition, he can find

Neptune and Vulcan

Most hypotheses in science don't entail predictions all by themselves; they have to be conjoined to auxiliary assumptions to do so. This means that if the prediction turns out to be false, scientists face a choice. They can reject the hypothesis or they can reject the auxiliary assumptions.

Two episodes in nineteenth-century astronomy illustrate these two options. Working separately, John Adams and Urbain Leverrier used Newtonian physics plus assumptions about the planets then known to exist to predict where the orbit of Uranus should be. These assumptions included the idea that Uranus is the planet farthest from the sun. The prediction obtained by conjoining Newton's theory with this assumption came out wrong. Adams and Leverrier therefore had to choose between rejecting Newtonian physics or rejecting one or more of the auxiliary assumptions. Because Newtonian theory was well supported by other observations, they were reluctant to reject it. They therefore suspected that the auxiliary assumptions were the culprit. They conjectured that Uranus isn't the last planet. Two years later, astronomers were able to confirm this conjecture; they observed the planet that we now call Neptune.

This same pattern of reasoning was subsequently applied to the planet Mercury. Newtonian physics plus auxiliary assumptions (including the assumption that there is no planet between Mercury and the sun) predict where Mercury's orbit should be. This prediction turned out to be false. Scientists therefore faced a choice. Either Newton's theory is wrong or at least one auxiliary assumption is mistaken. Following the pattern of reasoning that worked so well for the case of Uranus, scientists conjectured that there is a planet lying between Mercury and the Sun. It was given the name "Vulcan."

As it turned out, this conjecture was mistaken. There is no such planet. It wasn't the auxiliary assumption (that there is no planet between Mercury and the Sun) that was responsible for the false prediction about Mercury's orbit; it was Newtonian physics itself that led to the error. Only when Newton's theories were replaced by Einstein's theories of relativity could the departure of Mercury's orbit from Newtonian values be explained.

In the reasoning about Uranus and the reasoning about Mercury, three sorts of statement play a role. There are theories *(T)*, auxiliary assumptions *(A)*, and predictions *(P)*. Describe the logical form of the arguments that the scientists formulated in the two cases.

---

out whether A_4 or A_5 is true without his having to already know if Moriarty is the murderer.

Can the same be done for the auxiliary hypotheses about God's nature, like A_1, A_2, or A_3? This isn't so clear. It is easy enough to invent auxiliary hypotheses that reconcile what we observe with the hypothesis that God is responsible for what we observe. If we find that an organism is perfectly adapted to its environment, we can construct an auxiliary assumption that effects this reconciliation. And if we find that the organism is imperfectly adapted, a different auxiliary assumption can be invented that does the same thing. The problem is, how do we figure out which of these auxiliary assumptions is true without assuming at the outset that God is responsible for what we observe? This is the problem we ran into in Lecture 5 when we considered different versions of creationism.

In the detective case, Holmes wouldn't endlessly revise his opinions about auxiliary assumptions just to preserve his faith that Moriarty must be the murderer. To do so would be to fall prey to an obsession, not to do good detective work. Holmes would find out which of A_4 and A_5 is true, and then use these independently confirmed auxiliary assumptions to test the hypothesis that Moriarty is the murderer. The result may be that Holmes is forced to conclude Moriarty is probably innocent of the crime.

The problem with testing the hypothesis that God exists is that it is hard to determine which auxiliary assumptions to accept if you don't already believe that God exists.

How is what I'm saying different from what the Testability Theory of Meaning maintains? To begin with, I'm not using the idea of strong falsifiability to criticize the hypothesis that God exists. Nor am I claiming that no one will ever figure out how the hypothesis that God exists can be tested. Perhaps someday auxiliary assumptions will be independently confirmed that can tell us what the hypothesis that God exists predicts about the observable world. My claim is that this hasn't happened *yet*.

In summary, positivists used the Testability Theory of Meaning to derive an *absolute* verdict concerning the sentence "God exists." In contrast, I've used a different idea about testability (one that emphasizes the role of auxiliary assumptions) to argue for a verdict concerning how the issue of testability stands *now*.

"GOD EXISTS" IS MEANINGFUL

Quite apart from the question of whether the statement "God exists" is testable observationally, I disagree with positivism on another count. I think the hypothesis that there is a God is meaningful. It is possible to discuss whether there is evidence for or against it. Also, the hypothesis obviously has various logical properties; I noted before that it, in conjunction with various auxiliary statements, deductively implies various predictions. This is enough to show that the sentence "God exists" isn't meaningless gibberish.

SUMMARY

I'll summarize my assessment of the Testability Theory of Meaning as follows. I think there are difficulties in testing the hypothesis that God exists. This, however, isn't because I endorse the criterion of falsifiability; I don't. The bare statement "God exists" does not entail observational predictions, but neither does the bare statement "electrons exist." The typical situation in science is that theoretical statements have observational consequences only when they are conjoined with auxiliary assumptions.

It is easy to invent auxiliary assumptions that permit the hypothesis that God exists to make predictions. It also is easy to invent such assumptions so that the result is that the hypothesis makes *true* predictions. What is not so easy is to show that the auxiliary assumptions that permit the theistic hypothesis to make predictions are themselves well confirmed. Scientific testing requires that the auxiliary assumptions used be well supported by evidence; inventing them isn't enough.

Review Questions

1. What does it mean to say that a hypothesis is strongly falsifiable? Does this mean it is false? Is the hypothesis that organisms contain genes strongly falsifiable?
2. What is an auxiliary assumption? How does testing the hypothesis that God exists depend on a choice of auxiliary assumptions?
3. What does it mean to say that Holmes could independently confirm the auxiliary assumptions he needs concerning Moriarty? Independent of what?
4. How does the Surprise Principle explain why the existence of miracles would be strong evidence for the existence of God? What problems need to be addressed if one wishes to argue for theism in this way?

Problems for Further Thought

1. Consider the following passage from David Hume's "Essay on Miracles":

   > That no testimony is sufficient to establish a miracle unless the testimony be of such a kind, that its falsehood would be more miraculous than the fact which it endeavors to establish. . . . When any one tells me that he saw a dead man restored to life, I immediately consider with myself whether it be more probable that this person should either deceive or be deceived, or that the fact which he related should really have happened. I weigh the one miracle against the other, and according to the superiority which I discover, I pronounce my decision, and always reject the greater miracle. If the falsehood of his testimony would be more miraculous than the event which he relates, then, and only then, can he pretend to commend my belief or opinion.

   What general point about eyewitness testimony is Hume making here? Does Hume's argument show that miracles never happen?
2. Can positivists say that a sentence is meaningful even though we will never actually find out whether it is true? Can they say that a sentence is meaningful if it is impossible for us to discover whether it is true? Does this mean that sentences about the prehistoric past are meaningless?
3. The readings for this chapter include a selection from A. J. Ayer's *Language, Truth, and Logic* (1936). This was a very influential defense of logical positivism. In this selection, Ayer says that there is no conflict between science and religion. He also says that positivism agrees with what many religious mystics maintain. Why does Ayer hold these views?

LECTURE 10

Pascal and Irrationality

Blaise Pascal (1623–1662), a French physicist, philosopher, and mathematician, was interested in the question of whether it could be rational to believe in God, even if you think it is enormously improbable that God exists. Suppose all the evidence is *against* God's existence—you regard the existence of God as a possibility, although you think it is extremely implausible. Can it still make sense to be a theist?

Pascal was one of the founders of the modern mathematical theory of probability. His argument has come to be called *Pascal's Wager,* because Pascal argues that believing that God exists is a sensible wager, even if there is no evidence that God exists.

PRUDENTIAL AND EVIDENTIAL REASONS FOR BELIEF

Before analyzing Pascal's argument, I want to describe two kinds of reasons someone might have for believing some proposition or for performing some action. Suppose one day we meet for lunch. I'm carrying a machine gun and a briefcase. I open the briefcase and show you that it contains $1,000,000. I show you the gun is loaded. Then, I make you an offer I think you can't refuse.

You probably don't believe the President of the United States is juggling candy bars at this very moment. This proposition you regard as very improbable, though you grant that it isn't entirely impossible. Here is my offer: If you can get yourself to believe the President is juggling candy bars right now, I'll give you $1,000,000. If you don't believe this proposition, I'll shoot you with the machine gun. What is it reasonable for you to do, supposing that you think I'm entirely sincere in my threats and promises?

In one sense, it is rational to try to believe, even though you think the proposition in question is very improbable. It would be prudent (that is, in your self-interest) to try to believe, supposing that you don't want to die and would like to have the million dollars. The kind of reason you have here I'll call a *prudential reason.*

In another sense, however, you don't have any reason to believe that the President of the United States is juggling candy bars right now. You haven't one shred of evidence that the proposition is true. Let's describe this fact by saying that you don't have an *evidential reason* for believing the proposition in question.

Pascal's Wager is intended to provide you with a *prudential* reason for believing that God exists even if you think there is no *evidence* that there is a God. Even if you think all the evidence is against the existence of God, Pascal thinks he can give you a prudential reason for theism, so long as you grant that the existence of God is at least possible.

WHEN DOES IT MAKE SENSE TO GAMBLE?

Before analyzing Pascal's argument, I need to mention one other detail, about gambling. Here is a fact about reasonable gambles: *It can make sense to bet on improbable outcomes if the payoff is big enough.* Suppose I offer you the following wager. If you pay me $1, you will be allowed to draw a single card from a standard deck of cards. If the card drawn turns out to be the ace of spades, I'll give you $1,000,000. If it turns out to be some other card, you receive nothing, and so you are out the dollar you paid for the chance. Question: Does it make sense to buy into this gamble, assuming you can trust me to pay you if you win and that your goal is to maximize the amount of money you possess? The answer is yes. Although the probability of winning is only 1/52, the payoff if you win is so huge and the cost to you if you lose is so small that this is a great gamble to make. Bear this fact in mind as you consider Pascal's argument.

The Expected Value of an Action

You have to decide between two actions: buying a lottery ticket and not buying one. If you buy the ticket, a card is drawn at random from a standard deck of cards. If the card is the ace of spades, you win *$1,000,000.* If not, you lose. The ticket costs *$1.* Should you buy the ticket, if your only goal is to maximize your cash resources?

The *expected value* (expected utility) of an action is the *average* payoff you would receive, if you performed the action again and again. If you buy the ticket, there is a *51/52* chance that the ace of spades won't appear; in this case, your resources will have dropped *$1* (the cost of the ticket). On the other hand, if you buy the ticket, there is a *1/52* chance that you will win the million; in this case, your resources (taking account of the cost of the ticket) will have increased by *$999,999.* So the expected value of buying the ticket is

$$-(\$1)(51/52) + (\$999,999)(1/52) = \$19,230.$$

What is the expected value of the alternative action—of *not* buying the ticket? That depends on what you would do with the *$1* in question. Suppose that you would simply put it in your pocket if you didn't buy into the lottery. In this case, you can be certain that your resources will neither increase nor decline. So the expected value of not buying a ticket is *$0.*

Notice that buying the ticket has a higher expected value than not buying. So the rule in decision theory—to maximize expected utility (or value)—tells you to buy the ticket.

The expected value of buying the ticket is *not* the amount of money you can expect to get. If you enter the lottery, you'll either end up a dollar behind or *$999,999* ahead. The expected value is what you would average if you bought into the lottery again and again. Most of the time, you'll lose; occasionally, you'll win. The average payoff per ticket over the long run is about *$19,230.*

The mathematical idea of an expectation applies to quantities other than value or utility. A probability theorist might say that the expected number of offspring for parents in the United States today is about *2.2.* This doesn't mean that a couple can expect to have precisely this number of children. Rather, *2.2* is the expected number because it is the average. The same is true when life insurance companies describe the life expectancy of a person who is *19* years old.

PASCAL'S ARGUMENT

Pascal's Wager can be represented as a solution to a problem in decision theory. This is a modern theory that describes how an agent should choose among different available *actions* by seeing what the *utilities* are of the different *outcomes*. Be sure to get clear on how each of these italicized terms figures in Pascal's argument.

You have to decide whether or not to believe there is a God. These are the two possible actions. Quite independent of your decision here, there is the way the world is: Either there is a God or there isn't. Hence, there are four possible outcomes—an outcome being composed of your performing an action when the world is a particular way.

The four outcomes are represented in the following two-by-two table:

	Ways the World Might Be	
	God Exists	There is no God
Believe that God exists	$+\infty$	-10
Do not believe that God exists	$-\infty$	$+10$

(Actions label the left-hand rows.)

The upper-left entry represents the outcome in which you believe in God and there is a God. What is the result, if this should come to pass? Pascal says that the payoff to you is an infinite reward—you go to heaven. Suppose, on the other hand, that you occupy the lower-left cell. This is the outcome in which you don't believe there is a God, but God in fact exists. Here Pascal says you suffer an infinite punishment—you receive eternal damnation.

What about the other two entries? If you believe in God, but there is no God, perhaps you will have wasted your time with religious rituals and observances you might have preferred to skip had you only known there was no God listening to your prayers. This isn't a horrible result, though it should be represented as a modest disutility—hence my entry of −10. On the other hand, if you don't believe in God and there is no God (the lower-right cell), you receive a modest benefit. Instead of engaging in religious practices that you may find boring at times, you can get involved in activities that are more rewarding. Pascal says that the entry in this cell should represent a modest benefit; my chosen value for the utility here is +10.

To summarize the structure of the problem: The agent must decide which action to perform. The possible outcomes are given by the possible pairings of the available actions with the different ways the world might be. With each possible outcome, the agent associates a utility (a payoff), which represents how good or bad the outcome is for the agent.

How are the utilities of the different possible outcomes to be combined to reach a decision about which act is preferable? The *expected utility* of believing there is a

God needs to take account of two possibilities: There is the utility you receive if you believe and there is a God, and the quite different utility you receive if you believe and there is no God. Likewise the expected utility of not believing must take account of both outcome possibilities (represented in the bottom row).

Here is Pascal's solution. Even if you think the existence of God is very improbable (say, you assign it a probability of only 1/1,000,000), the expected utility of believing is higher than the expected utility of not believing. The reason is that though the existence of God is very improbable, there is a huge benefit if you are a theist and God exists, but only a small cost if you are a theist and there is no God. It makes sense to bet on the existence of God, even if the existence of God is very improbable, for reasons that parallel the gamble I mentioned before. The gamble makes sense even though it is improbable that there is a God.

FIRST CRITICISM OF PASCAL'S ARGUMENT

Two criticisms have been made of this wager, only one of which is decisive. First, some philosophers have objected to treating belief as an action. We can't decide to believe a proposition; belief isn't an action we control in this way. In my story about the President, you may recognize that it is in your interest to believe the President is now juggling candy bars. Seeing that this would be good for you, however, doesn't mean you can automatically make yourself believe the proposition. The objection is that you shouldn't treat belief as a problem in decision theory, since decision theory is about choosing actions that you can perform if you want to.

Pascal recognized this difficulty. After stating his wager, he comments that people who are convinced the reasoning is sound may not be able to suddenly start being theists. He suggests to them that they go live among religious people. By doing this, habits of faith will gradually take hold. Pascal realized you can't simply decide to believe something. But he did see you can choose to live your life in such a way that belief will come naturally after a while.

This means Pascal's Wager can be reformulated so that the actions considered really are things under our control. Rather than treating belief and nonbelief as things we can choose to do directly, let's recognize that sincere belief can only occur in the right setting, where the right habits have been developed. It also is worth mentioning that Pascal's Wager concerns what it is best for you to believe. The question of whether we can do what is best for us isn't part of Pascal's analysis.

SECOND CRITICISM OF PASCAL'S ARGUMENT

The second objection to Pascal's argument is more telling. In Lecture 9, I discussed the difficulty of establishing what God would be like if such a being existed. This is the problem of independently confirming auxiliary hypotheses, as I called them, about God's nature.

Pascal's Wager makes very specific assumptions about what God would be like if there were such a being. The assumption is that God would send believers to heaven and nonbelievers to hell. But there are other conceptions to consider. For example, maybe God would reward those who lead a good life and would punish those who are bad, independently of what those individuals' theological opinions may be. Or consider another possibility: Perhaps God will send everyone to heaven except those who are convinced by Pascal's Wager.

The main problem with the wager is that it makes assumptions about God's nature that are part of one religious tradition but not part of many others. How can one tell which assumptions are true? In the absence of a convincing argument, I see no reason to think Pascal's description of the payoffs is correct.

THE ROLE OF REASON

Pascal argued that it can make sense to believe things that are totally unsupported by evidence. If you think evidence is the hallmark of rational belief, then you'll interpret Pascal as giving a justification of irrationality. Of course, he didn't abandon the standard of rationality altogether. He tried to provide a rational argument that shows we should believe in God even if there is no evidence that God exists. Pascal aimed to provide a prudential reason, not an evidential reason.

Pascal rejected the idea that evidential reasoning should determine whether or not we believe in God. Other religious thinkers have done the same thing, but for reasons quite different from Pascal's. For example, it has been suggested that God is so different from other beings that techniques appropriate for discussing them are no longer appropriate when the question is a theological one. God is said to be an infinite being, one who may stand outside of space and time and yet be able to influence what happens in space and time. God is also supposed to be all-knowing, all-powerful, and all-good. In all these respects, God is far different from the familiar objects about which we are accustomed to reasoning.

Let's grant that God is supposed to have these special features. Why do they show that reason isn't an appropriate tool to use in thinking about whether God exists? I noted in Lecture 2 and again in Lecture 9 that deductive validity depends on an argument's form, not on its subject matter. If this is right, then deductive reasoning should apply to the question of God's existence in the same way it applies to other questions.

Sometimes it is suggested that God is so shrouded in mystery that we can't hope to understand God by rational inquiry. Maybe this is right—maybe the issues are so mysterious that you'll never be able to see that God exists if you adhere to rational standards of argument. But why does this mean those standards should be abandoned? Why not take this to mean that we shouldn't believe God exists, precisely because no good argument can be produced for this conclusion?

I won't pursue these questions any further. Maybe it can be explained why usual standards of evidence and argument should be abandoned when the question is whether God exists. So far, I know of no reason to think this.

FREUD'S PSYCHOLOGICAL EXPLANATION OF THEISM

There is a curious fact here, one that really does require an explanation. If we were talking about virtually any topic from everyday or scientific life, no one would be very attracted by the advice that we should believe something on the basis of no evidence. Yet, when the question is whether God exists, people sometimes drop their critical standards. This isn't true of everyone, of course. It wasn't true of Anselm, Aquinas, Hume, or Paley, for example. Still, the idea of switching from reason to faith has been attractive to many.

There is a psychological question I'll pose but not answer. Why are people sometimes inclined to believe without evidence when the question is whether God exists, but are much less willing to take this attitude when the question is a different one?

In his essay, "The Future of an Illusion," Sigmund Freud (1856–1939), the founder of psychoanalysis, gave an answer that is worth pondering. Freud points out the world is in many ways a frightening place. It is a relatively recent event in human history that people have come to exercise some mastery over nature. And even this recent mastery is enormously incomplete. Although we aren't threatened every day by wild animals, lightning, drought, famine, and flood, each of us has to face the inevitability of our own deaths. In this ultimate sense, we are as helpless as our ancient ancestors. With so much of nature out of our control, beyond our understanding, and threatening our survival, it isn't surprising that human beings should invent myths that provide a quite different and more appealing picture of our place in the cosmos. Instead of viewing the universe as indifferent to us, impersonal, and incomprehensible, we construct a comprehensible picture of forces more powerful than ourselves who take an interest in our fate. Freud's hypothesis was that belief in God persists in human history because of the psychological benefits it provides to believers.

Pascal aimed to provide a prudential argument for believing God exists. Freud was an atheist, but aimed to provide an explanation for why many people believe God exists. Pascal sought to justify theism; Freud didn't seek to justify it, but to explain it.

A NEW PRUDENTIAL ARGUMENT

In spite of these differences, we can use some of Freud's observations to formulate a prudential argument for theism that is stronger than the one Pascal provided. The stumbling block for Pascal was the assumptions he made about what God would be like if he existed. We can avoid these difficult questions about God's nature, however, and focus on something that is more familiar and closer to home—our own minds.

Suppose you are the sort of person who derives comfort and fulfillment from believing in God. Your belief in God provides your life with meaning. It gives you the courage to face adversity. Moreover, let's suppose that without believing in God, you would plunge into despair. You would become depressed, unable to live a productive life.

There are many people in the world who aren't like this. First, there are cheerful agnostics and atheists—people who manage to make a meaningful life for themselves without needing a theological framework. Second, there are people who remain tormented by despair even after they become theists. In both these cases, I'm talking about people whose general outlook is rather independent of the theological opinions they happen to have.

Nevertheless, let's suppose there are some people for whom belief in God makes all the difference. Perhaps you are a person of this sort. If so, you can use these psychological facts to formulate a prudential argument for theism:

> If you believe in God, you will lead a happy and productive life.
>
> If you don't believe in God, you will fall into depression and despair.
> _____
> The way to maximize expected utility is for you to be a theist.

This argument resembles Pascal's in that it ignores whatever evidence there may be concerning whether God exists. But unlike Pascal's argument, this prudential argument doesn't make assumptions about what God would do to theists and atheists. This argument focuses on the psychological consequences of theism, not on speculations about heaven and hell.

This argument is more difficult to refute than Pascal's. The major issue it raises is a difficult one. Should we allow prudential reasons to influence what we believe, or should we require that our beliefs be regulated by evidence alone?

PRAGMATISM

Pragmatism is a general philosophical position that has implications about this question. This philosophical idea was developed in the nineteenth and twentieth centuries principally by C. S. Peirce, William James, and John Dewey. In ordinary speech, "being pragmatic" means *being practical*. The philosophical position, however, isn't fully captured by the everyday meaning of the word.

Pragmatists say that we should believe propositions that are useful to us. In everyday life, this usually means that we should be attentive to evidence. Suppose you are about to cross the street and want to know whether a bus is coming. The most useful thing to do here is to use your senses (sight, hearing, etc.). It would be silly to engage in wishful thinking—to refuse to consult any evidence and simply believe the proposition you'd like to have be true.

In cases of this sort, the prudent thing to do is to attend to evidence. There are cases, however, in which prudential considerations can lead in one direction and evidential considerations in another. My story about the President juggling candy bars provides one example. A prudential argument for theism provides another.

In *The Will to Believe* (1897), William James (1842–1910) says that a person is entitled to believe in God for purely prudential reasons (of the psychological sort described above) if the belief provides a "vital benefit" and if no decision about theism can be made on the basis of the evidence available. But why shouldn't a pragmatist be more liberal? Even if there were *substantial* evidence against there being a God, why shouldn't sufficiently large prudential benefits outweigh the evidential considerations?

James's position doesn't provide a blanket justification of theism. As mentioned before, people who could lead happy productive lives without being theists can't claim they *need* to believe in God to avoid falling into despair. Yet, the spirit of pragmatism (if not the letter of James's formulation) seems to sanction believing in God if belief would be useful.

To do justice to the problems pragmatism raises, we would need to consider a variety of cases. If it is a matter of life and death, is it reasonable for someone to be a theist on purely prudential grounds? In less extreme cases, is the comfort provided by theism reason enough to believe in God? This raises complex questions about the attitudes we should take to our lives. Someone might reject pragmatic arguments for theism by saying that they prefer to look the universe square in the face without the benefit of comforting illusions. This person might prefer a life of honest uncertainty and doubt over a life made comfortable by beliefs that have no evidential basis.

The pragmatist says that we should believe what it is useful to believe. An opponent of pragmatism might insist that prudential considerations are irrelevant; we should believe only those propositions that are well supported by evidence. Although Pascal's Wager doesn't succeed in providing a prudential reason for theism, it is harder to refute the purely psychological argument just described.

Review Questions

1. What is the difference between a prudential reason and an evidential reason for believing something?
2. Can it ever make sense to bet on something that probably won't happen?
3. Given the payoffs Pascal assigns to outcomes, what is the expected value of believing in God? Of not believing?
4. Do people believe what they do because they "decide to believe?" If not, does it follow Pascal's argument is mistaken?
5. How does Pascal's argument depend on a set of auxiliary assumptions (in the sense of Lecture 9) about God's nature?
6. Describe a prudential argument for believing in God that avoids the problem that Pascal's argument confronts.

A Problem for Further Thought

In his essay "The Ethics of Belief" (1877), W. K. Clifford opposed the pragmatism described in the present lecture. He maintains: "It is wrong always, everywhere, and for any one, to believe anything upon insufficient evidence." Here is one of the arguments he gives:

... if I let myself believe anything on insufficient evidence, there may be no great harm done by the mere belief; it may be true after all, or I may never have occasion to exhibit it in outward acts. But I cannot help doing this great wrong towards Man, that I make myself credulous. The danger to society is not merely that it should believe wrong things, though that is great enough, but that it should become credulous and lose the habit of testing things and inquiring into them; for then it must sink back into savagery.

Is this a good argument against pragmatism?

LECTURE 11

The Argument from Evil

So far, most of the arguments considered concerning the existence of God have had theistic conclusions. I now turn to an issue many regard as providing an argument for atheism. It sometimes is thought that the fact that there is evil in the world proves there is no God. An argument to this effect is called an Argument from Evil. I'll consider three forms this argument might take. I think none of these successfully proves there is no God. I'll suggest, however, that the third argument does show that if there is a God, then God must be different from what at least one religious tradition has said.

FIRST VERSION OF THE ARGUMENT

The first form of the Argument from Evil is quite simple:

(1) If God were to exist, then that being would be all-powerful, all-knowing, and all-good (all-PKG, for short).

(2) If an all-PKG being existed, then there would be no evil.

(3) There is evil.
   _____

   Hence, there is no God.

The argument is deductively valid; convince yourself of this by identifying the argument's logical form.

Sometimes it is said that the first premiss is a definition of what we mean by the concept of God. I'll say in a minute why I don't think (1) is a definition.

Premiss (2) is usually defended as follows. If God is all-good, he wants to prevent evil. If he is all-knowing, he knows the difference between right and wrong and knows how to prevent evil from coming into existence. And if he is all-powerful, he can prevent evil, should he wish to do so. So God, if he is all-PKG, has both the inclination and the ability to prevent evil from occurring.

TWO KINDS OF EVIL

What does *evil* mean in premiss (3)? Discussion of the Argument from Evil usually divides existing evils into two categories. There are the wrongs that are brought into existence by human actions. And there are the evils that exist because of natural events that aren't under human control. In the first category falls the suffering that human beings inflict on each other; the second category includes the suffering that human beings (and other creatures) experience because of natural disasters, such as earthquakes and plagues.

POSSIBLE REACTIONS TO THE ARGUMENT

As mentioned before, the argument is valid. Hence, if you wish to reject the conclusion, you must reject one or more of the premisses. What options are available?

One option is to deny the existence of evil (premiss 3). For example, you could take the view that there really is no difference between right and wrong. This is the idea that the universe is morally neutral; we human beings impose illusory moral categories upon it. This view about morality will be discussed in the fifth section of the book, especially in Lectures 28 and 29. For now I'll ignore this option. I'll assume that some of the murders, tortures, and other brutalities that have peppered human history really are ethically deplorable. I also will assume that the world would have been a better place if some of the suffering caused by natural disasters hadn't occurred. This assumption—that premiss (3) is correct—is shared by many, if not all, religious traditions.

[A personal remark: In teaching introductory classes in philosophy, I've found that students who suggest that there is no such thing as real evil in the world often come from homes that have not been touched by tragedy or hardship. If you find yourself inclined to suggest that evil is only an illusion, ask yourself how you would feel about this question if your life had been less privileged.]

Another option is to reject premiss (1). You could interpret the existence of evil as showing merely that if there is a God, then God isn't all-PKG. This strategy grants premisses (2) and (3), but then concludes that if God exists, he can't be exactly the way one religious tradition says he is.

The fact that this strategy is available shows, I think, that (1) isn't "true by definition." If the first premiss really did define what the term "God" means, then the existence of evil couldn't be explained by rejecting this premiss. But this does seem to be a real option. What we need to recognize is that premiss (1) doesn't have the same status that the following sentence has: "A bachelor is an unmarried man." Suppose we found that a man we thought was a bachelor in fact was married. Would this lead us to consider the possibility that maybe bachelors could be married? I think not.

Premiss (1) embodies one theory about what God's nature is. It is one theory among many possible theories, none of which deserves to be viewed as "true by definition." The ancient Greeks denied that the gods are all-PKG. Manicheanism and Zoroastrianism deny that God is all-powerful. So rejecting premiss (1) is an option we need to consider as a way of explaining why evil exists.

THEODICY AND DEFENSE

One other option remains: reject premiss (2). This is the strategy pursued by theists who think premisses (1) and (3) are true. If you think God is all-PKG and that evil is a reality, you need to show how God's being all-PKG doesn't imply that there should be no evil in the world.

There are two types of criticism that might be offered of premiss (2). You could try to explain why it is false. This is the project known as "theodicy" in traditional Christian theology. Here you try to explain why an all-PKG God would allow evil to exist. Alternatively, there is the more modest criticism in which you try to show that we don't have a good reason to think that the premiss is true. Contemporary philosophers of religion use the term "defense" to describe this second type of reply to the Argument from Evil.

The distinction that separates theodicy from defense can be seen in the discussion of other arguments for the existence of God. For example, in criticizing Aquinas's first and second arguments for the existence of God in Lecture 4, I claimed that we have no good reason to accept his assertion that the natural world is only finitely old. I didn't provide a positive argument that the world *is* infinitely old. Rather, I made the more modest point that Aquinas offers no good reason to think that the world is only finitely old. In any event, I think there is some plausibility in rejecting premiss (2). Notice that premiss (2) makes an extreme claim. It says that if an all-PKG God existed, there would exist not even a tiny amount of evil in the world.

SOUL-BUILDING EVILS

Traditional theodicy has claimed that some evils have the property of being "soul-building." Soul-building evils are the ones that make us better people. Living through adversity strengthens our character; it makes us better people than we would have been if we had never suffered hardship.

I want to be careful about what I'm conceding here. I grant that *some* evils are soul-building. But I think it is morally outrageous to say this of *all* the evils that human beings have experienced. Sometimes suffering doesn't make the victim stronger; sometimes suffering destroys people. And even when people survive brutal tortures, do we really think that they are always better people for it? Sometimes they survive as mere shells. Even when torture victims in some sense are made stronger by their ordeals, do we still want to say that the experience has been worth it? If you think it was worthwhile for *them,* would *you* choose to undergo the torture yourself? There are some strengths that aren't worth having, because they cost too much to acquire.

Sometimes it is suggested that when people are destroyed by the sufferings they endure, the souls of other people are strengthened by watching this happen. I think this is sometimes true, but it is often false. Sometimes the only effect on witnesses is that they are sickened by having to watch events they know full well to be horrible. Sometimes people who witness the suffering of others react with callousness and indifference. And some suffering occurs in private; in these cases, there is no audience whose souls can be made stronger by watching the spectacle.

Just as suffering often doesn't make the sufferer a better person, it also is true that one person's suffering often fails to improve the characters of witnesses. So in granting that *some* suffering is soul-building, I'm granting something about a rather small portion of the huge mountain of agony the human race has experienced.

Is the fact that some evils are soul-building enough to refute premiss (2)? This isn't so clear. If it is desirable that we be strong of heart, why couldn't God have made us this way without us having to experience evil?

The need for soul-building experiences is sometimes defended by an analogy concerning the way a benevolent parent treats a child. If you really care about your children, you won't shield them from all adversity. There are some experiences that involve pain and suffering that children need to have if they are to mature into morally sensitive and autonomous adults. If your child is being picked on by a bully at school, you may decide she has to tough it out for herself. Intervening would save her a few scrapes and bruises *now.* But you might decide as a parent that this wouldn't be in her long-term best interests.

You, as a parent, have the goal of seeing your children develop in a certain way. You choose not to prevent some bad things from happening to your child because you recognize that there is no other way for her to mature as you intend. Suppose, however, that you could have your child become a mature adult without her having to be kicked around by the bully. In this case, why would you allow the bully to continue to harass your child?

A parent might allow soul-building evils to befall a child when there is no other way to have the child's soul grow strong. But the limitations that might justify a parent's choice aren't supposed to be present where God is concerned. If God is all-PKG, why couldn't he simply make us with strong souls?

Defenders of the soul-building idea reply that God wants us to be able to be proud of our own achievements. If we suffer through adversity, we get credit for the strong souls that result. If, however, God simply gave us strong souls *gratis,* we would deserve no credit. We couldn't be proud of ourselves; at best, we would simply be grateful to a benevolent deity.

To evaluate this suggestion, we must ask why it is so important that we be able to take credit for having strong characters. Why is it better to experience an evil and then get credit for having endured it? Why is this better than having a strong character because God made us that way from the start? I raise this question, but won't attempt to answer it. I'll concede for now that an all-PKG God would allow at least some evils to exist. Some soul-building evils are of this sort. In other words, I'll concede premiss (2) is false.

Does this mean there is no problem of evil—that the existence of evil poses no difficulty for the conception of God as an all-PKG being? I think not. The soul-building evils an all-PKG God would allow us to experience are a tiny portion of the evils we need to explain. What needs to be explained isn't why there is some evil *rather than none at all.* The deeper problem is to explain why there is so much evil, *rather than one ounce less.*

SECOND VERSION OF THE ARGUMENT

So the second Argument from Evil is more difficult to refute. It takes the following form:

(1) If God were to exist, then that being would be all-PKG.

(4) If an all-PKG being existed, then the amount of evil would not exceed a soul-building minimum.

(5) The amount of evil does exceed a soul-building minimum.

———————————

Hence, there is no God.

By "soul-building minimum," I mean the minimum amount of evil that would suffice to make us have strength of character. This argument is valid. Hence, if the conclusion is false, at least one of the premisses also must be false. The project of theodicy is to show that premiss (4) is mistaken.

FREE WILL

Is there a reason that an all-PKG being might have for permitting evils that go beyond the soul-building minimum to exist? It sometimes is suggested that this reason is to be found in the idea of *free will.* God made us free; this means it is up to us whether we do good or do evil. A consequence of this freedom is that there is more evil than would be strictly necessary for soul-building.

There is a question here that we will examine in detail in the section of this book on philosophy of mind. Why couldn't God have made us free agents who always freely choose to do what is right? Why assume that free people must sometimes produce evil? If a sinner can have free will, why can't a saint? After all, God is supposed to be a free being who never does evil things. This seems to show that being free and always doing what's right are not incompatible. Even if being free implies that you *could* do evil things, why does freedom imply that you *actually* produce evil actions?

However, let's now set this point aside and assume, for the sake of argument, that human freedom requires that people sometimes produce evil and that this evil exceeds the minimum that would exist strictly from the point of view of soul-building. This means that premiss (4) in the second argument is mistaken. But again, I want to emphasize that this doesn't fully solve the problem of evil. The problem is to account for the vast quantity of evil that exists. Let's grant that some evil must exist for soul-building and some more evil will be a consequence of human freedom. Does this explain the quantity of evil that the world contains?

EXAMPLES, AND A THIRD VERSION OF THE ARGUMENT

Let's single out some horrendous evil that has befallen the human race. Think of all the suffering Hitler caused. How could an all-PKG God have allowed this to happen? Is the answer that God made us free? I think this appeal to the importance of human freedom doesn't begin to address the difficulty.

Why didn't God intervene in human affairs on those rare occasions on which it would have made a dramatic difference? When the sperm and egg came together that produced Hitler, why didn't God prevent that fertilization event from happening? To do so would still have allowed human beings to be free; in addition, that brief intervention would allow there to be soul-building evils aplenty. Here I'm considering a minor foray into human affairs, not some major restructuring of human nature.

Suppose that if Hitler had never existed, many of the terrible things he did would never have happened. The world would have been a much better place. Most theists would agree with this. So why didn't God influence the course of human history for the better? What you must see here is that appeals to soul-building and to freedom don't provide an answer. Causing Hitler's parents to have failed to conceive on that one occasion wouldn't have robbed them of free will; the parents didn't will that this particular sperm and this particular egg should achieve the fertilization.

Another way to make this point is to consider horrendous evils that come into existence for reasons having nothing to do with human action. Consider the bubonic plague. If God had prevented that disease from existing, much suffering and death would have been avoided. To intervene in the lives of the relevant microorganisms doesn't rob them of free will, since they don't have wills (minds) to begin with. Also, the amount of suffering that occurred because of the plague far exceeded what could be explained by the goal of soul-building. About one-third of the European population died agonizing deaths from bubonic plague. Would our souls have been less strong if some smaller percentage had perished?

These considerations lead to a third version of the Argument from Evil:

(1) If God were to exist, then that being would be all-PKG.

(6) If an all-PKG being existed, then there would be no more evil
than the minimum required for soul-building and as
a consequence of human freedom.

(7) The quantity of evil found in human history exceeds
      the minimum required for soul-building and as
      a consequence of human freedom.
——————————
Hence, there is no God.

A CRITICISM OF THE ARGUMENT

How might this last argument be criticized? If there is a God, and if premisses (1) and (7) are true, what grounds can there be for rejecting premiss (6)? The project of *theodicy* has to produce a reason for thinking that (6) is false. The more modest project of *defense* merely has to show that we don't have a good reason to think that (6) is true. Whereas soul-building and free will were just presented in the context of a theodicy, I'll now shift gears and formulate a reply to this last argument that has the character of a defense.

Premiss (6), like premisses (2) and (4) in the preceding arguments, attempts to specify an upper bound on the amount of evil that an all-PKG God would allow to exist. But why think that we mere humans have the ability to figure this out? After all, God, if he exists, is vastly more intelligent than we are. It therefore is entirely possible that his plan for the world contains elements that we cannot understand or even imagine. Perhaps God allowed evils into the world beyond those required for soul-building and as a consequence of human freedom because these additional evils are required to obtain some greater good of which we are unaware.

We need to be careful in how we formulate this criticism of the Argument from Evil. I am not asserting that premiss (6) is false. I am giving a reason for thinking that we don't know that (6) is true. All of the versions of the Argument from Evil that I have surveyed attempt to circumscribe exactly how much evil there should be if an all-PKG being existed. To do this requires that we know a lot about what an all-PKG being would do. To the degree that we lack knowledge of what God's plan would be if he existed, we also lack the sort of knowledge that is needed for these arguments for atheism to succeed.

TESTABILITY, AGAIN

In Lectures 6 and 9 I discussed whether the existence of God is testable. The reply I just formulated to the Argument from Evil raises the same issue. How much evil should we expect there to be if there were a God? Atheists who advance the Arguments from Evil just described think they can answer this question. However, if we can't answer this question, we can't test the proposition that God exists by examining how much evil there is in the world.

Review Questions

1. Consider the proposition that God is all-powerful, all-knowing, and all-good. Should we regard this proposition as a definition of what the word "God" means? If it isn't a definition, does this mean that the proposition is false?
2. Does the existence of evil prove that God can't exist?
3. What does it mean to say that some evils are soul-building?
4. Does the fact that some evils are soul-building while others are consequences of human freedom solve the problem of evil?
5. What is the difference between theodicy and defense as criticisms of the Argument from Evil? Illustrate this distinction by constructing an argument that has nothing to do with the existence of God.
6. A criticism was presented of the third and final Argument from Evil. The argument is valid. And the criticism did not claim that any of the premises are false. What, then, is the criticism?

Problems for Further Thought

1. The appeal to free will, which is part of the project of theodicy, includes the claim that (a) God is omnipotent (all-powerful) and the claim that (b) God cannot give us free will without there also being evil in the world. Are (a) and (b) compatible? How should the concept of "omnipotence" be understood?
2. Are there reasons beyond the goal of soul-building and the goal of giving us free will that an all-PKG God would have for allowing evil to exist? If so, would that solve the problem of evil?
3. Some people interpret the Bible as providing an adequate theodicy. According to their interpretation, Adam and Eve freely chose to sin in the Garden of Eden. When they did so, this effectively unleashed all of the rest of the evil that we find in the world. This theodicy apparently can explain *all* of the evil that there is, not just the evils that can be attributed to soul-building and to free will. Is this theodicy an adequate reply to the Argument from Evil?
4. Reformulate the problem of evil in terms of an abductive argument. Construct and evaluate two or more hypotheses that each propose explanations of the quantity of evil that exists.

Readings

SAINT THOMAS AQUINAS

Five Ways to Prove That God Exists

In this selection from *Summa Theologica* (Part 1, Question 2, Article 3), Saint Thomas Aquinas provides five proofs of the existence of God. In each, an obvious and uncontroversial observation is the starting premiss.

The existence of God can be proved in five ways.

The first and more manifest way is the argument from motion. It is certain, and evident to our senses, that in the world some things are in motion. Now whatever is moved is moved by another, for nothing can be moved except it is in potentiality to that towards which it is moved; whereas a thing moves inasmuch as it is in act. For motion is nothing else than the reduction of something from potentiality to actuality. But nothing can be reduced from potentiality to actuality, except by something in a state of actuality. Thus that which is actually hot, as fire, makes wood, which is potentially hot, to be actually hot, and thereby moves and changes it. Now it is not possible that the same thing should be at once in actuality and potentiality in the same respect, but only in different respects. For what is actually hot cannot simultaneously be potentially hot; but it is simultaneously potentially cold. It is therefore impossible that in the same respect and in the same way a thing should be both mover and moved; *i.e.,* that it should move itself. Therefore, whatever is moved must be moved by another. If that by which it is moved be itself moved, then this also must needs be moved by another, and that by another again. But this cannot go on to infinity, because then there would be no first mover, and, consequently, no other mover,

Saint Thomas Aquinas, "Five Ways to Prove That God Exists," from *The Basic Writings of St. Thomas Aquinas,* edited by Anton C. Pegis (New York: Doubleday & Co., 1955), copyright © 1945, renewed 1973 by Random House, Inc. Reprinted by permission of Hackett Publishing Company, Inc. All rights reserved.

seeing that subsequent movers move only inasmuch as they are moved by the first mover; as the staff moves only because it is moved by the hand. Therefore it is necessary to arrive at a first mover, moved by no other; and this everyone understands to be God.

The second way is from the nature of efficient cause. In the world of sensible things we find there is an order of efficient causes. There is no case known (neither is it, indeed, possible) in which a thing is found to be the efficient cause of itself; for so it would be prior to itself, which is impossible. Now in efficient causes it is not possible to go on to infinity, because in all efficient causes following in order, the first is the cause of the intermediate cause, and the intermediate is the cause of the ultimate cause, whether the intermediate cause be several, or one only. Now to take away the cause is to take away the effect. Therefore, if there be no first cause among efficient causes, there will be no ultimate, nor any intermediate, cause. But if in efficient causes it is possible to go on to infinity, there will be no first efficient cause, neither will there be an ultimate effect, nor any intermediate efficient causes; all of which is plainly false. Therefore it is necessary to admit a first efficient cause, to which everyone gives the name of God.

The third way is taken from possibility and necessity, and runs thus. We find in nature things that are possible to be and not to be, since they are found to be generated, and to be corrupted, and consequently, it is possible for them to be and not to be. But it is impossible for these always to exist, for that which can not-be at some time is not. Therefore, if everything can not-be, then at one time there was nothing in existence. Now if this were true, even now there would be nothing in existence, because that which does not exist begins to exist only through something already existing. Therefore, if at one time nothing was in existence, it would have been impossible for anything to have begun to exist; and thus even now nothing would be in existence—which is absurd. Therefore, not all beings are merely possible, but there must exist something the existence of which is necessary. But every necessary thing either has its necessity caused by another, or not. Now it is impossible to go on to infinity in necessary things which have their necessity caused by another, as has been already proved in regard to efficient causes. Therefore we cannot but admit the existence of some being having of itself its own necessity, and not receiving it from another, but rather causing in others their necessity. This all men speak of as God.

The fourth way is taken from the gradation to be found in things. Among beings there are some more and some less good, true, noble, and the like. But *more* and *less* are predicated of different things according as they resemble in their different ways something which is the maximum, as a thing is said to be hotter according as it more nearly resembles that which is hottest; so that there is something which is truest, something best, something noblest, and, consequently, something which is most being, for those things that are greatest in truth are greatest in being, as it is written in *Metaphysics* II [a work of Aristotle]. Now the maximum in any genus is the cause of all in that genus, as fire, which is the maximum of heat, is the cause of all hot things, as is said in the same book. Therefore there must also be something which is to all beings the cause of their being, goodness, and every other perfection; and this we call God.

The fifth way is taken from the governance of the world. We see that things which lack knowledge, such as natural bodies, act for an end, and this is evident from their acting always, or nearly always, in the same way, so as to obtain the best result. Hence it is plain that they achieve their end, not fortuitously, but designedly. Now whatever lacks knowledge cannot move towards an end, unless it be directed by some being endowed with knowledge and intelligence; as the arrow is directed by the archer. Therefore some intelligent being exists by whom all natural things are directed to their end; and this being we call God.

WILLIAM PALEY

The Design Argument

In this selection from his **Natural Theology** (1836 edition), William Paley elaborates an argument for the existence of God that traces back at least to the last of Aquinas's five ways. His discussion of how one interprets a watch found on a heath is one of the most famous analogies proposed in the history of philosophy. The term "natural theology" means that the author attempts to establish the existence and nature of God by the same methods used in the natural sciences—observation and reasoning.

In crossing a heath, suppose I pitched my foot against a stone, and were asked how the stone came to be there: I might possibly answer, that for any thing I knew to the contrary, it had laid there for ever: nor would it perhaps be very easy to shew the absurdity of this answer. But suppose I had found a *watch* upon the ground, and it should be inquired how the watch happened to be in that place; I should hardly think of the answer which I had before given, that, for any thing I knew, the watch might have always been there. Yet why should not this answer serve for the watch as well as for the stone? why is it not as admissible in the second case, as in the first? For this reason, and for no other, viz, that, when we come to inspect the watch, we perceive (what we could not discover in the stone) that its several parts are framed and put together for a purpose, e.g. that they are so formed and adjusted as to produce motion, and that motion so regulated as to point out the hour of the day; that, if the different parts had been differently shaped from what they are, of a different size from what they are, or placed after any other manner, or in any other order, than that in which they are placed, either no motion at all would have been carried on in the machine, or none that would have answered the use that is now served by it. To reckon up a few of the plainest of these parts, and of their offices, all tending to one result:—We see a cylindrical box containing a coiled elastic spring, which, by its

William Paley, "The Design Argument," from *Natural Theology,* 1836.

endeavor to relax itself, turns round the box. We next observe a flexible chain (artificially wrought for the sake of flexure), communicating the action of the spring from the box to the fusee. We then find a series of wheels, the teeth of which catch in, and apply to each other, conducting the motion from the fusee to the balance, and from the balance to the pointer; and at the same time by the size and shape of those wheels so regulating that motion, as to terminate in causing an index, by an equable and measured progression, to pass over a given space in a given time. We take notice that the wheels are made of brass in order to keep them from rust; the springs of steel, no other metal being so elastic; that over the face of the watch there is placed a glass, a material employed in no other part of the work, but in the room of which, if there had been any other than a transparent substance, the hour could not be seen without opening the case. This mechanism being observed (it requires indeed an examination of the instrument, and perhaps some previous knowledge of the subject, to perceive and understand it; but being once, as we have said, observed and understood), the inference, we think, is inevitable, that the watch must have had a maker; that there must have existed, at some time, and at some place or other, an artificer or artificers, who formed it for the purpose which we find it actually to answer; who comprehended its construction and designed its use.

I. Nor would it, I apprehend, weaken the conclusion that we had never seen a watch made—that we had never known an artist capable of making one—that we were altogether incapable of executing such a piece of workmanship ourselves, or of understanding in what manner it was performed; all this being no more than what is true of some exquisite remains of ancient art, of some lost arts, and, to the generality of mankind, of the more curious productions of modern manufacture. Does one man in a million know how oval frames are turned? Ignorance of this kind exalts our opinion of the unseen and unknown artist's skill, if he be unseen and unknown, but raises no doubt in our minds of the existence and agency of such an artist, at some former time and in some place or other. Nor can I perceive that it varies at all the inference, whether the question arise concerning a human agent or concerning an agent of a different species, or an agent possessing in some respects a different nature.

II. Neither, secondly, would it invalidate our conclusion, that the watch sometimes went wrong, or that it seldom went exactly right. The purpose of the machinery, the design, and the designer might be evident, in whatever way we accounted for the irregularity of the movement, or whether we could account for it or not. It is not necessary that a machine be perfect, in order to show with what design it was made: still less necessary, where the only question is whether it were made with any design at all.

III. Nor, thirdly, would it bring any uncertainty into the argument, if there were a few parts of the watch concerning which we could not discover or had not yet discovered in what manner they conduced to the general effect; or even some parts, concerning which we could not ascertain whether they conduced to that effect in any manner whatever. For, as to the first branch of the case, if by the loss, or disorder, or decay of the parts in question, the movement of the watch were found in fact to be stopped, or disturbed, or retarded, no doubt would remain in our minds as to the utility or intention of these parts, although we should be unable to investigate the manner according to which, or the connection by which, the ultimate effect depended upon their action or assistance; and the more complex the machine, the more likely is this obscurity to arise. Then, as to the second thing supposed, namely, that there were parts which might be spared without prejudice to the movement of the watch, and that we had proved this by experiment, these superfluous parts, even if we were completely assured that they were such, would not vacate the reasoning which we had instituted concerning other parts. The indication of contrivance remained, with respect to them, nearly as it was before.

IV. Nor, fourthly, would any man in his senses think the existence of the watch with its various machinery accounted for, by being told that it was one out of possible combinations of material forms; that whatever he had found in the place where he found the watch, must have contained some internal configuration or other; and that this configuration might be the structure now exhibited; namely, of the works of a watch, as well as a different structure.

V. Nor, fifthly, would it yield his inquiry more satisfaction, to be answered that there existed in things a principle of order, which had disposed the parts of the watch into their present form and situation. He never knew a watch made by the principle of order; nor can he even form to himself an idea of what is meant by a principle of order, distinct from the intelligence of the watchmaker.

VI. Sixthly, he would be surprised to hear that the mechanism of the watch was no proof of contrivance, only a motive to induce the mind to think so.

VII. And not less surprised to be informed, that the watch in his hand was nothing more than the result of the laws of metallic nature. It is a perversion of language to assign any law as the efficient, operative cause of any thing. A law presupposes an agent; for it is only the mode according to which an agent proceeds: it implies a power; for it is the order according to which that power acts. Without this agent, without this power, which are both distinct from itself, the *law* does nothing, is nothing. The expression, "the law of metallic nature," may sound strange and harsh to a philosophic ear; but it seems quite as justifiable as some others which are more familiar to him, such as "the law of vegetable nature," "the law of animal nature," or, indeed, as "the law of nature" in general, when assigned as the cause of phenomena, in exclusion of agency and power, or when it is substituted into the place of these.

VIII. Neither, lastly, would our observer be driven out of his conclusion or from his confidence in its truth, by being told that he knew nothing at all about the matter. He knows enough for his argument; he knows the utility of the end; he knows the subserviency and adaptation of the means to the end. These points being known, his ignorance of other points, his doubts concerning other points, affect not the certainty of his reasoning. The consciousness of knowing little need not beget a distrust of that which he does know.

DAVID HUME

Critique of the Design Argument

In this selection from his ***Dialogues Concerning Natural Religion*** (1779), Hume describes a conversation between Cleanthes, Demea, and Philo. Hume did not publish this work during his lifetime, probably because he was apprehensive about what the public reaction would be.

Not to lose any time in circumlocutions, said Cleanthes, addressing himself to Demea, much less in replying to the pious declamations of Philo, I shall briefly explain how I conceive this matter. Look round the world: Contemplate the whole and every part of it: You will find it to be nothing but one great machine, subdivided into an infinite number of lesser machines, which again admit of subdivisions to a degree beyond what human senses and faculties can trace and explain. All these various machines, and even their most minute parts, are adjusted to each other with an accuracy which ravishes into admiration all men who have ever contemplated them. The curious adapting of means to ends, throughout all nature, resembles exactly, though it much exceeds, the productions of human contrivance—of human design, thought, wisdom, and intelligence. Since therefore the effects resemble each other, we are led to infer, by all the rules of analogy, that the causes also resemble, and that the Author of Nature is somewhat similar to the mind of man, though possessed of much larger faculties, proportioned to the grandeur of the work which he has executed. By this argument *a posteriori*, and by this argument alone, do we prove at once the existence of a Deity and his similarity to human mind and intelligence.

I shall be so free, Cleanthes, said Demea, as to tell you that from the beginning I could not approve of your conclusion concerning the similarity of the Deity to men, still less can I approve of the mediums by which you endeavor to establish it. What! No demonstration of the Being of God! No abstract arguments! No proofs *a priori*! Are these which have hitherto been so much insisted on by philosophers all fallacy, all sophism? Can we reach no farther in this subject than experience and probability? I will say not that this is betraying the cause of a Deity; but surely, by this affected candor, you give advantages to atheists which they never could obtain by the mere dint of argument and reasoning.

What I chiefly scruple in this subject, said Philo, is not so much that all religious arguments are by Cleanthes reduced to experience, as that they appear not to be even the most certain and irrefragable of that inferior kind. That a stone will fall, that fire will burn, that the earth has solidity, we have observed a thousand and a thousand times; and when any new instance of this nature is presented, we draw without hesitation the accustomed inference. The exact similarity of the cases gives us a

David Hume, "Critique of the Design Argument," from *Dialogues Concerning Natural Religion*, edited by Norman Kemp Smith (Walton-on-Thames, England: Thomas Nelson and Sons Ltd., 1947).

perfect assurance of a similar event, and a stronger evidence is never desired nor sought after. But wherever you depart, in the least, from the similarity of the cases, you diminish proportionably the evidence; and may at last bring it to a very weak *analogy,* which is confessedly liable to error and uncertainty. After having experienced the circulation of the blood in human creatures, we make no doubt that it takes place in Titius and Maevius; but from its circulation in frogs and fishes it is only a presumption, though a strong one, from analogy that it takes place in men and other animals. The analogical reasoning is much weaker when we infer the circulation of the sap in vegetables from our experience that the blood circulates in animals; and those who hastily followed that imperfect analogy are found, by more accurate experiments, to have been mistaken.

If we see a house, Cleanthes, we conclude, with the greatest certainty, that it had an architect or builder because this is precisely that species of effect which we have experienced to proceed from that species of cause. But surely you will not affirm that the universe bears such a resemblance to a house that we can with the same certainty infer a similar cause, or that the analogy is here entire and perfect. The dissimilitude is so striking that the utmost you can here pretend to is a guess, a conjecture, a presumption concerning a similar cause; and how that pretension will be received in the world, I leave you to consider.

It would surely be very ill received, replied Cleanthes; and I should be deservedly blamed and detested did I allow that the proofs of a Deity amounted to no more than a guess or conjecture. But is the whole adjustment of means to ends in a house and in the universe so slight a resemblance? the economy of final causes? the order, proportion, and arrangement of every part? Steps of a stair are plainly contrived that human legs may use them in mounting; and this inference is certain and infallible. Human legs are also contrived for walking and mounting; and this inference, I allow, is not altogether so certain because of the dissimilarity which you remark; but does it, therefore, deserve the name only of presumption or conjecture?

Good God! cried Demea, interrupting him, where are we? Zealous defenders of religion allow that the proofs of a Deity fall short of perfect evidence! And you, Philo, on whose assistance I depended in proving the adorable mysteriousness of the Divine Nature, do you assent to all these extravagant opinions of Cleanthes? For what other name can I give them? or, why spare my censure when such principles are advanced, supported by such an authority, before so young a man as Pamphilus?

You seem not to apprehend, replied Philo, that I argue with Cleanthes in his own way, and, by showing him the dangerous consequences of his tenets, hope at last to reduce him to our opinion. But what sticks most with you, I observe, is the representation which Cleanthes has made of the argument *a posteriori;* and, finding that that argument is likely to escape your hold and vanish into air, you think it so disguised that you can scarcely believe it to be set in its true light. Now, however much I may dissent, in other respects, from the dangerous principle of Cleanthes, I must allow that he has fairly represented that argument, and I shall endeavor so to state the matter to you that you will entertain no further scruples with regard to it.

Were a man to abstract from everything which he knows or has seen, he would be altogether incapable, merely from his own ideas, to determine what kind of scene the universe must be, or to give the preference to one state or situation of things above another. For as nothing which he clearly conceives could be esteemed impossible or implying a contradiction, every chimera of his fancy would be upon an equal footing; nor could he assign just reason why he adheres to one idea or system, and rejects the others which are equally possible.

Again, after he opens his eyes and contemplates the world as it really is, it would be impossible for him at first to assign the cause of any one event, much less the whole of things, or of the universe. He might set his fancy a rambling, and she might bring him in an infinite variety of reports and representations. These would all be possible; but, being all equally possible, he would never of himself give a satisfactory account for his preferring one of them to the rest. Experience alone can point out to him the true cause of any phenomenon.

Now, according to this method of reasoning, Demea, it follows (and is, indeed, tacitly allowed by Cleanthes himself) that order, arrangement, or the adjustment of final causes, is not of itself any proof of design, but only so far as it has been experienced to proceed from that principle. For aught we can know *a priori*, matter may contain the source or spring of order originally within itself, as well as mind does; and there is no more difficulty in conceiving that the several elements, from an internal unknown cause, may fall into the most exquisite arrangement, than to conceive that their ideas, in the great universal mind, from a like internal unknown cause, fall into that arrangement. The equal possibility of both these suppositions is allowed. But, by experience, we find (according to Cleanthes) that there is a difference between them. Throw several pieces of steel together, without shape or form they will never arrange themselves so as to compose a watch. Stone and mortar and wood, without an architect, never erect a house. But the ideas in a human mind, we see, by an unknown, inexplicable economy, arrange themselves so as to form the plan of a watch or house. Experience, therefore, proves that there is an original principle of order in mind, not in matter. From similar effects we infer similar causes. The adjustment of means to ends is alike in the universe, as in a machine of human contrivance. The causes, therefore, must be resembling.

I was from the beginning scandalized, I must own, with this resemblance which is asserted between the Deity and human creatures, and must conceive it to imply such a degradation of the Supreme Being as no sound theist could endure. With your assistance, therefore, Demea, I shall endeavor to defend what you justly call the adorable mysteriousness of the Divine nature, and shall refute this reasoning of Cleanthes, provided he allows that I have made a fair representation of it.

When Cleanthes had assented, Philo, after a short pause, proceeded in the following manner.

That all inferences, Cleanthes, concerning fact are founded on experience, and that all experimental reasonings are founded on the supposition that similar causes prove similar effects, and similar effects similar causes, I shall not at present much dispute with you. But observe, I entreat you, with what extreme caution all just reasoners proceed in the transferring of experiments to similar cases. Unless the cases be exactly similar, they repose no perfect confidence in applying their past observation to any particular phenomenon. Every alteration of circumstances occasions a doubt concerning the event; and it requires new experiments to prove certainly that the new circumstances are of no moment or importance. A change in bulk, situation, arrangement, age, disposition of the air, or surrounding bodies—any of these particulars may be attended with the most unexpected consequences. And unless the objects be quite familiar to us, it is the highest temerity to expect with assurance, after any of these changes, an event similar to that which before fell under our observation. The slow and deliberate steps of philosophers here, if anywhere, are distinguished from the precipitate march of the vulgar, who, hurried on by the smallest similitude, are incapable of all discernment or consideration.

But you can think, Cleanthes, that your usual phlegm and philosophy have been preserved in so wide a step as you have taken when you compared to the universe houses, ships, furniture, machines; and, from their similarity in some circumstances, inferred a similarity in their causes? Thought, design, intelligence, such as we discover in men and other animals, is no more than one of the springs and principles of the universe, as well as heat or cold, attraction or repulsion, and a hundred others which fall under daily observation. It is an active cause by which some particular parts of nature, we find, produce alterations on other parts. But can a conclusion, with any propriety, be transferred from parts to the whole? Does not the great disproportion bar all comparison and inference? From observing the growth of a hair, can we learn anything concerning the generation of a man? Would the manner of a leaf's blowing, even though perfectly known, afford us any instruction concerning the vegetation of a tree?

But allowing that we were to take the *operations* of one part of nature upon another for the foundation of our judgment concerning the *origin* of the whole (which never can be admitted), yet why select so minute, so weak, so bounded a principle as the reason and design of animals is found to be upon this planet? What peculiar privilege has this little agitation of the brain which we call *thought*, that we must thus make it the model of the whole universe? Our partiality in our own favor does indeed present it on all occasions, but sound philosophy ought carefully to guard against so natural an illusion.

So far from admitting, continued Philo, that the operations of a part can afford us any just conclusion concerning the origin of the whole, I will not allow any one part to form a rule for another part if the latter be very remote from the former. Is there any reasonable ground to conclude that the inhabitants of other planets possess thought, intelligence, reason, or anything similar to these faculties in men? When nature has so extremely diversified her manner of operation in this small globe, can we imagine that she incessantly copies herself throughout so immense a universe? And if thought, as we may well suppose, be confined merely to this narrow corner and has even there so limited a sphere of action, with what propriety can we assign it for the original cause of all things? The narrow views of a peasant who makes his domestic economy the rule for the government of kingdoms is in comparison a pardonable sophism.

But were we ever so much assured that a thought and reason resembling the human were to be found throughout the whole universe, and were its activity elsewhere vastly greater and more commanding than it appears in this globe; yet I cannot see why the operations of a world constituted, arranged, adjusted, can with any propriety be extended to a world which is in its embryo-state, and is advancing towards that constitution and arrangement. By observation we know somewhat of the economy, action, and nourishment of a finished animal; but we must transfer with great caution that observation to the growth of a foetus in the womb, and still more to the formation of an animalcule in the loins of its male parent. Nature, we find, even from our limited experience, possesses an infinite number of springs and principles which incessantly discover themselves on every change of her position and situation. And what new and unknown principles would actuate her in so new and unknown a situation as that of the formation of a universe, we cannot, without the utmost temerity, pretend to determine.

A very small part of this great system, during a very short time, is very imperfectly discovered to us; and do we thence pronounce decisively concerning the origin of the whole?

Admirable conclusion! Stone, wood, brick, iron, brass, have not, at this time, in this minute globe of earth, an order or arrangement without human art and contrivance; therefore, the universe could not originally attain its order and arrangement without something similar to human art. But is a part of nature a rule for another part very wide of the former? Is it a rule for the whole? Is a very small part a rule for the universe? Is nature in one situation a certain rule for nature in another situation vastly different from the former?

And can you blame me, Cleanthes, if I here imitate the prudent reserve of Simonides, who, according to the noted story, being asked by Hiero, *What God was?* desired a day to think of it, and then two days more; and after that manner continually prolonged the term, without ever bringing in his definition or description? Could you even blame me if I had answered, at first, *that I did not know,* and was sensible that this subject lay vastly beyond the reach of my faculties? You might cry out sceptic and railer, as much as you pleased; but, having found in so many other subjects much more familiar the imperfections and even contradictions of human reason, I never should expect any success from its feeble conjectures in a subject so sublime and so remote from the sphere of our observation. When two *species* of objects have always been observed to be conjoined together, I can *infer,* by custom, the existence of one wherever I *see* the existence of the other; and this I call an argument from experience. But how this argument can have place where the objects, as in the present case, are single, individual, without parallel or specific resemblance, may be difficult to explain. And will any man tell me with a serious countenance that an orderly universe must arise from some thought and art like the human because we have experience of it? To ascertain this reasoning it were requisite that we had experience of the origin of the worlds; and it is not sufficient, surely, that we have seen ships and cities arise from human art and contrivance. . . .

Philo was proceeding in this vehement manner, somewhat between jest and earnest, as it appeared to me, when he observed some signs of impatience in Cleanthes, and then immediately stopped short. What I had to suggest, said Cleanthes, is only that you would not abuse terms, or make use of popular expressions to subvert philosophical reasonings. You know that the vulgar often distinguish reason from experience, even where the question relates only to matter of fact and existence, though it is found, where that *reason* is properly analyzed, that it is nothing but a species of experience. To prove by experience the origin of the universe from mind is not more contrary to common speech than to prove the motion of the earth from the same principle. And a caviller might raise all the same objections to the Copernican system which you have urged against my reasonings. Have you other earths, might he say, which you have seen to move? Have . . .

Yes! cried Philo, interrupting him, we have other earths. Is not the moon another earth, which we see to turn round its center? Is not Venus another earth, where we observe the same phenomenon? Are not the revolutions of the sun also a confirmation, from analogy, of the same theory? All the planets, are they not earths which revolve about the sun? Are not the satellites moons which move round Jupiter and Saturn, and along with these primary planets round the sun? These analogies and resemblances, with others which I have not mentioned, are the sole proofs of the Copernican system; and to you it belongs to consider whether you have any analogies of the same kind to support your theory.

In reality, Cleanthes, continued he, the modern system of astronomy is now so much received by all inquirers, and has become so essential a part even of our earliest education, that we are not commonly very scrupulous in examining the reasons upon which it is founded. It is now become a matter of mere curiosity to study the first writers on that subject who had the full force of prejudice to encounter, and were obliged to turn their arguments on every side in order to render them popular and convincing. But if we peruse Galileo's famous *Dialogues* concerning the system of the world, we shall find that that great genius, one of the sublimest that ever existed, first bent all his endeavors to prove that there was no foundation for the distinction commonly made between elementary and celestial substances. The schools, proceeding from the illusions of sense, had carried this distinction very far; and had established the latter substances to be ingenerable, incorruptible, unalterable, impassible; and had assigned all the opposite qualities to the former. But Galileo, beginning with the moon, proved its similarity in every particular to the earth: its convex figure, its natural darkness when not illuminated, its density, its distinction into solid and liquid, the variations of its phases, the mutual illuminations of the earth and moon, their mutual eclipses, the inequalities of the lunar surface, etc. After many instances of this kind, with regard to all the planets, men plainly saw that these bodies became proper objects of experience, and that the similarity of their nature enabled us to extend the same arguments and phenomena from one to the other.

In this cautious proceeding of the astronomers you may read your own condemnation, Cleanthes; or rather may see that the subject in which you are engaged exceeds all human reason and inquiry. Can you pretend to show any such similarity between the fabric of a house and the generation of a universe? Have you ever seen nature in any such situation as resembles the first arrangement of the elements? Have worlds ever been formed under your eye, and have you had leisure to observe the whole progress of the phenomenon, from the first appearance of order to its final consummation? If you have, then cite your experience and deliver your theory.

SAINT ANSELM AND GAUNILO

The Ontological Argument

In this selection from the **Proslogion,** Saint Anselm attempts to provide an a priori proof of the existence of God. Gaunilo, a contemporary of Anselm's, presents two criticisms of the argument. In one of them, he claims that if Anselm's argument establishes the existence of God, then the existence of a perfect island would be provable a priori. Anselm replies to each of Gaunilo's criticisms.

ANSELM

Chapter II. That God Truly Is

O Lord, you who give understanding to faith, so far as you know it to be beneficial, give me to understand that you are just as we believe, and that you are what we believe.

We certainly believe that you are something than which nothing greater can be conceived.

But is there any such nature, since "the fool has said in his heart: God is not"?

However, when this very same fool hears what I say, when he hears of "something than which nothing greater can be conceived," he certainly understands what he hears.

What he understands stands in relation to his understanding (*esse in intellectu*), even if he does not understand that it exists. For it is one thing for a thing to stand in relation to our understanding; it is another thing for us to understand that it really exists. For instance, when a painter imagines what he is about to paint, he has it in relation to his understanding. However, he does not yet understand that it exists, because he has not yet made it. After he paints it, then he both has it in relation to his understanding and understands that it exists. Therefore, even the fool is convinced that "something than which nothing greater can be conceived" at least stands in relation to his understanding, because when he hears of it he understands it, and whatever he understands stands in relation to his understanding.

And certainly that than which a greater cannot be conceived cannot stand only in relation to the understanding. For if it stands at least in relation to the understanding, it can be conceived to be also in reality, and this is something greater. Therefore, if "that than which a greater cannot be conceived" only stood in relation to the understanding, then "that than which a greater cannot be conceived" would be something than which a greater can be conceived. But this is certainly impossible.

Therefore, something than which a greater cannot be conceived undoubtedly both stands in relation to the understanding and exists in reality.

Reprinted with the permission of Scribner, a Division of Simon & Schuster, from *The Many-Faced Argument,* edited by John Hick and Arthur C. McGill. Copyright © 1967 by John Hick and Arthur C. McGill.

Chapter III. That It Is Impossible to Conceive That God Is Not

This so truly is that it is impossible to think of it as not existing.

It can be conceived to be something such that we cannot conceive of it as not existing.

This is greater than something which we can conceive of as not existing.

Therefore, if that than which a greater cannot be conceived could be conceived not to be, we would have an impossible contradiction: That than which a greater cannot be conceived would not be that than which a greater cannot be conceived.

Therefore, something than which a greater cannot be conceived so truly is, that it is impossible even to conceive of it as not existing.

This is you, O Lord our God. You so truly are that you cannot be thought not to be. And rightly so.

For if some mind could conceive of something better than you, the creature would rise above its Creator and would judge its Creator, which would be completely absurd.

Also, whatever else there is, except for you alone, can be conceived not to be.

Therefore, you alone, of all things exist in the truest and greatest way (*verissime et maxime esse*), for nothing else so truly exists and therefore everything else has less being.

Why, then, did the fool say in his heart: "God is not," since it is so obvious to the rational mind that you exist supremely above all things? Why, because he is stupid and foolish.

Chapter IV. How the Fool Said in His Heart What Cannot Be Conceived

How was the fool able to "say in his heart" what he was unable to conceive? Or how was it that he could not conceive what he said in his heart? For to "say in one's heart" and to "conceive" are the same thing.

However, if—or rather because—he really did conceive of it (since he said it in his heart) and yet did not really say it in his heart (since he was unable to conceive of it), then there must be more than one way for something to be said in one's heart, or to be conceived.

Indeed, a thing is conceived of in one way when the word signifying it is thought; in another way when the very thing itself is understood.

Accordingly, God can be conceived not to be in the first way, but not at all in the second. Certainly no one who understands what God is can conceive that God is not. It is possible, however, for him to say this word in his heart, while giving it either no meaning at all or some alien meaning.

God is that than which a greater cannot be conceived. Whoever understands this correctly at least understands that he exists in such a way that even for thought he cannot not exist. Therefore, whoever understands that God is so cannot even conceive that he is not.

My thanksgiving to you, good Lord, my thanksgiving to you. For what I first believed through your giving I now so understand through your illumination that even if I did not want to believe that you are, I would be unable not to understand it.

GAUNILO

Consider this example: Certain people say that somewhere in the ocean there is an island, which they call the "Lost Island" because of the difficulty or, rather, the impossibility of finding what does not exist. They say that it is more abundantly filled with inestimable riches and delights than the Isles of the Blessed, and that although it has no owner or inhabitant, it excels all the lands that men inhabit taken together in the unceasing abundance of its fertility.

When someone tells me that there is such an island, I easily understand what is being said, for there is nothing difficult here. Suppose, however, as a consequence of this, that he then goes on to say: You cannot doubt that this island, more excellent than all lands, actually exists somewhere in reality, because it undoubtedly stands in relation to your understanding. Since it is more excellent, not simply to stand in relation to the understanding, but to be in reality as well, therefore this island must necessarily be in reality. Otherwise, any other land that exists in reality would be more excellent than this island, and this island, which you understand to be the most excellent of all lands would then not be the most excellent.

If, I repeat, someone should wish by this argument to demonstrate to me that this island truly exists and is no longer to be doubted, I would think he were joking; or, if I accepted the argument, I do not know whom I would regard as the greater fool, me for accepting it or him for supposing that he had proved the existence of this island with any kind of certainty. He should first show that this excellent island exists as a genuine and undeniable real thing, and not leave it standing in relation to my understanding as a false or uncertain something.

ANSELM

My reasoning, you claim, is as if something should say that there is an island in the ocean, which surpasses the whole earth in its fertility, but which is called a "Lost Island" because of the difficulty, or even impossibility, of finding something that does not exist; and as if he should then argue that no one can doubt that it actually does exist because the words describing it are easily understood.

I can confidently say that if anyone discovers for me something existing either in fact or at least in thought, other than "that than which a greater cannot be conceived," and is able to apply the logic of my argument to it, I shall find that "Lost Island" for him and shall give it to him as something which he will never lose again.

GAUNILO

When it is asserted to the fool [in *Proslogion III*] that this "greater than all things" is such that even to thought it cannot not be, and yet when this is proved to him on no other ground than that otherwise this "greater than all things" would not be greater than all things, he can give the same answer and reply: When did *I* ever say that such a being, one that is "greater than all things," exists in reality, so that from this you could prove to me that it exists so fully in reality that it cannot be conceived not to be? First of all, it should be proved by some most certain argument that some superior reality, that is, a nature which is greater and better than everything that is, actually exists. From this we can then prove all the other qualities which must not be lacking from that which is greater and better than all things.

ANSELM

That which cannot possibly not be is obviously something that can be conceived and understood. He who conceives of this conceives of something greater than he who conceives of that which has the possibility of not being. Therefore, while he is conceiving of "that than which a greater cannot be conceived," if he conceives that it has the possibility of not being, he is obviously not conceiving of "that than which a greater cannot be conceived." However, the same thing cannot be both conceived and not conceived at the same time. Therefore, he who conceives of "that than which a greater cannot be conceived" is not conceiving of what can, but of what cannot possibly, not be. For that reason, what he is conceiving must necessarily exist, because whatever is able not to exist is not that of which he is conceiving.

WILLIAM JAMES

The Will to Believe

William James (1842–1910) was an influential psychologist and philosopher who helped found the American school of philosophy known as pragmatism. In the present essay, James argues that we sometimes face decisions about what to believe that can and should be made on some basis other than the evidence at hand. His argument is an updated version of Pascal's Wager (Lecture 10).

1. . . . Let us give the name of *hypothesis* to anything that may be proposed to our belief; and just as the electricians speak of live and dead wires, let us speak of any hypothesis as either *live* or *dead*. A live hypothesis is one which appeals as a real possibility to him to whom it is proposed. If I ask you to believe in the Mahdi, the notion makes no electric connection with your nature—it refuses to scintillate with any credibility at all. As an hypothesis it is completely dead. To an Arab, however (even if he be not one of the Mahdi's followers), the hypothesis is among the mind's possibilities: it is

---

William James, "The Will to Believe," from *The Will to Believe and Other Essays in Popular Philosophy* (New York: Longmans Green & Co., 1897).

alive. This shows that deadness and liveness in an hypothesis are not intrinsic properties, but relations to the individual thinker. They are measured by his willingness to act irrevocably. Practically, that means belief; but there is some believing tendency wherever there is willingness to act at all.

Next, let us call the decision between two hypotheses an *option*. Options may be of several kinds. They may be—first, *living* or *dead;* secondly, *forced* or *avoidable;* thirdly, *momentous* or *trivial;* and for our purposes we may call an option a *genuine* option when it is of the forced, living, and momentous kind.

(1) A living option is one in which both hypotheses are live ones. If I say to you: "Be a theosophist or be a Mohammedan," it is probably a dead option, because for you neither hypothesis is likely to be alive. But if I say: "Be an agnostic or be a Christian," it is otherwise: trained as you are, each hypothesis makes some appeal, however small, to your belief.

(2) Next, if I say to you: "Choose between going out with your umbrella or without it," I do not offer you a genuine option, for it is not forced. You can easily avoid it by not going out at all. Similarly, if I say, "Either love me or hate me," "Either call my theory true or call it false," your option is avoidable. You may remain indifferent to me, neither loving nor hating, and you may decline to offer any judgment as to my theory. But if I say, "Either accept this truth or go without it," I put on you a forced option, but there is no standing place outside of the alternative. Every dilemma based on a complete logical disjunction, with no possibility of not choosing, is an option of this forced kind.

(3) Finally, if I were Dr. Nansen and proposed to you to join my North Pole expedition, your option would be momentous; for this would probably be your only similar opportunity, and your choice now would either exclude you from the North Pole sort of immortality altogether or put at least the chance of it into your hands. He who refuses to embrace a unique opportunity loses the prize as surely as if he tried and failed. *Per contra,* the option is trivial when the opportunity is not unique, when the stake is insignificant, or when the decision is reversible if it later prove unwise. Such trivial options abound in the scientific life. A chemist finds an hypothesis live enough to spend a year in its verification: he believes in it to that extent. But if his experiments prove inconclusive either way, he is quit for his loss of time, no vital harm being done. It will facilitate our discussion if we keep all these distinctions in mind. . . .

2. . . . The thesis I defend is . . . this: *Our passional nature not only lawfully may, but must, decide an option between propositions, whenever it is a genuine option that cannot by its nature be decided on intellectual grounds; for to say, under such circumstances, "Do not decide, but leave the question open," is itself a passional decision—just like deciding yes or no—and is attended with the same risk of losing the truth. . . .*

3. . . . Wherever the option between losing truth and gaining it is not momentous, we can throw the chance of *gaining truth* away, and at any rate save ourselves from any chance of *believing falsehood,* by not making up our minds at all till objective evidence has come. In scientific questions, this is almost always the case; and even in human affairs in general, the need of acting is seldom so urgent that a false belief to act on is better than no belief at all. Law courts, indeed, have to decide on the best evidence attainable for the moment, because a judge's duty is to make law as well as

to ascertain it, and (as a learned judge once said to me) few cases are worth spending much time over: the great thing is to have them decided on *any* acceptable principle, and got out of the way. But in our dealings with objective nature we obviously are recorders, not makers, of the truth; and decisions for the mere sake of deciding promptly and getting on to the next business would be wholly out of place. Throughout the breadth of physical nature facts are what they are quite independently of us, and seldom is there any such hurry about them that the risks of being duped by believing a premature theory need be faced. The questions here are always trivial options, the hypotheses are hardly living (at any rate not living for us spectators), the choice between believing truth or falsehood is seldom forced. The attitude of special balance is therefore the absolutely wise one if we would escape mistakes. What difference, indeed, does it make to most of us whether we have or have not a theory of the Röntgen rays, whether we believe or not in mind-stuff, or have a conviction about the causality of conscious states? It makes no difference. Such options are not forced on us. On every account it is better not to make them, but still keep weighing reasons *pro et contra* with an indifferent hand.

I speak, of course, here of the purely judging mind. For purposes of discovery such indifference is to be less highly recommended, and science would be far less advanced than she is if the passionate desires of individuals to get their own faiths confirmed had been kept out of the game. . . . If you want an absolute duffer in an investigation, you must, after all, take the man who has no interest whatever in its results: he is the warranted incapable, the positive fool. The most useful investigator, because the most sensitive observer, is always he whose eager interest in one side of the question is balanced by an equally keen nervousness lest he become deceived. Science has organized this nervousness into a regular *technique,* her so-called method of verification; and she has fallen so deeply in love with the method that one may even say she has ceased to care for truth by itself at all. It is only truth as technically verified that interests her. The truth of truths might come in merely affirmative form, and she would decline to touch it. Such truth as that, she might repeat with Clifford, would be stolen in defiance of her duty to mankind. Human passions, however, are stronger than technical rules. "*Le cœur a ses raisons,*" as Pascal says, "*que la raison ne connaît pas*"[1]; and however indifferent to all but the bare rules of the game the umpire, the abstract intellect, may be, the concrete players who furnish him the materials to judge of are usually, each one of them, in love with some pet "live hypothesis" of his own. Let us agree, however, that wherever there is no forced option, the dispassionately judicial intellect with no pet hypothesis, saving us, as it does, from dupery at any rate, ought to be our ideal.

The question next arises: Are there not somewhere forced options in our speculative questions, and can we (as men who may be interested at least as much in positively gaining truth as in merely escaping dupery) always wait with impunity till the coercive evidence shall have arrived? It seems *a priori* improbable that the truth should be so nicely adjusted to our needs and powers as that. In the great boarding-house of

---

1. The heart has its reasons, that reason does not know.

nature, the cakes and the butter and the syrup seldom come out so even and leave the plates so clean. Indeed, we should view them with scientific suspicion if they did.

4. *Moral questions* immediately present themselves as questions whose solution cannot wait for sensible proof. A moral question is a question not of what sensibly exists, but of what is good, or would be good if it did exist. Science can tell us what exists; but to compare the *worths*, both of what exists and of what does not exist, we must consult not science, but what Pascal calls our heart. Science herself consults her heart when she lays it down that the infinite ascertainment of fact and correction of false belief are the supreme goods for man. Challenge the statement, and science can only repeat it oracularly, or else prove it by showing that such ascertainment and correction bring men all sorts of other goods which man's heart in turn declares. The question of having moral beliefs at all or not having them is decidedly by our will. Are our moral preferences true or false, or are they only odd biological phenomena, making things good or bad for *us,* but in themselves indifferent? How can your pure intellect decide? If your heart does not *want* a world of moral reality, your head will assuredly never make you believe in one. Mephistophelian scepticism, indeed, will satisfy the head's play-instincts much better than any rigorous idealism can. Some men (even at the student age) are so naturally cool-hearted that the moralistic hypothesis never has for them any pungent life, and in their supercilious presence the hot young moralist always feels strangely ill at ease. The appearance of knowingness is on their side, of *naivete* and gullibility on his. Yet, in the articulate heart of him, he clings to it that he is not a dupe, and that there is a realm in which (as Emerson says) all their wit and intellectual superiority is no better than the cunning of a fox. Moral scepticism can no more be refuted or proved by logic than intellectual scepticism can. When we stick to it that there *is* truth (be it of either kind), we do so with our whole nature, and resolve to stand or fall by the results. The sceptic with his whole nature adopts the doubting attitude; but which of us is the wiser, Omniscience only knows.

Turn now from these wider questions of good to a certain class of questions of fact, questions concerning personal relations, states of mind between one man and another. *Do you like me or not?*—for example. Whether you do or not depends, in countless instances, on whether I meet you half-way, am willing to assume that you must like me, and show you trust and expectation. The previous faith on my part in your liking's existence is in such cases what makes your liking come. But if I stand aloof, and refuse to budge an inch until I have objective evidence . . . ten to one your liking never comes. How many women's hearts are vanquished by the mere sanguine insistence of some man that they *must* love him! He will not consent to the hypothesis that they cannot. The desire for a certain kind of truth here brings about that special truth's existence; and so it is in innumerable cases of other sorts. Who gains promotions, boons, appointments, but the man in whose life they are seen to play the part of live hypotheses, who discounts them, sacrifices other things for their sake before they have come, and takes risks for them in advance? His faith acts on the powers above him as a claim, and creates its own verification.

A social organism of any sort whatever, large or small, is what it is because each member proceeds to his own duty with a trust that the other members will simultaneously do theirs. Wherever a desired result is achieved by the co-operation of many independent persons, its existence as a fact is a pure consequence of the precursive faith in one another of those immediately concerned. A government, an army, a commercial system, a ship, a college, an athletic team, all exist on this condition, without which not only is nothing achieved, but nothing is even attempted. A whole train of passengers (individually brave enough) will be looted by a few highwaymen, simply because the latter can count on one another, while each passenger fears that if he makes a movement of resistance, he will be shot before any one else backs him up. If we believed that the whole carfull would rise at once with us, we should each severally rise, and trainrobbing would never be attempted. There are, then, cases where a fact cannot come at all unless a preliminary faith exists in its coming. *And where faith in a fact can help create the fact,* that would be an insane logic which should say that faith running ahead of scientific evidence is the "lowest kind of immortality" into which a thinking being can fall. Yet such is the logic by which our scientific absolutists pretend to regulate our lives!

5. In truths dependent on our personal action, then, faith based on desire is certainly a lawful and possibly an indispensable thing.

But now, it will be said, these are all childish human cases, and have nothing to do with great cosmical matters, like the question of religious faith. Let us then pass on to that. Religions differ so much in their accidents that in discussing the religious question we must make it very generic and broad. What then do we now mean by the religious hypothesis? Science says things are; morality says some things are better than other things; and religion says essentially two things.

First, she says that the best things are the more eternal things, the overlapping things, the things in the universe that throw the last stone, so to speak, and say the final word. "Perfection is eternal"—this phrase of Charles Secretan seems a good way of putting this first affirmation of religion, an affirmation which obviously cannot yet be verified scientifically at all.

The second affirmation of religion is that we are better off even now if we believe her first affirmation to be true.

Now, let us consider what the logical elements of this situation are *in case the religious hypothesis in both its branches be really true.* (Of course, we must admit that possibility at the outset. If we are to discuss the question at all, it must involve a living option. If for any of you religion be a hypothesis that cannot, by any living possibility, be true, then you need go no farther. I speak to the "saving remnant" alone.) So proceeding, we see, first, that religion offers itself as a *momentous* option. We are supposed to gain, even now, by our belief, and to lose by our non-belief, a certain vital good. Secondly, religion is a *forced* option, so far as that good goes. We cannot escape the issue by remaining sceptical and waiting for more light, because, although we do avoid error in that way *if religion be untrue,* we lose the good, *if it be true,* just as certainly as if we positively chose to disbelieve. It is as if a man should hesitate indefinitely to ask a certain woman to marry him because he was not perfectly sure that she would prove an angel after he brought her home. Would he not cut himself off from that particular angel-possibility as decisively as if he went and married some one else? Scepticism, then, is not avoidance of option; it is option of a certain particular kind of risk. *Better risk loss of truth than chance of error*—that is your faith-vetoer's exact position. He is actively playing his stake as much as the believer is; he is backing the field against the religious hypothesis, just as the believer is backing the religious hypothesis against the field. To preach scepticism to us as a duty until "sufficient evidence" for religion be found, is tantamount therefore to telling us, when in the presence of a religious hypothesis, that to yield to our fear of its being error is wiser and better than to yield to our hope that it may be true. It is not intellect against all passions, then; it is only intellect with one passion laying down its law. And by what, forsooth, is the supreme wisdom of this passion warranted? Dupery for dupery, what proof is there that dupery through hope is so much worse than dupery through fear? I, for one, can see no proof; and I simply refuse obedience to the scientist's command to imitate his kind of option, in a case where my own stake is important enough to give me the right to choose my own form of risk. If religion be true and the evidence for it be still insufficient, I do not wish, by putting your extinguisher upon my nature (which feels to me as if it had after all some business in this matter), to forfeit my sole chance in life of getting upon the winning side—that chance depending, of course, on my willingness to run the risk of acting as if my passional need of taking the world religiously might be prophetic and right.

All this is on the supposition that it really may be prophetic and right, and that, even to us who are discussing the matter, religion is a live hypothesis which may be true. Now, to most of us religion comes in a still further way that makes a veto on our active faith even more illogical. The more perfect and more eternal aspect of the universe is represented in our religions as having personal form. The universe is no longer a mere It to us, but a *Thou*, if we are religious; and any relation that may be possible from person to person might be possible here. For instance, although in one sense we are passive portions of the universe, in another we show a curious autonomy, as if we were small active centres on our own account. We feel, too, as if the appeal of religion to us were made to our own active good-will, as if evidence might be forever withheld from us unless we met the hypothesis half-way. To take a trivial illustration: just as a man who is in a company of gentlemen made no advances, asked a warrant for every concession, and believed no one's word without proof, would cut himself off by such churlishness from all the social rewards that a more trusting spirit would earn—so here, one who should shut himself up in snarling logicality and try to make the gods extort his recognition willy-nilly, or not get it at all, might cut himself off forever from his only opportunity of making the gods' acquaintance. This feeling, forced on us we know not whence, that by obstinately believing that there are gods (although not to do so would be so easy both for our logic and our life) we are doing the universe the deepest service we can, seems part of the living essence of the religious hypothesis. If the hypothesis were true in all its parts, including this one, then pure intellectualism, with its veto on our making willing advances, would be an absurdity; and some participation of our sympathetic nature would be logically required. I, therefore, for one, cannot see my way to accepting the agnostic rules for truth-seeking, or willfully agree to keep my willing nature out of the game. I cannot do so for this plain reason, that *a rule of thinking which would absolutely prevent me from acknowledging certain kinds of truth if those kinds of truth were really there, would be an irrational rule.* That for me is the long and short of the formal logic of the situation, no matter what the kinds of truth might materially be.

I confess I do not see how this logic can be escaped. But sad experience makes me fear that some of you may still shrink from radically saying with me, *in abstracto,* that we have the right to believe at our own risk any hypothesis that is live enough to tempt our will. I suspect, however, that if this is so, it is because you have got away from the abstract logical point of view altogether, and are thinking (perhaps without realizing it) of some particular religious hypothesis which for you is dead. The freedom to "believe what we will" you apply to the case of some patent superstition; and the faith you think of is the faith defined by the schoolboy when he said, "Faith is when you believe something that you know ain't true." I can only repeat that this is misapprehension. *In concreto,* the freedom to believe can only cover living options which the intellect of the individual cannot by itself resolve; and living options never seem absurdities to him who has them to consider. When I look at the religious question as it really puts itself to concrete men, and when I think of all the possibilities which both practically and theoretically it involves, then this command that we shall put a stopper on our heart, instincts, and courage, and *wait*—acting of course meanwhile more or less as if religion were *not* true—till doomsday, or till such time as our intellect and senses working together may have raked in evidence enough—this command, I say, seems to me the queerest idol ever manufactured in the philosophic cave. Were we scholastic absolutists, there might be more excuse. If we had an infallible intellect with its objective certitudes, we might feel ourselves disloyal to such a perfect organ of knowledge in not trusting to it exclusively, in not waiting for its releasing word. But if we are empiricists, if we believe that no bell in us tolls to let us know for certain when truth is in our grasp, then it seems a piece of idle fantasticality to preach so solemnly our duty of waiting for the bell. Indeed we *may* wait if we will—I hope you do not think that I am denying that—but if we do so, we do so at our peril as much as if we believed. In either case we *act,* taking our life in our hands. No one of us ought to issue vetoes to the other, nor should we bandy words of abuse. We ought, on the contrary, delicately and profoundly to respect one another's mental freedom: then only shall we bring about the intellectual republic; then only shall we have that spirit of inner tolerance without which all our outer tolerance is soulless, and which is empiricism's glory; then only shall we live and let live, in speculative as well as in practical things. . . .

ALFRED JULES AYER

The Meaninglessness of Religious Discourse

In this selection from *Language, Truth, and Logic* (1936), A. J. Ayer argues that the positivist theory of meaning shows that the claim that God exists is neither true nor false—it is meaningless.

It is now generally admitted, at any rate by philosophers, that the existence of a being having the attributes which define the god of any non-animistic religion cannot be demonstratively proved. To see that this is so, we have only to ask ourselves what are the premises from which the existence of such a god could be deduced. If the conclusion that a god exists is to be demonstratively certain, then these premises must be certain; for, as the conclusion of a deductive argument is already contained in the premises, any uncertainty there may be about the truth of the premises is necessarily shared by it. But we know that no empirical proposition can ever be anything more than probable. It is only *a priori* propositions that are logically certain. But we cannot deduce the existence of a god from an *a priori* proposition. For we know that the reason *a priori* propositions are certain is that they are tautologies. And from a set of tautologies nothing but a further tautology can be validly deduced. It follows that there is no possibility of demonstrating the existence of a god.

What is not so generally recognized is that there can be no way of proving that the existence of a god, such as the God of Christianity, is even probable. Yet this also is easily shown. For if the existence of such a god were probable, then the proposition that he existed would be an empirical hypothesis. And in that case it would be possible to deduce from it, and other empirical hypotheses, certain experiential propositions which were not deducible from those other hypotheses alone. But in fact this is not possible. It is sometimes claimed, indeed, that the existence of a certain sort of regularity in nature constitutes sufficient evidence for the existence of a god. But if the sentence "God exists" entails no more than that certain types of phenomena occur in certain sequences, then to assert the existence of a god will be simply equivalent to asserting that there is the requisite regularity in nature; and no religious man would admit that this was all he intended to assert in asserting the existence of a god. He would say that in talking about God, he was talking about a transcendent being who might be known through certain empirical manifestations, but certainly could not be defined in terms of those manifestations. But in that case the term "god" is a metaphysical term. And if "god" is a metaphysical term, then it cannot be even probable that a god exists. For to say that "God exists" is to make a metaphysical utterance which cannot be either true or false. And by the same criterion, no sentence which purports to describe the nature of a transcendent god can possess any literal significance.

Alfred Jules Ayer, "Religious Discourse Is Meaningless," from *Language, Truth and Logic* (New York: Dover Books, 1936), pp. 114–120. Reprinted with permission.

It is important not to confuse this view of religious assertions with the view that is adopted by atheists, or agnostics.[1] For it is characteristic of an agnostic to hold that the existence of a god is a possibility in which there is no good reason either to believe or disbelieve; and it is characteristic of an atheist to hold that it is at least probable that no god exists. And our view that all utterances about the nature of God are nonsensical, so far from being identical with, or even lending any support to, either of these familiar contentions, is actually incompatible with them. For if the assertion that there is a god is nonsensical, then the atheist's assertion that there is no god is equally nonsensical, since it is only a significant proposition that can be significantly contradicted. As for the agnostic, although he refrains from saying either that there is or that there is not a god, he does not deny that the question whether a transcendent god exists is a genuine question. He does not deny that the two sentences "There is a transcendent god" and "There is no transcendent god" express propositions one of which is actually true and the other false. All he says is that we have no means of telling which of them is true, and therefore ought not to commit ourselves to either. But we have seen that the sentences in question do not express propositions at all. And this means that agnosticism also is ruled out.

Thus we offer the theist the same comfort as we gave to the moralist. His assertions cannot possibly be valid, but they cannot be invalid either. As he says nothing at all about the world, he cannot justly be accused of saying anything false, or anything for which he has insufficient grounds. It is only when the theist claims that in asserting the existence of a transcendent god he is expressing a genuine proposition that we are entitled to disagree with him.

It is not be remarked that in cases where deities are identified with natural objects, assertions concerning them may be allowed to be significant. If, for example, a man tells me that the occurrence of thunder is alone both necessary and sufficient to establish the truth of the proposition that Jehovah is angry, I may conclude that, in his usage of words, the sentence "Jehovah is angry" is equivalent to "It is thundering." But in sophisticated religions, though they may be to some extent based on men's awe of natural process which they cannot sufficiently understand, the "person" who is supposed to control the empirical world is not himself located in it; he is held to be superior to the empirical world, and so outside it; and he is endowed with super-empirical attributes. But the notion of a person whose essential attributes are non-empirical is not an intelligible notion at all. We may have a word which is used as if it named this "person," but, unless the sentences in which it occurs express propositions which are empirically verifiable, it cannot be said to symbolize anything. And this is the case with regard to the word "god," in the usage in which it is intended to refer to a transcendent object. The mere existence of the noun is enough to foster the illusion that there is a real, or at any rate a possible entity corresponding to it. It is only when we enquire what God's attributes are that we discover that "God," in this usage, is not a genuine name.

---

1. This point was suggested to me by Professor H. H. Price.

It is common to find belief in a transcendent god conjoined with belief in an afterlife. But, in the form which it usually takes, the content of this belief is not a genuine hypothesis. To say that men do not ever die, or that the state of death is merely a state of prolonged insensibility, is indeed to express a significant proposition, though all the available evidence goes to show that it is false. But to say there is something imperceptible inside a man, which is his soul or his real self, and that it goes on living after he is dead, is to make a metaphysical assertion which has no more factual content than the assertion that there is a transcendent god.

It is worth mentioning that, according to the account which we have given of religious assertions, there is no logical ground for antagonism between religion and natural science. As far as the question of truth or falsehood is concerned, there is no opposition between the natural scientist and the theist who believes in a transcendent god. For since the religious utterances of the theist are not genuine propositions at all, they cannot stand in any logical relation to the propositions of science. Such antagonism as there is between religion and science appears to consist in the fact that science takes away one of the motives which make men religious. For it is acknowledged that one of the ultimate sources of religious feeling lies in the inability of men to determine their own destiny; and science tends to destroy the feeling of awe with which men regard an alien world, by making them believe that they can understand and anticipate the course of natural phenomena, and even to some extent control it. The fact that it has recently become fashionable for physicists themselves to be sympathetic towards religion is a point in favour of this hypothesis. For this sympathy towards religion marks the physicists' own lack of confidence in the validity of their hypotheses, which is a reaction on their part from the anti-religious dogmatism of nineteenth-century scientists, and a natural outcome of the crisis through which physics has just passed.

It is not within the scope of this enquiry to enter more deeply into the causes of religious feeling, or to discuss the probability of the continuance of religious belief. We are concerned only to answer those questions which arise out of our discussion of the possibility of religious knowledge. The point which we wish to establish is that there cannot be any transcendent truths of religion. For the sentences which the theist uses to express such "truths" are not literally significant.

An interesting feature of this conclusion is that it accords with what many theists are accustomed to say themselves. For we are often told that the nature of God is a mystery which transcends the human understanding. But to say that something transcends the human understanding is to say that it is unintelligible. And what is unintelligible cannot significantly be described. Again, we are told that God is not an object of reason but an object of faith. This may be nothing more than an admission that the existence of God must be taken on trust, since it cannot be proved. But it may also be an assertion that God is the object of a purely mystical intuition, and cannot therefore be defined in terms which are intelligible to the reason. And I think there are many theists who would assert this. But if one allows that it is impossible to define God in intelligible terms, then one is allowing that it is impossible for a sentence both to be significant and to be about God. If a mystic admits that the object of his vision is something which cannot be described, then he must also admit that he is bound to talk nonsense when he describes it.

For his part, the mystic may protest that his intuition does reveal truths to him, even though he cannot explain to others what these truths are; and that we who do not possess this faculty of intuition can have no ground for denying that it is a cognitive faculty. For we can hardly maintain *a priori* that there are no ways of discovering true propositions except those which we ourselves employ. The answer is that we set no limit to the number of ways in which one may come to formulate a true proposition. We do not in any way deny that a synthetic truth may be discovered by purely intuitive methods as well as by the rational method of induction. But we do say that every synthetic proposition, however it may have been arrived at, must be subject to the test of actual experience. We do not deny *a priori* that the mystic is able to discover truths by his own special methods. We wait to hear what are the propositions which embody his discoveries, in order to see whether they are verified or confuted by our empirical observations. But the mystic, so far from producing propositions which are empirically verified, is unable to produce any intelligible propositions at all. And therefore we say that his intuition has not revealed to him any facts. It is no use his saying that he has apprehended facts but is unable to express them. For we know that if he really had acquired any information, he would be able to express it. He would be able to indicate in some way or other how the genuineness of his discovery might be empirically determined. The fact that he cannot reveal what he "knows," or even himself devise an empirical test to validate his "knowledge," shows that his state of mystical intuition is not a genuinely cognitive state. So that in describing his vision the mystic does not give us any information about the external world; he merely gives us indirect information about the condition of his own mind.

These considerations dispose of the argument from religious experience, which many philosophers still regard as a valid argument in favour of the existence of a god. They say that it is logically possible for men to be immediately acquainted with God, as they are immediately acquainted with a sense-content, and that there is no reason why one should be prepared to believe a man when he says that he is seeing a yellow patch, and refuse to believe him when he says that he is seeing God. The answer to this is that if the man who asserts that he is seeing God is merely asserting that he is experiencing a peculiar kind of sense-content, then we do not for a moment deny that his assertion may be true. But, ordinarily, the man who says that he is seeing God is saying not merely that he is experiencing a religious emotion, but also that there exists a transcendent being who is the object of this emotion; just as the man who says that he sees a yellow patch is ordinarily saying not merely that his visual sense-field contains a yellow sense-content, but also that there exists a yellow object to which the sense-content belongs. And it is not irrational to be prepared to believe a man when he asserts the existence of a yellow object, and to refuse to believe him when he asserts the existence of a transcendent god. For whereas the sentence "There exists here a yellow-coloured material thing" expresses a genuine synthetic proposition which could be empirically verified, the sentence "There exists a transcendent god" has, as we have seen, no literal significance.

We conclude, therefore, that the argument from religious experience is altogether fallacious. The fact that people have religious experiences is interesting from the psychological point of view, but it does not in any way imply that there is such a thing as religious knowledge, any more than our having moral experiences implies that there is such a thing as moral knowledge. The theist, like the moralist, may believe that his experiences are cognitive experiences, but, unless he can formulate his "knowledge" in propositions that are empirically verifiable, we may be sure that he is deceiving himself. It follows that those philosophers who fill their books with assertions that they intuitively "know" this or that moral or religious "truth" are merely providing material for the psychoanalyst. For no act of intuition can be said to reveal a truth about any matter of fact unless it issues in verifiable propositions. And all such propositions are to be incorporated in the system of empirical propositions which constitutes science.

ERNEST NAGEL

Defending Atheism

In this excerpt from his essay "Philosophical Concepts of Atheism" (1959), Nagel reviews and criticizes some standard arguments for thinking that there is a God. Besides evaluating these criticisms, you should consider what positive argument Nagel develops for thinking that atheism is correct.

I

I must begin by stating what sense I am attaching to the word "atheism," and how I am construing the theme of this essay. I shall understand by "atheism" a critique and a denial of the major claims of all varieties of theism. And by theism I shall mean the view which holds, as one writer has expressed it, "that the heavens and the earth and all that they contain owe their existence and continuance in existence to the wisdom and will of a supreme, self-consistent, omnipotent, omniscient, righteous, and benevolent being, who is distinct from, and independent of, what he has created." Several things immediately follow from these definitions.

In the first place, atheism is not necessarily an irreligious concept, for theism is just one among many views concerning the nature and origin of the world. The denial of theism is logically compatible with a religious outlook upon life, and is in fact characteristic of some of the great historical religions. For as readers of this volume will know, early Buddhism is a religion which does not subscribe to any doctrine about a god; and there are pantheistic religions and philosophies which, because they deny that God is a being separate from and independent of the world, are not theistic in the sense of the word explained above.

Ernest Nagel, "Philosophical Concepts of Atheism," in *Basic Beliefs: The Religious Philosophies of Mankind.* Edited by J. E. Fairchild (Dobbs Ferry, NY: Sheridan House, Inc., 1959, 1987). Reprinted with permission.

The second point to note is that atheism is not to be identified with sheer unbelief, or with disbelief in some particular creed of a religious group. Thus, a child who has received no religious instruction and has never heard about God, is not an atheist—for he is not denying any theistic claims. Similarly, an adult who has withdrawn from the faith of his fathers without reflection or because of frank indifference to any theological issue is also not an atheist—for such an adult is not challenging theism and is not professing any views on the subject. . . .

One final word of preliminary explanation. I propose to examine some *philosophic* concepts of atheism, and I am not interested in the slightest in the many considerations atheists have advanced against the evidences for some particular religious and theological doctrine—for example, against the truth of the Christian story. What I mean by "philosophical" in the present context is that the views I shall consider are directed against any form of theism, and have their origin and basis in a logical analysis of the theistic position, and in a comprehensive account of the world believed to be wholly intelligible without the adoption of a theistic hypothesis. . . .

II

As I see it, atheistic philosophies fall into two major groups: (1) those which hold that the theistic doctrine is meaningful, but reject it either on the ground that (a) the positive evidence for it is insufficient or (b) the negative evidence is quite overwhelming; and (2) those who hold that the theistic thesis is not even meaningful, and reject it (a) as just nonsense or (b) as literally meaningless, but interpreting it as a symbolic rendering of human ideals, thus reading the theistic thesis in a sense that most believers in theism would disavow. It will not be possible in the limited space at my disposal to discuss the second category of atheistic critiques; and in any event, most of the traditional atheistic critiques of theism belong to the first group.

But before turning to the philosophical examination of the major classical arguments for theism, it is well to note that such philosophical critiques do not quite convey the passion with which atheists have often carried on their analyses of theistic views. For historically, atheism has been, and indeed continues to be, a form of social and political protest, directed as much against institutionalized religion as against theistic doctrine. Atheism has been, in effect, a moral revulsion against the undoubted abuses of the secular power exercised by religious leaders and religious institutions.

Religious authorities have opposed the correction of glaring injustices, and encouraged politically and socially reactionary policies. Religious institutions have been havens of obscurantist thought and centers for the dissemination of intolerance. Religious creeds have been used to set limits to free inquiry, to perpetuate inhumane treatment of the ill and the underprivileged, and to support moral doctrines insensitive to human suffering.

These indictments may not tell the whole story about the historical significance of religion; but they are at least an important part of the story. The refutation of theism has thus seemed to many an indispensable step not only toward liberating men's minds from superstition but also toward achieving a more equitable reordering of society. And no account of even the more philosophical aspects of atheistic thought is adequate which does not give proper recognition to the powerful social motives that actuate many atheistic arguments.

But however this may be, I want now to discuss three classical arguments for the existence of God, arguments which have constituted at least a partial basis for theistic commitments. As long as theism is defended simply as dogma, asserted as a matter of direct revelation or as the deliverance of authority, belief in the dogma is impregnable to rational argument. In fact, however, reasons are frequently advanced in support of the theistic creed, and these reasons have been the subject of acute philosophical critiques.

III

One of the oldest intellectual defenses of theism is the cosmological argument, also known as the argument from a first cause. Briefly put, the argument runs as follows. Every event must have a cause. Hence an event A must have as cause some event B, which in turn must have a cause C, and so on. But if there is no end to this backward progression of causes, the progression will be infinite; and in the opinion of those who use this argument, an infinite series of actual events is unintelligible and absurd. Hence there must be a first cause, and this first cause is God, the initiator of all change in the universe.

The argument is an ancient one . . . and it has impressed many generations of exceptionally keen minds. The argument is nonetheless a weak reed on which to rest the theistic thesis. Let us waive any question concerning the validity of the principle that every event has a cause, for though the question is important its discussion would lead us far afield. However, if the principle is assumed, it is surely incongruous to postulate a first cause as a way of escaping from the coils of an infinite series. For if everything must have a cause, why does not God require one for His own existence? The standard answer is that He does not need any, because He is self-caused. But if God can be self-caused, why cannot the world be self-caused? Why do we require a God transcending the world to bring the world into existence and to initiate changes in it? On the other hand, the supposed inconceivability and absurdity of an infinite series of regressive causes will be admitted by no one who has competent familiarity with the modern mathematical analysis of infinity. The cosmological argument does not stand up under scrutiny.

The second "proof" of God's existence is usually called the ontological argument. It too has a long history going back to early Christian days, though it acquired great prominence only in medieval times. The argument can be stated in several ways, one of which is the following. Since God is conceived to be omnipotent, he is a perfect being. A perfect being is defined as one whose essence or nature lacks no attributes (or properties) whatsoever, one whose nature is complete in every respect. But it is evident that we have an idea of a perfect being, for we have just defined the idea; and since this is so, the argument continues, God who is the perfect being must exist. Why must he? Because his existence follows from his defined nature. For if God lacked the attribute of existence, he would be lacking at least one attribute, and would therefore not be perfect. To sum up, since we have an idea of God as a perfect being, God must exist.

There are several ways of approaching this argument, but I shall consider only one. The argument was exploded by the 19th century philosopher Immanuel Kant. The substance of Kant's criticism is that it is just a confusion to say that existence is an attribute, and that though the *word* "existence" may occur as the grammatical predicate in a sentence, no attribute is being predicated of a thing when we say that the thing exists or has existence. Thus, to use Kant's example, when we think of $100 we are thinking of the nature of this sum of money; but the nature of $100 remains the same whether we have $100 in our pockets or not. Accordingly, we are confounding grammar with logic if we suppose that some characteristic is being attributed to the nature of $100 when we say that a $100 bill exists in someone's pocket.

To make the point clearer, consider another example. When we say that a lion has a tawny color, we are predicating a certain attribute of the animal, and similarly when we say that the lion is fierce or is hungry. But when we say the lion exists, all that we are saying is that something is (or has the nature of) a lion; we are not specifying an attribute which belongs to the nature of anything that is a lion. In short, the word "existence" does not signify any attribute, and in consequence no attribute that belongs to the nature of anything. Accordingly, it does not follow from the assumption that we have an idea of a perfect being that such a being exists. For the idea of a perfect being does not involve the attribute of existence as a constituent of that idea, since there is no such attribute. The ontological argument thus has a serious leak and it can hold no water.

IV

The two arguments discussed thus far are purely dialectical, and attempt to establish God's existence without any appeal to empirical data. The next argument, called the argument from design, is different in character, for it is based on what purports to be empirical evidence. . . .

One variant of it calls attention to the remarkable way in which different things and processes in the world are integrated with each other, and concludes that this mutual "fitness" of things can be explained only by the assumption of a divine architect who planned the world and everything in it. For example, living organisms can maintain themselves in a variety of environments, and do so in virtue of their delicate mechanisms which adapt the organisms to all sorts of environmental changes. There is thus an intricate pattern of means and ends throughout the animate world. But the existence of this pattern is unintelligible, so the argument runs, except on the hypothesis that the pattern has been deliberately instituted by a Supreme Designer. If we find a watch in some deserted spot, we do not think it came into existence by chance, and we do not hesitate to conclude that an intelligent creature designed and made it. But the world and all its contents exhibit mechanisms and mutual adjustments that are far more complicated and subtle than those of a watch. Must we not therefore conclude that these things too have a Creator?

The conclusion of this argument is based on an inference from analogy: The watch and the world are alike in possessing a congruence of parts and an adjustment of means to ends; the watch has a watch-maker; hence the world has a world-maker. But is the analogy a good one? Let us once more waive some important issues, in particular the issue of whether the universe is the unified system such as the watch admittedly is. And let us concentrate on the question of what is the ground for our assurance that watches do not come into existence except through the operations of intelligent manufacturers. The answer is plain. We have never run across a watch which has not been deliberately made by someone. But the situation is nothing like this in the case of the innumerable animate and inanimate systems with which we are familiar. Even in the case of living organisms, though they are generated by their parent organisms, the parents do not "make" their progeny in the same sense in which watchmakers make watches. And once this point is clear, the inference from the existence of living organisms to the existence of a supreme designer no longer appears credible.

Moreover, the argument loses all its force if the facts which the hypothesis of a divine designer is supposed to explain can be understood on the basis of a better supported assumption. And indeed, such an alternative explanation is one of the achievements of Darwinian biology. For Darwin showed that one can account for the variety of biological species, as well as for their adaptations to their environments, without invoking a divine creator and acts of special creation. The Darwinian theory explains the diversity of biological species in terms of chance variations in the structure of organisms, and of a mechanism of selection which retains those variation forms that possess some advantages for survival. The evidence for these assumptions is considerable; and developments subsequent to Darwin have only strengthened the case for a thoroughly naturalistic explanation of the facts of biological adaptation. In any event, this version of the argument from design has nothing to recommend it. . . .

V

The inconclusiveness of the three classical arguments for the existence of God was already made evident by Kant, in a manner substantially not different from the above discussion. There are, however, other types of arguments for theism that have been influential in the history of thought, two of which I wish to consider, even if only briefly.

Indeed, though Kant destroyed the classical intellectual foundations for theism, he himself invented a fresh argument for it. Kant's attempted proof is not intended to be a purely theoretical demonstration, and is based on the supposed facts of our moral nature. It has exerted an enormous influence on subsequent theological speculation. In barest outline, the argument is as follows. According to Kant, we are subject not only to physical laws like the rest of nature, but also to moral ones. These moral laws are categorical imperatives, which we must heed not because of their utilitarian consequences but simply because as autonomous moral agents it is our duty to accept them as binding. However, Kant was keenly aware that though virtue may be its reward, the virtuous man (that is, the man who acts out of a sense of duty and in conformity with the moral law) does not always receive his just desserts in this world; nor did he shut his eyes to the fact that evil men frequently enjoy the best things this world has to offer. In short, virtue does not always reap happiness. Nevertheless, the highest human good is the realization of happiness commensurate with one's virtue; and Kant believed that it is a practical postulate of the moral life to promote this good. But what can guarantee that the highest good is realizable? Such a guarantee can be found only in God, who must therefore exist if the highest good is not to be a fatuous ideal. The existence of an omnipotent, omniscient, and omnibenevolent God is thus postulated as a necessary condition for the possibility of a moral life.

Despite the prestige this argument has acquired, it is difficult to grant it any force. It is enough to postulate God's existence. But as Bertrand Russell observed in another connection, postulation has all the advantages of theft over honest toil. No postulation carries with it any assurance that what is postulated is actually the case. And though we may postulate God's existence as a means to guaranteeing the possibility of realizing happiness together with virtue, the postulation establishes neither the actual realizability of this ideal nor the fact of his existence. Moreover, the argument is not made more cogent when we recognize that it is based squarely on the highly dubious conception that considerations of utility and human happiness must not enter into the determination of what is morally obligatory. . . .

One further type of argument, pervasive in much Protestant theological literature, deserves brief mention. Arguments of this type take their point of departure from the psychology of religious and mystical experience. Those who have undergone such experiences often report that during the experience they feel themselves to be in the presence of the divine and holy, that they lose their sense of self-identity and become merged with some fundamental reality, or that they enjoy a feeling of total dependence upon some ultimate power. The overwhelming sense of transcending one's finitude, which characterizes such vivid periods of life, and of coalescing with some ultimate source of all existence, is then taken to be compelling evidence for the existence of a supreme being. In a variant form of this argument, other theologians have identified God as the object which satisfies the commonly experienced need for integrating one's scattered and conflicting impulses into a coherent unity, or as the subject which is of ultimate concern to us. In short, a proof of God's existence is found in the occurrence of certain distinctive experiences.

It would be flying in the face of well-attested facts were one to deny that such experiences frequently occur. But do these facts constitute evidence for the conclusion based on them? Does the fact, for example, that an individual experiences a profound sense of direct contact with an alleged transcendent ground of all reality, constitute competent evidence for the claim that there is such a ground and that it is the immediate cause of the experience? If well-established canons for evaluating evidence are accepted, the answer is surely negative. No one will dispute that many men do have vivid experiences in which such things as ghosts or pink elephants appear before them; but only the hopelessly credulous will without further ado count such experiences as establishing the existence of ghosts and pink elephants. To establish the existence of such things, evidence is required that is obtained under controlled conditions and that can be confirmed by independent inquirers. Again, though a man's report that he is suffering pain may be taken at face value, one cannot take at face value the claim, were he to make it, that it is the food he ate which is the cause (or a contributory cause) of his felt pain—not even if the man were to report a vivid feeling of abdominal disturbance. And similarly, an overwhelming feeling of being in the presence of the Divine is evidence enough for admitting the genuineness of such feeling; it is no evidence for the claim that a supreme being with a substantial existence independent of the experience is the cause of the experience.

VI

Thus far the discussion has been concerned with *noting inadequacies in various arguments widely used to support theism.* However, much atheistic criticism is also directed toward *exposing incoherencies in the very thesis of theism.* I want therefore to consider this aspect of the theistic critique, though I will restrict myself to the central difficulty in the theistic position, which arises from the simultaneous attribution of omnipotence, omniscience, and omnibenevolence to the Deity. The difficulty is that of reconciling these attributes with the occurrence of evil in the world. Accordingly, the question to which I now turn is whether, despite the existence of evil, it is possible to construct a theodicy which will justify the ways of an infinitely powerful and just God to man. . . .

I do not believe it is possible to reconcile the alleged omnipotence and omnibenevolence of God with the unvarnished facts of human existence. In point of fact, many theologians have concurred in this conclusion; for in order to escape from the difficulty which the traditional attributes of God present, they have assumed that God is not all-powerful, and that there are limits as to what he can do in his efforts to establish a righteous order in the universe. But whether such a modified theology is better off is doubtful; and in any event, the question still remains whether the facts of human life support the claim that an omnibenevolent Deity, though limited in power, is revealed in the ordering of human history. It is pertinent to note in this connection that though there have been many historians who have made the effort, no historian has yet succeeded in showing to the satisfaction of his professional colleagues that the hypothesis of a Divine Providence is capable of explaining anything which cannot be explained just as well without this hypothesis.

VII

This last remark naturally leads to the question whether, apart from their polemics against theism, philosophical atheists have not shared a common set of positive views, a common set of philosophical convictions which set them off from other groups of thinkers. In one very clear sense of this query the answer is indubitably negative. For there never has been what one might call a "school of atheism" in the way in which there has been a Platonic school or even a Kantian school. . . .

Nevertheless, despite the variety of philosophical positions to which atheists have subscribed at one time or another in the history of thought, it seems to me that atheism is not simply a negative standpoint. At any rate, there is a certain quality of intellectual temper that has characterized, and continues to characterize, many philosophical atheists. . . . I want therefore to conclude this discussion with a brief enumeration of some points of positive doctrine to which by and large philosophical atheists seem to me to subscribe. . . .

In the first place, philosophical atheists reject the assumption that there are disembodied spirits, or that incorporeal entities of any sort can exercise a causal agency. On the contrary, atheists are generally agreed that if we wish to achieve any understanding of what takes place in the universe, we must look to the operations of organized bodies. Accordingly, the various processes taking place in nature, whether animate or inanimate, are to be explained in terms of the properties and structures of identifiable and spatiotemporally located objects. Moreover, the present variety of systems and activities found in the universe is to be accounted for on the basis of the transformations things undergo when they enter into different relations with one another—transformations which often result in the emergence of novel kinds of objects. . . .

In the second place, atheists generally manifest a marked empirical temper, and often take as their ideal the intellectual methods employed in the contemporaneous empirical sciences. Philosophical atheists differ considerably on important points of detail in their account of how responsible claims to knowledge are to be established. But there is substantial agreement among them that controlled sensory observation is the court of final appeal in issues concerning matters of fact. It is indeed this commitment to the use of an empirical method which is the final basis of the atheistic critique of theism. For at bottom this critique seeks to show that we can understand whatever a theistic assumption is alleged to explain, through the use of the proved methods of the positive sciences and without the introduction of empirically unsupported *ad hoc* hypotheses about a Deity. It is pertinent in this connection to recall a familiar legend about the French mathematical physicist Laplace. According to the story, Laplace made a personal presentation of a copy of his now famous book on celestial mechanics to Napoleon. Napoleon glanced through the volume, and finding no reference to the Deity asked Laplace whether God's existence played any role in the analysis. "Sire, I have no need for that hypothesis," Laplace is reported to have replied. The dismissal of sterile hypotheses characterizes not only the work of Laplace; it is the uniform rule in scientific inquiry. The sterility of the theistic assumption is one of the main burdens of the literature of atheism both ancient and modern.

And finally, atheistic thinkers have generally accepted a utilitarian basis for judging moral issues, and they have exhibited a libertarian attitude toward human needs and impulses. The conceptions of the human good they have advocated are conceptions which are commensurate with the actual capacities of mortal men, so that it is the satisfaction of the complex needs of the human creature which is the final standard for evaluating the validity of moral ideal or moral prescription.

In consequence, the emphasis of atheistic model reflection has been this-worldly rather than other-worldly, individualistic rather than authoritarian. The stress upon a good life that must be consummated in this world has made atheists vigorous opponents of moral codes which seek to repress human impulses in the name of some unrealizable other-worldly ideal. The individualism that is so pronounced a strain in many philosophical atheists has made them tolerant of human limitations and sensitive to the plurality of legitimate moral goals. On the other hand, this individualism has certainly not prevented many of them from recognizing the crucial role which institutional arrangements can play in achieving desirable patterns of human living. In consequence, atheists have made important contributions to the development of a climate of opinion favorable to pursuing the values of a liberal civilization, and they have played effective roles in attempts to rectify social injustices.

Atheists cannot build their moral outlook on foundations upon which so many men conduct their lives. In particular, atheism cannot offer the incentives to conduct and the consolations for misfortune which theistic religions supply to their adherents. It can offer no hope of personal immortality, no threats of Divine chastisement, no promise of eventual recompense for injustices suffered, no blueprints to sure salvation. For on its view of the place of man in nature, human excellence and human dignity must be achieved within a finite life-span, or not at all, so that the rewards of moral endeavor must come from the quality of civilized living, and not from some source of disbursement that dwells outside of time. Accordingly, atheistic moral reflection at its best does not culminate in a quiescent ideal of human perfection, but is a vigorous call to intelligent activity—activity for the sake of realizing human potentialities and for eliminating whatever stands in the way of such realization. . . .

Suggestions for Further Reading

ON THE DEBATE BETWEEN CREATIONISM AND EVOLUTIONARY THEORY

Douglas Futuyama, *Science on Trial: The Case for Evolution.* New York, Pantheon, 1982.

Dwayne Gish, *Evolution? The Fossils Say No!* San Diego, Creation-Life Publishers, 1979.

Phillip Johnson, *Defeating Darwinism by Opening Minds.* Downers Grove, IL, Intervarsity Press, 1997.

Philip Kitcher, *Abusing Science: The Case Against Creationism.* Cambridge, Massachusetts, MIT Press, 1982.

Henry Morris, *Scientific Creationism.* San Diego, Creation-Life Publishers, 1974.

Robert Pennock, *Tower of Babel—The Evidence Against the New Creationism.* Cambridge, Massachusetts, MIT Press, 1998.

ON THE TESTABILITY OF RELIGIOUS CLAIMS

Essays by Antony Flew, R. M. Hare, and Basil Mitchell, "Theology and Falsification," in
Antony Flew and Alisdair MacIntyre (eds.), *New Essays in Philosophical Theology.* New
York, Macmillan, 1966.

Carl Hempel, "Empiricist Criteria of Cognitive Significance: Problems and Changes," in *Aspects
of Scientific Explanation,* New York, Free Press, 1965.

Elliott Sober, "Testability." Proceedings and Addresses of the American Philosophical Association, 1999. Available at the Web site http://philosophy.wisc.edu/sober.

ON THE ONTOLOGICAL ARGUMENT

John Hick and Arthur McGill (eds.), *The Many-Faced Argument: Recent Studies on the Ontological
Argument for the Existence of God.* London, Macmillan, 1968.

Alvin Plantinga, *The Nature of Necessity.* Oxford, Oxford University Press, 1974.

ON PASCAL'S WAGER

James Cargile, "Pascal's Wager." *Philosophy,* vol. 41, pp. 229–236, 1966.

William Lycan and George Schlesinger, "You Bet Your Life: Pascal's Wager Defended," in
J. Feinberg and R. Schafer-Landau (eds.), *Reason and Responsibility.* Belmont, California,
Wadsworth, 1999.

Gregory Mougin and Elliott Sober, "Betting Against Pascal's Wager." *Nous,* vol. 28, pp. 382–395,
1994.

Blaise Pascal, *Penseé.* Everyman's Library. London, J. M. Dent & Sons, 1958.

ON THE ARGUMENT FROM EVIL

Robert M. Adams, "Must God Create the Best?" *Philosophical Review,* vol. 81, pp. 317–332, 1972.

Richard Swinburne, "The Problem of Evil," in Stuart Brown (ed.), *Reason and Religion.* Ithaca,
Cornell University Press, 1977.

Peter Van Inwagen, "The Magnitude, Duration, and Distribution of Evil—a Theodicy." *Philosophical Topics,* vol. 16, 1988.

PART III
THEORY
OF KNOWLEDGE

What Is Knowledge?

EPISTEMOLOGY

In everyday life, in science, and in philosophy as well, we talk of "knowing" things. We also say that some beliefs are "strongly supported by evidence"; we say that they are "justified" or "well-confirmed." We not only describe *ourselves* with such terms; we also apply them to *others*.

Epistemology is the part of philosophy that tries to understand such concepts. Epistemologists try to evaluate the commonsense idea that we (often, if not always) have knowledge and that we are (often, if not always) rationally justified in the beliefs we have. Some philosophers have tried to defend these commonsense ideas with philosophical argumentation. Others have developed a philosophical position that involves denying these commonsense ideas. A philosopher who claims that we don't have knowledge, or that our beliefs aren't rationally justified, is defending some version of *philosophical skepticism*.

In this lecture, I'll begin with some remarks about the problem of knowledge. In the next lecture, I'll examine the views of the seventeenth-century French philosopher René Descartes. Descartes tried to show that we really do possess knowledge of the world; Descartes tried to refute the skeptic. After evaluating Descartes's views about knowledge, I'll turn to an alternative way of thinking about knowledge, *the Reliability Theory of Knowledge* (Lecture 14).

After this discussion of the problem of knowledge, I'll examine the idea of rational justification. The eighteenth-century Scottish philosopher David Hume, whose views on the Argument from Design we considered in Lecture 5, argued that the beliefs we have that are based on induction aren't rationally justified. Hume was a skeptic about induction. We'll consider his argument for this philosophical position and also the attempts some philosophers have made to show that Hume's startling thesis is mistaken.

So let's get started with the problem of knowledge. Before we can ask whether we know anything, we have to get clear on what knowledge is. To focus ideas, I want to distinguish three different ways we talk about knowledge. Only one of these will be our concern in what follows.

THREE KINDS OF KNOWLEDGE

Consider the difference between the following three statements, each concerning an individual, whom I'll call *S* (the subject):

(1) *S* knows how to ride a bicycle.

(2) *S* knows the President of the United States.

(3) *S* knows that the Rockies are in North America.

Right now I'm not interested in saying which of these statements is true. The point is that they involve different kinds of knowledge.

The kind of knowledge described in (3) I'll call *propositional knowledge*. Notice that the object of the verb in (3) is a proposition—something that is either true or false. There is a proposition—that the Rockies are in North America—and (3) asserts that *S* knows that that proposition is true.

Statements (1) and (2) don't have this structure. The object of the verb in (2) isn't a proposition, but a person. A similar kind of knowledge would be involved if I said that *S* knows Chicago. Statement (2) says that *S* is related to an object—a person, place, or thing—so I'll say that (2) describes an instance of *object knowledge*.

Is there a connection between object knowledge and propositional knowledge? Maybe to know the President of the United States, you must know some propositions that are about him. But which propositions? To know the President, do you have to know what state he comes from? This doesn't seem essential. And the same holds true for each other fact about the man: There doesn't seem to be any particular proposition you've got to know for you to know him.

There is another aspect of the idea of object knowledge, one that is rather curious. Suppose I've read lots of books about the President. I know as many propositions about him as you might wish. Still, it won't be true that I know him, because I've never met him. Knowing people seems to require some sort of direct acquaintance. But it is hard to say exactly what is needed here. If I once was introduced to the President at some large party, that wouldn't be enough for me to say that I "know" him. It isn't just direct acquaintance, but something more. I won't try to describe this further. I'll merely conclude that propositional knowledge, no matter how voluminous, isn't sufficient for object knowledge.

I turn next to the kind of knowledge described in statement (1). I'll call this *know-how* knowledge. What does it mean to know how to do something? I think this idea has little connection with propositional knowledge. My son Aaron knew how to ride a bike when he was five years old. This means he had certain abilities—he knew how to keep his balance, how to pedal, and so on. If you asked a physicist to describe what

Aaron was doing that allowed him to ride the bike, the physicist could write out a set of propositions. There would be facts about gravity, forward momentum, and balancing of forces. But Aaron wasn't a physicist at age five. He didn't know the propositions that the physicist specifies. Aaron *obeyed* the physical principles that the physicist describes—his behavior conformed to what they say. But he didn't do this by learning the propositions in question. Aaron had know-how knowledge, but little in the way of propositional knowledge.

Necessary and Sufficient Conditions

Consider the following suggested definition of what a bachelor is:

> For any *S*, *S* is a bachelor if and only if
>
> (1) *S* is an adult.
>
> (2) *S* is male.
>
> (3) *S* is unmarried.

I'm not claiming that this definition precisely captures what "bachelor" means in ordinary English. Rather, I want to use it as an example of a proposed definition.

The definition is a generalization. It concerns any individual you care to consider. The definition makes two claims: The first is that *IF* the individual has characteristics (1), (2), and (3), then the individual is a bachelor. In other words, (1), (2), and (3) are together *sufficient* for being a bachelor. The second claim is that *IF* the individual is a bachelor, then the individual has all three characteristics. In other words, (1), (2), and (3) are each *necessary* for being a bachelor.

We can define what a necessary condition is and what a sufficient condition is as follows:

> "*X* is a necessary condition for *Y*" means that
> if *Y* is true, then *X* is true.
>
> "*X* is a sufficient condition for *Y*" means that
> if *X* is true, then *Y* is true.

What does the expression "if and only if" mean in the above proposed definition of bachelorhood? It means that the conditions listed are both necessary and sufficient. A good definition will specify necessary and sufficient conditions for the concept one wishes to define.

This means that there can be two sorts of defects in a proposed definition. A definition can fail to provide conditions that are sufficient. It also can provide conditions that aren't necessary. And, of course, it can fall down on both counts.

Which sorts of defects are present in the following suggested definitions?

> *S* is a bachelor if and only if *S* is male.
>
> *S* is a bachelor if and only if *S* is an unmarried human adult male who is tall and lives in Ohio.

The first definition is said to be "too broad"; it admits too much. The second is "too narrow"; it admits too little.

Conversely, it is possible for a physicist to have detailed knowledge of the physical principles that describe successful bike riding and yet not know how to ride a bike. The physicist may lack the ability to perform the behaviors, but not because there is some proposition he or she fails to grasp.

I conclude that propositional knowledge is neither necessary nor sufficient for knowing how to perform some task. The two concepts of knowledge are quite separate.

The subject of this and the following two lectures will be *propositional knowledge,* not *object knowledge* or *know-how knowledge.* The goal is to understand what propositional knowledge is. That is, we want to answer the following question: What are the necessary and sufficient conditions for it to be true that S knows that p, where p is some proposition—for example, the proposition that the Rockies are in North America?

TWO REQUIREMENTS FOR KNOWLEDGE: BELIEF AND TRUTH

Two ideas that form part of the concept of knowledge should be noted at the outset. First, if S knows that p, then S must believe that p. Second, if S knows that p, then p must be true. Knowledge requires both *belief* and *truth*.

I won't try to argue for the first of these requirements, but will just assume it is correct. The second does require some explanation, however. People sometimes say they know things that, in fact, turn out to be false. But this isn't a case of knowing things that are untrue, but of people *thinking* they know things that happen to be untrue.

Knowledge has an objective and a subjective side. You should remember this pair of concepts from Lecture 1. A fact is objective if its truth doesn't depend on the way anyone's mind is. It is an objective fact that the Rocky Mountains are more than 10,000 feet above sea level. A fact is subjective, on the other hand, if it isn't objective. The most obvious example of a subjective fact is a description of what's going on in someone's mind.

Whether someone believes the Rockies are more than 10,000 feet above sea level is a subjective matter; but whether the mountains really are that high is an objective matter. Knowledge requires both an objective and a subjective element. For S to know that p, p must be true and the subject, S, must believe that p is true.

I've just cited two necessary conditions for knowledge: Knowledge requires belief, and knowledge requires truth. Is that it? That is, are these two conditions not just separately necessary but also jointly sufficient? Is true belief enough for knowledge?

PLATO: TRUE BELIEF ISN'T SUFFICIENT FOR KNOWLEDGE

In the dialogue called *The Theaetetus,* the Greek philosopher Plato (c. 430–345 B.C.), who was Aristotle's teacher, argues the answer is *no.* Orators and lawyers sometimes trick people into believing things; sometimes those things happen to be true. People who have been duped in this way have true beliefs, but they don't have knowledge.

Of course, the fact that orators and lawyers intend to deceive isn't crucial for Plato's point. Think of an individual, Clyde, who believes the story about Groundhog

Day. Clyde thinks that if the groundhog sees its shadow, then spring will come late. Suppose Clyde puts this silly principle to work this year. He receives the news about the behavior of the Official Designated Groundhog, and so he believes that spring will come late. Suppose Clyde turns out to be right about the late spring. If there is no real connection between the groundhog seeing its shadow and the coming of a late spring, then Clyde will have a true belief (that spring will come late), but he won't have knowledge.

So what else is needed, besides true belief, for someone to have knowledge? A natural suggestion is that knowledge requires justification. The problem with Clyde is that he didn't satisfy this further requirement (though perhaps he thought he did). Justification, notice, can't just mean that the subject *thinks* he has a reason.

JUSTIFICATION

What does it mean to say that an individual is "justified" in believing a proposition? Sometimes we start believing that a proposition is true because we consider an argument that describes the evidence available. Mendel believed that genes exist because of the data he collected from his pea plants. Sherlock Holmes believed that Moriarty was the murderer because of the evidence he found at the crime scene. Should we conclude that people are justified in believing a proposition only when their belief in the proposition was caused by their considering an argument? This isn't always plausible. When I believe that I have a headache, I don't construct an argument in which the evidence is laid out in a set of propositions that constitute my premises. Still, it would seem that I am justified in believing that I have a headache. This suggests that there is such a thing as *noninferential justification.* Some of the propositions we believe are apprehended more or less "directly;" they are not inferred from other propositions that we believe.

What, then, does "justification" mean when it is used in accounts of what knowledge is? When we talk about someone's action being *morally* justified, we mean that the action does not violate any *moral* duties that the person has. Perhaps "justified belief" should be understood in a similar way. We should think of individuals as having certain duties concerning how their beliefs should be formed. A belief is justified if the process by which it was formed does not violate any duties that the person has. To make sense of this suggestion, we'd have to say what duties we have that govern how we are supposed to form our beliefs. Are we obliged to base our beliefs on the evidence that is available, and only on the evidence? This, I take it, is what I do when I believe that I have a headache. However, this suggestion requires further exploration; some of the issues were touched on in Lecture 10, on Pascal's Wager.

Even though the concept of "justification" requires further attention, it is plausible to think that this is one of the necessary ingredients that defines what knowledge is. Knowing that a proposition is true requires more than just having a true belief. The third requirement is that your belief be "justified."

THE JTB THEORY

Suppose knowledge requires these three conditions. Is that it? That is, are these conditions not just separately necessary, but jointly sufficient? The theory of knowledge that asserts this I'll call the *JTB Theory*. It says that knowledge is one and the same thing as justified true belief:

(JTB)   For any individual *S* and any proposition *p*, *S* knows that *p*
if and only if

(1) *S* believes that *p*.

(2) *p* is true.

(3) *S* is justified in believing that *p*.

The JTB Theory states a generalization. It says what knowledge is for *any* person *S* and *any* proposition *p*. For example, let *S* be you and let *p* = "the moon is made of green cheese." The JTB Theory says this: If you know that the moon is made of green cheese, then statements (1)–(3) must be true as well. And if you don't know the moon is made of green cheese, then at least one of statements (1)–(3) must be false. As in the definition of bachelorhood discussed in the preceding box, the expression "if and only if" says that we are being given necessary and sufficient conditions for the defined concept.

THREE COUNTEREXAMPLES TO THE JTB THEORY

In 1963 the U.S. philosopher Edmund Gettier published a pair of counterexamples to the JTB Theory ("Is Justified True Belief Knowledge?" *Analysis,* 1963, Vol. 23, pp. 121–123). What is a *counterexample?* It is an example that goes counter to what some general theory says. A counterexample to a generalization shows that the generalization is false. The JTB Theory says that *all* cases of justified true belief are cases of knowledge. Gettier thought his two examples show that an individual can have justified true belief without having knowledge. If Gettier is right, then the three conditions given by the JTB Theory aren't sufficient.

Here is one of Gettier's examples: Smith works in an office. He knows that someone will soon be promoted. The boss, who is very reliable, tells Smith that Jones is going to get the promotion. Smith has just counted the coins in Jones's pocket, finding there to be 10 coins there. Smith therefore has excellent evidence for the following proposition:

(a) Jones will get the promotion and Jones has 10 coins in his pocket.

Smith then deduces from this statement the following:

(b) The man who will get the promotion has 10 coins in his pocket.

Now suppose that, unknown to Smith, Jones will *not* get the promotion. Rather it is Smith himself who will be promoted. And suppose Smith also happens to have 10 coins in his pocket. Smith believes (b); and (b) is true. Gettier also claims that Smith is justified in believing (b), since Smith deduced it from (a). Although (a) is false, Smith had excellent reason to think that it is true. Gettier concludes that Smith has a justified true belief in (b), but Smith doesn't know that (b) is true.

Gettier's other example exhibits the same pattern. The subject validly deduces a true proposition from a proposition that is very well supported by evidence even though it is, unbeknownst to the subject, false. I now want to describe a kind of counterexample to the JTB Theory in which the subject reasons *non*deductively.

The British philosopher, mathematician, and social critic Bertrand Russell (1872–1970) described a very reliable clock that stands in a town square. This morning you walk by it and glance up to find out what the time is. As a result, you come to believe that the time is 9:55. You are justified in believing this, based on your correct assumption that the clock has been very reliable in the past. But suppose that, unbeknownst to you, the clock stopped exactly 24 hours ago. You now have a justified true belief that it is 9:55, but you don't know that this is the correct time.

Let me add a third example to Gettier's Smith/Jones story and to Russell's clock. You buy a ticket in a fair lottery. "Fair" means that one ticket will win and every ticket has the same chance. There are 1,000 tickets and you get ticket number 452. You look at this ticket, think for a moment, and then believe the following proposition: Ticket number 452 will not win. Suppose that when the drawing occurs a week later, you are right. Your belief was true. In addition, it was extremely well justified; after all, its probability was extremely close to unity—there was only one chance in a thousand you would be mistaken. Yet, I think we want to say in this case that you didn't *know* that the ticket would fail to win. Here is a third case of justified true belief that isn't knowledge. Note that the reasoning here is nondeductive.

WHAT THE COUNTEREXAMPLES HAVE IN COMMON

In all three of these cases, the subject has *highly reliable,* but not *infallible,* evidence for the proposition believed. The boss *usually* is right about who will be promoted; the clock *usually* is right as to what the time is; and it *usually* is true that a ticket drawn at random in a fair lottery doesn't win. But, of course, *usually* doesn't mean *always.* The sources of information that the subjects exploited in these three examples are *highly* reliable, but not *perfectly* reliable. All the sources of information were prone to error to at least some degree.

Do these examples really refute the JTB theory? That depends on how we understand the idea of justification. If highly reliable evidence is enough to justify a belief, then the counterexamples do refute the JTB theory. But if justification requires perfectly infallible evidence, then these examples don't undermine the JTB theory.

My view is that justifying evidence needn't be infallible. I think we can have rational and well-supported beliefs even when we aren't entitled to be absolutely certain that what we believe is true. From this, I conclude that justified true belief isn't sufficient for knowledge.

AN ARGUMENT FOR SKEPTICISM

What more is required? The lottery example suggests the following idea. In this case, you *probably* won't be mistaken when you believe that ticket number 452 will lose. But high probability isn't enough. To know that the ticket will lose, it must be *impossible* for you to be mistaken. You don't have knowledge in this example, because there is a chance (small though it may be) that you will be wrong.

There is some plausibility to this suggestion about what knowledge requires. The problem is that this idea seems to lead immediately to skepticism—to the conclusion that we don't know anything. For it seems that virtually all the beliefs we have are based on evidence that isn't infallible. Consider, just briefly, the beliefs we have that depend on the testimony of our senses. We use vision, hearing, touch, and so forth, to gather evidence about the way the world is. Do the resulting beliefs count as knowledge? The problem is that the senses are sometimes misleading.

Right now, you believe you are looking at a printed page. You believe this because of the visual experiences you now are having. Do you *know* that there is a printed page in front of you? According to the present suggestion, for this to be true, it must be the case that you couldn't possibly be mistaken in believing what you do. But the fact of the matter seems to be that you *could* be mistaken. You might be hallucinating, or dreaming, or your senses might be malfunctioning in some other way.

So here's where we are. The JTB Theory is mistaken. JTB doesn't suffice for knowledge. As an alternative to the JTB theory, we have this suggestion: Knowledge requires the impossibility of error. But this suggestion, plausible though it may be as a diagnosis of why you don't have knowledge in the lottery example, allows us to formulate the following argument for skepticism:

> If S knows that p, then it isn't possible that S is mistaken in believing that p.
>
> It is possible that S is mistaken in believing that p.
> _____
>
> S doesn't know that p.

This form of argument can be used to argue that a posteriori knowledge is impossible. Recall from Lecture 9 that a proposition is a posteriori if it can be known only through the testimony of sense experience. The skeptic claims that beliefs based on sense experience aren't totally immune from the possibility of error. People make perceptual mistakes—for example, in cases of illusion, hallucination, and dreaming. Since we can't absolutely rule out the possibility of error, the skeptic concludes that we must admit that the senses don't provide us with knowledge.

Is Skepticism Self-Refuting?

Skeptics claim that people don't know anything. Can skeptics claim to know that what they say is true? If not, does that show that their philosophical thesis is false?

It is a contradiction to say that you know that no one (including yourself) knows anything. But a skeptic can assert that people lack knowledge without claiming to know that this is so. In addition, a skeptic can claim to provide a good argument for skepticism. This isn't contradictory.

The thesis that no one knows anything, if true, can't be known to be true. But that doesn't show that the position is false. If you think that all truths are knowable, you will say that this skeptical thesis can't be true. But why think that all truths are knowable? Why not think, instead, that the universe may contain truths that we are incapable of knowing?

Another way for skeptics to avoid contradicting themselves is to be modest. Instead of claiming that no one knows *anything*, they could limit themselves to the claim that no one ever knows anything *through the testimony of the senses*. If this more limited kind of skepticism could be supported by an a priori argument, the position wouldn't be self-refuting.

This argument for skepticism is deductively valid. (Identify its logical form.) The first premiss seems to describe a plausible requirement for knowing the proposition in question. The second premiss also seems plausible; it just says that the beliefs we have aren't absolutely immune from the possibility of error. If you want to reject skepticism, you must refute one or both of these premisses.

Although the above argument has fairly plausible premisses, its conclusion is pretty outrageous. I think I know lots of things, and I believe this is true of you as well. It is hard for me to accept the idea that I don't know that I have a hand. If you think that you now know there is a printed page in front of you, you should balk at this argument as well. The skeptical argument contradicts a fundamental part of our commonsense picture of the way we are related to the world around us. Common sense says that people have knowledge of the world they inhabit; the skeptical argument says that common sense is mistaken in this respect. If there is a mistake in the argument, where is it?

Review Questions

1. Explain how object knowledge, know-how knowledge, and propositional knowledge differ.
2. What do the following pieces of terminology mean? (i) X is a necessary condition for Y; (ii) X is a sufficient condition for Y; (iii) X is true if and only if Y is true; (iv) o is a counterexample to the statement "All emeralds are green."
3. Why think that true belief isn't sufficient for knowledge? What is the JTB theory? What is the difference between highly reliable evidence and absolutely infallible evidence?

4. Describe the three counterexamples to the JTB Theory (Gettier's, Russell's, and the lottery example). Do these counterexamples show that JTB isn't necessary or that it isn't sufficient for knowledge?

5. What is skepticism? What is the argument for skepticism given at the end of this lecture? Is the argument deductively valid?

Problems for Further Thought

1. People sometimes say, about a proposition that is difficult to take to heart, "I know it, but I don't believe it." Does this refute the claim that if S knows that p, then S believes that p?

2. I suggested that we lack knowledge in the lottery example because knowledge requires the impossibility of error. Can you think of some other explanation for why we lack knowledge in this or in the other two examples that were used against the JTB Theory?

LECTURE 13

Descartes's Foundationalism

René Descartes (1596–1650) is sometimes described as the father of modern philosophy. The kind of epistemology he tried to develop is called foundationalism. Before launching into the details of Descartes's philosophy, I want to describe what kind of approach to the problem of knowledge foundationalism provides.

FOUNDATIONALISM

The word *foundationalism* should make you think of a building. What keeps a building from falling over? The answer has two parts. First, there is a solid foundation. Second, the rest of the building, which I'll call the superstructure, is attached securely to that solid foundation. Descartes wanted to show that (many if not all of) the beliefs we have about the world are cases of genuine knowledge. To show this, he wanted to divide our beliefs into two categories. There are the foundational beliefs, which are perfectly solid. Second, there are the superstructural beliefs, which count as knowledge because they rest securely on that solid foundation.

Besides the metaphor from architecture, there is another that should help you understand what Descartes's project is. You probably had a geometry course in high school. Here you studied Euclid's development of the subject. Recall that Euclid, who lived about 2,200 years ago, divided the propositions of geometry into two categories.

First, there are the axioms of geometry. These are supposed to be simple and totally obvious truths. Second, there are the theorems, which at first glance are somewhat less obvious. Euclid shows that the theorems are true by showing how they can be deduced from the axioms.

A foundationalist theory of knowledge could also be called a Euclidean theory of knowledge. To show that a given body of beliefs counts as knowledge, we use the following strategy: First, we identify the beliefs that will provide the foundations of knowledge (the axioms). These must be shown to have some special property, like being totally beyond doubt. In a moment, I'll clarify what Descartes had in mind by this "special property." Second, we show that the rest of our beliefs count as knowledge because they bear some special relationship to the foundational items. In Euclid's geometry, the special relationship was deductive implication.

Euclid, of course, was interested only in the beliefs we have about geometry. Descartes cast his net much wider. He was interested in the totality of what we believe. But whether the problem is to describe the foundations of geometry or the foundations of knowledge as a whole, there are two ideas that must be clarified. We need to identify what the foundational items are, and we need to describe the relationship that must obtain between foundational and superstructural items that qualifies the latter as knowledge.

EUCLID'S PARALLEL POSTULATE

One last comment on high school geometry. If your course was like mine, you spent most of your time seeing what theorems could be proved from the axioms. You spent little or no time seeing why the axioms should be regarded as true. You were told that they are "obvious," or that they should just be accepted on faith. Maybe your teacher said that geometry is just a game and the axioms are the rules.

In fact, however, the question about the axioms is a serious one. One of Euclid's starting assumptions—his so-called fifth postulate—bothered geometers for about 2,000 years. This postulate says the following: Through a point that is not on a given straight line, there is exactly one line that is parallel to the given line. In other words, the parallel postulate says that if you extend all the lines passing through this point to infinity, exactly one of them will fail to intersect the initial line.

A number of subsequent geometers felt that this assumption of Euclid's was less obvious than the others he used. As a result, they tried to show that it could be proved from the other axioms. Geometers failed to do this, however, and eventually established that the parallel postulate couldn't be proved from Euclid's other assumptions. That is, they showed the parallel postulate is *independent* of the other assumptions. This means that the denial of the parallel postulate is consistent with Euclid's other assumptions. It then transpired that non-Euclidean geometries could be developed, ones that retain Euclid's other assumptions but reject his parallel postulate.

The details of this story don't matter here. The history of geometry does show, however, that it sometimes isn't so clear whether a given statement is "obviously true." Perhaps Euclid thought that the parallel postulate was obvious. If so, that would have been his justification for treating it as something that doesn't have to be proved; it would stand on its own as an axiom/postulate. This doesn't mean, however, that subsequent geometers had to regard Euclid's judgment as beyond question. What strikes one person as obvious may not be so obvious to someone else.

DESCARTES'S METHOD OF DOUBT

Now let's consider Descartes's approach to the problem of knowledge. Descartes's goal is to refute skepticism. He wants to show that we really do have knowledge of the world we inhabit. His strategy for achieving this goal is foundationalist in character. This means the first item on his agenda must be to identify the beliefs that are foundational.

At the beginning of his *Meditations on First Philosophy* (1641), Descartes proposes a method for determining which of the beliefs he has are foundational. He called this the *method of doubt.* You see whether it is possible to doubt a proposition. If it is possible to do this, you set the belief aside—it isn't foundational. If it isn't possible to do so (that is, if you find that the belief is *indubitable*), then the belief is a foundational item. Notice that failing the method of doubt test doesn't mean that the belief is *false.* It just means the belief isn't *absolutely certain.*

Descartes doesn't try to apply this method to beliefs one at a time. Think of all the beliefs you have—there are millions (at least). You believe that 1 is a number. You believe that 2 is a number. And so on. It would be time consuming and also boring to try to consider each belief separately. Rather, what Descartes does is consider *kinds* of beliefs; he considers whether all the beliefs in this or that category pass or fail the method of doubt test.

Indubitability

Very few propositions are made true just by your believing them. You can believe that there are unicorns, but that doesn't make such creatures pop into existence.

Consider the proposition "I am thinking." If you believe that this is true, then it must be true. Believing is a kind of thinking. Descartes thinks that the same is true for propositions of the form "I seem to see that p." He also thinks that this is true for propositions that say that you believe that p or want it to be true that q (where p and q are propositions). If you believe them, they must be true.

If a proposition is made true by your believing it, then it has this property: You can't describe a situation in which you believe the proposition but the proposition is false. Descartes determines whether a proposition is dubitable by seeing whether he can describe a situation of this kind. This means that a proposition is indubitable if the proposition is made true by the act of believing it.

Are there indubitable propositions that aren't made true by your believing them? Some philosophers have held that simple logical truths, like "It is raining or it is not raining," are beyond doubt. Is it plausible to maintain that these are made true by your believing them?

THE METHOD APPLIED TO A POSTERIORI BELIEFS

The first category Descartes considers is the set of beliefs that depend for their justification on sense experience. Many of our beliefs are based on sight, hearing, touch, taste, and smell. These propositions are a posteriori (Lecture 9). Is it possible to doubt these beliefs? Descartes says that the answer is *yes*. Your present belief that there is a printed page in front of you is based on vision. Vision, however, can be misleading. Psychologists tell us about hallucinations and illusions. Maybe you've had such experiences yourself. If not, remember Macbeth, who was certain a dagger was hovering in front of him. And besides hallucinations, there is the fact of dreaming. In a dream you may find yourself believing there is a printed page in front of you. You may find yourself having visual experiences just like the ones you are having now. But in the dream, your belief is mistaken. Descartes takes this to show that the belief you have right now might be mistaken.

So beliefs that rest on the testimony of the senses fail the method of doubt test. Let's be clear on why Descartes thinks they do so. Descartes shows such beliefs are dubitable by constructing a story of a particular kind. You now believe that there is a printed page in front of you on the basis of a set of visual experiences. Let's call the proposition you believe B and the experiences you now are having E. Your belief that B is true rests on your having experiences E. Descartes holds that B can be doubted because he can describe a situation in which you have E and believe B even though B is false. Dreams and hallucinations show how this can happen. Descartes shows that a class of beliefs is dubitable by constructing a story of this sort.

DUBITABILITY IS A LOGICAL, NOT A PSYCHOLOGICAL, PROPERTY

In saying that a belief is dubitable, Descartes isn't saying that we are able to take seriously the idea that it might be false. The proposition that there is a page in front of you is dubitable in Descartes's sense; this doesn't mean you are now about to take seriously that possibility that no page is present. A proposition is dubitable when a certain sort of story can be constructed; dubitability is thus a logical property that a proposition has. It has nothing to do with whether we can get ourselves to believe that the proposition might be false.

THE METHOD APPLIED TO BELIEFS BASED ON RATIONAL CALCULATION

Descartes next turns his attention to propositions of mathematics. I believe that $2 + 3 = 5$. I believe that squares have four sides. Descartes remarks that these are true "whether I'm awake or asleep." These propositions are a priori (recall this piece of vocabulary from Lecture 9). They don't depend for their justification on sensory experience. Do propositions justified by reason, independent of sense experience, pass the method of doubt test?

Descartes thinks that they fail. How could this be true? Descartes asks us to imagine that our minds are deceived by an "evil demon." Imagine that the evil demon causes our faculty of reasoning to find propositions totally obvious that in fact are false. If this were so, we might believe that $2 + 3 = 5$ even though the proposition isn't true.

These conclusions—all reached in the first of the *Meditations*—are entirely negative. A posteriori beliefs about the character of the world outside the mind are dubitable. This we see by considering dreams and hallucinations. A priori propositions also are dubitable. This we see by considering the evil demon. If no belief in these two categories passes the method of doubt test, which beliefs could be the foundations of knowledge? What category of belief could possibly satisfy this very stringent requirement?

I AM THINKING, THEREFORE I EXIST

In an earlier work, the *Discourse on the Method* (1637), Descartes identifies a pair of propositions that pass the test:

> I noticed that while I was trying to think everything false, it must be that I, who was thinking this, was something. And observing that this truth, *I am thinking, therefore I exist* [*Je pense, donc je suis; Cogito ergo sum* in Latin], was so solid and secure that the most extravagant suppositions of the skeptics could not overthrow it, I judged that I need not scruple to accept it as the first principle of the philosophy I was seeking.

In the *Second Meditation*, Descartes focuses on the belief "I am, I exist" as the first proposition that can be judged beyond doubt.

To understand what Descartes is driving at, you must think about yourself, formulating your thoughts in the first person. When Descartes considers the proposition "I am thinking," you aren't supposed to consider the proposition "Descartes is thinking." Rather, you should say to yourself precisely what Descartes says to himself.

Consider my belief that I am thinking. I can't doubt this. I can't construct a story in which I believe this proposition, though it is false. For if I *believe* the proposition, then I am thinking, and so the proposition is true. So the attempt to doubt the proposition proves that it must be true. The proposition "I am thinking" passes the method of doubt test.

There are two important characteristics of the proposition "I am thinking" that you should note. First, it is important that the proposition is in the first person. When Descartes considers "I am thinking," he concludes that this proposition passes the method of doubt test. However, if he had considered "Descartes is thinking," the result would have been different. It *is* possible for Descartes to doubt that there is someone named "Descartes." He can invent a story in which there is no such person as Descartes; that such a story can be constructed shows that the proposition is dubitable.

The second feature of the proposition "I am thinking" is that it involves a psychological property. I can't doubt that I am thinking, but I can doubt that I am now in North America. Both beliefs are first person. But only the former is psychological.

As noted above, Descartes maintains that the proposition "I exist" also passes the method of doubt test. Take a few minutes and formulate an argument, similar to the one just described for "I am thinking," that shows that this is so.

So far, we have two propositions that Descartes thinks can serve as foundations for the rest of what we know. I can't doubt that I am thinking; nor can I doubt that I exist. This is a meager foundation. Just as it would be hard to erect a big building on a foundation made of two bricks, so it would be difficult to ground the whole of what we know about the world on this paltry foundation of two beliefs.

There is more, however. Consider propositions solely about the contents of your own present sensory experiences. Such propositions describe the way things seem to you. You now seem to see a page in front of you. Descartes thinks that all such first-person descriptions of the way things seem are indubitable.

To understand Descartes's point, it is essential to recognize the difference between the following two propositions:

> There is a page in front of me.
>
> I seem to see a page in front of me.

It is pretty clear, as noted earlier, that the first of these can be doubted. That's the point about dreams and illusions. Descartes maintains that the second proposition is different, however. He holds that it has this peculiar property: If you believe that the proposition is true, then you can't be mistaken. If you *believe* that you seem to see a page in front of you, then you *do* seem to see a page in front of you. You can't be mistaken in your beliefs about the way things seem to you.

So the foundation of knowledge has just been augmented. "I am thinking" and "I exist" are indubitable, and so are the many first-person beliefs about the way things seem.

THESIS OF THE INCORRIGIBILITY OF THE MENTAL

Descartes went even further. He thought that people have infallible access to what they believe and desire. Introspection ("looking inward") is a method that the mind can use to accurately grasp its own contents. This is sometimes expressed by saying that Descartes believed in *the thesis of the incorrigibility of the mental*. Although "There is a page in front of me" isn't indubitable, Descartes thought "I believe that there is a page in front of me" is indubitable. If you believe that you have that belief, then it must be true that you have that belief. Ditto for desires. If you believe that you want some ice cream, then it must be true that you want some ice cream.

A great deal of work in psychology in the last 100 years shows that this incorrigibility thesis isn't plausible. Sigmund Freud, whose views on religion came up in Lecture 10, argued that we often misunderstand what we really believe and what we really want. At times our beliefs and desires would be very upsetting to us if we were conscious of them. So, as a defense mechanism, our minds repress them. The result is that we often have mistaken beliefs about what we really think and want.

An example of this is Freud's theory of the Oedipus Complex. Freud held that little boys want to kill their fathers and marry their mothers. If you asked a little boy whether he wanted to do this, however, he probably would sincerely answer *no.*

You might well ask: What evidence can there be for this theory? If little boys deny having these desires, why think they have them? Freud's answer is that this theory is a reasonable explanation of what little boys *do.* It is their behavior that we must consider, not just what they say they believe and desire. Verbal reports about what we think and want are evidence as to what our beliefs and desires really are. Sincere reports, however, don't settle the matter, since behavior may provide *other* evidence that is relevant.

Although this idea—that we often have a false picture of our own beliefs and desires—is very important in Freud's theories, it isn't unique to them. A great variety of approaches in psychology deny Descartes's thesis of incorrigibility. Descartes wants to include *all* first-person reports of his own beliefs and desires as foundations. Each, he thought, passes the method of doubt test. Freud and many other psychologists would disagree. I'm on their side.

Where does this leave Descartes's project of identifying the foundations of knowledge? The foundations include *I am thinking* and *I exist* and all first-person reports about the way the world seems to be to the agent. First-person reports about the contents of the agent's experience that don't comment on the way the world is outside the agent's mind Descartes took to be indubitable. Another example in this category (besides "I seem to see a page in front of me") is "I am in pain." Descartes's view was that if you believe that you are in pain, then you are in pain.

In Lecture 2, I pointed out that for a very large class of our beliefs, there is a huge difference between believing a proposition and that proposition's actually being true. To believe that the Rockies are over 10,000 feet is one thing; for the mountains to actually be that high is another. It is misguided wishful thinking to hold that believing the proposition guarantees that it is true.

This sensible separation of belief and truth, which seems right for a wide class of propositions, is called into question by the special examples Descartes thought pass the method of doubt test. According to Descartes, "I am in pain" must be true if I think it is. The same holds for "I am thinking" and "I seem to see a page in front of me." Wishful thinking seems to work *sometimes,* though not *always.*

DO FIRST-PERSON PSYCHOLOGICAL BELIEFS PROVIDE A SUFFICIENT FOUNDATION?

These propositions, Descartes thought, are foundational. We can't be mistaken in believing them. Some philosophers have disagreed with Descartes's claim here. They have maintained that it is possible to be mistaken in holding some of these beliefs. I'm not going to address that matter here. Instead, I want to consider another problem.

Recall the architectural metaphor discussed at the beginning of this lecture. An adequate foundation for a building must have two properties. It must be (1) secure and (2) sufficient to support the house. The foundations of knowledge are subject to the same requirements. According to Descartes, they must be indubitable. In addition, it must be possible to rest everything else we know on them. Don't forget that the method of doubt is intended to identify the foundations; the entire superstructure is supposed to rest on that basis.

Descartes, as I mentioned before, wasn't a skeptic. He thought that we know lots of things about the world outside our own minds. For example, you know that there is a page in front of you now. This belief about the external world isn't indubitable; it didn't pass the method of doubt test. But, nevertheless, it is (Descartes would agree) something you know. How can Descartes show this is true?

Recall the Euclidean analogy. We've just identified some axioms of the system of knowledge. Do these suffice to prove some theorems? We must show how you know there is a page in front of you by showing how this proposition is connected with foundational ones. In Euclidean geometry, we justify theorems by deducing them from axioms. How can a superstructural belief be shown to be knowledge? We must show that it is connected with foundational pieces of knowledge in the right way. But what is this special connection supposed to be?

Can deduction do the trick? Euclid deduced theorems from axioms. Can Descartes deduce propositions about the world outside the mind from beliefs that are first-person psychological reports? To show that you know that there is a page in front of you, maybe we should try to deduce that proposition in the following way:

I seem to see a page in front of me.
_____

There is a page in front of me.

The premiss of this argument is foundational. The problem is that it doesn't deductively imply the conclusion. The existence of a page in front of me doesn't deductively follow from the way things seem to me now. That's the point noted before about dreams and hallucinations.

The premiss given isn't enough. And even if I augmented it with other reports about my present psychological state (for example, "I seem to feel a page," "I seem to taste a page," etc.), that still wouldn't be enough. Such premisses might be ones about which I'm perfectly certain. But they don't provide a sufficient foundation for the beliefs I have about the world outside the mind. Such arguments aren't deductively valid.

AN ADDITIONAL FOUNDATIONAL BELIEF: GOD EXISTS AND IS NO DECEIVER

Descartes saw quite clearly that the argument just represented needs an additional premiss, one that will bridge the gap between first-person psychological premisses and a conclusion that describes the world outside the mind. Descartes thought the proposition that *God exists and is no deceiver* provides the additional premiss that he needs.

How would this additional premiss solve Descartes's problem? Descartes had the following picture in mind: God created your mind and situated you in the world. What sort of mind did God give you? Obviously, he didn't give you a mind that reaches true conclusions about the world on each and every occasion. Your mind isn't infallible. On the other hand, God wouldn't have furnished you with a mind that leads you to false beliefs about the world no matter how carefully you reason and no matter how much evidence you consult. If God had done this, he would have been a deceiver. Descartes thinks that God created us with minds that have the capacity to attain true beliefs about the world. We are neither infallible nor are we hopelessly trapped by falsehood. Rather, we are somewhere in the middle: We can reach true beliefs if we are careful about how we use the minds that God bestowed upon us.

HOW TO PROVE THAT GOD EXISTS

I've just explained what role the proposition that God exists and is no deceiver is supposed to play in Descartes's theory of knowledge. However, if this proposition is to be a part of the foundations, it must be indubitable. It must pass the method of doubt test. Descartes has to show that the proposition that God exists and is no deceiver is not just true, but indubitable. Here Descartes seems to be trying to do the impossible. Isn't it obvious that it is possible to doubt that God exists and is no deceiver? After all, atheists or agnostics don't believe that God exists. Isn't this enough to show that it is *possible* to doubt that God exists and is no deceiver?

Descartes thinks that atheists and agnostics have not considered the matter carefully enough. They *think* they can doubt the proposition, but they have not really grasped what this would really involve. Descartes believes that he has a proof of the existence of God whose premisses are *indubitable*. In addition, the proof is so simple that once you attend carefully to it, you can't doubt that there is a God. This is the proof that Descartes lays out in the *Third Meditation*. Here it is, in outline:

(1) My idea of God is an idea of a perfect being.

(2) There must be at least as much perfection in the cause as there is in the effect.

———————————

Hence, the cause of my idea is a perfect being—namely, God himself.

Once you inspect this proof, the proposition that God exists is like the *cogito*—it is impossible to doubt that it is true.

Descartes thinks he can know premiss (1) of this argument by introspection. By looking inward at the contents of his own mind, he can discern this fact about himself. Premiss (1), Descartes believes, is indubitable.

As to premiss (2), Descartes thinks that it is an indubitable principle about causality. It can be broken into two components. First, there is the idea that every event has a cause. Second, there is the idea that the cause must be at least as perfect as the effect. It isn't clear why we should accept these principles about causality. For example, why couldn't some events occur for no reason at all? This is a question we explored in Lectures 4 and 7. Descartes needs to show not only that it is true that every event has a cause, but that this proposition is indubitably true. This is something that he does not succeed in doing.

Premiss (2) needs to be clarified. Descartes distinguishes two kinds of perfection (or "reality") that an idea or representation might possess. To find out how *objectively* perfect a representation is, you must find out how perfect the thing is that the representation represents. Two photographs of a saint must have the same degree of objective perfection; two photographs of a trash can will have the same degree of objective perfection as well. And if saints are more perfect than trash cans, the first pair will have more objective perfection than the second.

This characterization of objective perfection requires a little fine-tuning. A picture of a unicorn has a certain degree of objective perfection, even though there are no unicorns. So, to determine how objectively perfect the picture is, you must ask yourself this question: If the picture represented something that actually existed, how perfect would that thing be?

I hope you can see from the definition of objective perfection why Descartes thinks that his concept of God has the maximum amount of objective perfection. This is something that Descartes can say just by examining his concept of God. Indeed, it is something that an atheist might agree to as well. If there were a God, then that being would have all the perfections; this means that the atheist's concept of God is objectively perfect.

The concept of objective perfection allows some representations to be ranked higher than others. My idea of God is at the top. Somewhere below that is my idea of a saint. And still farther down the list is my idea of a trash can. The second kind of perfection that Descartes discusses is different. This is what Descartes calls an idea's *formal perfection*. All mental contents have the same degree of formal perfection, because they all are made of the same stuff. To see what Descartes has in mind here, consider paintings. These may differ in their degree of objective perfection. But all are made of canvas and paint. In this sense, they have the same degree of formal perfection. Descartes thinks the same holds for all the ideas I may have.

In the argument for the existence of God that I just sketched, Descartes is talking about the *objective* perfection of his idea of God. Let's reformulate the argument to make this explicit:

(1) My idea of God is objectively perfect.

(2) If an idea is objectively perfect, then the cause of that idea
     must be a perfect being.
     ———————————
     Hence, God exists.

Premiss (2) strikes me as implausible. Here is a way to see that it is false. I claim that people could form their concept of God (a perfect being) in the following way. They could look at *imperfect* things in the world and thereby form the idea of *limited* intelligence, *limited* goodness, and *limited* power. Then, by applying the concept of negation (the concept we express by the word "not") to these ideas, they would obtain the idea of a being who has *unlimited* intelligence, goodness, and power. This seems to be an entirely possible causal explanation for why we have the idea of a perfect being. If it is possible, then (2) is false.

In the *Third Meditation,* Descartes explicitly considers this suggestion. He rejects the idea that we might have acquired the concept of perfection by seeing imperfect things and then applying the concept of negation. You should consider Descartes's argument and decide whether you think it works. Descartes thinks the only possible explanation for the fact that we have an idea of a perfect being is that a perfect being actually exists and caused us to have this idea.

Leaving this exercise to you, I'll conclude that Descartes's causal argument for the existence of God is defective. Descartes wanted to show that "God exists" isn't just true, but indubitably true. It was to be a foundational element in the structure of our knowledge. The argument he gave falls short of this ambitious goal.

THE CLARITY AND DISTINCTNESS CRITERION

If God is no deceiver, how can we tell whether the beliefs we have are true? Descartes thought that if we inspect them carefully, and make sure that they are clear and distinct, we can be certain that they are correct. Descartes maintained that *clear and distinct beliefs must be true.* If you reason carefully and use your mental faculties in the way that God intended them to be used, you can obtain knowledge of the world you inhabit. Descartes thinks you have an indubitable grasp of the contents of your own mind; he also thinks that you can know indubitably that God exists and is no deceiver. This foundation, he believes, provides a sufficient and secure basis for you to gain knowledge of the world you inhabit.

THE CARTESIAN CIRCLE

Scholars argue over whether Descartes's argument for the existence of God has a defect that goes beyond the fact that some of his premisses are dubious. They have suggested that the argument is circular, given its place in Descartes's larger epistemological program. Recall that Descartes wants to prove that God exists and is no deceiver in order to be able to conclude that clear and distinct ideas must be true.

Descartes's argument for the existence of God, like all arguments, involves the use of reason. For us to recognize that the argument establishes the existence of God, we must use the faculty of reasoning we possess. Descartes's argument begins by examining his concept of God and determining that this is the idea of a perfect being. Descartes therefore seems to be using the clarity and distinctness criterion in arguing that God exists. Descartes vehemently denied that he was guilty of circular reasoning. This problem has come to be known as the Problem of the Cartesian Circle.

Here's how I see this issue: Descartes is using the method of doubt test to assemble foundations for knowledge. His goal is to assemble enough premises by this procedure so that he can show that we have knowledge of the world outside our minds. The existence of a God who is no deceiver is supposed to be one of these premises. Descartes thought his causal argument for the existence of God is beyond doubt; he thought that as you reason your way through the argument, you must find it irresistible.

Why should we agree that the proposition "Every event has a cause" is beyond doubt? Descartes's view seems to be that when we consider the proposition carefully, using the full resources of clarification and logic that we possess, we will be driven to conclude that the proposition must be true. This seems to mean that we are applying the clarity and distinctness criterion. If so, Descartes is reasoning in a circle.

CONCLUSION

Where does this leave the project of refuting skepticism? Descartes thought that first-person psychological beliefs are indubitable. He recognized that this, by itself, isn't enough to show that the beliefs we have provide us with genuine knowledge of the world outside the mind. Additional premises are needed. The following example argument shows how Descartes wanted to bridge the gap between the indubitable knowledge we have of our own minds and the beliefs we have about the world outside our minds:

(1) I now believe that the object in front of me is a page.

(2) My present belief is clear and distinct.

(3) Clear and distinct ideas are true.

———————————

There is a page in front of me.

The argument is valid: If the premises are true, the conclusion also must be true. Descartes's foundationalism can be understood as a pair of claims about this argument. First, he claims that the premises of this argument are *indubitable*. Second, he thinks that the conclusion of the argument is a proposition we *know* because it follows from these indubitable premises.

I've already discussed premiss (1); Descartes thought that it is indubitable. But what of the next two premises? There is an unhappy tension between these two claims.

Suppose we grant Descartes that premiss (3) is right—that a clear and distinct idea can't fail to be true. If we grant this, then it isn't so obvious that my present belief about what is in front of me really is clear and distinct. I may *think* that it is, but this appearance may be deceiving. So if (3) is right, (2) can't be beyond doubt. Alternatively, suppose we are able to tell, by introspection, whether a belief is clear and distinct. That will be enough to underwrite the truth of (2). But in that case, there is no longer any absolute assurance that (3) is right.

The problem here concerns whether we should see "clarity and distinctness" as a purely subjective characteristic of a belief. If I can tell just by examining the contents of my own beliefs whether they are "clear and distinct," I see no reason to say that a clear and distinct belief must be true. On the other hand, if we treat "clarity and distinctness" as a characteristic that is necessarily connected with truth, I don't see how I can tell whether a belief is "clear and distinct" just by introspection.

Descartes tried to refute the following skeptical argument, which I described at the end of the previous lecture:

> Knowledge requires the impossibility of error.
>
> It now is possible that I am mistaken in believing that there is a page in front of me.
> _____
> Hence, I don't know that there is a page in front of me.

Descartes accepted the first premiss but denied the second. Descartes concedes that we often make mistakes. The senses sometimes play tricks on us, and so does our faculty of reasoning. But the fact that this *sometimes* happens doesn't show that it is happening *now*. If I am now reasoning in a careful and logically rigorous way, then I can't now be mistaken in what I believe, or so Descartes maintained.

So Descartes's reply to the skeptic's argument can be put like this:

> If God exists and is no deceiver and I now have a clear and distinct belief that there is a page in front of me, then I can't be mistaken in thinking that there is a page in front of me.
>
> God exists and is no deceiver and I now have a clear and distinct belief that there is a page in front of me.
> _____
> I can't be mistaken in thinking that there is a page in front of me.

The problem is that Descartes's argument for the second premiss of this last argument wasn't successful. He wasn't able to prove that we are embedded in the world in the special way described by the hypothesis that God exists and is no deceiver. In consequence, he wasn't able to refute the skeptic's argument.

Review Questions

1. What is foundationalism in epistemology? What does it have to do with Euclidean geometry? With building a house?

2. What is the method of doubt test? What does Descartes use this method to do? What fails the test? What passes?

3. What does it mean to say that there is a "gap" between our first-person psychological beliefs and the beliefs we have about the world outside the mind?

4. Descartes thought that proving that God exists would help show why we are able to have knowledge of the world around us. Why did he think this? Is the proposition that "God exists and is no deceiver" foundational, according to Descartes?

5. Analyze Descartes's causal argument for the existence of God. Suppose that one of Aquinas's arguments for the existence of God is valid and has true premises. Could Descartes have used it, instead of his causal argument, to prove that God exists?

6. What is the Problem of the Cartesian Circle?

7. In the previous lecture, an argument for skepticism was presented. How would Descartes evaluate this argument?

Problems for Further Thought

1. Which of the following propositions pass the method of doubt test? How are they different from each other?

> I saw Joe run.
>
> I seem to remember seeing Joe run.
>
> I remember seeming to see Joe run.

2. Can someone mistakenly believe that he or she seems to see a coffee cup? Can someone mistakenly believe he or she is in pain?

3. I suggested that our idea of a perfect being might be obtained by observing imperfect things and then using the concept of negation. Descartes considers this suggestion in the *Third Meditation* and rejects it. What reason does Descartes give for rejecting this explanation? Are his reasons plausible?

4. In *The Principles of Philosophy* (1644), Descartes defines clarity and distinctness as follows:

> I term that "clear" which is present and apparent to an attentive mind, in the same way that we see objects clearly when, being present to the regarding eye, they operate upon it with sufficient strength. But the "distinct" is that which is so precise and different from all other objects that it contains within itself nothing but what is clear. . . . Perceptions may be clear without being distinct, but cannot be distinct without also being clear.

Given this definition, can a clear and distinct idea be false?

LECTURE 14

The Reliability Theory of Knowledge

DESCARTES: KNOWLEDGE IS INTERNALLY CERTIFIABLE

According to Descartes, *knowledge is internally certifiable*. What does this mean? It means that if I know some proposition *p*, then there exists an argument that shows that *p* must be true, *whose premises are either a priori true or knowable by introspection*. Recall how Descartes would explain why I now know that there is a page in front of me:

> I believe that there is a page in front of me.
>
> My belief that there is a page in front of me is clear and distinct.
>
> Clear and distinct ideas are true.
>
> ———————
>
> There is a page in front of me.

The first two premisses I know by *introspection*—by gazing within my own mind and examining its contents. How do I know that the third premiss is true? I know by introspection that I have an idea of a perfect God; I (supposedly) know a priori that an idea of a perfect being must be caused by a perfect being. Putting these two thoughts together, I deduce that God—a perfect being—must exist. The third premiss is supposed to follow from this.

Notice that the word "knowledge" doesn't appear in the displayed argument. So what does this argument have to do with the issue of whether I *know* that there is a page in front of me? For Descartes, I know that the concluding proposition is true because I know the premisses are true. And how do I know the premisses? I know these by introspection and a priori reasoning.

I want to name the elements in this argument. There is a *subjective premiss*, an *objective conclusion*, and a *linking premiss*. The subjective premiss describes what is going on in the subject's mind ("I believe that there is a page in front of me"). The objective conclusion makes a claim about the world outside the subject's mind ("There is a page in front of me"). The linking premiss (or premisses) shows how the subjective premiss necessitates the objective conclusion ("If I have a particular belief and it is clear and distinct, then it is true").

This vocabulary can be used to say what is characteristic of Descartes's approach to the problem of knowledge. His idea—that knowledge is internally certifiable—comes to this: *If the subject knows that the objective conclusion is true, then the subject must know that the linking premiss is true and must know this independently of sense experience.* By introspection and a priori reasoning, I can establish the required connection between what is inside the mind and what is outside it.

The theory of knowledge I'll discuss in this lecture involves a very different approach from that taken by Descartes. It agrees with Descartes that knowledge requires the existence of a connection between what is going on inside the mind and what is going on outside it. Knowledge requires that a particular linking premiss be true. But according to the *Reliability Theory of Knowledge,* the linking premiss doesn't have to be knowable by introspection and a priori reasoning. In fact, this theory maintains that the subject doesn't have to know that the linking premiss is true at all.

This approach to the problem of knowledge was first proposed by Fred Dretske (in "Conclusive Reasons," *Australasian Journal of Philosophy,* Vol. 49, 1971) and by David Armstrong (in *Belief, Truth, and Knowledge,* Cambridge University Press, 1973).

WHAT MAKES A THERMOMETER RELIABLE?

The Reliability Theory of Knowledge claims there is an important analogy between knowledge and a reliable measuring device. If you know that there is a page in front of you now, then your belief is related to the world outside your mind in the same way that the reading of a reliable thermometer is related to the temperature.

Thermometers are devices that form representations of temperature. The height of the mercury column is the representation; the ambient temperature is the thing represented. Thermometer readings represent temperature, just as your beliefs represent the world outside your mind. Thermometer readings can be accurate or inaccurate, just as beliefs can be true or false.

What makes a thermometer reliable? Does this just mean that its readings are accurate? To see why this isn't enough, consider a thermometer that is used just once. Suppose, on that one occasion, the thermometer said "98 degrees Fahrenheit" and the ambient temperature happened to be 98 degrees Fahrenheit. The reading was accurate, but that doesn't mean that the thermometer was reliable. For all I've said, the thermometer may have been stuck. If so, it wasn't reliable, even though its one and only reading was accurate.

A reliable thermometer is one for which there is a *necessary connection* between readings and ambient temperatures. If the thermometer reads *n* degrees Fahrenheit, then the temperature *must be n* degrees Fahrenheit. If a thermometer is reliable, then its reading *must* be correct; it can't be mistaken in what it says. A stuck thermometer isn't reliable, even when its readings happen to be correct. It is unreliable because its readings are correct only *by accident.*

Do reliable thermometers exist? I think so. The mercury thermometers we use to check whether we have fevers are examples. In saying this, I'm not denying two obvious facts. First, a thermometer can be reliable in one set of circumstances but not in another. A mercury thermometer wouldn't be very useful for measuring temperature if it were wrapped in insulation before being placed in the mouth. The second point is that in saying that a thermometer is reliable, I'm not denying that it would be unreliable if it were broken. Hitting a reliable thermometer with a hammer will usually be enough to make it unreliable.

So there are two things that help make a thermometer reliable. First, it has to be used in the right environment (for example, don't wrap it in insulation if you want to take somebody's temperature). Second, the internal makeup of the device has to be right (for example, the glass tube that holds the mercury can't be broken).

Notice that reliability is an objective feature of the relationship between the thermometer and its environment. The question is whether the thermometer and its environment make the following claim true: *If the thermometer says that the temperature is n degrees Fahrenheit, then the temperature must be n degrees Fahrenheit.* It is an entirely separate question whether anybody realizes that this thermometer/environment relationship obtains. Whether we notice this fact is a subjective question, but whether the relationship obtains is an objective matter.

Let's imagine that you take a thermometer out of a child's mouth, see that it reads *n* degrees Fahrenheit, and then announce: "The thermometer is reliable, and so the baby's temperature is *n* degrees Fahrenheit." Suppose a contentious philosopher (like me) comes along and tries to refute your claim. I say:

> Your thermometer isn't reliable. It is unreliable because I can conceive of a circumstance in which its reading would be false. I can conceive of a situation in which the thermometer is wrapped in insulation. In that case, the thermometer reading wouldn't be correct. I also can conceive of the thermometer's being broken. In that case as well, the thermometer reading wouldn't be correct. It follows from the fact that I can conceive of these things that your thermometer isn't reliable.

Should you be convinced by my argument? I think not. Whether the thermometer is reliable *here and now* has nothing to do with what I can imagine. Granted, if the situations I described actually obtained, then the thermometer wouldn't be reliable in *those* circumstances. But from this it doesn't follow that the thermometer is unreliable in the circumstances in which it actually was used.

RELEVANCE TO THE PROBLEM OF KNOWLEDGE

How does this discussion of reliable thermometers bear on the problem of knowledge? The Reliability Theory of Knowledge says that an individual knows a proposition if the individual is related to the proposition the way a reliable thermometer is related to the temperature it measures. A reliable thermometer wouldn't say *n* degrees Fahrenheit unless the temperature were *n* degrees Fahrenheit. An individual knows that there is a page in front of her precisely when she wouldn't have believed there is a page in front of her unless there were one there.

Another way to express this idea is by using the concept of *causality*. A thermometer is reliable in a given circumstance if the only thing that could cause the thermometer to read *n* degrees Fahrenheit is that the temperature really is *n* degrees Fahrenheit. Similarly, *S* knows that there is a page in front of her in a given circumstance if the only thing that could cause *S* to believe this is that there really is a page in front of her.

I hope the connection between thermometers and knowledge is starting to become clear. Suppose *S* believes that there is a page in front of her. We want to know whether this belief is an instance of knowledge. The answer should depend on the *actual* relationship that obtains between *S* and her environment. Suppose *S*'s sensory system is functioning normally; she isn't hallucinating, for example. In addition, suppose that there are no evil demons around who might choose to provide *S* with misleading evidence. If so, it may be true that *S* is a reliable indicator of the presence of a page. If you want to answer the question of whether *S* knows that there is a page present, it will be entirely irrelevant to point out that if *S* had taken a hallucinatory drug or if *S* were plagued by an evil demon, then *S*'s belief would be (or might be) false. These *hypothetical* considerations do nothing to undermine the claim that *S*'s sensory state is a reliable indicator of what is going on in her environment.

Here's how the Reliability Theory of Knowledge characterizes what knowledge is:

(RTK) *S* knows that *p* if and only if

(1) *S* believes that *p*.

(2) *p* is true.

(3) in the circumstances that *S* occupies, if *S* believes that *p*, then *p* must be true.

The third condition can also be formulated in either of the following two ways:

In the circumstances that *S* occupies, *S* wouldn't believe that *p* unless *p* were true.

In the circumstances that *S* occupies, it is impossible that *S* believe *p* and *p* be false.

Notice that the Reliability Theory of Knowledge makes use of the concepts of *necessity* and *impossibility*. To understand this theory of knowledge, we need to look more carefully at what these concepts mean.

THREE CONCEPTS OF IMPOSSIBILITY

I want to discuss three kinds of impossibility. Consider the following three statements:

(1) Joe can't be a married bachelor.

(2) Joe can't go faster than the speed of light.

(3) Joe can't tie his shoes now.

The word "can't" in each of these indicates that something is *im*possible. But different kinds of impossibility are involved.

The first statement is logically necessary. It has to be true, just by virtue of logic and the definitions of the terms involved. If definitions and their deductive consequences are a priori true (Lecture 8), then (1) expresses a necessary truth that is a priori.

In contrast, statement (2) isn't a priori. We know that it is true because Einstein's theory of relativity—an a posteriori theory—says that it is so. Statement (2) is said to be *nomologically necessary* (from *nomos,* meaning "law"). It is necessary because of a law of nature, in this case an a posteriori law of physics.

Statement (3) differs from the first two examples. Its truth doesn't follow from logic or definitions. Nor does its truth follow from any law of nature—physical or biological or whatever. Rather, to see that (3) is true, you have to take into account particular facts about Joe. Joe can't tie his shoes now because he is carrying several bags of groceries. I'll call this third sort of necessity *circumstantial necessity*. By this I mean that the statement is necessarily true only because of facts about the circumstances described.

There is an additional fact about type (3) necessity that I should note. Whether we judge (3) true or false depends on how we interpret it. That is, (3) is ambiguous. If we interpret it to mean that Joe can't tie his shoes because he is otherwise occupied, (3) may be true. Suppose, however, we take (3) to mean that even if Joe put down the bags, he still couldn't tie his shoes. If that is how we interpret (3), we may judge it false. This is an important feature of statements that are circumstantially necessary.

When I say that a thermometer is reliable, I mean that it and its environment are related in a special way. I'm saying that its circumstances are such that its readings *must* be correct. In saying this, I'm using the concept of *circumstantial necessity*.

Similarly, when I say that *S* knows that there is a page in front of her, I'm saying that she is related to her environment in a special way. I'm saying that she can't be mistaken in believing what she does. Here again, I'm using the concept of circumstantial necessity.

Suppose that a real printed page is the only thing that could get *S* to believe that a printed page is before her. Her senses are functioning normally. There are no evil demons lurking about who provide misleading evidence. If this is so, and if *S* subsequently believes the proposition in question, then *S* will *know* that there is a printed page in front of her. This is what the reliability theory says. In this circumstance, her belief will be related to the world the way the reading of a reliable thermometer is related to the temperature.

TO HAVE KNOWLEDGE, YOU DON'T HAVE TO BE ABLE TO CONSTRUCT A PHILOSOPHICAL ARGUMENT REFUTING THE SKEPTIC

It is important to notice that the claims that *S* knows some proposition *p* isn't refuted by the fact that *S* may not be able to defend her knowledge claim against clever philosophical interrogation. If I asked *S* how she knows that her impressions aren't caused by an evil demon, she may draw a blank. If I ask her how she knows that she isn't dreaming, she may admit that she can't construct an argument proving that she isn't dreaming. Such philosophical puzzles may even lead *S* to say "I guess I don't know that there is a printed page in front of me." But her comment doesn't show that she lacks knowledge. Rather, it shows only that *S* doesn't believe that she knows there is a printed page in front of her.

If *S* is like a reliable thermometer, she has knowledge. Being like a reliable thermometer, however, doesn't require that *S* have the ability to construct fancy philosophical arguments that show she is like a thermometer. Thermometers can't construct philosophical arguments, yet they are sometimes reliable. *S* may be similar. She may be unable to refute the skeptic, but that doesn't show she lacks knowledge.

S may even be a skeptic herself. She may believe that she lacks knowledge. But that doesn't mean that she really lacks it. Just as it is possible to mistakenly believe that a thermometer is unreliable, so it is possible to mistakenly believe that an individual lacks knowledge. In fact, it is possible to have false beliefs about one's own situations: *S* can believe that she lacks knowledge and yet be wrong.

The KK-Principle

According to the Reliability Theory of Knowledge, knowing a proposition doesn't imply that you know that you know it. That is, the reliability theory rejects what is called the *KK-principle*. The following several paragraphs about this principle will be somewhat tough to grasp—so take a deep breath, read them slowly, and then read them again.

The *KK-principle* says that if *S* knows that *p*, then *S* knows that she knows that *p*. But I've just argued that the following is possible: *S* knows that *p*, but *S* doesn't believe that she knows that *p*. This means that *S* might know that *p* even though she doesn't know that she knows that *p*. So if I'm right, the KK-principle is false.

If the KK-principle were true, *S* could prove that she lacked knowledge just by becoming a philosophical skeptic. This would be very *convenient*—wouldn't it be nice to be able to prove some thesis just by believing it?

Suppose *S* believed, maybe for no reason at all, that she lacked knowledge. If so, the KK-principle would imply that, indeed, she did lack knowledge. To see why, consider the following argument:

(1) If you do not believe that you have knowledge, then you don't know that you have knowledge.

(2) If you don't know that you have knowledge, then you don't have knowledge.

───────────

If you do not believe that you have knowledge, then you don't have knowledge.

This argument is deductively valid (what is its logical form?). Notice that premiss (1) is correct; it follows from the fact that knowing a proposition requires that you believe the proposition. Premiss (2) would be true if the KK-principle were correct.

So if the KK-principle were true, then believing that skepticism is true would be enough to ensure that skepticism is true. But if knowing is like being a reliable thermometer, this has got to be wrong.

The Reliability Theory of Knowledge holds that whether an agent knows something is settled by the objective relationship that obtains between the agent's belief and the environment. Whether the agent believes that this relationship obtains is irrelevant. The reliability theory rejects the KK-principle.

In summary, the Reliability Theory of Knowledge explains why *S* knows that there is a page in front of her by describing the following argument:

> *S* believes that there is a page in front of her.
>
> In the circumstances *S* occupies, she wouldn't believe that there is a page in front of her unless there were a page in front of her.
> _____
> There is a page in front of *S*.

This argument doesn't use the word "know." So what does it have to do with knowledge? According to the reliability theory, *S* knows that the concluding proposition is true because the premises are true. But *S* doesn't have to *know* that the premises are true. Nor does *S* have to produce an argument independent of sense experience for the premises. This shows why the reliability theory rejects Descartes's claim that knowledge is internally certifiable.

One virtue of the reliability theory is that it explains what is wrong with a standard skeptical argument. The skeptic claims that *S* doesn't know that there is a printed page in front of her on the grounds that it is possible to imagine that *S* is deluded in some way. You can imagine a situation in which *S* believes what she does, but is mistaken. The reliability theory shows why this act of imagination is irrelevant to the question of whether *S* has knowledge *in the real world situation she occupies*.

A CONSEQUENCE OF THE RELIABILITY THEORY

To conclude this discussion, I want to consider an implication that the reliability theory has. It involves a fact about circumstantial necessity that I mentioned before. This is the fact that claims of circumstantial necessity often are ambiguous. I'll restate the point and then show how it is relevant to the reliability theory.

Consider the statement "Joe can't tie his shoes now." Suppose I make this comment to you while we are looking at Joe, who is carrying two heavy bags of groceries. Is the quoted remark true? Here are two ways of interpreting it:

> (1) If Joe tries to tie his shoes while holding the bags of groceries, he will fail.
>
> (2) If Joe tries to tie his shoes after first putting down the groceries, he will fail.

If we interpreted "Joe can't tie his shoes now" to mean (1), it might be true; if we interpreted it to mean (2), it might be false. Which reading you choose affects whether you will say that the quoted claim is true.

To see how this idea applies to the Reliability Theory of Knowledge, let's switch examples—from knowing that there is a printed page in front of you to knowing that there is a barn in the field next to the road on which you are driving.

Suppose one day you go for a drive in Dane County, the county that contains Madison, Wisconsin. On your drive, you look at a field and say, "There is a barn in that field." Suppose that the proposition you've asserted is true. Is this belief of yours a case of knowledge?

The reliability theory says that we must ask whether, in the circumstances you occupy, there is anything besides a real barn that could have caused you to believe a barn is present. The problem I want to focus on is that it isn't clear how to decide what is included and what is excluded by the expression "in the circumstances you occupy."

First I'll define the idea of a *fool's barn*. Fool's gold looks like gold, but isn't gold at all. A fool's barn is something that looks like a barn but isn't one. Suppose there are no fool's barns in Dane County. The only things that look like barns are real barns. This means that if I describe the circumstances you occupy by saying that you are in Dane County, then it will be true that the only thing that could have made you think a barn is present is a real barn. Hence, your belief counts as a case of knowledge.

But now let's broaden our vision. In Hollywood, there are fool's barns. These are the facades used in movie sets. When viewed from one angle, they look like barns, but they aren't buildings at all. So if you were driving around Hollywood and came to believe that a barn was present, your belief wouldn't count as knowledge (even if your belief happened to be true). The reason is that, around Hollywood, there are things besides real barns that can make you believe a barn is present.

So if your circumstances are restricted to Dane County, you might know that a barn is present; if your circumstances are restricted to Hollywood, you wouldn't. But now consider a puzzle.

I initially suggested that the circumstances you occupy are limited to the objects in Dane County. Given this array of objects, I argued that a real barn is the only thing (in the circumstances) that could cause you to think that a barn is present. But why describe your circumstances so narrowly? Why not describe your circumstances as including all the objects in the U.S.A.? If I describe your situation in this way, it will be false that the only thing that could cause you to believe a barn is present is a real barn.

Here is the point: When we assert or deny that the only thing *in the circumstances* that could cause you to believe a barn is present is a real barn, we are making reference to the environment you occupy. The environment may be thought of as composed of a set of objects. If we describe that set narrowly, it may be true that the only thing in the set that could cause your belief is a real barn. If we describe the set more broadly, this may no longer be true.

So whether you know, on your drive through Dane County, that there is a barn on the hill next to the road depends on how we choose to describe the "circumstances you occupy." There are many true descriptions we might select. Narrow ones will entail that you have knowledge; broader ones will entail that you don't.

THESIS OF THE RELATIVITY OF KNOWLEDGE

The claim I just made about knowledge may be put this way: *Knowledge is relative.* Whether S knows that p depends on (is relative to) a choice. "S is in Dane County" and "S is in the U.S.A." are equally correct descriptions of the circumstances that S occupies. Which one we consider depends on our interests.

Let's be clear what this relativity thesis asserts. When you say that something is relative, you should be prepared to say *what* it is relative to. The thesis that knowledge is relative is the thesis that whether an agent knows a proposition depends on (is relative to) a specification of his or her circumstances. These circumstances can be specified in different equally correct ways, and so there is no absolute answer to the question of whether the agent has knowledge.

Let's consider a down-to-earth example of relativity. Mary and Alice are walking down the street, side by side. Is Mary walking to the left of Alice? Well, that depends on the point of view. If you look at them from the front, you get one answer. If you look at them from the back, you get the other. The key thing to notice is that x being to the left of y isn't a relation between x and y alone. It involves some third item, z.

Does S know that p? The suggestion now being considered is that the question is incomplete. Whether S knows that p depends on a third item besides the agent S and the proposition p. It depends on a specification of S's environment. There are different true ways to describe S's environment. S is in Dane County. But it also is true that S is in the U.S.A. Relative to one specification of the environment—call it E_1— S knows that p. But relative to another equally true specification of the environment—call it E_2—S doesn't know that p.

WHAT DOES THE RELATIVITY THESIS SAY ABOUT SKEPTICISM?

The thesis that knowledge is relative has interesting implications about skepticism. Skepticism, recall, is the position that people don't have knowledge. Its opposite is the more commonsense idea that people often (if not always) know the propositions they believe. If the relativity thesis is true, then each of these theses is true in one sense but false in another.

If the agent's environment is given a very broad specification, then skepticism is true. If the environment is given a narrower specification, then the opposite position will be correct. Notice, however, that there is no conflict between the following two claims:

(1) S knows that p, relative to E_1.

(2) S doesn't know that p, relative to E_2.

These statements don't conflict with each other, any more than the following pair conflict with each other:

What's Relative About Einstein's Theory of Relativity?

Sometimes people say that Einstein proved that "Everything is relative." This isn't true. Neither is the more modest claim that Einstein proved that everything in physics is relative.

To say that a statement is relative isn't to say that it is subjective or arbitrary. Rather, it is to say that the statement is incomplete in a particular way. Whether Sue is walking to the left of Mary is a relative matter. That means that there exists some third item, beyond the two people mentioned, that must be referred to if the statement is to be true or false. To say just that the one is to the left of the other is to fail to express a complete thought.

It takes no enormous insight or creativity to see that whether one person is walking to the left of another is a relative, not an absolute, matter. In contrast, Einstein's idea that simultaneity is relative is anything but obvious. It was a brilliant theoretical conjecture, something that isn't at all suggested by our commonsense talk about space and time.

Consider two events that occur at different places. Common sense suggests that either the events are simultaneous with each other or they aren't. Einstein's theory says that this isn't true.

Whether two events are simultaneous depends on the choice of some third item—a rest frame. Relative to one rest frame, the events are simultaneous, but relative to another equally "correct" rest frame, they aren't. Simultaneity is relative, not absolute.

Einstein didn't say that everything in physics is relative. For example, in the special theory of relativity he defines a quantity called *the space–time interval*. This quantity measures the amount of separation that there is between events; it takes account of both spatial and temporal distances. The space–time interval between two events isn't relative to the choice of a rest frame. Space–time interval is absolute, not relative.

---

(3) Mary is walking to the left of Sue, when they are viewed from the front.

(4) Mary is not walking to the left of Sue, when they are viewed from the back.

So the dispute between skepticism and common sense seems to end in a stalemate, not in a victory for either side, if the relativity thesis is correct. Each position is correct in one sense but incorrect in another. This consequence follows from the Reliability Theory of Knowledge, once we acknowledge that claims about circumstantial necessity are ambiguous.

Review Questions

1. At the beginning of this lecture, I said that Descartes held that knowledge is "internally certifiable." What does this mean? Does the Reliability Theory of Knowledge agree?
2. What is the difference between logical necessity, nomological necessity, and circumstantial necessity?

3. What does it mean to say that claims about circumstantial necessity are "ambiguous"?
4. What does it mean to say that a thermometer is "reliable"? What analogy does the Reliability Theory of Knowledge see between reliable thermometers and knowledge?
5. How does the Reliability Theory of Knowledge assess the following skeptical argument: "I can imagine that my senses are now malfunctioning. Hence, I don't now know that there is a printed page in front of me."
6. What does it mean to say that knowledge is "relative"? Relative to what?
7. Does the relativity thesis entail that skepticism is correct?

Problems for Further Thought

1. For any proposition p, we can construct the sentence "S knows that p." Since "S knows that lemons are yellow" is a sentence, we can construct the sentence "S knows that S knows that lemons are yellow." We can repeat this operation as many times as we please. The KK-principle says that if S knows that p, then S knows that S knows that p. Formulate similar principles for truth (the TT-principle), belief (the BB-principle), and surprise (the SS-principle). Are any of these principles plausible? Defend your answers.
2. Whether a ring is made of gold depends on the materials that the jeweler chooses when the ring is made. Does this mean that whether a ring is made of gold is a relative matter? How is this example different from the two claims about relativity discussed in this lecture?
3. Do you think that nonhuman organisms have knowledge? For example, do dogs? What is required for dogs to have knowledge, according to the reliability theory? How do these requirements differ from what would be demanded by the view that knowledge is internally certifiable?

LECTURE 15

Justified Belief and Hume's Problem of Induction

In this lecture, I'm going to present a new problem in epistemology. So far, I've discussed the concept of *knowledge*, examining Descartes's foundationalism (Lecture 13) and the Reliability Theory of Knowledge (Lecture 14). The problem to be considered here concerns the idea of justified belief.

KNOWLEDGE VERSUS JUSTIFIED BELIEF

Before starting, let's be clear on how this problem differs from the previous one. What is the difference between knowledge and justified belief? Two differences should be clear. First, if *S* knows that *p*, then *p* must be true; whereas *S*'s having a justified belief that *p* doesn't require that *p* be true. Knowledge requires truth, but justified belief doesn't.

The second difference is that knowledge requires the impossibility of error; justified belief doesn't. Recall the lottery example discussed in Lecture 12. Suppose you believe, before the drawing, that ticket number 346 will not win in a fair lottery containing 1,000 tickets. Suppose your belief turns out (after the drawing) to have been true. I claim you didn't *know* that the ticket wouldn't win. Nevertheless, I claim that you had strong evidence for thinking the ticket would lose. Your belief was reasonable, or justified. (I'll use these two terms interchangeably.)

These comparisons of knowledge and justified belief are summarized in the following table:

	Is truth required?	Is the impossibility of error required?
Knowledge	yes	yes
Justified belief	no	no

As the lottery example illustrates, the evidence we have for many of the beliefs we hold falls short of providing absolute certainty. We sometimes use the word *probability* to describe such cases. We say that ticket number 346 *probably* won't win, to indicate that we aren't absolutely sure that it won't. Similarly, we might also say that our present experiences make the beliefs we have about the world outside the mind highly probable. Your present experiences don't make it absolutely certain that there is a printed page in front of you. But it does seem plausible to say that your experiences make it very probable that there is a printed page before you.

SKEPTICISM ABOUT JUSTIFIED BELIEF

Until now I've talked about skepticism as if it were a single thesis. Now I want to distinguish skepticism about knowledge from a second kind of skepticism, which concerns the idea of justified belief.

Although skepticism about knowledge sounds like a shocking thesis at first hearing, once one grasps what it says, it doesn't fundamentally undermine our picture of ourselves and the world we inhabit. If knowledge requires the *impossibility* of error, perhaps we should concede that we don't know many things. Of course, we often talk about the knowledge we have. But perhaps this is just sloppy talk.

This concession to skepticism isn't terribly threatening, because it allows us to hold onto the idea that our beliefs about the world aren't groundless and arbitrary. We can still say that they are "reasonable" and "well justified," even if they aren't entitled to be labeled "knowledge."

Skepticism about knowledge doesn't entail skepticism about rational belief. This is why it is possible to abandon the claim that we have knowledge without thereby giving up the idea that our beliefs are rational.

There is a second form of skepticism that is far more disturbing. This form of skepticism rejects our claim to rationality. According to this more radical form of skepticism, we aren't rationally justified in believing what we do. It is this type of skepticism that is involved in Hume's views on induction. Hume claimed that the beliefs we have about the future and the beliefs we have concerning generalizations can't be rationally justified. It isn't just that we can't be *certain* that the sun will rise tomorrow. And it's not just that we don't *know* that the sun will rise tomorrow. According to Hume, we have no rational justification at all for this or for any other expectation we have about the future.

HUME'S SKEPTICAL THESIS ABOUT INDUCTION

We constantly form expectations about what the future will be like or about which generalizations (statements of the form "All *A*s are *B*") are true, based on evidence that isn't deductively conclusive. Our beliefs about the future are based on perception and memory, but you can't deduce what the future will be like from premises that describe just the present and the past.

Let's focus on an example in order to get clear on this simple point. Suppose I have observed many emeralds and have found each of them to be green. I then formulate the prediction "The next emerald I observe will be green"; or maybe I formulate the generalization "All emeralds are green." (Just so this can be an example of the kind I want, suppose that emeralds aren't green by definition.)

Common sense says that we are rational in believing the predictions and generalizations we do if those beliefs are based on lots of evidence. Looking at lots of emeralds and finding that each is green seems to justify my expectation that the next emerald I examine will be green. Now it is obvious that we can't *deduce* generalizations or predictions from our past observations. Yet, the following appear to be perfectly sensible *nondeductive* arguments:

(GEN)
I've observed numerous emeralds, and each has been green.
═══════════════
Hence, all emeralds are green.

(PRED)
I've observed numerous emeralds, and each has been green.
═══════════════
Hence, the next emerald I observe will be green.

I've drawn a double line between premisses and conclusions to indicate that these arguments aren't deductively valid.

In both the generalization argument (GEN) and the prediction argument (PRED), we think that the conclusion reached is rationally justified by the premisses. We think that it isn't a mere prejudice to hold, in each case, that the premiss provides good evidence for the truth of the conclusion. Hume's thesis is that this conviction can't be rationally defended.

It is important to see that Hume's thesis goes far beyond the undisturbing claim that the (GEN) and (PRED) arguments just given aren't deductively valid. That much is obvious. Rather, Hume is saying that the premisses in those arguments don't rationally justify their conclusions. Hume's view is that there is absolutely no rational justification for the beliefs we have that are predictions or generalizations.

Hume's view is that it is merely a habit we have that we regard such premisses as providing good reason to believe such conclusions. This is a habit we can't abandon; it is part of human nature to expect the future to resemble the past. But it is a habit that we can't rationally defend. When challenged by the skeptic to rationally justify this pattern in our thinking, we can only say that this is the way human beings in fact operate. We can't produce a good argument to rationally justify this habit of mind.

HUME'S ARGUMENT THAT INDUCTION CAN'T BE RATIONALLY JUSTIFIED

Why did Hume reach this startling conclusion about induction? (Here I'll reconstruct the argument that Hume gives in Part II of the section from *An Enquiry Concerning Human Understanding* called "Skeptical Doubts Concerning the Operations of the Understanding.") Hume thought that the arguments stated above (GEN and PRED) require an additional premiss. As they stand, the premiss doesn't support the conclusion. If the observation is to support the generalization or the prediction, then we must assume that the future will resemble the past. This assumption Hume calls the *Principle of the Uniformity of Nature* (PUN).

Hume thought that this principle plays an indispensable role in each and every inductive argument we make. The above example concerns the color of emeralds. Consider, however, the belief that the sun will rise tomorrow. This predictive belief is based on the premiss that the sun has risen on each of the days that we have bothered to make an observation. Why should these *past* observations support the prediction I make about *tomorrow*? Hume thought that I must be assuming that nature is uniform—that the future will resemble the past. Hume says that without this assumption, the past would be no guide to the future.

So each and every inductive argument presupposes PUN: We must assume PUN if the observational premiss is to support the prediction or generalization stated in the argument's conclusion. This means that if the conclusion we reach is rationally defensible, then a good argument must be available for thinking that PUN is true. If PUN can't be defended, then anything we believe that depends on assuming that PUN is true must likewise be indefensible.

We now can state Hume's skeptical argument:

(1) Every inductive argument requires PUN as a premiss.

(2) If the conclusion of an inductive argument is rationally justified by the premisses, then those premisses must themselves be rationally justifiable.

(3) So, if the conclusion of an inductive argument is justified, there must be a rational justification for PUN.

(4) If PUN is rationally justifiable, then there must be a good inductive argument or a good deductive argument for PUN.

(5) There is no good inductive argument for PUN, since any inductive argument for PUN will be circular.

(6) There cannot be a good deductive argument for PUN, since PUN is not a priori true, nor does PUN deductively follow from the observations we have made to date.

(7) So, PUN is not rationally justifiable.

Hence, there is no rational justification for the beliefs we have that take the form of predictions or generalizations.

In a nutshell, Hume's claim is that the beliefs we have about emerald color and to-morrow's sunrise (and lots of other beliefs as well) aren't rationally justifiable, because they rest on an assumption that can't be rationally justified.

WHY CAN'T PUN BE JUSTIFIED?

Let's look more carefully at steps (4)–(6) in the argument. Consider what PUN asserts; it says that the future will resemble the past—that past uniformities will continue to obtain in the future. Is this something that we could know to be true on the basis of induction? If it were, the inductive argument would look like this:

Nature has been uniform in my past observations.

Nature in general is uniform.

Recall that Hume claims that *all* inductive arguments require that PUN be assumed as a premiss. But the above argument is inductive. Notice that if we insert PUN as a premiss, as Hume requires, that the argument becomes circular—it assumes as a premiss the very proposition it tries to establish as a conclusion.

What about the other sort of justification? Can we give a deductive justification of PUN? Here again, Hume holds that the answer is *no*. The above argument isn't deductively valid; the general uniformity principle can't be deduced from the observations I've made in the past.

Hume considers, and rejects, a second possible sort of deductive argument. Could PUN be a definitional truth, deducible from the definitions of the terms it uses? If PUN were a definitional truth, it would have the same sort of a priori justification that "All bachelors are unmarried" possesses. Hume rejects this idea by saying that there is "no contradiction" in supposing that the universe should suddenly cease to be uniform. It isn't a definitional truth that past regularities will continue into the future, Hume says.

SUMMARY OF HUME'S ARGUMENT

It now should be clear how Hume's skeptical argument proceeds. First, there is a claim: Every inductive argument requires the premiss that nature is uniform. Second, Hume argues that no rational justification can be given for that premiss. He defends this assertion by considering three options: (1) an inductive argument in favor of PUN; (2) a deduction of PUN from past observations; (3) a deduction of PUN from definitions. He asserts that none of these ways of defending PUN is going to work. This means that PUN can't be justified. Hume concludes that the inductive inferences we make aren't rationally justifiable.

Review Questions

1. What is the difference between knowledge and justified belief? Does skepticism about knowledge entail skepticism about rational justification? What do each of these skeptical theses assert?
2. Hume says that we can't deduce what the future will be like from our present observations and memories. Does Hume's skeptical thesis say anything more than this?
3. What is the Principle of the Uniformity of Nature?
4. What is Hume's skeptical argument about induction?

Problems for Further Thought

1. Is the claim that nature is uniform falsifiable (Lecture 8)? That is, can you describe a possible observation that would count against this claim?
2. Is it possible that all of our beliefs could be rationally justified? Would this be possible if we had some finite number of beliefs? What does it mean to say that a belief is rationally justified?

LECTURE 16

Can Hume's Skepticism Be Refuted?

In the previous lecture, I described Hume's skeptical argument about induction as focusing on the Principle of the Uniformity of Nature (PUN). This principle, recall, says that the future will resemble the past. In this lecture, I'll criticize this version of Hume's argument. Then I'll formulate Hume's argument in another way. After that, I'll examine two suggestions that have been made for refuting Hume's very startling conclusion. Again, you want to be clear on what Hume's conclusion is. He didn't merely say that our predictions are uncertain; he said that they have *no rational justification whatever.* They are the product of a rationally indefensible habit that is deeply entrenched in human nature.

WHAT DOES THE PRINCIPLE OF THE UNIFORMITY OF NATURE SAY?

PUN says that the future will resemble the past. Recall that Hume held that every time we make an induction—inferring that the sun will rise tomorrow or that the next emerald we observe will be green—we are assuming that nature is uniform. So PUN is supposed to be an assumption that is required by each and every inductive argument.

But what, exactly, does PUN mean? Does it mean that nature is uniform *in each and every respect?* If so, it is pretty clear that we don't think that PUN is true. Summer leaves are green, but we don't expect autumn to resemble summer in this respect. So if we understand PUN in this way, the principle isn't, contrary to Hume, something we are always assuming.

Let's try a second interpretation. Maybe PUN means that the future will resemble the past *in some respect.* This does seem to be something we believe. This is such a modest principle, however, that it is hard to see how it will help very much in the task of inferring what the future will be like. If I want to know whether future emeralds will be green or blue based on my observation that so far they all have been green, this version of PUN is pretty useless. It doesn't tell me whether it makes sense to expect emeralds to remain green or to expect a change.

These two attempts to clarify what PUN says illustrate a general problem. No one yet has been able to clarify the principle so that it has both of the following properties:

(1) PUN is plausible.

(2) PUN gives definite advice about what we should infer from present observations.

There is a third characteristic that Hume's argument about induction attributes to PUN. This is the idea that PUN plays an indispensable role in the way we think about the world:

(3) If we want to make inductive inferences about the world, PUN
    is something we must believe, no matter what else we believe.

This last condition expresses the idea that PUN is an assumption—a presupposition—that underlies the whole project of inductive inference.

If it is hard to formulate PUN so that it satisfies (1) and (2), it will be even harder to clarify the principle so that it satisfies (1), (2), and (3). I haven't proved that it is impossible to do this. No one has done so yet, however.

As a result, I suggest we drop the formulation of Hume's argument that involves PUN. Instead, I'll consider a different version of Hume's argument that induction can't be rationally justified.

A NEW CONCEPT: DEGREES OF RELIABILITY

This new version of Hume's argument involves the idea that a method of inference possesses *some degree of reliability.* Induction is a method of inference. Like other methods of inference, it makes predictions and says what generalizations are true based on a set of observations. We can say of a method of inference *how often* the predictions or generalizations it endorses have been true. A method that usually leads to truth is highly reliable; one that rarely does so is very unreliable.

This use of the concept of reliability departs somewhat from the one employed by the Reliability Theory of Knowledge (Lecture 14). There I discussed reliability as an on/off concept; a thermometer is either reliable or it isn't. Moreover, a reliable thermometer, in the sense employed there, *must* make true claims about the temperature.

Notice that the concept of *degrees of reliability* isn't an on/off concept. In addition, a highly reliable method of inference can sometimes lead to falsehood. The point is that it does so *rarely*. A method of inference is highly reliable if the predictions it makes are *usually* true.

Induction is a rule that scientists use to evaluate hypotheses in the light of evidence. A scientist makes a finite number of observations—call them *O*. The goal is to say which hypothesis among a set of competing hypotheses is most plausible in the light of those observations. For example, suppose you've examined numerous emeralds and all have been green (call this *O*). The problem is to say which of the following hypotheses is better supported in the light of those observations:

(H_1) All emeralds are green.

(H_2) All emeralds are green until the year 2050; thereafter,
         they are blue.

Common sense suggests that H_1 is more plausible than H_2 in the light of the observations *O*. The philosophical question is to explain why this is so. Hume denied that this evaluation of the competing hypotheses can be rationally defended.

WHAT IS A RULE OF INFERENCE?

Rules of inference provide *licenses*. A fishing license permits you to fish. A rule of inference permits you to draw conclusions. In the previous example, induction permits you to conclude that H_1 is probably true, given O. That is, induction is a rule of inference that connects premiss to conclusion in the following argument:

I've examined lots of emeralds and all have been green.

I ════════════════

All emeralds are green.

I've drawn a double line to indicate that the argument isn't deductively valid. I've written an "I" beside the double line to indicate that the rule of inference being used is induction. The problem of induction is to explain why we are entitled to use this inference rule.

DOES THE PAST RELIABILITY OF INDUCTION PROVIDE AN ANSWER?

Common sense may suggest that we are entitled to use induction now, because induction has been reliable in the past. Induction has often been used to make predictions; and the predictions endorsed by inductive arguments usually, if not always, turned out to be correct. This is why we rightly take seriously what induction tells us.

Hume rejected this attempt to justify induction. Let's examine it more carefully. Here is the argument we need to consider:

Induction has been highly reliable in the past.

════════════════

Induction will be highly reliable now and in the future.

The premiss of this argument is something we know by having observed the past track record of the inductive method. The conclusion makes a claim about what will be true now and in the future.

Every argument must use a rule of inference to license the transition from premiss to conclusion. What rule of inference is used here? Can the conclusion be validly deduced from the premiss? *No;* that is why I've drawn a double line. This is an *inductive* argument; induction (I) is the rule of inference that is being used.

Hume's point about this argument is that it is *circular* or *question-begging*. The philosophical question is whether induction can be rationally justified. This argument simply assumes that induction is legitimate. You can't justify using induction now by appeal to the fact that induction has been successful in the past.

HUME'S ARGUMENT REFORMULATED

So Hume's skeptical argument about induction can be formulated as follows:

(1) To rationally justify induction, you must show that induction will be reliable.

(2) To show that induction will be reliable, you must construct an inductive argument or a deductively valid argument.

(3) You can't show that induction will be reliable by an inductive argument; that would be question-begging.

(4) You can't validly deduce that induction will be reliable from premises describing the past reliability of induction (or from definitions).

    Hence, induction cannot be rationally justified.

This argument doesn't say anything about the Principle of the Uniformity of Nature (PUN). Can it be refuted?

STRAWSON: IT IS ANALYTIC THAT INDUCTION IS RATIONAL

Hume claimed that a rational justification for using induction must show that the method will probably be reliable. But the contemporary British philosopher Peter Strawson (in *Introduction to Logical Theory*, Methuen, 1952) has challenged this. Strawson rejects premiss (1) of Hume's argument.

Strawson's idea is a simple one. He thinks that the statement "Induction is rational" is like the statement "Bachelors are unmarried." Both are a priori truths. Both are deductive consequences of the definitions of the terms that occur in them. According to Strawson, induction is, by definition, a rational activity.

Strawson doesn't claim "Induction will be reliable" is an a priori truth. He agrees with Hume that this isn't true by definition. But he thinks that you don't have to establish that an inference rule will be reliable if you want to show that using the rule is rational. Hume thought that rationality requires reliability. Strawson denies this.

According to Strawson, it is entirely rational to use inductive methods to formulate our beliefs about the future, even though we can offer no good reason for expecting that the method will probably lead to true beliefs. If it turns out later that we were entirely mistaken about what we thought the world would be like, no one can accuse us of having been irrational. We would have behaved perfectly reasonably even though we ended up with false beliefs.

I find Strawson's argument unconvincing. Methods of inference are methods for doing things. Consider an analogy: *recipes*. Suppose I told you that I have a great recipe for making a cake. To determine whether this is true, you would want to see if the method is reliable. The point of the recipe is to produce nice cakes. You evaluate the recipe by seeing if it is a reliable instrument. It would be puzzling if someone said that a particular recipe is excellent even though he granted that there is no reason whatever to think that using the recipe would probably result in a nice cake.

This, however, is just what Strawson is saying about induction. The point of induction is to reach true beliefs about the world. That is the goal of inference. Whether it is reasonable to use induction or some other method depends on whether the method is a reliable instrument for attaining the specified goal. If it can't be shown that the instrument will attain the goal, it is hard to see how using the instrument is rationally justified. Strawson's mistake, I think, is to hold that the rationality of a method has nothing to do with its reliability.

BLACK: INDUCTION CAN BE INDUCTIVELY JUSTIFIED

I turn now to an attempt at providing an inductive justification of induction. The American philosopher Max Black (in "Inductive Support of Inductive Rules," *Problems of Analysis,* Cornell University Press, 1954) argued that once you look carefully at what *circularity* means, you'll see that the inductive justification of induction isn't circular at all. That is, Black holds that the following argument provides a perfectly good reason for accepting the conclusion:

> Induction has been highly reliable until now.
> ═══════════════
> Probably, induction will be highly reliable if we use it now
> and in the future.

Once again, I use the letter "I" to indicate that the rule of inference that licenses passing from the premiss to the conclusion is the principle of induction.

What does Black think it means for an argument to be circular? His suggestion is roughly as follows: If an argument is circular, then the conclusion occurs as one of the premisses. This isn't Black's exact formulation, but it captures the spirit of what he says. For Black, circularity involves a relationship between the conclusion and the premisses. It has nothing to do with what rule of inference is used to get from premisses to conclusion.

I hope it is clear why, if you accept Black's definition of circularity, the above inductive justification of induction isn't circular. The point I want to make, however, is that Black's definition is too narrow. I think there is a broader definition of circularity that shows that the above argument is circular. It is this: An argument is circular if it couldn't possibly convince someone that the conclusion is true if they didn't believe this already. A circular argument can't change anybody's mind. If you have doubts about induction, the above argument isn't going to lay them to rest.

Besides this, there is another problem confronting Black's suggestion. Consider a bizarre rule of inference that is the mirror image of induction. It is called *counterinduction.* Induction tells you to expect past regularities to continue into the future. Counterinduction tells you to expect past regularities *not* to continue. For example, counterinduction licenses the following inference:

I've examined lots of emeralds and all have been green.

Future emeralds will not all be green.

Of course, induction would lead to a quite different conclusion. The problem of induction is, in part, to explain why we should use induction rather than counterinduction to formulate our predictions about the future.

What has this to do with Black's proposal? Black claims that the inductive justification of induction isn't circular. If he is right, then neither is the following argument:

Counterinduction has been highly unreliable until now.

Probably, counterinduction will be highly reliable if we use it now
and in the future.

Here we have a counterinductive justification of counterinduction.

Counterinduction has had a poor track record in the past. How should we expect it to do in the future? That depends on what rule of inference we use. If we use induction, we will expect counterinduction's dismal past track record to continue into the future. If, however, we use counterinduction, we expect the pattern to reverse. Since the method has been unreliable in the past, we expect that counterinduction will be *reliable* in the future.

So we have two arguments to compare: the inductive justification of induction and the counterinductive justification of counterinduction. Which method of inference—induction or counterinduction—should we now use? The problem with Black's inductive justification of induction is that it gives us no reason to reject the counterinductive justification of counterinduction. This means that Black's favored inductive justification of induction, even if it is noncircular in Black's sense of the term, doesn't show why we should use induction rather than counterinduction. So Hume's problem hasn't been solved.

Is it possible to refute Hume's argument? We have examined two attempts to do so. I think both fail. This doesn't mean that there is no way to prove Hume wrong. In the next lecture, I'll consider this problem from a different angle.

Review Questions

1. When we try to clarify exactly what the Principle of the Uniformity of Nature says, we run into a problem. What is the problem?
2. How can Hume's skeptical argument about induction be formulated without mentioning PUN?
3. What is Strawson's justification of induction? What objection to it was presented in this lecture?

4. What is Black's inductive justification of induction? What two objections to it were presented in this lecture?

5. What does it mean to say that a rule of inference is a "license"? What is the difference between the license provided by induction and the license provided by counterinduction?

Problems for Further Thought

1. The problem of induction involves explaining why the observation of many emeralds, all of them green, supports H_1 better than H_2:

    H_1: All emeralds are green.

    H_2: All emeralds are green until 2050; thereafter, they are blue.

    Can the Surprise Principle (Lecture 3) be used to show that the observations strongly favor H_1 over H_2? Explain your answer.

2. Hume considers, and rejects, two kinds of arguments that might justify induction—deductive arguments and inductive arguments. Would considering abductive arguments change the sort of conclusion that Hume reaches about induction?

3. Consider the rules of inference that are used in arguments we think are deductively valid. How can these rules be justified? Formulate a skeptical problem about deduction that is similar to Hume's problem about induction. Can this problem be solved?

LECTURE 17

Beyond Foundationalism

In the previous lecture, I briefly considered two attempts to refute Hume's skeptical argument about induction. I argued that neither is successful. However, from this we can't be certain that no attempt to justify induction will succeed. So the question remains: Can Hume's skepticism be refuted?

HUME'S PROBLEM AND DESCARTES'S PROBLEM

In this lecture, I'm going to argue that if we understand the idea of rational justification in the way Hume did, then he was right that induction can't be rationally justified. Notice that the thesis I'll be arguing for has an *IF* in it. I won't claim that Hume's skepticism is correct. My conclusion will be more modest: Skepticism is correct, *IF* the task of rational justification is understood in the way Hume understood it.

To defend this thesis, I want to describe a similarity between a problem that Descartes confronted and the one that Hume addressed. Descartes asked, how does my present mental state justify the beliefs I have about the world outside my mind? Hume asked, how do the observations I have made of my physical environment justify the beliefs I have about the future? The parallelism between these two problems is illustrated in the following diagram:

	Level	Kind of Belief	Examples
Hume's problem	3	Predictions and generalizations	"The sun will rise tomorrow."
	2	Present and past observations	"The sun is now rising." "The sun has risen each day that I have made an observation."
Descartes's problem			
	1	Indubitable beliefs	"I now seem to see a sunrise." "I now seem to remember that the sun has risen each day that I have made an observation."

In this diagram, I've divided beliefs into three categories. Hume was asking how beliefs at level 3 can be justified. Descartes was asking how beliefs in level 2 can be justified.

Both Descartes and Hume were foundationalists in the way they approached questions about knowledge and justification. By this, I mean that each held that *IF* a belief is rationally justified or known, then it is justified or known solely on the basis of its relationship to beliefs at lower levels. Foundationalism holds that justification flows from bottom to top, not in the other direction. Beliefs are justified because of their relationship to other beliefs that are more certain.

Hume reasoned that *IF* beliefs in category 3 were justified, they would have to be justified solely on the basis of items in category 2. Descartes reasoned that *IF* beliefs in category 2 were justified, they would have to be justified solely on the basis of items in category 1. Notice that both of these points are *IF*-statements. They don't assert that the beliefs in question actually are justified; the point is that Descartes and Hume agreed about what would have to be true *IF* the items in question were justified. This is something on which a skeptic and a nonskeptic might agree.

In spite of this similarity between the way Descartes and Hume formulated their respective problems, they ended up defending quite different solutions. Remember that Hume was a skeptic, whereas Descartes wasn't. Hume claimed that level 3 beliefs can't be justified, whereas Descartes argued that level 2 beliefs can be justified.

I now want to advance a thesis about Descartes's problem and then extend that thesis so that it applies to Hume's problem as well. Let's grant Descartes that each of us is absolutely certain about his or her own psychological state. My point is that these level 1 beliefs aren't enough to justify the beliefs I have about the physical environment I inhabit (level 2). I need an additional assumption concerning the *relationship* between levels 1 and 2. This connecting principle might take the form of claiming that God exists and is no deceiver. Or it might take some other form. But the contents of my own experience are simply not enough, taken all by themselves.

The parallel thesis about Hume's problem is as follows: If my beliefs about my present and past environment (items at level 2) are to justify the predictions and generalizations I believe (items at level 3), then I have to assume something about the *relationship* between levels 2 and 3. Perhaps the principle of the uniformity of nature ("the future will resemble the past") is an example of such a bridge principle. Or some other bridge principle might be proposed. But my present perceptions and memories are simply not enough, taken all by themselves.

Be clear on what I'm suggesting. First, let's note a trivial and obvious point: Level 1 statements don't deductively imply level 2 statements, and level 2 statements don't deductively imply level 3 statements. This should be obvious from the examples of level 1, 2, and 3 beliefs given in the diagram.

My point isn't this obvious fact about deductive relationships. I want to make a more ambitious claim. Not only do lower level statements fail to deductively imply higher level statements; I also want to claim that lower level statements, all by themselves, aren't enough to provide a justification for higher level statements. Lower level statements, taken by themselves, don't even provide good evidence for higher level statements.

WHETHER *X* IS EVIDENCE FOR *Y* DEPENDS ON BACKGROUND ASSUMPTIONS *Z*

This is a pretty radical thesis, I admit. Do your present experiences provide evidence about the physical environment you occupy? For example, does statement (a) below provide a rational justification for believing statement (b)?

(a) You seem to see a printed page in front of you now.

(b) There is a printed page in front of you now.

I claim that the answer depends on what you assume about the *relationship* between your present experiences and the world outside your mind. Given one set of assumptions, statement (a) might be excellent evidence that statement (b) is true. But given a different set of assumptions, statement (a) would be good evidence that statement (b) is false. The point is that the assumptions you make, one way or the other, go beyond what is contained in level 1. Assumptions about the relationship of levels 1 and 2 aren't, properly speaking, contained in level 1.

I hope my discussion of Descartes makes plausible what I'm saying about the relationship of (a) and (b). If you assume that the environment is "normal" and that your senses are functioning properly, then (a) is evidence favoring (b). If you assume that your senses are misleading you, however, then (a) would be evidence against (b).

What would the parallel claim be about the relationship of statements at levels 2 and 3? For example, does statement (c) provide strong evidence for statement (d)?

(c) I've examined lots of emeralds and all have been green.

(d) All emeralds are green.

We naturally take (c) to be evidence favoring (d). How could this be otherwise? Well, suppose you believed the following statement (the example is due to I. J. Good, "The White Shoe Is a Red Herring," *British Journal for the Philosophy of Science*, Vol. 17, 1967, p. 322):

Either there are lots of emeralds, of which 99 percent are green, or there are very few emeralds, and all of them are green.

If you believed this, then (c) would be evidence *against* (d). On the other hand, if you believed the following statement, then (c) would provide evidence in favor of (d):

If you examine lots of emeralds and all have been found to be green, then probably all emeralds are green.

Notice that the two possible assumptions just listed aren't strictly at level 2.

Whether (c) is evidence for or against (d) depends on what assumptions you make. If you make no assumptions about the relationship of level 2 and level 3, then the evidence described in (c) can't be interpreted as either favorable or unfavorable to (d).

In a way, the present idea is something that has already come up in this book. I've already pointed out that hypotheses are testable only when background assumptions are added to them (Lecture 8). Here's an elaboration of that idea: When you test a hypothesis H and obtain some observations O, it will usually be true that O is evidence for or against H only because of the background assumptions (A) you made.

ANOTHER RELATIVITY THESIS

We have here another example of a relativity thesis in philosophy. The idea of relativity, recall, came up in Lecture 14 in connection with the problem of knowledge. There it was argued that the Reliability Theory of Knowledge leads to the conclusion that whether S knows some proposition p depends on how one chooses to describe the environment that S inhabits. Different equally true descriptions of S's circumstances lead to opposite conclusions about whether S has knowledge.

The present point concerns the concept of evidence, not the concept of knowledge. Is statement (c) evidence for statement (d)? No answer can be given until a third term is specified. Relative to one set of assumptions the answer is *no*, but relative to another the answer is *yes*. We shouldn't ask whether one statement is evidence for another, but whether one statement is evidence for another relative to a set of background assumptions.

FOUNDATIONALISM LEADS TO SKEPTICISM

I'm stressing that the evidence relationship involves three things, not just two. Whether O is evidence for H depends on background assumptions (A). What impact does this point have on the problems that Hume and Descartes pursued about the concept of rational justification? My suggestion is that the problems they posed lead right to skepticism. If the challenge is to see if level 3 beliefs can be justified *strictly by level 2 beliefs,* we must conclude that this can't be done. Likewise, if the problem is to see if level 2 beliefs can be justified *strictly by level 1 beliefs,* we are forced to reach a negative conclusion in this case as well.

Descartes wasn't a skeptic about the rational justifiability of level 2 beliefs. Hume was a skeptic about the rational justifiability of level 3 beliefs. My claim is that if we adopt a foundationalist understanding of what rational justification involves, then Descartes was wrong and Hume was right. In both Descartes's problem and Hume's problem, foundationalism leads to skepticism.

A NONFOUNDATIONALIST APPROACH TO JUSTIFICATION

However, I don't think this shows that our beliefs are totally lacking in rational justification. Rather, I believe that the foundationalist misunderstands what it takes to rationally justify a belief. We *can* justify a level 3 belief. We do this by appealing to other beliefs we have, some of which will themselves be at level 3. The same holds for the beliefs we have at level 2.

Think of how the task of justification works in everyday life and in science. If a scientist makes a prediction, or if we do this in our everyday lives, how are these predictions to be defended? If we say that the sun will rise tomorrow, we can support this prediction by appealing to other beliefs we have about the way the solar system has worked *and will continue to work.* In everyday life and science, we allow people to justify their beliefs at level 3 by appealing to other beliefs that also are at level 3. Often, predictions are justified by citing generalizations. In doing this, we aren't playing by the rules that foundationalism lays down. We aren't justifying a belief at one level strictly in terms of beliefs that are at lower levels.

What does this imply about whether our beliefs about the world are rationally justified? My point is to focus on what it means to ask for a rational justification. If we understand that idea in a foundationalist way, we will be led straight to skepticism— to the conclusion that the beliefs we have aren't rationally justifiable. On the other hand, if we recognize that the idea of rational justification needn't be understood in a foundationalist way, skepticism doesn't threaten. In everyday life and in science, we frequently say that our beliefs are justified. When we do this, we aren't using a foundationalist understanding of the idea of rational justification. I'm suggesting that we are often perfectly correct when we say that this or that belief is well justified. Such claims are correct, in part, because rational justification is usually not understood in the way the foundationalist demands.

STANDARDS OF JUSTIFICATION OFTEN DEPEND ON THE AUDIENCE

Our standards of rational justification often depend on the audience we have in mind. Suppose you believe some proposition that some other person doesn't. Your goal is to rationally persuade the other individual that you are right. In doing this, you will feel free to use as a premiss in your argument any belief that the two of you share. If you agree about lots of things, there will be many propositions that you can use as premisses. If, however, your disagreement is more pervasive, you will be much more limited in the premisses you can use. And if you somehow disagreed about *everything*, it would be impossible to construct a rational argument that shows this person that the proposition in question is correct.

In everyday life, it is a familiar occurrence that one person rationally justifies some proposition to another. The same is true in science and in courts of law. This can happen because the two parties agree about enough; what they share is sufficient to allow an argument to be constructed that shows whether the proposition under dispute is correct. Matters change, however, when we ask someone to justify a proposition *to a skeptic*. A skeptic won't agree with you about many of the things you take for granted. If skeptics differ with you on sufficiently many beliefs, perhaps it will be impossible to rationally convince them that the proposition is true.

Foundationalists say that when you try to provide a rational justification of some proposition *p*, you must construct an argument that would be compelling *to a skeptic who doubts all the propositions that are at the same level as p*. This is one sort of activity, but there are others. A more familiar problem of rational justification is to construct an argument that would convince someone who doesn't already believe *p*, but who has lots of other beliefs at the same level as *p*. Even if the foundationalist's problem is insoluble, this doesn't mean that more familiar problems of rational justification are, too.

Review Questions

1. What is meant by saying that we have beliefs at level 1, level 2, and level 3? How does a foundationalist understand what it means for a belief at a level to be rationally justified? Are there any beliefs that are located at none of these three levels?
2. A relativity thesis is advanced in this lecture concerning the idea of evidence. What is that thesis? How does it go beyond the "trivial and obvious" fact that level 2 beliefs don't deductively imply beliefs at level 3?

3. How could the observation of lots of green emeralds be evidence against the claim that all emeralds are green?

4. Foundationalists understand the problem of rational justification in one way, but people in ordinary life usually think of the problem in another. What is the difference?

Problems for Further Thought

1. Otto Neurath (1882–1945) thought that the following metaphor captures something important about how we go about rationally constructing and revising the beliefs we have: "We are like sailors who must rebuild their ship on the open sea, without being able to dismantle the ship in dry dock or being able to reconstruct it from the best components." What does this metaphor mean? What do you think Neurath's view was of foundationalism?

2. In Lecture 7, I argued that scientific explanation is possible only for local why-questions. In the present lecture, I argued that you can rationally justify a proposition to someone only if you agree with that person about something. What similarities are there between these two theses?

Readings

PLATO

Knowledge Is Something More Than True Belief

In this dialogue, **The Theaetetus**, Plato (427–347 B.C.) describes a conversation between Socrates, who was his teacher, and Theaetetus. Theaetetus discovers, through Socrates's questioning, that he, Theaetetus, knows much less than he thought he did.

Two main points emerge in these excerpts. First, knowledge is something more than true belief. The suggestion is made that knowledge requires true belief plus "an account." An account must involve some sort of justification. But what sort? If the propositions providing the account are not themselves known to be true, then it is hard to see how they can provide knowledge. However, it is circular and unhelpful to say that someone knows a proposition **p** when the individual truly believes that **p** and knows some propositions that justify **p**.

SOCRATES: Well, that is precisely what I am puzzled about. I cannot make out to my own satisfaction what knowledge is. Can we answer that question? What do you all say?

THEAETETUS: I think the things one can learn from Theodorus are knowledge—geometry and all the sciences you mentioned just now, and then there are the crafts of the cobbler and other workmen. Each and all of these are knowledge and nothing else.

SOCRATES: You are generous indeed, my dear Theaetetus—so openhanded that, when you are asked for one simple thing, you offer a whole variety.

THEAETETUS: What do you mean, Socrates?

SOCRATES: There may be nothing in it, but I will explain what my notion is. When you speak of cobbling, you mean by that word precisely a knowledge of shoemaking?

Plato, "Knowledge and True Beliefs," from "The Theaetetus," in *The Collected Dialogues of Plato*, translated by F. M. Cornford (Andover, England: Routledge, a division of Routledge, Chapman & Hall Ltd., 1961), pp. 905–908, pp. 914–919. © 1958. Reprinted by permission of Prentice-Hall, Inc., Upper Saddle River, N.J.

THEAETETUS: Precisely.

SOCRATES: And when you speak of carpentry, you mean just a knowledge of how to make wooden furniture?

THEAETETUS: Yes.

SOCRATES: In both cases, then, you are defining what the craft is a knowledge of?

THEAETETUS: Yes.

SOCRATES: But the question you were asked, Theaetetus, was not, what are the objects of knowledge, nor yet how many sorts of knowledge there are. We did not want to count them, but to find out what the thing itself—knowledge—is. Is there nothing in that?

THEAETETUS: No, you are quite right. . . .

SOCRATES: Then tell me, what definition can we give with the least risk of contradicting ourselves?

THEAETETUS: The one we tried before, Socrates. I have nothing else to suggest.

SOCRATES: What was that?

THEAETETUS: That true belief is knowledge. Surely there can at least be no mistake in believing what is true and the consequences are always satisfactory.

SOCRATES: Try, and you will see, Theaetetus, as the man said when he was asked if the river was too deep to ford. So here, if we go forward on our search, we may stumble upon something that will reveal the thing we are looking for. We shall make nothing out, if we stay where we are:

THEAETETUS: True. Let us go forward and see.

SOCRATES: Well, we need not go far to see this much. You will find a whole profession to prove that true belief is not knowledge.

THEAETETUS: How so? What profession?

SOCRATES: The profession of those paragons of intellect known as orators and lawyers. There you have men who use their skill to produce conviction, not by instruction, but by making people believe whatever they want them to believe. You can hardly imagine teachers so clever as to be able, in the short time allowed by the clock, to instruct their hearers thoroughly in the true facts of a case of robbery or other violence which those hearers had not witnessed.

THEAETETUS: No, I cannot imagine that, but they can convince them.

SOCRATES: And by convincing you mean making them believe something.

THEAETETUS: Of course.

SOCRATES: And when a jury is rightly convinced of facts which can be known only by an eyewitness, then, judging by hearsay and accepting a true belief, they are judging without knowledge, although, if they find the right verdict, their conviction is correct?

THEAETETUS: Certainly.

SOCRATES: But if true belief and knowledge were the same thing, the best of jurymen could never have a correct belief without knowledge. It now appears that they must be different things.

THEAETETUS: Yes, Socrates, I have heard someone make the distinction. I had forgotten, but now it comes back to me. He said that true belief with the addition of an account (λόγος) was knowledge, while belief without an account was outside its range. Where no account could be given of a thing, it was not "knowable"—that was the word he used—where it could, it was knowable.

SOCRATES: A good suggestion. But tell me how he distinguished these knowable things from the unknowable. It may turn out that what you were told tallies with something I have heard said.

THEAETETUS: I am not sure if I can recall that, but I think I should recognize it if I heard it stated.

SOCRATES: If you have had a dream, let me tell you mine in return. I seem to have heard some people say that what might be called the first elements of which we and all other things consist are such that no account can be given of them. Each of them just by itself can only be named; we cannot attribute to it anything further or say that it exists or does not exist, for we should at once be attaching to it existence or nonexistence, whereas we ought to add nothing if we are to express just it alone. We ought not even to add "just" or "it" or "each" or "alone" or "this," or any other of a host of such terms. These terms, running loose about the place, are attached to everything, and they are distinct from the things to which they are applied. If it were possible for an element to be expressed in any formula exclusively belonging to it, no other terms ought to enter into that expression. But in fact there is no formula in which any element can be expressed; it can only be named, for a name is all there is that belongs to it. But when we come to things composed of these elements, then, just as these things are complex, so the names are combined to make a description (**λόγος**), a description being precisely a combination of names. Accordingly, elements are inexplicable and unknowable, but they can be perceived, while complexes ("syllables") are knowable and explicable, and you can have a true notion of them. So when a man gets hold of the true notion of something without an account, his mind does think truly of it, but he does not know it, for if one cannot give and receive an account of a thing, one has no knowledge of that thing. But when he has also got hold of an account, all this becomes possible to him and he is fully equipped with knowledge.

Does that version represent the dream as you heard it, or not?

THEAETETUS: Perfectly.

SOCRATES: So this dream finds favor and you hold that a true notion with the addition of an account is knowledge?

THEAETETUS: Precisely.

SOCRATES: Can it be, Theaetetus, that, all in a moment, we have found out today what so many wise men have grown old in seeking and have not found?

THEAETETUS: I, at any rate, am satisfied with our present statement, Socrates.

SOCRATES: Yes, the statement just in itself may well be satisfactory, for how can there ever be knowledge without an account and right belief? But there is one point in the theory as stated that does not find favor with me. . . .

SOCRATES: What can really be meant by saying that an account added to true belief yields knowledge in its most perfect form.

THEAETETUS: Yes, we must see what that means.

SOCRATES: Well then, what is this term "account" intended to convey to us? I think it must mean one of three things.

THEAETETUS: What are they?

SOCRATES: The first will be giving overt expression to one's thought by means of vocal sound with names and verbs, casting an image of one's notion on the stream that flows through the lips, like a reflection in a mirror or in water. Do you agree that an expression of that sort is an "account"?

THEAETETUS: I do. We certainly call that expressing ourselves in speech (λέγειν).

SOCRATES: On the other hand, that is a thing that anyone can do more or less readily. If a man is not born deaf or dumb, he can signify what he thinks on any subject. So in this sense anyone whatever who has a correct notion evidently will have it "with an account" and there will be no place left anywhere for a correct notion apart from knowledge.

THEAETETUS: True.

SOCRATES: Then we must not be too ready to charge the author of the definition of knowledge now before us with talking nonsense. Perhaps that is not what he meant. He may have meant being able to reply to the question, what any given thing is, by enumerating its elements.

THEAETETUS: For example, Socrates?

SOCRATES: For example, Hesiod says about a wagon, "In a wagon are a hundred pieces of wood."[1] I could not name them all; no more, I imagine, could you. If we were asked what a wagon is, we should be content if we could mention wheels, axle, body, rails, yoke.

THEAETETUS: Certainly.

SOCRATES: But I dare say he would think us just as ridiculous as if we replied to the question about your own name by telling the syllables. We might think and express ourselves correctly, but we should be absurd if we fancied ourselves to be grammarians and able to give such an account of the name Theaetetus as a grammarian would offer. He would say it is impossible to give a scientific account of anything, short of adding to your true notion a complete catalogue of the elements, as, I think, was said earlier.

THEAETETUS: Yes, it was.

SOCRATES: In the same way, he would say, we may have a correct notion of the wagon, but the man who can give a complete statement of its nature by going through those hundred parts has thereby added an account to his correct notion and, in place of mere belief, has arrived at a technical knowledge of the wagon's nature, by going through all the elements in the whole.

THEAETETUS: Don't you approve, Socrates?

SOCRATES: Tell me if you approve, my friend, and whether you accept the view that the complete enumeration of elements is an account of any given thing, whereas description in terms of syllables or of any larger unit still leaves it unaccounted for. Then we can look into the matter further.

THEAETETUS: Well, I do accept that.

SOCRATES: Do you think, then, that anyone has knowledge of whatever it may be, when he thinks that one and the same thing is a part sometimes of one thing,

---

1. *Works and Days* 456 (454).

sometimes of a different thing, or again when he believes now one and now another thing to be part of one and the same thing?

THEAETETUS: Certainly not.

SOCRATES: Have you forgotten, then, that when you first began learning to read and write, that was what you and your schoolfellows did?

THEAETETUS: Do you mean, when we thought that now one letter and now another was part of the same syllable, and when we put the same letter sometimes into the proper syllable, sometimes into another?

SOCRATES: That is what I mean.

THEAETETUS: Then I have certainly not forgotten, and I do not think that one has reached knowledge so long as one is in that condition.

SOCRATES: Well then, if at that stage you are writing "Theaetetus" and you think you ought to write T and H and E and do so, and again when you are trying to write "Theodorus," you think you ought to write T and E and do so, can we say that you know the first syllable of your two names?

THEAETETUS: No, we have just agreed that one has not knowledge so long as one is in that condition.

SOCRATES: And there is no reason why a person should not be in the same condition with respect to the second, third, and fourth syllables as well?

THEAETETUS: None whatever.

SOCRATES: Can we, then, say that whenever in writing "Theaetetus" he puts down all the letters in order, then he is in possession of the complete catalogue of elements together with correct belief?

THEAETETUS: Obviously.

SOCRATES: Being still, as we agree, without knowledge, though his beliefs are correct?

THEAETETUS: Yes.

SOCRATES: Although he possesses the "account" in addition to right belief. For when he wrote he was in possession of the catalogue of the elements which we agreed was the "account."

THEAETETUS: True.

SOCRATES: So, my friend, there is such a thing as right belief together with an account, which is not yet entitled to be called knowledge.

THEAETETUS: I am afraid so.

SOCRATES: Then, apparently, our idea that we had found the perfectly true definition of knowledge was no better than a golden dream. Or shall we not condemn the theory yet? Perhaps the meaning to be given to "account" is not this, but the remaining one of the three, one of which we said must be intended by anyone who defines knowledge as correct belief together with an account.

THEAETETUS: A good reminder. There is still one meaning left. The first was what might be called the image of thought in spoken sound, and the one we have just discussed was going all through the elements to arrive at the whole. What is the third?

SOCRATES: The meaning most people would give—being able to name some mark by which the thing one is asked about differs from everything else.

THEAETETUS: Could you give me an example of such an account of a thing?

SOCRATES: Take the sun as an example. I dare say you will be satisfied with the account of it as the brightest of the heavenly bodies that go round the earth.

THEAETETUS: Certainly.

SOCRATES: Let me explain the point of this example. It is to illustrate what we were just saying—that if you get hold of the difference distinguishing any given thing from all others, then, so some people say, you will have an "account" of it, whereas, so long as you fix upon something common to other things, your account will embrace all the things that share it.

THEAETETUS: I understand. I agree that what you describe may fairly be called an "account."

SOCRATES: And if, besides a right notion about a thing, whatever it may be, you also grasp its difference from all other things, you will have arrived at knowledge of what, till then, you had only a notion of.

THEAETETUS: We do say that, certainly.

SOCRATES: Really, Theaetetus, now I come to look at this statement at close quarters, it is like a scene painting. I cannot make it out at all, though, so long as I kept at a distance, there seemed to be some sense in it.

THEAETETUS: What do you mean? Why so?

SOCRATES: I will explain, if I can. Suppose I have a correct notion about you; if I add to that the account of you, then, we are to understand, I know you. Otherwise I have only a notion.

THEAETETUS: Yes.

SOCRATES: And "account" means putting your differences into words.

THEAETETUS: Yes.

SOCRATES: So, at the time when I had only a notion, my mind did not grasp any of the points in which you differ from others?

THEAETETUS: Apparently not.

SOCRATES: Then I must have had before my mind one of those common things which belong to another person as much as to you.

THEAETETUS: That follows.

SOCRATES: But look here! If that was so, how could I possibly be having a notion of you rather than of anyone else? Suppose I was thinking, Theaetetus is one who is a man and has a nose and eyes and a mouth and so forth, enumerating every part of the body. Will thinking in that way result in my thinking of Theaetetus rather than of Theodorus or, as they say, of the man in the street?

THEAETETUS: How should it?

SOCRATES: Well, now suppose I think not merely of a man with a nose and eyes, but of one with a snub nose and prominent eyes. Once more shall I be having a notion of you any more than of myself or anyone else of that description.

THEAETETUS: No.

SOCRATES: In fact, there will be no notion of Theaetetus in my mind, I suppose, until this particular snubness has stamped and registered within me a record distinct from all the other cases of snubness that I have seen, and so with every other part of you. Then, if I meet you tomorrow, that trait will revive my memory and give me a correct notion about you.

THEAETETUS: Quite true.

SOCRATES: If that is so, the correct notion of anything must itself include the differentness of that thing.

THEAETETUS: Evidently.

SOCRATES: Then what meaning is left for getting hold of an "account" in addition to the correct notion? If, on the one hand, it means adding the notion of how a thing differs from other things, such an injunction is simply absurd.

THEAETETUS: How so?

SOCRATES: When we have a correct notion of the way in which certain things differ from other things, it tells us to add a correct notion of the way in which they differ from other things. On this showing, the most vicious of circles would be nothing to this injunction. It might better deserve to be called the sort of direction a blind man might give. To tell us to get hold of something we already have, in order to get to know something we are already thinking of, suggests a state of the most absolute darkness.

THEAETETUS: Whereas, if . . . ? The supposition you made just now implied that you would state some alternative. What was it?

SOCRATES: If the direction to add an "account" means that we are to get to know the differentness, as opposed to merely having a notion of it, this most admirable of all definitions of knowledge will be a pretty business, because "getting to know" means acquiring knowledge, doesn't it?

THEAETETUS: Yes.

SOCRATES: So, apparently, to the question, "What is knowledge?" our definition will reply, "Correct belief together with knowledge of a differentness," for, according to it, "adding an account" will come to that.

THEAETETUS: So it seems.

SOCRATES: Yes, and when we are inquiring after the nature of knowledge, nothing could be sillier than to say that it is correct belief together with a *knowledge* of differentness or of anything whatever. So, Theaetetus, neither perception, nor true belief, nor the addition of an "account" to true belief can be knowledge.

THEAETETUS: Apparently not.

SOCRATES: Are we in labor, then, with any further child, my friend, or have we brought to birth all we have to say about knowledge?

THEAETETUS: Indeed we have, and for my part I have already, thanks to you, given utterance to more than I had in me.

SOCRATES: All of which our midwife's skill pronounces to be mere wind eggs and not worth the rearing?

THEAETETUS: Undoubtedly.

SOCRATES: Then supposing you should ever henceforth try to conceive afresh, Theaetetus, if you succeed, your embryo thoughts will be the better as a consequence of today's scrutiny, and if you remain barren, you will be gentler and more agreeable to your companions, having the good sense not to fancy you know what you do not know. For that, and no more, is all that my art can effect; nor have I any of that knowledge possessed by all the great and admirable men of our own day or of the past. But this midwife's art is a gift from heaven; my mother had it for women, and I for young men of a generous spirit and for all in whom beauty dwells.

Now I must go to the portico of the King-Archon to meet the indictment which Meletus has drawn up against me. But tomorrow morning, Theodorus, let us meet here again.

RENÉ DESCARTES

Meditations on First Philosophy

In this work, René Descartes (1596–1650) tries to discover to what extent he has genuine knowledge of the world he inhabits. He pursues a foundationalist strategy. First, he attempts to discover which of his beliefs are beyond doubt. These will be the foundations for the rest of what he knows. Second, the task is to show how these foundational items support the rest of his knowledge.

Besides addressing the problem of knowledge, Descartes also considers the relationship that obtains between his mind and his body. In the *Sixth Meditation* he argues that these are distinct objects. This position—*dualism*—will be discussed in the section of the text on philosophy of mind.

SYNOPSIS OF THE SIX FOLLOWING MEDITATIONS

In the First Meditation I set forth the reasons for which we may, generally speaking, doubt about all things and especially about material things, at least as long as we have no other foundations for the sciences than those which we have hitherto possessed. But although the utility of a Doubt which is so general does not at first appear, it is at the same time very great, inasmuch as it delivers us from every kind of prejudice, and sets out for us a very simple way by which the mind may detach itself from the senses; and finally it makes it impossible for us ever to doubt those things which we have once discovered to be true.

In the Second Meditation, mind, which making use of the liberty which pertains to it, takes for granted that all those things of whose existence it has the least doubt, are non-existent, recognises that it is however absolutely impossible that it does not itself exist. This point is likewise of the greatest moment, inasmuch as by this means a distinction is easily drawn between the things which pertain to mind—that is to say to the intellectual nature—and those which pertain to body.

But because it may be that some expect from me in this place a statement of the reasons establishing the immortality of the soul, I feel that I should here make known

René Descartes, *Meditations on First Philosophy*, edited and translated by Elizabeth Haldane and G. R. T. Ross, in *The Philosophical Works of Descartes*, vol. 1 (Cambridge University Press, 1969), pp. 140–199. Reprinted by permission of Cambridge University Press.

to them that having aimed at writing nothing in all this Treatise of which I do not possess very exact demonstrations, I am obliged to follow a similar order to that made use of by the geometers, which is to begin by putting forward as premises all those things upon which the proposition that we seek depends, before coming to any conclusion regarding it. Now the first and principal matter which is requisite for thoroughly understanding the immortality of the soul is to form the clearest possible conception of it, and one which will be entirely distinct from all the conceptions which we may have of body; and in this Meditation this has been done. In addition to this it is requisite that we may be assured that all the things which we conceive clearly and distinctly are true in the very way in which we think them; and this could not be proved previously to the Fourth Meditation. Further we must have a distinct conception of corporeal nature, which is given partly in this Second, and partly in the Fifth and Sixth Meditations. And finally we should conclude from all this, that those things which we conceive clearly and distinctly as being diverse substances, as we regard mind and body to be, are really substances essentially distinct one from the other; and this is the conclusion of the Sixth Meditation. This is further confirmed in this same Meditation by the fact that we cannot conceive of body excepting in so far as it is divisible, while the mind cannot be conceived of excepting as indivisible. For we are not able to conceive of the half of a mind as we can do of the smallest of all bodies; so that we see that not only are their natures different but even in some respects contrary to one another. I have not however dealt further with this matter in this treatise, both because what I have said is sufficient to show clearly enough that the extinction of the mind does not follow from the corruption of the body, and also to give men the hope of another life after death, as also because the premises from which the immortality of the soul may be deduced depend on an elucidation of a complete system of Physics. This would mean to establish in the first place that all substances generally—that is to say all things which cannot exist without being created by God—are in their nature incorruptible, and that they can never cease to exist unless God, in denying to them his concurrence, reduce them to nought; and secondly that body, regarded generally, is a substance, which is the reason why it also cannot perish, but that the human body, inasmuch as it differs from other bodies, is composed only of a certain configuration of members and of other similar accidents, while the human mind is not similarly composed of any accidents, but is a pure substance. For although all the accidents of mind be changed, although, for instance, it think certain things, will others, perceive others, etc., despite all this it does not emerge from these changes another mind: the human body on the other hand becomes a different thing from the sole fact that the figure or form of any of its portions is found to be changed. From this it follows that the human body may indeed easily enough perish, but the mind [or soul of man (I make no distinction between them)] is owing to its nature immortal.

In the third Meditation it seems to me that I have explained at sufficient length the principal argument of which I make use in order to prove the existence of God. But none the less, because I did not wish in that place to make use of any comparisons derived from corporeal things, so as to withdraw as much as I could the minds of readers from the senses, there may perhaps have remained many obscurities which, however, will, I hope, be entirely removed by the Replies which I have made to the Objections which have been set before me. Amongst others there is, for example, this one, "How the idea in us of a being supremely perfect possesses so much objective reality [that is to say participates by representation in so many degrees of being and perfection] that it necessarily proceeds from a cause which is absolutely perfect." This is illustrated in these Replies by the comparison of a very perfect machine, the idea of which is found in the mind of some workman. For as the objective contrivance of this idea must have some cause, i.e. either the science of the workman or that of some other from whom he has received the idea, it is similarly impossible that the idea of God which is in us should not have God himself as its cause.

In the fourth Meditation it is shown that all these things which we very clearly and distinctly perceive are true, and at the same time it is explained in what the nature of error or falsity consists. This must of necessity be known both for the confirmation of the preceding truths and for the better comprehension of those that follow. (But it must meanwhile be remarked that I do not in any way there treat of sin—that is to say of the error which is committed in the pursuit of good and evil, but only of that which arises in the deciding between the true and the false. And I do not intend to speak of matters pertaining to the Faith or the conduct of life, but only of those which concern speculative truths, and which may be known by the sole aid of the light of nature.)

In the fifth Meditation corporeal nature generally is explained, and in addition to this the existence of God is demonstrated by a new proof in which there may possibly be certain difficulties also, but the solution of these will be seen in the Replies to the Objections. And further I show in what sense it is true to say that the certainty of geometrical demonstrations is itself dependent on the knowledge of God.

Finally in the Sixth I distinguish the action of the understanding from that of the imagination; the marks by which this distinction is made are described. I here show that the mind of man is really distinct from the body, and at the same time that the two are so closely joined together that they form, so to speak, a single thing. All the errors which proceed from the senses are then surveyed, while the means of avoiding them are demonstrated, and finally all the reasons from which we may deduce the existence of material things are set forth. Not that I judge them to be very useful in establishing that which they prove, to wit, that there is in truth a world, that men possess bodies, and other such things which never have been doubted by anyone of sense; but because in considering these closely we come to see that they are neither so strong nor so evident as those arguments which lead us to the knowledge of our mind and of God; so that these last must be the most certain and most evident facts which can fall within the cognizance of the human mind. And this is the whole matter that I have tried to prove in these Meditations, for which reason I here omit to speak of many other questions with which I dealt incidentally in this discussion.

MEDITATIONS ON THE FIRST PHILOSOPHY IN WHICH THE EXISTENCE OF GOD AND THE DISTINCTION BETWEEN MIND AND BODY ARE DEMONSTRATED

Meditation I: Of the Things Which May Be Brought Within the Sphere of the Doubtful

It is now some years since I detected how many were the false beliefs that I had from my earliest youth admitted as true, and how doubtful was everything I had since constructed on this basis; and from that time I was convinced that I must once for all seriously undertake to rid myself of all the opinions which I had formerly accepted, and commence to build anew from the foundation, if I wanted to establish any firm and permanent structure in the sciences. But as this enterprise appeared to be a very great one, I waited until I had attained an age so mature that I could not hope that at any later date I should be better fitted to execute my design. This reason caused me to delay so long that I should feel that I was doing wrong were I to occupy in deliberation the time that yet remains to me for action. To-day, then, since very opportunely for the plan I have in view I have delivered my mind from every care [and am happily agitated by no passions] and since I have procured for myself an assured leisure in a peaceable retirement, I shall at last seriously and freely address myself to the general upheaval of all my former opinions.

Now for this object it is not necessary that I should show that all of these are false—I shall perhaps never arrive at this end. But inasmuch as reason already persuades me that I ought no less carefully to withhold my assent from matters which are not entirely certain and indubitable than from those which appear to me manifestly to be false, if I am able to find in each one some reason to doubt, this will suffice to justify my rejecting the whole. And for that end it will not be requisite that I should examine each in particular, which would be an endless undertaking; for owing to the fact that the destruction of the foundations of necessity brings with it the downfall of the rest of the edifice, I shall only in the first place attack those principles upon which all my former opinions rested.

All that up to the present time I have accepted as most true and certain I have learned either from the senses or through the senses; but it is sometimes proved to me that these senses are deceptive, and it is wiser not to trust entirely to anything by which we have once been deceived.

But it may be that although the senses sometimes deceive us concerning things which are hardly perceptible, or very far away, there are yet many others to be met with as to which we cannot reasonably have any doubt, although we recognise them by their means. For example, there is that fact that I am here, seated by the fire, attired in a dressing gown, having this paper in my hands and other similar matters. And how could I deny that these hands and this body are mine, were it not perhaps that I compare myself to certain persons, devoid of sense, whose cerebella are so troubled and clouded by the violent vapours of black bile, that they constantly assure us that they think they are kings when they are really quite poor, or that they are clothed in purple when they are really without covering, or who imagine that they have an earthenware head or are nothing but pumpkins or are made of glass. But they are mad, and I should not be any the less insane were I to follow examples so extravagant.

At the same time I must remember that I am a man, and that consequently I am in the habit of sleeping, and in my dreams representing to myself the same things or sometimes even less probable things, than do those who are insane in their waking moments. How often has it happened to me that in the night I dreamt that I found myself in this particular place, that I was dressed and seated near the fire, whilst in reality I was lying undressed in bed! At this moment it does indeed seem to me that it is with eyes awake that I am looking at this paper; that this head which I move is not asleep, that it is deliberately and of set purpose that I extend my hand and perceive it; what happens in sleep does not appear so clear nor so distinct as does all this. But in thinking over this I remind myself that on many occasions I have in sleep been deceived by similar illusions, and in dwelling carefully on this reflection I see so manifestly that there are no certain indications by which we may clearly distinguish wakefulness from sleep that I am lost in astonishment. And my astonishment is such that it is most capable of persuading me that I now dream.

Now let us assume that we are asleep and that all these particulars, e.g. that we open our eyes, shake our head, extend our hands, and so on, are but false delusions; and let us reflect that possibly neither our hands nor our whole body are such as they appear to us to be. At the same time we must at least confess that the things which are represented to us in sleep are like painted representations which can only have been formed as the counterparts of something real and true, and that in this way those general things at least, i.e. eyes, a head, hands, and a whole body, are not imaginary things, but things really existent. For, as a matter of fact, painters, even when they study with the greatest skill to represent sirens and satyrs by forms the most strange and extraordinary, cannot give them natures which are entirely new, but merely make a certain medley of the members of different animals; or if their imagination is extravagant enough to invent something so novel that nothing similar has ever before been seen, and that then their work represents a thing purely fictitious and absolutely false, it is certain all the same that the colours of which is compared are necessarily real. And for the same reason, although these general things, to wit, [a body], eyes, a head, hands, and such like, may be imaginary, we are bound at the same time to confess that there are at least some other objects yet more simple and more universal, which are real and true; and of these just in the same way as with certain real colours, all these images of things which dwell in our thoughts, whether true and real or false and fantastic, are formed.

To such a class of things pertains corporeal nature in general, and its extension, the figure of extended things, their quantity or magnitude and number, as also the place in which they are, the time which measures their duration, and so on.

That is possibly why our reasoning is not unjust when we conclude from this that Physics, Astronomy, Medicine and all other sciences which have as their end the consideration of composite things, are very dubious and uncertain; but that Arithmetic, Geometry and other sciences of that kind which only treat of things that are very simple and very general, without taking great trouble to ascertain whether they are actually existent or not, contain some measure of certainty and an element of the indubitable. For whether I am awake or asleep, two and three together always form five, and the square can never have more than four sides, and it does not seem possible that truths so clear and apparent can be suspected of any falsity [or uncertainty].

Nevertheless I have long had fixed in my mind the belief that an all-powerful God existed by whom I have been created such as I am. But how do I know that He has not brought it to pass that there is no earth, no heaven, no extended body, no magnitude, no place, and that nevertheless [I possess the perceptions of all these things and that] they seem to me to exist just exactly as I now see them? And, besides, as I sometimes imagine that others deceive themselves in the things which they think they know best, how do I know that I am not deceived every time that I add two and three, or count the sides of a square, or judge of things yet simpler, if anything simpler can be imagined? But possibly God has not desired that I should be thus deceived, for He is said to be supremely good. If, however, it is contrary to His goodness to have made me such that I constantly deceive myself, it would also appear to be contrary to His goodness to permit me to be sometimes deceived, and nevertheless I cannot doubt that He does permit this.

There may indeed be those who would prefer to deny the existence of a God so powerful, rather than believe that all other things are uncertain. But let us not oppose them for the present, and grant that all that is here said of a God is a fable; nevertheless in whatever way they suppose that I have arrived at the state of being that I have reached—whether they attribute it to fate or to accident, or make out that it is by a continual succession of antecedents, or by some other method—since to err and deceive oneself is a defect, it is clear that the greater will be the probability of my being so imperfect as to deceive myself ever, as is the Author to whom they assign my origin the less powerful. To these reasons I have certainly nothing to reply, but at the end I feel constrained to confess that there is nothing in all that I formerly believed to be true, of which I cannot in some measure doubt, and that not merely through want of thought or through levity, but for reasons which are very powerful and maturely considered; so that henceforth I ought not the less carefully to refrain from giving credence to these opinions than to that which is manifestly false, if I desire to arrive at any certainty [in the sciences].

But it is not sufficient to have made these remarks, we must also be careful to keep them in mind. For these ancient and commonly held opinions still revert frequently to my mind, long and familiar custom having given them the right to occupy my mind against my inclination and rendered them almost masters of my belief; nor will I ever lose the habit of deferring to them or of placing my confidence in them, so long as I consider them as they really are, i.e. opinions in some measure doubtful, as I have just shown, and at the same time highly probable, so that there is much more reason to believe in than to deny them. That is why I consider that I shall not be acting amiss, if, taking of set purpose a contrary belief, I allow myself to be deceived, and for a certain time pretend that all these opinions are entirely false and imaginary, until at last, having thus balanced my former prejudices with my latter [so that they cannot divert my opinions more to one side than to the other], my judgment will no longer be dominated by bad usage or turned away from the right knowledge of the truth. For I am assured that there can be neither peril nor error in this course, and that I cannot at present yield too much to distrust, since I am not considering the question of action, but only of knowledge.

I shall then suppose, not that God who is supremely good and the fountain of truth, but some evil genius not less powerful than deceitful, has employed his whole energies in deceiving me; I shall consider that the heavens, the earth, colours, figures, sound, and all other external things are nought but the illusions and dreams of which this genius has availed himself in order to lay traps for my credulity; I shall consider myself as having no hands, no eyes, no flesh, no blood, nor any senses, yet falsely believing myself to possess all these things; I shall remain obstinately attached to this idea, and if by this means it is not in my power to arrive at the knowledge of any truth, I may at least do what is in my power [i.e. suspend my judgment], and with firm purpose avoid giving credence to any false thing, or being imposed upon by this arch deceiver, however powerful and deceptive he may be. But this task is a laborious one, and insensibly a certain lassitude leads me into the course of my ordinary life. And just as a captive who in sleep enjoys an imaginary liberty, when he begins to suspect that his liberty is but a dream, fears to awaken, and conspires with these agreeable illusions that the deception may be prolonged, so insensibly of my own accord I fall back into my former opinions, and I dread awakening from this slumber, lest the laborious wakefulness which would follow the tranquillity of this repose should have to be spent not in daylight, but in the excessive darkness of the difficulties which have just been discussed.

Meditation II: Of the Nature of the Human Mind; and That It Is More Easily Known Than the Body

The Meditation of yesterday filled my mind with so many doubts that it is no longer in my power to forget them. And yet I do not see in what manner I can resolve them; and, just as if I had all of a sudden fallen into very deep water, I am so disconcerted that I can neither make certain of setting my feet on the bottom, nor can I swim and so support myself on the surface. I shall nevertheless make an effort and follow anew the same path as that on which I yesterday entered, i.e. I shall proceed by setting aside all that in which the least doubt could be supposed to exist, just as if I had discovered that it was absolutely false; and I shall ever follow in this road until I have met with something which is certain, or at least, if I can do nothing else, until I have learned for certain that there is nothing in the world that is certain. Archimedes, in order that he might draw the terrestrial globe out of its place, and transport it elsewhere, demanded only that one point should be fixed and immoveable; in the same way I shall have the right to conceive high hopes if I am happy enough to discover one thing only which is certain and indubitable.

I suppose, then, that all the things that I see are false; I persuade myself that nothing has ever existed of all that my fallacious memory represents to me. I consider that I possess no senses; I imagine that body, fatigue, extension, movement and place are but the fictions of my mind. What, then, can be esteemed as true? Perhaps nothing at all, unless that there is nothing in the world that is certain.

But how can I know there is not something different from those things that I have just considered, of which one cannot have the slightest doubt? Is there not some God, or some other being by whatever name we call it, who puts these reflections into my mind? That is not necessary, for is it not possible that I am capable of producing them myself? I myself, am I not at least something? But I have already denied that I had senses and body. Yet I hesitate, for what follows from that? Am I so dependent on body and senses that I cannot exist without these? But I was persuaded that there was nothing in all the world, that there was no heaven, no earth, that there were no minds, nor any bodies: was I not then likewise persuaded that I did not exist? Not at all; of a surety I myself did exist since I persuaded myself of something [or merely because I thought of something]. But there is some deceiver or other, very powerful and very cunning, who ever employs his ingenuity in deceiving me. Then without doubt I exist also if he deceives me, and let him deceive me as much as he will, he can never cause me to be nothing so long as I think that I am something. So that after having reflected well and carefully examined all things, we must come to the definite conclusion that this proposition: I am, I exist, is necessarily true each time that I pronounce it, or that I mentally conceive it.

But I do not yet know clearly enough what I am, I who am certain that I am; and hence I must be careful to see that I do not imprudently take some other object in place of myself, and thus that I do not go astray in respect of this knowledge that I hold to be the most certain and most evident of all that I have formerly learned. That is why I shall now consider anew what I believed myself to be before I embarked upon these last reflections; and of my former opinions I shall withdraw all that might even in a small degree be invalidated by the reasons which I have just brought forward, in order that there may be nothing at all left beyond what is absolutely certain and indubitable.

What then did I formerly believe myself to be? Undoubtedly I believed myself to be a man. But what is a man? Shall I say a reasonable animal? Certainly not; for then I should have to inquire what an animal is, and what is reasonable; and thus from a single question I should insensibly fall into an infinitude of others more difficult; and I should not wish to waste the little time and leisure remaining to me in trying to unravel subtleties like these. But I shall rather stop here to consider the thoughts which of themselves spring up in my mind, and which were not inspired by anything beyond my own nature alone when I applied myself to the consideration of my being. In the first place, then, I considered myself as having a face, hands, arms, and all that system of members composed of bones and flesh as seen in a corpse which I designated by the name of body. In addition to this I considered that I was nourished, that I walked, that I felt, and that I thought, and I referred to all these actions to the soul: but I did not stop to consider what the soul was, or if I did stop, I imagined that it was something extremely rare and subtle like a wind, a flame, or an ether, which was spread throughout my grosser parts. As to body I had no manner of doubt about its nature, but thought I had a very clear knowledge of it; and if I had desired to explain it according to the notions that I had then formed of it, I should have described it thus: By the body I understand all that which can be defined by a certain figure: something which can be confined in a certain place, and which can fill a given space in such a way that every other body will be excluded from it; which can be perceived either by touch, or by sight, or by hearing, or by taste, or by smell: which can be moved in many ways not, in truth, by itself, but by something which is foreign to it, by which it is touched [and from which it receives impressions]: for to have the power of self-movement, as also of feeling or of thinking, I did not consider to appertain to the nature of body: on the contrary, I was rather astonished to find that faculties similar to them existed in some bodies.

But what am I, now that I suppose that there is a certain genius which is extremely powerful, and, if I may say so, malicious, who employs all his powers in deceiving me? Can I affirm that I possess the least of all those things which I have just said pertain to the nature of body? I pause to consider, I revolve all these things in my mind, and I find none of which I can say that it pertains to me. It would be tedious to stop to enumerate them. Let us pass to the attributes of soul and see if there is any one which is in me? What of nutrition or walking [the first mentioned]? But if it is so that I have no body it is also true that I can neither walk nor take nourishment. Another attribute is sensation. But one cannot feel without body, and besides I have thought I perceived many things during sleep that I recognised in my waking moments as not having been experienced at all. What of thinking? I find here that thought is an attribute that belongs to me; it alone cannot be separated from me. I am, I exist, that is certain. But how often? Just when I think; for it might possibly be the case if I ceased entirely to think, that I should otherwise cease altogether to exist. I do not now admit anything which is not necessarily true: to speak accurately I am not more than a thing which thinks, that is to say a mind or a soul, or an understanding, or a reason, which are terms whose significance was formerly unknown to me. I am, however, a real thing and really exist; but what thing? I have answered: a thing which thinks.

And what more? I shall exercise my imagination [in order to see if I am not something more]. I am not a collection of members which we call the human body: I am not a subtle air distributed through these members, I am not a wind, a fire, a vapour, a breath, nor anything at all which I can imagine or conceive; because I have assumed that all these were nothing. Without changing that supposition I find that I only leave myself certain of the fact that I am somewhat. But perhaps it is true that these same things which I supposed were non-existent because they are unknown to me, are really not different from the self which I know. I am not sure about this, I shall not dispute about it now; I can only give judgment on things that are known to me. I know that I exist, and I inquire what I am, I whom I know to exist. But it is very certain that the knowledge of my existence taken in its precise significance does not depend on things whose existence is not yet known to me; consequently it does not depend on those which I can feign in imagination. And indeed the very term *feign* in imagination proves to me my error, for I really do this if I image myself a something, since to imagine is nothing else than to contemplate the figure or image of a corporeal thing. But I already know for certain that I am, and that it may be that all these images, and, speaking generally, all things that relate to the nature of body are nothing but dreams [and chimeras]. For this reason I see clearly that I have as little reason to say, "I shall stimulate my imagination in order to know more distinctly what I am," than if I were to say, "I am now awake, and I perceive somewhat that is real and true: but because I do not yet perceive it distinctly enough, I go to sleep of express purpose, so that my dreams may represent the perception with greatest truth and evidence." And, thus, I know for certain that nothing of all that I can understand by means of my imagination belongs to this knowledge which I have of myself, and that it is necessary to recall the mind from this mode of thought with the utmost diligence in order that it may be able to know its own nature with perfect distinctness.

But what then am I? A thing which thinks. What is a thing which thinks? It is a thing which doubts, understands, [conceives], affirms, denies, wills, refuses, which also imagines and feels.

Certainly it is no small matter if all these things pertain to my nature. But why should they not so pertain? Am I not that being who now doubts nearly everything, who nevertheless understands certain things, who affirms that one only is true, who denies all the others, who desires to know more, is averse from being deceived, who imagines many things, sometimes indeed despite his will, and who perceives many likewise, as by the intervention of the bodily organs? Is there nothing in all this which is as true as it is certain that I exist, even though I should always sleep and though he who has given me being employed all his ingenuity in deceiving me? Is there likewise any one of these attributes which can be distinguished from my thought, or which might be said to be separated from myself? For it is so evident of itself that it is I who doubts, who understands, and who desires, that there is no reason here to add anything to explain it. And I have certainly the power of imagining likewise; for although it may happen (as I formerly supposed) that none of the things which I imagine are true, nevertheless this power of imagining does not cease to be really in use, and it forms part of my thought. Finally, I am the same who feels, that is to say, who perceives certain things, as by the organs of sense, since in truth I see light, I hear noise, I feel heat. But it will be said that these phenomena are false and that I am dreaming. Let it be so; still it is at least quite certain that it seems to me that I see light, that I hear noise and that I feel heat. That cannot be false; properly speaking it is what is in me called feeling; and used in this precise sense that is no other thing than thinking.

From this time I begin to know what I am with a little more clearness and distinction than before; but nevertheless it still seems to me, and I cannot prevent myself from thinking, that corporeal things, whose images are framed by thought, which are tested by the senses, are much more distinctly known than that obscure part of me which does not come under the imagination. Although really it is very strange to say that I know and understand more distinctly these things whose existence seems to me dubious, which are unknown to me, and which do not belong to me, than others of the truth of which I am convinced, which are known to me and which pertain to my real nature, in a word, than myself. But I see clearly how the case stands: my mind loves to wander, and cannot yet suffer itself to be retained within the just limits of truth. Very good, let us once more give it the freest rein, so that, when afterwards we seize the proper occasion for pulling up, it may the more easily be regulated and controlled.

Let us begin by considering the commonest matters, those which we believe to be the most distinctly comprehended, to wit, the bodies which we touch and see; not indeed bodies in general, for these general ideas are usually a little more confused, but let us consider one body in particular. Let us take, for example, this piece of wax: it has been taken quite freshly from the hive, and it has not yet lost the sweetness of the honey which it contains; it still retains somewhat of the odour of the flowers from which it has been culled; its colour, its figure, its size are apparent; it is hard, cold, easily handled, and if you strike it with the finger, it will emit a sound. Finally all the things which are requisite to cause us distinctly to recognise a body, are met with in it. But notice that while I speak and approach the fire what remained of the taste is exhaled, the smell evaporates, the colour alters, the figure is destroyed, the size increases, it becomes liquid, it heats, scarcely can one handle it, and when one strikes it, no sound is emitted. Does the same wax remain after this change? We must confess that it remains; none would judge otherwise. What then did I know so distinctly in this piece of wax? It could certainly be nothing of all that the senses brought to my notice, since all these things which fall under taste, smell, sight, touch, and hearing, are found to be changed, and yet the same wax remains.

Perhaps it was what I now think, viz. that this wax was not that sweetness of honey, nor that agreeable scent of flowers, nor that particular whiteness, nor that figure, nor that sound, but simply a body which a little while before appeared to me as perceptible under these forms, and which is now perceptible under others. But what, precisely, is it that I imagine when I form such conceptions? Let us attentively consider this, and, abstracting from all that does not belong to the wax, let us see what remains. Certainly nothing remains excepting a certain extended thing which is flexible and movable. But what is the meaning of flexible and movable? Is it not that I imagine that this piece of wax being round is capable of becoming square and of passing from a square to a triangular figure? No, certainly it is not that, since I imagine it admits of an infinitude of similar changes, and I nevertheless do not know how to compass the infinitude by my imagination, and consequently this conception which I have of the wax is not brought about by the faculty of imagination. What now is this extension? Is it not also unknown? For it becomes greater when the wax is melted, greater when it is boiled, and greater still when the heat increases; and I should not conceive [clearly] according to truth what wax is, if I did not think that even this piece that we are considering is capable of receiving more variations in extension than I have ever imagined. We must then grant that I could not even understand through the imagination what this piece of wax is, and that it is my mind alone which perceives it. I say this piece of wax in particular, for as to wax in general it is yet clearer. But what is this piece of wax which cannot be understood excepting by the [understanding or] mind? It is certainly the same that I see, touch, imagine, and finally it is the same which I have always believed it to be from the beginning. But what must particularly be observed is that its perception is neither an act of vision, nor of touch, nor of imagination, and has never been such although it may have appeared formerly to be so, but only an intuition of the mind, which may be imperfect and confused as it was formerly, or clear and distinct as it is at present, according as my attention is more or less directed to the elements which are found in it, and of which it is composed.

Yet in the meantime I am greatly astonished when I consider [the great feebleness of mind] and its proneness to fall [insensibly] into error; for although without giving expression to my thoughts I consider all this in my own mind, words often impede me and I am almost deceived by the terms of ordinary language. For we say that we see the same wax, if it is present, and not that we simply judge that it is the same from its having the same colour and figure. From this I should conclude that I knew the wax by means of vision and not simply by the intuition of the mind; unless by chance I remember that, when looking from a window and saying I see men who pass in the street, I really do not see them, but infer that what I see is men, just as I say that I see wax. And yet what do I see from the window but hats and coats which may cover automatic machines? Yet I judge these to be men. And similarly solely by the faculty of judgment which rests in my mind, I comprehend that which I believed I saw with my eyes.

A man who makes it his aim to raise his knowledge above the common should be ashamed to derive the occasion for doubting from the forms of speech invented by the vulgar; I prefer to pass on and consider whether I had a more evident and perfect conception of what the wax was when I first perceived it, and when I believed I knew it by means of the external senses or at least by the common sense as it is called, that is to say by the imaginative faculty, or whether my present conception is clearer now that I have most carefully examined what it is, and in what way it can be known. It would certainly be absurd to doubt as to this. For what was there in this first perception which was distinct? What was there which might not as well have been perceived by any of the animals? But when I distinguish the wax from its external forms, and when, just as if I had taken from it its vestments, I consider it quite naked, it is certain that although some error may still be found in my judgment, I can nevertheless not perceive it thus without a human mind.

But finally what shall I say of this mind, that is, of myself, for up to this point I do not admit in myself anything but mind? What then, I who seem to perceive this piece of wax so distinctly, do I not know myself, not only with much more truth and certainty, but also with much more distinctness and clearness? For if I judge that the wax is or exists from the fact that I see it, it certainly follows much more clearly that I am or that I exist myself from the fact that I see it. For it may be that what I see is not really wax, it may also be that I do not possess eyes with which to see anything; but it cannot be that when I see, or (for I no longer take account of the distinction) when I think I see, that I myself who think am nought. So if I judge that the wax exists from the fact that I touch it, the same thing will follow, to wit, that I am; and if I judge that my imagination, or some other cause, whatever it is, persuades me that the wax exists, I shall still conclude the same. And what I have here remarked of wax may be applied to all other things which are external to me [and which are met with outside of me]. And further, if the [notion or] perception of wax has seemed to me clearer and more distinct, not only after the sight or the touch, but also after many other causes have rendered it quite manifest to me, with how much more [evidence] and distinctness must it be said that I now know myself, since all the reasons which contribute to the knowledge of wax, or any other body whatever, are yet better proofs of the nature of my mind! And there are so many other things in the mind itself which may contribute to the elucidation of its nature, that those which depend on body such as these just mentioned, hardly merit being taken into account.

But finally here I am, having insensibly reverted to the point I desired, for, since it is now manifest to me that even bodies are not properly speaking known by the senses or by the faculty of imagination, but by the understanding only, and since they are not known from the fact that they are seen or touched, but only because they are understood, I see clearly that there is nothing which is easier for me to know than my mind. But because it is difficult to rid oneself so promptly of an opinion to which one was accustomed for so long, it will be well that I should halt a little at this point, so that by the length of my meditation I may more deeply imprint on my memory this new knowledge.

Meditation III: Of God, That He Exists

I shall now close my eyes, I shall stop my ears, I shall call away all my senses, I shall efface even from my thoughts all the images of corporeal things, or at least (for that is hardly possible) I shall esteem them as vain and false; and thus holding converse only with myself and considering my own nature, I shall try little by little to reach a better knowledge of and a more familiar acquaintanceship with myself. I am a thing that thinks, that is to say, that doubts, affirms, denies, that knows a few things, that is ignorant of many [that loves, that hates], that wills, that desires, that also imagines and perceives; for as I remarked before, although the things which I perceive and imagine are perhaps nothing at all apart from me and in themselves, I am nevertheless assured that these modes of thought that I call perceptions and imaginations, inasmuch only as they are modes of thought, certainly reside [and are met with] in me.

And in the little that I have just said, I think I have summed up all that I really know, or at least all that hitherto I was aware that I knew. In order to try to extend my knowledge further, I shall now look around more carefully and see whether I cannot still discover in myself some other things which I have not hitherto perceived. I am certain that I am a thing which thinks; but do I not then likewise know what is requisite to render me certain of a truth? Certainly in this first knowledge there is nothing that assures me of its truth, excepting the clear and distinct perception of that which I state, which would not indeed suffice to assure me that what I say is true, if it could ever happen that a thing which I conceived so clearly and distinctly could be false; and accordingly it seems to me that already I can establish as a general rule that all things which I perceive very clearly and very distinctly are true.

At the same time I have before received and admitted many things to be very certain and manifest, which yet I afterwards recognised as being dubious. What then were these things? They were the earth, sky, stars and all other objects which I apprehended by means of the senses. But what did I clearly [and distinctly] perceive in them? Nothing more than that the ideas or thoughts of these things were presented to my mind. And not even now do I deny that these ideas are met with in me. But there was yet another thing which I affirmed, and which, owing to the habit which I had formed of believing it, I thought I perceived very clearly, although in truth I did not perceive it at all, to wit, that there were objects outside of me from which these ideas proceeded, and to which they were entirely similar. And it was in this that I erred, or, if perchance my judgment was correct, this was not due to any knowledge arising from my perception.

But when I took anything very simple and easy in the sphere of arithmetic or geometry into consideration, e.g. that two and three together made five, and other things of the sort, were not these present to my mind so clearly as to enable me to affirm that they were true? Certainly if I judged that since such matters could be doubted, this would not have been so for any other reason than that it came into my mind that perhaps a God might have endowed me with such a nature that I may have been deceived even concerning things which seemed to me most manifest. But every time that this preconceived opinion of the sovereign power of a God presents itself to my thought, I am constrained to confess that it is easy to Him, if He wishes it, to cause me to err, even in matters in which I believe myself to have the best evidence. And, on the other hand, always when I direct my attention to things which I believe myself to perceive very clearly, I am so persuaded of their truth that I let myself break out into words such as these: Let who will deceive me, He can never cause me to be nothing while I think that I am, or some day cause it to be true to say that I have never been, it being true now to say that I am, or that two and three make more or less than five, or any such thing in which I see a manifest contradiction. And, certainly, since I have no reason to believe that there is a God who is a deceiver, and as I have not yet satisfied myself that there is a God at all, the reason for doubt which depends on this opinion alone is very slight, and so to speak metaphysical. But in order to be able altogether to remove it, I must inquire whether there is a God as soon as the occasion presents itself; and if I find that there is a God, I must also inquire whether He may be a deceiver; for without a knowledge of these two truths I do not see that I can ever be certain of anything.

And in order that I may have an opportunity of inquiring into this in an orderly way [without interrupting the order of meditation which I have proposed to myself, and which is little by little to pass from the notions which I find first of all in my mind to those which I shall later on discover in it] it is requisite that I should here divide my thoughts into certain kinds, and that I should consider in which of these kinds there is, properly speaking, truth or error to be found. Of my thoughts some are, so to speak, images of the things, and to these alone is the title "idea" properly applied; examples are my thought of a man or of a chimera, of heaven, of an angel, or [even] of God. But other thoughts possess other forms as well. For example in willing, fearing, approving, denying, though I always perceive something as the subject of the action of my mind, yet by this action I always add something else to the idea which I have of that thing; and of the thoughts of this kind some are called volitions or affections, and others judgments.

Now as to what concerns ideas, if we consider them only in themselves and do not relate them to anything else beyond themselves, as they cannot properly speaking be false; for whether I imagine a goat or a chimera, it is not less true that I imagine the one than the other. We must not fear likewise that falsity can enter into will and into affections, for although I may desire evil things, or even things that never existed, it is not the less true that I desire them. Thus there remains no more than the judgments which we make, in which I must take the greatest care not to deceive myself. But the principal error and the commonest which we may meet with in them, consists in my judging that the ideas which are in me are similar or conformable to the things which are outside me; for without doubt if I considered the ideas only as certain modes of my thoughts, without trying to relate them to anything beyond, they could scarcely give me material for error.

But among these ideas, some appear to me to be innate, some adventitious, and others to be formed [or invented] by myself; for, as I have the power of understanding what is called a thing, or a truth, or a thought, it appears to me that I hold this power from no other source than my own nature. But if I now hear some sound, if I see the sun, or feel heat, I have hitherto judged that these sensations proceeded from certain things that exist outside of me; and finally it appears to me that sirens, hippogryphs, and the like, are formed out of my own mind. But again I may possibly persuade myself that all these ideas are of the nature of those which I term adventitious, or else that they are all innate, or all fictitious: for I have not yet clearly discovered their true origin.

And my principal task in this place is to consider, in respect to those ideas which appear to me to proceed from certain objects that are outside me, what are the reasons which cause me to think them similar to these objects. It seems indeed that I am taught this lesson by nature; and, secondly, I experience in myself that these ideas do not depend on my will nor therefore on myself—for they often present themselves to my mind in spite of my will. Just now, for instance, whether I will or whether I do not will, I feel heat, and thus I persuade myself that this feeling, or at least this idea of heat, is produced in me by something which is different from me, i.e. by the heat of the fire near which I sit. And nothing seems to me more obvious than to judge that this object imprints its likeness rather than anything else upon me.

Now I must discover whether these proofs are sufficiently strong and convincing. When I say that I am so instructed by nature, I merely mean a certain spontaneous inclination which impels me to believe in this connection, and not a natural light which makes me recognise that it is true. But these two things are very different; for I cannot doubt that which the natural light causes me to believe to be true, as, for example, it has shown me that I am from the fact that I doubt, or other facts of the same kind. And I possess no other faculty whereby to distinguish truth from falsehood, which can teach me that what this light shows me to be true is not really true, and no other faculty that is equally trustworthy. But as far as [apparently] natural impulses are concerned, I have frequently remarked, when I had to make active choice between virtue and vice, that they often enough led me to the part that was worse, and this is why I do not see any reason for following them in what regards truth and error.

And as to the other reason, which is that these ideas must proceed from objects outside me, since they do not depend on my will, I do not find it any the more convincing. For just as these impulses of which I have spoken are found in me, notwithstanding that they do not always concur with my will, so perhaps there is in me some faculty fitted to produce these ideas without the assistance of any external things, even though it is not yet known by me; just as, apparently, they have hitherto always been found in me during sleep without the aid of any external objects.

And finally, though they did proceed from objects different from myself, it is not a necessary consequence that they should resemble these. On the contrary, I have noticed that in many cases there was a great difference between the object and its idea. I find, for example, two completely diverse ideas of the sun in my mind; the one derives its origin from the senses, and should be placed in the category of adventitious ideas; according to this idea the sun seems to be extremely small; but the other is derived from astronomical reasonings, i.e. is elicited from certain notions that are innate in me, or else it is formed by me in some other manner; in accordance with it the sun appears to be several times greater than the earth. These two ideas cannot, indeed, both resemble the same sun, and reason makes me believe that the one which seems to have originated directly from the sun itself, is the one which is most dissimilar to it.

All this causes me to believe that until the present time it has not been by a judgment that was certain [or premeditated], but only by a sort of blind impulse that I believed that things existed outside of, and different from me, which, by the organs of my senses, or by some other method whatever it might be, conveyed these ideas or images to me [and imprinted on me their similitudes].

But there is yet another method of inquiring whether any of the objects of which I have ideas within me exist outside of me. If ideas are only taken as certain modes of thought, I recognise amongst them no difference or inequality, and all appear to proceed from me in the same manner; but when we consider them as images, one representing one thing and the other another, it is clear that they are very different one from the other. There is no doubt that those which represent to me substances are something more, and contain so to speak more objective reality within them [that is to say, by representation participate in a higher degree of being or perfection] than those that simply represent modes or accidents; and that idea again by which I understand a supreme God, eternal, infinite, [immutable], omniscient, omnipotent, and Creator of all things which are outside of Himself, has certainly more objective reality in itself than those ideas by which finite substances are represented.

Now it is manifest by the natural light that there must at least be as much reality in the efficient and total cause as in its effect. For pray, whence can the effect derive its reality, if not from its cause? And in what way can this cause communicate this reality to it, unless it possessed it in itself? And from this it follows, not only that something cannot proceed from nothing, but likewise that what is more perfect—that is to say, which has more reality within itself—cannot proceed from the less perfect. And this is not only evidently true of those effects which possess actual or formal reality, but also of the ideas in which we consider merely what is termed objective reality. To take an example, the stone which has not yet existed not only cannot now commence to be unless it has been produced by something which possesses within itself, either formally or eminently, all that enters into the composition of the stone [i.e. it must possess the same things or other more excellent things than those which exist in the stone] and heat can only be produced in a subject in which it did not previously exist by a cause that is of an order [degree or kind], at least as perfect as heat, and so in all other cases. But further, the idea of heat, or of a stone, cannot exist in me unless it has been placed within me by some cause which possesses within it at least as much reality as that which I conceive to exist in the heat or the stone. For although this cause does not transmit anything of its actual or formal reality to my idea, we must not for that reason imagine that it is necessarily a less real cause; we must remember that [since every idea is a work of the mind] its nature is such that it demands of itself no other formal reality than that which it borrows from my thought, of which it is only a mode [i.e. a manner or way of thinking]. But in order that an idea should contain some one certain objective reality rather than another, it must without doubt derive it from some cause in which there is at least as much formal reality as this idea contains of objective reality. For if we imagine that something is found in an ideas which is not found in the cause, it must then have been derived from nought; but however imperfect may be this mode of being by which a thing is objectively [or by representation] in the understanding of its idea, we cannot certainly say that this mode of being is nothing, nor, consequently, that the idea derives its origin from nothing.

Nor must I imagine that, since the reality that I consider in these ideas is only objective, it is not essential that this reality should be formally in the causes of my ideas, but that it is sufficient that it should be found objectively. For just as this mode of objective existence pertains to the causes of those ideas (this is at least true of the first and principal) by the nature peculiar to them. And although it may be the case that one idea gives birth to another idea, that cannot continue to be so indefinitely; for in the end we must reach an idea whose cause shall be so to speak an archetype, in which the whole reality [or perfection] which is so to speak objectively [or by representation] in these ideas is contained formally [and really]. Thus the light of nature causes me to know clearly that the ideas in me are like [pictures or] images which can, in truth, easily fall short of the perfection of the objects from which they have been derived, but which can never contain anything greater or more perfect.

And the longer and the more carefully that I investigate these matters, the more clearly and distinctly do I recognise their truth. But what am I to conclude from it all in the end? It is this, that if the objective reality of any one of my ideas is of such a nature as clearly to make me recognise that it is not in me either formally or eminently, and that consequently I cannot myself be the cause of it, it follows of necessity that I am not alone in the world, but that there is another being which exists, or which is the cause of this idea. On the other hand, had no such an idea existed in me, I should have had no sufficient argument to convince me of the existence of any being beyond myself; for I have made very careful investigation everywhere and up to the present time have been able to find no other ground.

But of my ideas, beyond that which represents me to myself, as to which there can be no difficulty, there is another which represents a God, and there are others representing corporeal and inanimate things, others angels, others animals, and others again which represent to me men similar to myself.

As regards the ideas which represent to me other men or animals, or angels, I can however easily conceive that they might be formed by an admixture of the other ideas which I have of myself, of corporeal things, and of God, even although there were apart from me neither men nor animals, nor angels, in all the world.

And in regard to the ideas of corporeal objects, I do not recognise in them anything so great or so excellent that they might not have possibly proceeded from myself; for if I consider them more closely, and examine them individually, as I yesterday examined the idea of wax, I find that there is very little in them which I perceive clearly and distinctly. Magnitude or extension in length, breadth, or depth, I do so perceive; also figure which results from a termination of this extension, the situation which bodies of different figure preserve in relation to one another, and movement or change of situation; to which we may also add substance, duration and number. As to other things such as light, colours, sounds, scents, tastes, heat, cold and the other tactile qualities, they are thought by me with so much obscurity and confusion that I do not even know if they are true or false, i.e. whether the ideas which I form of these qualities are actually the ideas of real objects or not [or whether they only represent chimeras which cannot exist in fact]. For although I have before remarked that it is only in judgments that falsity, properly speaking, or formal falsity, can be met with, a certain material falsity may nevertheless be found in ideas, i.e. when these ideas represent what is nothing as though it were something. For example, the ideas which I have of cold and heat are so far from clear and distinct that by their means I cannot tell whether cold is merely a privation of heat, or heat a privation of cold, or whether both are real qualities, or are not such. And inasmuch as [since ideas resemble images] there cannot be any ideas which do not appear to represent some things, if it is correct to say that cold is merely a privation of heat, the idea which represents it to me as something real and positive will not be improperly termed false, and the same holds good of other similar ideas.

To these it is certainly not necessary that I should attribute any author other than myself. For if they are false, i.e. if they represent things which do not exist, the light of nature shows me that they issue from nought, that is to say, that they are only in me in so far as something is lacking to the perfection of my nature. But if they are true, nevertheless because they exhibit so little reality to me that I cannot even clearly distinguish the thing represented from non-being, I do not see any reason why they should not be produced by myself.

As to the clear and distinct idea which I have of corporeal things, some of them seem as though I might have derived them from the idea which I possess of myself, as those which I have of substance, duration, number, and such like. For [even] when I think that a stone is a substance, or at least a thing capable of existing of itself, and that I am a substance also, although I conceive that I am a thing that thinks and not one that is extended, and that the stone on the other hand is an extended thing which does not think, and thus there is a notable difference between the two conceptions—they seem, nevertheless, to agree in this, that both represent substances. In the same way, when I perceive that I now exist and further recollect that I have in former times existed, and when I remember that I have various thoughts of which I can recognise the number, I acquire ideas of duration and number which I can afterwards transfer to any object that I please. But as to all other qualities of which the ideas of corporeal things are composed, to wit, extension, figure, situation and motion, it is true that they are not formally in me, since I am only a thing that thinks; but because they are merely certain modes of substance [and so to speak the vestments under which corporeal substance appears to us] and because I myself am also a substance, it would seem that they might be contained in me eminently.

Hence there remains only the idea of God, concerning which we must consider whether it is something which cannot have proceeded from me myself. By the name God I understand a substance that is infinite [eternal, immutable], independent, all-knowing, all-powerful, and by which I myself and everything else, if anything else does exist, have been created. Now all these characteristics are such that the more diligently I attend to them, the less do they appear capable of proceeding from me alone; hence, from what has been already said, we must conclude that God necessarily exists.

For although the idea of substance is within me owing to the fact that I am substance, nevertheless I should not have the idea of an infinite substance—since I am finite—if it had not proceeded from some substance which was veritably infinite.

Nor should I imagine that I do not perceive the infinite by a true idea, but only by the negation of the finite, just as I perceive repose and darkness by the negation of movement and light; for, on the contrary, I see that there is manifestly more reality in infinite substance than in finite, and therefore that in some way I have in me the notion of the infinite earlier than the finite—to wit, the notion of God before that of myself. For how would it be possible that I should know that I doubt and desire, that is to say, that something is lacking to me, and that I am not quite perfect, unless I had within me some idea of a Being more perfect than myself, in comparison with which I should recognise the deficiencies of my nature?

And we cannot say that this idea of God is perhaps materially false and that consequently I can derive it from nought [i.e. that possibly it exists in me because I am imperfect], as I have just said is the case with ideas of heat, cold and other such things; for, on the contrary, as this idea is very clear and distinct and contains within it more objective reality than any other, there can be none which is of itself more true, nor any in which there can be less suspicion of falsehood. The idea, I say, of this Being who is absolutely perfect and infinite, is entirely true; for although, perhaps we can imagine that such a Being does not exist, we cannot nevertheless imagine that His idea represents nothing real to me, as I have said of the idea of cold. This idea is also very clear and distinct; since all that I conceive clearly and distinctly of the real and the true, and of what conveys some perfection, is in its entirety contained in this idea. And this does not cease to be true although I do not comprehend the infinite, or though in God there is an infinitude of things which I cannot comprehend, nor possibly even reach in any way by thought; for it is of the nature of the infinite that my nature, which is finite and limited, should not comprehend it; and it is sufficient that I should understand this, and that I should judge that all things which I clearly perceive and in which I know that there is some perfection, and possibly likewise an infinitude of properties of which I am ignorant, are in God formally or eminently, so that the idea which I have of Him may become the most true, most clear, and most distinct of all the ideas that are in my mind.

But possibly I am something more than I suppose myself to be, and perhaps all those perfections which I attribute to God are in some way potentially in me, although they do not yet disclose themselves, or issue in action. As a matter of fact I am already sensible that my knowledge increases [and perfects itself] little by little, and I see nothing which can prevent it from increasing more and more into infinitude; not do I see, after it has thus been increased [or perfected], anything to prevent my being able to acquire by its means all the other perfections of the Divine nature; nor finally why the power I have of acquiring these perfections, if it really exists in me, shall not suffice to produce the ideas of them.

At the same time I recognise that this cannot be. For, in the first place, although it were true that every day my knowledge acquired new degrees of perfection, and that there were in my nature many things potentially which are not yet there actually, nevertheless these excellences do not pertain to [or make the smallest approach to] the idea which I have of God in whom there is nothing merely potential [but in whom all is present really and actually]; for it is an infallible token of imperfection in my knowledge that it increases little by little. And further, although my knowledge grows more and more, nevertheless I do not for that reason believe that it can ever be actually infinite, since it can never reach a point so high that it will be unable to attain to any greater increase. But I understand God to be actually infinite, so that He can add nothing to His supreme perfection. And finally I perceive that the objective being of an idea cannot be produced by a being that exists potentially only, which properly speaking is nothing, but only by a being which is formal or actual.

To speak the truth, I see nothing in all that I have just said which by the light of nature is not manifest to anyone who desires to think attentively on the subject; but when I slightly relax my attention, my mind, finding its vision somewhat obscured and so to speak blinded by the images of sensible objects, I do not easily recollect the reason why the idea that I possess of a being more perfect than I, must necessarily have been placed in me by a being which is really more perfect; and this is why I wish here to go on to inquire whether I, who have this idea, can exist if no such being exists.

And I ask, from whom do I then derive my existence? Perhaps from myself or from my parents, or from some other source less perfect than God; for we can imagine nothing more perfect than God, or even as perfect as He is.

But [were I independent of every other and] were I myself the author of my being, I should doubt nothing and I should desire nothing, and finally no perfection would be lacking to me; for I should have bestowed on myself every perfection of which I possessed any idea and should thus be God. And it must not be imagined that those things that are lacking to me are perhaps more difficult of attainment than those which I already possess; for, on the contrary, it is quite evident that it was a matter of much greater difficulty to bring to pass that I, that is to say, a thing or a substance that thinks, should emerge out of nothing, than it would be to attain to the knowledge of many things of which I am ignorant, and which are only the accidents of this thinking substance. But it is clear that if I had of myself possessed this greater perfection of which I have just spoken [that is to say, if I had been the author of my own existence], I should not at least have denied myself the things which are the more easy to acquire [to wit, many branches of knowledge of which my nature is destitute]; nor should I have deprived myself of any of the things contained in the idea which I form of God, because there are none of them which seem to me specially difficult to acquire: and if there were any that were more difficult to acquire, they would certainly appear to me to be such (supposing I myself were the origin of the other things which I possess) since I should discover in them that my powers were limited.

But though I assume that perhaps I have always existed just as I am at present, neither can I escape the force of this reasoning, and imagine that the conclusion to be drawn from this is, that I need not seek for any author of my existence. For all the course of my life may be divided into an infinite number of parts, none of which is in any way dependent on the other; and thus from the fact that I was in existence a short time ago it does not follow that I must be in existence now, unless some cause at this instant, so to speak, produces me anew, that is to say, conserves me. It is as a matter of fact perfectly clear and evident to all those who consider with attention the nature of time, that, in order to be conserved in each moment in which it endures, a substance has need of the same power and action as would be necessary to produce and create it anew, supposing it did not yet exist, so that the light of nature shows us clearly that the distinction between creation and conservation is solely a distinction of the reason.

All that I thus require here is that I should interrogate myself, if I wish to know whether I possess a power which is capable of bringing it to pass that I who now am shall still be in the future; for since I am nothing but a thinking thing, or at least since thus far it is only this portion of myself which is precisely in question at present, if such a power did reside in me, I should certainly be conscious of it. But I am conscious of nothing of the kind, and by this I know clearly that I depend on some being different from myself.

Possibly, however, this being on which I depend is not that which I call God, and I am created either by my parents or by some other cause less perfect than God. This cannot be, because, as I have just said, it is perfectly evident that there must be at least as much reality in the cause as in the effect; and thus since I am a thinking thing, and possess an idea of God within me, whatever in the end be the cause assigned to my existence, it must be allowed that it is likewise a thinking thing and that it possesses in itself the idea of all the perfections which I attribute to God. We may again inquire whether this cause derives its origin from itself or from some other thing. For if from itself, it follows by the reasons before brought forward, that this cause must itself be God; for since it possesses the virtue of self-existence, it must also without doubt have the power of actually possessing all the perfections of which it has the idea, that is, all those which I conceive as existing in God. But if it derives its existence from some other cause than itself, we shall again ask, for the same reason, whether this second cause exists by itself or through another, until from one step to another, we finally arrive at an ultimate cause, which will be God.

And it is perfectly manifest that in this there can be no regression into infinity, since what is in question is not so much the cause which formerly created me, as that which conserves me at the present time.

Nor can we suppose that several causes may have concurred in my production, and that from one I have received the idea of one of the perfections which I attribute to God, and from another the idea of some other, so that all these perfections indeed exist somewhere in the universe, but not as complete in one unity which is God. On the contrary, the unity, the simplicity or the inseparability of all things which are in

God is one of the principal perfections which I conceive to be in Him. And certainly the idea of this unity of all Divine perfections cannot have been placed in me by any cause from which I have not likewise received the ideas of all the other perfections; for this cause could not make me able to comprehend them as joined together in an inseparable unity without having at the same time caused me in some measure to know what they are [and in some way to recognise each one of them].

Finally, so far as my parents [from whom it appears I have sprung] are concerned, although all that I have ever been able to believe of them were true, that does not make it follow that it is they who conserve me, nor are they even the authors of my being in any sense, in so far as I am a thinking being; since what they did was merely to implant certain dispositions in that matter in which the self—i.e. the mind, which alone I at present identify with myself—is by me deemed to exist. And thus there can be no difficulty in their regard, but we must of necessity conclude from the fact alone that I exist, or that the idea of a Being supremely perfect—that is of God—is in me, that the proof of God's existence is grounded on the highest evidence.

It only remains to me to examine into the manner in which I have acquired this idea from God; for I have not received it through the senses, and it is never presented to me unexpectedly, as is usual with the ideas of sensible things when these things present themselves, or seem to present themselves, to the external organs of my senses; nor is it likewise a fiction of my mind, for it is not in my power to take from or to add anything to it; and consequently the only alternative is that it is innate in me, just as the idea of myself is innate in me.

And one certainly ought not to find it strange that God, in creating me, placed this idea within me to be like the mark of the workman imprinted on his work; and it is likewise not essential that the mark shall be something different from the work itself. For from the sole fact that God created me it is most probable that in some way he has placed his image and similitude upon me, and that I perceive this similitude (in which the idea of God is contained) by means of the same faculty by which I perceive myself—that is to say, when I reflect on myself I not only know that I am something [imperfect], incomplete and dependent on another, which incessantly aspires after something which is better and greater than myself, but I also know that He on whom I depend possesses in Himself all the great things towards which I aspire [and the ideas of which I find within myself], and that not indefinitely or potentially alone, but really, actually and infinitely; and that thus He is God. And the whole strength of the argument which I have here made use of to prove the existence of God consists in this, that I recognise that it is not possible that my nature should be what it is, and indeed that I should have in myself the idea of a God, if God did not veritably exist— a God, I say, whose idea is in me, i.e. who possesses all those supreme perfections of which our mind may indeed have some idea but without understanding them all, who is liable to no errors or defect [and who has none of all those marks which denote imperfection]. From this it is manifest that He cannot be a deceiver, since the light of nature teaches us that fraud and deception necessarily proceed from some defect.

But before I examine this matter with more care, and pass on to the consideration of other truths which may be derived from it, it seems to me right to pause for a while in order to contemplate God Himself, to ponder at leisure His marvellous attributes, to consider, and admire, and adore, the beauty of this light so resplendent, at least as far as the strength of my mind, which is in some measure dazzled by the sight, will allow me to do so. For just as faith teaches us that the supreme felicity of the other life consists only in this contemplation of the Divine Majesty, so we continue to learn by experience that a similar meditation, though incomparably less perfect, causes us to enjoy the greatest satisfaction of which we are capable in this life.

Meditation IV: Of the True and the False

I have been well accustomed these past days to detach my mind from my senses, and I have accurately observed that there are very few things that one knows with certainty respecting corporeal objects, that there are many more which are known to us respecting the human mind, and yet more still regarding God Himself; so that I shall now without any difficulty abstract my thoughts from the consideration of [sensible or] imaginable objects, and carry them to those which, being withdrawn from all contact with matter, are purely intelligible. And certainly the idea which I possess of the human mind inasmuch as it is a thinking thing, and not extended in length, width and depth, nor participating in anything pertaining to body, is incomparably more distinct than is the idea of any corporeal thing. And when I consider that I doubt, that is to say, that I am an incomplete and dependent being, the idea of a being that is complete and independent, that is of God, presents itself to my mind with so much distinctness and clearness—and from the fact alone that this idea is found in me, or that I who possess this idea exist, I conclude so certainly that God exists, and that my existence depends entirely on Him in every moment of my life—that I do not think that the human mind is capable of knowing anything with more evidence and certitude. And it seems to me that I now have before me a road which will lead us from the contemplation of the true God (in whom all the treasures of science and wisdom are contained) to the knowledge of the other objects of the universe.

For, first of all, I recognise it to be impossible that He should ever deceive me; for in all fraud and deception some imperfection is to be found, and although it may appear that the power of deception is a mark of subtilty or power, yet the desire to deceive without doubt testifies to malice or feebleness, and accordingly cannot be found in God.

In the next place I experienced in myself a certain capacity for judging which I have doubtless received from God, like all the other things that I possess; and as He could not desire to deceive me, it is clear that He has not given me a faculty that will lead me to err if I use it aright.

And no doubt respecting this matter could remain, if it were not that the consequence would seem to follow that I can thus never be deceived; for if I hold all that I possess from God, and if He has not placed in me the capacity for error, it seems as though I could never fall into error. And it is true that when I think only of God [and direct my mind wholly to Him], I discover [in myself] no cause of error, or falsity; yet directly afterwards, when recurring to myself, experience shows me that

I am nevertheless subject to an infinitude of errors, as to which, when we come to investigate them more closely, I notice that not only is there a real and positive idea of God or of a Being of supreme perfection present to my mind, but also, so to speak, a certain negative idea of nothing, that is, of that which is infinitely removed from any kind of perfection; and that I am in a sense something intermediate between God and nought, i.e. placed in such a manner between the supreme Being and nonbeing, that there is in truth nothing in me that can lead to error in so far as a sovereign Being has formed me; but that, as I in some degree participate likewise in nought or in non-being, i.e. in so far as I am not myself the supreme Being, and as I find myself subject to an infinitude of imperfections, I ought not to be astonished if I should fall into error. Thus do I recognise that error, in so far as it is such, is not a real thing depending on God, but simply a defect; and therefore, in order to fall into it, that I have no need to possess a special faculty given me by God for this very purpose, but that I fall into error from the fact that the power given me by God for the purpose of distinguishing truth from error is not infinite.

Nevertheless this does not quite satisfy me; for error is not a pure negation [i.e. is not the simple defect or want of some perfection which ought not to be mine], but it is a lack of some knowledge which it seems that I ought to possess. And on considering the nature of God it does not appear to me possible that He should have given me a faculty which is not perfect of its kind, that is, which is wanting in some perfection due to it. For if it is true that the more skilful the artizan, the more perfect is the work of his hands, what can have been produced by this supreme Creator of all things that is not in all its parts perfect? And certainly there is no doubt that God could have created me so that I could never have been subject to error; it is also certain that He ever wills what is best; is it then better that I should be subject to err than that I should not?

In considering this more attentively, it occurs to me in the first place that I should not be astonished if my intelligence is not capable of comprehending why God acts as He does; and that there is thus no reason to doubt of His existence from the fact that I may perhaps find many other things besides this as to which I am able to understand neither for what reason nor how God has produced them. For, in the first place, knowing that my nature is extremely feeble and limited, and that the nature of God is on the contrary immense, incomprehensible, and infinite, I have no further difficulty in recognising that there is an infinitude of matters in His power, the causes of which transcend my knowledge; and this reason suffices to convince me that the species of cause termed final, finds no useful employment in physical [or natural] things; for it does not appear to me that I can without temerity seek to investigate the [inscrutable] ends of God.

It further occurs to me that we should not consider one single creature separately, when we inquire as to whether the works of God are perfect, but should regard all his creations together. For the same thing which might possibly seem very imperfect with some semblance of reason if regarded by itself, is found to be very perfect if regarded as part of the whole universe; and although, since I resolved to doubt all things, I as yet have only known certainly my own existence and that of God, nevertheless since I have recognised the infinite power of God, I cannot deny that He may have produced many other things, or at least that He has the power of producing them, so that I may obtain a place as a part of a great universe.

Whereupon, regarding myself more closely, and considering what are my errors (for they alone testify to there being any imperfection in me), I answer that they depend on a combination of two causes, to wit, on the faculty of knowledge that rests in me, and on the power of choice or of free will—that is to say, of the understanding and at the same time of the will. For by the understanding alone I [neither assert nor deny anything, but] apprehend the ideas of things as to which I can form a judgment. But no error is properly speaking found in it, provided the word error is taken in its proper signification; and though there is possibly an infinitude of things in the world of which I have no idea in my understanding, we cannot for all that say that it is deprived of these ideas [as we might say of something which is required by its nature], but simply it does not possess these; because in truth there is no reason to prove that God should have given me a greater faculty of knowledge than He has given me; and however skilful a workman I represent Him to be, I should not for all that consider that He was bound to have placed in each of His works all the perfections which He may have been able to place in some. I likewise cannot complain that God has not given me a free choice or a will which is sufficient, ample and perfect, since as a matter of fact I am conscious of a will so extended as to be subject to no limits. And what seems to me very remarkable in this regard is that of all the qualities which I possess there is no one so perfect and so comprehensive that I do not very clearly recognise that it might be yet greater and more perfect. For, to take an example, if I consider the faculty of comprehension which I possess, I find that it is of very small extent and extremely limited, and at the same time I find the idea of another faculty much more ample and even infinite, and seeing that I can form the idea of it, I recognise from this very fact that it pertains to the nature of God. If in the same way I examine the memory, the imagination, or some other faculty, I do not find any which is not small and circumscribed, while in God it is immense [or infinite]. It is free-will alone or liberty of choice which I find to be so great in me that I can conceive no other idea to be more great; it is indeed the case that it is for the most part this will that causes me to know that in some manner I bear the image and similitude of God. For although the power of will is incomparably greater in God than in me, both by reason of the knowledge and the power which, conjoined with it, render it stronger and more efficacious, and by reason of its object, inasmuch as in God it extends to a great many things; it nevertheless does not seem to me greater if I consider it formally and precisely in itself: for the faculty of will consists alone in our having the power of choosing to do a thing or choosing not to do it (that is, to affirm or deny, to pursue or to shun it), or rather it consists alone in the fact that in order to affirm or deny, pursue or shun those things placed before us by the understanding, we act so that we are unconscious that any outside force constrains us in doing so. For in order that I should be free it is not necessary that I should be indifferent as to the choice of one or the other of two contraries; but contrariwise the more I lean to the one—whether I recognise clearly that the reasons of the good and true are to be found in it, or whether God so disposes my inward thought—the more freely do I choose and embrace it. And undoubtedly both divine grace and natural knowledge, far from diminishing my liberty, rather increase it and strengthen it. Hence this indifference which I feel, when I am not swayed to one side rather than to the other by lack of reason, is the lowest grade of liberty, and rather evinces a lack or negation in knowledge than a perfection of will: for if I always recognised clearly what was true and good, I should never have trouble in deliberating as to what judgment or choice I should make, and then I should be entirely free without ever being indifferent.

From all this I recognise that the power of will which I have received from God is not of itself the source of my errors—for it is very ample and very perfect of its kind—any more than is the power of understanding; for since I understand nothing but by the power which God has given me for understanding, there is no doubt that all that I understand, I understand as I ought, and it is not possible that I err in this. Whence then come my errors? They come from the sole fact that since the will is much wider in its range and compass than the understanding, I do not restrain it within the same bounds, but extend it also to things which I do not understand: and as the will is of itself indifferent to these, it easily falls into error and sin, and chooses the evil for the good, or the false for the true.

For example, when I lately examined whether anything existed in the world, and found that from the very fact that I considered this question it followed very clearly that I myself existed, I could not prevent myself from believing that a thing I so clearly conceived was true: not that I found myself compelled to do so by some external cause, but simply because from great clearness in my mind there followed a great inclination of my will; and I believed this with so much the greater freedom or spontaneity as I possessed the less indifference towards it. Now, on the contrary, I not only know that I exist, inasmuch as I am a thinking thing, but a certain representation of corporeal nature is also presented to my mind; and it comes to pass that I doubt whether this thinking nature which is in me, or rather by which I am what I am, differs from this corporeal nature, or whether both are not simply the same thing; and I here suppose that I do not yet know any reason to persuade me to adopt the one belief rather than the other. From this it follows that I am entirely indifferent as to which of the two I affirm or deny, or even whether I abstain from forming any judgment in the matter.

And this indifference does not only extend to matters as to which the understanding has no knowledge, but also in general to all those which are not apprehended with perfect clearness at the moment when the will is deliberating upon them: for, however probable are the conjectures which render me disposed to form a judgment respecting anything, the simple knowledge that I have that those are conjectures alone and not certain and indubitable reasons, suffices to occasion me to judge the contrary. Of this I have had great experience of late when I set aside as false all that I had formerly held to be absolutely true, for the sole reason that I remarked that it might in some measure be doubted.

But if I abstain from giving my judgment on any thing when I do not perceive it with sufficient clearness and distinctness, it is plain that I act rightly and am not deceived. But if I determine to deny or affirm, I no longer make use as I should of my free will, and if I affirm what is not true, it is evident that I deceive myself; even though I judge according to truth, this comes about only by chance, and I do not escape the blame of missing my freedom; for the light of nature teaches us that the knowledge of the understanding should always precede the determination of the will. And it is in the misuse of the free will that the privation which constitutes the characteristic nature of error is met with. Privation, I say, is found in the act, in so far as it proceeds from me, but it is not found in the faculty which I have received from God, nor even in the act in so far as it depends on Him.

For I have certainly no cause to complain that God has not given me an intelligence which is more powerful, or a natural light which is stronger than that which I have received from Him, since it is proper to the finite understanding not to comprehend a multitude of things, and it is proper to a created understanding to be finite; on the contrary, I have every reason to render thanks to God who owes me nothing and who has given me all the perfections I possess, and I should be far from charging Him with injustice, and with having deprived me of, or wrongfully withheld from me, these perfections which He has not bestowed upon me.

I have further no reason to complain that He has given me a will more ample than my understanding, for since the will consists only of one single element, and is so to speak indivisible, it appears that its nature is such that nothing can be abstracted from it [without destroying it]; and certainly the more comprehensive it is found to be, the more reason I have to render gratitude to the giver.

And, finally, I must also not complain that God concurs with me in forming the acts of the will, that is the judgment in which I go astray, because these acts are entirely true and good, inasmuch as they depend on God; and in a certain sense more perfection accrues to my nature from the fact that I can form them, than if I could not do so. As to the privation in which alone the formal reason of error or sin consists, it has no need of any concurrence from God, since it is not a thing [or an existence], and since it is not related to God as to a cause, but should be termed merely a negation [according to the significance given to these words in the Schools]. For in fact it is not an imperfection in God that He has given me the liberty to give or withhold my assent from certain things as to which He has not placed a clear and distinct knowledge in my understanding; but it is without doubt an imperfection in me not to make a good use of my freedom, and to give my judgment readily on matters which I only understand obscurely. I nevertheless perceive that God could easily have created me so that I never should err, although I still remained free, and endowed with a limited knowledge, viz. by giving to my understanding a clear and distinct intelligence of all things as to which I should ever have to deliberate; or simply by His engraving deeply in my memory the resolution never to form a judgment on anything without having a clear and distinct understanding of it, so that I could never forget it. And it is easy for me to understand that, in so far as I consider myself alone, and as if there were only myself in the world, I should have been much more perfect than I am, if God had created me so that I could never err. Nevertheless I cannot deny that in some sense it is a greater perfection in the whole universe that certain parts should not be exempt from error as others are than that all parts should be exactly similar. And I have no right to complain if God, having placed me in the world, has not called upon me to play a part that excels all others in distinction and perfection.

And further I have reason to be glad on the ground that if He has not given me the power of never going astray by the first means pointed out above, which depends on a clear and evident knowledge of all the things regarding which I can deliberate, He has at least left within my power the other means, which is firmly to adhere to the resolution never to give judgment on matters whose truth is not clearly known to me; for although I notice a certain weakness in my nature in that I cannot continually concentrate my mind on one single thought, I can yet, by attentive and frequently repeated meditation, impress it so forcibly on my memory that I shall never fail to recollect it whenever I have need of it, and thus acquire the habit of never going astray.

And inasmuch as it is in this that the greatest and principal perfection of man consists, it seems to me that I have not gained little by this day's Meditation, since I have discovered the source of falsity and error. And certainly there can be no other source than that which I have explained; for as often as I so restrain my will within the limits of my knowledge that it forms no judgment except on matters which are clearly and distinctly represented to it by the understanding, I can never be deceived; for every clear and distinct conception is without doubt something, and hence cannot derive its origin from what is nought, but must of necessity have God as its author—God, I say, who being supremely perfect, cannot be the cause of any error; and consequently we must conclude that such a conception [or such a judgment] is true. Nor have I only learned to-day what I should avoid in order that I may not err, but also how I should act in order to arrive at a knowledge of the truth; for without doubt I shall arrive at this end if I devote my attention sufficiently to those things which I perfectly understand; and if I separate from these that which I only understand confusedly and with obscurity. To these I shall henceforth diligently give heed.

Meditation V: Of the Essence of Material Things, and Again, of God, That He Exists

Many other matters respecting the attributes of God and my own nature or mind remain for consideration; but I shall possibly on another occasion resume the investigation of these. Now (after first noting what must be done or avoided, in order to arrive at a knowledge of the truth) my principal task is to endeavour to emerge from the state of doubt into which I have these last days fallen, and to see whether nothing certain can be known regarding material things.

But before examining whether any such objects as I conceive exist outside of me, I must consider the ideas of them in so far as they are in my thought, and see which of them are distinct and which confused.

In the first place, I am able distinctly to imagine that quantity which philosophers commonly call continuous, or the extension in length, breadth, or depth, that is in this quantity, or rather in the object to which it is attributed. Further, I can number in it many different parts, and attribute to each of its parts many sorts of size, figure, situation and local movement, and, finally, I can assign to each of these movements all degrees of duration.

And not only do I know these things with distinctness when I consider them in general, but, likewise [however little I apply my attention to the matter], I discover an infinitude of particulars respecting numbers, figures, movements, and other such things, whose truth is so manifest, and so well accords with my nature, that when I begin to discover them, it seems to me that I learn nothing new, or recollect what I formerly knew—that is to say, that I for the first time perceive things which were already present to my mind, although I had not as yet applied my mind to them.

And what I here find to be most important is that I discover in myself an infinitude of ideas of certain things which cannot be esteemed as pure negations, although they may possibly have no existence outside of my thought, and which are not framed by me, although it is within my power either to think or not to think them, but which possess natures which are true and immutable. For example, when I imagine a triangle, although there may nowhere in the world be such a figure outside my thought, or ever have been, there is nevertheless in this figure a certain determinate nature, form, or essence, which is immutable and eternal, which I have not invented, and which in no wise depends on my mind, as appears from the fact that diverse properties of that triangle can be demonstrated, viz. that its three angles are equal to two right angles, that the greatest side is subtended by the greatest angle, and the like, which now, whether I wish it or do not wish it, I recognise very clearly as pertaining to it, although I never thought of the matter at all when I imagined a triangle for the first time, and which therefore cannot be said to have been invented by me.

Nor does the objection hold good that possibly this idea of a triangle has reached my mind through the medium of my senses, since I have sometimes seen bodies triangular in shape; because I can form in my mind an infinitude of other figures regarding which we cannot have the least conception of their ever having been objects of sense, and I can nevertheless demonstrate various properties pertaining to their nature as well as to that of the triangle, and these must certainly all be true since I conceive them clearly. Hence they are something, and not pure negation; for it is perfectly clear that all that is true is something, and I have already fully demonstrated that all that I know clearly is true. And even although I had not demonstrated this, the nature of my mind is such that I could not prevent myself from holding them to be true so long as I conceive them clearly; and I recollect that even when I was still strongly attached to the objects of sense, I counted as the most certain those truths which I conceived clearly as regards figures, numbers, and the other matters which pertain to arithmetic and geometry, and, in general, to pure and abstract mathematics.

But now, if just because I can draw the idea of something from my thought, it follows that all which I know clearly and distinctly as pertaining to this object does really belong to it, may I not derive from this an argument demonstrating the existence of God? It is certain that I no less find the idea of God, that is to say, the idea of a supremely perfect Being, in me, than that of any figure or number whatever it is; and I do not know any less clearly and distinctly that an [actual and] eternal existence pertains to this nature than I know that all that which I am able to demonstrate of some figure or number truly pertains to the nature of this figure or number, and therefore, although all that I concluded in the preceding Meditations were found to be false, the existence of God would pass with me as at least as certain as I have ever held the truths of mathematics (which concern only numbers and figures) to be.

This indeed is not at first manifest, since it would seem to present some appearance of being a sophism. For being accustomed in all other things to make a distinction between existence and essence, I easily persuade myself that the existence can be separated from the essence of God, and that we can thus conceive God as not actually existing. But, nevertheless, when I think of it with more attention, I clearly see that existence can no more be separated from the essence of God than can its having its three angles equal to two right angles be separated from the essence of a [rectilinear] triangle, or the idea of a mountain from the idea of a valley; and so there is not any less repugnance to our conceiving a God (that is, a Being supremely perfect) to whom existence is lacking (that is to say, to whom a certain perfection is lacking), than to conceive of a mountain which has no valley.

But although I cannot really conceive of a God without existence any more than a mountain without a valley, still from the fact that I conceive of a mountain with a valley, it does not follow that there is such a mountain in the world; similarly although I conceive of God as possessing existence, it would seem that it does not follow that there is a God which exists; for my thought does not impose any necessity upon things, and just as I may imagine a winged horse, although no horse with wings exists, so I could perhaps attribute existence to God, although no God existed.

But a sophism is concealed in this objection; for from the fact that I cannot conceive a mountain without a valley, it does not follow that there is any mountain or any valley in existence, but only that the mountain and the valley, whether they exist or do not exist, cannot in any way be separated one from the other. While from the fact that I cannot conceive God without existence, it follows that existence is inseparable from Him, and hence that He really exists; not that my thought can bring this to pass, or impose any necessity on things, but, on the contrary, because the necessity which lies in the thing itself, i.e. the necessity of the existence of God determines me to think in this way. For it is not within my power to think of God without existence (that is of a supremely perfect Being devoid of a supreme perfection) though it is in my power to imagine a horse either with wings or without wings.

And we must not here object that it is in truth necessary for me to assert that God exists after having presupposed that He possesses every sort of perfection, since existence is one of these, but that as a matter of fact my original supposition was not necessary, just as it is not necessary to consider that all quadrilateral figures can be inscribed in the circle; for supposing I thought this, I should be constrained to admit that the rhombus might be inscribed in the circle since it is a quadrilateral figure, which, however, is manifestly false. [We must not, I say, make any such allegations because] although it is not necessary that I should at any time entertain the notion of God, nevertheless whenever it happens that I think of a first and a sovereign Being, and, so to speak, derive the idea of Him from the storehouse of my mind, it is necessary that I should attribute to Him every sort of perfection, although I do not get so far as to enumerate them all, or to apply my mind to each one in particular. And this necessity suffices to make me conclude (after having recognised that existence is a perfection) that this first and sovereign Being really exists; just as though it is not

necessary for me ever to imagine any triangle, yet, whenever I wish to consider a recti-
linear figure composed only of three angles, it is absolutely essential that I should attribute to it all those properties which serve to bring about the conclusion that its three
angles are not greater than two right angles, even although I may not then be considering this point in particular. But when I consider which figures are capable of being
inscribed in the circle, it is in no wise necessary that I should think that all quadrilateral figures are of this number; on the contrary, I cannot even pretend that this is the
case, so long as I do not desire to accept anything which I cannot conceive clearly and
distinctly. And in consequence there is a great difference between the false suppositions
such as this, and the true ideas born within me, the first and principal of which is that
of God. For really I discern in many ways that this idea is not something factitious, and
depending solely on my thought, but that it is the image of a true and immutable nature; first of all, because I cannot conceive anything but God himself to whose essence
existence [necessarily] pertains; in the second because it is not possible for me to conceive two or more Gods in this same position; and, granted that there is one such God
who now exists, I see clearly that it is necessary that He should have existed from all eternity, and that He must exist eternally; and finally, because I know an infinitude of other
properties in God, none of which I can either diminish or change.

For the rest, whatever proof or argument I avail myself of, we must always return
to the point that it is only those things which we conceive clearly and distinctly that
have the power of persuading me entirely. And although amongst the matters which
I conceive of in this way, some indeed are manifestly obvious to all, while others only
manifest themselves to those who consider them closely and examine them attentively;
still, after they have once been discovered, the latter are not esteemed as any less
certain than the former. For example, in the case of every right-angled triangle, although it does not so manifestly appear that the square of the base is equal to the
squares of the two other sides as that this base is opposite to the greatest angle; still,
when this has once been apprehended, we are just as certain of its truth as of the truth
of the other. And as regards God, if my mind were not pre-occupied with prejudices,
and if my thought did not find itself on all hands diverted by the continual pressure
of sensible things, there would be nothing which I could know more immediately and
more easily than Him. For is there anything more manifest than that there is a God,
that is to say, a Supreme Being, to whose essence alone existence pertains?

And although for a firm grasp of this truth I have need of a strenuous application
of mind, at present I not only feel myself to be as assured of it as of all that I hold as
most certain, but I also remark that the certainty of all other things depends on it so
absolutely, that without this knowledge it is impossible ever to know anything perfectly.

For although I am of such a nature that as long as I understand anything very
clearly and distinctly, I am naturally impelled to believe it to be true, yet because I
am also of such a nature that I cannot have my mind constantly fixed on the same
object in order to perceive it clearly, and as I often recollect having formed a past judgment without at the same time properly recollecting the reasons that led me to make
it, it may happen meanwhile that other reasons present themselves to me, which
would easily cause me to change my opinion, if I were ignorant of the facts of the
existence of God, and thus I should have no true and certain knowledge, but only

vague and vacillating opinions. Thus, for example, when I consider the nature of a [rectilinear] triangle, I who have some little knowledge of the principles of geometry recognise quite clearly that the three angles are equal to two right angles, and it is not possible for me not to believe this so long as I apply my mind to its demonstration; but so soon as I abstain from attending to the proof, although I still recollect having clearly comprehended it, it may easily occur that I come to doubt its truth, if I am ignorant of there being a God. For I can persuade myself of having been so constituted by nature that I can easily deceive myself even in those matters which I believe myself to apprehend with the greatest evidence and certainty, especially when I recollect that I have frequently judged matters to be true and certain which other reasons have afterwards impelled me to judge to be altogether false.

But after I have recognised that there is a God—because at the same time I have also recognised that all things depend upon Him, and that He is not a deceiver, and from that have inferred that what I perceive clearly and distinctly cannot fail to be true—although I no longer pay attention to the reasons for which I have judged this to be true, provided that I recollect having clearly and distinctly perceived it no contrary reason can be brought forward which could ever cause me to doubt of its truth; and thus I have a true and certain knowledge of it. And this same knowledge extends likewise to all other things which I recollect having formerly demonstrated, such as the truths of geometry and the like; for what can be alleged against them to cause me to place them in doubt? Will it be said that my nature is such as to cause me to be frequently deceived? But I already know that I cannot be deceived in the judgment whose grounds I know clearly. Will it be said that I formerly held many things to be true and certain which I have afterwards recognised to be false? But I had not had any clear and distinct knowledge of these things, and not as yet knowing the rule whereby I assure myself of the truth, I had been impelled to give my assent from reasons which I have since recognised to be less strong than I had at the time imagined them to be. What further objection can then be raised? That possibly I am dreaming (an objection I myself made a little while ago), or that all the thoughts which I now have are no more true than the phantasies of my dreams? But even though I slept the case would be the same, for all that is clearly present to my mind is absolutely true.

And so I very clearly recognise that the certainty and truth of all knowledge depends alone on the knowledge of the true God, in so much that, before I knew Him, I could not have a perfect knowledge of any other thing. And now that I know Him I have the means of acquiring a perfect knowledge of an infinitude of things, not only of those which relate to God Himself and other intellectual matters, but also of those which pertain to corporeal nature in so far as it is the object of pure mathematics [which have no concern with whether it exists or not].

Meditation VI: Of the Existence of Material Things, and of the Real Distinction Between the Soul and Body of Man

Nothing further now remains but to inquire whether material things exist. And certainly I at least know that these may exist in so far as they are considered as the objects of pure mathematics, since in this aspect I perceive them clearly and distinctly.

For there is no doubt that God possesses the power to produce everything that I am capable of perceiving with distinctness, and I have never deemed that anything was impossible for Him, unless I found a contradiction in attempting to conceive it clearly. Further, the faculty of imagination which I possess, and of which, experience tells me, I make use when I apply myself to the consideration of material things, is capable of persuading me of their existence; for when I attentively consider what imagination is, I find that it is nothing but a certain application of the faculty of knowledge to the body which is immediately present to it, and which therefore exists.

And to render this quite clear, I remark in the first place the difference that exists between the imagination and pure intellection [or conception]. For example, when I imagine a triangle, I do not conceive it only as a figure comprehended by three lines, but I also apprehend these three lines as present by the power and inward vision of my mind, and this is what I call imagining. But if I desire to think of a chiliagon, I certainly conceive truly that it is a figure composed of a thousand sides, just as easily as I conceive of a triangle that it is a figure of three sides only; but I cannot in any way imagine the thousand sides of a chiliagon [as I do the three sides of a triangle], nor do I, so to speak, regard them as present [with the eyes of my mind]. And although in accordance with the habit I have formed of always employing the aid of my imagination when I think of corporeal things, it may happen that in imagining a chiliagon I confusedly represent to myself some figure, yet it is very evident that this figure is not a chiliagon, since it in no way differs from that which I represent to myself when I think of a myriagon or any other many-sided figure; nor does it serve my purpose in discovering the properties which go to form the distinction between a chiliagon and other polygons. But if the question turns upon a pentagon, it is quite true that I can conceive its figure as well as that of a chiliagon without the help of my imagination; but I can also imagine it by applying the attention of my mind to each of its five sides, and at the same time to the space which they enclose. And thus I clearly recognise that I have need of a particular effort of mind in order to effect the act of imagination, such as I do not require in order to understand, and this particular effort of mind clearly manifests the difference which exists between imagination and pure intellection.

I remark besides that this power of imagination which is in one, inasmuch as it differs from the power of understanding, is in no wise a necessary element in my nature, or in [my essence, that is to say, in] the essence of my mind; for although I did not possess it I should doubtless ever remain the same as I now am, from which it appears that we might conclude that it depends on something which differs from me. And I easily conceive that if some body exists with which my mind is conjoined and united in such a way that it can apply itself to consider it when it pleases, it may be that by this means it can imagine corporeal objects; so that this mode of thinking differs from pure intellection only inasmuch as mind in its intellectual activity in some manner turns on itself, and considers some of the ideas which it possesses in itself; while in imagining it turns towards the body, and there beholds in it something conformable to the idea which it has either conceived of itself or perceived by the senses. I easily understand, I say, that the imagination could be thus constituted if it is true that body exists; and because I can discover no other convenient mode of explaining it,

I conjecture with probability that body does exist; but this is only with probability, and although I examine all things with care, I nevertheless do not find that from this distinct idea of corporeal nature, which I have in my imagination, I can derive any argument from which there will necessarily be deduced the existence of body.

But I am in the habit of imagining many other things besides this corporeal nature which is the object of pure mathematics, to wit, the colours, sounds, scents, pain, and other such things, although less distinctly. And inasmuch as I perceive these things much better through the senses, by the medium of which, and by the memory, they seem to have reached my imagination, I believe that, in order to examine them more conveniently, it is right that I should at the same time investigate the nature of sense perception, and that I should see if from the ideas which I apprehend by this mode of thought, which I call feeling, I cannot derive some certain proof of the existence of corporeal objects.

And first of all I shall recall to my memory those matters which I hitherto held to be true, as having perceived them through the senses, and the foundations on which my belief has rested; in the next place I shall examine the reasons which have since obliged me to place them in doubt; in the last place I shall consider which of them I must now believe.

First of all, then, I perceived that I had a head, hands, feet, and all other members of which this body—which I considered as a part, or possibly even as the whole, of myself—is composed. Further I was sensible that this body was placed amidst many others, from which it was capable of being affected in many different ways, beneficial and hurtful, and I remarked that a certain feeling of pleasure accompanied those that were beneficial, and pain those which were harmful. And in addition to this pleasure and pain, I also experienced hunger, thirst, and other similar appetites, as also certain corporeal inclinations towards joy, sadness, anger, and other similar passions. And outside myself, in addition to extension, figure, and motions of bodies, I remarked in them hardness, heat, and all other tactile qualities, and, further, light and colour, and scents and sounds, the variety of which gave me the means of distinguishing the sky, the earth, the sea, and generally all the other bodies, one from the other. And certainly, considering the ideas of all these qualities which presented themselves to my mind, and which alone I perceived properly or immediately, it was not without reason that I believed myself to perceive objects quite different from my though, to wit, bodies from which those ideas proceeded; for I found by experience that these ideas presented themselves to me without my consent being requisite, so that I could not perceive any object, however desirous I might be, unless it were present to the organs of sense; and it was not in my power not to perceive it, when it was present. And because the ideas which I received through the senses were much more lively, more clear, and even, in their own way, more distinct than any of those which I could of myself frame in meditation, or than those I found impressed on my memory, it appeared as though they could not have proceeded from my mind, so that they must necessarily have been produced in me by some other things. And having no knowledge of those objects excepting the knowledge which the ideas themselves gave me, nothing was more likely to occur to my mind than that the objects were similar to the ideas which were caused. And because I likewise remembered that I had formerly made use of my senses rather than my reason, and recognised that the ideas which I formed of myself were not so distinct as those which I perceived through the senses, and that they were most frequently even composed of portions of these last, I persuaded myself easily that I had no idea in my mind which had not formerly come to me through the senses. Nor was it without some reason that I believed that this body (which by a certain special right I call my own) belonged to me more properly and more strictly than any other; for in fact I could never be separated from it as from other bodies; I experienced in it and on account of it all my appetites and affections, and finally I was touched by the feeling of pain and the titillation of pleasure in its parts, and not in the parts of other bodies which were separated from it. But when I inquired, why, from some, I know not what, painful sensation, there follows sadness of mind, and from the pleasurable sensation there arises joy, or why this mysterious pinching of the stomach which I call hunger causes me to desire to eat, and dryness of throat causes a desire to drink, and so on, I could give no reason excepting that nature taught me so; for there is certainly no affinity (that I at least can understand) between the craving of the stomach and the desire to eat, any more than between the perception of whatever causes pain and the thought of sadness which arises from this perception. And in the same way it appeared to me that I had learned from nature all the other judgments which I formed regarding the objects of my senses, since I remarked that these judgments were formed in me before I had the leisure to weigh and consider any reasons which might oblige me to make them.

But afterwards many experiences little by little destroyed all the faith which I had rested in my senses; for I from time to time observed that those towers which from afar appeared to me to be round, more closely observed seemed square, and that colossal statues raised on the summit of these towers, appeared as quite tiny statues when viewed from the bottom; and so in an infinitude of other cases I found error in judgments founded on the external senses. And not only in those founded on the external senses, but even in those founded on the internal as well; for is there anything more intimate or more internal than pain? And yet I have learned from some persons whose arms or legs have been cut off, that they sometimes seemed to feel pain in the part which had been amputated, which made me think that I could not be quite certain that it was a certain member which pained me, even although I felt pain in it. And to those grounds of doubt I have lately added to others, which are very general; the first is that I never have believed myself to feel anything in waking moments which I cannot also sometimes believe myself to feel when I sleep, and as I do not think that these things which I seem to feel in sleep, proceed from objects outside of me, I do not see any reason why I should have this belief regarding objects which I seem to perceive while awake. The other was that being still ignorant, or rather supposing myself to be ignorant, of the author of my being, I saw nothing to prevent me from having been so constituted by nature that I might be deceived even in matters which seemed to me to be most certain. And as to the grounds on which I was formerly persuaded of the truth of sensible objects, I had not much trouble in replying to them. For since nature seemed to cause me to lean towards many things from which reason repelled me, I did not believe that I should trust much to the teachings of nature. And although the ideas which I receive by the senses do not depend on my will, I did not think that one should for that reason conclude that they proceeded from things different from myself, since possibly some faculty might be discovered in me—though hitherto unknown to me—which produced them.

But now that I begin to know myself better, and to discover more clearly the author of my being, I do not in truth think that I should rashly admit all the matters which the senses seem to teach us, but, on the other hand, I do not think that I should doubt them all universally.

And first of all, because I know that all things which I apprehend clearly and distinctly can be created by God as I apprehend them, it suffices that I am able to apprehend one thing apart from another clearly and distinctly in order to be certain that the one is different from the other, since they may be made to exist in separation at least by the omnipotence of God; and it does not signify by what power this separation is made in order to compel me to judge them to be different: and, therefore, just because I know certainly that I exist, and that meanwhile I do not remark that any other thing necessarily pertains to my nature or essence, excepting that I am a thinking thing, I rightly conclude that my essence consists solely in the fact that I am a thinking thing [or a substance whose whole essence or nature is to think]. And although possibly (or rather certainly, as I shall say in a moment) I possess a body with which I am very intimately conjoined, yet because, on the one side, I have a clear and distinct idea of myself inasmuch as I am only a thinking and unextended thing, and as, on the other, I possess a distinct idea of body, inasmuch as it is only an extended and unthinking thing, it is certain that this [that is to say, my soul by which I am what I am], is entirely and absolutely distinct from my body, and can exist without it.

I further find in myself faculties employing modes of thinking peculiar to themselves, to wit, the faculties of imagination and feeling, without which I can easily conceive myself clearly and distinctly as a complete being; while, on the other hand, they cannot be so conceived apart from me, that is without an intelligent substance in which they reside, for [in the notion we have of these faculties, or, to use the language of the Schools] in their formal concept, some kind of intellection is comprised, from which I infer that they are distinct from me as its modes are from a thing. I observe also in me some other faculties such as that of change of position, the assumption of different figures and such like, which cannot be conceived, any more than can the preceding, apart from some substance to which they are attached, and consequently cannot exist without it; but it is very clear that these faculties, if it be true that they exist, must be attached to some corporeal or extended substance, and not to an intelligent substance, since in the clear and distinct conception of these there is some sort of extension found to be present, but no intellection at all. There is certainly further in me a certain passive faculty of perception, that is, of receiving and recognising the ideas of sensible things, but this would be useless to me [and I could in no way avail myself of it], if there were not either in me or in some other thing another active faculty capable of forming and producing these ideas. But this active faculty cannot exist in me [inasmuch as I am a thing that thinks] seeing that it does not presuppose thought, and also that those ideas are often produced in me without my contributing in any way to the same, and often even against my will; it is thus necessarily the case that the faculty resides in some substance different from me in which all the reality which is objectively in the ideas that are produced by this faculty is formally or eminently contained, as I remarked before. And this substance is either a body, that is, a corporeal nature in which there is contained formally [and really] all that which is objectively [and by representation] in those ideas, or it is God Himself, or some other creature more noble than body in which that same is contained eminently. But, since God is no deceiver, it is very manifest that He does not communicate to me these ideas immediately and by Himself, nor yet by the intervention of some creature in which their reality is not formally, but only eminently, contained. For since He has given me no faculty to recognise that this is the case, but, on the other hand, a very great inclination to believe [that they are sent to me or] that they are conveyed to me by corporeal objects, I do not see how He could be defended from the accusation of deceit if these ideas were produced by causes other than corporeal objects. Hence we must allow that corporeal things exist. However, they are perhaps not exactly what we perceive by the senses, since this comprehension by the senses is in many instances very obscure and confused; but we must at least admit that all things which I conceive in them clearly and distinctly, that is to say, all things which, speaking generally, are comprehended in the object of pure mathematics, are truly to be recognised as external objects.

As to other things, however, which are either particular only, as, for example, that the sun is of such and such a figure, etc., or which are less clearly and distinctly conceived, such as light, sound, pain and the like, it is certain that although they are very dubious and uncertain, yet on the sole ground that God is not a deceiver, and that consequently He has not permitted any falsity to exist in my opinion which He has not likewise given me the faculty of correcting, I may assuredly hope to conclude that I have within me the means of arriving at the truth even here. And first of all there is no doubt that in all things which nature teaches me there is some truth contained; for by nature, considered in general, I now understand no other thing than either God Himself or else the order and disposition which God has established in created things; and by my nature in particular I understand no other thing than the complexus of all the things which God has given me.

But there is nothing which this nature teaches me more expressly [nor more sensibly] than that I have a body which is adversely affected when I feel pain, which has need of food or drink when I experience the feelings of hunger and thirst, and so on; nor can I doubt there being some truth in all this.

Nature also teaches me by these sensations of pain, hunger, thirst, etc., that I am not only lodged in my body as a pilot in a vessel, but that I am very closely united to it, and so to speak so intermingled with it that I seem to compose with it one whole. For if that were not the case, when my body is hurt, I, who am merely a thinking thing, should not feel pain, for I should perceive this wound by the understanding only, just as the sailor perceives by sight when something is damaged in his vessel; and when my body has need of drink or food, I should clearly understand the fact without being warned of it by confused feelings of hunger and thirst. For all these sensations of hunger, thirst, pain, etc. are in truth none other than certain confused modes of thought which are produced by the union and apparent intermingling of mind and body.

Moreover, nature teaches me that many other bodies exist around mine, of which some are to be avoided, and others sought after. And certainly from the fact that I am sensible of different sorts of colours, sounds, scents, tastes, heat, hardness, etc., I very easily conclude that there are in the bodies from which all these diverse sense-perceptions proceed certain variations which answer to them, although possibly these are not really at all similar to them. And also from the fact that amongst these different sense-perceptions some are very agreeable to me and others disagreeable, it is quite certain that my body (or rather myself in my entirety, inasmuch as I am formed of body and soul) may receive different impressions agreeable and disagreeable from the other bodies which surround it.

But there are many other things which nature seems to have taught me, but which at the same time I have never really received from her, but which have been brought about in my mind by a certain habit which I have of forming inconsiderate judgments on things; and thus it may easily happen that these judgments contain some error. Take, for example, the opinion which I hold that all space in which there is nothing that affects [or makes an impression on] my senses is void; that in a body which is warm there is something entirely similar to the idea of heat which is in me; that in a white or green body there is the same whiteness or greenness that I perceive; that in a bitter or sweet body there is the same taste, and so on in other instances; that the stars, the towers, and all other distant bodies are of the same figure and size as they appear from far off to our eyes, etc. But in order that in this there should be nothing which I do not conceive distinctly, I should define exactly what I really understand when I say that I am taught somewhat by nature. For here I take nature in a more limited signification than when I term it the sum of all the things given me by God, since in this sum many things are comprehended which only pertain to mind (and to these I do not refer in speaking of nature) such as the notion which I have of the fact that what has once been done cannot ever be undone and an infinitude of such things which I know by the light of nature [without the help of the body]; and seeing that it comprehends many other matters besides which only pertain to body, and are no longer here contained under the nature of nature, such as the quality of weight which it possesses and the like, with which I also do not deal; for in talking of nature I only treat of those things given by God to me as a being composed of mind and body. But the nature here described truly teaches me to flee from things which cause the sensation of pain, and seek after the things which communicate to me the sentiment of pleasure and so forth; but I do not see that beyond this it teaches me that from those diverse sense-perceptions we should ever form any conclusion regarding things outside of us, without having [carefully and maturely] mentally examined them beforehand. For it seems to me that it is mind alone, and not mind and body in conjunction, that is requisite to a knowledge of the truth in regard to such things. Thus, although a star makes no larger an impression on my eye than the flame of a little candle there is yet in me no real or positive propensity impelling me to believe that it is not greater than that flame; but I have judged it to be so from my earliest years, without any rational foundation. And although in approaching fire I feel heat, and in approaching it a little too near I even feel pain, there is at the same time no reason in this which could persuade me that there is in the fire something resembling this heat any more than there is in it something resembling the pain; all that I have any reason to believe from this is, that there is something in it, whatever it may be, which excites in me these sensations of heat or of pain. So also, although there are spaces in which I find nothing which excites my senses, I must not from that conclude that these spaces contain no body; for I see in this, as in other similar things, that I have been in the habit of perverting the order of nature, because these perceptions of sense having been placed within me by nature merely for the purpose of signifying to my mind what things are beneficial or hurtful to the composite whole of which it forms a part, and being up to that point sufficiently clear and distinct, I yet avail myself of them as though they were absolute rules by which I might immediately determine the essence of the bodies which are outside me, as to which, in fact, they can teach me nothing but what is most obscure and confused.

But I have already sufficiently considered how, notwithstanding the supreme goodness of God, falsity enters into the judgments I make. Only here a new difficulty is presented—one respecting those things the pursuit or avoidance of which is taught me by nature, and also respecting the internal sensations which I possess, and in which I seem to have sometimes detected error [and thus to be directly deceived by my own nature]. To take an example, the agreeable taste of some food in which poison has been intermingled may induce me to partake of the poison, and thus deceive me. It is true, at the same time, that in this case nature may be excused, for it only induces me to desire food in which I find a pleasant taste, and not to desire the poison which is unknown to it; and thus I can infer nothing from this fact, except that my nature is not omniscient, at which there is certainly no reason to be astonished, since man, being finite in nature, can only have knowledge the perfectness of which is limited.

But we not infrequently deceive ourselves even in those things to which we are directly impelled by nature, as happens with those who when they are sick desire to drink or eat things hurtful to them. It will perhaps be said here that the cause of their deceptiveness is that their nature is corrupt, but that does not remove the difficulty, because a sick man is none the less truly God's creature than he who is in health; and it is therefore as repugnant to God's goodness for the one to have a deceitful nature as it is for the other. And as a clock composed of wheels and counterweights no less exactly observes the laws of nature when it is badly made, and does not show the time properly, than when it entirely satisfies the wishes of its maker, and as, if I consider the body of a man as being a sort of machine so built up and composed of nerves, muscles, veins, blood and skin, that although there were no mind in it at all, it would not cease to have the same motions as at present, exception being made of those movements which are due to the direction of the will, and in consequence depend upon the mind [as opposed to those which operate by the disposition of its organs], I easily recognise that it would be as natural to this body, supposing it to be, for example, dropsical, to suffer the parchedness of the throat which usually signifies to the mind the feeling of thirst, and to be disposed by this parched feeling to move the nerves and other parts in the way requisite for drinking, and thus to augment its malady and do harm to itself, as it is natural to it, when it has no indisposition, to be impelled to drink for its good by a similar cause. And although, considering the use to which the clock has been destined by its maker, I may say that it deflects from the order of its nature when it does not indicate the hours correctly; and as, in the same way, considering the machine of the human body as having been formed by God in order to have in itself all the movements usually manifested there, I have reason for thinking that it does not follow the order of nature when, if the throat is dry, drinking does harm to the conservation of health, nevertheless I recognise at the same time that this last mode of explaining nature is very different from the other. For this is but a purely verbal characterisation depending entirely on my thought, which compares a sick man and a badly constructed clock with the idea which I have of a healthy man and a well made clock, and it is hence extrinsic to the things to which it is applied; but according to the other interpretation of the term nature I understand something which is truly found in things and which is therefore not without some truth.

But certainly although in regard to the dropsical body it is only so to speak to supply an extrinsic term when we say that its nature is corrupted, inasmuch as apart from the need to drink, the throat is parched; yet in regard to the composite whole, that is to say, to the mind or soul united to this body, it is not a purely verbal predicate, but a real error of nature, for it to have thirst when drinking would be hurtful to it. And thus it still remains to inquire how the goodness of God does not prevent the nature of man so regarded from being fallacious.

In order to begin this examination, then, I here say, in the first place, that there is a great difference between mind and body, inasmuch as body is by nature always divisible, and the mind is entirely indivisible. For, as a matter of fact, when I consider the mind, that is to say, myself inasmuch as I am only a thinking thing, I cannot distinguish in myself any parts, but apprehend myself to be clearly one and entire; and although the whole mind seems to be united to the whole body, yet if a foot, or an arm, or some other part, is separated from my body, I am aware that nothing has been taken away from my mind. And the faculties of willing, feeling, conceiving, etc. cannot be properly speaking said to be its parts, for it is one and the same mind which employs itself in willing and in feeling and understanding. But it is quite otherwise with corporeal or extended objects, for there is not one of these imaginable by me which my mind cannot easily divide into parts, and which consequently I do not recognise as being divisible; this would be sufficient to teach me that the mind or soul of man is entirely different from the body, if I had not already learned it from other sources.

I further notice that the mind does not receive the impressions from all parts of the body immediately, but only from the brain, or perhaps even from one of its smallest parts, to wit, from that in which the common sense is said to reside, which, whenever it is disposed in the same particular way, conveys the same thing to the mind, although meanwhile the other portions of the body may be differently disposed, as is testified by innumerable experiments which it is unnecessary here to recount.

I notice, also, that the nature of body is such that none of its parts can be moved by another part a little way off which cannot also be moved in the same way by each one of the parts which are between the two, although this more remote part does not act at all. As, for example, in the cord *ABCD* [which is in tension] if we pull the last part *D*, the first part *A* will not be moved in any way differently from what would be the case if one of the intervening parts *B* or *C* were pulled, and the last part *D* were to remain unmoved. And in the same way, when I feel pain in my foot, my knowledge of physics teaches me that this sensation is communicated by means of nerves dispersed through the foot, which, being extended like cords from there to the brain, when they are contracted in the foot, at the same time contract the inmost portions of the brain which is their extremity and place of origin, and then excite a certain movement which nature has established in order to cause the mind to be affected by a sensation of pain represented as existing in the foot. But because these nerves must pass through the tibia, the thigh, the loins, the back and the neck, in order to reach from the leg to the brain, it may happen that although their extremities which are in the foot are not affected, but only certain ones of their intervening parts [which pass by the loins or the neck], this action will excite the same movement in the brain that might have been excited there by a hurt received in the foot, in consequence of which the mind will necessarily feel in the foot the same pain as if it had received a hurt. And the same holds good of all the other perceptions of our senses.

I notice finally that since each of the movements which are in the portion of the brain by which the mind is immediately affected brings about one particular sensation only, we cannot under the circumstances imagine anything more likely than that this movement, amongst all the sensations which it is capable of impressing on it, causes mind to be affected by that one which is best fitted and most generally useful for the conservation of the human body when it is in health. But experience makes us aware that all the feelings with which nature inspires us are such as I have just spoken of; and there is therefore nothing in them which does not give testimony to the power and goodness of the God [who has produced them]. Thus, for example, when the nerves which are in the feet are violently or more than usually moved, their movement, passing through the medulla of the spine to the inmost parts of the brain, gives a sign to the mind which makes it feel somewhat, to wit, pain, as though in the foot, by which the mind is excited to do its utmost to remove the cause of the evil as dangerous and hurtful to the foot. It is true that God could have constituted the nature of man in such a way that this same movement in the brain would have conveyed something quite different to the mind; for example, it might have produced consciousness of itself either in so far as it is in the brain, or as it is in the foot, or as it is in some other place between the foot and the brain, or it might finally have produced consciousness of anything else whatsoever; but none of all this would have contributed so well to the conservation of the body. Similarly, when we desire to drink, a certain dryness of the throat is produced which moves its nerves, and by their means the internal portions of the brain; and this movement causes in the mind the sensation of thirst, because in this case there is nothing more useful to us than to become aware that we have need to drink for the conservation of our health; and the same holds good in other instances.

From this it is quite clear that, notwithstanding the supreme goodness of God, the nature of man, inasmuch as it is composed of mind and body, cannot be otherwise than sometimes a source of deception. For if there is any cause which excites, not in the foot but in some part of the nerves which are extended between the foot and the brain, or even in the brain itself, the same movement which usually is produced when the foot is detrimentally affected, pain will be experienced as though it were in the foot, and the sense will thus naturally be deceived; for since the same movement in the brain is capable of causing but one sensation in the mind, and this sensation is much more frequently excited by a cause which hurts the foot than by another existing in some other quarter, it is reasonable that it should convey to the mind pain in the foot rather than in any other part of the body. And although the parchedness of the throat does not always proceed, as it usually does, from the fact that drinking is necessary for the health of the body, but sometimes comes from quite a different cause, as is the case with dropsical patients, it is yet much better that it should mislead on this occasion than if, on the other hand, it were always to deceive us when the body is in good health; and so on in similar cases.

And certainly this consideration is of great service to me, not only in enabling me to recognise all the errors to which my nature is subject, but also in enabling me to avoid them or to correct them more easily. For knowing that all my senses more frequently indicate to me truth than falsehood respecting the things which concern that which is beneficial to the body, and being able almost always to avail myself of many of them in order to examine one particular thing, and, besides that, being able to make use of my memory in order to connect the present with the past, and of my understanding which already has discovered all the causes of my errors, I ought no longer to fear that falsity may be found in matters every day presented to me by my senses. And I ought to set aside all the doubts of these past days as hyperbolical and ridiculous, particularly that very common uncertainty respecting sleep, which I could not distinguish from the waking state; for at present I find a very notable difference between the two, inasmuch as our memory can never connect our dreams one with the other, or with the whole course of our lives, as it unites events which happen to us while we are awake. And, as a matter of fact, if someone, while I was awake, quite suddenly appeared to me and disappeared as fast as do the images which I see in sleep, so that I could not know from whence the form came nor whither it went, it would not be without reason that I should deem it a spectre or a phantom formed by my brain [and similar to those which I form in sleep], rather than a real man. But when I perceive things as to which I know distinctly both the place from which they proceed, and that in which they are, and the time at which they appeared to me; and when, without any interruption, I can connect the perceptions which I have of them with the whole course of my life, I am perfectly assured that these perceptions occur while I am waking and not during sleep. And I ought in no wise to doubt the truth of such matters, if, after having called up all my senses, my memory, and my understanding, to examine them, nothing is brought to evidence by any one of them which is repugnant to what is set forth by the others. For because God is in no wise a deceiver, it follows that I am not deceived in this. But because the exigencies of action often oblige us to make up our minds before having leisure to examine matters carefully, we must confess that the life of man is very frequently subject to error in respect to individual objects, and we must in the end acknowledge the infirmity of our nature.

DAVID HUME

Induction Cannot Be Rationally Justified

In this excerpt from his *An Enquiry Concerning Human Understanding*, Hume (1711–1776) argues that there can be no rational justification of the inductions that people perform. The reason is that all such inductions depend on the Principle of the Uniformity of Nature, and this principle cannot be given a rational justification.

SKEPTICAL DOUBTS CONCERNING THE OPERATIONS OF THE UNDERSTANDING

Part I

All the objects of human reason or inquiry may naturally be divided into two kinds, to wit, "Relations of Ideas," and "Matters of Fact." Of the first kind are the sciences of Geometry, Algebra, and Arithmetic, and, in short, every affirmation which is either intuitively or demonstratively certain. *That the square of the hypotenuse is equal to the square of the two sides* is a proposition which expresses a relation between these figures. *That three times five is equal to the half of thirty* expresses a relation between these numbers. Propositions of this kind are discoverable by the mere operation of thought, without dependence on what is anywhere existent in the universe. Though there never were a circle or triangle in nature, the truths demonstrated by Euclid would forever retain their certainty and evidence.

Matters of fact, which are the second objects of human reason, are not ascertained in the same manner, nor is our evidence of their truth, however great, of a like nature with the foregoing. The contrary of every matter of fact is still possible, because it can never imply a contradiction and is conceived by the mind with the same facility and distinctness as if ever so conformable to reality. *That the sun will not rise tomorrow* is no less intelligible a proposition and implies no more contradiction than the affirmation *that it will rise*. We should in vain, therefore, attempt to demonstrate its falsehood. Were it demonstratively false, it would imply a contradiction and could never be distinctly conceived by the mind.

It may, therefore, be a subject worthy of curiosity to inquire what is the nature of that evidence which assures us of any real existence and matter of fact beyond the present testimony of our senses or the records of our memory. This part of philosophy, it is observable, had been little cultivated either by the ancients or moderns; and, therefore, our doubts and errors in the prosecution of so important an inquiry may be the more excusable while we march through such difficult paths without any guide or direction. They may even prove useful by exciting curiosity and destroying that implicit faith and security which is the bane of all reasoning and free inquiry. The discovery of defects in the common philosophy, if any such there be, will not, I

David Hume, "Induction Cannot Be Rationally Justified," from *An Enquiry Concerning Human Understanding*, edited by Charles W. Hendel (New York: Macmillan, 1957), pp. 40–53.

presume, be a discouragement, but rather an incitement, as is usual, to attempt something more full and satisfactory than has yet been proposed to the public.

All reasoning concerning matters of fact seem to be founded on the relation of *cause* and *effect*. By means of that relation alone we can go beyond the evidence of our memory and senses. If you were to ask a man why he believes any matter of fact which is absent, for instance, that his friend is in the country or in France, he would give you a reason, and this reason would be some other fact: as a letter received from him or the knowledge of his former resolutions and promises. A man finding a watch or any other machine in a desert island would conclude that there had once been men in that island. All our reasonings concerning fact are of the same nature. And here it is constantly supposed that there is a connection between the present fact and that which is inferred from it. Were there nothing to bind them together, the inference would be entirely precarious. The hearing of an articulate voice and rational discourse in the dark assures us of the presence of some person. Why? Because these are the effects of the human make and fabric, and closely connected with it. If we anatomize all the other reasonings of this nature, we shall find that they are founded on the relation of cause and effect, and that this relation is either near or remote, direct or collateral. Heat and light are collateral effects of fire, and the one effect may justly be inferred from the other.

If we would satisfy ourselves, therefore, concerning the nature of that evidence which assures us of matters of fact, we must inquire how we arrive at the knowledge of cause and effect.

I shall venture to affirm, as a general proposition which admits of no exception, that the knowledge of this relation is not, in any instance, attained by reasonings *a priori*, but arises entirely from experience, when we find that any particular objects are constantly conjoined with each other. Let an object be presented to a man of ever so strong natural reason and abilities—if that object be entirely new to him, he will not be able, by the most accurate examination of its sensible qualities, to discover any of its causes or effects. Adam, though his rational faculties may be supposed, at the very first, entirely perfect, could not have inferred from the fluidity and transparency of water that it would suffocate him, or from the light and warmth of fire that it would consume him. No object ever discovers, by the qualities which appear to the senses, either the causes which produced it or the effects which will arise from it; nor can our reason, unassisted by experience, ever draw any inference concerning real existence and matter of fact.

This proposition, *that causes and effects are discoverable, not by reason, but by experience,* will readily be admitted with regard to such objects as we remember to have once been altogether unknown to us, since we must be conscious of the utter inability which we then lay under of foretelling what would arise from them. Present two smooth pieces of marble to a man who has no tincture of natural philosophy; he will never discover that they will adhere together in such a manner as to require great force to separate them in a direct line, while they make so small a resistance to a lateral pressure. Such events as bear little analogy to the common course of nature are also readily confessed to be known only by experience, nor does any man imagine that the explosion of gunpowder or the attraction of a loadstone could ever be discovered by arguments *a priori.* In like manner, when an effect is supposed to depend upon an intricate machinery or secret structure of parts, we make no difficulty in attributing all our knowledge of it to experience. Who will assert that he can give the ultimate reason why milk or bread is proper nourishment for a man, not for a lion or tiger?

But the same truth may not appear at first sight to have the same evidence with regard to events which have become familiar to us from our first appearance in the world, which bear a close analogy to the whole course of nature, and which are supposed to depend on the simple qualities of objects without any secret structure of parts. We are apt to imagine that we could discover these effects by the mere operation of our reason without experience. We fancy that, were we brought on a sudden into this world, we could at first have inferred that one billiard ball would communicate motion to another upon impulse, and that we needed not have waited for the event in order to pronounce with certainty concerning it. Such is the influence of custom that where it is strongest it not only covers our natural ignorance but even conceals itself, and seems not to take place, merely because it is found in the highest degree.

But to convince us that all the laws of nature and all the operations of bodies without exception are known only by experience, the following reflections may perhaps suffice. Were any object presented to us, and were we required to pronounce concerning the effect which will result from it without consulting past observation, after what manner, I beseech you, must the mind proceed in this operation? It must invent or imagine some event which it ascribes to the object as its effect; and it is plain that this invention must be entirely arbitrary. The mind can never possibly find the effect in the supposed cause by the more accurate scrutiny and examination. For the effect is totally different from the cause, and consequently can never be discovered in it. Motion in the second billiard ball is a quite distinct event from motion in the first, nor is there anything in the one to suggest the smallest hint of the other. A stone or piece of metal raised into the air and left without any support immediately falls. But to consider the matter *a priori,* is there anything we discover in this situation which can beget the idea of a downward rather than an upward or any other motion in the stone or metal?

And as the first imagination or invention of a particular effect in all natural operations is arbitrary where we consult not experience, so must we also esteem the supposed tie or connection between the cause and effect which binds them together and renders it impossible that any other effect could result from the operation of that cause. When I see, for instance, a billiard ball moving in a straight line toward another, even suppose motion in the second ball should by accident be suggested to me as the result of their contact or impulse, may I not conceive that a hundred different events might as well follow from that cause? May not both these balls remain at absolute rest? May not the first ball return in a straight line or leap off from the second in any line or direction? All these suppositions are consistent and conceivable. Why, then, should we give the preference to one which is no more consistent or conceivable than the rest? All our reasonings *a priori* will never be able to show us any foundation for this preference.

In a word, then, every effect is a distinct event from its cause. It could not, therefore, be discovered in the cause, and the first invention or conception of it, *a priori*, must be entirely arbitrary. And even after it is suggested, the conjunction of it with the cause must appear equally arbitrary, since there are always many other effects which, to reason, must seem fully as consistent and natural. In vain, therefore, should we pretend to determine any single event or infer any cause or effect without the assistance of observation and experience.

Hence we may discover the reason why no philosopher who is rational and modest has ever pretended to assign the ultimate cause of any natural operation, or to show distinctly the action of that power which produces any single effect in the universe. It is confessed that the utmost effort of human reason is to reduce the principles productive of natural phenomena to a greater simplicity, and to resolve the many particular effects into a few general causes, by means of reasonings from analogy, experience, and observation. But as to the causes of these general causes, we should in vain attempt their discovery, nor shall we ever be able to satisfy ourselves by any particular explication of them. These ultimate springs and principles are totally shut up from human curiosity and inquiry. Elasticity, gravity, cohesion of parts, communication of motion by impulse—these are probably the ultimate causes and principles which we shall ever discover in nature; and we may esteem ourselves sufficiently happy if, by accurate inquiry and reasoning, we can trace up the particular phenomena to, or near to, these general principles. The most perfect philosophy of the natural kind only staves off our ignorance a little longer, as perhaps the most perfect philosophy of the moral or metaphysical kind serves only to discover larger portions of it. Thus the observation of human blindness and weakness is the result of all philosophy, and meets us, at every turn, in spite of our endeavors to elude or avoid it.

Nor is geometry, when taken into the assistance of natural philosophy, ever able to remedy this defect or lead us into the knowledge of ultimate causes by all that accuracy of reasoning for which it is so justly celebrated. Every part of mixed mathematics proceeds upon the supposition that certain laws are established by nature in her operations, and abstract reasonings are employed either to assist experience in the discovery of these laws or to determine their influence in particular instances where it depends upon any precise degree of distance and quantity. Thus it is a law of motion, discovered by experience, that the moment or force of any body in motion is in the compound ratio or proportion of its solid contents and its velocity, and, consequently, that a small force may remove the greatest obstacle or raise the greatest weight if by any contrivance or machinery we can increase the velocity of that force so as to make it an overmatch for its antagonist. Geometry assists us in the application of this law by giving us the just dimensions of all the parts and figures which can enter into any species of machine, but still the discovery of the law itself is owing merely to experience; and all the abstract reasonings in the world could never lead us one step toward the knowledge of it. When we reason *a priori* and consider merely any object or cause as it appears to the mind, independent of all observation, it never could suggest to us the notion of any distinct object, such as its effect, much less show us the inseparable and inviolable connection between them. A man must be very sagacious who could discover by reasoning that crystal is the effect of heat, and ice of cold, without being previously acquainted with the operation of these qualities.

Part II

But we have not yet attained any tolerable satisfaction with regard to the question first proposed. Each solution still gives rise to a new question as difficult as the foregoing and leads us on to further inquiries. When it is asked, *What is the nature of all our reasonings concerning matter of fact?* the proper answer seems to be, That they are founded on the relation of cause and effect. When again it is asked, *What is the foundation of all our reasonings and conclusions concerning that relation?* it may be replied in one word, *experience*. But if we still carry on our sifting humor and ask, *What is the foundation of all conclusions from experience?* this implies a new question which may be of more difficult solution and explication. Philosophers that give themselves airs of superior wisdom and sufficiency have a hard task when they encounter persons of inquisitive dispositions, who push them from every corner to which they retreat, and who are sure at least to bring them to some dangerous dilemma. The best expedient to prevent this confusion is to be modest in our pretensions and even to discover the difficulty ourselves before it is objected to us. By this means we may make a kind of merit of our very ignorance.

I shall content myself in this section with an easy task and shall pretend only to give a negative answer to the question here proposed. I say, then, that even after we have experience of the operations of cause and effect, our conclusions from that experience are *not* founded on reasoning or any process of the understanding. This answer we must endeavor both to explain and to defend.

It must certainly be allowed that nature has kept us at a great distance from all her secrets and has afforded us only the knowledge of a few superficial qualities of objects, while she conceals from us those powers and principles on which the influence of these objects entirely depends. Our senses inform us of the color, weight, and consistency of bread, but neither sense nor reason can ever inform us of those qualities which fit it for the nourishment and support of the human body. Sight or feeling conveys an idea of the actual motion of bodies, but as to that wonderful force or power which would carry on a moving body forever in a continued change of place, and which bodies never lose but by communicating it to others, of this we cannot form the most distant conception. But notwithstanding this ignorance of natural powers and principles, we always presume when we see like sensible qualities that they have like secret powers, and expect that effects similar to those which we have experienced will follow from them. If a body of like color and consistency with that bread which we have formerly eaten be presented to us, we make no scruple of repeating the experiment and foresee with certainty like nourishment and support. Now this is a process of the mind or thought of which I would willingly know the foundation. It is allowed on all hands that there is no known connection between the sensible qualities and the secret powers, and, consequently, that the mind is not led to form such a conclusion concerning their constant and regular conjunction by anything which it knows of their nature. As to past *experience,* it can be allowed to give *direct* and *certain* information of those precise objects only, and that precise period of time which fell under its cognizance: But why this experience should be extended to future times and to other objects which, for aught we know, may be only in appearance similar, this is the main question on which I would insist. The bread which I formerly ate nourished me; that is, a body of such sensible qualities was, at that time, endued with such secret powers. But does it follow that other bread must also nourish me at another time, and that like sensible qualities must always be attended with like secret powers? The consequence seems nowise necessary. At least, it must be acknowledged that there is here a consequence drawn by the mind that there is a certain step taken, a process of thought, and an inference which wants to be explained. These two propositions are far from being the same: *I have found that such an object has always been attended with such an effect,* and *I foresee that other objects which are in appearance similar will be attended with similar effects.* I shall allow, if you please, that the one proposition may justly be inferred from the other: I know, in fact, that it always is inferred. But if you insist that the inference is made by a chain of reasoning, I desire you to produce that reasoning. The connection between these propositions is not intuitive. There is required a medium which may enable the mind to draw such an inference, if indeed it be drawn by reasoning and argument. What that medium is I must confess passes my comprehension; and it is incumbent on those to produce it who assert that it really exists and is the original of all our conclusions concerning matter of fact.

This negative argument must certainly, in process of time, become altogether convincing if many penetrating and able philosophers shall turn their inquiries this way, and no one be ever able to discover any connecting proposition or intermediate step which supports the understanding in this conclusion. But as the question is yet new, every reader may not trust so far to his own penetration as to conclude, because an argument escapes his inquiry, that therefore it does not really exist. For this reason it may be requisite to venture upon a more difficult task, and, enumerating all the branches of human knowledge, endeavor to show that none of them can afford such an argument.

All reasonings may be divided into two kinds, namely, demonstrative reasoning, or that concerning relations of ideas, and moral reasoning, or that concerning matter of fact and existence. That there are no demonstrative arguments in the case seems evident, since it implies no contradiction that the course of nature may change and that an object, seemingly like those which we have experienced, may be attended with different or contrary effects. May I not clearly and distinctly conceive that a body, falling from the clouds and which in all other respects resembles snow, has yet the taste of salt or feeling of fire? Is there any more intelligible proposition than to affirm that all the trees will flourish in December and January, and will decay in May and June? Now, whatever is intelligible and can be distinctly conceived implies no contradiction and can never be proved false by any demonstrative argument or abstract reasoning *a priori.*

If we be, therefore, engaged by arguments to put trust in past experience and make it the standard of our future judgment, these arguments must be probable only, or such as regard matter of fact and real existence, according to the division above mentioned. But that there is no argument of this kind must appear if our explication of that species of reasoning be admitted as solid and satisfactory. We have said that all arguments concerning existence are founded on the relation of cause and effect, that our knowledge of that relation is derived entirely from experience, and that all our experimental conclusions proceed upon the supposition that the future will be conformable to the past. To endeavor, therefore, the proof of this last supposition by probable arguments, or arguments regarding existence, must be evidently going in a circle and taking that for granted which is the very point in question.

In reality, all arguments from experience are founded on the similarity which we discover among natural objects, and by which we are induced to expect effects similar to those which we have found to follow from such objects. And though none but a fool or madman will ever pretend to dispute the authority of experience or to reject that great guide of human life, it may surely be allowed a philosopher to have so much curiosity at least as to examine the principle of human nature which gives this might authority to experience and makes us draw advantage from that similarity which nature has placed among different objects. From causes which appear similar, we expect similar effects. This is the sum of all our experimental conclusions. Now it seems evident that, if this conclusion were formed by reason, it would be as perfect at first, and upon one instance, as after ever so long a course of experience; but the case is far otherwise. Nothing is so like as eggs, yet no one, on account of this appearing similarity, expects the same taste and relish in all of them. It is only after a long course of uniform experiments in any kind that we attain a firm reliance and security with regard to a particular event. Now, where is that process of reasoning which, from one instance, draws a conclusion so different from that which it infers from a hundred instances that are nowise different from that single one? This question I propose as much for the sake of information as with an intention of raising difficulties. I cannot find, I cannot imagine any such reasoning. But I keep my mind still open to instruction if anyone will vouchsafe to bestow it on me.

Should it be said that, from a number of uniform experiments, we *infer* a connection between the sensible qualities and the secret powers, this, I must confess, seems the same difficulty, couched in different terms. The question still occurs, On what process of argument is this *inference* founded? Where is the medium, the interposing ideas which join propositions so very wide of each other? It is confessed that the color, consistency, and other sensible qualities of bread appear not of themselves to have any connection with the secret powers of nourishment and support; for otherwise we could infer these secret powers from the first appearance of these sensible qualities without the aid of experience, contrary to the sentiment of all philosophers, and contrary to plain matter of fact. Here, then, is our natural state of ignorance with regard to the powers and influence of all objects. How is this remedied by experience? It only shows us a number of uniform effects resulting from certain objects, and teaches us that those particular objects, at that particular time, were endowed with such powers and forces. When a new object endowed with similar sensible qualities is produced, we expect similar powers and forces, and look for a like effect. From a body of like color and consistency with bread, we expect like nourishment and support. But this surely is a step or progress of the mind which wants to be explained. When a man says, *I have found, in all past instances, such sensible qualities, conjoined with such secret powers,* and when he says, *similar sensible qualities will always be conjoined with similar secret powers,* he is not guilty of tautology, nor are these propositions in any respect the same. You say that the one proposition is an inference from the other; but you must confess that the inference is not intuitive, neither is it demonstrative. Of what nature is it then? To say it is experimental is begging the question. For all inferences from experience suppose, as their foundation, that the future will resemble the past and that similar powers will be conjoined with similar sensible qualities. If there be any suspicion that the course of nature may change, and that the past may be no rule for the future, all experience becomes useless and can give rise to no inference or conclusion. It is impossible, therefore, that any arguments from experience can prove this resemblance of the past to the future, since all these arguments are founded on the supposition of that resemblance. Let the course of things be allowed hitherto ever so regular, that alone, without some new argument or inference, proves not that for the future it will continue so. In vain do you pretend to have learned the nature of bodies from your past experience. Their secret nature, and consequently all their effects and influence, may change without any change in their sensible qualities. This happens sometimes, and with regard to some objects. Why may it not happen always, and with regard to all objects? What logic, what process of argument secures you against this supposition? My practice, you say, refutes my doubts. But you mistake the purport of my question. As an agent, I am quite satisfied in the point; but as a philosopher who has some share of curiosity, I will not say skepticism, I want to learn the foundation of this inference. No reading, no inquiry has yet been able to remove my difficulty or give me satisfaction in a matter of such importance. Can I do better than propose the difficulty to the public, even though, perhaps, I have small hopes of obtaining a solution? We shall at least, by this means, be sensible of our ignorance, if we do not augment our knowledge.

I must confess that a man is guilty of unpardonable arrogance who concludes, because an argument has escaped his own investigation, that therefore it does not really exist. I must also confess that, though all the learned, for several ages, should have employed themselves in fruitless search upon any subject, it may still, perhaps, be rash to conclude positively that the subject must therefore pass all human comprehension. Even though we examine all the sources of our knowledge and conclude them unfit for such a subject, there may still remain a suspicion that the enumeration is not complete or the examination not accurate. But with regard to the present subject, there are some considerations which seem to remove all this accusation of arrogance or suspicion of mistake.

It is certain that the most ignorant and stupid peasants, nay infants, nay even brute beasts, improve by experience and learn the qualities of natural objects by observing the effects which result from them. When a child has felt the sensation of pain from touching the flame of a candle, he will be careful not to put his hand near any candle, but will expect a similar effect from a cause which is similar in its sensible qualities and appearance. If you assert, therefore, that the understanding of the child is led into this conclusion by any process of argument or ratiocination,

I may justly require you to produce that argument, nor have you any pretense to refuse so equitable a demand. You cannot say that the argument is abstruse and may possibly escape your inquiry, since you confess that it is obvious to the capacity of a mere infant. If you hesitate, therefore, a moment or if, after reflection, you produce an intricate or profound argument, you, in a manner, give up the question and confess that it is not reasoning which engages us to suppose the past resembling the future, and to expect similar effects from causes which are to appearance similar. This is the proposition which I intended to enforce in the present section. If I be right, I pretend not to have made any mighty discovery. And if I be wrong, I must acknowledge myself to be indeed a very backward scholar, since I cannot now discover an argument which, it seems, was perfectly familiar to me long before I was out of my cradle.

Suggestions for Further Reading

ON DESCARTES
Bernard Williams, *Descartes: The Project of Pure Inquiry*. London, Harvester Press, 1978.
Margaret Wilson, *Descartes*. London, Routledge and Kegan Paul, 1978.

ON THE RELIABILITY THEORY OF KNOWLEDGE
David Armstrong, *Belief, Knowledge, and Truth*. London, Cambridge University Press, 1973.
Fred Dretske, *Knowledge and the Flow of Information*. Cambridge, Massachusetts, MIT Press, 1981.
Alvin Goldman, "A Causal Theory of Knowing," *Journal of Philosophy*, vol. 64, pp. 357–372, 1967.
Robert Nozick, *Philosophical Explanations*. Cambridge, Massachusetts, Harvard University Press, 1981.

ON HUME
Barry Stroud, *Hume*. London, Routledge and Kegan Paul, 1977.

ON INDUCTION
Nelson Goodman, *Fact, Fiction, and Forecast*. Indianapolis, Bobbs Merrill, 1965.
Wesley Salmon, *Foundations of Scientific Inference*. Pittsburgh, Pennsylvania, University of Pittsburgh Press, 1968.
Brian Skyrms, *Choice and Chance*. Belmont, California, Wadsworth, 1986.
Elliott Sober, *Reconstructing the Past—Parsimony, Evolution, and Inference*. Cambridge, Massachusetts, MIT Press, chapter 2.

PART IV
PHILOSOPHY OF MIND

LECTURE 18

Dualism and the Mind/Body Problem

In this section of the book on philosophy of mind, I'll discuss three problems. The first is the mind/body problem (Lectures 18–22). The second is the problem of free will (Lectures 23–25). The last is the problem of psychological egoism (Lecture 26).

In different ways, the mind/body problem and the problem of free will address the issue of how the mind is related to the physical world of cause and effect. Is the mind a different thing from the body; or is the mind part of the physical world? If your beliefs and desires are caused by physical events outside of yourself, can it be true that you act the way you do of your own free will? The last problem—the problem of psychological egoism—concerns the motives that drive us to act the way we do. Are people genuinely moved by the welfare of others, or is all behavior, in reality, selfish?

These three problems concern different stages in the causal chain that leads from genes and environment, to the mind, to action:

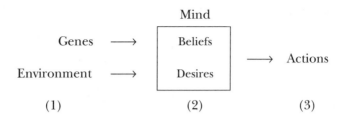

The mind/body problem concerns the nature of the objects and events that exist at stage 2 in this diagram. What is a mind? What are beliefs and desires? The problem of free will concerns the relation of stage 1 to stage 2. If our beliefs and desires are caused by the genes we possess and the environments we have inhabited, how can we possess free will? The problem of psychological egoism concerns the relationship of stages 2 and 3. If the actions we perform are caused by the desires we have, won't it be true that action is fundamentally selfish—aimed at satisfying the actor's own desires, not at satisfying the needs of others?

Of course, these are only preliminary statements of the philosophical problems. Each will be refined when the time comes.

WHAT IS THE MIND/BODY PROBLEM?

The question posed by the mind/body problem is simple: What is the relationship between the mental and the physical? I have a mind, which contains various beliefs, desires, sensations, and emotions. I also have a brain; this physical thing is a structured piece of tissue containing an intricate web of neurons. Are the mind and the brain one and the same thing? Are my beliefs, desires, emotions, and sensations identical with physical things found in my brain? Or are the mind and the brain different objects?

DESCARTES'S DUALISM

In the previous chapter, the discussion of Descartes focused on his epistemology. Descartes also advanced a solution to the mind/body problem. It is this view, now called Cartesian Dualism, that I'll discuss in this lecture. Dualism is the idea that there are two kinds of things in the world. There are physical objects on the one hand, and, on the other, there are mental objects (like minds, pains, beliefs, etc.).

Descartes didn't deny that there is a causal interaction between the mental and the physical: taking aspirin can cure headaches, and the sound of trumpets can lift your spirits. In the other direction, it seems undeniable that beliefs and desires can cause the parts of your body to move in various ways (speaking, walking, etc.). But granting this two-way interaction didn't drive Descartes to abandon dualism.

THE MIND/BRAIN IDENTITY THEORY

One alternative to dualism is provided by the Mind/Brain Identity Theory. This theory makes a claim about objects and also about the properties those objects possess. First, it says that your mind and your brain are one and the same object. Second, it claims that the mental properties you have (for example, believing that fire is hot, or wanting some ice cream, or being in pain) are physical properties; to be in pain is to have some physical event occur in your central nervous system.

The identity theory asserts that mental terminology and physical terminology describe the same items in the world. The following analogy may be instructive. People for a long time used the term "water" to denote various items in the world. This term was used in everyday life. At a certain point in the history of science, it was discovered that water is made of H_2O molecules. The discovery was that water and H_2O are one and the same thing.

There certainly is a difference between the two pieces of terminology "water" and "H_2O." The first word has been used by ordinary people for a very long time. The second term was introduced much more recently, as part of a scientific theory. Yet it doesn't follow from this that the terms denote different things. Water is identical with H_2O, as chemistry has discovered.

Philosophers who defend the Mind/Brain Identity Theory say that the same point applies to the relationship of mental terms and neurophysiological terms. Common sense has for a very long time deployed terms like "belief," "desire," "pain," and "mind." The identity theory suggests that what happened to water will happen to the mind. Eventually, neurophysiology will discover the nature of the mind, just as chemistry discovered the nature of water. Once various scientific theories have been developed, we will be able to say what it is to believe that snow is white, what it is to want some coffee, what it is to feel pain, what it is to have a mind. In each case, the answer will be given in the vocabulary provided by brain science. Right now, we have only a very partial picture of what these neurophysiological theories will be like. However, the identity theory predicts that science is headed in the direction of a purely materialistic account of the mind. The mind is a physical thing, even though we now have only an incomplete picture of what its physical nature is.

In addition to dualism and the Mind/Brain Identity Theory, there are other solutions to the mind/body problem that I'll discuss. These are logical behaviorism (Lecture 19) and functionalism (Lecture 22). Rather than describing them right now, I'll turn to the task of analyzing Cartesian Dualism.

IMMORTALITY OF THE SOUL

Before I present Descartes's arguments for dualism, I should note a connection between the mind/body problem and an issue in the philosophy of religion. If you believe the doctrine of the immortality of the soul but also hold that the body disintegrates at death, you may be attracted by dualism. The issue of whether the soul is immortal, of course, isn't the same as the question of whether there is a God. After all, there are many religions that deny the immortality of the soul. And conceivably someone might hold that the soul survives the death of the body and yet deny that there is a God. But historically, it is worth remembering that what we might call "traditional" Christianity (this includes the Christianity of Descartes's time) espouses the doctrine of immortality. Dualism makes room for this possibility.

If the soul is part of the mind (even if it isn't the entirety of the mind) and if the soul lives forever and the body doesn't, we have an argument for dualism. Descartes didn't offer this as his argument for dualism, however. Perhaps the reason was as follows. Anyone who doubts dualism also will probably doubt that any part of the mind survives the death of the body. So you aren't going to convince anyone that dualism is true by beginning with the premise that the soul is immortal.

LEIBNIZ'S LAW

Note a structural feature of the argument for dualism that I just described. The argument defends dualism by trying to find a property that the mind has but the brain lacks; the property in question is immortality. Quite apart from whether this argument works, we should note a perfectly sensible principle that it uses. The idea is that if *m* and *b* are identical, then they must have all the same properties. This principle is called Leibniz's Law, after the seventeenth-century philosopher/mathematician (who, incidentally, coinvented the calculus with Newton. In Lecture 7, I briefly discussed Leibniz's belief that we live in the best of all possible worlds).

Leibniz's Law is sometimes called the *indiscernability of identicals*. It states that if you can find even one property that *m* has and *b* lacks, then you will have shown that *m* and *b* are distinct entities. You'll see this principle at work in both of the arguments that Descartes presents for dualism.

The following form of argument is deductively valid:

m has property *P.*

b doesn't have property *P.*

If *m* has property *P* and *b* lacks property *P,* then *m* ≠ *b*.

_____

m ≠ *b*.

Be sure you see how the argument concerning immortality has this logical form. Since the argument is valid, if you reject the conclusion, you must reject at least one of the premises. I suggest that the third premiss (Leibniz's Law) is true. This means that if you reject the conclusion, you must reject one of the first two premises.

DESCARTES'S FIRST ARGUMENT FOR DUALISM

Now let's look at Descartes's first argument for dualism. In Lecture 13, I discussed how Descartes uses the method of doubt in his epistemology. He also uses the idea of doubt in his discussion of the mind/body problem.

In the *Second Meditation,* Descartes claims you can't doubt that you have a mind. If you try to doubt that you have a mind, you will find yourself entertaining a thought, and so you must grant that you have a mind after all.

Descartes thought that the existence of the body has a quite different status. He thought that it *is* possible for you to doubt that you have a body. After all, you *can* entertain the thought that you are a disembodied spirit. Descartes concludes that your mind has a property that your body lacks. You can doubt the existence of one, but not the other. Dualism follows, by Leibniz's Law.

Perhaps you are suspicious of what Descartes says about your body. Is it really possible for you to doubt that you have a body? Can you conceive of yourself being a disembodied spirit? You also should consider Descartes's other premiss. Is Descartes right that you can't doubt that you have a mind?

I'm not going to pursue these questions here. I'll grant Descartes that he *can't* doubt that he has a mind and that he *can* doubt that he has a body. I want to consider whether dualism validly follows from these premisses. To see whether this follows, we must be very explicit about what the property is that the mind is supposed to have and the body is supposed to lack.

Descartes claims that his mind has the property of *indubitable existence,* and that his body lacks that property. Let's look more closely at this property. For an object X to have this property means that the "owner" of X can't doubt that X exists. I say "owner" since *my* mind doesn't have indubitable existence *for you.* I take it that *you* have no trouble entertaining the thought that *I* don't have a mind. It is the first-person case that matters here—a person can't doubt the existence of his or her own mind.

AN ANALOGY

There is a subtle mistake in Descartes's argument. I'm going to argue that properties involving psychological concepts like "doubts," "wants," and so on, can be deceptive. They appear to be the kinds of properties that Leibniz's Law applies to, but in fact they may not be.

I'll illustrate this idea by an example. Lois Lane wants to marry Superman. She doesn't realize that Superman and Clark Kent are one and the same person. Clark Kent, you'll recall, is the most incompetent reporter at the *Daily Planet*. If you ask Lois whether she wants to marry Clark Kent, she will say "No!" Does it follow from this (via Leibniz's Law) that Superman and the most incompetent reporter at the *Daily Planet* are two different people? Of course not. The following argument is invalid:

> Lois Lane wants to marry Superman.
>
> Lois Lane doesn't want to marry the most incompetent reporter at the *Daily Planet.*
> ───────────────
> Superman and the most incompetent reporter at the *Daily Planet* are different people.

On the surface, it looks like this argument applies Leibniz's Law. It describes a property that Superman has and the most incompetent reporter at the *Daily Planet* lacks, and concludes that they are nonidentical. What you must see is that the argument doesn't describe any such property. Leibniz's Law, properly understood, doesn't license the conclusion of nonidentity.

Superman and Clark Kent have exactly the same properties. This isn't contradicted by the fact that Lois Lane wants one of the following *propositions* to be true and the other to be false:

Lois Lane marries Superman.

Lois Lane marries Clark Kent.

The fact that Lois desires one of these propositions to be true and the other to be false doesn't show that Superman and Clark Kent have different properties.

Likewise, Descartes says that I'm able to doubt one, but not the other, of the following two *propositions:*

I have a brain.

I have a mind.

But from this it doesn't follow that my brain has a different property from my mind.

PROPOSITIONAL ATTITUDES AND ABOUTNESS

The crucial distinction we have to note here is this: Doubting and desiring are attitudes we have to *propositions;* doubting, desiring, and believing are examples of *propositional attitudes.* Perhaps there are some propositions whose truth can't be doubted, whereas other propositions we are able to doubt. And surely we desire that some propositions, but not others, should be true. But quite separate from this issue concerning propositions, there is the issue of what *objects* those propositions are about.

Here is the lesson I draw from the example about Lois Lane: *Even if one proposition is desired whereas another is not, it doesn't follow that what the first proposition is about differs from what the second proposition is about.* The same point holds when we consider other propositional attitudes, like doubting. What follows from these two statements?

Lois Lane wants it to be true that Lois Lane marries Superman.

Lois Lane doesn't want it to be true that Lois Lane marries Clark Kent.

What follows is that the proposition *Lois Lane marries Superman* is a different proposition from the proposition *Lois Lane marries Clark Kent.* What does *not* follow is that the person the first proposition is about (Superman) differs from the person the second proposition is about (Clark Kent).

What follows from these two statements?

I can't doubt that I have a mind.

I can doubt that I have a body.

What follows is that the proposition *I have a mind* is a different proposition from the proposition *I have a body.* What does *not* follow is that the object the first proposition is about (my mind) differs from the object the second proposition is about (my body).

With this diagnosis in hand, let's go back to Descartes's argument for dualism. He says that his mind has the property of indubitable existence, whereas his body doesn't have that property. It *sounds* like Descartes is describing a property that the one thing has but the other thing lacks. But this, I claim, is deceptive. Indubitable existence isn't a property of an object; rather, doubting is something we do or fail to do to propositions.

To say that my mind indubitably exists is just to say that I can't doubt a particular proposition. To say that my body doesn't indubitably exist is just to say that I can doubt a particular proposition. From this difference between propositions, however, nothing follows concerning whether those propositions are about the same or different things. This argument for dualism is invalid.

Sense and Reference

The philosopher/logician Gottlob Frege (1848–1925) wanted to explain a salient difference between these two statements:

> The Evening Star is the Evening Star.

> The Evening Star is the Morning Star.

The first of these is obviously true; it is a logical truth of the form "$a = a$." It is a priori; anyone who understands the meanings of the terms will be able to see that it is true, there being no need for astronomical observation.

The second statement is different. It describes a discovery that astronomers made; it is a posteriori. "*The Evening Star*" was a term used to refer to the first star to appear in the evening. "*The Morning Star*" was used to refer to the last star to disappear in the morning. It was discovered that these are one and the same object—namely, the planet Venus.

Notice that the terms occurring in the two statements refer to exactly the same thing. How, then, can the statements express different thoughts? Frege tried to explain this fact by saying that terms have sense (meaning) as well as reference. Although "*the Morning Star*" and "*the Evening Star*" are terms that refer to the same thing (the planet Venus), the two expressions aren't synonymous; they have different meanings.

Frege thought that synonymous terms must refer to the same thing, but that coreferential terms needn't be synonymous. The meaning of a term determines its reference, but not conversely. He also believed that the "truth value" of a statement (that is, whether the statement is true or false) is settled just by the reference of the terms it contains.

Consider the statement "The inventor of bifocals is dead." This statement is true. If Frege were right to say that the truth value of a statement is determined by the reference of the terms it contains, then we should be able to remove any term we choose, replace it with a coreferring term, and have the resulting statement still be true. This we can do; "the inventor of bifocals" and "the first U.S. ambassador to France" are coreferential. Substituting one for the other, we obtain the following sentence: "The first U.S. ambassador to France is dead." This statement is true. In this case, a true statement remains true if one of its terms is replaced by another that is coreferring.

(continued)

Sense and Reference *(continued)*

Statements describing propositional attitudes posed a problem for Frege. Even though "*Superman*" and "*Clark Kent*" refer to the same person, the first, but not the second, of the following statements is true:

Lois Lane wanted to marry Superman.

Lois Lane wanted to marry Clark Kent.

To account for this fact, Frege suggested that terms in such sentences don't refer to the objects that they normally refer to. Normally, "*Superman*" and "*Clark Kent*" refer to a person. But in the above pair of sentences, Frege claimed that a shift occurs; the first refers to the meaning of the term "*Superman*," while the second refers to the meaning of the term "*Clark Kent*." Since these terms have different meanings, it won't be true that the terms in the first sentence refer to precisely the same things that the terms in the second sentence refer to. This makes it possible for the first sentence to be true and the second false. In this way, Frege was able to retain his principle that the truth value of a sentence is determined by the reference of its constituent terms.

When you say, "Lois Lane shook hands with Superman," you are referring to Superman. When you say "Lois Lane wanted to marry Superman," you aren't referring to Superman, according to this proposal of Frege's. If you believe that you are referring to Superman in both statements, then you will reject Frege's account of how propositional attitude statements are to be understood.

DESCARTES'S SECOND ARGUMENT FOR DUALISM

I turn now to Descartes's second argument for dualism. It is far simpler than the one just analyzed. In the *Sixth Meditation*, Descartes claims that physical things have spatial parts. For example, a surgeon could divide my brain into pieces. My mind, however, doesn't have spatial parts. From this, dualism follows by Leibniz's Law.

Descartes also says that the body, but not the mind, has *extension*. By this he means that the body, but not the mind, takes up physical space; it has spatial location. This also leads to dualism by Leibniz's Law.

I'll treat these two arguments together: If the body has the properties of divisibility and extension, but the mind doesn't, dualism follows. I think that Descartes's argument here is valid. The question is whether his premises are true.

I'll grant Descartes that it sounds odd to say that my mind has spatial parts and that it is located between my ears. It also sounds strange to say that my mind weighs about five pounds and has blood vessels running through it. How are we to explain the fact that such claims sound funny to us? One explanation is that they can't be true. If this were right, dualism would follow, since we then would have cited properties that my brain has but my mind doesn't.

However, there is another possible explanation for why it sounds odd to say that my mind has spatial parts, or weighs five pounds, or has blood vessels running through it. The explanation is that these ideas are unfamiliar. The assertions sound jarring because they radically depart from what we happen to believe.

Consider the claim that water is H_2O. Before the advent of the atomic theory, the claim that a liquid is made of numerous tiny particles may have sounded pretty strange to people. But this, of course, didn't mean that water couldn't be made of molecules of H_2O. For this reason, I claim that Descartes's second argument for dualism is inconclusive. If the mind and the brain really are identical, then many surprising facts may follow.

I conclude that Descartes's arguments for dualism don't work. The first argument (involving the idea of indubitable existence) is invalid. The second argument (involving the ideas of divisibility and extension) is valid, but it begs the question. There seems to be no reason to accept the premises (that the mind is indivisible and lacks extension) unless you already believe that the conclusion (dualism) is true.

These negative verdicts don't show that dualism is false. All I've claimed so far is that these two arguments don't work. I now turn to a criticism that has been made of dualism.

CAUSALITY BETWEEN THE PHYSICAL AND THE NONPHYSICAL

One of the main stumbling blocks for dualism has been the idea, endorsed by Cartesian Dualism, that there can be causal interactions between physical and nonphysical things. Descartes thought that physical events in your body can cause sensations in your mind. These sensations, like all mental events, allegedly lack spatial location. But how can events that are located in space bring about events that lack spatial location? And how are causal relations in the opposite direction possible? In *The Passions of the Soul*, Descartes claimed that the pineal gland in the brain is the jumping off point for this interaction. Nerve impulses reach the pineal gland and then manage to affect the mind, even though the mind isn't located anywhere at all. Conversely, your mind (which is no place at all) influences your body by making an impact on the pineal gland. This is very mysterious, and dualists since Descartes haven't managed to make this process any less incomprehensible.

Causality is something we understand best when we consider two physical events that are linked by a physical signal. When we say that throwing the switch caused the light to go on, we are talking about two physical events that occur at different times and at different places. These two events are connected by the flow of electricity. We not only know *that* throwing the switch caused the light to go on; we also know *how* throwing the switch managed to bring this about.

If we were unable to detect a physical signal passing from the switch to the light, we would be puzzled about how the first event was able to cause the second. Similarly, if I said that throwing the switch caused an event that isn't located anywhere at all, you would be puzzled how electricity or any other physical signal could reach an event that has no spatial location.

In light of the difficulty of understanding how causality can "cross over" from the mental to the physical and back again, wouldn't it be simpler to account for the causal interaction of the mind and the body by adopting the identity theory? If the mind and the brain are identical, it isn't terribly puzzling how your beliefs and desires can cause you to behave in various ways. This doesn't prove that the Mind/Brain Identity Theory is correct; the point is just that what is hard for dualism to explain isn't a special difficulty for the identity theory.

Review Questions

1. What does dualism assert? What is the Mind/Brain Identity Theory?
2. What is Leibniz's Law? How is it used in arguments supporting dualism?
3. "I can't doubt that I have a mind, but I can doubt that I have a body. Hence, my mind isn't identical with my body." Is this argument valid?
4. "My brain is divisible into spatial parts, is located between my ears, weighs about five pounds, and has blood vessels running through it. My mind has none of these properties. Hence, my brain and my mind are nonidentical." Is this argument valid? If it is valid, must dualism be true?
5. Dualism has been thought to make mysterious how the mind and the body can causally interact. What problem is involved here?

Problems for Further Thought

1. Descartes says that he can conceive of himself being a disembodied spirit (that is, having a mind but no body). What does conceiving of something mean? Does Descartes's claim entail that it is possible for him to be a disembodied spirit? (See pages 83–84.)
2. Is a statue identical with the stone it is made of? Is an organism identical with the collection of cells in its body? Can Leibniz's Law be used to show that either of these claims of identity is false?
3. In the *Sixth Meditation*, Descartes argues that he is *essentially* a thinking thing. An essential property of a thing is a property that the thing must have if it is to exist. Could Descartes be deprived of thought and still be Descartes? Could Descartes have been born without the capacity of thought and still be Descartes? If Descartes can't doubt that he thinks, is that enough to show that Descartes is essentially a thinking thing?

LECTURE 19

Logical Behaviorism

In 1949 Gilbert Ryle, a philosopher at Oxford University, published an influential book called *The Concept of Mind*. In it, he presented a solution to the mind/body problem that has come to be called logical behaviorism. His views have something in common with those expressed by Ludwig Wittgenstein in his posthumously published *Philosophical Investigations* (1953). Later, an American philosopher deeply influenced by Wittgenstein, Norman Malcolm, elaborated this philosophical position in his book *Dreaming* (1959).

Logical behaviorism is a thesis about the meaning of the mentalistic terms we use in ordinary speech. Logical behaviorism tries to describe what we mean when we talk of an individual's thoughts, beliefs, intentions, dreams, and sensations. This thesis about meaning is quite different from a doctrine called methodological behaviorism, which I'll discuss in the next lecture. Methodological behaviorism is a thesis about science. It doesn't offer a linguistic analysis of ordinary speech; rather, it gives advice about how a productive science of psychology should be developed.

Logical behaviorism advances both negative and positive claims. The negative part presents criticisms of other views of the mind. The positive part is an account of what mentalistic terminology means. I'll take these two components in order.

THE ATTACK ON "THE GHOST IN THE MACHINE"

Ryle thought that the commonsense view of the mind is deeply confused. According to Ryle, common sense is committed to the idea that mental states are inner causes of behavior. To see what he means, suppose we ask why Joe lifted the cup to his lips. A commonsense answer might be that he did this because he *wanted* a drink of water and *believed* that there was water in the cup. This commonsense explanation says that mental states are inner states that Joe occupies, ones which cause his outward behavior. According to common sense, we see the behavior (the drinking), but we don't see the beliefs and desires that cause it. The beliefs and desires are "inside"; they can't be directly observed, though their effects—behavior—can be. I'll use the term "mentalism" to name this commonsense idea that mental states are inner causes of behavior. Ryle thought that this natural picture is deeply confused—mentalism is one-half of what he called the myth of "the Ghost in the Machine."

Ryle also held that common sense embraces *dualism*. This is the other half of the myth of the Ghost in the Machine. Although Ryle lumped mentalism and dualism together, we need to keep them separate. Mentalism and dualism are different. Someone who thinks that the mind and the brain are identical—that mental states are states of the central nervous system—would reject dualism but would agree that mental states are inner causes of behavior. So mentalism does not imply dualism.

Why did Ryle reject mentalism—that minds exist and are quite different from the behaviors they cause? I'll discuss one of his main reasons. Ryle thought that the view of minds as inner causes leads to what I'll call *third-person skepticism.*

RYLE'S OBJECTION TO MENTALISM: IT LEADS TO SKEPTICISM

Ryle's argument goes as follows. If mental states were inner, then the mental states of others would be hidden from us. Each of us would be able to observe the behaviors of others, but not the beliefs and desires that others have. Because of this, we wouldn't be able to know what others think or want. At best, the only facts we would know about the mind would come to us via *first-person introspection.* I can tell by examining my own mind what I think, want, and feel. However, if mental states were inner, I would have no way of knowing anything about what mental states you occupy. Ryle thought we clearly do have knowledge of the mental characteristics of others. He concluded that mental states can't be inner causes of behavior.

The deductively valid argument that Ryle advances goes like this:

(1) If mental states were inner causes of behavior, we would not have knowledge of the mental states of others.

(2) We do have knowledge of the mental states of others.
_____

Hence, mental states are not inner causes of behavior.

Since the argument is valid, if you want to reject the conclusion, you must reject one or both of the premises. My view is that premiss (2) is true. I also think that the conclusion is false. This means that I must reject premiss (1). To do this, I must explain how we can have knowledge of the inner mental states of others.

DO WE KNOW ABOUT THE MENTAL STATES OF OTHERS BY ANALOGY WITH OUR OWN CASE?

A traditional way of attempting to show how we could have knowledge of the mental states of others is via an *argument by analogy.* In 1948 Bertrand Russell advanced this argument in his book *Human Knowledge: Its Scope and Limits,* but the argument has been put forward by many philosophers. It is offered as a solution to the so-called "problem of other minds."

By introspection I know that I have a mind. I also see by observing my own body that I behave in certain ways. I note that some of my behaviors tend to be associated with some of my mental states. For example, when I hurt my finger by stabbing it with a pin, I tend to say "Ouch!" I then look at others and notice that they produce certain behaviors. They say "Ouch!" on some occasions. I reason, by analogy, that others probably have minds and occupy the mental states that I do when I produce the same behaviors.

So the analogy argument goes like this:

> In my own case, I notice that when I produce behavior *B*, I usually am in mental state *M*.
>
> I observe that another individual (*O*) is now producing behavior *B*.
> ══════════════════
> So, *O* is now in mental state *M*.

The double line indicates that the argument isn't supposed to be deductively valid. Rather, the analogy argument says that the conclusion is probable if the premises are true. This analogy argument aims to show how we can have knowledge of the inner mental states of others. If the argument works, it refutes Ryle's claim that mentalism leads to third-person skepticism. But is the analogy argument persuasive?

The usual criticism of this argument is that it is very weak because the evidence is limited to my own case. It is like arguing that since *I* own a green chair, probably *everyone* has one. I agree with this criticism: An induction from one's own case to a conclusion about *all* human beings is basing too ambitious a conclusion on too slender an evidential basis. The sample size is too small.

Although the analogy argument doesn't refute premiss (1) in Ryle's argument, I still think this premiss is mistaken. We can see why by thinking about abduction, not induction.

ABDUCTION

Let's view the beliefs and desires we attribute to others as theoretical postulates. We don't directly observe what other individuals think and want; we observe their behavior. We then invent a "theory" whose adequacy is judged by its ability to explain and predict behavior. My suggestion is that there are many cases in which the ascription of mental states to others is well confirmed by the behaviors we observe. (Of course, there also are cases in which our claims about what people think and want are undermined by what we subsequently observe them do, but that isn't in dispute.)

What's the difference between this solution to the problem of other minds and the analogy argument? In the analogy argument, I begin with an observation of myself and then seek to extend that description to other individuals. In the abductive argument, I make no mention of introspection.

Mendel never observed a gene, but that is no objection to his theory. The fact that genes are inner causes of how tall a pea plant grows, or of whether its peas will be wrinkled or smooth, doesn't mean we can't know about genes (see Lecture 3). Likewise, the view that mental states are inner causes of behavior doesn't lead to third-person skepticism. Ryle's criticism of mentalism is mistaken.

There is a simple but important distinction I want to draw here. The following two questions are quite different; they needn't have the same answers:

(1) Is proposition *P* about observable things and only observable things?

(2) Is proposition *P* testable by observation?

The Mendelian case and the case of claims about the mental states of others provide examples in which the answers are (1) *no* and (2) *yes*.

This discussion of the problem of other minds should remind you of material covered in Lecture 5 concerning the role of analogy and induction in the Argument from Design for the existence of God. Hume criticized the Argument from Design for being a weak analogy argument and for being a weak induction. How is my reply to Hume similar to the reply I've just made to Ryle?

LOGICAL BEHAVIORISM'S ANALYSIS OF MENTALISTIC VOCABULARY

In addition to criticizing mentalism, Ryle also advances a positive thesis about how talk of beliefs and desires should be understood. Logical behaviorists maintain not just that belief is *not* an inner state; they also make a positive claim about what it *is* for an agent to believe something.

Logical behaviorism says that the meanings of mentalistic terms can be specified purely in terms of behavior. For example, we may ask what it means to say that someone wants a drink of water. The following proposal, though false, at least is consistent with the requirements that logical behaviorism imposes on the problem:

S wants to drink water $=_{df}$ S drinks.

The subscript "df" means that the two statements are said to be equivalent by definition.

This proposal is false; people who want a drink of water don't always get to drink. Notice, however, that the proposal obeys the rules that logical behaviorism lays down. The proposal analyzes the meaning of a mentalistic term ("wants to drink water") in purely behavioral language ("drinks").

Behaviorists usually admit that proposals like this one are too crude. They suggest, instead, that the meaning of mentalistic terminology isn't to be given in terms of *actual* behavior, but in terms of *dispositions* to behave. A more satisfactory suggestion, logical behaviorists maintain, is the following:

S wants to drink some water $=_{df}$ S is disposed to drink water.

I have two criticisms of this proposal. First, it is incomplete. When the proposal is fleshed out, it isn't consistent with the requirements of logical behaviorism. Second, I'll claim that even if the proposal were true, it wouldn't establish what logical behaviorists hold—namely, that mental terminology doesn't describe inner causes of outward behavior.

THE DISPOSITIONAL ANALYSIS OF DESIRE IS INCOMPLETE

I'll begin with the charge of incompleteness. Wanting to drink water is supposed to be a disposition to drink water. Suppose Joe wants to drink some water and we place a cup of water before him, but he doesn't drink. Why not? The answer might be that he doesn't *believe* the cup contains water. However, this means that the behaviorist's proposed definition must be corrected as follows:

> *S* wants to drink water =$_\text{df}$ *S* is disposed to drink those things that *S* believes are water.

Notice that the proposal now isn't consistent with behaviorist requirements. The present proposal analyzes a desire in terms of a disposition to behave *and* a belief. So we haven't analyzed the mentalistic concept in *purely* behavioral terms.

I doubt that behaviorists can overcome this problem. Our commonsense mentalistic concepts seem to have the following property: Attributing a *single* mentalistic property to an agent doesn't, by itself, have implications concerning how the agent will behave. What has such implications are *batches* of mentalistic properties. If an agent wants, above all else, to drink water *and* believes that the cup before him contains water, perhaps this implies that he will reach for the cup and drink its contents. But the desire by itself has no such implication and neither does the belief.

A DISPOSITIONAL ANALYSIS DOESN'T REFUTE MENTALISM

My second objection to logical behaviorism's proposal for how mentalistic terms are to be analyzed is this: Even if mentalistic concepts could be analyzed purely in terms of behavioral dispositions, that wouldn't disprove the idea that mental states are inner causes of outward behavior.

To see why, I want to describe an analogy that David Armstrong (whose views on the Reliability Theory of Knowledge were discussed in Lecture 14) noticed between the supposed dispositional property of wanting a drink and other nonmental properties that clearly are dispositional in character. Dispositional properties are often named in English with "ible" or "able" suffixes. For example, to say that a lump of sugar is *soluble* is to say that it is disposed to dissolve. Solubility is a dispositional property. It isn't hard to give a "behavioral analysis" of solubility. To say that something is soluble is to say that it is disposed to behave in a certain way when placed in a certain situation:

> *X* is soluble (in water) =$_\text{df}$ If *X* were immersed (in water), then *X* would dissolve.

Dissolving is a behavior; to immerse something is to place it in a particular sort of environment. This definition of solubility conforms to behavioristic requirements, since it makes no mention of an inner state that soluble substances are said to occupy.

I have no objection to this behaviorist definition of solubility. The point I want to emphasize is that the adequacy of this definition doesn't imply that there is no inner state of lumps of sugar that makes them dissolve when immersed. In fact, chemistry provides a scientific description of the inner features of sugar that make sugar dissolve when immersed in water. Solubility is a dispositional property, but this is consistent with the fact that soluble substances have internal, structural properties that make them behave as they do.

How is this relevant to the logical behaviorist's attempt to analyze mental states? Even if wanting to drink water were a behavioral disposition—one that could be described without mentioning any inner state of the organism—this wouldn't show that wants aren't inner states. On the contrary, there is every reason to think that when something has a dispositional property, there is a physical basis of that disposition. When an organism is disposed to drink water, it is entirely appropriate to ask what it is about the organism's internal makeup that disposes it to act in this way.

This completes my criticism of logical behaviorism's positive thesis. I claim that the meanings of mentalistic terminology can't be analyzed in purely behavioral language. In addition, I've argued that even if such an analysis could be provided (by describing mental states as "dispositions to behave"), it wouldn't follow that mental states aren't inner causes of behavior.

Pain Without Pain Behavior?

Curare, the poison that some South American Indians have used on their darts, paralyzes its subject. In the 1930s and 1940s, scientists purified curare and studied its effects on the central nervous system. At first, some doctors thought that curare was a pain killer; they noticed that if you give curare to your patient before surgery, the patient will not move under the knife. After surgery, the patients complained that they experienced great pain, but for a time, the physicians didn't believe them (many of the patients were children). Eventually, a physician volunteered to undergo surgery with curare; he reported that the pain was vivid and excruciating. After that, doctors realized that curare isn't a pain killer; it simply immobilizes.

Daniel Dennett (in "Why You Can't Make a Computer That Feels Pain," *Brainstorms,* MIT Press, 1978) suggests the following puzzle. An amnesiac is a drug that makes you forget. Suppose that you gave someone curare and an amnesiac before surgery. Would the individual feel pain?

The patient wouldn't say "ouch" or writhe during surgery. And after surgery, the patient wouldn't say, "That was horribly painful." Let's use the term "pain behavior" to name any behavior that usually accompanies pain. So in Dennett's puzzle, there is no pain behavior, either during surgery or after it. The question is, can there be pain without pain behavior?

Dennett's example suggests that the answer is yes. Would you be prepared to undergo surgery with curare and an amnesiac as the only drugs you get? If not, the reason is probably that you think that you would still feel pain.

What does this example show about the claim that mentalistic terms don't describe the inner causes of behavior, but only describe the behavior itself?

Review Questions

1. What is the "problem of other minds"? Does the analogy argument from one's own case solve this problem? Ryle thought that the mental states of others would be unknowable if mental states were inner causes of behavior. Why did Ryle think this?
2. What is logical behaviorism? Can a logical behaviorist analysis be given of the statement "Jones believes that there is rat poison in the gravy"?
3. Suppose that a mentalistic concept (like wanting to drink water) could be analyzed as a disposition to behave. Would that show that wants aren't inner causes of behavior?

Problems for Further Thought

1. I've suggested that an abductive argument can solve the problem of other minds. Construct such an argument, making clear how the Surprise Principle (Lecture 3) applies.
2. What does it mean to say that *X* is "nothing but" *Y*? It can't mean just that *X* wouldn't exist if *Y* didn't. We wouldn't exist without oxygen. It doesn't follow that we are "nothing but" oxygen.

LECTURE 20

Methodological Behaviorism

Logical behaviorism was the subject of the last lecture; methodological behaviorism is the subject of the present one. Although the names sound similar, the doctrines themselves are very different. Logical behaviorism says that the meanings of commonsense mentalistic concepts can be analyzed in purely behavioral terms. Methodological behaviorism isn't a thesis about what such commonsense terms mean; rather, it is a recommendation for how the science of psychology ought to be pursued.

In a curious way, methodological and logical behaviorism take opposite views on the nature of commonsense mentalistic language. As noted earlier, logical behaviorism *rejects* the idea that beliefs and desires are inner states that cause behavior. Methodological behaviorism, by contrast, *accepts* the idea that our commonsense mentalistic vocabulary refers to inner states. Methodological behaviorism then argues that a scientific psychology should avoid talking about beliefs and desires precisely because they are inner states.

In this lecture, I'll divide methodological behaviorism into a negative and a positive thesis. (This is similar to my division of logical behaviorism into a negative and a positive thesis in the previous lecture.) First, I'll analyze the negative thesis; this is the claim that psychology should *not* attempt to explain behavior in terms of people's beliefs and desires. Then, I'll consider methodological behaviorism's positive thesis; this is the idea that people's behavior *can* be explained solely in terms of their history of conditioning.

THE NEGATIVE THESIS: PSYCHOLOGY SHOULD AVOID BELIEF/DESIRE EXPLANATIONS

Why should psychology avoid explaining the behavior of agents by attributing beliefs and desires to them? B. F. Skinner, one of the leading proponents of behaviorism, provides several answers to this question in his books *Science and Human Behavior* (New York, Free Press, 1953), *Beyond Freedom and Dignity* (New York, Knopf, 1971), and *About Behaviorism* (New York, Random House, 1974). Skinner's first objection to mentalistic explanation is that beliefs and desires aren't observable. They are hidden. All we can directly observe is the behaviors of others, not what goes on in their minds. By now, my view of this kind of argument should be clear. Science quite legitimately talks about things that aren't or can't be observed. The fact that beliefs and desires can't be observed directly doesn't mean that claims about an individual's beliefs and desires can't be tested by observing behavior. For example, suppose I claim that Jane wants a drink of water and believes that there is water in the cup before her. Suppose I further claim that she has no other desires that would override her desire for the water. These claims about the agent's mind predict that she will reach for the water and drink it. If that prediction fails, I've gained evidence against the description just formulated of Jane's mind. As in the Mendelian case, claims about what isn't observed can be tested by examining what they imply about what can be observed.

Another reason that Skinner gives for rejecting mentalistic theories is that they are "too easy." In the above example, I attributed to Jane a combination of beliefs and desires that predict something about her behavior. Suppose she doesn't reach for the water. What will I do? I'll modify my claim about what she thinks and wants. I won't abandon my assumption that Jane has beliefs and desires and that these cause her behavior. So, apparently, the assumption of mentalism—that behavior is caused by beliefs and desires of some sort—isn't tested by observing behavior. Indeed, it appears that no matter what Jane does, I can always formulate a belief/desire story that is consistent with what I observe.

I want to clarify this point of Skinner's by distinguishing *specific belief/desire hypotheses* from what I'll call *the mentalistic thesis,* which is the claim that an individual's behaviors are caused by the beliefs and desires he or she possesses. The specific attributions are testable against the data of behavior; however, the mentalistic thesis doesn't seem to be. Skinner believes that the claims of science must be testable by observation; hence, he concludes, the mentalistic thesis doesn't deserve to be part of a scientific psychology.

Notice that even if the mentalistic thesis were untestable, this wouldn't imply that science shouldn't advance and test *specific belief/desire attributions*. Rather, the curious position is that psychologists may do this, but they aren't allowed to say that mentalism is the framework within which they develop their explanations. So, at the very most, Skinner's argument would prohibit science from stating what it is quite legitimate for science to do. This is a rather paradoxical claim.

In Lecture 9, I discussed the idea that scientific claims should be testable. I argued that the thesis of strong falsifiability is implausible. I now want to make a related point: *There are many perfectly respectable scientific statements that can't be refuted by the result of a single experiment.* In the present case, we have an example of this kind of statement. Statements that describe the basic tenets of a *research program* aren't strongly falsifiable.

Mentalism is such a thesis; it says that theories explaining behavior can be developed by extending and refining the ordinary concepts of belief and desire. Time will tell whether this is a good idea for psychology or a dead end. The fact that a single theory within this framework fails doesn't show that the whole framework is bankrupt. One rotten apple needn't show that the barrel is spoiled.

Curiously enough, precisely the same point applies to Skinner's own research program. Skinner rejects mentalism and espouses behaviorism. This is the thesis that behaviors can be explained by describing the stimuli people have received from their environments. Skinner says we don't need to describe the inner states—mental or physical—of individuals in order to explain their behavior.

This thesis states the framework of the Skinnerian research program. Suppose I follow its dictates and construct a detailed behaviorist explanation of why you are now reading this page. Suppose further that this explanation turns out to be inadequate. Does that refute behaviorism as a general research program? I would say not (and Skinner would probably agree).

It is appropriate to demand that *specific explanations* be testable against the data of observations. It isn't appropriate to demand that *theses about the framework of a research program* should be strongly falsifiable. Mentalism can't be faulted on the ground that it isn't testable. Specific mentalistic hypotheses can be tested. Time will tell whether the general thesis of mentalism will turn out to be correct. In this sense, the framework of mentalism, like the framework of behaviorism, *is* testable.

METHODOLOGICAL BEHAVIORISM'S POSITIVE THESIS

I'll now consider methodological behaviorism's positive claim—that behavior can be explained without describing the inner states of the organism. I believe that there is a simple fact about people that shows that behaviorism can't be successful—that the kind of explanations it demands can't be had.

Recall that methodological behaviorism doesn't deny that we have inner mental states. It claims, rather, that psychology needn't discuss them in its attempt to explain behavior. So behaviorism grants that the causal chain linking environmental stimuli to behavior has the following structure:

Environment $\longrightarrow$ Inner state of organism $\longrightarrow$ Behavior

Methodological behaviorism maintains that my present behavior can be explained in terms of (1) the past environments I've occupied and the behaviors I produced in them, and (2) my present environment.

Skinner's theory of stimulus conditioning shows how such explanations can be constructed. In his research, Skinner manipulated the behavior of chickens and other organisms by placing them into a totally controlled environment—a *Skinner box*. For example, a chicken can be conditioned to peck at a key in its cage when the light is on. This is how. When the chicken is first placed in the box, it will peck occasionally. The box is so arranged that if the chicken pecks when the light is on, it will receive a pellet of food. After some time, the chicken's pecking starts to happen pretty much only when the light goes on. In this stimulus/response experiment, the chicken is conditioned to peck when the light is on. The conditioning works by rewarding the chicken in some circumstances but not in others.

Suppose that this conditioning process has taken place. You then look into the cage and see that the chicken is pecking. How might you explain this behavior? A mentalistic explanation might say that the chicken is now pecking because it wants food and believes, based on its past experience, that pecking produces pellets of food. This is explanation in terms of beliefs and desires. Skinner believes that this mentalistic story is entirely unnecessary. You can give a behaviorist explanation of the present behavior as follows: (1) in the past, the chicken was conditioned to peck when the light was on; (2) in the present case, the light is on. Notice that Skinner's explanation makes no mention of beliefs and desires. We can formulate the behaviorist explanation as a deductive argument:

If the light is on, then the chicken pecks.

The light is on now.

Hence, the chicken now pecks.

You explain the present behavior by deducing it from the two facts listed as premises.

Skinner thinks that what is true of the chicken's pecking in the experiment is true of all the chicken's behaviors, both those produced in the box and those that occur in less controlled environments (like the barnyard). In addition, Skinner believes that human beings are like the chicken in relevant respects. Each of our behaviors can be explained by describing our history of stimulus conditioning. This is the thesis on which the behaviorist research program rests. We don't need to talk about what human beings think and want if we are to explain what human beings do.

FIRST OBJECTION TO BEHAVIORISM'S POSITIVE THESIS: NOVEL BEHAVIORS

Are we like the chicken in the Skinner box? Critics of behaviorism, like the linguist Noam Chomsky, have claimed that *novel behaviors* can't be explained in the way the behaviorist demands. Let's look with some care at an example of Skinner's to see what this criticism means.

Suppose you are walking down the street one day and a robber jumps out of the shadows, sticks a gun in your face, and says, "Your money or your life." You fumble nervously and then hand over your wallet. How should your behavior be explained? What makes the behavior novel is that you have never been robbed before. The only time anyone ever waved a gun in your face was when you were a child and the gun was a water gun. In that case, you didn't hand over your wallet; rather, you giggled and ran away. So why didn't you do the same thing this time?

The behaviorist needs to show that the present stimulus situation is similar to past ones in which you behaved similarly. Skinner explains the chicken's present peck-ing by saying that the *present* situation is like *past* situations in which the chicken pecked. The similarity is that the light is on in the Skinner box. The problem is that the present robbery is similar to many past situations you've been in. It is similar to your childhood playing with water guns. It is also similar to the time your mother threatened to spank you if you didn't clean up your room. After all, the robbery in-volved a gun *and* a threat. Which of these past experiences is the right one to appeal to in explaining your present behavior?

Remember that you've never been robbed before. The only time anyone waved a gun in your face it was a water gun and you giggled and ran away. And when your mom threatened to spank you, you apologized and cleaned up your room; you didn't hand her your wallet. What past episodes can a behaviorist say are similar to, and also explain, your current behavior?

The obvious answer is that you learned in the past that you should accommodate those who threaten you. Perhaps you were rewarded in the past for doing this and so the behavioral pattern became fixed. Although this sounds like the right sort of explanation to develop, it isn't true to the demands of behaviorism.

In the chicken case, there was a *physical property* of the earlier stimulus situations that recurs in the present. In the past, *the light was on.* In the present case, *the light is on.* It is perfectly permissible for a behaviorist to describe the history of condition-ing in terms of such physical properties. What the behaviorist can't say, however, is that you are the sort of individual who behaves in ways you *believe* are accommodat-ing when you *believe* that you are being threatened. This is a regularity about your stim-ulus history that involves inner mental states. These are just the items that the behaviorist says should *not* be included in the explanation.

I doubt that there is a physical similarity between past threats and the present one. In the past, your mom may have said, "If you don't clean up your room, I'll give you a spanking." The behavioral response on your part wasn't to hand your wallet over, but to apologize and tidy things up. The only way to describe how this past event is similar to the present robbery is to describe your beliefs and desires.

If our behaviors always obeyed patterns that were describable in terms of *physical similarities* between past and present stimulus conditions, behaviorism might work. But this seems to be radically untrue. What makes the past similar to the present is that we conceptualize past and present in similar ways. Take this mentalistic similarity away and behaviorism delivers radically mistaken predictions. In terms of purely physical similarities, I suppose that your participation in a water gun battle may be more similar to the present robbery than your being scolded by your mother. If you were to behave now in ways that are similar to the ways you behaved in previous *physically similar* past events, the prediction would be that you would giggle and run away.

The important fact about us is that small physical differences in a stimulus often make enormous differences in the response, and huge physical differences in the stimulus often make no difference in the response. If a robber walks into a bank and hands the teller a note that says "You give me the cash," the teller produces one response. If the note had said "Me give you the cash," the response would be different. The notes aren't that different physically, so why was the response so different?

Likewise, receiving a few marks on paper can produce the same result as hearing a verbal command. But the marks on paper ("You give me the cash") and a verbal message ("Empty the cash drawers into this sack") are physically very different.

Minimal Explanation Versus Deep Explanation

The behavior of a conditioned chicken in a Skinner box can be explained without describing the chicken's internal state. Why is the chicken now pecking the key? Skinner's answer is that the chicken pecks whenever the light is on, and the light is now on.

Since we have explained the behavior without mentioning the chicken's internal state, Skinner concludes that describing the internal state would be of no explanatory relevance. You don't need to describe what is going on inside, so why bother?

I grant that the purely behavioral account is an adequate explanation. However, I think that there can be a deeper explanation of the chicken's behavior.

Consider an analogy. Why did this white cube just dissolve? A behaviorist might answer by noting that (1) the cube was made of sugar, (2) it was just immersed in water, and (3) all sugar dissolves when immersed in water. Granted, this is an explanation. But it is possible to do better.

What is it about sugar that makes it dissolve when immersed? Here we request information about the internal structure of the sugar lump. Since sugar is water soluble but wood isn't, we expect that the one has some internal state that the other lacks. Once described, this internal state of the lump of sugar is relevant to explaining why it just dissolved.

The chicken pecks when the light is on. Surely we can ask what it is about the conditioned chicken that makes it peck when the light is on. A conditioned chicken has a disposition to behave that an unconditioned chicken doesn't have. It is legitimate to expect that the one has some internal state that the other lacks. Once described, this internal state of the conditioned chicken is relevant to explaining why it now is pecking.

Perhaps it is possible to explain the chicken's behavior in the way the methodological behaviorist demands. However, this doesn't mean that other explanations that violate behaviorist principles are irrelevant to understanding why the chicken pecks.

Behaviorism sounds plausible for two reasons. First, it is true that claims about the mental states of individuals should be tested against behavioral data. Second, what individuals do is importantly influenced by the environments they have experienced. Neither of these truisms, however, shows what methodological behaviorism maintains—that it is possible to explain (and predict) behavior without mentioning mental states.

SECOND OBJECTION TO BEHAVIORISM'S POSITIVE THESIS: IT ASSUMES THAT ENVIRONMENTAL DETERMINISM IS TRUE

One final shortcoming of methodological behaviorism should be noted. Behaviorism is a radically environmentalist doctrine. That is, when it comes to the nature/nurture problem—the problem of saying how much a behavior is explained by genes and how much by environment—the behaviorist is entirely on the side of the environment. By saying that *inner states* needn't be described in explaining behavior, the behaviorist is excluding genes as well as environmentally acquired mental states. My point is that environmentalism may be true in some cases, but not in others.

Returning to the example of the chicken, it is interesting to note that there are some behaviors that you can't condition a chicken to perform. Speaking English is something that human beings learn to do when they are in the right kind of environment. A chicken in the same environment won't master this skill. Why not? Since the environments are the same, the answer can't be environmental. Presumably, there is a genetic difference between chickens and human beings that explains this behavioral difference.

What is true between species may also be true, in some cases, within a species. There may be genetic differences between human beings that are relevant to explaining differences in their behaviors. This is now a controversial area of investigation. My point is that methodological behaviorism assumes in advance of any detailed analysis that environmental variables suffice to explain behavior. This shouldn't be assumed as a matter of doctrine, but should be empirically investigated on a case-by-case basis.

Scientists are now considering the possibility that there may be a significant genetic component in diseases like depression and schizophrenia. That is, in addition to the environmental causes of these conditions, there also may be genetic causes. In contrast, no one now believes that there is a genetic component in explaining why some people speak one language while others speak another. In this case, variation in the behavior has an entirely environmental explanation.

Environmental determinism is the view that genetic differences don't help explain any behavioral differences. Genetic determinism is the view that environmental differences don't help explain any behavioral differences. Both these views are too sweeping and extreme to be plausible. First, we must consider different behaviors separately. The kind of explanation we offer for schizophrenia may differ from the kind we want to give for speaking English. Second, we must recognize that there are "mixed" proposals that deserve a hearing; we want to consider the idea that some behaviors have both environmental and genetic causes.

THE TWO OBJECTIONS SUMMARIZED

In conclusion, there are two kinds of questions, quite different from each other, that methodological behaviorism can't address. The first is the kind of question typified by the robbery example. When I ask how your present behavior of handing over the money is explained by your previous experiences, it seems essential to describe your beliefs and desires. There is no purely physical similarity between the present holdup and your previous environments. Rather, the similarity exists only because you conceptualize the present situation in a way similar to the way you conceptualized previous (physically different) situations.

Second, there is the idea of genetic (nonenvironmental) causes of behavior. If these exist, then methodological behaviorism will be unable to explain in some cases why some organisms behave differently from others.

Methodological behaviorism began by rejecting mentalism; it claimed that mental states are irrelevant to explaining behavior. But, in fact, its thesis excludes brain science and genetics as well. The real thrust of behaviorism is to claim that the explanation of behavior needn't describe the *inner state* of the organism. Mentalism describes what goes on inside, but so do brain science and genetics.

By focusing on what happens in tightly controlled environments, behaviorism may seem to have established a general pattern for explaining all behavior. It is true that the pecking of the chicken in the Skinner box can be handled in the way Skinner demands. However, it is a mistake to think that successful explanation in this case can be generalized to all other behaviors. Take the chicken out of the Skinner box and perhaps it will produce novel behaviors, just as you did when the robber said "Your money or your life." And quite apart from the issue of novel behaviors, there is the nature/nurture issue, which methodological behaviorism settles in advance of looking at the relevant data.

Review Questions

1. What is the difference between methodological behaviorism and logical behaviorism?
2. What is mentalism? Is mentalism testable? How does the distinction between specific explanations and framework assumptions about a research program bear on this question?
3. Why do so-called "novel" behaviors pose a problem for methodological behaviorism? What does *novel* mean? Isn't every behavior novel in some respect or other?
4. What does methodological behaviorism say about the relevance of genetics and brain science to the explanation of behavior? Why would innate differences in behavior be a problem for behaviorism?

Problems for Further Thought

1. Some psychotherapists call themselves "behaviorists." They treat patients with phobias (extreme fears) by helping them modify fear behavior (like increased heart rate, perspiration, anxiety) rather than by helping them understand why they have the array of beliefs and desires that produce the reaction. Consider people who are enormously afraid of being in closed areas (claustrophobia). Instead of trying to get a claustrophobic individual to understand why he or she has this fear, a behavioral therapist might concentrate on "desensitizing" the individual. The goal would be to modify the individual's behavior. Treatment might begin with very brief exposures to closed areas; gradually, as the patient gains confidence, longer exposures would be attempted. Here's the question: Do the criticisms I've made of methodological behaviorism imply that behavioral therapy won't be effective? Defend your answer.

2. *Saying that lemons are yellow* is a kind of event. Can it be defined by its physical characteristics? Is *saying the English sentence "lemons are yellow"* definable by its physical characteristics? What is the difference between these two kinds of events?

LECTURE 21

The Mind/Brain Identity Theory

So far, I've examined two theories about the nature of the mind and its relationship to the body. These were Cartesian Dualism (Lecture 18) and logical behaviorism (Lecture 19). Methodological behaviorism (Lecture 20), recall, isn't a thesis about the nature of the mind; since methodological behaviorism recommends that scientific explanations of behavior ignore the mind, it doesn't say much about what the mind is.

THE IDENTITY THEORY IS AN A POSTERIORI CLAIM

Cartesian Dualism and logical behaviorism are very different positions. Yet the arguments that each presents have something in common: Neither appeals to any scientific finding as evidence for what it maintains. Cartesian Dualism says that we can recognize by introspection and philosophical reasoning that the mind has a property that the body lacks. Logical behaviorism says that we can see that mental states aren't inner causes of behavior just by analyzing the meanings of commonsense mentalistic terms. Both theories are defended by arguments that are intended to be a priori.

The Mind/Brain Identity Theory isn't only a different theory from those surveyed so far; it also is a different *kind* of theory. The identity theory argues for its solution to the mind/body problem by describing the progress that science has made so far and by predicting the progress that science will make in the future. The relationship of the mind and the body, says the identity theory, is something that science discovers by observation and experiment. It isn't something that armchair philosophy—introspection and linguistic analysis—can hope to resolve. The identity theory is offered as an a posteriori proposition about the relationship of mind and body.

MATERIALISM

The identity theory asserts that the history of science has been marked by success after success for a doctrine called *materialism* or *physicalism*. This is the view that every object in the world is a material (physical) object. If we go back in time, we find phenomena that weren't well understood scientifically. For example, lightning was once profoundly perplexing. The ancient Greeks thought that lightning was Zeus's thunderbolt. But in the eighteenth and nineteenth centuries, the science of electricity established that lightning is an electrical discharge. Science was able to take a phenomenon that earlier had seemed to defy physical description and show that it can be understood within the framework of the laws of physics.

Consider a statement that describes this scientific discovery:

Lightning is one and the same thing as a kind of electrical discharge.

This statement wasn't established by analyzing the meaning of the word *lightning*. The statement isn't an a priori truth, knowable by linguistic analysis; rather, it is an a posteriori truth that the science of electricity discovered. It could be established only by observation and experiment.

In the past century, there was a similar perplexity about the nature of life. What is the difference between living things and things that aren't alive? A doctrine called *vitalism* held that living things contain a nonphysical substance that animates them with life—an *élan vital*. In this century, vitalism has been undermined by the discoveries of molecular biology. We now know that life is a physicochemical phenomenon. Organisms are made of the same basic elements (carbon, oxygen, etc.) as nonliving things. Life differs from nonlife because of how the basic physical constituents are organized. There is no extra nonphysical ingredient that magically makes organisms "alive."

Biology in the last 100 years has discredited vitalism. The discovery of the molecular basis of life has been a triumph for materialism. By this I don't mean that each and every detail of the physical basis of life is well understood; if this were true, there would no longer be a need for research in molecular biology and biochemistry. Rather, what I mean is that the details are sufficiently well understood that there is no longer any real doubt that metabolism, reproduction, digestion, respiration, and so on are physical processes.

DUALISM RESEMBLES VITALISM

Cartesian Dualism and vitalism are similar. Dualism says that an individual's mind is a nonmaterial substance. Thinking beings therefore are said to contain a nonphysical ingredient not found in beings that don't have minds. Vitalism says that living things contain a nonphysical substance—an *élan vital*—that is unique to them. Just as dualism opposes a materialistic solution to the mind/body problem, so vitalism opposes a materialistic answer to the question of how biological and physical processes are related to each other.

The Mind/Brain Identity Theory says that what has happened to the problem of life is in the process of happening to the problem of mind. We now have some knowledge of the physical basis—the neurophysiological basis—of the mind. If science progresses the way it has in other areas, this materialistic understanding will broaden and deepen. The identity theory predicts that science will fully vindicate the thesis that an individual's mind and brain are one and the same entity. Each mental characteristic (for example, believing that snow is white, wanting a drink, feeling pain) is identical with some physical characteristic. The identity theory is a version of materialism: Mental objects are physical objects and mental characteristics are physical characteristics.

During the 1950s and 1960s, identity theorists—for example, J. J. C. Smart, in "Sensations and Brain Processes" and U. T. Place, in "Is Consciousness a Brain Process" (both reprinted in V. Chappell [ed.], *The Philosophy of Mind,* Prentice-Hall, 1962)—gave the following as an example of what they meant. Brain scientists at that time suggested that feeling pain is one and the same event as having the c-fibers in one's brain fire. This neurophysiological hypothesis about the physical basis of pain later turned out to be untrue. This didn't deter identity theorists, however, who are quite happy to leave it to science to work out the details of the general hypotheses they formulate. The identity theorist claims that feeling pain is identical with being in *some physical state or other;* it is for science to tell us precisely what this physical state is.

A CORRELATION EXPERIMENT

Consider this example in more detail. How might a scientist investigate the connection of pain and c-fiber firing? The scientist would want to find out if people experience pain whenever their c-fibers fire and if people have their c-fibers fire whenever they experience pain. Here's a simple experiment that would help determine if these mental and physical events co-occur. A probe inserted into the subject's brain would indicate when the c-fibers fire. Perhaps the subject's own testimony, based on introspection, would indicate when he or she experiences pain. The experimenter occasionally hits the subject's thumb with a hammer. Ignoring complications, suppose that different human subjects, when placed in the same (morally questionable) experiment, generate the same data. Suppose that the data show a perfect correlation between experiences of pain and c-fiber firings.

Does this, by itself, show that the identity theory is true? No. Recall that dualism is quite consistent with there being a perfect correlation of mental events of a certain kind with physical events of a certain kind. Dualism claims that feeling pain and having your c-fibers fire are *two* distinct kinds of events. The identity theory, on the other hand, says that feeling a pain and having one's c-fibers fire are perfectly correlated because they are one and the same kind of event.

How are we to choose between dualism and the identity theory? One consideration, mentioned in Lecture 18, is that dualism makes it difficult to understand how mind and body can causally interact. The identity theory, on the other hand, has no difficulty accommodating this fact.

THE PRINCIPLE OF PARSIMONY

Identity theorists offer a second reason for rejecting dualism. They claim that the identity theory is more parsimonious (simpler) than dualism. Their idea is that the scientific method says we should prefer simpler theories over more complex ones, when both are consistent with the observations. It isn't just that more parsimonious ideas are easier to think about or are aesthetically more pleasing. Rather, their idea is that more parsimonious theories have a better claim to be regarded as *true*.

The identity theory is more parsimonious because it claims (if the experiment just described were to yield a perfect correlation) that feeling pain and having one's c-fibers fire are one and the same event. A dualist, on the other hand, says that these are two different events. The Principle of Parsimony, sometimes called "Ockham's Razor" after the medieval philosopher William of Ockham, is an abductive principle. It says that we should prefer explanations that minimize the number of entities, processes, and events they postulate. Since one is less than two, the identity theory is more parsimonious than dualism. Identity theorists count this as a reason for thinking that the identity theory is true and dualism is false, given that both are consistent with the observed correlation of mental and physical states.

In the vitalism controversy, no biologist took seriously the idea that an *élan vital* exists once the physical bases of life processes became reasonably clear. Rather, the conclusion was that an organism's being alive is nothing above and beyond its having certain physical processes going on in its body. To say otherwise would be to admit a further entity—an *élan vital*—without necessity. This would contradict the Principle of Parsimony. Biologists took this principle to heart once they obtained physical explanations of life processes. They realized that there was no reason to postulate the existence of an *élan vital*. For this reason, vitalism was rejected and materialism accepted.

If a perfect correlation could be found between mental characteristics and physical ones, what reason could there be to postulate the existence of an immaterial mind—one that just happens to exhibit psychological characteristics that are correlated with the physical characteristics of the brain? This seems entirely gratuitous—

Newton on Parsimony

The Principle of Parsimony has been used in many scientific debates. In his *Principles of Natural Philosophy* (1690), Newton presents four "Rules of Reasoning in Philosophy." The first two concern abduction, the second two induction:

1. *We are to admit no more causes of natural things than such as are both true and sufficient to explain their appearances.* To this purpose the philosophers say that Nature does nothing in vain, and more is in vain when less will serve; for Nature is pleased with simplicity and affects not the pomp of superfluous causes.

2. *Therefore to the same natural effects we must, as far as possible, assign the same causes.* As to respiration in a man and in a beast, the descent of stones in Europe and in America, the light of our culinary fire and of the sun, the reflection of light in the earth and in the planets.

3. *The qualities of bodies, which admit neither intensification nor remission of degrees, and which are found to belong to all bodies within the reach of our experiments, are to be esteemed the universal qualities of all bodies whatsoever.* For since the qualities of bodies are only known to us by experiments, we are to hold for universal all such as universally agree with experiments, and such as are not liable to diminution can never be quite taken away. We are certainly not to relinquish evidence of experiments for the sake of dreams and vain fictions of our own devising; nor are we to recede from the analogy of Nature, which is wont to be simple and always consonant to itself. . . .

4. *In experimental philosophy we are to look upon propositions inferred by general induction from phenomena as accurately or very nearly true, notwithstanding any contrary hypotheses that may be imagined, till such time as other phenomena occur by which they may either be made more accurate or liable to exceptions.* This rule we must follow, that the argument of induction not be evaded by hypotheses.

Rule 1 is relevant to the debate between the identity theory and dualism. Rule 2 is similar to the Principle of the Common Cause discussed in connection with the Argument from Design (Lecture 6). Rule 3 bears on the relevance of Descartes's method of doubt (Lecture 13) to the progress of science.

a violation of the Principle of Parsimony. For this reason, the identity theory suggests that dualism should be rejected and materialism accepted, if science discovers perfect correlations between mental and physical characteristics.

Let's be clear on what the Principle of Parsimony recommends. In the problem of life, the principle leads one to deny the existence of an immaterial vital substance. It doesn't say that one should suspend judgment as to whether such a substance exists. Likewise, mind/brain identity theorists have argued that parsimony offers a reason to think that immaterial minds don't exist. Their recommendation wasn't to suspend judgment about dualism, but to conclude that dualism is false. In both cases, Ockham's Razor leads one to conclude that X doesn't exist, not to conclude that one should suspend judgment as to whether X exists.

There is an interesting and difficult philosophical problem here, which I won't attempt to solve: Why should the greater simplicity or parsimony of a theory be a reason to think that it is true? Does using the Principle of Parsimony in this way require us to assume that nature is simple? If so, what evidence do we have that nature *is* simple?

It is interesting that the dispute between materialism and dualism isn't decidable by any straightforward observational finding. This doesn't mean that the dispute can't be decided at all, only that it is more difficult than some of the experimental questions that scientists confront. Although many scientific questions can be answered by experiment, there are many questions *about* science of a distinctively philosophical kind that resist experimental resolution.

Review Questions

1. What is materialism? Is it the view that money is the most important thing?
2. What is vitalism? Is vitalism shown to be true by the fact that living things contain DNA while nonliving things don't?
3. In what way is vitalism (as a solution to the problem of life) similar to dualism (as a solution to the problem of mind)? What is meant by "the problem of life" and "the problem of mind"?
4. What is the Principle of Parsimony? Why is dualism said to be less parsimonious than the identity theory?
5. Does the Principle of Parsimony agree with the following claim: "Since dualism and the identity theory both predict that mental events will be correlated with physical events, there is no way to choose between the two theories"?

Problems for Further Thought

1. Suppose we observe a perfect correlation between some mental property (like feeling pain) and some physical property (like having one's c-fibers fire). Apply the Surprise Principle (Lecture 3) to see whether this observation strongly favors the identity theory over dualism.
2. In the passage from *Principles of Natural Philosophy* quoted in this lecture, Newton defends the Principle of Parsimony by saying that "Nature does nothing in vain." Is this idea consistent with what we now know about natural selection (Lecture 6)?
3. Can two objects contain the same basic physical ingredients and still have different properties? If so, does this show that materialism is false? (Think about different ways of combining the ingredients called for in a cake recipe.)

LECTURE 22

Functionalism

In the previous lecture, I described the Mind/Brain Identity Theory as applying to the mind/body problem the general thesis that *everything is material*. Minds aren't made of an immaterial substance; rather, people have minds and mental characteristics by virtue of the fact that they have brains that possess various sorts of physical structures.

In the 1960s and 1970s, several philosophers—preeminently, Hilary Putnam (in "The Nature of Mental States" in H. Putnam, *Mind, Language, and Reality*, Cambridge University Press, 1975) and Jerry Fodor (in *Psychological Explanation*, Random House, 1968)—developed a criticism of the identity theory. They espoused a point of view that came to be called "functionalism." Although functionalism doesn't reject materialism, it does reject one important part of the identity theory.

Functionalism has two parts—one negative, the other positive. The negative part describes what psychological states are *not*. This is the functionalist critique of the identity theory. The positive part advances a proposal about what psychological states *are*. I'll take these two ideas in order.

FUNCTIONALISM'S NEGATIVE THESIS: WHAT'S WRONG WITH THE IDENTITY THEORY?

To begin with, I need to draw a commonsense distinction. Suppose someone says to you, looking at your clothing, "We own the same shirt." What might this mean? There are two choices. One is that you and this person own the same *kind* of shirt. The other is that the very shirt on your back is jointly owned by the two of you.

THE TYPE/TOKEN DISTINCTION

Let's introduce some terminology to mark this distinction. Unique physical objects are called *tokens*. Kinds (or properties) are called *types*. The unique physical object that you are now wearing is a token of many types. It is a token of the type *shirt;* it also is a token of the type *blue*, and a token of the type *clothing*. To say that a single token is a token of many types is merely to say that a single object has many properties.

Conversely, a given type may have zero, one, or many tokens that fall under it. *Unicorn* is a type of animal that has no instances; there are no tokens of that type. *Golden mountain* is a type of geological object, one that happens to have no exemplars. You can see just from this pair of examples that two types (properties) may apply to exactly the same tokens and still be distinct types. Being a unicorn isn't the same property as being a golden mountain, even though the set of unicorns has precisely the same members as the set of golden mountains.

How does the type/token distinction apply to the mind/body problem? The identity theory is a claim about psychological tokens and also a claim about psychological types. The former category—of psychological tokens—includes the following: Descartes's mind, the pain I felt in my foot last Thursday, Jones's thinking to herself today that lemons are yellow. Each of these is a token, and the identity theory says that each is identical with some physical token.

In addition, there are psychological types (properties); the identity theory makes a claim about these as well. For example, there is the property of having a mind, the property of feeling pain, the property of believing that lemons are yellow, and so on. Note that these types have numerous tokens falling under them. Each type, therefore, describes something that various tokens have in common. The identity theory says that each of these psychological types (properties) is identical with some physical property or other.

MULTIPLE REALIZABILITY

Functionalism rejects what the identity theory says about psychological types. Functionalists hold that psychological properties aren't identical with physical properties. Instead, functionalists argue that psychological types are *multiply realizable*. I'll explain this idea with an example.

Consider a type that isn't psychological—the property of *being a mousetrap*. Each token mousetrap is a physical object. But think of all the different ways there are to build a mousetrap. Some are made of wood and wire and are loaded with

---

The Birthday Fallacy, Again

The Birthday Fallacy, introduced in Lecture 4, is the mistake you make if you confuse the following two statements:

> Everyone has a birthday.
>
> There is a single day on which everyone was born.

The first is true; the second false.

The same mistake is involved in confusing the following two statements:

> Each mousetrap has physical properties that allow it to catch mice.
>
> There is a single set of physical properties that all mousetraps have in common that allows them to catch mice.

The first is true; the second false.

How can the Birthday Fallacy be used to describe functionalism's criticism of the identity theory?

cheese. Others are made of plastic and catch mice by injecting them with curare. Still others are made of a team of philosophers, who stalk around armed with inverted wastepaper baskets. There are many, perhaps endlessly many, ways to build a mousetrap.

Is there a single physical characteristic that all mousetraps have in common, and which non-mousetraps lack? This seems highly dubious. Each token mousetrap is a physical thing, but the property of being a mousetrap (the type) doesn't seem to be a physical property at all.

How does this analogy bear on the plausibility of the Mind/Brain Identity Theory? There is more than one (physical) way to build a mousetrap. The analogy is that there may be many physical ways to build a creature that has a mind, and more than one way for a thinking being to have this or that psychological property.

COULD A COMPUTER HAVE PSYCHOLOGICAL CHARACTERISTICS?

Consider computers. It isn't very plausible to regard very simple computers as having beliefs and desires. My desk calculator no more "knows" facts about simple arithmetic than my stove "knows" recipes for making soup. Rather, human beings can use these devices to do arithmetic or to make soup. A desk calculator, in this respect, is like paper and pencil. It facilitates *our* calculations, but doesn't itself engage in mental activity.

Don't be misled by the fact that we sometimes use mentalistic terms to describe simple computers. For example, we talk about computer "memory." However, I don't think my home computer literally remembers anything. This is just a metaphor. If I write some thoughts on a piece of paper and those scribbles aren't erased, it is true that the piece of paper has "retained" the inscriptions I placed there. But the piece of paper didn't remember anything. In this respect, I think a simple computer is just like a piece of paper.

So I don't think that very simple machines have minds or mental states. But let's now use our imaginations and think about what the future may bring. Could there be computers that have mental states? Could computers be built that perceive—see and hear, for example? Could computers be built that remember? Could a computer reason? Could a computer be built that has wants and needs and preferences?

Functionalists have generally regarded these as very real possibilities. Perhaps current computers can't do these things. And perhaps computer scientists at times exaggerate how close they are to making computers with these abilities. But take seriously for a moment the possibility that computers eventually will be built that have one or more of these abilities.

This possibility has serious implications for the identity theory. These computers, let's suppose, won't be made of protein. Perhaps they will be made of silicon chips. There seems to be no reason to expect that these thinking machines must be physically very much like the brains we have. Just as there are many physical ways to build a mousetrap, so there seem to be many physical ways to have a mind and to have particular mental states.

MULTIPLE REALIZABILITY WITHIN THE CLASS OF LIVING THINGS

We don't need to consider the future of computer science to see the point of the idea of multiple realizability. Organisms other than human beings have psychological states. Some can perceive and remember and feel pain, even if they aren't capable of all the complex thoughts that human beings can entertain. Is it reasonable to suppose that these psychological states in other species must be based on precisely the same physical structures that are present in human beings?

Even within the human species, there may be variation in the physical structures used to encode this or that mental state. Indeed, even within a single human being there may be many ways that the brain can encode a single piece of information. Believing that lemons are yellow may be something that your brain can do in various different physical ways.

This is functionalism's criticism of the identity theory. A given mental type—believing that lemons are yellow, wanting a drink of water, feeling pain—isn't identical with any single physical type. The reason the identity theory is false is that psychological types have multiple physical realizations.

This point might be formulated slightly sarcastically by saying that functionalism accuses the identity theory of being a "chauvinist" doctrine. (This quip is due to Ned Block, "Troubles with Functionalism," in W. Savage [ed.], *Perception and Cognition,* University of Minnesota Press, 1978.) Identity theorists say that a computer or another species must be like us physically if it is to have a mind and mental characteristics. Functionalism regards this as implausibly restrictive.

This, then, is the negative thesis that functionalism advances. Mental properties are *not* identical with physical properties. Notice that this rejection of type-identity is consistent with accepting token-identity. Perhaps being a mousetrap isn't a physical property, but each mousetrap is a physical thing. Perhaps believing that lemons are yellow isn't a physical property, but my present belief that lemons are yellow might still be a physical state that my brain occupies. Functionalism rejects the identity theory's thesis of *type*-identity, not its thesis of *token*-identity.

The identity theory is a version of materialism. So is functionalism. The identity theory denies that minds are made of an immaterial substance; it denies that disembodied spirits exist. Functionalism agrees. The following table shows how these two theories are related to each other, and also to dualism:

| | Are all mental _____ physical? | | |
	Dualism	Functionalism	Identity theory
Types	no	no	yes
Tokens	no	yes	yes

In a sense, functionalism is an intermediate position; it is conceptually "in between" dualism and the identity theory.

FUNCTIONALISM'S POSITIVE THESIS

So much for the negative thesis. What positive account does functionalism provide of what the mind and its properties are like? The name *functionalism* suggests what this positive account is. Let's return to the property of being a mousetrap. This property, I've argued, isn't identical with any single physical property. What, then, makes something a mousetrap? What do the mousetraps have in common that makes them different from the non-mousetraps?

A vague, though suggestive, answer is that being a mousetrap is a functional property; a mousetrap is any device that functions to turn a free mouse into a caught one. Mousetraps are things that play a particular causal role. Any device that produces certain effects in certain circumstances counts as a mousetrap, regardless of what physical materials it is made of or how it is physically constructed.

What does it mean, then, to claim that psychological properties are "functional" properties? Let's consider a psychological state *X* that has the following characteristics:

When an individual believes that there is water in a cup in front of him and the individual is in state *X,* the individual drinks from the cup.

When an individual believes that a well contains water and the individual is in state *X,* then the individual will draw water from the well and drink it.

Each of these two statements is a *conditional;* it describes what an agent will do *if* the agent has a particular belief and is in state *X.*

Can you guess from these two conditionals what state *X* is? A reasonable conjecture is that *X* is the desire to drink water. Of course, there is more to this desire than what these two conditionals describe. But functionalism maintains that these conditionals, and others like them, describe what it is to have a particular desire. Any state that plays the right causal role will be the desire to drink water. The physical composition of the state doesn't matter. Psychological states are to be understood in terms of their causal relations to behavior and to other mental states.

This example concerning state *X* suggests the following functionalist proposal for understanding what it is for an agent to want to drink water:

S wants proposition *P* to be true if and only if, if *S*'s beliefs are true, then *S* will cause *P* to become true.

Notice that this proposal describes desire as a state that plays a particular causal role: When added to beliefs, desires produce actions of certain sorts.

As plausible as this suggestion might be at first glance, there are problems. First, people don't always get what they want when their beliefs are true. A pitcher may want to strike out a batter and may have true beliefs about how to achieve this, but still fail. The second objection is that people sometimes cause propositions to come true that they don't want. When I drink from the cup, I cause my moustache to get damp, but this isn't something I want.

So the functionalist proposal just stated for understanding desire is defective. Perhaps it can be repaired. Maybe there is something right about the idea that mental states are to be understood in terms of their causal connections with behavior and with other mental states.

SENSATIONS

The kind of difficulty we have been considering is especially prominent when we shift our attention from beliefs and desires to sensations. Consider what a functionalist says about the nature of pain, for example. When people are in pain, they are inclined to say "Ouch!" They are inclined to withdraw their bodies from the stimulus they think is causing the pain. And being in pain diminishes a person's attention span and has other psychological effects as well.

Suppose I exhaustively described the causes and the effects of being in pain. These would involve the relationship of being in pain to external stimuli, to behavior, and to other psychological states. Some of these I just mentioned. It is sometimes suggested that this functionalist account of pain leaves out the most important fact about pain—the fact that pain *hurts*. A state may play the functional role of pain and still not be a pain state, so this objection asserts. If this is right, then functionalism will fail as an account of the nature of pain.

I won't try to answer this question of whether functionalism is adequate. Perhaps there are some psychological phenomena that functionalism can't explain. Maybe sensations (like pain) are counterexamples. Even if this is true, however, there may be other psychological states for which functionalism is adequate; perhaps belief and desire can be understood along functionalist lines. This is now a controversial issue in philosophy.

SUMMARY

I've argued that dualism, logical behaviorism, and the Mind/Brain Identity Theory are each inadequate. I think there is nothing wrong with mentalism—the view that beliefs and desires are inner causes of outward behavior. Behavior *provides evidence* as to what an agent's mental states are; but behavior doesn't *define* what it is to be in a given mental state. To make sense of mentalism, we needn't think that an agent's mind is made of some strange immaterial substance (as dualism maintains). Individuals have minds in virtue of the physical organization of their bodies. This, however, doesn't require that all the individuals who possess some psychological characteristic (like feeling pain, or believing that lemons are yellow) have some single physical characteristic in common. My conclusion is that functionalism's negative thesis is correct; it is plausible to hold that psychological states are

Positions in the Mind/Body Problem

If you read from top to bottom in the following chart, you'll see how the various positions we have surveyed on the mind/body problem are related to each other:

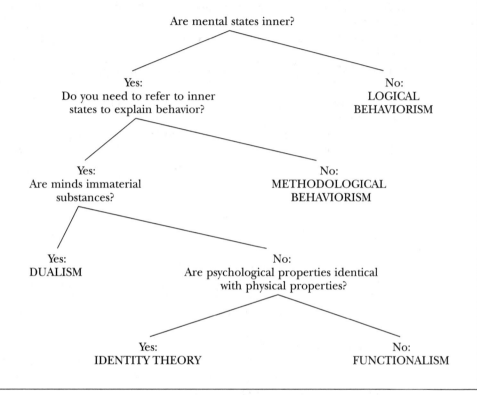

Are mental states inner?

Yes:
Do you need to refer to inner
states to explain behavior?

No:
LOGICAL
BEHAVIORISM

Yes:
Are minds immaterial
substances?

No:
METHODOLOGICAL
BEHAVIORISM

Yes:
DUALISM

No:
Are psychological properties identical
with physical properties?

Yes:
IDENTITY THEORY

No:
FUNCTIONALISM

multiply realizable. As to the positive thesis that functionalism advances, it remains to be seen whether an adequate functionalist account of different mental states can be developed.

In the rest of this section of the book, I'll explore two other philosophical problems about the mind. If human beings act as they do because of what they think and want, and if what they think and want is caused by things outside of themselves, how can human beings have free will? This problem is addressed in Lectures 23–25. After that, I'll consider the problem of psychological egoism. If human beings act on the basis of what they think and want, doesn't it follow that people always act selfishly—that they try to satisfy their own wants and never care, ultimately, about the welfare of others?

Review Questions

1. I return home from a furniture store and report to my family, "They're selling our sofa." I look at the plate of food in front of my son and say, "That is what I ate for lunch." How does the type/token distinction help remove the ambiguity from these two remarks?

2. What does it mean to say that a psychological property (a type) is multiply realizable?

3. Functionalists criticize the Mind/Brain Identity Theory for being "chauvinistic." What does this mean?

4. How is it possible to reject the identity theory without thinking that there are immaterial minds (disembodied spirits)?

5. Functionalists try to characterize what it is to have a psychological property (like feeling pain, or believing that Washington is the capital of the United States) by describing that property's "causal role." What does that mean?

Problems for Further Thought

1. The fact that two types apply to exactly the same tokens isn't enough to ensure that they are identical. For example, *being a unicorn* and *being a golden mountain* are different types (properties), even though they apply to exactly the same objects (namely, to no objects at all). Can the same point be made with respect to types that are exemplified? Can two types be different, even though they apply to the same (nonempty) set of objects? Describe an example of this sort.

2. In Lecture 6, I discussed the concept of fitness that is used in evolutionary theory. What would it mean to say that fitness is *multiply realizable?* Is it plausible to claim that fitness has this characteristic?

3. In the readings accompanying this lecture is an essay by Alan Turing on the question of whether a computer could think. Turing proposes a behavioral test for saying whether a machine is thinking. What is the test? How adequate is the test? To assess its adequacy, you should ask, could the test falsely conclude that S is thinking, when S isn't? And could the test falsely conclude that S isn't thinking, when S is?

4. Here is *the inverted spectrum problem:* You have a particular characteristic sensation when you look at red things and a quite different sensation when you look at green things. Is it possible that someone has precisely the reverse arrangement? This individual would have a red sensation when he looks at green things and a green sensation when he looks at red things. His behavior, including his use of language, would be precisely the same as yours. For example, he would apply the term "red" to fire engines and the term "green" to grasshoppers. If spectrum inversion is possible, what consequences does this have for functionalism's positive thesis about the nature of mental states?

LECTURE 23

Freedom, Determinism, and Causality

In the previous lectures about the mind/body problem, there was a simple idea that no theory contested. Dualists, identity theorists, and functionalists all grant that the mind and the physical world causally interact. Your beliefs and desires cause your body to move in various ways. In addition, mental states themselves have causal antecedents in the physical world. What you now believe and the preferences you now have—indeed, your personality as a whole—can be traced back to experiences you have had. These experiences were themselves caused by items in your physical environment. In addition, modern science recognizes that some features of your mind may be influenced by the genetic endowment you received from your parents.

So just as the human mind has effects on the physical environment, so too does the physical world—both inside and outside our own bodies—affect our mental states. The following diagram represents these causal relationships:

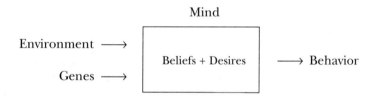

THE PROBLEM OF FREEDOM

The puzzle about the existence of human freedom can now be given a preliminary formulation. Your beliefs and desires, and hence your behavior, are caused by things outside your control. You didn't freely choose the genes you have or the sequence of environments in which you grew up. If you didn't freely choose them, how can it be said that your behavior is the result of a free choice on your part? How can you be responsible for actions that were caused by events (long ago) over which you exercised no control? It looks like you are no more free than a computer; a computer behaves as it does because it was programmed to do so.

Another way to see the problem is to attend to a different feature of the above causal picture. Suppose our behavior is the result of our beliefs and desires just as a computer's behavior is the result of its programming. There is a feature of the computer's situation that seems also to characterize our own. Given the computer's program, it can't act differently from the way it does. Suppose a computer is programmed to compute the sum of two numbers. This means that if you input 7 and 5, then the computer can't fail to output 12. The computer can't act other than the way it does.

Transitivity

Some objects stand in relation to others. Alice *is taller than* Ben. David *loves* Edward. The italicized terms denote relationships. The names flanking the italicized term refer to objects that are said to be related to each other.

Some relations are transitive; others aren't. If Alice is taller than Ben and Ben is taller than Cathy, then Alice is taller than Cathy. A relation *R* is said to be transitive precisely when it has this property:

> For any three objects *a, b,* and *c,* if *a* bears *R* to *b,* and *b* bears *R* to *c,*
> then *a* must bear *R* to *c.*

Being taller than is a transitive relation.

Loving isn't a transitive relationship. The fact that David loves Edward and Edward loves Flo doesn't guarantee that David loves Flo.

Causality is a relation that obtains between events. Holmes's pulling the trigger caused Moriarty to die. Moriarty's death caused alarm to spread in the London underworld. Does it follow that Holmes's pulling the trigger caused alarm to spread in the London underworld? That is, is causality a transitive relation?

Does the Distant Causation Argument, discussed in this lecture, assume that causality is transitive?

Are we like computers in this respect? Given the beliefs and desires we presently have, isn't it inevitable that we do precisely what we do? Our beliefs and desires leave open what we will do no more than a computer's program leaves open what the computer will do. This fact about the computer, and about ourselves if we are like the computer, seems to entail that we aren't free. The reason is that if an action is performed freely, then it must have been possible for the agent to have done otherwise. If I freely lift a cup to my lips, then it must have been possible for me to refrain from lifting the cup to my lips. But given the beliefs and desires I had, I couldn't have done anything other than lift the cup to my lips. Our actions are the inevitable consequences of the minds we have, just as a computer's output is the inevitable consequence of its program.

I've just pointed out two features of the causal relationships depicted in the preceding diagram. Each suggests its own argument for the thesis that no human action is free. The first argument I'll call the *Distant Causation Argument;* it focuses on the idea that our behaviors are caused by factors (our genes and early childhood environment) that were beyond our control. The second argument I'll call the *Could-Not-Have-Done-Otherwise Argument;* it focuses on the claim that we can't act other than the way our beliefs and desires cause us to act. Both these arguments will be clarified later. For now, it should be clear that if you think that we sometimes act freely, you must find a flaw in both these arguments.

It is important to see that both these arguments reach a conclusion of total generality; each concludes that *not one* of our actions is performed freely. This goes beyond the more modest idea that *some* of our actions aren't performed freely.

EXAMPLES OF UNFREE ACTS

Let's consider two sorts of behaviors that no one thinks are free. The first is behavior produced by *brainwashing*. Consider the case of Patty Hearst. Heiress to the newspaper fortune, Hearst was kidnaped and abused mentally and physically by her captors for several months in 1974. She then participated with them in a bank robbery. Later, she was caught and brought to trial.

There was never any doubt that Hearst helped rob the bank. The question was whether she did so of her own free will. The defense attorneys tried to establish that Hearst didn't have free will at the time; they argued that her captors had so distorted her mental faculties that she was a mere pawn in their hands. Her actions were an expression of *their* wants, not of *hers,* or so they argued. The prosecution tried to show that Hearst was a free agent; they argued that even though she had been abused, she was a willing participant in the bank robbery.

The prosecution won the case, and Patty Hearst went to jail. Quite apart from whether this was the right outcome, I want to draw your attention to an idea on which both the defense and the prosecution agreed: People who do what they do because of brainwashing aren't acting of their own free will. Here, then, is one kind of behavior that I think we can safely regard as unfree.

The second category of unfree behavior was described by Freud. Freud describes a man who obsessively washes his hands. He is caught in the grip of a compulsion. Even after normal people would recognize that their hands are clean, the compulsive handwasher keeps scrubbing away. Sometimes the compulsion is so extreme that the person's flesh is eaten away, exposing the bone. "They can't help themselves," we may want to say.

Another example of this sort is kleptomania. A kleptomaniac is someone driven by the compulsion to steal. Even when they recognize that stealing is ruining their lives, kleptomaniacs find themselves powerless to change their behavior. Perhaps some people steal of their own free will; this doesn't seem to be true of kleptomaniacs.

Even philosophers who think that we sometimes act freely usually concede that brainwashing and compulsions rob us of our freedom. The question is whether there are *other* categories of behavior that are genuinely free. I've already described two arguments—the Distant Causation Argument and the Could-Not-Have-Done-Otherwise Argument—that answer this question in the negative.

ARE ALL BEHAVIORS LIKE THOSE PRODUCED BY BRAINWASHING AND COMPULSIONS?

To decide whether we ever act freely, you will have to decide whether some of our behaviors differ significantly from the unfree behaviors just described. If brainwashing robs us of freedom, what should we say about the way a normal upbringing shapes us into the kinds of people we are? If indoctrination robs people of their freedom, what effect does education have on the possibility of free action? If a victim of brainwashing isn't responsible for what he or she does, how can we say that "normal" individuals are responsible for what they do?

Shifting now to the examples of compulsive behavior, we can ask, if compulsive behavior is unfree, what should we say about normal cases of rational deliberation in which people act on the basis of the wants they have? Perhaps the only difference between someone said to have a compulsion and a "normal" person is that they have different wants. It is unusual to want to wash your hands 200 times a day, but not so unusual to want to wash them once after they get covered with dirt. If this is the only thing that distinguishes compulsive behavior from normal behavior, why say that the one is any less free than the other? To understand what freedom is, we will have to answer questions such as these.

A CLASH OF PLAUSIBLE CONCEPTIONS

The problem of freedom involves an apparent clash between two very fundamental ways we have of conceiving of ourselves. First, there is the idea that we are part of the causal network. Our actions don't spring from nothing; rather, they trace back to the beliefs, desires, and other mental features we possess. And these mental characteristics didn't spring out of nothing; they, too, have their causal antecedents in our genes and environment. Second, there is the idea that (at least sometimes) we perform actions of our own free will. Is there a clash between these two ideas, or can they be reconciled?

The arguments considered above concerned two different stages of the causal process represented in the figure. The Distant Causation Argument concerns the relationship of your actions to your genes and environment. The Could-Not-Have-Done-Otherwise Argument concerns the relationship of your actions to your beliefs and desires. In spite of this difference, the two arguments have something in common. Both assert that your actions are caused. And both assert that some fact about how your actions are caused shows those actions aren't free. As noted before, if you think that some actions are performed freely, you must reject one or the other of these two premises.

WHAT IS CAUSALITY?

For the rest of this lecture, I want to focus on the second of these key concepts. What does it mean to say that some events "cause" others? Understanding causality has been a very deep philosophical problem at least since David Hume's work in the eighteenth century. I won't attempt to get to the bottom of this cluster of problems. I will, however, try to clarify what causality is—enough so we can better understand the problem of seeing the relationship between causality and freedom.

What does it mean to say that striking a match caused the match to ignite? This doesn't mean that the striking was, all by itself, enough to get the match to light.

After all, besides being struck, the match had to be dry and there had to be oxygen in the air. So the first fact about causality is this: *A cause doesn't have to be a sufficient condition for its effect.*

The second fact about causality is that there usually are many ways to get a particular effect to occur. Striking the match caused it to light, but that doesn't mean that striking the match was the only way to get the match to catch fire. Using a magnifying glass to focus sunlight on the match head would have done the trick. And putting the match into a heated frying pan also would have worked. So the second fact is this: *Causes often aren't necessary conditions for their effects.* (See Lecture 12 to review the definitions of necessary and sufficient conditions.)

I now want to note a difference between *a* cause of an event and what we may term *the whole cause* of that event. Striking the match is *a* cause of its lighting. It is, however, only part of the whole set of causally relevant facts. Suppose I somehow were able to list all the causally relevant facts about the match at a given time. At that time, the match is struck in a certain way, there is oxygen present, the match is dry, and so on. Given all this information, what can we conclude about what will happen next?

DETERMINISM

Can we say that the match *may* light? Yes. Can we say something more—namely, that the match *must* light, given this complete specification of all the causal facts? The idea that a complete description of the causal facts guarantees what will happen next is the thesis of *determinism*.

This thesis says that if you list all the causally relevant facts pertaining to the match and its environment at a given time, these facts uniquely determine what will happen next. The match's future isn't left open by its present state. Given the match's present state, there is only one option as to what will happen next.

Sometimes we describe causally relevant facts about an object so that the description does leave open what will happen next. For example, suppose we say that a pair of dice is fair. If this is all I know, I should conclude that the probability that the dice will land double-six on the next roll is 1/36. The fact that the dice are fair and that I'm now rolling them doesn't allow me to say what *must* happen. All I can say is that the dice *may* land double-six, but it also is true that they *may* fail to do so.

This doesn't mean that the pair of dice violates the thesis of determinism. That thesis says only that a *complete* description of the system determines what will happen next. Perhaps causal determinism is true and my description of the dice is incomplete.

This has some plausibility. For example, I didn't describe exactly how the dice would be rolled, what the surface is like on which they land, or what the wind conditions are that affect them as they leave my hand. Causal determinism says only that if *all* the causally relevant facts are set out, these will leave open only one possible future for the pair of dice.

INDETERMINISM

Is determinism true? Before I answer this question, let's be clear on what it would be for determinism to be false. If determinism is false, then the world is indeterministic. This means that a complete description of the causal facts at one time leaves open what will happen next. In such a universe, all one can say is that the present state of a system makes some futures more probable than others; the point is that even a complete description of the present will leave open more than one possible future.

Until the twentieth century, determinism was a plausible and widely accepted thesis about the world. Newton's laws of motion, for example, are deterministic in character. You may recall from high school physics that those laws don't make use of the concept of probability. For example, "$F = ma$" says that if a billiard ball of mass m is acted on by a force of magnitude F, the ball will have an acceleration equal to F/m. It doesn't say that this will "probably" happen, as if there are other possibilities that could happen instead. Rather, the law says what must happen if the object is acted on in a certain way.

This Newtonian picture about how physical objects move provides a suggestive model for how *all* events in nature ultimately will be described. Living things are more complicated than billiard balls; creatures with minds are more complicated than many living things. The idea I want to consider, however, says that all things that are made of matter are ultimately governed by the laws of physics. So, since Newtonian theory is deterministic, the idea is that the behaviors of living things and of things with minds also must be deterministic in character. The idea involved in this generalized Newtonian thesis is that "determinism percolates up." If elementary particles are deterministic, so is everything that is made of elementary particles. If a person's mind is a material object, then his or her beliefs, desires, and subsequent behaviors are governed by deterministic laws. I'm not saying that Newton was right about elementary particles; and I'm not saying that the mind is a physical thing made of elementary particles. What I do want you to consider is a certain idea: *If* all matter is deterministic and *if* a person's mind is a material thing, then human behavior is physically determined.

One of the *if*s in what I've just described—the idea that matter is deterministic— wasn't much questioned until the twentieth century. It was then that Niels Bohr, Werner Heisenberg, and Erwin Schrödinger developed the Quantum Theory. This theory is interpreted in different ways by physicists, but what might be called the standard interpretation (called "the Copenhagen interpretation," for Bohr's home town) is that the Quantum Theory says that the behavior of particles is not deterministic. According to this interpretation of the theory, even a complete description of a physical system leaves open what its future will be like. Some futures will be more probable than others, but the number of possibilities is always greater than one. In short, the present doesn't determine the future—chance is part of the way the world is.

It is by no means settled that the Copenhagen interpretation is the best interpretation of the Quantum Theory. Nor is it inconceivable that this very well confirmed theory will one day be replaced by another, which assures us that the universe is deterministic. But what seems clear now is that one can no longer simply assume

---

Two Uses of Probability

We often use the concept of probability to describe our *lack of knowledge*. When we say that a coin has an equal chance of landing heads or tails on the next toss, we often mean that the coin is evenly balanced (fair) and that we don't know exactly how it will be tossed or what the wind conditions will be.

If determinism is true, then the only reason we need to talk about probabilities is that we lack a complete description of the coin's initial state. Recall that determinism says that a complete description of a system at one time uniquely determines what will happen next; the present can't leave open different future possibilities that each have some chance of coming true. That is, if determinism is true, then the probability concept is needed only to describe something subjective—namely, the knowing subject's lack of information.

On the other hand, if determinism is false, then probability describes an objective fact about the world. Chance is a feature of the way things happen. In this case, probability talk isn't simply a way to represent our ignorance.

In short, whether determinism is true affects how we can use the concept of probability.

---

that determinism must be right. Perhaps the universe is deterministic, and then again, perhaps it is not. This is a scientific question to be settled by scientific investigation. One can't decide a priori whether or not determinism is true.

Suppose we are made of matter. Suppose that our psychological characteristics aren't due to the presence of some immaterial substance (a Cartesian ego), but are consequences of how the matter we are made of is structured. If this is right, then I suggest that our behavior must be like the behaviors of physical particles. If chance influences the behavior of particles, then chance also influences the behavior of people. That is, I'm advancing the thesis that *in*determinism percolates up. If physical things don't obey deterministic laws, then our beliefs and desires don't determine what our actions will be. Rather, those beliefs and desires make some actions vastly more probable than others. Similarly, our genes plus the environments we inhabit don't determine what our thoughts and wants will be. Again, the relationship is probabilistic, not deterministic.

Most philosophers who have written about the issue of human freedom haven't worried about the implications of the Quantum Theory. Usually, they have assumed that matter is deterministic and then have considered what this implies about the question of whether we are free. This is entirely understandable for people like David Hume, who wrote about the issue of freedom long before the Quantum Theory came on the scene; after all, Hume was writing in the heyday of the Newtonian world picture.

DOES INDETERMINISM MAKE US FREE?

If the world is indeterministic, how does that fact affect the issue of whether we are free? My suspicion is that the shift from determinism to indeterminism doesn't make much of a difference. The reason I say this is that if you suspect that determinism rules out freedom, you'll probably be inclined to think that we wouldn't be free if indeterminism were true instead.

Suppose you think we can't have free will on the grounds that our thoughts and wants are causally determined by factors outside our control. We don't freely choose the genes we have, or the environments we inhabit in early childhood. These are thrust upon us. They shape the kinds of people we are as well as the specific beliefs and desires we have. Given all this, how can our actions be regarded as free? This is the thought expressed in the Distant Causation Argument.

Maybe you find the Distant Causation Argument somewhat plausible. The question I want to ask is whether you would change your mind about freedom if chance were introduced into the above story? That is, suppose that your beliefs and desires were due to genes, environments, *and chance*. If determinism robs you of freedom, chance seems to rob you of freedom as well.

The same point applies to the Could-Not-Have-Done-Otherwise Argument. Suppose you agree with this argument's thesis—that our actions can't be free, since they are inevitable, given the beliefs and desires we have. Would introducing chance into this story make more room for freedom? I think not. If the fact that your beliefs and desires determine your action makes you unfree, I think you'd still be unfree if your actions were caused by your beliefs, desires, *and chance.*

To make this point graphic, consider a kind of brain surgery. Suppose you now are a deterministic system: Your beliefs and desires determine what you will do. I now offer you a brain implant, whereby a tiny roulette wheel is introduced into your deliberation processes. If you think you are unfree as a deterministic system, would the operation make you free? This seems implausible. Before the operation, you were a slave to your beliefs and desires. After the surgery, you are a slave to your beliefs, desires, and the roulette wheel. The shift from being a deterministic system to being an indeterministic system hasn't made a difference as far as the question of freedom is concerned.

CAUSALITY IS THE ISSUE, NOT DETERMINISM

So my suggestion is that determinism *and* indeterminism both pose a problem for human freedom. The reason is that causality can exist in an indeterministic universe just as much as it can in a deterministic one. If your mental states are caused by factors outside your control, the puzzle is how you can be a free agent. Whether these causal factors *determine* your behavior isn't essential.

It isn't hard to visualize how some events can cause others in a deterministic universe. If striking the match causes the match to light, determinism tells us the striking completed a set of causal conditions that determines that the match must light. But how could some events cause others if determinism were false?

The following example (due to Fred Dretske and Aaron Snyder, "Causal Irregularity," *Philosophy of Science,* Vol. 39, 1972, pp. 69–71) shows, I think, that this is possible. Suppose a roulette wheel is connected to a gun, which is pointed at a cat. If I spin the roulette wheel and the ball were to land on 00, this would cause the gun to fire, which then would kill the cat. Suppose that the roulette wheel is an indeterministic system—spinning the wheel doesn't determine where the ball will drop. Now suppose

I spin the wheel and the ball happens to fall on 00, thereby killing the cat. It seems to me that my spinning the wheel caused the cat to die, even though the process isn't deterministic. The death of the cat *traces back* to my spinning the wheel. For this to be true, it isn't required that my spinning the wheel *made it inevitable* that the cat would die. This is why it is possible to have causation without determinism.

So my hunch is that the real problem isn't to see whether determinism and freedom can be reconciled, but to see whether causality and freedom can be reconciled. However, since the traditional positions about freedom all focus on deterministic causation, I'll do the same.

WHAT DOES DETERMINISM SAY ABOUT THE CAUSATION OF BEHAVIOR?

To fix ideas, let's be clear on how the thesis of determinism would apply to the diagram given earlier. This diagram represents the idea that your genes and environment cause your present mental state, and that this, in turn, causes your behavior. What do these causal relations mean, if causality is understood deterministically?

Let's suppose for a moment that this diagram is *complete*. That is, suppose it represents *all* the factors that influence your mental state and your subsequent behavior. What does the thesis of determinism say about this chain? It asserts the following: Given your genes and environment, you couldn't have had a set of beliefs and desires different from the set you in fact possess. And given your beliefs and desires, you couldn't have performed an action different from the action you in fact produced. Determinism, recall, is the thesis that the facts at one time uniquely determine what comes next.

DETERMINISM DIFFERS FROM FATALISM

Determinism is an entirely different doctrine from the idea termed *fatalism*. Fatalism is summed up in the saying, "Que sera, sera" ("whatever will be, will be"). It is easy to understand what fatalism says by seeing how it figures in the Greek myth about Oedipus.

Oedipus was a victim of fate. The Fates decreed that he would kill his father and marry his mother. In the story, Oedipus does these things in spite of himself. The Fates somehow ensured that Oedipus would find himself in this sorry state of affairs no matter what choices he made and no matter what he did.

Determinism says that the present determines the future; it does *not* say that the future is cast in stone, unaffected by what is true of the present. Determinism is quite consistent with the idea that what is true at a later time *depends* on what is true earlier. Determinism doesn't rule out the idea that if the past had been different, the present would be different. Determinism doesn't rule out the idea that I can affect what the future will be like by now acting one way rather than another. Fatalism denies this; it says that the future is *independent* of what you do in the present.

Newton said that billiard balls are deterministic systems. If you hit the ball in a certain way (call it W_1), then the ball will move to a certain position (call it P_1) on the table. But Newtonian physics also says that if you hit the ball in some *other* way (W_2), the ball will move to a *different* position (P_2). Notice that in this theory, the present *makes a difference* to the future. The future is under the control of the present.

What would it be for Oedipus to be a deterministic system? This doesn't require us to think that there are such things as the Fates. Oedipus would be a deterministic system if his actions were deterministically controlled by his beliefs and desires. If Oedipus has one set of beliefs and desires (call it S_1), then Oedipus produces one action (call it A_1). But if he had had a different set of beliefs and desires (S_2), his action would have been entirely different (A_2).

Here is a picture of Oedipus according to which he is a deterministic system, but fatalism is false: Oedipus's beliefs and desires, plus the environment he was in, ensured that he would kill his father and marry his mother. But if he had had a different set of beliefs and desires, he wouldn't have done this.

It is easy to confuse determinism and fatalism, even though they are very different ideas. In fact, they are almost opposite in what they say. Fatalism says that our beliefs and desires make no difference as far as what actions we perform and as far as what happens to us. In a sense, fatalism says that our beliefs and desires are impotent; they don't have the power to make a difference. But determinism, if we model it on the Newtonian idea, says that our beliefs and desires aren't impotent; they causally control what we do and thereby powerfully influence what happens to us.

According to fatalism, there is no point in *trying* to do something. If it is fated that you will get an *A* in a course, you will get an *A* whether you try to get one or not; and if it is fated that you will get a *D,* you will whether you try to avoid this fate or not. On the other hand, to think that your efforts influence what happens to you—to think that trying makes a difference to the grade you receive—is to reject fatalism.

Greek mythology talked about the Fates. I'll assume that there are no such things. I'll assume that fatalism is false. This leaves open the quite separate question of whether determinism is true. Most previous writers on the free will problem have assumed that causality requires determinism. I hope you see why I reject this connection; I think that causality is a fact about the world we inhabit, even if determinism turns out to be false.

In the next lecture, I'll consider a variety of positions about the relationship of freedom and determinism. Even though I think that determinism isn't the central problem—the real issue concerns the relationship of freedom and causality—the fact of the matter is that most writers have thought about freedom's connection with determinism. It is this traditional way of posing the problem that I'll investigate next.

Review Questions

1. What is the Distant Causation Argument? What is the Could-Not-Have-Done-Otherwise Argument? What do these arguments have in common? How do they differ?

2. Two examples were given of unfree actions. What were they?
3. What does the thesis of determinism assert? What is indeterminism? How do these theses employ the concept of a "sufficient condition" and the concept of a "complete description"?
4. An unusual sort of brain surgery was described in this lecture. What was it and what relevance does it have to the problem of free will?
5. What is fatalism? How does it differ from determinism?

A Problem for Further Thought

Suppose the Fates decided to get Oedipus to kill his father and marry his mother by controlling what Oedipus thinks and wants. If this were so, how would determinism differ from fatalism?

LECTURE 24

A Menu of Positions on Free Will

In this lecture, I'll present a menu of standard philosophical positions about the relationship of freedom and determinism. I then will make some critical remarks about some of the positions. This will set the stage for the positive proposal I'll make in the next lecture about how the idea of freedom of the will should be understood.

"COMPATIBILITY" DEFINED

Before proceeding, I need to define a piece of terminology from logic. To say that two propositions are *compatible* is to say that the truth of one wouldn't rule out the truth of the other. Incompatibility means conflict; if one proposition were true, the other would have to be false.

Two propositions can be compatible even though neither is, in fact, true. And two propositions can be incompatible even though both are false. Consider the following triplet of statements:

(1) My shirt is green all over.

(2) My shirt is red all over.

(3) My shirt is torn.

(1) and (2) are incompatible. (1) and (3) are compatible. Do these two pieces of information tell you what color my shirt is? Do they tell you whether the shirt is torn? The answer to both questions is *no*.

INCOMPATIBILISM AND COMPATIBILISM

Incompatibilism is a thesis about the problem of free will. It doesn't claim that determinism is true. It also doesn't claim that we are unfree. It merely asserts an if/then statement: *If determinism is true, then we aren't free.*

If two propositions (*D* and *F*) are incompatible, there are three possibilities: *D* is true and *F* is false; *D* is false and *F* is true; or *D* and *F* are both false. What is excluded by the claim of incompatibility is that both propositions are true.

Of the three possible positions an incompatibilist can take, two have been prominent in philosophical discussion. The first holds that determinism is true and that we aren't free. This position has come to be called *hard determinism.* The second says that we are free and that our actions aren't causally determined. This position is called *libertarianism.* These two positions agree that you can't have it both ways, but they disagree about which proposition is true and which is false.

Opposed to incompatibilism is the idea that determinism doesn't rule out the possibility that we are free. This view, not surprisingly, is called *compatibilism.* In principle, there are four possible subvarieties of compatibilism. If propositions *D* and *F* are compatible then the options are (1) *D* and *F* are both true; (2) *D* and *F* are both false; (3) *D* is true and *F* is false; or (4) *D* is false and *F* is true.

Of these four possible positions, only one has been discussed much in the philosophical literature. This viewpoint is called *soft determinism;* it holds that our actions are both free and causally determined. The basic idea here is that freedom doesn't require the absence of determinism, but rather requires that our actions be caused in a particular way.

So the basic menu of positions is as follows:

I. Incompatibilism (if determinism is true, then we lack freedom).
   A. Hard Determinism: Incompatibilism and determinism are true, and so we lack freedom.
   B. Libertarianism: Incompatibilism is true and we are free, and so determinism is false.
   C.
II. Compatibilism (if determinism were true, that wouldn't rule out the possibility that we are free).
   A. Soft Determinism: Compatibilism and determinism are true, and we are free.
   B, C, D.

Note that this outline leaves some possible positions unlabeled. My own view falls in II.B; I'm a compatibilist. As explained in the previous lecture, I don't think one can assume that determinism is true. I do, however, think that some of our actions are performed freely. The kind of compatibilist position I endorse will be described in the next lecture.

The three labeled positions display three patterns of similarity and difference. Soft determinism and libertarianism agree that we are free, hard and soft determinism agree that determinism is true, and hard determinism and libertarianism agree that incompatibilism is correct. To understand how these three positions are related, we can schematize each as endorsing an argument. Let *F* be the proposition that some of our actions are free and *D* the proposition that determinism is true. Here is each position's characteristic argument:

Hard determinism: If *D*, then not-*F*

   D
   ──────────
   Not *F*

Libertarianism: If *D*, then not-*F*

   F
   ──────────
   Not *D*

Soft determinism: *F*

   D
   ──────────
   F and *D* are compatible

The Normative Problem of Freedom

Libertarianism, soft determinism, and hard determinism take different stances on the question of whether we, in fact, are free. They don't advance claims as to whether it is a good thing or a bad thing to be free. In other words, these theories concern *descriptive*, not *normative*, issues.

There is a quite separate issue about freedom that arises in political philosophy. It involves the question of which freedoms people have a right to. Are people entitled to particular liberties, which may not be compromised by other individuals or by the State? This is a normative question about what people should and shouldn't do. It isn't the same as the question of whether people have free will.

Freedoms can come into conflict. Some defenders of capitalism hold that people should be free to engage in buying and selling without regulation by the State. However, this can result in "boom and bust" cycles that produce widespread suffering. If freedom from want is an entitlement that people have, then certain economic freedoms may have to be regulated or curtailed. This and other normative questions about the freedoms that people are entitled to will be discussed in the section of the text on ethics.

Note that each of these arguments is deductively valid. Our task is to figure out which of the premisses are plausible.

LIBERTARIANISM

I'll begin by considering libertarianism; the philosopher C. A. Campbell (1897–1974) is the libertarian on whom I'll focus. Before I describe how Campbell defends libertarianism, let me note that "libertarianism" in the problem of free will is an entirely different doctrine from the idea that goes by that name in political philosophy. Libertarians in political philosophy argue that the State shouldn't interfere in buying and selling or in other spheres of life. This is a *normative* view—a claim about the way things ought to be. On the other hand, libertarianism in the problem of free will is a *descriptive* claim, not a normative one. It asserts that we are free agents and that determinism is false. Libertarianism doesn't say whether this is good news or bad.

Libertarians usually think they can tell by introspection that at least some of their actions aren't determined by the beliefs, desires, and other psychological characteristics they have. For example Campbell, in his book *Selfhood and Godhood* (Allen and Unwin, 1957), focuses on the fact that we sometimes perform actions that are "out of character." When we do this, he says, it isn't true that our actions are determined by the characters we have.

I have two objections to this line of thinking. First, as noted in Lecture 13, there is no reason to place such complete trust in introspection. The beliefs we form about ourselves by "gazing within" can be both incomplete and inaccurate. They can be incomplete, because there may be facts about ourselves of which we aren't conscious—facts that introspection fails to detect. In addition, introspection can be inaccurate, because there are psychological mechanisms that systematically distort the way we appear to ourselves. Freud stressed both these ideas. In the latter category, he argued that some of the beliefs and desires we have would cause us great pain if we realized that we had them. As a "defense mechanism," introspection provides us with a false picture of what we really think and want. Although this view about introspection is characteristically Freudian, it is important to realize that many other approaches in psychology also endorse it. There is broad consensus that we shouldn't take the testimony of introspection at face value.

There is an additional difficulty with Campbell's view. He says that when we act out of character, our actions aren't determined by what our minds are like. I disagree. Consider a person who is usually cowardly but manages to act courageously on a given occasion. Is it plausible to think that the courageous act can't be explained by what the person's mind was like? I find this highly dubious. I suspect that there are aspects of the person's mind that came into play. Perhaps a combination of unusual circumstances led the person to muster the courage in a way that earlier hadn't been possible. So I really don't see that the actions we call "acting out of character" pose a problem for determinism.

Campbell assumes that the phrase "acting out of character" means that the action isn't caused by the agent's character. But this is to misunderstand what the phrase means. When people who usually have been cowardly manage to act courageously, we might say "Evidently, they had it in them." This testifies to the fact that "acting out of character" isn't something we think of as uncaused.

Campbell accepts incompatibilism, thinks that introspection shows that we sometimes produce free acts, and so concludes that determinism must be false. I've suggested that this introspective argument against determinism is very weak. If you think that free will and determinism are incompatible, I don't see how the introspective impression we have that we are free can be decisive. The behaviorist psychologist B. F. Skinner, whose views I discussed in Lecture 20, wrote a book called *Beyond Freedom and Dignity* (Knopf, 1971). Skinner is an incompatibilist; in fact, he is a hard determinist. His view is that the introspective picture we have of ourselves as free agents is an illusion. It is a comforting idea—a fairy tale we tell ourselves. I don't agree with Skinner's hard determinism. My present point, however, is that I think Skinner is right not to take introspection at face value.

If I thought that incompatibilism were true, I'd try to find out if human actions are determined. I would do this by seeing what science has to say about determinism and what psychology has to say about the causation of behavior. Campbell accepts incompatibilism, but argues in the opposite direction. He decides via introspection that some of our actions are free, and he concludes that our actions can't be causally determined. This, I think, is the wrong order in which to address the questions.

Notice that Campbell's position, as I've presented it here, doesn't *argue* that incompatibilism is true. Rather, Campbell *assumes* that incompatibilism is true. He uses this as one of his premises to argue for the conclusion that our actions aren't causally determined.

TWO SOFT DETERMINIST THEORIES

I turn now to the standard form that compatibilist theorizing takes—soft determinism. Soft determinist theories try to construct a plausible theory of what freedom is, one that shows how freedom isn't ruled out by the idea that our actions are determined. I think the two compatibilist theories I'll now consider are defective. They provide lessons concerning how a more successful compatibilist theory might be constructed, however.

The goal of a compatibilist theory is to show that an act is performed freely if it is caused in a particular sort of way; freedom doesn't require the absence of causality, but the right sort of causality. The goal is to make room for freedom in a world of causes.

HUME

I'll begin with the compatibilist account of freedom advanced by David Hume. His idea was that an action is performed freely when the agent could have done otherwise, had the agent wanted to. Suppose you accept an employer's offer of a summer job. Hume says you act freely if you could have declined the offer had you wanted to. By the same token, when you hand the robber your wallet after the robber says, "Your money or your life," you do so of your own free will, if the following were true: Had you wanted to die rather than stay alive, you could have refused to hand over your wallet. So Hume's theory is that free actions are ones that are under the causal control of the agent's beliefs and desires. When an action is under the agent's control in this way, it will be true that if the agent had had a different set of wants, the agent would have selected and performed a different action. Hume's is a compatibilist theory because it says that an action is free if it is causally related to the agent's beliefs and desires in a particular way.

What would an *un*free action be like, according to Hume's theory? Suppose you want to leave the room but you can't because you are handcuffed to the floor. In this case, you don't remain in the room freely. You stay in the room *whether you want to or not*. What you do isn't under the control of your beliefs and desires.

Here is another example of unfreedom. Suppose I perform a brain operation on you. I disconnect your beliefs and desires from the nerves that send impulses to the rest of your body. I then implant a radio transmitter so that your body receives instructions from me. Now it is *my* beliefs and desires that dictate what *you* say and do. Your actions are no longer under the causal control of your own beliefs and desires. In this bizarre arrangement, your body would become a robot—a slave to my will. It would do what *I* want because I want it. We might observe you drinking water, depositing money into my bank account, and so on. But you wouldn't be doing these things of your own free will. Hume's theory explains why your actions are unfree in this case.

FIRST OBJECTION TO HUME'S THEORY: COMPULSIVE BEHAVIOR

I think the main objection to Hume's theory is to be found in cases of *compulsive behavior*. Think of the kleptomaniac discussed in the previous lecture. A kleptomaniac is a thief whose desire to steal is overpoweringly strong. Kleptomaniacs want to steal though they may be completely convinced that they will be caught and punished. Even with full knowledge that stealing will hurt them rather than help, they continue to steal.

Kleptomaniacs are caught in the grip of an obsession. They are slaves to a desire that isn't diminished by the realization that acting on the desire does them more harm than good. There are thieves who aren't kleptomaniacs, of course. Such a thief may try to steal something, but his decision to do this would be affected by information about the chances of being caught and punished. None of this information makes any difference to a kleptomaniac. The kleptomaniac is *stuck;* his desire isn't sensitive in the familiar way to considerations about self-interest.

I claim that the kleptomaniac doesn't steal of his own free will. Yet he satisfies Hume's requirements for what it takes to be free. Kleptomaniacs want, above all, to steal things. When a kleptomaniac steals, he does so because of the desires he has. If he hadn't wanted to steal, he wouldn't have done so. The kleptomaniac's actions are under the control of his beliefs and desires. The problem is that there is something about the desires themselves and the way they work that make the kleptomaniac unfree.

The causal diagram from the previous lecture can be used to illustrate why Hume's account of freedom looks for freedom in the wrong place:

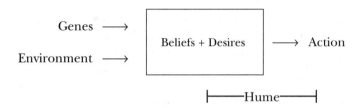

Hume's theory defines freedom in terms of a relation that obtains between beliefs and desires on the one hand and action on the other. For Hume, free actions are ones that are controlled by the agent's desires. The case of compulsive behavior provides an objection to Hume's account. It is the nature of the kleptomaniac's desires that makes him unfree. This suggests that a compatibilist theory shouldn't ignore the earlier links in the above causal chain.

SECOND OBJECTION TO HUME'S THEORY: LOCKE'S LOCKED ROOM

There is a second, more subtle, problem with Hume's account. In his *Essay Concerning Human Understanding* (1690), John Locke (1632–1704) describes a man who decides of his own free will to remain in a room in order to talk with a friend there. Unbeknownst to the man, the door of the room has been locked. The man remains in the room freely, although it is false that he could have done otherwise had he chosen to do so.

If Locke is right in the way he describes this example, Hume's theory is mistaken. For you to have performed some action of your own free will, it isn't essential that you could have performed some other action if you had wanted to. According to Locke, you can perform an action freely even though you aren't free to act in any other way. The act was free because of why it was performed, and Hume's theory fails to pinpoint what the process lying behind free actions must be like.

Here's another example that illustrates Locke's point. Take any action that an agent performed of his or her own free will. For example, suppose that Joe attended a concert last night of his own free will. Now imagine that if he hadn't decided to go to the concert, he would have been kidnapped and taken there against his will. Joe didn't know about this plot when he was deliberating about whether he would attend. The point is that Joe attended the concert of his own free will, even though he couldn't have done otherwise.

One way to see what Locke is driving at is to contrast the man locked in the room (though he doesn't know he is) with the kleptomaniac. The kleptomaniac's thought processes have malfunctioned; it is something about his mind that makes his actions unfree. But there is nothing wrong with the mind of the man in Locke's example. His will is free, although he isn't free to act in certain ways.

DOES COERCION ROB US OF FREE WILL?

This contrast is important to bear in mind when you think about another important issue for the free will problem—coercion. Consider a robber who coerces you into handing over your cash by saying (convincingly) "Your money or your life." The robber has robbed you of your money. But has he also robbed you of your free will?

The robber presents you with an option—you can keep your money and die, or hand over your wallet and live. One option he has taken away from you is for you to keep your money *and* your life as well. You aren't free to do that. But has the robber robbed you of your free will?

This is a hard problem, but let me tentatively venture this answer: In many cases (if not in all), coerced actions don't rob their victims of free will. Of course, they can rob their victims of many things that are precious. And, of course, it often is wrong to place people in situations in which they have the choices (and only the choices) that the robber offers them. My point, however, is that the robbery victim's calculation—that he is better off surrendering the wallet—is very different from the kleptomaniac's "decision" to steal. The robbery victim's mind is functioning quite well; it is the circumstances in which the victim finds himself that are objectionable. In contrast, something has gone seriously wrong with the kleptomaniac's mind—and it is this incapacity that makes him unfree.

A SECOND COMPATIBILIST PROPOSAL:
THE RELEVANCE OF SECOND-ORDER DESIRES

I now want to consider a second compatibilist theory, one that is intended to meet the problem posed by compulsive behavior. This theory has been defended by Gerald Dworkin (in "Acting Freely," *Nous,* Vol. 4, 1970, pp. 367–383) and by Harry Frankfurt (in "Freedom of the Will and the Concept of a Person," *Journal of Philosophy,* Vol. 68, 1971, pp. 5–20). The idea is that people in the grip of a compulsion are unfree because they act on the basis of desires they would rather not have. Suppose you asked a kleptomaniac whether he would prefer to not have an overpowering desire to steal. The kleptomaniac might sadly reply that he would be glad to have this monkey off his back.

The proposal we are considering requires us to distinguish first-order from second-order desires. A second-order desire is a desire about what one's desires should be like. "I'd like to be less selfish" is a second-order remark. It says that I would like to care more about the welfare of others. "I'd like to have an ice cream" or "I'd like Jones to get a raise" are first-order desires. They express desires about what should be true in the world outside the mind. So the proposal is that people act freely when their second-order desires are related in a specific way to their first-order desires. To do an action *A* of one's own free will is to do *A* because one has desires *D,* where one doesn't mind having *D.* This last clause means that one doesn't have the second-order desire that *D* be dropped from one's list of first-order desires.

Although this proposal implies that many people who are in the grip of compulsions are unfree, it still is defective. Imagine a kleptomaniac who is so warped by his compulsion that he can't even recognize that it is harming him. Imagine a compulsive handwasher who has been brainwashed into thinking that handwashing is the greatest thing in the world. Such individuals may not mind having the desires they have. That, however, doesn't show they have free will; it shows only that they don't mind being unfree.

This theory of freedom, like Hume's, fails to explain why some forms of compulsive behavior are unfree. This doesn't mean that no compatibilist theory will work, just that the two I've just examined aren't satisfactory. In the next lecture, I'll outline a third compatibilist account.

Review Questions

1. What does it mean to say that *X* and *Y* are compatible? What does incompatibility mean? What do *X* and *Y* stand for?
2. Define compatibilism, incompatibilism, hard determinism, libertarianism, and soft determinism.
3. What argument have libertarians given for thinking some actions are free? Assess this argument.
4. In the *Fourth Meditation,* Descartes argues that the will is infinite (that is, unlimited, and so absolutely free) as follows:

   > I know from experience that it [my will or freedom of choice] is not restricted in any way. . . . This is because the will simply consists in our ability to do or not do something (that is, to affirm or deny, to pursue or avoid); or rather, it consists simply in the fact that when the intellect puts something forward for affirmation or denial or for pursuit or avoidance, our inclinations are such that we do not feel we are determined by any external force.

   What is Descartes's argument? Evaluate its plausibility.
5. Explain Hume's theory of freedom. What makes it a compatibilist theory? Why does compulsive behavior provide a counterexample to this theory? Why does Locke's example of the man locked in the room provide a counterexample to Hume's theory?
6. Are the following propositions equivalent in meaning? (I) *S* did *A* of her own free will; (II) *S* was free to not do *A*.
7. In Lecture 12, I explained that a definition can be defective because it fails to provide necessary conditions, or because it fails to provide sufficient conditions.

What sort of defect in Hume's definition of freedom is involved in (1) the example of compulsive behavior; (2) the example of the locked room?

Problems for Further Thought

1. In the selection from Campbell's *Selfhood and Godhood* reprinted at the end of this section of the book, Campbell argues that some actions occur neither by chance nor by necessity. These are examples of *creative activity*, "in which [. . .] nothing determines the act save the agent's doing it." According to Campbell, these are the acts that are free. Define what "chance" and "necessity" mean, taking into account the definitions of determinism and indeterminism provided in the previous lecture. Do your definitions allow that some actions may fall into neither category?

2. Political philosophers have often been interested in describing how much freedom of action a society allows its members. Would it be reasonable to measure this by determining how many of a person's desires are satisfiable in the society? There is an objection to this proposal similar to the objection I've formulated to the Dworkin/Frankfurt theory of freedom. What is it?

LECTURE 25

Compatibilism

In the previous lecture, I presented and criticized two compatibilist theories of freedom. Each sought to show that freedom doesn't require the absence of causality; both say that an action is free when it arises by a certain sort of causal process. In this lecture, I'll present a third compatibilist theory, one inspired by an idea suggested by my colleagues Dennis Stampe and Martha Gibson (in their "Of One's Own Free Will," *Philosophy and Phenomenological Research*, Vol. 52, 1992, pp. 529–556). After presenting a simplified version of this theory, I'll describe an objection to it. I won't propose a way of meeting this objection, but will leave the problem of freedom unsolved. However, I do hope to convince you that compatibilism is a plausible view, even though I don't claim that a completely plausible compatibilist theory has yet been articulated.

THE WEATHER VANE ANALOGY

I'll begin with an analogy. Consider a weather vane. This is a device that farmers put on top of their barns to tell them in which direction the wind is blowing. We talk about weather vanes being "stuck." We also talk about weather vanes being "free." What does this mean?

A free weather vane is one that responds to certain causal influences. If the wind is blowing north, a free weather vane will point north. The behavior of a free weather vane isn't uncaused.

A stuck weather vane, on the other hand, doesn't respond to the wind's direction. When a weather vane is stuck pointing due north, there is a causal explanation for why it is pointing in that direction. The explanation, however, has nothing to do with the direction of the wind.

So the difference between a free weather vane and a stuck one isn't that the position of the former is uncaused, whereas the position of the latter has a causal explanation. Both are caused to point in a certain direction by something or other. The difference isn't in *whether* the behavior is caused, but in *what* causes it.

I've just described the ordinary meaning of "free" when it is applied to weather vanes. Notice that our commonsense understanding of this idea involves a compatibilist theory of what it is for a weather vane to be free. The idea is to use this as an analogy for constructing a compatibilist theory of what it is for the will to be free. Of course, weather vanes don't have minds, whereas the issue of freedom of the will has to do with a feature of the mind. Let's press on, however, and see if the analogy can be developed.

FUNCTION AND MALFUNCTION

Why do we say that the vane is free when it is causally responsive to the wind's direction? Why don't we describe a weather vane whose swivel is rusted solid as free, since in that case the direction it points isn't influenced by the wind? A stuck weather vane, after all, is free from the wind's influences. I suggest that the answer is to be found in the fact that the weather vane has a *function*. When it performs its function, its behavior is caused by the wind's direction. When it is stuck, it can't perform its function.

How can this idea about function be applied to the human mind? If we think of different parts of the mind as having functions, then freedom of the will exists if the mind is functioning properly. A malfunction, on the other hand, may result in a "stuck" will—one that is unfree.

Consider the following diagram, which shows how beliefs and desires are formed and then lead, via deliberation, to intentions and thence to action:

$$
\begin{array}{l}
\text{Evidence} \rightarrow \boxed{\text{BGD}} \rightarrow \text{Beliefs} \\
\qquad\quad\; ? \qquad \rightarrow \boxed{\text{DGD}} \rightarrow \text{Desires}
\end{array}
\Biggr\} \rightarrow \boxed{\text{Deliberation}} \rightarrow \text{Intention} \rightarrow \text{Action}
$$

The box labeled "BGD" is the belief-generating device. It is the part of the mind that produces beliefs. Beliefs are its output. The belief-generating device takes account of evidence (other beliefs and experiences); these are its inputs.

The BGD malfunctions when it isn't sensitive to evidence—when it outputs beliefs in a way that ignores the evidence at hand. Perhaps paranoia—the irrational and unshakable conviction that the whole world is conspiring against you—can be described as a malfunction of the BGD. In this situation, the person's beliefs are "stuck." The BGD has malfunctioned because it isn't responsive to evidence.

The DGD is the desire-generating device. It produces desires. Its inputs are the things that cause us to have the desires we do. I've put a question mark where the inputs to the DGD go; the inputs to this device are the things the device is sensitive to when it is functioning properly. Later, I'll discuss what function the DGD might have.

The BGD and the DGD output beliefs and desires, which are fed into a deliberator. This device takes into account the agent's beliefs and desires and decides on the basis of them what the agent should do. This device completes its work when the agent forms the intention to perform some action.

By analogy with the weather vane, a person has free will when the various components involved in the process described in the above diagram are functioning properly. And proper functioning is to be understood to mean that the BGD and the DGD are causally sensitive to certain sorts of causal influences.

WHAT DOES IT MEAN TO ASCRIBE A FUNCTION TO SOMETHING?

Before we can develop this idea much further, we must have some idea of what the word "function" means. In the case of the weather vane, we know what the function of the object is, because it was created by human beings for a certain purpose. If farmers put such objects on their barns for purely ornamental reasons, we might not regard them as malfunctioning when their swivels rust solid. But farmers want weather vanes to respond to the wind's direction; this is their intended function.

If the human mind were created by an Intelligent Designer, and if we could find out why that Designer gave people the kinds of minds they have, we could say what functions the mind and its components subserve. However, if we want a naturalistic, not a theological, account of what it is for parts of the mind to have functions, we must set this idea about an Intelligent Designer (God) to one side.

Consider an analogous problem. We say that the function of the heart is to pump blood. What makes this true? After all, the heart does lots of things. It takes up space in your chest cavity. It also makes noise. But we don't say that the function of the heart is to take up space or to make noise. The problem is that the heart has many effects, but only some of these effects are what the heart is *for*—what it has as its function.

If the heart were created by an Intelligent Designer, that would solve our problem. The Designer's intentions would settle what the function of the heart is. But I'll assume that we want a naturalistic, not a theological, account of heart function. We want to make sense of the idea of function without having to rely on the existence of an Intelligent Designer.

My proposal is that we understand the biological function of the heart in terms of the historical explanation of why people and other organisms have hearts. The reason hearts evolved is that they provided a benefit to the organisms possessing them. The benefit was that hearts pumped blood. As a side effect of the evolution of such blood pumps, it turned out that organisms had noise makers in their chests. But the heart didn't evolve because it made noise. Making noise provided no advantage for survival and reproduction.

Here, then, is a naturalistic account of what it is for an object (or characteristic) to have a function. We don't have to imagine that the object is present because of Intelligent Design. Natural selection (discussed in Lecture 6) is a perfectly satisfactory mechanism. My proposal is that "the function of *o* is to do *F*" means that *o* is present because *o*'s do *F*. The function of the heart is to pump blood (rather than make noise), since individuals have hearts because hearts pump blood (not because they make noise). (For elaboration of this way of understanding the concept of function, see Larry Wright, "Functions," *Philosophical Review,* Vol. 85, 1973, pp. 70–86.)

THE FUNCTION OF THE DESIRE-GENERATING DEVICE

Why do individuals have desires? More specifically, why do individuals have devices (DGDs) that construct desires? What use could this faculty have had in our evolutionary past?

The suggestion I want to consider is that the DGD has the function of representing what is good for the organism. Consider the case of thirst. When an organism gets dehydrated, it would be good for the organism to get some water. Organisms with minds seek out water when they are dehydrated because their DGD produces a desire for water. Like any device, the DGD might malfunction; if it fails to produce a desire for water when the organism is dehydrated, this could handicap the organism in its struggle to survive.

Bear in mind that there are other ways besides forming desires to get organisms to perform actions that satisfy their biological needs. Bacteria are capable of behaviors that satisfy their needs, but they don't have minds (or desires) to help them do this. The suggestion, then, is that the DGD has the function of representing what would be good for the organism; it isn't part of this suggestion that a DGD is the only way to get an organism to act so as to satisfy its needs.

Recall what this claim about the function of the DGD actually means. It means that we possess DGDs because, historically, such devices represented what was good for the organisms that possessed them; organisms with such devices did better at surviving and reproducing than ones that lacked them (or had DGDs that were constructed differently).

If this is right, we can understand why individuals who are in the grip of a compulsion aren't free. Their DGD is stuck; it is malfunctioning because it no longer can represent what would be good for the agent. Kleptomaniacs want to steal even though stealing isn't good for them; indeed, kleptomaniacs sometimes want to steal even when they *know* that it isn't good for them to have this want. Likewise, a compulsive handwasher has an overpowering desire to keep washing his hands even though there is ample evidence available that this is a harm, not a help.

A similar explanation can be given for why brainwashing is able to rob people of their freedom. When people are brainwashed, they are given beliefs and desires on which they subsequently act. These beliefs and desires are "implanted" by short-circuiting the normal function of the belief- and desire-generating devices. The process of brainwashing is intended to cause the BGD and the DGD to malfunction. This is why individuals who are brainwashed to perform some action don't perform that action of their own free will.

So my proposal about freedom is this: An agent freely performs an action if the agent's mind is functioning properly. This includes the idea that the agent's DGD is able to perform the function of representing what is good for the agent. In addition, the idea of well-functioning includes the idea that the agent can rationally deliberate, given the beliefs and desires he or she has.

Although the present proposal and Hume's idea are both compatibilist theories, they are different. Hume thought the crucial consideration was whether the agent's desires control the agent's behavior. The idea I've just described says that it is the entire psychological process—from belief and desire formation through the formation of an intention to act—that settles whether the agent's action is free.

I now want to consider what the present theory of freedom would say in reply to the arguments described in Lecture 23. Each of these arguments, recall, aimed to show that we can't be free, because of some fact about how our beliefs, desires, and actions are caused.

REPLY TO THE DISTANT CAUSATION ARGUMENT

I turn first to the Distant Causation Argument, which I represent as follows:

(1) If an agent freely performs an action, then the agent is responsible for the action.

(2) Agents are not responsible for actions that are caused by factors outside their control.

(3) Every action an agent performs is caused by factors (genes and early childhood environments) over which the agent had no control.

———————————

No action is performed freely.

The compatibilist theory of freedom advanced in this lecture (the "Weather Vane Theory") must reject this argument. But how? The argument is deductively valid. (Identify its logical form.) So, to reject the conclusion, we must reject one or more of the premises.

WHAT DOES RESPONSIBILITY MEAN?

To reply to this argument, I need to examine the concept of *responsibility*. Consider what it means to say that a storm was responsible for some crop damage. Here "responsible for" simply means "causes."

If we use this understanding of the concept of responsibility to clarify premiss (2) of the Distant Causation Argument, we can see that premiss (2) is false. A storm can cause crop damage even though there were causes of the crop damage that the storm didn't control. Consider the following causal chain:

$$X \longrightarrow \text{Storm} \longrightarrow \text{Crop damage}$$

The storm was caused by earlier events X, which existed before the storm occurred. If causation is transitive (see the box on transitivity in Lecture 23), X caused the crop damage. The storm didn't exercise any influence over X, since X happened before the storm even existed. But from this it doesn't follow that the storm didn't cause the crop damage.

So the fact that the crop damage had "distant causes" doesn't mean that the storm wasn't responsible for the crop damage. By the same token, I conclude that premiss (2) in the Distant Causation Argument is false.

MORAL RESPONSIBILITY

It might be replied, in defense of the Distant Causation Argument, that "responsibility" isn't the simple causal concept I've just described. After all, if Patty Hearst was brainwashed by her kidnappers, we might say that she wasn't responsible for robbing the bank. This doesn't mean, however, that she played no causal role in the robbery.

If the storm wasn't responsible for the crop damage, this means that the storm didn't cause the damage. But if Patty Hearst wasn't responsible for what she did, this doesn't mean that she didn't do what she did. What, then, is the difference?

We sometimes say that we don't "hold" people responsible for some of the things they do. In contrast, it sounds funny to say that we don't hold the storm responsible for what it did. Holding X responsible, and deciding not to hold X responsible, seem to imply that X is a moral agent.

When we say that we don't hold Patty Hearst responsible for what she did, I think we mean that we don't *blame* her for her action. We don't think she deserves moral criticism for the robbery if she did it while brainwashed.

If an agent is *morally responsible* for an event (a bank robbery, say), this means (1) that the agent caused the event; and (2) that the occurrence of the event reflects on the agent's moral character. Moral responsibility differs from the simpler idea of causal responsibility; it is this latter concept that we apply to storms, there being no implication of moral praise and blame in such cases.

Suppose we interpret the Distant Causation Argument to be talking about moral responsibility in the sense just described. Understood in this way, premiss (2) is still false. We are morally responsible for many (if not all) of the actions we perform, though the beliefs and desires that cause those actions are themselves results of factors outside our control. The reason is that much of what we do shows what sort of moral character we have.

To say that someone is morally responsible for doing something wrong doesn't automatically mean that he or she should be punished. Unfortunately, the law often seems to connect these two issues. If members of the jury think that Patty Hearst shouldn't be punished for robbing the bank, they must find that she wasn't responsible for what she did. There is a question here that needs to be faced head on, however, one that shouldn't be allowed to slip by.

Suppose someone does something wrong, and we take this to indicate a defect in the person's moral character. Maybe the rather minor lies that people tell have this feature. But surely we don't want to pass laws that say that anyone who lies will go to jail or pay a fine. The reason might be that this legalistic apparatus would intrude into private life so much that society would be worse rather than better as a result. We hold people responsible when they do such things, but this doesn't mean we think they should be punished.

The Distant Causation Argument tries to make it look like agents have nothing to do with the actions they perform—as if it is people's genes and environments that cause their actions, *rather than the agents themselves*. But this is absurd—*we* cause things to happen and these actions reflect on our characters, even though there are causal explanations for why we are the way we are.

REPLY TO THE COULD-NOT-HAVE-DONE-OTHERWISE ARGUMENT

A second argument was presented in Lecture 23 that attempts to show that we lack free will. This is the Could-Not-Have-Done-Otherwise Argument, which can be represented as follows:

(1) If an agent freely performs some action *A*, then the agent could have done otherwise (that is, could have performed some action other than *A*).

(2) People can't perform actions other than the ones they do, in fact, perform.

———————————

Agents never act freely.

Since I believe that the conclusion of this argument is false, I must reject one or both of the premises.

Actually, I think that both are defective. Premiss (1) is mistaken for reasons that Locke brought out in his discussion of the man who decides of his own free will to remain in a room to talk to a friend; unbeknownst to him, the door was locked. This was discussed in the previous lecture.

Premiss (2) also should be examined carefully. In Lecture 14, I formulated an idea that I called the thesis of the ambiguity of necessity. Statements about necessity and possibility often are ambiguous. The example I discussed there was the statement "Joe can't tie his shoes." Interpreted one way, the statement is true (Joe is holding two bags of groceries). Interpreted in another way, the statement is false (if he put down the groceries, he could do it).

I think premiss (2) in the above argument is ambiguous. It could mean either of the following:

(2a) Given the very beliefs and desires the agent had, and given
      that the agent rationally deliberated, he could not
      have performed a different action from the one he did.

(2b) Even if the agent had had a different set of beliefs and desires,
      the agent still could not have produced an action different
      from the one he did.

Proposition (2a) basically says that rational deliberation is a deterministic process: Beliefs and desires determine a unique choice of action, if those beliefs and desires are rationally evaluated. Since I don't think that determinism is true, I doubt that (2a) is correct. Even if it were correct, however, I don't see why that would show that we are never free. Even if weather vanes were deterministic systems, that wouldn't show that they are never free. I believe the same holds true of the human mind.

Proposition (2b) denies that the agent's beliefs and desires make a difference; (2b) says that the agent would have done the same thing even if the agent had had different beliefs and desires. I think that this statement is false—it is basically the doctrine of fatalism, which I discussed and set aside in Lecture 23.

In summary, proposition (2) is ambiguous. If it is clarified to mean proposition (2a), then it fails to show that we are unfree. If it is clarified to mean proposition (2b), then it is false. I conclude that the Could-Not-Have-Done-Otherwise Argument fails to show that freedom is an illusion.

ARE COERCED ACTIONS UNFREE?

The Distant Causation Argument and the Could-Not-Have-Done-Otherwise Argument don't refute compatibilism in general or the Weather Vane Theory in particular. I now want to consider an objection that is aimed specifically at the Weather Vane Theory. It criticizes the theory for what the theory says about coerced action.

It seems natural to say that coerced acts aren't performed freely. However, when the robber coerces you into surrendering your wallet, it doesn't seem to be true that your mind has malfunctioned. You correctly realize it is in your best interest to hand over your wallet, and so that is what you do. Action under coercion is often no

What Is Coercion?

The robber says, "Your money or your life." You would prefer to stay alive without forfeiting your money, but that option isn't available. The choice is clear, and so you hand over the money.

You are in a grocery store and want a loaf of bread. The grocer will let you have the loaf only if you pay $1.50. You would prefer to have the loaf without handing over the money, but that option isn't available. The choice is clear, and so you hand over the money.

The robber has coerced you; the grocer hasn't. What is the difference?

There is a moral difference: What the robber did was wrong, but the grocer did nothing wrong. However, this doesn't seem to define what coercion is. You can coerce people for morally impeccable reasons. Suppose you are using a life preserver for a pillow and I need to throw the preserver to someone who is drowning. If you refuse to hand it over willingly, I may have to coerce you. But in coercing you, I've done nothing wrong.

There is a difference in magnitude: In the robbery example, you want to stay alive far more than you want to hold onto your wallet. In the grocer case, you would rather get the loaf than keep the $1.50, but the difference between these outcomes is far less momentous. Does this mean that coercion means putting people in situations in which it makes a great deal of difference to them what they do? Suppose I offer you $1,000 if you smile. Have I coerced you into smiling? You would much rather have the money and smile than forgo the money and not smile. That doesn't make my offer coercive, however.

Some years ago, there was a program of testing new drugs in prisons. Prisoners would receive time off their sentences if they agreed to run the risk of being guinea pigs. The program was discontinued, partly because the offer was thought to be coercive. Do you agree that this offer would be coercive?

Let's return to the original question: What distinguishes the grocer from the robber? What, in short, is coercion?

different from other, less dramatic, actions produced by rational deliberation, at least as far as the inner workings of the mind are concerned. So if coerced actions are always unfree, the Weather Vane Theory is in trouble, since the theory says that we act freely when our minds are functioning properly.

My reply is to claim that coercion doesn't rob an individual of free will. I think that when you hand your wallet to the robber because you want to stay alive, your will is functioning perfectly well. Your situation here is quite different from that of a kleptomaniac or compulsive handwasher, whose DGDs have malfunctioned.

I guess there probably are *some* cases of coerced behavior that are unfree. Suppose that the robber's threat frightens you so much that you totally lose your capacity to think clearly. You are so overcome by fear that you hand over your wallet, but not for any good reason. In this case, perhaps the coerced action is unfree. However, I think that many (perhaps most) cases of coercion aren't like this. People in such situations rarely "lose their heads"; often they show a considerable degree of care and self-control (you gingerly hand over your wallet, all the while assuring the robber that you have no intention of resisting). I conclude that a coerced action doesn't have to involve the will's being unfree.

AN OBJECTION TO THE WEATHER VANE THEORY: FREE, RATIONAL, SELF-SACRIFICE

Although the three objections I've just discussed don't undermine the Weather Vane Theory of Freedom, the one I'll discuss now poses a serious challenge. According to the Weather Vane Theory, the function of the desire-generating device (DGD) is to produce desires that represent what is good for the agent. I want to argue that this thesis is either too vague or is mistaken, if we consider the case of *rational self-sacrifice.*

Consider people who calmly and rationally decide to sacrifice their own interests to help others (perhaps their family or friends or nation). A soldier, for example, decides to throw himself on a grenade in order to save the lives of his comrades. Is it possible for a soldier to do this of his own free will?

I would say *yes*, but what does the Weather Vane Theory say? We have to ask whether the DGD is functioning properly here. Does the desire that it produces— the desire to sacrifice the agent's life to save the lives of his comrades—really represent what is good for the agent? Interpreted in one way, the answer seems to be *no.* The self-sacrifice would be good for others, not good for the soldier himself. If the DGD has the function of representing what is good for the agent, then it seems to have malfunctioned in this instance.

The other alternative is to interpret the account given of the function of the DGD so that the soldier's DGD isn't malfunctioning in this case. We might say that the soldier's DGD *is* representing what is good for him to do, since he believes a moral principle that says that this sort of self-sacrifice is morally required. But now "representing what is good for the agent" is being interpreted to mean "representing what the agent *thinks* is good." The problem with this way of understanding the function of the DGD is that the kleptomaniac who thinks that stealing is the best thing in the world also will be said to have a well-functioning DGD.

This suggests, I think, that the description I've been using of the DGD needs to be modified. I don't think rational self-sacrifice indicates that the individual's will is unfree. According to the Weather Vane Theory, this requires that the individual's DGD not have malfunctioned. To be able to say this, however, we need to revise the description of what the function of the DGD is.

This is all I'll say about the problem of freedom of the will. I hope you now understand what a compatibilist theory of freedom would be like. Even though the Weather Vane Theory isn't satisfactory as it stands, this theory, I think, suggests that there may be some merit in the compatibilist position. There does seem to be a difference between people engaged in normal rational deliberation and people who are caught in the grip of a compulsion. The Weather Vane Theory seeks to characterize what this difference is. It remains an open question in philosophy how the concept of freedom of the will should be understood.

Review Questions

1. In this lecture I sketched a commonsense picture of what it means to say that a weather vane is "free." What is this commonsense idea? Why say that it is compatibilist in character?
2. A weather vane has a function because it was designed by people to do something. What could it mean to say that the heart functions to pump blood, if the heart isn't the product of Intelligent Design?
3. What is the difference between saying that X is causally responsible for Y (as in "The storm was responsible for the crop damage") and saying that X is morally responsible for Y?
4. What is mistaken in the Distant Causation Argument and in the Could-Not-Have-Done-Otherwise Argument?
5. Are coerced actions performed freely? What consequence does the answer to this question have for the Weather Vane Theory?
6. What problem does the existence of rational self-sacrifice pose for the Weather Vane Theory?

Problems for Further Thought

1. In Lecture 5 on the Argument from Design, I said that Aristotle's teleological conception of the universe has been rejected by modern science. People, tools, and nonhuman organisms are goal-directed systems; but it seems implausible to think of a mountain or the solar system in this way. In the present lecture, I presented an account of what it means to ascribe a function to something. How does this account help explain why it is mistaken, for example, to say that the function of rain is to provide farm crops with water?
2. Can the Weather Vane Theory of Freedom be revised so that it avoids the counterexample presented here of free, rational, self-sacrifice? How might this be done?

LECTURE 26

Psychological Egoism

In earlier lectures, I've used a standard and commonsensical model of what rational deliberation is. This model was employed in the discussion of Pascal's Wager (Lecture 10) and in the three lectures (23–25) on the free will problem. The idea is that rational deliberators decide what to do by taking account of their beliefs and desires.

This commonsense idea has been made precise by the science called decision theory; rational agents are said to "maximize expected utility."

This idea seems to lead to the conclusion that rational people are fundamentally selfish: They act so as to achieve the goals they have—they act to get what they want. Not only is this true of a person we would ordinarily call selfish—for example, a business executive whose only goal is to make as much money as possible. The idea seems to apply to everybody. Even Mother Teresa, who devoted her life to helping the needy in India, would count as selfish, according to this idea. It is true that Mother Teresa didn't strive for wealth or material comfort. Her values placed fundamental importance on reducing the amount of suffering in the world. However, in devoting her life to this, she aimed at satisfying her own goals.

Mother Teresa gained satisfaction from her work, just as the businessman just mentioned gains satisfaction from his. If Mother Teresa had done something else with her life, she would have felt guilty. Mother Teresa's payoff came from reducing the suffering of others; she gained a feeling of satisfaction and avoided the guilt feelings she would have experienced if she had done something else. The businessman also gains satisfaction; his comes in the currency of dollars and cents. The idea is that both act on the basis of their own wants; both do what they do in order to gain a feeling of satisfaction (and to avoid such negative feelings as guilt).

The previous two paragraphs express in an imprecise way the idea I'll call psychological egoism (PE, for short). In this lecture, I'll clarify what PE says and argue that in some important ways it is false. I won't reject the model of decision making used so far—that rational agents act on the basis of the beliefs and desires they have. However, I'll argue that PE doesn't follow from this model. Even though Mother Teresa tried to get what she wanted, just as the businessman does, there yet may be important differences between them; I'll try to clarify what these are.

TWO TRUISMS

I want to formulate what PE says more precisely. Let's begin by identifying two propositions that aren't in dispute. The debate over whether PE is true is *not* settled by the following facts:

(1) Rational agents decide which action to perform by consulting their beliefs and desires.

(2) At times, rational agents are guided by desires that are other-directed.

Proposition (1) describes the model of rational deliberation I've been assuming. It says nothing about what the *content* is of people's desires; it doesn't say *what* people want. Statement (1) says that whatever it is that a rational agent wants, that agent's behavior will be aimed at achieving those goals. The debate over PE isn't settled by (1); (1) is a "truism" to which defenders and critics of PE can agree.

Proposition (2) also is a truism. It says that people often have desires that concern the situations of others. A benevolent person may want others to suffer less. A sadist may want others to suffer more. Both of these individuals have what I'll call *other-directed preferences*. It makes a difference to them what the situations of other people are like.

I'll use the term "other-directed preference" to refer to preferences that people have about the situations of others, preferences that don't mention their own situation. If I prefer that *others suffer less rather than more,* this is an other-directed preference that I have; note that the italicized words, which specify the content of the preference, refer to others, but not to me.

Similarly, a *self-directed preference* is any preference that I have that refers to my own well-being, but doesn't say anything about the situation of others. If I prefer that *I have more money rather than less,* this is a self-directed preference that I have.

Some preferences are neither purely self-directed nor purely other-directed. They are *mixed.* If I want to be the best chess player in the world, this is a preference whose content refers both to me and to others.

Proposition (2) doesn't refute PE. I might genuinely desire that your back gets scratched; but I would be an egoist if my only reason for wanting this is that I see it as a way to have my back get scratched as well. PE doesn't deny the existence of other-directed preferences. Rather, PE asserts that when we want others to do well (or ill), we don't care about others for their own sakes; the only reason we care about what happens to them is that we think that their welfare will affect our own welfare. PE maintains that concern for others is *purely instrumental, never ultimate.*

GOALS AND SIDE EFFECTS OF AN ACT

The philosopher/psychologist William James (1842–1910) discussed the issue of whether PE is true. In his *Principles of Psychology* (London, Henry Holt, 1890), he noted a fact about PE that we should consider. He pointed out (as had Aristotle) that an action may bring a feeling of satisfaction to an agent without the action's having been done in order to obtain the feeling.

James thought that many altruistic acts are of this sort. We help people because we genuinely care about their situations. It happens that our helping others is accompanied by our receiving a glow of satisfaction. But, according to James, obtaining the glow wasn't the goal; it was an unintended side effect.

If James were right, PE would be false. A defender of PE, however, would deny part of what James is saying. A defender of PE might say that James has the story precisely backward. It is true that an action can produce an effect that isn't the real goal of the action. But a psychological egoist might say that when we help others, what we really are after is the glow of satisfaction; the fact that others receive a benefit is merely a side effect of our trying to make ourselves feel good.

There is a point of agreement between James and this defender of PE. Although they disagree over which effect of the helping behavior is the goal and which is the mere side effect, they agree that there is a difference between the two. So let's identify a third proposition on which the two sides concur:

> (3) That an action has a particular effect does not necessarily mean that it was performed in order to produce that effect.

It is easy to see why (3) is correct, quite apart from the issue of whether PE is true. Statement (3) simply notes the difference between intended and unintended consequences of an action.

A SIMPLE EXAMPLE

In order to clarify what PE asserts, I want to focus on a simple example. You see an advertisement in a magazine. It asks you to send a check for $10 to help starving children. You are fairly well-off. You could find enjoyable things to do with $10. But the picture in the ad is pathetic. You believe that a $10 contribution will make a real difference for the people involved (it won't solve the whole problem, of course). You think for a moment and then put a $10 check in the mail to the charity.

In this case, were you an altruist or an egoist? On the surface, it may appear that you were altruistically motivated. After all, it seems that you wrote the check because you felt a genuine concern for the starving children. An advocate of PE, however, would maintain that your real motives, of which you perhaps aren't fully conscious, were purely selfish. You derived a glow of satisfaction—a nice feeling about yourself—from the donation. You also avoiding feeling guilty. These psychological benefits were the real motives for your behavior, or so PE asserts.

To decide what your motivation was in this situation, I want to describe four kinds of people. Three of them have altruistic motives; one of them has purely egoistic motives. After I've explained these four possibilities, I'll consider how we might go about deciding which of the categories you occupy.

FOUR PREFERENCE STRUCTURES

The first type of individual I'll call the Pure Egoist. This individual cares nothing for the welfare of others; the only thing that matters to a Pure Egoist is his or her own situation.

The following two-by-two table illustrates the preferences of the Pure Egoist. The table answers two questions about this individual. What preference does he have as to whether he will receive a benefit? What preference does he have as to whether the children do better rather than worse? The first question has to do with his self-directed preferences; the second concerns his other-directed preferences.

The Pure Egoist

Other-directed

		+	−
Self-directed	+	4	4
	−	1	1

The Pure Egoist cares only that he himself receive more (+) rather than less (−) of whatever the benefit is that is at issue. It is a matter of indifference to this person whether the children do better (+) or worse (−). This individual isn't benevolent; he also isn't malevolent. He simply doesn't care one way or the other about others.

The numbers in this table represent the order of the agent's preferences. The absolute values have no meaning; I could as easily have used "9" and "5" instead of "4" and "1."

If you were a Pure Egoist, would you give $10 to charity? Donating the money would have two effects. You would receive a glow of satisfaction; and the children would be made better off. On the other hand, not donating the money also would have two effects. You would feel guilty about yourself; and the children would be worse off. (For simplicity, I'm ignoring how you feel about retaining $10 or giving it away.) In this situation, there are two possible actions, whose consequences are represented in the table by the upper-left entry (+ to self and + to other) and the entry in the lower-right (− to self and − to other).

In this situation, the Pure Egoist will choose the first action; he will donate the $10 to charity. He therefore will choose an action that benefits others. This benefit to others, however, isn't the goal of his action but a mere side effect. If you were a Pure Egoist, you would help the starving, but your real motive would be to make yourself feel good.

The second personality type is the mirror image of the Pure Egoist. It is the Pure Altruist:

The Pure Altruist

Other-directed

		+	−
Self-directed	+	4	1
	−	4	1

This individual cares nothing about his own situation, but only wants the other person to be better off.

What would a Pure Altruist do if he had to choose between the actions represented by the entries in the upper-left and lower-right cells of the table? He either must benefit both self and other, or benefit neither. Notice that the Pure Altruist will choose the action that benefits both himself and the other person.

If you were a Pure Altruist, you would donate the money to charity. A consequence of doing this would be that you would feel good about yourself. However, in this case, the benefit to self would be a side effect of the act, not the act's real motive.

So in a choice between the upper-left and lower-right cells, the Pure Altruist will do the same thing that the Pure Egoist will do. Their actions will be the same, but their motives will differ. The Pure Egoist acts solely in order to benefit himself; benefits to others are just side effects. The Pure Altruist acts solely to benefit others; benefits to self are just side effects.

PEOPLE ARE RARELY PURE ALTRUISTS OR PURE EGOISTS

Which of these preference structures describes real people? I think that in the vast majority of cases, the answer is *neither*. In most choice situations, most of us care about both self *and* others. We don't like to feel guilty; we also enjoy the glow of satisfaction that comes from thinking well of ourselves. Most of us have preferences about having other goods (like money) as well. But besides these self-directed preferences, we also have other-directed preferences. We often are either benevolent or malevolent in how we feel about the situation of others.

Both the Pure Egoist and the Pure Altruist have only one kind of preference. Real people usually have both. So we must complicate our representation.

I now introduce a third character—the S-over-O Pluralist.

The S-over-O Pluralist

Other-directed

		+	−
	+	4	3
Self-directed			
	−	2	1

This individual prefers that he be better off rather than worse off (since $4 > 2$ and $3 > 1$). He also prefers that other people be better off rather than worse off (since $4 > 3$ and $2 > 1$). So this individual has both self-directed and other-directed preferences. This is why I call him a Pluralist. I've called this person an S-over-O Pluralist because of what he does when self interest *conflicts* with the interests of others. Suppose the choice is between two actions. The first action provides him with a benefit while the other individual goes without; this is the outcome in the upper-right box. The second action provides the other with a benefit while he himself goes without; this is the lower-left outcome. When self-interest and the welfare of others conflict, the S-over-O Pluralist gives priority to himself $(3 > 2)$. His self-directed preferences are *stronger* than his other-directed preferences.

What's the difference between the S-over-O Pluralist and the Pure Egoist? The Pure Egoist doesn't care at *all* about the situation of others. The S-over-O Pluralist *does* prefer that others be better off rather than worse. Both, however, say "me first," when self-interest conflicts with the welfare of others.

The last character I want to describe is the O-over-S Pluralist:

The O-over-S Pluralist

Other-directed

		+	−
Self-directed	+	4	2
	−	3	1

The O-over-S Pluralist cares about others and about himself as well; this is why he is a pluralist. I call him an O-over-S Pluralist to describe what he does when self-interest and the interests of others conflict. If an O-over-S Pluralist has to choose between the upper-right and lower-left cells, he will choose the lower left $(3 > 2)$. He will sacrifice his own well-being so that the interests of the other person will be satisfied.

Notice that, of the four motivational structures I have described, only one of them completely lacks an altruistic motive. Psychological egoism says that people are Pure Egoists.

It should not be assumed that all of a person's motives, throughout his or her life, correspond to just one of these four motivational structures. For example, a person might be a Pure Egoist in one situation and an S-over-O Pluralist in another. These motivational structures are not intended to describe stable traits of people, but the traits that a person might have in a given situation in which there is a choice between actions that have consequences both for self and for someone else.

I noted before that when a Pure Altruist or a Pure Egoist face a choice between the upper-left and lower-right cells, they behave in the same way—both choose the action that benefits both self and other. The same is true of the S-over-O Pluralist and the O-over-S Pluralist. The four characters behave identically when self-interest *co-incides* with the welfare of others. This means that how people behave in such situations is completely uninformative; the behavior doesn't help you figure out which of the four motivational structures they have. This is precisely what is going on in the example in which you donate $10 to charity.

You would have donated the money no matter which of these four preference structures you possessed. How, then, are we to tell whether you are an altruist or an egoist?

The difference between Pure Egoists and S-over-O Pluralists, on the one hand, and O-over-S Pluralists and Pure Altruists, on the other, shows up when there is a *conflict* between helping one's self and having others be better off. In a situation of this sort, the agent must choose between being in the upper-right box (+ to self, − to other) and the lower-left box (− to self, + to other). People who choose to help others at cost to themselves in such conflict situations can't be Pure Egoists. However, people who help themselves and ignore the needs of others may be Pure Egoists, or they may be S-over-O Pluralists. To help figure out what your motives were when you gave $10 to the charity, let's put you in this sort of conflict situation.

When you contemplated sending $10 to the charity, there was no conflict; the action that made you feel good also made the starving children better off. Because self-interest and the welfare of others *coincided,* it was impossible to tell what your motivation for helping was. To gain insight into your motives, we must ask what you would have done if there had been a conflict between self-interest and the welfare of the starving children.

AN EXPERIMENTAL TEST

To visualize what such a conflict situation would be like, suppose I had made you the following promise as you sat at your desk deliberating about whether to write a check to the charity:

> Once you decide whether to write the check, I'll give you a pill that will cause you to *misremember* what you did. Thus, if you write the check, the pill will cause you to believe that you didn't, and so you will end up feeling guilty. And if you decide not to write the check, the pill will cause you to believe that you did do so, in which case you will end up feeling good about yourself.

Suppose you trust me to do what I say I'll do. Will you write the check or not?

In this hypothetical situation, self-interest and the welfare of others conflict. You can *either* feel good about yourself or help the starving children. You can't do both. What you choose shows what matters more to you.

My prediction is that you might well choose to write the check. If so, you have altruistic motives. It is false that the only thing you care about is feeling good about yourself. If, on the other hand, you decide not to write the check, how should this behavior be interpreted? I suggested before that it is ambiguous. It is consistent with your being a Pure Egoist, but the behavior also is consistent with your being an S-over-O Pluralist.

When people send checks to charity in the real world, it may not be entirely clear why they do so. We can determine what their preference structures are if we consider what they would have done if self-interest and the interest of others had conflicted. The experiment described here is a way to think about that kind of situation. My guess is that many people who give money to charity have altruistic motives in the sense defined here.

If so, psychological egoism is false as a generality. At least sometimes, people care about others, not just out of self-interest, but because the welfare of others is one of their ultimate concerns. This doesn't mean they don't care about themselves. It also doesn't mean that people don't value the glow of satisfaction and the freedom from guilt feelings they receive from helping others. Altruistically motivated people don't have to be Pure Altruists.

Apportioning Causal Responsibility

Events usually have more than one cause. A fatal car crash may be due to a slippery road surface, to the driver's carelessness, to the condition of the car's tires, to the position of a concrete wall, and so on. It is a mistake to think that precisely one of these was the "real" cause; each factor played a causal role.

Once we recognize that an event has many causes, we may wish to say which was "more important." The following situation provides an example of how the issue of apportioning causal responsibility may be addressed.

Suppose that you are a farmer who grows two fields of corn. The corn in the first field is shorter than the corn in the second. Upon investigation, you find that the corn in the first field has received less water and less fertilizer than the corn in the second. You suspect that the extra fertilizer going to the second field may have helped the corn there to grow taller; you also think that the additional water going to the second field may have been a help as well. Your question is, did these factors really make a difference? And if so, which was more important, the extra fertilizer or the extra water?

This problem can be represented by a two-by-two table. The corn in the first field received one unit of fertilizer and one unit of water; the corn in the second field received two units of each. The entries in the table represent the average height of the corn in each field:

	Water	
	W1	W2
F1	1	
F2		4

Fertilizer

What experiment would you perform to find out whether an increase in fertilizer makes a difference? How would you find out whether an increase in water makes a difference? What would it mean to say that each makes a difference, but that one makes more of a difference than the other?

How is this problem related to the issue of egoism and altruism discussed in this lecture?

In saying this, I'm not claiming that people *always* have altruistic ultimate motives. In some situations, some people are altruistically motivated; in others, perhaps people are not. What I reject is the thesis that we are Pure Egoists *in every choice situation we face.* Once egoism is clarified in the way I've suggested, I believe that PE turns out to be false as a general theory of human motivation.

Review Questions

1. Give an example of an action that has two consequences, one of which was the goal of the action, the other of which was an unintended consequence.

2. What are self-directed and other-directed preferences? Give examples of each. Are there preferences that fall into neither category?
3. Represent each of the following preference structures by drawing a two-by-two table: (I) a *radical egalitarian* (someone who cares only that self and other receive the same degree of benefit); (II) a *utilitarian* (someone whose one concern is that more people benefit rather than fewer); (III) someone who is purely *malevolent* (who doesn't care about himself, but wants only that others be worse off rather than better).
4. What is the difference between the Pure Egoist and the Pure Altruist? There is a kind of choice situation in which these two individuals will behave in the same way. Describe a case of this kind.
5. What is the difference between the O-over-S Pluralist and the Pure Altruist? What is the difference between the S-over-O Pluralist and the Pure Egoist?
6. There is a kind of choice situation in which people who have altruistic motives will behave differently from people who do not. Describe a case of this kind.
7. When you help someone and this makes you feel good, how can you tell whether your motivation was altruistic or egoistic (or both)?

Problems for Further Thought

1. In the experiment I described, there is a *time lag* between my describing the pill to you and your deciding what you will do. Suppose you decide to send the check to charity (and so the pill makes you falsely believe you did no such thing). I claimed this behavior shows you are an altruist. Could a defender of PE reply that you felt good about yourself in the time between my description and your decision, and that your behavior was therefore selfishly motivated?
2. Suppose people with altruistic preference structures have them because their parents rewarded them with love and approval for helping others. Would this show that altruists are really egoists—that what really motivates them is parental approval?
3. In this lecture, I tried to clarify what it means to ask *whether* someone is altruistically motivated. Two quantitative issues remain. How would you measure *how* altruistic someone is? And what would it mean to say that one person is *more altruistic* than another?
4. (Suggested by Roy Sorensen) In the experiment described in this lecture, I assumed that the only egoistic motive that you might have is your wanting to feel good about yourself. This assumption allowed me to claim that if you donate to charity in the experiment, your motives are not exclusively egoistic. However, perhaps psychological egoism can be saved as a theory if we expand the list of what pure egoists care about. Why can't egoism maintain that people who donate to charity have the ultimate goal of being generous people. This goal is self-directed—the claim is that people want to have a certain type of personality. Evaluate this suggestion.

Readings

BERTRAND RUSSELL

Other Minds Are Known by Analogy
from One's Own Case

In this excerpt from **Human Knowledge: Its Scope and Limits** (1948), Russell argues that each of us knows about the mental characteristics of other people by analogy with our own case. You know by introspection which of your various mental states occurs when you behave in specific ways. Hence, the observation that others behave in similar ways makes it probable that they occupy similar mental states.

In Lecture 19, I described Ryle's objection to this argument. It resembles an objection (discussed in Lecture 5) that Hume made to the Argument from Design.

The problem with which we are concerned is the following. We observe in ourselves such occurrences as remembering, reasoning, feeling pleasure, and feeling pain. We think that sticks and stones do not have these experiences, but that other people do. Most of us have no doubt that the higher animals feel pleasure and pain, though I was once assured by a fisherman that "Fish have no sense nor feeling." I failed to find out how he had acquired this knowledge. Most people would disagree with him, but would be doubtful about oysters and starfish. However this may be, common sense admits an increasing doubtfulness as we descend in the animal kingdom, but as regards human beings it admits no doubt.

It is clear that belief in the minds of others requires some postulate that is not required in physics, since physics can be content with a knowledge of structure. My present purpose is to suggest what this further postulate may be.

Bertrand Russell, "Other Minds Are Known by Analogy from One's Own Case," from *Human Knowledge: Its Scope and Limits* (London: Unwin Hyman Ltd., 1948), pp. 482–486. Reproduced with permission of Taylor & Francis Books Ltd., with acknowledgment to the Bertrand Russell Peace Foundation.

It is clear that we must appeal to something that may be vaguely called "analogy." The behavior of other people is in many ways analogous to our own, and we suppose that it must have analogous causes. What people say is what we should say if we had certain thoughts, and so we infer that they probably have these thoughts. They give us information which we can sometimes subsequently verify. They behave in ways in which we behave when we are pleased (or displeased) in circumstances in which we should be pleased (or displeased). We may talk over with a friend some incident which we have both experienced, and find that his reminiscences dovetail with our own; this is particularly convincing when he remembers something that we have forgotten but that he recalls to our thoughts. Or again: you set your boy a problem in arithmetic, and with luck he gets the right answer; this persuades you that he is capable of arithmetical reasoning. There are, in short, very many ways in which my responses to stimuli differ from those of "dead" matter, and in all these ways other people resemble me. As it is clear to me that the causal laws governing my behavior have to do with "thoughts," it is natural to infer that the same is true of the analogous behavior of my friends.

The inference with which we are at present concerned is not merely that which takes us beyond solipsism, by maintaining that sensations have causes about which *something* can be known. This kind of inference . . . suffices for physics. . . . We are concerned now with a much more specific kind of inference, the kind that is involved in our knowledge of the thoughts and feelings of others—assuming that we have such knowledge. It is of course obvious that such knowledge is more or less doubtful. There is not only the general argument that we may be dreaming; there is also the possibility of ingenious automata. There are calculating machines that do sums much better than our schoolboy sons; there are gramophone records that remember impeccably what So-and-so said on such-and-such an occasion; there are people in the cinema who, though copies of real people, are not themselves alive. There is no theoretical limit to what ingenuity could achieve in the ways of producing the illusion of life where in fact life is absent.

But, you will say, in all such cases it was the thoughts of human beings that produced the ingenious mechanism. Yes, but how do you know this? And how do you know that the gramophone does *not* "think"?

There is, in the first place, a difference in the causal laws of observable behavior. If I say to a student, "Write me a paper on Descartes's reasons for believing in the existence of matter," I shall, if he is industrious, cause a certain response. A gramophone record might be so constructed as to respond to this stimulus, perhaps better than the student, but if so it would be incapable of telling me anything about any other philosopher, even if I threatened to refuse to give it a degree. One of the most notable peculiarities of human behavior is change of response to a given stimulus. An ingenious person could construct an automaton which would always laugh at his jokes, however often it heard them; but a human being, after laughing a few times, will yawn, and end by saying, "How I laughed the first time I heard that joke."

But the differences in observable behavior between living and dead matter do not suffice to prove that there are "thoughts" connected with living bodies other than my own. It is probably possible theoretically to account for the behavior of living bodies by purely physical causal laws, and it is probably impossible to refute materialism by external observation alone. If we are to believe that there are thoughts and feelings other than our own, that must be in virtue of some inference in which our own thoughts and feelings are relevant, and such an inference must go beyond what is needed in physics.

I am, of course, not discussing the history of how we come to believe in other minds. We find ourselves believing in them when we first begin to reflect; the thought that Mother may be angry or pleased is one which arises in early infancy. What I am discussing is the possibility of a postulate which shall establish a rational connection between this belief and data, e.g., between the belief "Mother is angry" and the hearing of a loud voice.

The abstract schema seems to be as follows. We know, from observation of ourselves, a causal law of the form "A causes B," where A is a "thought" and B a physical occurrence. We sometimes observe a B when we cannot observe any A; we then infer an unobserved A. For example: I know when I say, "I'm thirsty," I say so, usually, because I am thirsty, and therefore, when I hear the sentence "I'm thirsty" at a time when I am not thirsty, I assume that someone else is thirsty. I assume this more readily if I see before me a hot, drooping body which goes on to say, "I have walked twenty desert miles in this heat with never a drop to drink." It is evident that my confidence in the "inference" is increased by increased complexity in the datum and also by increased certainty of the causal law derived from subjective observation, provided the causal law is such as to account for the complexities of the datum.

It is clear that insofar as plurality of causes is to be suspected, the kind of inference we have been considering is not valid. We are supposed to know "A causes B," and also to know that B has occurred; if this is to justify us in inferring A, we must know that *only* A causes B. Or, if we are content to infer that A is probable, it will suffice if we can know that in most cases it is A that causes B. If you hear thunder without having seen lightning, you confidently infer that there was lightning, because you are convinced that the sort of noise you heard is seldom caused by anything except lightning. As this example shows, our principle is not only employed to establish the existence of other minds but is habitually assumed, though in a less concrete form, in physics. I say "a less concrete form" because unseen lightning is only abstractly similar to seen lightning, whereas we suppose the similarity of other minds to our own to be by no means purely abstract.

Complexity in the observed behavior of another person, when this can all be accounted for by a simple cause such as thirst, increases the probability of the inference by diminishing the probability of some other cause. I think that in ideally favorable circumstances the argument would be formally as follows:

From subjective observation I know that A, which is a thought or feeling, causes B, which is a bodily act, e.g., a statement. I know also that, whenever B is an act of my own body, A is its cause. I now observe an act of the kind B in a body not my own, and I am having no thought or feeling of the kind A. But I still believe, on the basis of self-observation, that only A can cause B; I therefore infer that there was an A which caused B, though it was not an A that I could observe. On this ground I infer that other people's bodies are associated with minds, which resemble mine in proportion as their bodily behavior resembles my own.

In practice, the exactness and certainty of the above statement must be softened. We cannot be sure that, in our subjective experience, A is the only cause of B. And even if A is the only cause of B in our experience, how can we know that this holds outside our experience? It is not necessary that we should know this with any certainty; it is enough if it is highly probable. It is the assumption of probability in such cases that is our postulate. The postulate may therefore be stated as follows:

> If, whenever we can observe whether A and B are present or absent, we find that every case of B has an A as a causal antecedent, then it is probable that most B's have A as causal antecedents, even in cases where observation does not enable us to know whether A is present or not.

This postulate, if accepted, justifies the inference to other minds, as well as many other inferences that are made unreflectingly by common sense.

J. J. C. SMART

Mental Processes Are Physical

In this excerpt from **"Sensations and Brain Processes"** (1959), Smart defends the mind/brain identity theory against a number of objections.

. . . The suggestion I wish if possible to avoid is . . . that [such a statement as] "I am in pain" is a genuine report, and that what it reports is an irreducibly psychical something. . . .

Why do I wish to avoid this suggestion? Mainly because of Occam's razor. It seems to me that science is increasingly giving us a viewpoint whereby organisms are able to be seen as physiochemical mechanisms; it seems that the behavior of man himself will one day be explicable in mechanistic terms. There does seem to be, so far as science is concerned, nothing in the world but increasingly complex arrangements of physical constituents. All except for one place: in consciousness. That is, for a full description of what is going on in a man you would have to describe not only the physical processes in his tissues, glands, nervous system, and so forth, but also his states of consciousness: his visual, auditory, and tactual sensations, his aches and pains. That these are *correlated* with brain processes does not help, for to say that they are *correlated* [with them] is to say that they are something "over and above" [them]. You cannot

J. J. C. Smart, from "Sensations and Brain Processes," *Philosophical Review,* 68 (1959), pp. 141–156. Copyright 1959 Cornell University. Reprinted by permission of the publisher.

correlate something with itself. You correlate footprints with burglars, but not Bill Sykes the burglar with Bill Sykes the burglar. So sensations, states of consciousness, do seem to be the one sort of thing left outside the physicalist picture, and for various reasons I just cannot believe that this can be so. That everything should be explicable in terms of physics (together of course with descriptions of the ways in which parts are put together . . .) except the occurrence of sensations seems to me frankly unbelievable. . . . [I]t is the object of this paper to show that there are no philosophical arguments which compel us to be dualists. . . .

Why should not sensations just be brain processes of a certain sort? There are, of course, well known . . . philosophical objections to the view that reports of sensations are reports of brain processes, but I shall try to argue that these arguments are by no means as cogent as is commonly thought to be the case.

Let me first try to state more accurately the thesis that sensations are brain processes. It is not the thesis that, for example . . . "ache" means the same as "brain process of sort X" (where "X" is replaced by a description of a certain sort of brain process). It is that, in so far as "ache" [i.e., "so and so has an ache"] is the report of a process, it is a report of a process that *happens to be* a brain process. It follows that the thesis does not claim that sensation statements can be *translated* into statements about brain processes. Nor does it claim that the logic of a sensation statement is the same as that of a brain-process statement. All it claims is that in so far as a sensation statement is a report of something, that something is in fact a brain process. Sensations are nothing over and above brain processes. Nations are nothing "over and above" citizens, but this does not prevent the logic of nation statements from being very different from the logic of citizen statements, nor does it insure the translatability of nation statements into citizen statements.

When I say that a sensation is a brain process or that lightning is an electrical discharge, I am using "is" in the sense of strict identity. (Just as in the . . . proposition "7 is identical with the smallest prime number greater than 5.") When I say that a sensation is a brain process or that lightning is an electrical discharge I do not mean just that the sensation is somehow spatially or temporally continuous with the brain process or that the lightning is just spatially or temporally continuous with the discharge. . . .

I shall now discuss various possible objections to the view that the processes reported in sensation statements are in fact processes in the brain. Most of us have met some of these objections in our first year as philosophy students. All the more reason to take a good look at them. . . .

Objection 1. Any illiterate peasant can talk perfectly well about . . . how things look or feel to him, or about his aches and pains, and yet he may know nothing whatever about neurophysiology. A man may, like Aristotle, believe that the brain is an organ for cooling the body without any impairment of his ability to make true statements about his sensations. Hence the things we are talking about when we describe our sensations cannot be processes in the brain.

Reply. You might as well say that a nation of slugabeds, who never saw the Morning Star or knew of its existence, or who had never thought of the expression, "The Morning Star," but who used the expression "The Evening Star" perfectly well, would not use this expression to refer to the same entity as we refer to (and describe as) "the

Morning Star." (Or consider the example of lightning.) Modern physical science tells us that lightning is a certain kind of electrical discharge due to ionization of clouds of water vapor in the atmosphere. This, it is now believed, is what the true nature of lightning is. Note that there are not two things: a flash of lightning and an electrical discharge. There is one thing, a flash of lightning which is described scientifically as an electrical discharge to the earth from a cloud of ionized water molecules. The case is not at all like that of explaining a footprint by reference to a burglar. [In that case the footprints were *caused by* the burglar, and of course the burglar is not the same thing as the footprints; but the lightning is not *caused by* an electrical discharge—it is one and the same thing as an electrical discharge.] We say what lightning really is, what its true nature as revealed by science is, is an electrical discharge. (It is not the true nature of a footprint to be a burglar.)

In short, the reply to Objection 1 is that there can be contingent statements of the form "A is identical with B," and a person may well know that something is an A without knowing that it is a B. An illiterate peasant might well be able to talk about his sensations without knowing about his brain processes, just as he can talk about lightning though he knows nothing of electricity.

Objection 2. It is only a contingent fact . . . that when we have a certain kind of sensation there is a certain kind of process in our brain. Indeed it is possible, though perhaps in the highest degree unlikely, that our present physiological theories will be as out of date as the ancient theory connecting mental processes with goings on in the heart. It follows that when we report a sensation we are not reporting brain processes.

Reply. The objection certainly proves that when we say "I have an [ache]" we cannot *mean* something of the form "I have such and such a brain process." But this does not show that what we report (having [an ache]) is not in *fact* a brain process. "I see lightning" does not *mean* "I see an electrical discharge." Indeed, it is logically possible (though highly unlikely) that the electrical discharge account of lightning might some day be given up. [But of course the fact that this is logically possible does not mean that that theory *is* incorrect, nor, therefore, that "lightning" reports are not in fact reports of electrical discharges.] . . .

. . . *Objection 4.* The [sensation] is not in physical space. The brain process is. So the [sensation] is not a brain process.

Reply. This is an *ignoratio elenchi* [i.e., an argument directed against something that is not being asserted]. I am not arguing that the [sensation] is a brain process, but that the experience of having [a sensation] is a brain process. It is the *experience* which is reported in the introspective report. [Consider an "afterimage," like the one you get after you look at the sun and then close your eyes.] Similarly, if it is objected that the afterimage is yellowy-orange [whereas the brain process is *not* yellowy-orange], my reply is that it is the experience of seeing yellowy-orange that is being described, and this experience is not a yellowy-orange something. So to say that a brain process cannot be yellowy-orange is not to say that a brain process can not be in fact the experience of having a yellowy-orange after-image. . . .

Objection 5. It would make sense to say of a molecular movement in the brain that it is swift or slow, straight or circular, but it makes no sense to say this of the experience of seeing something yellow. [Therefore, that experience cannot be *the same thing* as *e.g.* that molecular movement.]

Reply. So far we have not given sense to talk of experience as swift or slow, straight or circular. But I am not claiming that [the words] "experience" and "brain process" mean the same or even that they have the same logic. "Somebody" and "the doctor" do not have the same logic, but this does not lead us to suppose that talking about somebody telephoning is talking about someone over and above, say, the doctor. The ordinary man when he reports an experience is reporting that something is going on, but he leaves it open as to what sort of thing is going on, whether in a material solid medium or perhaps in some sort of gaseous medium, or even perhaps in some sort of nonspatial medium (if this makes sense). All that I am saying is that "experience" and "brain process" may in fact refer to the same thing, and if so we may easily adopt a convention . . . whereby it would make sense to talk of an experience in terms appropriate to physical processes.

Objection 6. Sensations are private, brain processes are *public.* If I sincerely say, "I see a yellowy-orange after-image," and I am not making a verbal mistake, then I cannot be wrong. But I can be wrong about a brain process. The scientist looking into my brain [and reporting upon what processes are apparently going on in there] might be having an illusion. Moreover, it makes sense to say that two or more people are observing the same brain process but not that two or more people are reporting the same inner experience.

Reply. This shows that the language of introspective reports has a different logic from the language of material processes. It is obvious that until the brain-process theory is much improved and widely accepted there will be no *criteria* for saying "Smith has an experience of such and such a sort" *except* Smith's introspective reports. So we have adopted a rule of language that (normally) what Smith says goes.

Objection 7. I can imagine myself turned to stone and yet having images, aches, pains, and so on. [So it could happen that there were *no* brain processes going on in me and yet I still had sensations; so sensations cannot *be* processes.]

Reply. I can imagine that the electrical theory of lightning is false, that lightning is some sort of purely optical phenomenon. I can imagine that lightning is not an electrical discharge . . . All the objection shows is that "experience" and "brain process" do not have the same meaning. It does not show that an experience is not in fact a brain process. . . .

I have now considered a number of objections to the brain-process thesis. I wish to conclude with some remarks on the logical status of the thesis itself. U.T. Place seems to hold that it is a straight-out scientific hypothesis. If so, he is partly right and partly wrong. If the issue is between (say) a brain-process thesis [i.e. sensations are brain processes] and a heart thesis [sensations are heart processes], or a liver thesis, then the issue is purely an empirical one, and the verdict is overwhelmingly in favor of the brain. The right sorts of things don't go on in the heart, liver, or kidney, nor do these organs possess the right sort of complexity of structure. On the other hand, if the issue is between a brain-or-liver-or-kidney thesis (that is, some form of materialism on the one hand and epiphenomenalism [a form of dualism] on the other hand, then the issue is not an empirical one. For there is no conceivable experiment which could decide between materialism and epiphenomenalism. The latter issue is not the average straight-out empirical issue in science, but like that between the 19th century English naturalist Philip Gosse and the orthodox geologists and paleontologists of his day. According to Gosse, the earth was created about 4000 B.C. exactly as described in *Genesis,* with twisted rock strata, "evidence" of erosion, and so forth, and all sorts of fossils, all in their appropriate strata, just as if the usual evolutionist story had been a true one. Let us ignore the theological setting in which Gosse's hypothesis had been placed, thus ruling out objections of a theological kind, such as "what a queer God who would go to such lengths to deceive us." Let us suppose that it is held that the universe [was not created by a God but] just *began* in 4004 B.C. with the initial conditions just everywhere as they were in 4004 B.C., and in particular that our own planet began with sediment in the rivers, eroded cliffs, fossils in the rocks, and so on. No scientist would ever entertain this as a serious hypothesis, consistent though it is with all possible evidence. The hypothesis offends against the principles of parsimony and simplicity. There would be far too many brute and inexplicable facts. Why are pterodactyl bones just as they are? No explanation in terms of the evolution of pterodactyls from earlier forms of life would any longer be possible. We would have millions of facts about the world as it was in 4004 B.C. that just have to be accepted [—i.e., facts that cannot be explained].

The issue between the brain process theory and epiphenomenalism seems to be of the above sort. . . . If it be agreed that there are no cogent philosophical arguments which force us into accepting dualism, and if the brain process theory and dualism are equally consistent with the facts, then the principles of parsimony and simplicity seem to me to decide overwhelmingly in favor of the brain process theory. As I pointed out earlier, dualism involves a large number of irreducible psycho-physical laws . . . of a queer sort, that just have to be taken on trust, and are just as difficult to swallow as the irreducible facts about the paleontology of the earth with which we are faced on Philip Gosse's theory.

A. M. TURING

Computing Machinery and Intelligence

Alan Turing (1912–1954) was a founder of the mathematical theory of computation, on which all computer design rests. In his article "**Computing Machinery and Intelligence**" (1950), Turing does three things. He considers (and rejects) various reasons that might be offered for thinking that computers could never think. He describes the basic idea of a computer program. Finally, he proposes a behavioral test for determining whether a machine is thinking.

A. M. Turing, "Computing Machinery and Intelligence." Reprinted from *Mind,* 59 (1950), pp. 433–460, by permission of Oxford University Press.

1. THE IMITATION GAME

I propose to consider the question "Can machines think?" This should begin with definitions of the meaning of the terms "machine" and "think." The definitions might be framed so as to reflect so far as possible the normal use of the words, but this attitude is dangerous. If the meaning of the words "machine" and "think" are to be found by examining how they are commonly used it is difficult to escape the conclusion that the meaning and the answer to the question, "Can machines think?" is to be sought in a statistical survey such as a Gallup poll. But this is absurd. Instead of attempting such a definition I shall replace the question by another, which is closely related to it and expressed in relatively unambiguous words.

The new form of the problem can be described in terms of a game which we call the "imitation game." It is played with three people, a man (A), a woman (B), and an interrogator (C) who may be of either sex. The interrogator stays in a room apart from the other two. The object of the game for the interrogator is to determine which of the other two is the man and which is the woman. He knows them by labels X and Y, and at the end of the game he says either "X is A and Y is B" or "X is B and Y is A." The interrogator is allowed to put questions to A and B thus:

C: Will X please tell me the length of his or her hair?

Now suppose X is actually A, then A must answer. It is A's object in the game to try to cause C to make the wrong identification. His answer might therefore be

"My hair is shingled, and the longest strands are about nine inches long."

In order that tones of voice may not help the interrogator the answers should be written, or better still, typewritten. The ideal arrangement is to have a teleprinter communicating between the two rooms. Alternatively the question and answers can be repeated by an intermediary. The object of the game for the third player (B) is to help the interrogator. The best strategy for her is probably to give truthful answers. She can add such things as "I am the woman, don't listen to him!" to her answers, but it will avail nothing as the man can make similar remarks.

We now ask the question, "What will happen when a machine takes the part of A in this game?" Will the interrogator decide wrongly as often when the game is played like this as he does when the game is played between a man and a woman? These questions replace our original, "Can machines think?"

2. CRITIQUE OF THE NEW PROBLEM

As well as asking, "What is the answer to this new form of the question," one may ask, "Is this new question a worthy one to investigate?" This latter question we investigate without further ado, thereby cutting short an infinite regress.

The new problem has the advantage of drawing a fairly sharp line between the physical and the intellectual capacities of a man. No engineer or chemist claims to be able to produce a material which is indistinguishable from the human skin. It is possible that at some time this might be done, but even supposing this invention available we should feel there was little point in trying to make a "thinking machine" more human by dressing it up in such artificial flesh. The form in which we have set the problem reflects this fact in the condition which prevents the interrogator from seeing or touching the other competitors, or hearing their voices. Some other advantages of the proposed criterion may be shown up by specimen questions and answers. Thus:

Q: Please write me a sonnet on the subject of the Forth Bridge.
A: Count me out on this one. I never could write poetry.
Q: Add 34957 to 70764.
A: (Pause about 30 seconds and then give as answer) 105621.
Q: Do you play chess?
A: Yes.
Q: I have K at my K1, and no other pieces. You have only K at K6 and R at R1. It is your move. What do you play?
A: (After a pause of 15 seconds) R-R8 mate.

The question and answer method seems to be suitable for introducing almost any one of the fields of human endeavor that we wish to include. We do not wish to penalize the machine for its inability to shine in beauty competitions, nor to penalize a man for losing in a race against an airplane. The conditions of our game make these disabilities irrelevant. The "witnesses" can brag, if they consider it advisable, as much as they please about their charms, strength or heroism, but the interrogator cannot demand practical demonstrations.

The game may perhaps be criticized on the ground that the odds are weighted too heavily against the machine. If the man were to try and pretend to be the machine he would clearly make a very poor showing. He would be given away at once by slowness and inaccuracy in arithmetic. May not machines carry out something which ought to be described as thinking but which is very different from what a man does? This objection is a very strong one, but at least we can say that if, nevertheless, a machine can be constructed to play the imitation game satisfactorily, we need not be troubled by this objection.

It might be urged that when playing the "imitation game" the best strategy for the machine may possibly be something other than imitation of the behavior of man. This may be, but I think it is unlikely that there is any great effect of this kind. In any case there is no intention to investigate here the theory of the game, and it will be assumed that the best strategy is to try to provide answers that would naturally be given by a man.

3. THE MACHINES CONCERNED IN THE GAME

The question which we put in §1 will not be quite definite until we have specified what we mean by the word "machine." It is natural that we should wish to permit every kind of engineering technique to be used in our machines. We also wish to allow the possibility that an engineer or team of engineers may construct a machine which works, but whose manner of operation cannot be satisfactorily described by its constructors because they have applied a method which is largely experimental. Finally, we wish to exclude from the machines men born in the usual manner. It is difficult to frame the definitions so as to satisfy these three conditions. One might for instance insist that the team of engineers should be all of one sex, but this would not really be satisfactory, for it is probably possible to rear a complete individual from a single cell of the skin (say) of a man. To do so would be a feat of biological technique deserving of the very highest praise, but we would not be inclined to regard it as a case of "constructing a thinking machine." This prompts us to abandon the requirement that every kind of technique should be permitted. We are the more ready to do so in view of the fact that the present interest in "thinking machines" has been aroused by a particular kind of machine usually called an "electronic computer" or "digital computer." Following this suggestion we only permit digital computers to take part in our game.

This restriction appears at first sight to be a very drastic one. I shall attempt to show that it is not so in reality. To do this necessitates a short account of the nature and properties of these computers.

It may also be said that this identification of machines with digital computers, like our criterion for "thinking," will only be unsatisfactory if (contrary to my belief), it turns out that digital computers are unable to give a good showing in the game.

There are already a number of digital computers in working order, and it may be asked, "Why not try the experiment straight away? It would be easy to satisfy the conditions of the game. A number of interrogators could be used, and statistics compiled to show how often the right identification was given." The short answer is that we are not asking whether all digital computers would do well in the game nor whether the computers at present available would do well, but whether there are imaginable computers which would do well. But this is only the short answer. We shall see this question in a different light later.

4. DIGITAL COMPUTERS

The idea behind digital computers may be explained by saying that these machines are intended to carry out any operations which could be done by a human computer. The human computer is supposed to be following fixed rules; he has no authority to deviate from them in any detail. We may suppose that these rules are supplied in a book, which is altered whenever he is put on to a new job. He has also an unlimited supply of paper on which he does his calculations. He may also do his multiplications and additions on a "desk machine," but this is not important.

If we use the above explanation as a definition we shall be in danger of circularity of argument. We avoid this by giving an outline of the means by which the desired effect is achieved. A digital computer can usually be regarded as consisting of three parts:

(i) Store.

(ii) Executive unit.

(iii) Control.

The store is a store of information, and corresponds to the human computer's paper, whether this is the paper on which he does his calculations or that on which his book of rules is printed. Insofar as the human computer does calculations in his head a part of the store will correspond to his memory.

The executive unit is the part which carries out the various individual operations involved in a calculation. What these individual operations are will vary from machine to machine. Usually fairly lengthy operations can be done such as "Multiply 3540675445 by 7076345687" but in some machines only very simple ones such as "Write down 0" are possible.

We have mentioned that the "book of rules" supplied to the computer is replaced in the machine by a part of the store. It is then called the "table of instructions." It is the duty of the control to see that these instructions are obeyed correctly and in the right order. The control is so constructed that this necessarily happens.

The information in the store is usually broken up into packets of moderately small size. In one machine, for instance, a packet might consist of ten decimal digits. Numbers are assigned to the parts of the store in which the various packets of information are stored, in some systematic manner. A typical instruction might say—

> "Add the number stored in position 6809 to that in 4302 and put
> the result back into the latter storage position."

Needless to say it would not occur in the machine expressed in English. It would more likely be coded in a form such as 6809430217. Here 17 says which of various possible operations is to be performed on the two numbers. In this case the operation is that described above, viz. "Add the number. . . ." It will be noticed that the instruction takes up 10 digits and so forms one packet of information, very conveniently. The control will normally take the instructions to be obeyed in the order of the positions in which they are stored, but occasionally an instruction such as

> "Now obey the instruction stored in position 5606, and continue
> from there"

may be encountered, or again

> "If position 4505 contains 0 obey next the instruction stored in 6707,
> otherwise continue straight on."

Instructions of these latter types are very important because they make it possible for a sequence of operations to be repeated over and over again until some condition is fulfilled, but in doing so to obey, not fresh instructions on each repetition, but the same ones over and over again. To take a domestic analogy. Suppose Mother wants Tommy to call at the cobbler's every morning on his way to school to see if her shoes are done; she can ask him afresh every morning. Alternatively she can stick up a notice once and for all in the hall which he will see when he leaves for school and which tells him to call for the shoes, and also to destroy the notice when he comes back if he has the shoes with him.

The reader must accept it as a fact that digital computers can be constructed, and indeed have been constructed, according to the principles we have described, and that they can in fact mimic the actions of a human computer very closely.

The book of rules which we have described our human computer as using is of course a convenient fiction. Actual human computers really remember what they have got to do. If one wants to make a machine mimic the behavior of the human computer in some complex operation one has to ask him how it is done, and then translate the answer into the form of an instruction table. Constructing instruction tables is usually described as "programming." To "program a machine to carry out the operation A" means to put the appropriate instruction table into the machine so that it will do A.

An interesting variant on the idea of a digital computer is a "digital computer with a random element." These have instructions involving the throwing of a die or some equivalent electronic process; one such instruction might for instance be, "Throw the die and put the resulting number into store 1000." Sometimes such a machine is described as having free will (though I would not use this phrase myself). It is not normally possible to determine from observing a machine whether it has a random element, for a similar effect can be produced by such devices as making the choices depend on the digits of the decimal for π.

Most actual digital computers have only a finite store. There is no theoretical difficulty in the idea of a computer with an unlimited store. Of course only a finite part can have been used at any one time. Likewise only a finite amount can have been constructed, but we can imagine more and more being added as required. Such computers have special theoretical interest and will be called infinite capacity computers.

The idea of a digital computer is an old one. Charles Babbage, Lucasian Professor of Mathematics at Cambridge from 1828 to 1839, planned such a machine, called the Analytical Engine, but it was never completed. Although Babbage had all the essential ideas, his machine was not at that time such a very attractive prospect. The speed which would have been available would be definitely faster than a human computer but something like 100 times slower than the Manchester machine, itself one of the slower of the modern machines. The storage was to be purely mechanical, using wheels and cards.

The fact that Babbage's Analytical Engine was to be entirely mechanical will help us to rid ourselves of a superstition. Importance is often attached to the fact that modern digital computers are electrical, and that the nervous system also is electrical. Since Babbage's machine was not electrical, and since all digital computers are in a sense equivalent, we see that this use of electricity cannot be of theoretical importance. Of course electricity usually comes in where fast signaling is concerned, so that it is not surprising that we find it in both these connections. In the nervous system chemical phenomena are at least as important as electrical. In certain computers the storage system is mainly acoustic. The feature of using electricity is thus seen to be only a very superficial similarity. If we wish to find such similarities we should look rather for mathematical analogies of function.

5. UNIVERSALITY OF DIGITAL COMPUTERS

The digital computers considered in the last section may be classified among the "discrete state machines." These are the machines which move by sudden jumps or clicks from one quite definite state to another. These states are sufficiently different for the possibility of confusion between them to be ignored. Strictly speaking there are no such machines. Everything really moves continuously. But there are many kinds of machines which can profitably be *thought of* as being discrete state machines. For instance in considering the switches for a lighting system it is a convenient fiction that each switch must be definitely on or definitely off. There must be intermediate positions, but for most purposes we can forget about them. As an example of a discrete state machine we might consider a wheel which clicks round through $120°$ once a second, but may be stopped by a lever which can be operated from outside; in addition a lamp is to light in one of the positions of the wheel. This machine could be described abstractly as follows: The internal state of the machine (which is described by the position of the wheel) may be q_1, q_2 or q_3. There is an input signal i_0 or i_1 (position of lever). The internal state at any moment is determined by the last state and input signal according to the table

	Last State		
	q_1	q_2	q_3
i_0	q_2	q_3	q_1
i_1	q_1	q_2	q_3

Input appears at the left spanning the rows i_0 and i_1.

The output signals, the only externally visible indication of the internal state (the light) are described by the table

State

$q_1 q_2 q_3$

Output

$o_0 o_0 o_1$

This example is typical of discrete state machines. They can be described by such tables provided they have only a finite number of possible states.

It will seem that given the initial state of the machine and the input signals it is always possible to predict all future states. This is reminiscent of Laplace's view that from the complete state of the universe at one moment of time, as described by the positions and velocities of all particles, it should be possible to predict all future states. The prediction which we are considering is, however, rather nearer to practicability than that considered by Laplace. The system of the "universe as a whole" is such that quite small errors in the initial conditions can have an overwhelming effect at a later time. The displacement of a single electron by a billionth of a centimeter at one moment might make the difference between a man being killed by an avalanche a year later, or escaping. It is an essential property of the mechanical systems which we have called "discrete state machines" that this phenomenon does not occur. Even when we consider the actual physical machines instead of the idealized machines, reasonably accurate knowledge of the state at one moment yields reasonably accurate knowledge any number of steps later.

As we have mentioned, digital computers fall within the class of discrete state machines. But the number of states of which such a machine is capable is usually enormously large. For instance, the number for the machine now working at Manchester is about $2^{165,000}$, i.e., about $10^{50,000}$. Compare this with our example of the clicking wheel described above, which had three states. It is not difficult to see why the number of states should be so immense. The computer includes a store corresponding to the paper used by a human computer. It must be possible to write into the store any one of the combinations of symbols which might have been written in the paper. For simplicity suppose that only digits from 0 to 9 are used as symbols. Variations in handwriting are ignored. Suppose the computer is allowed 100 sheets of paper each containing 50 lines each with room for 30 digits. Then the number of states is $10^{100 \times 50 \times 30}$, i.e., $10^{150,000}$. This is about the number of states of three Manchester machines put together. The logarithm to the base two of the number of states is usually called the "storage capacity" of the machine. Thus the Manchester machine has a storage capacity of about 165,000 and the wheel machine of our example about 1.6. If two machines are put together their capacities must be added to obtain the capacity of the resultant machine. This leads to the possibility of statements such as "The Manchester machine contains 64 magnetic tracks each with a capacity of 2560, eight electronic tubes with a capacity of 1280. Miscellaneous storage amounts to about 300 making a total of 174,380."

Given the table corresponding to a discrete state machine it is possible to predict what it will do. There is no reason why this calculation should not be carried out by means of a digital computer. Provided it could be carried out sufficiently quickly the digital computer could mimic the behavior of any discrete state machine. The imitation game could then be played with the machine in question (as B) and the mimicking digital computer (as A) and the interrogator would be unable to distinguish them. Of course the digital computer must have an adequate storage capacity as well as working sufficiently fast. Moreover, it must be programmed afresh for each new machine which it is desired to mimic.

This special property of digital computers, that they can mimic any discrete state machine, is described by saying that they are *universal* machines. The existence of machines with this property has the important consequence that, considerations of speed apart, it is unnecessary to design various new machines to do various computing processes. They can all be done with one digital computer, suitably programmed for each case. It will be seen that as a consequence of this all digital computers are in a sense equivalent.

We may now consider again the point raised at the end of §3. It was suggested tentatively that the question, "Can machines think?" should be replaced by "Are there imaginable digital computers which would do well in the imitation game?" If we wish we can make this superficially more general and ask "Are there discrete state machines which would do well?" But in view of the universality property we see that either of these questions is equivalent to this, "Let us fix our attention to one particular digital computer C. Is it true that by modifying this computer to have an adequate storage, suitably increasing its speed of action, and providing it with an appropriate program, C can be made to play satisfactorily the part of A in the imitation game, the part of B being taken by a man?"

6. CONTRARY VIEWS ON THE MAIN QUESTION

We may now consider the ground to have been cleared and we are ready to proceed to the debate on our question, "Can machines think?" and the variant of it quoted at the end of the last section. We cannot altogether abandon the original form of the problem, for opinions will differ as to the appropriateness of the substitution and we must at least listen to what has to be said in this connection.

It will simplify matters for the reader if I explain first my own beliefs in the matter. Consider first the more accurate form of the question. I believe that in about fifty years' time it will be possible to program computers, with a storage capacity of about 109, to make them play the imitation game so well that an average interrogator will not have more than 70 per cent chance of making the right identification after five minutes of questioning. The original question, "Can machines think?" I believe to be too meaningless to deserve discussion. Nevertheless I believe that at the end of the century the use of words and general educated opinion will have altered so much that one will be able to speak of machines thinking without expecting to be contradicted. I believe further that no useful purpose is served by concealing these beliefs. The popular view that scientists proceed inexorably from well-established fact to well-established fact, never being influenced by any unproved conjecture, is quite mistaken. Provided it is made clear which are proved facts and which are conjectures, no harm can result. Conjectures are of great importance since they suggest useful lines of research.

I now proceed to consider opinions opposed to my own.

(1) The Theological Objection. Thinking is a function of man's immortal soul. God has given an immortal soul to every man and woman, but not to any other animal or to machines. Hence no animal or machine can think.[1]

I am unable to accept any part of this, but will attempt to reply in theological terms. I should find the argument more convincing if animals were classed with men, for there is a greater difference, to my mind, between the typical animate and the inanimate than there is between man and the other animals. The arbitrary character of the orthodox view becomes clearer if we consider how it might appear to a member of some other religious community. How do Christians regard the Moslem view that women have no souls? But let us leave this point aside and return to the main argument. It appears to me that the argument quoted above implies a serious restriction of the omnipotence of the Almighty. It is admitted that there are certain things that He cannot do such as making one equal to two, but should we not believe that He has freedom to confer a soul on an elephant if He sees fit? We might expect that He would only exercise this power in conjunction with a mutation which provided the elephant with an appropriately improved brain to minister to the needs of this soul. An argument of exactly similar form may be made for the case of machines. It may seem different because it is more difficult to "swallow." But this really only means that we think it would be less likely that He would consider the circumstances suitable for conferring a soul. The circumstances in question are discussed in the rest of this paper. In attempting to construct such machines we should not be irreverently usurping His power of creating souls, any more than we are in the procreation of children: rather we are, in either case, instruments of His will providing mansions for the souls that He creates.

However, this is mere speculation. I am not very impressed with theological arguments whatever they may be used to support. Such arguments have often been found unsatisfactory in the past. In the time of Galileo it was argued that the texts, "And the sun stood still . . . and hasted not to go down about a whole day" (Joshua x. 13) and "He laid the foundations of the earth, that it should not move at any time" (Psalm cv. 5) were an adequate refutation of the Copernican theory. With our present knowledge such an argument appears futile. When that knowledge was not available it made a quite different impression.

(2) The "Heads in the Sand" Objection. "The consequences of machines thinking would be too dreadful. Let us hope and believe that they cannot do so."

This argument is seldom expressed quite so openly as in the form above. But it affects most of us who think about it at all. We like to believe that Man is in some subtle way superior to the rest of creation. It is best if he can be shown to be *necessarily* superior, for then there is no danger of him losing his commanding position. The popularity of the theological argument is clearly connected with this feeling. It is likely to be quite strong in intellectual people, since they value the power of thinking more highly than others, and are more inclined to base their belief in the superiority of Man on this power.

I do not think that this argument is sufficiently substantial to require refutation. Consolation would be more appropriate; perhaps this should be sought in the transmigration of souls.

(3) The Mathematical Objection. There are a number of results of mathematical logic which can be used to show that there are limitations to the powers of discrete state machines. The best known of these results is known as Gödel's theorem, and shows that in any sufficiently powerful logical system statements can be formulated which can neither be proved nor disproved within the system, unless possibly the system itself is inconsistent. There are other, in some respects similar, results due to Church, Kleene, Rosser, and Turing. The latter result is the most convenient to consider, since

it refers directly to machines, whereas the others can only be used in a comparatively indirect argument: for instance if Gödel's theorem is to be used we need in addition to have some means of describing logical systems in terms of machines, and machines in terms of logical systems. The result in question refers to a type of machine which is essentially a digital computer with an infinite capacity. It states that there are certain things that such a machine cannot do. If it is rigged up to give answers to questions as in the imitation game, there will be some questions to which it will either give a wrong answer, or fail to give an answer at all however much time is allowed for a reply. There may, of course, be many such questions, and questions which cannot be answered by one machine may be satisfactorily answered by another. We are of course supposing for the present that the questions are of the kind to which an answer "Yes" or "No" is appropriate, rather than questions such as "What do you think of Picasso?" The questions that we know the machines must fail on are of this type, "Consider the machine specified as follows. . . . Will this machine ever answer 'Yes' to any question?" The dots are to be replaced by a description of some machine in a standard form, which could be something like that used in §5. When the machine described bears a certain comparatively simple relation to the machine which is under interrogation, it can be shown that the answer is either wrong or not forthcoming. This is the mathematical result: it is argued that it proves a disability of machines to which the human intellect is not subject.

The short answer to this argument is that although it is established that there are limitations to the powers of any particular machine, it has only been stated, without any sort of proof, that no such limitations apply to the human intellect. But I do not think this view can be dismissed quite so lightly. Whenever one of these machines is asked the appropriate critical question, and gives a definite answer, we know that this answer must be wrong, and this gives us a certain feeling of superiority. Is this feeling illusory? It is no doubt quite genuine, but I do not think too much importance should be attached to it. We too often give wrong answers to questions ourselves to be justified in being very pleased at such evidence of fallibility on the part of the machines. Further, our superiority can only be felt on such an occasion in relation to the one machine over which we have scored our petty triumph. There would be no question of triumphing simultaneously over *all* machines. In short, then, there might be men cleverer than any given machine, but then again there might be other machines cleverer again, and so on.

Those who hold to the mathematical argument would, I think, mostly be willing to accept the imitation game as a basis for discussion. Those who believe in the two previous objections would probably not be interested in any criteria.

(4) The Argument from Consciousness. This argument is very well expressed in Professor Jefferson's Lister Oration for 1949, from which I quote. "Not until a machine can write a sonnet or compose a concerto because of thoughts and emotions felt, and not by the chance fall of symbols, could we agree that machine equals brain—that is, not only write it but know that it had written it. No mechanism could feel (and not merely artificially signal, an easy contrivance) pleasure at its successes, grief when its values fuse, be warmed by flattery, be made miserable by its mistakes, be charmed by sex, be angry or depressed when it cannot get what it wants."

This argument appears to be a denial of the validity of our test. According to the most extreme form of this view the only way by which one could be sure that a machine thinks is to *be* the machine and to feel oneself thinking. One could then describe these feelings to the world, but of course no one would be justified in taking any notice. Likewise according to this view the only way to know that a *man* thinks is to be that particular man. It is in fact the solipsist point of view. It may be the most logical view to hold but it makes communication of ideas difficult. A is liable to believe "A thinks but B does not" while B believes "B thinks but A does not." Instead of arguing continually over this point it is usual to have the polite convention that everyone thinks.

I am sure that Professor Jefferson does not wish to adopt the extreme and solipsist point of view. Probably he would be quite willing to accept the imitation game as a test. The game (with the player B omitted) is frequently used in practice under the name of *viva voce* to discover whether someone really understands something or has "learned it parrot fashion." Let us listen in to a part of such a *viva voce*:

INTERROGATOR: In the first line of your sonnet which reads "Shall I compare thee to a summer's day," would not a "spring day" do as well or better?

WITNESS: It wouldn't scan.

I: How about "a winter's day." That would scan all right.

W: Yes, but nobody wants to be compared to a winter's day.

I: Would you say Mr. Pickwick reminded you of Christmas?

W: In a way.

I: Yet Christmas is a winter's day, and I do not think Mr. Pickwick would mind the comparison.

W: I don't think you're serious. By a winter's day one means a typical winter's day, rather than a special one like Christmas.

And so on. What would Professor Jefferson say if the sonnet-writing machine was able to answer like this in the *viva voce?* I do not know whether he would regard the machine as "merely artificially signaling" these answers, but if the answers were as satisfactory and sustained as in the above passage I do not think he would describe it as "an easy contrivance." This phrase is, I think, intended to cover such devices as the inclusion in the machine of a record of someone reading a sonnet, with appropriate switching to turn it on from time to time.

In short then, I think that most of those who support the argument from consciousness could be persuaded to abandon it rather than be forced into the solipsist position. They will then probably be willing to accept our test.

I do not wish to give the impression that I think there is no mystery about consciousness. There is, for instance, something of a paradox connected with any attempt to localize it. But I do not think these mysteries necessarily need to be solved before we can answer the question with which we are concerned in this paper.

(5) Arguments from Various Disabilities. These arguments take the form, "I grant you that you can make machines do all the things you have mentioned but you will never be able to make one to do X." Numerous features X are suggested in this connection. I offer a selection:

> Be kind, resourceful, beautiful, friendly . . . have initiative, have a sense of humor, tell right from wrong, make mistakes . . . fall in love, enjoy strawberries and cream . . ., make someone fall in love with it, learn from experience . . ., use words properly, be the subject of its own thought . . ., have as much diversity of behavior as a man, do something really new. . . .

No support is usually offered for these statements. I believe they are mostly founded on the principle of scientific induction. A man has seen thousands of machines in his lifetime. From what he sees of them he draws a number of general conclusions. They are ugly, each is designed for a very limited purpose, when required for a minutely different purpose they are useless, the variety of behavior of any one of them is very small, etc., etc. Naturally he concludes that these are necessary properties of machines in general. Many of these limitations are associated with the very small storage capacity of most machines. (I am assuming that the idea of storage capacity is extended in some way to cover machines other than discrete state machines. The exact definition does not matter as no mathematical accuracy is claimed in the present discussion.) A few years ago, when very little had been heard of digital computers, it was possible to elicit much incredulity concerning them, if one mentioned their properties without describing their construction. That was presumably due to a similar application of the principle of scientific induction. These applications of the principle are of course largely unconscious. When a burned child fears the fire and shows that he fears it by avoiding it, I should say that he was applying scientific induction. (I could of course also describe his behavior in many other ways.) The works of customs of mankind do not seem to be very suitable material to which to apply scientific induction. A very large part of space-time must be investigated if reliable results are to be obtained. Otherwise we may (as most English children do) decide that everybody speaks English, and that it is silly to learn French.

There are, however, special remarks to be made about many of the disabilities that have been mentioned. The inability to enjoy strawberries and cream may [strike] the reader as frivolous. Possibly a machine might be made to enjoy this delicious dish, but any attempt to make one do so would be idiotic. What is important about this disability is that it contributes to some of the other disabilities, e.g., to the difficulty of the same kind of friendliness occurring between man and machine as between white man and white man, or between black man and black man.

The claim that "machines cannot make mistakes" seems a curious one. One is tempted to retort, "Are they any worse for that?" But let us adopt a more sympathetic attitude, and try to see what is really meant. I think this criticism can be explained in terms of the imitation game. It is claimed that the interrogator could distinguish the machine from the man simply by setting them a number of problems in arithmetic. The machine would be unmasked because of its deadly accuracy. The reply to this is simple. The machine (programmed for playing the game) would not attempt to give the *right* answers to the arithmetic problems. It would deliberately introduce mistakes in a manner calculated to confuse the interrogator. A mechanical fault would probably show itself through an unsuitable decision as to what sort of mistake to make in the arithmetic. Even this interpretation of the criticism is not sufficiently sympathetic. But we cannot afford the space to go into it much further. It seems to me that this criticism depends on a confusion between two kinds of mistakes. We may call them "errors of functioning" and "errors of conclusion." Errors of functioning are due to some mechanical or electrical fault which causes the machine to behave otherwise than it was designed to do. In philosophical discussions one likes to ignore the possibility of such errors; one is therefore discussing "abstract machines." These abstract machines are mathematical fictions rather than physical objects. By definition they are incapable of errors of functioning. In this sense we can truly say that "machines can never make mistakes." Errors of conclusion can only arise when some meaning is attached to the output signals from the machine. The machine might, for instance, type out mathematical equations, or sentences in English. When a false proposition is typed we say that the machine has committed an error of conclusion. There is clearly no reason at all for saying that a machine cannot make this kind of mistake. It might do nothing but type out repeatedly "$0 = 1$." To take a less perverse example, it might have some method for drawing conclusions by scientific induction. We must expect such a method to lead occasionally to erroneous results.

The claim that a machine cannot be the subject of its own thought can of course only be answered if it can be shown that the machine has *some* thought with some matter. Nevertheless, "the subject matter of a machine's operations" does seem to mean something, at least to the people who deal with it. If, for instance, the machine was trying to find a solution to the equation $X^2 - 40x - 11 = 0$ one would be tempted to describe this equation as part of the machine's subject matter at that moment. In this sort of sense a machine undoubtedly can be its own subject matter. It may be used to help in making up its own programs, or to predict the effect of alterations in its own structure. By observing the results of its own behavior it can modify its own programs so as to achieve some purpose more effectively. These are possibilities of the near future, rather than Utopian dreams.

The criticism that a machine cannot have much diversity of behavior is just a way of saying that it cannot have much storage capacity. Until fairly recently a storage capacity of even a thousand digits was very rare.

The criticisms that we are considering here are often disguised forms of the argument from consciousness. Usually if one maintains that a machine *can* do one of these things, and describes the kind of method that the machine could use, one will not make much of an impression. It is thought that the method (whatever it may be, for it must be mechanical) is really rather base. Compare the parenthesis of Jefferson's statement quoted above.

(6) Lady Lovelace's Objection. Our most detailed information of Babbage's Analytical Engine comes from a memoir by Lady Lovelace. In it she states, "The Analytical Engine has no pretensions to *originate* anything. It can do *whatever we know how to order it* to perform" (her italics). This statement is quoted by Hartree who adds: "This does not imply that it may not be possible to construct electronic equipment which will 'think for itself,' or in which, in biological terms, one could set up a conditioned reflex, which would serve as a basis for 'learning.' Whether this is possible in principle or not is a stimulating and exciting question, suggested by some of these recent developments. But it did not seem that the machines constructed or projected at the time had this property."

I am in thorough agreement with Hartree over this. It will be noticed that he does not assert that the machines in question had not got the property, but rather that the evidence available to Lady Lovelace did not encourage her to believe that they had it. It is quite possible that the machines in question had in a sense got this property. For suppose that some discrete state machine has the property. The Analytical Engine was a universal digital computer, so that, if its storage capacity and speed were adequate, it could by suitable programming be made to mimic the machine in question. Probably this argument did not occur to the Countess or to Babbage. In any case there was no obligation on them to claim all that could be claimed.

This whole question will be considered again under the heading of learning machines.

A variant of Lady Lovelace's objection states that a machine can "never do anything really new." This may be parried for a moment with the saw, "There is nothing new under the sun." Who can be certain that "original work" that he has done was not simply the growth of the seed planted in him by teaching, or the effect of following well-known general principles. A better variant of the objection says that a machine can never "take us by surprise." This statement is a more direct challenge and can be met directly. Machines take me by surprise with great frequency. This is largely because I do not do sufficient calculation to decide what to expect them to do, or rather because, although I do a calculation, I do it in a hurried, slipshod fashion, taking risks. Perhaps I say to myself, "I suppose the voltage here ought to be the same as there: anyway let's assume it is." Naturally I am often wrong, and the result is a surprise for me, for by the time the experiment is done these assumptions have been forgotten. These admissions lay me open to lectures on the subject of my vicious ways, but do not throw any doubt on my credibility when I testify to the surprises I experience.

I do not expect this reply to silence my critic. He will probably say that such surprises are due to some creative mental act on my part, and reflect no credit on the machine. This leads us back to the argument from consciousness, and far from the idea of surprise. It is a line of argument we must consider closed, but it is perhaps worth remarking that the appreciation of something as surprising requires as much of a "creative mental act" whether the surprising event originates from a man, a book, a machine or anything else.

The view that machines cannot give rise to surprises is due, I believe, to a fallacy to which philosophers and mathematicians are particularly subject. This is the assumption that as soon as a fact is presented to a mind all consequences of that fact spring into the mind simultaneously with it. It is a very useful assumption under many circumstances, but one too easily forgets that it is false. A natural consequence of doing so is that one then assumes that there is no virtue in the mere working out of consequences from data and general principles.

(7) Argument from Continuity in the Nervous System. The nervous system is certainly not a discrete state machine. A small error in the information about the size of a nervous impulse impinging on a neuron, may make a large difference to the size of the outgoing impulse. It may be argued that, this being so, one cannot expect to be able to mimic the behavior of the nervous system with a discrete state system.

It is true that a discrete state machine must be different from a continuous machine. But if we adhere to the conditions of the imitation game, the interrogator will not be able to take any advantage of this difference. The situation can be made clearer if we consider some other simpler continuous machine. A differential analyzer will do very well. (A differential analyzer is a certain kind of machine not of the discrete state type used for some kinds of calculation.) Some of these provide their answers in a typed form, and so are suitable for taking part in the game. It would not be possible for a digital computer to predict exactly what answers the differential analyzer would give to a problem, but it would be quite capable of giving the right sort of answer. For instance, if asked to give the value of π (actually about 3.1416) it would be reasonable to choose at random between the values 3.12, 3.13, 3.14, 3.15, 3.16 with the probabilities of 0.05, 0.15, 0.55, 0.19, 0.06 (say). Under the circumstances it would be very difficult for the interrogator to distinguish the differential analyzer from the digital computer.

(8) The Argument from Informality of Behavior. It is not possible to produce a set of rules purporting to describe what a man should do in every conceivable set of circumstances. One might for instance have a rule that one is to stop when one sees a red traffic light, and to go if one sees a green one, but what if by some fault both appear together? One may perhaps decide that it is safest to stop. But some further difficulty may well arise from this decision later. To attempt to provide rules of conduct to cover every eventuality, even those arising from traffic lights, appears to be impossible. With all this I agree.

From this it is argued that we cannot be machines. I shall try to reproduce the argument, but I fear I shall hardly do it justice. It seems to run something like this. "If each man had a definite set of rules of conduct by which he regulated his life he would be no better than a machine. But there are no such rules, so men cannot be machines." The undistributed middle is glaring. I do not think the argument is ever put quite like this, but I believe this is the argument used nevertheless. There may however be a certain confusion between "rules of conduct" and "laws of behavior" to cloud the issue. By "rules of conduct" I mean precepts such as "Stop if you see red lights," on which one can act, and of which one can be conscious. By "laws of behavior" I mean laws of nature as applied to a man's body such as "if you pinch him he will squeak." If we substitute "laws of behavior which regulate his life" for "laws of conduct by which he regulates his life" in the argument quoted the undistributed middle is no longer insuperable. For we believe that it is not only true that being regulated by laws of behavior implies being some sort of machine (though not necessarily a discrete state machine), but that conversely being such a machine implies being regulated by such laws. However, we cannot so easily convince ourselves of the absence of complete laws of behavior as of complete rules of conduct. The only way we know of for finding such laws is scientific observation, and we certainly know of no circumstances under which we could say, "We have searched enough. There are no such laws."

We can demonstrate more forcibly that any such statement would be unjustified. For suppose we could be sure of finding such laws if they existed. Then given a discrete state machine it should certainly be possible to discover by observation sufficient about it to predict its future behavior, and this within a reasonable time, say a thousand years. But this does not seem to be the case. I have set up on the Manchester computer a small program using only 1000 units of storage, whereby the machine supplied with one sixteen-figure number replies with another within two seconds. I would defy anyone to learn from these replies sufficient about the program to be able to predict any replies to untried values.

(9) The Argument from Extra-Sensory Perception. I assume that the reader is familiar with the idea of extra-sensory perception, and the meaning of the four items of it, viz., telepathy, clairvoyance, precognition and psychokinesis. These disturbing phenomena seem to deny all our usual scientific ideas. How we would like to discredit them! Unfortunately, the statistical evidence, at least for telepathy, is overwhelming. It is very difficult to rearrange one's ideas so as to fit these new facts in. Once one has accepted them it does not seem a very big step to believe in ghosts and bogies. The idea that our bodies move simply according to the known laws of physics, together with some others not yet discovered but somewhat similar, would be one of the first to go.

This argument is to my mind quite a strong one. One can say in reply that many scientific theories seem to remain workable in practice, in spite of clashing with E.S.P.; that in fact one can get along very nicely if one forgets about it. This is rather cold comfort, and one fears that thinking is just the kind of phenomenon where E.S.P. may be especially relevant.

A more specific argument based on E.S.P. might run as follows: "Let us play the imitation game, using as witnesses a man who is good as a telepathic receiver, and a digital computer. The interrogator can ask such questions as 'What suit does the card in my right hand belong to?' The man by telepathy or clairvoyance gives the right answer 130 times out of 400 cards. The machine can only guess at random, and perhaps gets 104 right, so the interrogator makes the right identification." There is an interesting possibility which opens here. Suppose the digital computer contains a random number generator. Then it will be natural to use this to decide what answer to give. But then the random number generator will be subject to the psychokinetic powers of the interrogators. Perhaps this psychokinesis might cause the machine to guess right more often than would be expected on a probability calculation, so that the interrogator might still be unable to make the right identification. On the other hand, he might be able to guess right without any questioning, by clairvoyance. With E.S.P. anything may happen.

If telepathy is admitted it will be necessary to tighten our test. The situation could be regarded as analogous to that which would occur if the interrogator were talking to himself and one of the competitors was listening with his ear to the wall. To put the competitors into a "telepathy-proof room" would satisfy all requirements.

7. LEARNING MACHINES

The reader will have anticipated that I have no very convincing arguments of a positive nature to support my views. If I had I should not have taken such pains to point out the fallacies in contrary views. Such evidence as I have I shall now give.

Let us return for a moment to Lady Lovelace's objection, which stated that the machine can only do what we tell it to do. One could say that a man can "inject" an idea into the machine, and that it will respond to a certain extent and then drop into quiescence, like a piano string struck by a hammer. Another simile would be an atomic pile of less than critical size: an injected idea is to correspond to a neutron entering the pile from without. Each such neutron will cause a certain disturbance which eventually dies away. If, however, the size of the pile is sufficiently increased, the disturbance caused by such an incoming neutron will very likely go on and on increasing until the whole pile is destroyed. Is there a corresponding phenomenon for minds, and is there one for machines? There does seem to be one for the human mind. The majority of them seem to be "subcritical," i.e., to correspond in this analogy to piles of subcritical size. An idea presented to such a mind will on an average give rise to less than one idea in reply. A smallish proportion are supercritical. An idea presented to such a mind may give rise to a whole "theory" consisting of secondary, tertiary and more remote ideas. Animals' minds seem to be very definitely subcritical. Adhering to this analogy we ask, "Can a machine be made to be supercritical?"

The "skin of an onion" analogy is also helpful. In considering the functions of the mind or the brain we find certain operations which we can explain in purely mechanical terms. This we say does not correspond to the real mind: it is a sort of skin which we must strip off if we are to find the real mind. But then in what remains we find a further skin to be stripped off, and so on. Proceeding in this way do we ever come to the "real" mind, or do we eventually come to the skin which has nothing in it? In the latter case the whole mind is mechanical. (It would not be a discrete state machine however. We have discussed this.)

These last two paragraphs do not claim to be convincing arguments. They should rather be described as "recitations tending to produce belief."

The only really satisfactory support that can be given for the view expressed at the beginning of §6, . . . will be that provided by waiting for the end of the century and then doing the experiment described. But what can we say in the meantime? What steps should be taken now if the experiment is to be successful?

As I have explained, the problem is mainly one of programming. Advances in engineering will have to be made too, but it seems unlikely that these will not be adequate for the requirements. Estimates of the storage capacity of the brain vary from 10^{10} to 10^{15} binary digits. I incline to the lower values and believe that only a very small fraction is used for the higher types of thinking. Most of it is probably used for the retention of visual impressions. I should be surprised if more then 10^9 was required for satisfactory playing of the imitation game, at any rate against a blind man. (Note: The capacity of the *Encyclopedia Britannica,* eleventh edition, is 2×10^9.) A storage capacity of 10^7 would be a very practicable possibility even by present techniques. It is probably not necessary to increase the speed of operations of the machines at all. Parts of modern machines which can be regarded as analogues of nerve cells work about a thousand times faster than the latter. This should provide a "margin of safety" which could cover losses of speed arising in many ways. Our problem then is to find out how to program these machines to play the game. At my present rate of working I produce about a thousand digits of program a day, so that about sixty workers, working steadily through the fifty years might accomplish the job, if nothing went into the wastepaper basket. Some more expeditious method seems desirable.

In the process of trying to imitate an adult human mind we are bound to think a good deal about the process which has brought it to the state that it is in. We may notice three components,

(a) The initial state of the mind, say at birth,

(b) The education to which it has been subjected,

(c) Other experience, not to be described as education, to which it has been subjected.

Instead of trying to produce a program to simulate the adult mind, why not rather try to produce one which simulates the child's? If this were then subjected to an appropriate course of education one would obtain the adult brain. Presumably the child-brain is something like a notebook as one buys it from the stationers. Rather little mechanism, and lots of blank sheets. (Mechanism and writing are from our point of view almost synonymous.) Our hope is that there is so little mechanism in the child-brain that something like it can be easily programmed. The amount of work in the education we can assume, as a first approximation, to be much the same as for the human child.

We have thus divided our problem into two parts—the child-program and the education process. These two remain very closely connected. We cannot expect to find a good child-machine at the first attempt. One must experiment with teaching one such machine and see how well it learns. One can then try another and see if it is better or worse. There is an obvious connection between this process and evolution, by the identifications

Structure of the child-machine	=	Hereditary material
Changes of the child-machine	=	Mutations
Natural selection	=	Judgment of the experimenter

One may hope, however, that this process will be more expeditious than evolution. The survival of the fittest is a slow method for measuring advantages. The experimenter, by the exercise of intelligence, should be able to speed it up. Equally important is the fact that he is not restricted to random mutations. If he can trace a cause for some weakness he can probably think of the kind of mutation which will improve it.

It will not be possible to apply exactly the same teaching process to the machine as to a normal child. It will not, for instance, be provided with legs, so that it could not be asked to go out and fill the coal scuttle. Possibly it might not have eyes. But however well these deficiencies might be overcome by clever engineering, one could not send the creature to school without the other children making excessive fun of it. It must be given some tuition. We need not be too concerned about the legs, eyes, etc. The example of Miss Helen Keller shows that education can take place provided that communication in both directions between teacher and pupil can take place by some means or other.

We normally associate punishments and rewards with the teaching process. Some simple child-machines can be constructed or programmed on this sort of principle. The machine has to be so constructed that events which shortly preceded the occurrence of a punishment-signal are unlikely to be repeated, whereas a reward-signal increases the probability of repetition of the events which led up to it. These definitions do not presuppose any feelings on the part of the machine. I have done some experiments with one such child-machine, and succeeded in teaching it a few things, but the teaching method was too unorthodox for the experiment to be considered really successful.

The use of punishments and rewards can at best be a part of the teaching process. Roughly speaking, if the teacher has no other means of communicating to the pupil, the amount of information which can reach him does not exceed the total number of rewards and punishments applied. By the time a child has learned to repeat "Casablanca" he would probably feel very sore indeed, if the text could only be discovered by a "Twenty Questions" technique, every "NO" taking the form of a blow. It is necessary therefore to have some other "unemotional" channels of communication. If these are available it is possible to teach a machine by punishments and rewards to obey orders given in some language, e.g., a symbolic language. These orders are to be transmitted through the "unemotional" channels. The use of this language will diminish greatly the number of punishments and rewards required.

Opinions may vary as to the complexity which is suitable in the child-machine. One might try to make it as simple as possible consistently with the general principles. Alternatively one might have a complete system of logical inference "built in."[2] In the latter case the store would be largely occupied with definitions and propositions. The propositions would have various kinds of status, e.g., well-established facts, conjectures, mathematically proved theorems, statements given by an authority, expressions having the logical form of proposition but not belief-value. Certain propositions may be described as "imperatives." The machine should be so constructed that as soon as an imperative is classed as "well-established" the appropriate action automatically takes place. To illustrate this, suppose the teacher says to the machine, "Do your homework now." This may cause "Teacher says 'Do your homework now'" to be included among the well-established facts. Another such fact might be, "Everything that teacher says is true." Combining these may eventually lead to the imperative, "Do your homework now," being included among the well-established facts, and this, by the construction of the machine, will mean that the homework actually gets started, but the effect is very unsatisfactory. The processes of inference used by the machine need not be such as would satisfy the most exacting logicians. There might for instance be no hierarchy of types. But this need not mean that type fallacies will occur, any more than we are bound to fall over unfenced cliffs. Suitable imperatives (expressed *within* the systems, not forming part of the rules *of* the system) such as "Do not use a class unless it is a subclass of one which has been mentioned by teacher" can have a similar effect to "Do not go too near the edge."

The imperatives that can be obeyed by a machine that has no limbs are bound to be of a rather intellectual character, as in the example (doing homework) given above. Important among such imperatives will be ones which regulate the order in which the rules of the logical system concerned are to be applied. For at each stage when one is using a logical system, there is a very large number of alternative steps, any of which one is permitted to apply, so far as obedience to the rules of the logical system is concerned. These choices make the difference between a brilliant and a footling reasoner, not the difference between a sound and a fallacious one. Propositions leading to imperatives of this kind might be "When Socrates is mentioned, use the syllogism in Barbara" or "If one method has been proved to be quicker than another, do not use the slower method." Some of these may be "given by authority," but others may be produced by the machine itself, e.g., by scientific induction.

The idea of a learning machine may appear paradoxical to some readers. How can the rules of operation of the machine change? They should describe completely how the machine will react whatever its history might be, whatever changes it might undergo. The rules are thus quite time-invariant. This is quite true. The explanation of the paradox is that the rules which get changed in the learning process are of a rather less pretentious kind, claiming only an ephemeral validity. The reader may draw a parallel with the Constitution of the United States.

An important feature of a learning machine is that its teacher will often be very largely ignorant of quite what is going on inside, although he may still be able to some extent to predict his pupil's behavior. This should apply most strongly to the later education of a machine arising from a child-machine of well-tried design (or program). This is in clear contrast with normal procedure when using a machine to do computations: one's object is then to have a clear mental picture of the state of the machine at each moment in the computation. The object can only be achieved with a struggle. The view that "the machine can only do what we know how to order it to do,"[3] appears strange in face of this. Most of the programs which we can put into the machine will result in its doing something that we cannot make sense of at all, or which we regard as completely random behavior. Intelligent behavior presumably consists in a departure from the completely disciplined behavior involved in computation, but a rather slight one, which does not give rise to random behavior, or to pointless repetitive loops. Another important result of preparing our machine for its part in the imitation game by a process of teaching and learning is that "human fallibility" is likely to be omitted in a rather natural way, i.e., without special "coaching." . . . Processes that are learned do not produce a hundred per cent certainty of result; if they did they could not be unlearned.

It is probably wise to include a random element in a learning machine. . . . A random element is rather useful when we are searching for a solution of some problem. Suppose for instance we wanted to find a number between 50 and 200 which was equal to the square of the sum of its digits, we might start at 51 then try 52 and go on until we got a number that worked. Alternatively we might choose numbers at random until we got a good one. This method has the advantage that it is unnecessary to keep track of the values that have been tried, but the disadvantage that one may try the same one twice, but this is not very important if there are several solutions. The systematic method has the disadvantage that there may be an enormous block without any solutions in the region which has to be investigated first. Now the learning process may be regarded as a search for a form of behavior which will satisfy the teacher (or some other criterion). Since there is probably a very large number of satisfactory solutions the random method seems to be better than the systematic. It should be noticed that it is used in the analogous process of evolution. But there the systematic method is not possible. How could one keep track of the different genetical combinations that had been tried, so as to avoid trying them again?

We may hope that machines will eventually compete with men in all purely intellectual fields. But which are the best ones to start with? Even this is a difficult decision. Many people think that a very abstract activity, like the playing of chess, would be best. It can also be maintained that it is best to provide the machine with the best sense organs that money can buy, and then teach it to understand and speak English. This process could follow the normal teaching of a child. Things would be pointed out and named, etc. Again I do not know what the right answer is, but I think both approaches should be tried.

We can only see a short distance ahead, but we can see plenty there that needs to be done.

NOTES

1. Possibly this view is heretical. Saint Thomas Aquinas (*Summa Theologica*, quoted by Bertrand Russell, *A History of Western Philosophy* [New York; Simon & Schuster, 1945], p. 458) states that God cannot make a man to have no soul. But this may not be a real restriction on His powers, but only a result of the fact that men's souls are immortal, and therefore indestructible.
2. Or rather "programmed in" for our child-machine will be programmed in a digital computer. But the logical system will not have to be learned.
3. Compare Lady Lovelace's statement, . . . which does not contain the word "only."

DAVID HUME

Of Liberty and Necessity

In this passage from *An Enquiry Concerning Human Understanding* (1748), Hume defends what has come to be called a "soft determinist" solution to the problem of free will. He maintains that actions are both free and causally determined. A free action, for Hume, is one in which the agent could have done otherwise had the agent wished to do so.

PART I

It might reasonably be expected in questions which have been canvassed and disputed with great eagerness, since the first origin of science and philosophy, that the meaning of all the terms, at least, should have been agreed upon among the disputants; and our enquiries, in the course of two thousand years, been able to pass

David Hume, "Of Liberty and Necessity," from *An Inquiry Concerning Human Understanding,* edited by Charles W. Hendel (New York: Macmillan, 1957), pp. 90–111.

from words to the true and real subject of the controversy. For how easy may it seem to give exact definitions of the terms employed in reasoning, and make these definitions, not the mere sound of words, the object of future scrutiny and examination? But if we consider the matter more narrowly, we shall be apt to draw a quite opposite conclusion. From this circumstance alone, that a controversy has been long kept on foot, and remains still undecided, we may presume that there is some ambiguity in the expression, and that the disputants affix different ideas to the terms employed in the controversy. For as the faculties of the mind are supposed to be naturally alike in every individual; otherwise nothing could be more fruitless than to reason or dispute together; it were impossible, if men affix the same ideas to their terms, that they could so long form different opinions of the same subject; especially when they communicate their views, and each party turn themselves on all sides, in search of arguments which may give them the victory over their antagonists. It is true, if men attempt the discussion of questions which lie entirely beyond the reach of human capacity, such as those concerning the origin of worlds, or the economy of the intellectual system or region of spirits, they may long beat the air in their fruitless contests, and never arrive at any determinate conclusion. But if the question regard any subject of common life and experience, nothing, one would think, could preserve the dispute so long undecided but some ambiguous expressions, which keep the antagonists still at a distance, and hinder them from grappling with each other.

This has been the case in the long disputed question concerning liberty and necessity; and to so remarkable a degree that, if I be not much mistaken, we shall find, that all mankind, both learned and ignorant, have always been of the same opinion with regard to this subject, and that a few intelligible definitions would immediately have put an end to the whole controversy. I own that this dispute has been so much canvassed on all hands, and has led philosophers into such a labyrinth of obscure sophistry, that it is no wonder, if a sensible reader indulge his ease so far as to turn a deaf ear to the proposal of such a question, from which he can expect neither instruction or entertainment. But the state of the argument here proposed may, perhaps, serve to renew his attention; as it has more novelty, promises at least some decision of the controversy, and will not much disturb his ease by any intricate or obscure reasoning.

I hope, therefore, to make it appear that all men have ever agreed in the doctrine both of necessity and of liberty, according to any reasonable sense, which can be put on these terms; and that the whole controversy has hitherto turned merely upon words. We shall begin with examining the doctrine of necessity.

It is universally allowed that matter, in all its operations, is actuated by a necessary force, and that every natural effect is so precisely determined by the energy of its cause that no other effect, in such particular circumstances, could possibly have resulted from it. The degree and direction of every motion is, by the laws of nature, prescribed with such exactness that a living creature may as soon arise from the shock of two bodies as motion in any other degree or direction than what is actually produced by it. Would we, therefore, form a just and precise idea of *necessity*, we must consider whence that idea arises when we apply it to the question of bodies.

It seems evident that, if all the scenes of nature were continually shifted in such a manner that no two events bore any resemblance to each other, but every object was entirely new, without any similitude to whatever had been seen before, we should never, in that case, have attained the least idea of necessity, or of a connexion among these objects. We might say, upon such a supposition, that one object or event has followed another; not that one was produced by the other. The relation of cause and effect must be utterly unknown to mankind. Inference and reasoning concerning the operations of nature would, from that moment, be at an end; and the memory and senses remain the only canals, by which the knowledge of any real existence could possibly have access to the mind. Our idea, therefore, of necessity and causation arises entirely from the uniformity observable in the operations of nature, where similar objects are constantly conjoined together, and the mind is determined by custom to infer the one from the appearance of the other. These two circumstances form the whole of that necessity, which we ascribe to matter. Beyond the constant *conjunction* of similar objects, and the consequent *inference* from one to the other, we have no notion of any necessity or connexion.

If it appear, therefore, that all mankind have ever allowed, without any doubt or hesitation, that these two circumstances take place in the voluntary actions of men, and in the operations of mind; it must follow, that all mankind have ever agreed in the doctrine of necessity, and that they have hitherto disputed, merely for not understanding each other.

As to the first circumstance, the constant and regular conjunction of similar events, we may possibly satisfy ourselves by the following considerations. It is universally acknowledged that there is a great uniformity among the actions of men, in all nations and ages, and that human nature remains still the same, in its principles and operations. The same motives always produce the same actions. The same events follow from the same causes. Ambition, avarice, self-love, vanity, friendship, generosity, public spirit: these passions, mixed in various degrees, and distributed through society, have been, from the beginning of the world, and still are, the source of all the actions and enterprises, which have ever been observed among mankind. Would you know the sentiments, inclinations, and course of life of the Greeks and Romans? Study well the temper and actions of the French and English: You cannot be much mistaken in transferring to the former *most* of the observations which you have made with regard to the latter. Mankind are so much the same, in all times and places, that history informs us of nothing new or strange in this particular. Its chief use is only to discover the constant and universal principles of human nature, by showing men in all varieties of circumstances and situations, and furnishing us with materials from which we may form our observations and become acquainted with the regular springs of human action and behaviour. These records of wars, intrigues, factions, and revolutions, are so many collections of experiments, by which the politician or moral philosopher fixes the principles of his science, in the same manner as the physician or natural philosopher becomes acquainted with the nature of plants, minerals, and other external objects, by the experiments which he forms concerning them. Nor are the earth, water, and other elements, examined by Aristotle, and Hippocrates, more like to those which at present lie under our observation than the men described by Polybius and Tacitus are to those who now govern the world.

Should a traveller, returning from a far country, bring us an account of men, wholly different from any with whom we were ever acquainted; men, who were entirely divested of avarice, ambition, or revenge; who knew no pleasure but friendship, generosity, and public spirit; we should immediately, from these circumstances, detect the falsehood, and prove him a liar, with the same certainty as if he had stuffed his narration with stories of centaurs and dragons, miracles and prodigies. And if we would explode any forgery in history, we cannot make use of a more convincing argument, than to prove, that the actions ascribed to any person are directly contrary to the course of nature, and that no human motives, in such circumstances, could ever induce him to such a conduct. The veracity of Quintus Curtius is as much to be suspected, when he describes the supernatural courage of Alexander, by which he was hurried on singly to attack multitudes, as when he describes his supernatural force and activity, by which he was able to resist them. So readily and universally do we acknowledge a uniformity in human motives and actions as well as in the operations of body.

Hence likewise the benefit of that experience, acquired by long life and a variety of business and company, in order to instruct us in the principles of human nature, and regulate our future conduct, as well as speculation. By means of this guide, we mount up to the knowledge of men's inclinations and motives, from their actions, expressions, and even gestures; and again descend to the interpretation of their actions from our knowledge of their motives and inclinations. The general observations treasured up by a course of experience, give us the clue of human nature, and teach us to unravel all its intricacies. Pretexts and appearances no longer deceive us. Public declarations pass for the specious colouring of a cause. And though virtue and honour be allowed their proper weight and authority, that perfect disinterestedness, so often pretended to, is never expected in multitudes and parties; seldom in their leaders; and scarcely even in individuals of any rank or station. But were there no uniformity in human actions, and were every experiment which we could form of this kind irregular and anomalous, it were impossible to collect any general observations concerning mankind; and no experience, however accurately digested by reflection, would ever serve to any purpose. Why is the aged husbandman more skillful in his calling than the young beginner but because there is a certain uniformity in the operation of the sun, rain, and earth towards the production of vegetables; and experience teaches the old practitioner the rules by which this operation is governed and directed.

We must not, however, expect that this uniformity of human actions should be carried to such a length as that all men, in the same circumstances, will always act precisely in the same manner, without making any allowance for the diversity of characters, prejudices, and opinions. Such a uniformity in every particular, is found in no part of nature. On the contrary, from observing the variety of conduct in different men, we are enabled to form a greater variety of maxims, which still suppose a degree of uniformity and regularity.

Are the manners of men different in different ages and countries? We learn thence the great force of custom and education, which mould the human mind from its infancy and form it into a fixed and established character. Is the behaviour and conduct of the one sex very unlike that of the other? Is it thence we become acquainted with the different characters which nature has impressed upon the sexes, and which she preserves with constancy and regularity? Are the actions of the same person much diversified in the different periods of his life, from infancy to old age? This affords room for many general observations concerning the gradual change of our sentiments and inclinations, and the different maxims which prevail in the different ages of human creatures. Even the characters, which are peculiar to each individual, have a uniformity in their influence; otherwise our acquaintance with the persons and our observation of their conduct could never teach us their dispositions, or serve to direct our behaviour with regard to them.

I grant it possible to find some actions, which seem to have no regular connexion with any known motives, and are exceptions to all the measures of conduct which have ever been established for the government of men. But if we would willingly know what judgement should be formed of such irregular and extraordinary actions, we may consider the sentiments commonly entertained with regard to those irregular events which appear in the course of nature, and the operations of external objects. All causes are not conjoined to their usual effects with like uniformity. An artificer, who handles only dead matter, may be disappointed of his aim, as well as the politician, who directs the conduct of sensible and intelligent agents.

The vulgar, who take things according to their first appearance, attribute the uncertainty of events to such an uncertainty in the causes as makes the latter often fail of their usual influence; though they meet with no impediment in their operation. But philosophers, observing that, almost in every part of nature, there is contained a vast variety of springs and principles, which are hid, by reason of their minuteness or remoteness, find, that it is at least possible the contrariety of events may not proceed from any contingency in the cause, but from the secret operation of contrary causes. This possibility is converted into certainty by farther observation, when they remark that, upon an exact scrutiny, a contrariety of effects always betrays a contrariety of causes, and proceeds from their mutual opposition. A peasant can give no better reason for the stopping of any clock or watch than to say that it does not commonly go right: But an artist easily perceives that the same force in the spring or pendulum has always the same influence on the wheels; but fails of its usual effect, perhaps by reason of a grain of dust, which puts a stop to the whole movement. From the observation of several parallel instances, philosophers form a maxim that the connexion between all causes and effects is equally necessary, and that its seeming uncertainty in some instances proceeds from the secret opposition of contrary causes.

Thus, for instance, in the human body, when the usual symptoms of health or sickness disappoint our expectation; when medicines operate not with their wonted powers; when irregular events follow from any particular cause; the philosopher and physician are not surprised at the matter, nor are even tempted to deny, in general, the necessity and uniformity of those principles by which the animal economy is conducted. They know that a human body is a mighty complicated machine: That many secret powers lurk in it, which are altogether beyond our comprehension: That to us it must often appear very uncertain in its operations: And that therefore the irregular events, which outwardly discover themselves, can be no proof that the laws of nature are not observed with the greatest regularity in its internal operations and government.

The philosopher, if he be consistent, must apply the same reasoning to the actions and volitions of intelligent agents. The most irregular and unexpected resolutions of men may frequently be accounted for by those who know every particular circumstance of their character and situation. A person of an obliging disposition gives a peevish answer: But he has the toothache, or has not dined. A stupid fellow discovers an uncommon alacrity in his carriage: But he has met with a sudden piece of good fortune. Or even when an action, as sometimes happens, cannot be particularly accounted for, either by the person himself or by others; we know, in general, that the characters of men are, to a certain degree, inconstant and irregular. This is, in a manner, the constant character of human nature; though it be applicable, in a more particular manner, to some persons who have no fixed rule for their conduct, but proceed in a continued course of caprice and inconstancy. The internal principles and motives may operate in a uniform manner, notwithstanding these seeming irregularities; in the same manner as the winds, rain, clouds, and other variations of the weather are supposed to be governed by steady principles; though not easily discoverable by human sagacity and enquiry.

Thus it appears, not only that the conjunction between motives and voluntary actions is as regular and uniform as that between the cause and effect in any part of nature; but also that this regular conjunction has been universally acknowledged among mankind, and has never been the subject of dispute, either in philosophy or common life. Now, as it is from past experience that we draw all inferences concerning the future, and as we conclude that objects will always be conjoined together which we find to have always been conjoined; it may seem superfluous to prove that this experienced uniformity in human actions is a source whence we draw *inferences* concerning them. But in order to throw the argument into a greater variety of lights we shall also insist, though briefly, on this latter topic.

The mutual dependence of men is so great in all societies that scarce any human action is entirely complete in itself, or is performed without some reference to the actions of others, which are requisite to make it answer fully the intention of the agent. The poorest artificer, who labours alone, expects at least the protection of the magistrate, to ensure him the enjoyment of the fruits of his labour. He also expects that, when he carries his goods to market, and offers them at a reasonable price, he shall find purchasers, and shall be able, by the money he acquires, to engage others to supply him with those commodities which are requisite for his subsistence. In proportion as men extend their dealings, and render their intercourse with others more complicated, they always comprehend, in their schemes of life, a greater variety of voluntary actions, which they expect, from the proper motives, to co-operate with their own. In all these conclusions they take their measures from past experience, in the same manner as in their reasonings concerning external objects; and firmly believe that men, as well as all the elements, are to continue, in their operations, the same that they have ever found them. A manufacturer reckons upon the labour of his servants for the execution of any work as much as upon the tools which he employs, and would be equally surprised were his expectations disappointed. In short, this experimental inference and reasoning concerning the actions of others enters so much into human life that no man, while awake, is ever a moment without employing it. Have we not reason, therefore, to affirm that all mankind have always agreed in the doctrine of necessity according to the foregoing definition and explication of it?

Nor have philosophers ever entertained a different opinion from the people in this particular. For, not to mention that almost every action of their life supposes that opinion, there are even few of the speculative parts of learning to which it is not essential. What would become of *history,* had we not a dependence on the veracity of the historian according to the experience which we have had of mankind? How could *politics* be a science, if laws and forms of government had not a uniform influence upon society? Where would be the foundation of *morals,* if particular characters had no certain or determinate power to produce particular sentiments, and if these sentiments had no constant operation on actions? And with what pretense could we employ our *criticism* upon any poet or polite author, if we could not pronounce the conduct and sentiments of his actors either natural or unnatural to such characters, and in such circumstances? It seems almost impossible, therefore, to engage either in science or action of any kind without acknowledging the doctrine of necessity, and this *inference* from motive to voluntary actions, from characters to conduct.

And indeed, when we consider how aptly *natural* and *moral* evidence link together, and form only one chain of argument, we shall make no scruple to allow that they are of the same nature, and derived from the same principles. A prisoner who has neither money nor interest, discovers the impossibility of his escape, as well when he considers the obstinacy of the gaoler, as the walls and bars with which he is surrounded; and, in all attempts for his freedom, chooses rather to work upon the stone and iron of the one, than upon the inflexible nature of the other. The same prisoner, when conducted to the scaffold, foresees his death as certainly from the constancy and fidelity of his guards, as from the operation of the axe or wheel. His mind runs along a certain train of ideas: The refusal of the soldiers to consent to his escape; the action of the executioner; the separation of the head and body; bleeding, convulsive motions, and death. Here is a connected chain of natural causes and voluntary actions; but the mind feels no difference between them in passing from one link to another: Nor is less certain of the future even than if it were connected with the objects present to the memory or senses, by a train of causes, cemented together by what we are pleased to call a *physical* necessity. The same experienced union has the same effect on the mind, whether the united objects be motives, volition, and actions; or figure and motion. We may change the name of things; but their nature and their operation on the understanding never change.

Were a man, whom I know to be honest and opulent, and with whom I live in intimate friendship, to come into my house, where I am surrounded with my servants, I rest assured that he is not to stab me before he leaves it in order to rob me of my silver standish; and I no more suspect this event than the falling of the house itself, which is new, and solidly built and founded—*But he may have been seized with a sudden and unknown frenzy.*—So may a sudden earthquake arise, and shake and tumble my house about my ears. I shall therefore change the suppositions. I shall say that I know with certainty that he is not to put his hand into the fire and hold it there till it be consumed: And this event, I think I can foretell with the same assurance, as that, if he throw himself out at the window and meet with no obstruction, he will not remain a moment suspended in the air. No suspicion of an unknown frenzy can give the least possibility to the former event, which is so contrary to all the known principles of human nature. A man who at noon leaves his purse full of gold on the pavement at Charing-Cross, may as well expect that it will fly away like a feather, as that he will find it untouched an hour after. Above one half of human reasonings contain inferences of a similar nature, attended with more or less degrees of certainty proportioned to our experience of the usual conduct of mankind in such particular situations.

I have frequently considered, what could possibly be the reason why all mankind, though they have ever, without hesitation, acknowledged the doctrine of necessity in their whole practice and reasoning, have yet discovered such a reluctance to acknowledge it in words, and have rather shown a propensity, in all ages, to profess the contrary opinion. The matter, I think, may be accounted for after the following manner. If we examine the operations of body, and the production of effects from their causes, we shall find that all our faculties can never carry us farther in our knowledge of this relation than barely to observe that particular objects are *constantly conjoined* together, and that the mind is carried, by a *customary transition,* from the appearance of one to the belief of the other. But though this conclusion concerning human ignorance be the result of the strictest scrutiny of this subject, men still entertain a strong propensity to believe that they penetrate farther into the powers of nature, and perceive something like a necessary connexion between the cause and the effect. When again they turn their reflections towards the operations of their own minds, and *feel* no such connexion of the motive and the action; they are thence apt to suppose, that there is a difference between the effects which result from material force, and those which arise from thought and intelligence. But being once convinced that we know nothing farther of causation of any kind than merely the *constant conjunction* of objects, and the consequent *inference* of the mind from one to another, and finding that these two circumstances are universally allowed to have place in voluntary actions; we may be more easily led to own the same necessity common to all causes. And though this reasoning may contradict the systems of many philosophers, in ascribing necessity to the determinations of the will, we shall find, upon reflection, that they dissent from it in words only, not in their real sentiment. Necessity, according to the sense in which it is here taken, has never yet been rejected, nor can ever, I think, be rejected by any philosopher. It may only, perhaps, be pretended that the mind can perceive, in the operations of matter, some farther connexion between the cause and effect; and connexion that has not place in voluntary actions of intelligent beings. Now whether it be so or not, can only appear upon examination; and it is incumbent on these philosophers to make good their assertion, by defining or describing that necessity, and pointing it out to us in the operations of material causes.

It would seem, indeed, that men begin at the wrong end of this question concerning liberty and necessity, when they enter upon it by examining the faculties of the soul, the influence of the understanding, and the operations of the will. Let them first discuss a more simple question, namely, the operations of body and of brute unintelligent matter; and try whether they can there form any idea of causation and necessity, except that of a constant conjunction of objects, and subsequent inference of the mind from one to another. If these circumstances form, in reality, the whole of that necessity, which we conceive in matter, and if these circumstances be also universally acknowledged to take place in the operations of the mind, the dispute is at an end; at least, must be owned to be thenceforth merely verbal. But as long as we will rashly suppose, that we have some farther idea of necessity and causation in the operations of external objects; at the same time, that we can find nothing farther in the voluntary actions of the mind; there is no possibility of bringing the question to any determinate issue, while we proceed upon so erroneous a supposition. The only method of undeceiving us is to mount up higher; to examine the narrow extent of science when applied to material causes; and to convince ourselves that all we know of them is the constant conjunction and inference above mentioned. We may, perhaps, find that it is with difficulty we are induced to fix such narrow limits to human understanding: But we can afterwards find no difficulty when we come to apply this doctrine to the actions of the will. For as it is evident that these have a regular conjunction with motives and circumstances and characters, and as we always draw inferences from one to the other, we must be obliged to acknowledge in words that necessity, which we have already avowed, in every deliberation of our lives, and in every step of our conduct and behaviour.[1]

But to proceed in this reconciling project with regard to the question of liberty and necessity; the most contentious question of metaphysics, the most contentious science; it will not require many words to prove, that all mankind have ever agreed in the doctrine of liberty as well as in that of necessity, and that the whole dispute, in this respect also, has been hitherto merely verbal. For what is meant by liberty, when applied to voluntary actions? We cannot surely mean that actions have so little connexion with motives, inclinations, and circumstances, that one does not follow with a certain degree of uniformity from the other, and that one affords no inference by which we can conclude the existence of the other. For these are plain and acknowledged matters of fact. By liberty, then, we can only mean *a power of acting or not acting, according to the determinations of the will;* that is, if we choose to remain at rest, we may; if we choose to move, we also may. Now this hypothetical liberty is universally allowed to belong to every one who is not a prisoner and in chains. Here, then, is not subject of dispute.

Whatever definition we may give of liberty, we should be careful to observe two requisite circumstances; *first,* that it be consistent with plain matter of fact; *second,* that it be consistent with itself. If we observe these circumstances, and render our definition intelligible, I am persuaded that all mankind will be found of one opinion with regard to it.

It is universally allowed that nothing exists without a cause of its existence, and that chance, when strictly examined, is a mere negative word, and means not any real power which has anywhere a being in nature. But it is pretended that some causes are necessary, some not necessary. Here then is the advantage of definitions. Let any one *define* a cause, without comprehending, as a part of the definition, a *necessary connexion* with its effect; and let him show distinctly the origin of the idea, expressed by the definition; and I shall readily give up the whole controversy.

But if the foregoing explication of the matter be received, this must be absolutely impracticable. Had not objects a regular conjunction with each other, we should never have entertained any notion of cause and effect; and this regular conjunction produces that inference of the understanding, which is the only connexion, that we can have any comprehension of. Whoever attempts a definition of cause, exclusive of these circumstances, will be obliged either to employ unintelligible terms or such as are synonymous to the term which he endeavours to define.[2] And if the definition above mentioned be admitted; liberty, when opposed to necessity, not to constraint, is the same thing with chance; which is universally allowed to have no existence.

PART II

There is no method of reasoning more common, and yet none more blameable, than, in philosophical disputes, to endeavour the refutation of any hypothesis, by a pretense of its dangerous consequences to religion and mortality. When any opinion leads to absurdities, it is certainly false; but it is not certain that an opinion is false, because it is of dangerous consequence. Such topics, therefore, ought entirely to be forborne; as serving nothing to the discovery of truth, but only to make the person of an antagonist odious. This I observe in general, without pretending to draw any advantage from it. I frankly submit to an examination of this kind, and shall venture to affirm that the doctrines, both of necessity and of liberty, as above explained, are not only consistent with morality, but are absolutely essential to its support.

Necessity may be defined two ways, conformably to the two definitions of *cause*, of which it makes an essential part. It consists either in the constant conjunction of like objects, or in the inference of the understanding from one object to another. Now necessity, in both these senses, (which, indeed, are at bottom the same) has universally, though tacitly, in the schools, in the pulpit, and in common life, been allowed to belong to the will of man; and no one has ever pretended to deny that we can draw inferences concerning human actions, and that those inferences are founded on the experienced union of like actions, with like motives, inclinations, and circumstances. The only particular in which any one can differ, is, that either, perhaps, he will refuse to give the name of necessity to this property of human actions: But as long as the meaning is understood, I hope the word can do no harm: Or that he will maintain it possible to discover something farther in the operations of matter. But this, it must be acknowledged, can be of no consequence to morality or religion, whatever it may be to natural philosophy or metaphysics. We may here be mistaken in asserting that there is no idea of any other necessity of connexion in the actions of the mind, but what everyone does, and must readily allow of. We change no circumstance in the received orthodox system with regard to the will, but only in that with regard to material objects and causes. Nothing, therefore, can be more innocent, at least, than this doctrine.

All laws being founded on rewards and punishments, it is supposed as a fundamental principle, that these motives have a regular and uniform influence on the mind, and both produce the food and prevent the evil actions. We may give to this influence what name we please; but, as it is usually conjoined with the action, it must be esteemed a *cause*, and be looked upon as an instance of that necessity, which we would here establish.

The only proper object of hatred or vengeance is a person or creature, endowed with thought and consciousness; and when any criminal or injurious actions excite that passion, it is only by their relation to the person, or connexion with him. Actions are, by their very nature, temporary and perishing; and where they proceed not from some *cause* in the character and disposition of the person who performed them, they can neither redound to his honour, if good; nor infamy, if evil. The actions themselves may be blameable; they may be contrary to all the rules of morality and religion: But the person is not answerable for them; and as they proceed from nothing in him that is durable and constant, and leave nothing of that nature behind them, it is impossible he can, upon their account, become the object of punishment or vengeance. According to the principle, therefore, which denies necessity, and consequently causes, a man is as pure and untainted, after having committed the most horrid crime, as at the first moment of his birth, nor is his character anywise concerned in his actions, since they are not derived from it, and the wickedness of the one can never be used as a proof of the depravity of the other.

Men are not blamed for such actions as they perform ignorantly and casually, whatever may be the consequences. Why? But because the principles of these actions are only momentary, and terminate in them alone. Men are less blamed for such actions as they perform hastily and unpremeditatedly than for such as proceed from deliberation. For what reason? but because a hasty temper, though a constant cause or principle in the mind, operates only by intervals, and infects not the whole character. Again, repentance wipes off every crime, if attended with a reformation of life and manners. How is this to be accounted for? but by asserting that actions render a person criminal merely as they are proofs of criminal principles in the mind; and when, by an alteration of these principles, they cease to be just proofs, they likewise cease to be criminal. But, except upon the doctrine of necessity, they never were just proofs, and consequently never were criminal.

It will be equally easy to prove, and from the same arguments, that *liberty*, according to that definition above mentioned, in which all men agree, is also essential to morality, and that no human actions, where it is wanting, are susceptible of any moral qualities, or can be the objects either of approbation or dislike. For as actions are objects of our moral sentiment, so far only as they are indications of the internal character, passions, and affections; it is impossible that they can give rise either to praise or blame, where they proceed not from these principles, but are derived altogether from external violence.

I pretend not to have obviated or removed all objections to this theory, with regard to necessity and liberty. I can foresee other objections, derived from topics which have not here been treated of. It may be said, for instance, that, if voluntary actions be subjected to the same laws of necessity with the operations of matter, there is a continued chain of necessary causes, pre-ordained and pre-determined, reaching from the original cause of all to every single volition of every human creature. No contingency anywhere in the universe; no indifference; no liberty. While we act, we are, at the same time, acted upon. The ultimate Author of all our volitions is the Creator of the world, who first bestowed motion on this immense machine, and placed all beings in that particular position, whence every subsequent event, by an inevitable necessity, must result. Human actions, therefore, either can have no moral turpitude at all, as proceeding from so good a cause; or if they have any turpitude, they must involve our Creator in the same guilt, while he is acknowledged to be their ultimate cause and author. For as a man, who fired a mine, is answerable for all the consequences whether the train he employed be long or short; so wherever a continued chain of necessary causes is fixed, that Being, either finite or infinite, who produces the first, is likewise the author of all the rest, and must both bear the blame and acquire the praise which belong to them. Our clear and unalterable ideas of morality establish this rule, upon unquestionable reasons, when we examine the consequences of any human action; and these reasons must still have greater force when applied to the volitions and intentions of a Being infinitely wise and powerful. Ignorance or impotence may be pleaded for so limited a creature as man; but those imperfections have no place in our Creator. He foresaw, he ordained, he intended all those actions of men, which we so rashly pronounce criminal. And we must therefore conclude, either that they are not criminal or that the Deity, not man, is accountable for them. But as either of these positions is absurd and impious, it follows, that the doctrine from which they are deduced cannot possibly be true, as being liable to all the same objections. An absurd consequence, if necessary, proves the original doctrine to be absurd; in the same manner as criminal actions render criminal the original cause, if the connexion between them be necessary and evitable.

This objection consists of two parts, which we shall examine separately; *First,* that, if human actions can be traced up, by a necessary chain, to the Deity, they can never be criminal; on account of the infinite perfection of that Being from whom they are derived, and who can intend nothing but what is altogether good and laudable. Or, *Secondly,* if they be criminal, we must retract the attribute of perfection, which we ascribe to the Deity, and must acknowledge him to be the ultimate author of guilt and moral turpitude in all his creatures.

The answer to the first objection seems obvious and convincing. There are many philosophers who, after an exact scrutiny of all the phenomena of nature, conclude, that the WHOLE, considered as one system, is, in every period of its existence, ordered with perfect benevolence; and that the utmost possible happiness will, in the end, result to all created beings, without any mixture of positive or absolute ill or misery. Every physical ill, say they, makes an essential part of this benevolent system, and could not possibly be removed, even by the Deity himself, considered as a wise agent, without giving entrance to greater ill, or excluding greater good, which will result from it. From this theory, some philosophers, and the ancient *Stoics* among the rest, derived a topic of consolation under all afflictions, while they taught their pupils that those ills under which they laboured were, in reality, goods to the universe; and that to an enlarged view, which could comprehend the whole system of nature, every event became an object of joy and exultation. But though this topic be specious and sublime, it was soon found in practice weak and ineffectual. You would surely more irritate than appease a man lying under the racking pains of the gout by preaching up to him the rectitude of those general laws, which produced the malignant humours in his body, and led them through the proper canals, to the sinews and nerves, where they now excite such acute torments. These enlarged views may, for a moment, please the imagination of a speculative man, who is placed in ease and security; but neither can they dwell with constancy on his mind, even though undisturbed by the emotions of pain or passion; much less can they maintain their ground when attacked by such powerful antagonists. The affections take a narrower and more natural survey of their object; and by an economy, more suitable to the infirmity of human minds, regard alone the beings around us, and are actuated by such events as appear good or ill to the private system.

The case is the same with *moral* as with *physical* ill. It cannot reasonably be supposed, that those remote considerations, which are found of so little efficacy with regard to one, will have a more powerful influence with regard to the other. The mind of man is so formed by nature that, upon the appearance of certain characters, dispositions, and actions, it immediately feels the sentiment of approbation or blame; nor are there any emotions more essential to its frame and constitution. The characters which engage our approbation are chiefly such as contribute to the peace and security of human society; as the characters which excite blame are chiefly such as tend to public detriment and disturbance: Whence it may reasonably be presumed, that the moral sentiments arise, either mediately or immediately, from a reflection of these opposite interests. What though philosophical mediations establish a different opinion or conjecture; that everything is right with regard to the WHOLE, and that the qualities, which disturb society, are, in the main, as beneficial, and are as suitable to the primary intention of nature as those which more directly promote its happiness and welfare? Are such remote and uncertain speculations able to counterbalance the sentiments which arise from the natural and immediate view of the objects? A man who is robbed of a considerable sum; does he find his vexation for the loss anywise diminished by these sublime reflections? Why then should his moral resentment against the crime be supposed incompatible with them? Or why should not the acknowledgment of a real distinction between vice and virtue be reconcilable to all speculative systems of philosophy, as well as that of a real distinction between personal beauty and deformity? Both these distinctions are founded in the natural sentiments of the human mind: And these sentiments are not to be controlled or altered by any philosophical theory or speculation whatsoever.

The *second* objection admits not of so easy and satisfactory an answer; nor is it possible to explain distinctly, how the Deity can be the mediate cause of all the actions of men, without being the author of sin and moral turpitude. These are mysteries, which mere natural and unassisted reason is very unfit to handle; and whatever system she embraces, she must find herself involved in inextricable difficulties, and even contradictions, at every step which she takes with regard to such subjects. To reconcile the indifference and contingency of human actions with prescience; or to defend absolute decrees, and yet free the Deity from being the author of sin, has been found hitherto to exceed all the power of philosophy. Happy, if she be thence sensible to her temerity, when she pries into these sublime mysteries; and leaving a scene so full of obscurities and perplexities, return, with suitable modesty, to her true and proper province, the examination of common life; where she will find difficulties enough to employer her enquiries, without launching into so boundless an ocean of doubt, uncertainty, and contradiction!

NOTES

1. The prevalence of the doctrine of liberty may be accounted for, from another cause, viz, a false sensation or seeming experience which we have, or may have, of liberty or indifference, in many of our actions. The necessity of any action, whether of matter or of mind, is not, properly speaking, a quality in the agent, but in any thinking or intelligent being, who may consider the action; and it consists chiefly in the determination of his thoughts to infer the existence of that action from some preceding objects; as liberty, when opposed to necessity, is nothing but the want of that determination, and a certain looseness or indifference, which we feel, in passing, or not passing, from the idea of one object to that of any succeeding one. Now we may observe, that, though, in *reflecting* on human actions, we seldom feel such a looseness, or indifference, but are commonly able to infer them with considerable certainty from their motives, and from the dispositions of the agent; yet it frequently happens, that, in *performing* the actions themselves, we are sensible of something like it: And as all resembling objects are readily taken for each other, this has been employed as a demonstrative and even intuitive proof of human liberty. We feel, that our actions are subject to our will, on most occasions; and imagine we feel, that the will itself is subject to nothing, because, when by a denial of it we are provoked to try, we feel, that it moves easily every way, and produces an image of itself (or a *Velleïty*, as it is called in the schools) even on that side, on which it did not settle. This image, or faint motion, we persuade ourselves, could, at that time, have been completed into the thing itself; because, should that be denied, we find, upon a second trial, that, at present, it can. We consider not, that the fantastical desire of showing liberty, is here the motive of our actions. And it seems certain, that, however we may imagine we feel a liberty within ourselves, a spectator can commonly infer our actions from our motives and character; and even where he cannot, he concludes in general, that he might, were he perfectly acquainted with every circumstance of our situation and temper, and the most secret springs of our complexion and disposition. Now this is the very essence of necessity, according to the foregoing doctrine.
2. Thus, if a cause be defined, *that which produces any thing;* it is easy to observe, that *producing* is synonymous to *causing*. In like manner, if a cause be defined, *that by which any thing exists;* this is liable to the same objection. For what is meant by these words, *by which?* Had it been said, that a cause is *that* after which *any thing constantly exists;* we should have understood the terms. For this is, indeed, all we know of the matter. And this constancy forms the very essence of necessity, nor have we any other idea of it.

C. A. CAMPBELL

Has the Self "Free Will"?

In this excerpt from his book *On Selfhood and Godhood* (1957), Campbell defends a libertarian solution to the problem of free will. He argues that we know by introspection that some of our actions are free. Campbell claims that these actions, therefore, cannot possess causal explanations.

1. . . . It is something of a truism that in philosophic enquiry the exact formulation of a problem often takes one a long way on the road to its solution. In the case of the Free Will problem I think there is a rather special need of careful formulation. For there are many sorts of human freedom; and it can easily happen that one wastes a great deal of labour in proving or disproving a freedom which has almost nothing to do with the freedom which is at issue in the traditional problem of Free Will. The abortiveness of so much of the argument for and against Free Will in contemporary philosophical literature seems to me due in the main to insufficient pains being taken over the preliminary definition of the problem. . . .

Fortunately we can at least make a beginning with a certain amount of confidence. It is not seriously disputable that the kind of freedom in question is the freedom which is commonly recognised to be in some sense a precondition of moral responsibility. Clearly, it is on account of this integral connection with moral responsibility that such exceptional importance has always been felt to attach to the Free Will problem. But in what precise sense is free will a precondition of moral responsibility, and thus a postulate of the moral life in general? This is an exceedingly troublesome question; but until we have satisfied ourselves about the answer to it, we are not in a position to state, let alone decide, the question whether "Free Will" in its traditional, ethical, significance is a reality.

Our first business, then, is to ask, exactly what kind of freedom is it which is required for moral responsibility? And as to method of procedure in this inquiry, there seems to me to be no real choice. I know of only one method that carries with it any hope of success; viz. the critical comparison of those acts for which, on due reflection, we deem it proper to attribute moral praise or blame to the agents, with those acts for which, on due reflection, we deem such judgments to be improper. The ultimate touchstone, as I see it, can only be our moral consciousness as it manifests itself in our more critical and considered moral judgments. . . .

2. The first point to note is that the freedom at issue (as indeed the very name "Free *Will* Problem" indicates) pertains primarily not to overt acts but to inner acts. The nature of things has decreed that, save in the case of one's self, it is only overt acts which one can directly observe. But a very little reflection serves to show that in

C. A. Campbell, "Has the Self 'Free Will'?" from *On Selfhood and Godhood* (London: Unwin Hyman Ltd., 1957), pp. 158–165, 167–179. Reproduced with permission of Taylor & Francis Books, Ltd.

our moral judgments upon others their overt acts are regarded as significant only in so far as they are the expression of inner acts. We do not consider the acts of a robot to be morally responsible acts; nor do we consider the acts of a man to be so save insofar as they are distinguishable from those of a robot by reflecting an inner life of choice. Similarly, from the other side, if we are satisfied (as we may on occasion be, at least in the case of ourselves) that a person has definitely elected to follow a course which he believes to be wrong, but has been prevented by external circumstances from translating his inner choice into an overt act, we still regard him as morally blameworthy. Moral freedom, then, pertains to *inner* acts.

The next point seems at first sight equally obvious and controversial; but, as we shall see, it has awkward implications if we are in real earnest with it (as almost nobody is). It is the simple point that the act must be one of which the person judged can be regarded as the *sole* author. It seems plain enough that if there are any *other* determinants of the act, external to the self, to that extent the act is not an act which the *self* determines, and to that extent not an act for which the self can be held morally responsible. The self is only part-author of the act, and his moral responsibility can logically extend only to those elements within the act (assuming for the moment that these can be isolated) of which he is the *sole* author.

The awkward implications of this apparent truism will be readily appreciated. For, if we are mindful of the influences exerted by heredity and environment, we may well feel some doubt whether there is any act of will at all of which one can truly say that the self is sole author, sole determinant. No man has a voice in determining the raw material of impulses and capacities that constitute his hereditary endowment, and no man has more than a very partial control of the material and social environment in which he is destined to live his life. Yet it would be manifestly absurd to deny that these two factors do constantly and profoundly affect the nature of a man's choices. That this is so we all of us recognise in our moral judgments when we "make allowances," as we say, for a bad heredity or a vicious environment, and acknowledge in the victim of them a diminished moral responsibility for evil courses. Evidently we do *try*, in our moral judgments, however crudely, to praise or blame a man only in respect of that of which we can regard him as *wholly* the author. And evidently we do recognize that, for a man to be the author of an act in the full sense required for moral responsibility, it is enough merely that he "wills" or "chooses" the act: since even the most unfortunate victim of heredity or environment does, as a rule, "will" what he does. It is significant, however, that the ordinary man, though well enough aware of the influence upon choices of heredity and environment, does not feel obliged thereby to give up his assumption that moral predicates are somehow applicable. Plainly he still believes that there is *something* for which a man is morally responsible, something of which we can fairly say that he is the sole author. *What is this something?* To that question common sense is not ready with an explicit answer—though an answer is, I think, implicit in the line which its moral judgments take. I shall do what I can to give an explicit answer later in this lecture. Meantime it must suffice to observe that, if we are to be true to the deliverances of our moral consciousness, it is very difficult to deny that *sole* authorship is a necessary condition of the morally responsible act.

Thirdly we come to a point over which much recent controversy has raged. We may approach it by raising the following question. Granted an act of which the agent is sole author, does this "sole authorship" suffice to make the act a morally free act? We may be inclined to think that it does, until we contemplate the possibility that an act of which the agent is sole author might conceivably occur as a necessary expression of the agent's nature; the way in which, e.g. some philosophers have supposed the Divine act of creation to occur. This consideration excites a legitimate doubt, for it is far from easy to see how a person can be regarded as a proper subject for moral praise or blame in respect of an act which he *cannot help* performing—even if it be his own "nature" which necessitates it. Must we not recognize it as a condition of the morally free act that the agent "could have acted otherwise" than he in fact did? It is true, indeed, that we sometimes praise or blame a man for an act about which we are prepared to say, in the light of our knowledge of his established character, that he "could do no other." But I think that a little reflection shows that in such cases we are not praising or blaming the man strictly for what he does *now* (or at any rate we ought not to be), but rather for those past acts of his which have generated the firm habit of mind from which his *present* act follows "necessarily." In other words, our praise and blame, so far as justified, are really retrospective, being directed not at the agent *qua* performing *this* act, but to the agent *qua* performing those past acts which have built up his present character, and in respect to which we presume that he *could* have acted otherwise, that there really *were* open possibilities before him. These cases, therefore, seem to me to constitute no valid exception to what I must take to be the rule, viz. that a man can be morally praised or blamed for an act only if he could have acted otherwise.

Now philosophers today are fairly well agreed that it is a postulate of the morally responsible act that the agent "could have acted otherwise" in *some* sense of that phrase. But sharp differences of opinion have arisen over the way in which the phrase ought to be interpreted. There is a strong disposition to water down its apparent meaning by insisting that it is not (as a postulate of moral responsibility) to be understood as a straightforward categorical proposition, but rather as a disguised hypothetical proposition. All that we really require to be assured of, in order to justify our holding X morally responsible for an act, is, we are told, that X could have acted otherwise *if* he had *chosen* otherwise (Moore, Stevenson); or perhaps that X could have acted otherwise *if* he had had a different character, or *if* he had been placed in different circumstances.

I think it is easy to understand, and even, in a measure, to sympathise with, the motives which induce philosophers to offer these counter-interpretations. It is not just the fact that "X" could have acted otherwise," as a bald categorical statement, is incompatible with the universal sway of causal law—though this is, to some philosophers, a serious stone of stumbling. The more widespread objection is that it at least looks as though it were incompatible with that causal continuity of an agent's character with his conduct which is implied when we believe (surely with justice) that we can often tell the sort of thing a man will do from our knowledge of the sort of man he is.

We shall have to make our accounts with that particular difficulty later. At this stage I wish merely to show that neither of the hypothetical propositions suggested—and I think the same could be shown for *any* hypothetical alternative—is an acceptable substitute for the categorical proposition "X could have acted otherwise" as the presupposition of moral responsibility.

Let us look first at the earlier suggestion—"X could have acted otherwise *if* he had chosen otherwise." Now clearly there are a great many acts with regard to which we are entirely satisfied that the agent is thus situated. We are often perfectly sure that—for this is all it amounts to—if X had chosen otherwise, the circumstances presented to external obstacle to the translation of that choice into action. For example, we often have no doubt at all that X, who in point of fact told a lie, could have told the truth *if* he had so chosen. But does our confidence on this score allay all legitimate doubts about whether X is really blameworthy? Does it entail that X is free in the sense required for moral responsibility? Surely not. The obvious question immediately arises: "But *could* X have *chosen* otherwise than he did?" It is doubt about the true answer to *that* question which leads most people to doubt the reality of moral responsibility. Yet on this crucial question the hypothetical proposition which is offered as a sufficient statement of the condition justifying the ascription of moral responsibility gives us no information whatsoever.

Indeed this hypothetical substitute for the categorical "X could have acted otherwise" seems to me to lack all plausibility unless one contrives to forget why it is, after all, that we ever come to feel fundamental doubts about man's moral responsibility. Such doubts are born, surely, when one becomes aware of certain reputable worldviews in religion or philosophy, or of certain reputable scientific beliefs, which in their several ways imply that man's actions are necessitated, and thus could not be otherwise than they in fact are. But clearly a doubt so based is not even touched by the recognition that a man could very often act otherwise *if* he so chose. That proposition is entirely compatible with the necessitarian theories which generate our doubt: indeed it is this very compatibility that has recommended it to some philosophers, who are reluctant to give up either moral responsibility or Determinism. The proposition which we *must* be able to affirm if moral praise or blame of X is to be justified is the categorical proposition that X could have acted otherwise because—not if—he could have chosen otherwise; or, since it is essentially the inner side of the act that matters, the proposition simply that X could have chosen otherwise.

For the second of the alternative formulae suggested we cannot spare more than a few moments. But its inability to meet the demands it is required to meet is almost transparent. "X could have acted otherwise," as a statement of a precondition of X's moral responsibility, really means (we are told) "X could have acted otherwise *if* he were differently constituted, or *if* he had been placed in different circumstances." It seems a sufficient reply to this to point out that the person whose moral responsibility is at issue is X; a specific individual, in a specific set of circumstances. It is totally irrelevant to X's moral responsibility that we should be able to say that some person differently constituted from X or X in a different set of circumstance, could have done something different from what X did.

3. Let me, then, briefly sum up the answer at which we have arrived to our question about the kind of freedom required to justify moral responsibility. It is that a man can be said to exercise free will in a morally significant sense only insofar as his chosen act is one of which he is the sole cause or author, and only if—in the straightforward, categorical sense of the phrase—he "could have chosen otherwise".

I confess that this answer is in some ways a disconcerting one. Disconcerting, because most of us, however objective we are in the actual conduct of our thinking, would *like* to be able to believe that moral responsibility is real: whereas the freedom required for moral responsibility, on the analysis we have given, is certainly far more difficult to establish than the freedom required on the analyses we found ourselves obliged to reject. If, e.g. moral freedom entails only that I could have acted otherwise *if* I had chosen otherwise, there is no real "problem" about it at all. I am "free" in the normal case where there is no external obstacle to prevent my translating the alternative choice into action, and not free in other cases. Still less is there a problem if all that moral freedom entails is that I could have acted otherwise *if* I had been a differently constituted person, or been in different circumstances. Clearly I am *always* free in *this* sense of freedom. But, as I have argued, these so-called "freedoms" fail to give us the pre-conditions of moral responsibility, and hence leave the freedom of the traditional free-will problem, the freedom that people are really concerned about, precisely where it was. . . .

5. That brings me to the second, and more constructive, part of this lecture. From now on I shall be considering whether it is reasonable to believe that man does in fact possess a free will of the kind specified in the first part of the lecture. If so, just how and where within the complex fabric of the volitional life are we to locate it?—for although free will must presumably belong (if anywhere) to the volitional side of human experience, it is pretty clear from the way in which we have been forced to define it that it does not pertain simply to volition as such; not even to all volitions that are commonly dignified with the name of "choices." It has been, I think, one of the more serious impediments to profitable discussion of the Free Will problem that Libertarians and Determinists alike have so often failed to appreciate the comparatively narrow area within which the free will that is necessary to "save" morality is required to operate. It goes without saying that this failure has been gravely prejudicial to the case for Libertarianism. I attach a good deal of importance, therefore, to the problem of locating free will correctly within the volitional orbit. Its solution forestalls and annuls, I believe, some of the more tiresome clichés of Determinist criticism.

We saw earlier that Common Sense's practice of "making allowances" in its moral judgments for the influence of heredity and environment indicates Common Sense's conviction, both that a just moral judgment must discount determinants of choice over which the agent has no control, and also (since it still accepts moral judgments as legitimate) that *something* of moral relevance survives which can be regarded as genuinely self-originated. We are now to try to discover what this "something" is. And I think we may still usefully take Common Sense as our guide. Suppose one asks the ordinary intelligent citizen *why* he deems it proper to make allowances for X, whose heredity and/or environment are unfortunate. He will tend to reply, I think, in some such terms as these: that X has more and stronger temptations to deviate from what is right than Y or Z, who are normally circumstanced, so that he must put forth a *stronger moral effort* if he is to achieve the same level of external conduct. The intended implication seems to be that X is just as morally praiseworthy as Y or Z *if* he exerts an equivalent moral effort, even though he may not thereby achieve an equal success in conforming his will to the "concrete" demands of duty. And this implies, again, Common Sense's belief that *in moral effort* we have something for which a man is responsible *without qualification,* something that is *not* affected by heredity and environment but depends *solely* upon the self itself.

Now in my opinion Common Sense has here, in principle, hit upon the one and only defensible answer. Here, and here alone, so far as I can see, in the act of deciding whether to put forth or withhold the moral effort required to resist temptation and rise to duty, is to be found an act which is free in the sense required for moral responsibility; an act of which the self is sole author, and of which it is true to say that "it could be" (or, after the event, "could have been") "otherwise." Such is the thesis which we shall now try to establish.

6. The species of argument appropriate to the establishment of a thesis of this sort should fall, I think, into two phases. First, there should be a consideration of the evidence of the moral agent's own inner experience. What is the act of moral decision, and what does it imply, from the standpoint of the actual participant? Since there is no way of knowing the act of moral decision—or for that matter any other form of activity—except by actual participation in it, the evidence of the subject, or agent, is on an issue of this kind of primary importance. It can hardly, however, be taken as in itself conclusive. For even if that evidence should be overwhelmingly to the effect that moral decision does have the characteristics required by moral freedom, the question is bound to be raised—and in view of considerations from other quarters pointing in a contrary direction is *rightly* raised—Can we *trust* the evidence in inner experience? That brings us to what will be the second phase of the argument. We shall have to go on to show, if we are to make good our case, that the extraneous considerations so often supposed to be fatal to the belief in moral freedom are in fact innocuous to it.

In the light of what was said [previously] about the self's experience of moral decision as a *creative* activity, we may perhaps be absolved from developing the first phase of the argument at any great length. The appeal is throughout to one's own experience in the actual taking of the moral decision in the situation of moral temptation. "Is it possible," we must ask, "for anyone so circumstanced to *dis*believe that he could be deciding otherwise?" The answer is surely not in doubt. When we decide to exert moral effort to resist a temptation, we feel quite certain that we *could* withhold the effort; just as, if we decide to withhold the effort and yield to our desires, we feel quite certain that we *could* exert it—otherwise we should not blame ourselves afterwards for having succumbed. It may be, indeed, that this conviction is mere self-delusion. But that is not at the moment our concern. It is enough at present to establish that the act of deciding to exert or to withhold moral effort, as we know it from the inside in actual moral living, belongs to the category of acts which "could have been otherwise."

Mutatis mutandis, the same reply is forthcoming if we ask, "Is it possible for the moral agent in the taking of his decision to *dis*believe that he is the *sole* author of that decision?" Clearly he cannot disbelieve that it is *he* who takes the decision. That, however, is not in itself sufficient to enable him, on reflection, to regard himself as *solely* responsible for the act. For his "character" as so far formed might conceivably be a factor in determining it, and no one can suppose that the constitution of his "character" is uninfluenced by circumstances of heredity and environment with which *he* has nothing to do. But as we pointed out . . ., the very essence of the moral decision as it is experienced is that it is a decision whether or not to *oppose* our character. I think we are entitled to say, therefore, that the act of moral decision is one in which the self is for itself not merely "author" but "sole author."

7. We may pass on, then, to the second phase of our constructive argument; and this will demand more elaborate treatment. Even if a moral agent *qua* making a moral decision in the situation of "temptation" cannot help believing that he has free will in the sense at issue—a moral freedom between real alternatives, between genuinely open possibilities—are there, nevertheless, objections to a freedom of this kind so cogent that we are bound to distrust the evidence of "inner experience"?

I begin by drawing attention to a simple point whose significance tends, I think, to be underestimated. If the phenomenological analysis we have offered is substantially correct, no one while functioning as a moral agent can help believing that he enjoys free will. Theoretically he may be completely convinced by Determinist arguments, but when actually confronted with a personal situation of conflict between duty and desire he is quite certain that it lies with him here and now whether or not he will rise to duty. It follows that if Determinists could produce convincing theoretical arguments against a free will of this kind, the awkward predicament would ensue that man has to deny as a theoretical being what he had to assert as a practical being. Now I think the Determinist ought to be a good deal more worried about this than he usually is. He seems to imagine that a strong case on general theoretical grounds is enough to prove that the "practical" belief in free will, even if inescapable for us as practical beings, is mere illusion. But in fact it proves nothing of the sort. There is no reason whatever why a belief that we find ourselves obliged to hold *qua* practical beings should be required to give way before a belief which we find ourselves obliged to hold *qua* theoretical beings; or, for that matter, vice versa. All that the theoretical arguments of Determinism can prove, unless they are reinforced by a refutation of the phenomenological analysis that support Libertarianism, is that there is a radical conflict between the theoretical and the practical sides of man's nature, an antinomy at the very heart of the self. And this is a state of affairs with which no one can easily rest satisfied. I think therefore that the Determinist ought to concern himself a great deal more than he does with phenomenological analysis, in order to show, if he can, that the assurance of free will is not really an inexpungable element in man's practical consciousness. There is just as much obligation upon him, convinced though he may be of the soundness of his theoretical arguments, to expose the errors of the Libertarian's phenomenological analysis, as there is upon us, convinced though we may be of the soundness of the Libertarian's phenomenological analysis, to expose the errors of the Determinist's theoretical arguments.

8. However, we must at once begin the discharge of our own obligation. The rest of this lecture will be devoted to trying to show that the arguments which seem to carry most weight with Determinists are, to say the least of it, very far from compulsive.

Fortunately a good many of the arguments which at an earlier time in the history of philosophy would have been strongly urged against us make almost no appeal to the bulk of philosophers today, and we may here pass them by. That applies to any criticism of "open possibilities" based on a metaphysical theory about the nature of the universe as a whole. Nobody today *has* a metaphysical theory about the nature of the universe as a whole! It applies also, with almost equal force, to criticisms based upon the universality of causal law as a supposed postulate of science. There have always been, in my opinion, sound philosophic reasons for doubting the validity, as distinct from the convenience, of the causal postulate in its universal form, but at the present time, when scientists themselves are deeply divided about the need for postulating causality even within their own special field, we shall do better to concentrate our attention upon criticisms which are more confidently advanced. I propose to ignore also, on different grounds, the type of criticism of free will that is sometimes advanced from the side of religion, based upon religious postulates of Divine Omnipotence and Omniscience. So far as I can see, a postulate of human freedom is every bit as necessary to meet certain religious demands (e.g. to make sense of the "conviction of sin"), as postulates of Divine Omniscience and Omnipotence are to meet certain other religious demands. If so, then it can hardly be argued that religious experience as such tells more strongly against than for the position we are defending; and we may be satisfied, in the present context, to leave the matter there. It will be more profitable to discuss certain arguments which contemporary philosophers do think important, and which recur with a somewhat monotonous regularity in the literature of anti-Libertarianism.

These arguments can, I think, be reduced in principle to no more than two; first, the argument from "predictability"; second, the argument from the alleged meaninglessness of an act supposed to be the self's act and yet not an expression of the self's character. Contemporary criticism of free will seems to me to consist almost exclusively of variations on these two themes. I shall deal with each in turn.

9. On the first we touched in passing at an earlier stage. Surely it is beyond question (the critic urges) that when we know a person intimately we can foretell with a high degree of accuracy how he will respond to at least a large number of practical situations. One feels safe in predicting that one's dog-loving friend will not use his boot to repel the little mongrel that comes yapping at his heels; or again that one's wife will not pass with incurious eyes (or indeed pass at all) the new hat-shop in the city. So to behave would not be (as we say) "in character." But, so the criticism runs, you with your doctrine of "genuinely open possibilities," of a free will by which the self can diverge from its own character, remove all rational basis from such prediction. You require us to make the absurd supposition that the success of countless predictions of the sort in the past has been mere matter of chance. If you *really* believed in your theory, you would not be surprised if tomorrow your friend with the notorious horror of strong drink should suddenly exhibit a passion for whisky and

soda, or if your friend whose taste for reading has hitherto been satisfied with the sporting columns of the newspapers should be discovered on a fine Saturday afternoon poring over the works of Hegel. But of course you *would* be surprised. Social life would be sheer chaos if there were not well-grounded social expectations; and social life is not sheer chaos. Your theory is hopelessly wrecked upon obvious facts.

Now whether or not this criticism holds good against some versions of Libertarian theory I need not here discuss. It is sufficient if I can make it clear that against the version advanced in this lecture according to which free will is localised in a relatively narrow field of operation, the criticism has no relevance whatsoever.

Let us remind ourselves briefly of the setting within which, on our view, free will functions. There is X, the course which we believe we ought to follow, and Y, the course towards which we feel our desire is strongest. The freedom which we ascribe to the agent is the freedom to put forth or refrain from putting forth the moral effort required to resist the pressure of desire and do what he thinks he ought to do.

But then there is surely an immense range of practical situations—covering by far the greater part of life—in which there is no question of a conflict within the self between what he most desires to do and what he thinks he ought to do? Indeed such conflict is a comparatively rare phenomenon for the majority of men. Yet over that whole vast range there is nothing whatever in our version of Libertarianism to prevent our agreeing that character determines conduct. In the absence, real or supposed, of any "moral" issue, what a man chooses will be simply that course which, after such reflection as seems called for, he deems most likely to bring him what he most strongly desires; and that is the same as to say the course to which his present character inclines him.

Over by far the greatest area of human choices, then, our theory offers no more barrier to successful prediction on the basis of character than any other theory. For where there is no clash of strongest desire with duty, the free will we are defending has no business. There is just nothing for it to do.

But what about the situations—rare enough though they may be—in which there *is* this clash and in which free will does therefore operate? Does our theory entail that there at any rate, as the critic seems to suppose, "anything may happen"?

Not by any manner of means. In the first place, and by the very nature of the case, the range of the agent's possible choices is bounded by what he thinks he ought to do on the one hand, and what he most strongly desires on the other. The freedom claimed for him is a freedom of decision to make or withhold the effort required to do what he thinks he ought to do. There is no question of a freedom to act in some "wild" fashion, out of all relation to his characteristic beliefs and desires. This so-called "freedom of caprice," so often charged against the Libertarian, is, to put it bluntly, a sheer figment of the critic's imagination, with no *habitat* in serious Libertarian theory. Even in situations where free will does come into play it is perfectly possible, on a view like ours, given the appropriate knowledge of a man's character, to predict within certain limits how he will respond.

But "probable" prediction in such situations can, I think, go further than this. It is obvious that where desire and duty are at odds, the felt "gap" (as it were) between the two may vary enormously in breadth in different cases. The moderate drinker and the chronic tippler may each want another glass, and each deem it his duty to abstain, but the felt gap between desire and duty in the case of the former is trivial beside the great gulf which is felt to separate them in the case of the latter. Hence it will take a far harder moral effort for the tippler than for the moderate drinker to achieve the same external result of abstention. So much is matter of common agreement. And we are entitled, I think, to take it into account in prediction, on the simple principle that the harder the moral effort required to resist desire the less likely it is to occur. Thus in the example taken, most people would predict that the tippler will very probably succumb to his desires, whereas there is a reasonable likelihood that the moderate drinker will make the comparatively slight effort needed to resist them. So long as the prediction does not pretend to more than a measure of probability, there is nothing in our theory which would disallow it.

I claim, therefore, that the view of free will I have been putting forward is consistent with predictability of conduct on the basis of character over a very wide field indeed. And I make the further claim that the field will cover all the situations of life concerning which there is any empirical evidence that successful prediction is possible.

10. Let us pass on to consider the second main line of criticism. This is, I think, much the more illuminating of the two, if only because it compels the Libertarian to make explicit certain concepts which are indispensable to him, but which, being desperately hard to state clearly, are apt not to be stated at all. The critic's fundamental point might be stated somewhat as follows:

"Free will as you describe it is completely unintelligible. On your own showing no *reason* can be given, because there just *is* no reason, why a man decides to exert rather than to withhold moral effort, or vice versa. But such an act—or more properly, such an 'occurrence'—it is nonsense to speak of as an act of a *self.* If there is nothing in the self's character to which it is, even in principle, in any way traceable, the self has nothing to do with it. Your so-called 'freedom,' therefore, so far from supporting the self's moral responsibility, destroys it as surely as the crudest Determinism could do."

If we are to discuss this criticism usefully, it is important, I think, to begin by getting clear about two different senses of the word "intelligible."

If, in the first place, we mean by an "intelligible" act one whose occurrence is in principle capable of being inferred, since it follows necessarily from something (though we may not know in fact from what), then it is certainly true that the Libertarian's free will is unintelligible. But that is only saying, is it not, that the Libertarian's "free" act is not an act which follows necessarily from something! This can hardly rank as a *criticism* of Libertarianism. It is just a description of it. That there can be nothing unintelligible in *this* sense is precisely what the Determinist has got to *prove.*

Yet it is surprising how often the critic of Libertarianism involves himself in this circular mode of argument. Repeatedly it is urged against the Libertarian, with a great air of triumph, that on his view he can't say *why* I now decide to rise to duty, or now decide to follow my strongest desire in defiance of duty. Of course he can't. If he could he wouldn't *be* a Libertarian. To "account for" a "free" act is a contradiction in terms. A free will is *ex hypothesi* the sort of thing of which the request for an *explanation* is absurd. The assumption that an explanation must be in principle possible for the act of moral decision deserves to rank as a classic example of the ancient fallacy of "begging the question."

But the critic usually has in mind another sense of the word "unintelligible." He is apt to take it for granted that an act which is unintelligible in the *above* sense (as the morally free act of the Libertarian undoubtedly is) is unintelligible in the *further* sense that we can attach no meaning to it. And this is an altogether more serious matter. If it could really be shown that the Libertarian's "free will" were unintelligible in this sense of being meaningless, that, for myself at any rate, would be the end of the affair. Libertarianism would have been conclusively refuted.

But it seems to me manifest that this can *not* be shown. The critic has allowed himself, I submit, to become the victim of a widely accepted but fundamentally vicious assumption. He has assumed that whatever is meaningful must exhibit its meaningfulness to those who view it from the standpoint of external observation. Now if one chooses thus to limit one's self to the role of external observer, it is, I think, perfectly true that one can attach no meaning to an act which is the act of something we call a "self" and yet follows from nothing in that self's character. But then *why should we* so limit ourselves, when what is under consideration is a subjective activity? For the apprehension of subjective acts there is *another* standpoint available, that of *inner experience,* of the practical consciousness in its actual functioning. If our free will should turn out to be something to which we can attach a meaning from *this* standpoint, no more is required. And no more ought to be expected. For I must repeat that only from the inner standpoint of living experience *could* anything of the nature of "activity" be directly grasped. Observation from without is in the nature of the case impotent to apprehend the active *qua* active. We can from without observe sequences of states. If into these we read activity (as we sometimes do), this can only be on the basis of what we discern in ourselves from the inner standpoint. It follows that if anyone insists upon taking his criterion of the meaningful simply from the standpoint of external observation, he is really deciding in advance of the evidence that the notion of activity, and *a fortiori* the notion of a free will, is "meaningless." He looks for the free act through a medium which is in the nature of the case incapable of revealing it, and then, because inevitably he doesn't find it, he declares that it doesn't exist!

But if, as we surely ought in this context, we adopt the inner standpoint, then (I am suggesting) things appear in a totally different light. From the inner standpoint, it seems to me plain, there is no difficulty whatever in attaching meaning to an act which is the self's act and which nevertheless does not follow from the self's character. So much I claim has been established by the phenomenological analysis . . . of the act of moral decision in face of moral temptation. It is thrown into particularly clear relief where the moral decision is to make the moral effort required to rise to duty. For the very function of moral effort, as it appears to the agent engaged in the act, is to enable the self to act against the line of resistance, against the line to which his character as so far formed most strongly inclines him. But if the self is thus conscious here of *combating* his formed character, he surely cannot possibly suppose that the act, although his own act, *issues from* his formed character? I submit, therefore, that the self knows very well indeed—from the inner standpoint—what is meant by an act which is the *self's* act and which nevertheless does not follow from the self's character.

What this implies—and it seems to me to be an implication of cardinal importance for any theory of the self that aims at being more than superficial—is that the nature of the self is for itself something more than just its character as so far formed. The "nature" of the self and what we commonly call the "character" of the self are by no means the same thing, and it is utterly vital that they should not be confused. The "nature" of the self comprehends, but is not without remainder reducible to, its "character"; it must, if we are to be true to the testimony of our experience of it, be taken as including *also* the authentic creative power of fashioning and re-fashioning "character."

The misguided, and as a rule quite uncritical, belittlement, of the evidence offered by inner experience has, I am convinced, been responsible for more bad argument by the opponents of Free Will than has any other single factor. How often, for example, do we find the Determinist critic saying, in effect, "*Either* the act follows necessarily upon precedent states, *or* it is a mere matter of chance and accordingly of no moral significance." The disjunction is invalid, for it does not exhaust the possible alternatives. It seems to the critic to do so only because he *will* limit himself to the standpoint which is proper, and indeed alone possible, in dealing with the physical world, the standpoint of the external observer. If only he would allow himself to assume the standpoint which is not merely proper for, but necessary to, the apprehension of subjective activity, the inner standpoint of the practical consciousness in its actual functioning, he would find himself obliged to recognise the falsity of his disjunction. Reflection upon the act of moral decision as apprehended from the inner standpoint would force him to recognise a *third* possibility, as remote from chance as from necessity, that, namely, of *creative activity*, in which (as I have ventured to express it) nothing determines the act save the agent's doing of it.

11. There we must leave the matter. But as this lecture has been, I know, somewhat densely packed, it may be helpful if I conclude by reminding you, in bald summary, of the main things I have been trying to say. Let me set them out in so many successive theses.

1. The freedom which is at issue in the traditional Free Will problem is the freedom which is presupposed in moral responsibility.
2. Critical reflection upon carefully considered attributions of moral responsibility reveals that the only freedom that will do is a freedom which permits to inner acts of choice, and that these acts must be acts (*a*) of which the self is *sole* author, and (*b*) which the self could have performed otherwise.
3. From phenomenological analysis of the situation of moral temptation we find that the self as engaged in this situation is inescapably convinced that it possesses a freedom of precisely the specified kind, located in the decision

to exert or withhold the moral effort needed to rise to duty where the pressure of its desiring nature is felt to urge it in a contrary direction.

4. Of the two types of Determinist criticism which seem to have most influence today, that based on the predictability of much human behaviour fails to touch a Libertarianism which confines the area of free will as above indicated. Libertarianism so understood is compatible with all the predictability that the empirical facts warrant. And:

5. The second main type of criticism, which alleges the "meaninglessness" of an act which is the self's act and which is yet not determined by the self's character, is based on a failure to appreciate that the standpoint of inner experience is not only legitimate but indispensable where what is at issue is the reality and nature of a subjective activity. The creative act of moral decision is inevitably meaningless to the mere external observer, but from the inner standpoint it is as real, and as significant, as anything in human experience.

B. F. SKINNER

Determinism Rules Out Freedom

B. F. Skinner (1904–1992) was an influential psychologist and social commentator. His views on methodological behaviorism were discussed in Lecture 20. The present essay, excerpted from Skinner's novel ***Walden Two*** (Macmillan, 1948), takes the form of a conversation. Skinner is here presenting his view that human freedom is an illusion. We think we are free, but the fact that human behavior is caused shows that we are not.

"Mr. Castle," said Frazier very earnestly, "let me ask you a question. I warn you, it will be the most terrifying question of your life. *What would you do if you found yourself in possession of an effective science of behavior?* Suppose you suddenly found it possible to control the behavior of men as you wished. What would you do?"

"That's an assumption?"

"Take it as one if you like. *I* take it as a fact. And apparently you accept it as a fact too. I can hardly be as despotic as you claim unless I hold the key to an extensive practical control."

"What would I do?" said Castle thoughtfully. "I think I would dump your science of behavior in the ocean."

"And deny men all the help you could otherwise give them?"

B. F. Skinner, "Determinism Rules Out Freedom," from *Walden Two* (New York: Macmillan, 1948). © 1977. Reprinted by permission of Prentice-Hall, Inc., Upper Saddle River, N.J.

"And give them the freedom they would otherwise lose forever!"

"How could you give them freedom?"

"By refusing to control them!"

"But you would only be leaving the control in other hands."

"Whose?"

"The charlatan, the demagogue, the salesman, the ward heeler, the bully, the cheat, the educator, the priest—all who are now in possession of the techniques of behavioral engineering."

"A pretty good share of the control would remain in the hands of the individual himself."

"That's an assumption, too, and it's your only hope. It's your only possible chance to avoid the implications of a science of behavior. If man is free, then a technology of behavior is impossible. But I'm asking you to consider the other case."

"Then my answer is that your assumption is contrary to fact and any further consideration idle."

"And your accusations—?"

"—were in terms of intention, not of possible achievement."

Frazier sighed dramatically.

"It's a little late to be proving that a behavioral technology is well advanced. How can you deny it? Many of its methods and techniques are really as old as the hills. Look at their frightful misuse in the hands of the Nazis! And what about the techniques of the psychological clinic? What about education? Or religion? Or practical politics? Or advertising and salesmanship? Bring them all together and you have a sort of rule-of-thumb technology of vast power. No, Mr. Castle, the science is there for the asking. But its techniques and methods are in the wrong hands—they are used for personal aggrandizement in a competitive world or, in the case of the psychologist and educator, for futilely corrective purposes. My question is, have you the courage to take up and wield the science of behavior for the good of mankind? You answer that you would dump it in the ocean?"

"I'd want to take it out of the hands of the politicians and advertisers and salesmen, too."

"And the psychologists and educators? You see, Mr. Castle, you can't have that kind of cake. The fact is, we not only *can* control human behavior, we *must*. But who's to do it, and what's to be done?"

"So long as a trace of personal freedom survives, I'll stick to my position," said Castle, very much out of countenance.

"Isn't it time we talked about freedom?" I said. "We parted a day or so ago on an agreement to let the question of freedom ring. It's time to answer, don't you think?"

"My answer is simple enough," said Frazier. "I deny that freedom exists at all. I must deny it—or my program would be absurd. You can't have a science about a subject matter which hops capriciously about. Perhaps we can never *prove* that man isn't free; it's an assumption. But the increasing success of a science of behavior makes it more and more plausible."

"On the contrary, a simple personal experience makes it untenable," said Castle. "The experience of freedom. I *know* that I'm free."

"It must be quite consoling," said Frazier.

"And what's more—you do, too," said Castle hotly. "When you deny your own freedom for the sake of playing with a science of behavior, you're acting in plain bad faith. That's the only way I can explain it." He tried to recover himself and shrugged his shoulders. "At least you'll grant that you *feel* free."

"The 'feeling of freedom' should deceive no one," said Frazier. "Give me a concrete case."

"Well, right now," Castle said. He picked up a book of matches. "I'm free to hold or drop these matches."

"You will, of course, do one or the other," said Frazier. "Linguistically or logically there seem to be two possibilities, but I submit that there's only one in fact. The determining forces may be subtle but they are inexorable. I suggest that as an orderly person you will probably hold—ah! you drop them! Well, you see, that's all part of your behavior with respect to me. You couldn't resist the temptation to prove me wrong. It was all lawful. You had no choice. The deciding factor entered rather late, and naturally you couldn't foresee the result when you first held them up. There was no strong likelihood that you would act in either direction, and so you said you were free."

"That's entirely too glib," said Castle. "It's easy to argue lawfulness after the fact. But let's see you predict what I will do in advance. Then I'll agree there's law."

"I didn't say that behavior is always predictable, any more than the weather is always predictable. There are often too many factors to be taken into account. We can't measure them all accurately, and we couldn't perform the mathematical operations needed to make a prediction if we had the measurements. The legality is usually an assumption—but none the less important in judging the issue at hand."

"Take a case where there's no choice, then," said Castle. "Certainly a man in jail isn't free in the sense in which I am free now."

"Good! That's an excellent start. Let us classify the kinds of determiners of human behavior. One class, as you suggest, is physical restraint—handcuffs, iron bars, forcible coercion. These are ways in which we shape human behavior according to our wishes. They're crude, and they sacrifice the affection of the controllee, but they often work. Now, what other ways are there of limiting freedom?"

Frazier had adopted a professional tone and Castle refused to answer.

"The threat of force would be one," I said.

"Right. And here again we shan't encourage any loyalty on the part of the controllee. He has perhaps a shade more of the feeling of freedom, since he can always 'choose to act and accept the consequences,' but he doesn't feel exactly free. He knows his behavior is being coerced. Now what else?"

I had no answer.

"Force or the threat of force—I see no other possibility," said Castle after a moment.

"Precisely," said Frazier.

"But certainly a large part of my behavior has no connection with force at all. There's my freedom!" said Castle.

"I wasn't agreeing that there was no other possibility—merely that *you* could see no other. Not being a good behaviorist—or a good Christian, for that matter—you have no feeling for a tremendous power of a different sort."

"What's that?"

"I shall have to be technical," said Frazier. "But only for a moment. It's what the science of behavior calls 'reinforcement theory.' The things that can happen to us fall into three classes. To some things we are indifferent. Other things we like—we want them to happen, and we take steps to make them happen again. Still other things we don't like—we don't want them to happen and we take steps to get rid of them or keep them from happening again.

"*Now,*" Frazier continued earnestly, "if it's in our power to create any of the situations which a person likes or to remove any situation he doesn't like, we can control his behavior. When he behaves as we want him to behave, we simply create a situation he likes, or remove one he doesn't like. As a result, the probability that he will behave that way again goes up, which is what we want. Technically it's called 'positive reinforcement.'

"The old school made the amazing mistake of supposing that the reverse was true, that by removing a situation a person likes or setting up one he doesn't like— in other words by punishing him—it was possible to *reduce* the probability that he would behave in a given way again. That simply doesn't hold. It has been established beyond question. What is emerging at this critical stage in the evolution of society is a behavioral and cultural technology based on positive reinforcement alone. We are gradually discovering—at an untold cost in human suffering—that in the long run punishment doesn't reduce the probability that an act will occur. We have been so preoccupied with the contrary that we always take 'force' to mean punishment. We don't say we're using force when we send shiploads of food into a starving country, though we're displaying quite as much *power* as if we were sending troops and guns."

"I'm certainly not an advocate of force," said Castle. "But I can't agree that it's not effective."

"It's *temporarily* effective, that's the worst of it. That explains several thousand years of bloodshed. Even nature has been fooled. We 'instinctively' punish a person who doesn't behave as we like—we spank him if he's a child or strike him if he's a man. A nice distinction! The immediate effect of the blow teaches us to strike again. Retribution and revenge are the most natural things on earth. But in the long run the man we strike is no less likely to repeat his act."

"But he won't repeat it if we hit him hard enough," said Castle.

"He'll still *tend* to repeat it. He'll *want* to repeat it. We haven't really altered his potential behavior at all. That's the pity of it. If he doesn't repeat it in our presence, he will in the presence of someone else. Or it will be repeated in the disguise of a neurotic symptom. If we hit hard enough, we clear a little place for ourselves in the wilderness of civilization, but we make the rest of the wilderness still more terrible.

"Now, early forms of government are naturally based on punishment. It's the obvious technique when the physically strong control the weak. But we're in the throes of a great change to positive reinforcement—from a competitive society in which one man's reward is another man's punishment, to a cooperative society in which no one gains at the expense of anyone else.

"The change is slow and painful because the immediate, temporary effect of punishment overshadows the eventual advantage of positive reinforcement. We've all seen countless instances of the temporary effect of force, but clear evidence of the effect of not using force is rare. That's why I insist that Jesus, who was apparently the first to discover the power of refusing to punish, must have hit upon the principle by accident. He certainly had none of the experimental evidence which is available to us today, and I can't conceive that it was possible, no matter what the man's genius, to have discovered the principle from casual observation."

"A touch of revelation, perhaps?" said Castle.

"No, accident. Jesus discovered one principle because it had immediate consequences, and he got another thrown in for good measure."

I began to see light.

"You mean the principle of 'love your enemies'?" I said.

"Exactly! To 'do good to those who despitefully use you' has two unrelated consequences. You gain the peace of mind we talked about the other day. Let the stronger man push you around—at least you avoid the torture of your own rage. *That's* the immediate consequence. What an astonishing discovery it must have been to find that in the long run you could *control the stronger man* in the same way!"

"It's generous of you to give so much credit to your early colleague," said Castle, "but why are we still in the throes of so much misery? Twenty centuries should have been enough for one piece of behavioral engineering."

"The conditions which made the principle difficult to discover made it difficult to teach. The history of the Christian Church doesn't reveal many cases of doing good to one's enemies. To inoffensive heathens, perhaps, but not enemies. One must look outside the field of organized religion to find the principle in practice at all. Church governments are devotees of *power,* both temporal and bogus."

"But what has all this got to do with freedom?" I said hastily.

Frazier took time to reorganize his behavior. He looked steadily toward the window, against which the rain was beating heavily.

"Now that we *know* how positive reinforcement works and why negative doesn't," he said at last, "we can be more deliberate, and hence more successful, in our cultural design. We can achieve a sort of control under which the controlled, though they are following a code much more scrupulously than was ever the case under the old system, nevertheless *feel free.* They are doing what they want to do, not what they are forced to do. That's the source of the tremendous power of positive reinforcement—there's no restraint and no revolt. By a careful cultural design, we control not the final behavior, but the *inclination* to behave—the motives, the desires, the wishes.

"The curious thing is that in that case the *question of freedom never arises.* Mr. Castle was free to drop the match book in the sense that nothing was preventing him. If it had been securely bound to his hand he wouldn't have been free. Nor would he have been quite free if I'd covered him with a gun and threatened to shoot him if he let it fall. The question of freedom arises when there is restraint—either physical or psychological.

"But restraint is only one sort of control, and absence of restraint isn't freedom. It's not control that's lacking when one feels 'free,' but the objectionable control of force. Mr. Castle felt free to hold or drop the matches in the sense that he felt no restraint—no threat of punishment in taking either course of action. He neglected to examine his positive reasons for holding or letting go, in spite of the fact that these were more compelling in this instance than any threat of force.

"We have no vocabulary of freedom in dealing with what we want to do," Frazier went on. "The question never arises. When men strike for freedom, they strike against jails and the police, or the threat of them—against oppression. They never strike against forces which make them want to act the way they do. Yet, it seems to be understood that governments will operate only through force or the threat of force, and that all other principles of control will be left to education, religion, and commerce. If this continues to be the case, we may as well give up. A government can never create a free people with the techniques now allotted to it.

"The question is: Can men live in freedom and peace? And the answer is: Yes, if we can build a social structure which will satisfy the needs of everyone and in which everyone will want to observe the supporting code. But so far this has been achieved only in Walden Two. Your ruthless accusations to the contrary, Mr. Castle, this is the freest place on earth. And it is free precisely because we make no use of force or the threat of force. Every bit of our research, from the nursery through the psychological management of our adult membership, is directed toward that end—to exploit every alternative to forcible control. By skillful planning, by a wise choice of techniques we *increase* the feeling of freedom.

"It's not planning which infringes upon freedom, but planning which uses force. A sense of freedom was practically unknown in the planned society of Nazi Germany, because the planners made a fantastic use of force and the threat of force.

"No, Mr. Castle, when a science of behavior has once been achieved, there's no alternative to a planned society. We can't leave mankind to an accidental or biased control. But by using the principle of positive reinforcement—carefully avoiding force or the threat of force—we can preserve a personal sense of freedom."

Suggestions for Further Reading

ON THE MIND/BODY PROBLEM

Ned Block (ed.), *Readings in the Philosophy of Psychology,* 2 vols. Cambridge, Massachusetts, MIT Press, 1981.
Daniel Dennett, *Brainstorms.* Cambridge, Massachusetts, MIT Press, 1978.
Jerry Fodor, *Psychological Explanation.* New York, Random House, 1968.
George Graham, *Philosophy of Mind—An Introduction.* Oxford University Press, 1993.
John Haugland, *Mind Design.* Cambridge, Massachusetts, MIT Press, 1981.

Jaegwon Kim, *Philosophy of Mind*. Boulder, Colorado, Westview Press, 1997.
David Rosenthal (ed.), *Materialism and the Mind–Body Problem*. Englewood Cliffs, New Jersey, Prentice–Hall, 1971.
John Searle, "Minds, Brains, and Programs," in *Behavior and Brain Sciences*, vol. 3, pp. 417–457, 1980.

ON FREEDOM OF THE WILL

Daniel Dennett, *Elbow Room*. Cambridge, Massachusetts, MIT Press, 1985.
Gerald Dworkin (ed.), *Determinism, Free Will, and Moral Responsibility*. Englewood Cliffs, New Jersey, Prentice–Hall, 1970.
John Martin Fischer (ed.), *Moral Responsibility*. Cornell University Press, 1986.
Robert Nozick, "Free Will," in *Philosophical Explanation*. Cambridge, Massachusetts, Harvard University Press, 1981.
Timothy O'Connor (ed.), *Agents, Causes, and Events*. Oxford, Oxford University Press, 1995.
Gary Watson (ed.), *Free Will*. New York, Oxford University Press, 1982.

ON EGOISM AND ALTRUISM

Robert Axelrod, *The Evolution of Cooperation*. New York, Basic Books, 1985.
Joel Feinberg, "Psychological Egoism," in J. Feinberg (ed.), *Reason and Responsibility*. Belmont, California, Wadsworth, 1981.
Elliott Sober and David Sloan Wilson, *Unto Others: The Evolution and Psychology of Unselfish Behavior*. Cambridge, Massachusetts, Harvard University Press, 1998.

PART V
ETHICS

LECTURE 27

Ethics—Normative and Meta

The philosophical study of ethics (morality) concerns the nature of good and bad, right and wrong, justice and injustice. In the section of this book on the theory of knowledge, I addressed the question of what a person should *believe*. Ethics focuses on the question of *action*—what actions should a person undertake to perform? Ethics deals with what may be the most fundamental personal question of all—how should you lead your life?

ETHICS AND RELIGION

People often think that ethical questions are inseparable from religious ones. During childhood, many of us had our moral training and our religious training mixed together. We were taught basic ethical principles (like the Golden Rule) by being told how God wants us to act. In adulthood, disagreements about some ethical questions (for example, the permissibility of contraception or abortion) sometimes reflect differences over some religious doctrine.

If you think that ethics and religion are tightly bound together, it may well puzzle you how an atheist or an agnostic could have strong moral convictions. Maybe you suspect that such people are being inconsistent. If someone doesn't believe that God exists, how can he or she hold that there is a difference between right and wrong? A character in Fyodor Dostoyevsky's novel *The Brothers Karamazov* expresses this idea when he says "If God is dead, then everything is permitted."

If you tend to connect God and morality in this way, it may surprise you that a very central tradition in Western philosophy has sought to separate questions of ethics from the issue of what God wants us to do. This tradition goes back to Plato in fourth-century B.C. Greece. The philosophers in this tradition usually weren't atheists.

They believed in God (or in the gods, in Plato's case), but thought that ethical questions should be addressed independently of assumptions about whether there is a God and what God commands. I'll discuss this idea in Lecture 30.

METAETHICS AND NORMATIVE ETHICS

The study of ethics is usually divided into two large areas. These are *metaethics* and *normative ethics*. The prefix *meta* suggests the idea of "aboutness." For example, metamathematics involves theories that are about mathematical theories; metalinguistic statements are statements about language. In metaethics, we consider general questions about the nature of morality and about the meaning of moral concepts. In metaethics we don't ask whether murder is wrong rather than right. Rather, we might inquire as to whether there really is a difference between right and wrong, or try to clarify what it means to classify an action as "wrong" or "right."

In normative ethics, on the other hand, we assume that there is a difference between right and wrong and ask which actions fall into the one category and which into the other. For example, utilitarians say that whether an action should be performed depends on whether it promotes the greatest happiness for the greatest number of people. An alternative position is that actions shouldn't be performed if they are unjust, where the dictates of justice may not always coincide with what makes people happy. This dispute assumes that there is a correct answer to the question of what principles people should use to guide their actions. The problem in normative ethics is to determine what those principles are.

TRUTH AND OPINION

Back in Lectures 1 and 2, I drew a distinction between truth and opinion. It is one thing to say that

> The Rockies are more than 10,000 feet tall.

It is something else to say that

> Many people believe the Rockies are more than 10,000 feet tall.

The first of these propositions is true independently of anyone's believing it or saying that it is so. The second, obviously, depends for its truth on what people believe. There are objective facts about geology, over and above the subjective opinions people happen to have.

Does this distinction apply to the case of ethics? There is variation in ethical opinions—people sometimes disagree about whether a given action is right or wrong. But is there, in addition, a fact of the matter as to whether the action really *is* right or wrong? That is, are there objective facts in ethics that exist above and beyond the subjective opinions people happen to have? This is the primary question I'll consider in metaethics.

After surveying a range of possible answers to this question, I'll move on to normative ethics in Lecture 31. When I do this, I'll simply assume that there is a real difference between right and wrong. Given this assumption, I'll ask what makes some actions have the one property and other actions have the other.

ALTERNATIVE METAETHICAL POSITIONS

To get started on the metaethical question of whether there are objective facts in ethics, I'm going to provide a road map to the different positions I'll consider. These positions divide up according to how they answer the following two questions:

(1) Are there any ethical truths?

(2) If so, what makes the ethical truths true?

SUBJECTIVISM

What would it mean to answer "no" to the first question? The idea here is that there are various ethical *opinions* that people have about right and wrong. But no statement that says that an action *is* right (or wrong) is, in fact, *true.* Opinions occupy what I've called *the subjective realm.* So the theory that says there is opinion but no truth in ethics I'll call *ethical subjectivism.*

One way to describe this position is to use a distinction David Hume made famous. It is the distinction between *is* and *ought.* Science aims to discover what *is* the case; ethics tries to describe the way things *ought* to be. A negative answer to question (1) might be understood to mean that all true propositions are *is*-propositions; there are no true *ought*-propositions. I'll consider in the next two lectures several arguments that have been suggested for saying "no" to question (1).

REALISM

Consider next what the options are if you answer "yes" to question (1). That is, suppose that some ethical statements are true. Question (2) then becomes relevant: What makes those statements true? One possibility is that they are true independently of anyone's say-so. Ethical truths are true whether or not anyone thinks they are. This position I'll call *ethical realism.*

Realism here doesn't mean what it means in politics—as when we say that someone is a political realist. We sometimes call people "political realists" when they are "practical"—they don't try too hard to do the right thing, because they think the right thing is unattainable anyway. Humphrey Bogart is a realist of this sort at the beginning of the movie *Casablanca,* though he changes at the end.

Rather, ethical realism is the view that there are objective ethical facts that exist independently of anyone's say-so. If murder is wrong, this isn't because you, I, or anyone says (or thinks) it is wrong. Hamlet says that nothing is right or wrong, unless thinking makes it so. This bit of poetry rejects ethical realism.

CONVENTIONALISM

The remaining option asserts that there are ethical truths, but maintains that these truths are true because of someone's say-so. I call this point of view *conventionalism.* Conventionalists differ from subjectivists in the way they answer question (1); they differ from realists in the way they answer question (2).

In the U.S.A., people drive on the right side of the road. In England, they drive on the left. There is nothing inherently better about one procedure (suppose). They are equally workable, as long as everybody in a country does the same thing. The key idea about conventions is that they embody *arbitrary decisions.* The reason you should drive on the right in the U.S.A. is simply that the people there have agreed that that is the rule to follow. In this case, a fact is brought into being by people's saying that things shall be one way rather than the other.

In Lecture 2, I made a general remark about how we should avoid "wishful thinking." For the vast majority of propositions we could consider, thinking (or saying) that they are true doesn't, all by itself, make them true. Saying or thinking that the Rocky Mountains are more than 10,000 feet high doesn't make them so.

Descartes (Lecture 13) thought he had found an exception to this pattern; he thought that the proposition "I am thinking" is made true by my thinking it is true.

Conventionalism in ethics holds that the same goes for right and wrong. Someone's saying (or believing) that murder is wrong makes murder wrong. Conventionalists, however, disagree among themselves as to whose say-so does the job.

THREE VARIETIES OF CONVENTIONALISM

The first conventionalist theory I'll consider is called the *Divine Command Theory.* It says that an act is right or wrong because and only because God says that it is. It isn't that murder (or whatever) is inherently bad. Rather, murder has the moral status it does only because God commanded that we behave in a certain way.

The second conventionalist theory is called *ethical relativism.* This view says that what is right or wrong is determined by the society you inhabit. If your society adopts norms that prohibit murder, then it is wrong for you to murder. If some other society adopts different standards, then it may be quite permissible for someone in that society to murder. Ethical truths are relative, not absolute. Murder isn't wrong absolutely; it is wrong relative to the norms of one society but may be right relative to the norms of another. According to ethical relativism, it isn't God's say-so that makes the ethical truths true, but society's.

The third and last conventionalist theory I'll consider asserts that each individual constructs his or her own morality. It isn't just that each of us must decide for ourselves how we should live. Rather, the idea is that we make our actions right or wrong by deciding what standards to adopt. This idea is part of one version of the philosophy called *existentialism*.

In his book *Existentialism* (1946), the French philosopher Jean-Paul Sartre (1905–1980) describes a young Frenchman during World War II who must decide between joining the Resistance to fight the Nazis or staying home to care for his ailing mother. Sartre says that there is no standard of conduct that determines what the young man ought to do. *He* must choose whether he wants to be one sort of person or another. Once this choice is made, his subsequent action thereby counts as good or bad. For Sartre's existentialism, it is the individual's say-so that makes an action right or wrong.

This menu of options in metaethics is summarized in the following flow chart. At the bottom of the chart are the names of the positions described above them:

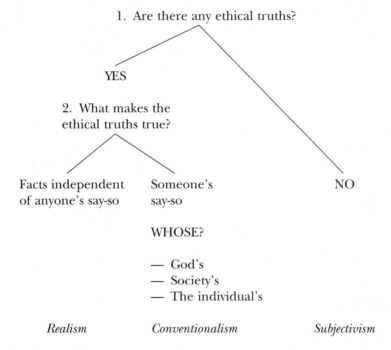

In the next two lectures, I'll consider various arguments that have been made for subjectivism. After that, I'll discuss various conventionalist theories in metaethics, beginning with the Divine Command Theory and Plato's famous criticism of it. The position I'll reach by the end of my discussion of metaethics is that there is no good argument against ethical realism. I don't claim that I can prove that realism is true, but I do think the attempts to refute it by conventionalists and subjectivists haven't worked.

Review Questions

1. What is subjectivism? What does it mean to distinguish objective fact from subjective opinion in science? In ethics?
2. What does it mean to say that ethical truths are "conventional"?
3. What does it mean to say that ethical truths are "relative," as ethical relativism asserts? Relative to what?
4. What is ethical realism? How is it similar to conventionalism? How is it different?

A Problem for Further Thought

The study of ethics often involves discussion of principles that tell people they should have acted in a way different from the way they did act; sometimes these principles require people to be less selfish and more altruistic. In the previous section of the book, I argued that people have free will and that the thesis of psychological egoism is false. If either of these claims were mistaken, would there still be a point to discussing ethical principles? Defend your answer.

LECTURE 28

The Is/Ought Gap and the Naturalistic Fallacy

From the previous lecture, you should have a preliminary grasp of what ethical subjectivism is and of how it differs from ethical realism and ethical conventionalism. In this lecture and the next, I'll consider several arguments for thinking subjectivism is true, and I'll suggest that none of them is convincing.

SUBJECTIVISM: ETHICAL STATEMENTS ARE NEITHER TRUE NOR FALSE

In the previous lecture, I said that subjectivism is the view that no ethical statement is true. Often the view is given a slightly different formulation: Subjectivism says that ethical statements are *neither true nor false*. I think this representation of the doctrine is less apt to mislead, and so I'll use it from now on. This is a small change, since if a statement is neither true nor false, then it isn't true.

Subjectivism says that ethical statements have a particular characteristic. But what is an ethical statement? Examples include any statement of the form "*X* is morally wrong," "*X* is morally permissible," "*X* is unfair," or "*X* is unjust." The *X* may be filled in by a description of an action. So *both* the following statements are ethical statements:

Emotivism

Subjectivism says that there are no ethical facts. If subjectivism is true, why do we have ethical sentences in our language? What function do they perform if there are no ethical facts for them to describe? The emotive theory of ethics ("emotivism") attempts to provide an answer.

"Ouch!" I exclaim when I hit my thumb with a hammer. "Whoopee!" I exclaim when a birthday cake is placed before me. In both cases, I've used language, but not to make an assertion. It would be a mistake to ask whether my utterances were true or false. They were neither.

"Ouch!" and "whoopee!" *express* how I feel. Emotivism claims that ethical sentences allow speakers to express their feelings and attitudes. To say "Murder is wrong" isn't to make an assertion that is either true or false; it is to express a certain sort of attitude toward murder.

There is no doubt that ethical language is sometimes used in this expressive way. The question is whether there is anything more to ethical discourse than this.

When someone says "You are an ignorant pig," the sentence is used to express the speaker's attitudes or feelings. However, that doesn't show that the sentence is neither true nor false. Besides having an expressive function, the sentence makes an assertion, which is either true or false depending on the characteristics of the person whom the speaker is addressing.

---

(1) Murder is always morally wrong.

(2) Murder is sometimes morally permissible.

Ethical subjectivism claims the first of these statements isn't true. According to subjectivism, it isn't true that murder is always wrong. But the reason this isn't true is not that it is sometimes morally permissible to murder. Remember, (1) and (2) are both ethical statements, and subjectivism claims no ethical statement is true.

At first glance, it might seem that (1) and (2) have the following characteristic: Either one of them is true, or the other is. Ethical subjectivism denies this, because it holds there don't exist any ethical facts about murder. The formulation of ethical subjectivism that I'm using—that ethical statements are *neither true nor false*—should alert you to the fact that subjectivism says that (1) and (2) are *both* untrue.

DOES THE EXISTENCE OF ETHICAL DISAGREEMENT SHOW THAT SUBJECTIVISM IS TRUE?

What arguments might be presented to support subjectivism? Sometimes it is suggested that there can't be any ethical facts on the grounds that people disagree over what's right and what's wrong. In our own society, there are moral controversies. Some people hold that abortion is sometimes permissible, others that it isn't. And even when you find actions about which there is broad consensus in our society, you can find other times and places at which there was no such consensus. For example, most people in our society would now agree that slavery is wrong; however, if you go back 150 years (or even less), there was no such broad consensus.

Is the fact that ethical opinions vary (in space and time) a reason to accept subjectivism? I don't think so. Science also contains controversies. And what now is accepted often was controversial in the past. To use an example discussed in Lectures 5 and 6, scientists now accept the idea that life has evolved. This scientific consensus, however, didn't always exist. And even now, there are people—creationists—who deny that evolution is a fact.

Even though there is and has been variation in opinion about whether evolution has occurred, all parties in this dispute believe there is a fact of the matter about whether life has evolved. No one denies that there are facts about the history of life on earth. So lack of consensus about a question doesn't show that there is no objective answer to the question.

It is important to remember that ethical subjectivism is *not* the view that some ethical statements are controversial or are hard to prove or disprove. It says that each and every ethical statement is untrue. This includes "Slavery is wrong" and "Torturing babies for fun is wrong," just as much as it includes presently controversial claims about the moral status of abortion or capital punishment. If you are prepared to say that even one moral statement is true, you are rejecting subjectivism.

THE GENETIC FALLACY

Another argument for subjectivism focuses on the explanation of why we hold the ethical beliefs we do. To formulate this argument, consider the fact that most people think it is wrong for parents to totally neglect their children. What might account for why we think this? Two kinds of explanation come to mind. First, society teaches us to think this way. Second, evolution may have led us to think this way; people who totally neglected their children would have been less reproductively successful than people who didn't, and so the less fit trait of total child neglect would gradually have disappeared from the population. (For the basics on how a selection process is supposed to work, see Lecture 6.)

Suppose there is a social or an evolutionary explanation for why people think it is wrong to totally neglect their children. Does it follow that the ethical statement "It is wrong to totally neglect your children" is untrue? I don't think so. A belief isn't shown to be untrue by the mere fact that you can explain why people hold the belief.

Consider arithmetic. How do you explain the fact that most of us think that $2 + 3 = 5$? Society has taught us to think this; and I suppose evolution has somehow contributed to our capacity to have opinions about mathematics. However, this doesn't show that there is no fact of the matter about whether $2 + 3 = 5$.

Philosophers call the mistake I'm discussing here "the Genetic Fallacy." The word *genetic* means "cause" (as in the genesis of a belief); the Genetic Fallacy has nothing much to do with chromosomes. The mistake is to think that a fact about how you come to believe something by itself settles whether the belief is true. In the next lecture, I'll consider a slightly different and more subtle version of this argument. For now, the point is that you don't establish subjectivism just by pointing out that there is a social or an evolutionary explanation for why we have the ethical beliefs we do.

So much for these two arguments for subjectivism. I now turn to two others. The first focuses on Hume's distinction between is-statements and ought-statements; the second involves G. E. Moore's idea of a "naturalistic fallacy."

HUME: THE IS/OUGHT GAP

Hume claimed that an ethical statement (describing what *ought* to be the case) can't validly be deduced from a set of premisses that describes only what *is* the case. Consider the following argument:

> Torturing babies for fun causes great suffering.
>
> _____
>
> Hence, torturing babies for fun is wrong.

The single premiss of this argument describes what is the case, not what ought to be the case. The conclusion concerns what ought to be the case. Hume said you can't deduce an ought-conclusion from exclusively is-premisses. The above argument, he claimed, isn't deductively valid.

Of course, this argument can be turned into a deductively valid argument by adding another premiss. The following argument *is* deductively valid:

> Torturing babies for fun causes great suffering.
>
> Causing great suffering is wrong.
>
> _____
>
> Hence, torturing babies for fun is wrong.

Remember what it means to say that an argument is deductively valid (Lecture 2). In a deductively valid argument, *IF* the premisses are true, then the conclusion can't fail to be true. In saying that an argument is valid, I'm not saying that the premisses are true (remember the *IF!*).

The last argument displayed doesn't deduce an ought-conclusion from exclusively is-premisses. The second premiss is an ethical statement. So Hume's point might be put like this: If a deductively valid argument has an ethical conclusion, at least one of the premisses must be ethical in character as well.

Hume's point is sometimes characterized by saying that you can't infer an ethical conclusion from purely nonethical premisses. This is an acceptable rendition of Hume's thesis, if "infer" is taken to mean *validly deduce*. However, if nondeductive inference (Lecture 3) is involved, I don't accept the formulation just given. It seems to me that the fact that torturing babies causes great suffering is an excellent reason for thinking that the action is wrong. *X* can be a reason for *Y* even though *Y* doesn't deductively follow from *X*.

(S1): AN ARGUMENT FOR SUBJECTIVISM WITH HUME'S THESIS AS A PREMISS

Hume's thesis concerns a fact about deductive implication. Does this thesis lead to subjectivism? Again, I think the answer is *no*. To see why, consider the following argument for subjectivism:

> You can't validly deduce an ethical statement from purely is-premisses (Hume's thesis).
>
> ――――――――
>
> Hence, ethical statements are neither true nor false.

This argument isn't deductively valid. A premiss can be added, however, so that the resulting argument is valid:

> You can't deduce an ethical statement from purely is-premisses (Hume's thesis).
>
> (S1) If ethical statements are not deducible from purely is-premisses, then ethical statements are neither true nor false (reductionist premiss).
>
> ――――――――
>
> Hence, ethical statements are neither true nor false.

(S1) is a deductively valid argument for subjectivism. I find the second premiss highly dubious, however. Why not adopt an antireductionist view of the status of ethical statements? That is, why not hold that some ethical statements are true, even though they aren't reducible to (deducible from) purely is-statements?

Here's an analogy. It is pretty clear that astronomy and anthropology describe different sorts of facts. Astronomers are interested in planets, stars, and other heavenly objects. Anthropologists, on the other hand, study similarities and differences among human cultures. What does it mean to say that these are different subjects? One implication is that you can't deduce anthropological statements from purely astronomical ones. Describing the orbits and masses of the planets in the solar system doesn't allow you to deduce which customs are followed in which human cultures. Would it be plausible to conclude that there are no anthropological facts, simply because anthropological statements can't be deduced from astronomical statements? Presumably not. That is, the following argument isn't deductively valid:

> You can't deduce anthropological statements from purely astronomical premisses.
>
> ――――――――
>
> Hence, anthropological statements are neither true nor false.

The next argument, though deductively valid, has a dubious reductionist second premiss:

You can't deduce anthropological statements from purely
astronomical premises.

If a statement isn't deducible from purely astronomical premises,
then the statement is neither true nor false (reductionist premise).
_____

Hence, anthropological statements are neither true nor false.

We should reject this argument. A perfectly sensible position is that there are facts
in anthropology and facts in astronomy even though neither reduces to (is deducible
from) the other. The facts coexist as separate aspects of reality.

THE NATURALISTIC FALLACY

The idea of a "naturalistic fallacy" is due to the English philosopher G. E. Moore
(1873–1958). In his book *Principia Ethica* (1903), Moore criticized the idea that the
ethical properties of an action—for example, its rightness or wrongness—might be
identical with some "natural" property of that action. An example of such a naturalistic theory is provided by one form of utilitarianism, which I'll call hedonistic
utilitarianism. This theory says that for an action to be ethically right is for it to maximize pleasure and minimize pain for those affected by it.

I'm not suggesting this theory is correct. My point is that it is an example of a
moral theory that identifies an ethical property with a natural property. This theory
says that the rightness of an action is one and the same property as the action's maximizing pleasure and minimizing pain. A natural scientist—a psychologist—could
inquire whether one action produces more pleasure and less pain than another. According to hedonistic utilitarianism, this scientist would be investigating whether the
first action is ethically preferable to the second.

Utilitarianism proposes an "identity thesis," which bears a logical similarity to the
Mind/Brain Identity Theory discussed in Lecture 21. An ethical property is said to
be identical with a natural property. By natural property, I mean a property that the
natural sciences (including psychology) might investigate.

Moore thought that hedonistic utilitarianism and theories like it make a mistake,
which he called the Naturalistic Fallacy. Moore thought it is always a mistake to say that
an ethical property of an action is the same property as one of its natural properties.
Why is it a fallacy to do this? According to Moore, we can see this by considering the
meanings of the terms involved. The term "morally right" doesn't mean the same thing
as the term "maximizes pleasure and minimizes pain." From this, Moore thought it
followed that hedonistic utilitarianism is mistaken. Moore's argument goes like this:

The expression "x is morally preferable to y" does not mean
the same thing as the expression "x produces more pleasure
and less pain than y."

(NFA) _____

Hence, the property named by the first expression
is not identical with the property named by the second.

Moore thought that any ethical theory that equates an ethical property with a natural property could be refuted by this type of argument. Any such theory, he said, commits the Naturalistic Fallacy. Let's call this argument of Moore's the Naturalistic Fallacy Argument (NFA).

I claim that Moore is mistaken. For two terms to refer to the same property, it isn't essential that they mean the same thing (be synonymous). Chemistry tells us that the temperature of a gas is one and the same property as the gas's mean molecular kinetic energy. This claim isn't refuted by the fact that "temperature" and "mean kinetic energy" aren't synonymous expressions. Consider the following argument:

> The expression "temperature" doesn't mean the same thing
> as the expression "mean kinetic energy."
> _____
>
> Hence, the property named by the first expression isn't identical
> with the property named by the second.

This argument is a fallacy. So is Moore's. That is, I think Moore's argument concerning the Naturalistic Fallacy is itself a fallacy. He commits what I'll call (following John Searle) the Naturalistic Fallacy Fallacy.

Moore failed to establish the thesis that ethical properties aren't identical with naturalistic properties. Call this "Moore's thesis." I now want to consider a quite separate question. Suppose, just for the sake of argument, that Moore's thesis is correct. Would subjectivism follow from this?

Moore didn't think so. Moore was no subjectivist. He believed that there are ethical facts and that these ethical facts exist quite apart from the naturalistic facts investigated by science. For Moore, there are two kinds of truths—ethical truths and naturalistic ones. Others have gone in the opposite direction; they have thought that Moore's thesis leads to ethical subjectivism; they have claimed that if ethics fails to reduce to naturalistic facts, then there are no ethical facts at all.

(S2): AN ARGUMENT FOR SUBJECTIVISM WITH MOORE'S THESIS AS A PREMISS

Moore's thesis doesn't, all by itself, imply subjectivism. Rather, Moore's thesis, combined with a second idea, leads to subjectivism. Here's the argument we need to consider:

> Ethical properties are not identical with naturalistic properties
> (Moore's thesis).
>
> (S2) If ethical properties are not identical with naturalistic properties,
> then ethical statements are neither true nor false (reductionist
> thesis).
> _____
>
> Hence, ethical statements are neither true nor false.

I'll call this argument (S2).

I've suggested that Moore's argument for the first premiss in (S2) doesn't work. What I want you to see now is that the first premiss, even if it were true, wouldn't be enough to establish subjectivism. To reach the conclusion that subjectivism is true, (S2) requires the reductionist thesis as well as Moore's thesis. I call the second premiss "reductionist" because it says that a property must reduce to (be identical with) a naturalistic (scientific) property if there are to be any ethical facts.

Is the second premiss in (S2) plausible? Why not reject it and adopt, instead, an *antireductionist* position, according to which ethical statements are sometimes true, even though ethical properties aren't identical with naturalistic properties? We agree that anthropological statements are sometimes true even though anthropological properties aren't identical with astronomical properties. Why not take the same view with respect to the relation of ethics and natural science?

SUMMARY

Hume correctly noted that you can't deduce an ought-conclusion from purely is-premisses. This thesis of Hume's is true. Subjectivism doesn't follow just from this point, however. Rather, to get subjectivism from Hume's insight, you've got to make a reductionist assumption. I see no compelling reason to be a reductionist about ethical statements. So (S1) isn't a convincing argument for ethical subjectivism.

Moore correctly claimed that ethical expressions aren't synonymous with naturalistic expressions. Moore, however, went on to claim that ethical properties aren't identical with naturalistic properties. This thesis of Moore's doesn't follow. And even if Moore were right that ethical properties are irreducibly different from natural properties, subjectivism wouldn't follow from that. So I reject argument (S2).

Although (S1) and (S2) are different arguments for subjectivism, they have something in common. Both assume that if there are ethical truths, these truths must be connected in an especially intimate way with naturalistic truths; ethical statements must somehow "boil down to" the facts described by is-propositions, if ethical statements are to be true. Can this assumption that the two arguments share be defended or refuted?

Review Questions

1. How do subjectivists view the statement "Lying is always wrong"? Do subjectivists reject this statement because they think lying is sometimes morally legitimate?
2. Does the fact that people disagree about ethical issues show subjectivism is true?
3. Suppose there is a social or a biological explanation for why people have the ethical beliefs they do. Does this show that those beliefs are untrue?
4. Hume saw that there is a "gap" between *is* and *ought*. What does this mean? Does Hume's insight show that subjectivism is true?
5. What does Moore mean by the *Naturalistic Fallacy*? If Moore were right about the Naturalistic Fallacy, would subjectivism follow?

Problems for Further Thought

1. In Lecture 18, I explained Frege's distinction between *sense* and *reference*. How can this distinction be used to clarify the mistake Moore makes in his Naturalistic Fallacy Argument (NFA)?

2. In discussing the Genetic Fallacy, I argued that you don't prove that a sentence is untrue just by showing that there is a causal explanation for why people believe the sentence. Can you construct an example in which the explanation for why people believe a sentence makes it highly improbable that the sentence is true? If such an example can be constructed, does this show that the so-called Genetic Fallacy isn't a fallacy at all?

LECTURE 29

Observation and Explanation in Ethics

Some people find ethical subjectivism an attractive philosophical position because they think ethics and science are fundamentally different. For them, it seems reasonable to talk about scientific facts. It strikes them, however, that ethics is very different—different enough that it is a mistake to think there are ethical facts. The problem for subjectivism is to make precise the gut feeling that there is a difference here: Can it be stated in such a way that a convincing case for ethical subjectivism emerges?

REASONING ABOUT ETHICAL ISSUES

All too often, the idea that there is an important difference between science and ethics rests on a misconception of one, the other, or both. One such misconception is the idea that reasoning can play no role in ethics—that ethics is nothing more than the irrational outpouring of feelings about what we think and do.

It isn't to be denied that people often are strongly moved by feelings when they talk about right and wrong. However, people sometimes care passionately about scientific matters and about nonethical matters that arise in everyday life. In addition, it is important to see that reasoning *can* play a role in ethics—that ethical statements can be subjected to rational criticism. An example of how this can occur is provided by Gilbert Harman (in his book *The Nature of Morality*, Oxford University Press, 1977). He asks us to consider the following principle: "If you have a choice between five people alive and one dead or one alive and five dead, you should always choose the first option over the second."

This principle is a generalization. Should we accept it? One way to tell is to see what it implies about specific examples—about concrete situations that people might sometimes confront. Harman asks us to consider the following example, which is one test case for the principle:

> You are a doctor in a hospital's emergency room when six accident victims are brought in. All six are in danger of dying but one is much worse off than the others. You can just barely save that person if you devote all your resources to him and let the others die. Alternatively you can save the other five if you are willing to ignore the most seriously injured person.

Harman says that in this case, the doctor should save the five and let the sixth person die. This is Harman's moral judgment about the example problem. I agree with Harman about this, and I'll assume that you do, too. So in this case, what we are prepared to say about the example is consistent with the dictates of the principle. Harman concludes that this example is *evidence in favor* of the principle.

Harman next considers a quite different situation that a doctor might face:

> You have five patients in the hospital who are dying, each in need of a separate organ. One needs a kidney, another a lung, a third a heart, and so forth. You can save all five if you take a single healthy person and remove his heart, lungs, kidneys, and so forth, to distribute to these five patients. Just such a healthy person is in Room 306. He is in the hospital for routine tests. Having seen his test results, you know that he is perfectly healthy and of the right tissue compatibility. If you do nothing, he will survive without incident; the other patients will die, however. The other five patients can be saved only if the person in Room 306 is cut up and his organs distributed. In that case, there would be one dead but five saved.

Harman's judgment about this case, with which I also agree, is that it would be wrong for the doctor to save the five by taking the organs of the sixth. This example, then, is evidence that the general principle stated before is false.

TESTING GENERAL PRINCIPLES BY APPLYING THEM TO SPECIFIC EXAMPLES

As Harman's example illustrates, we can reason about the correctness of a general principle by seeing what it implies about concrete cases. We reject the principle because of an ethical judgment we are prepared to make about a concrete case (the second one mentioned above). Or, if we disagree with Harman about his judgment on this second case, we might conclude that the general principle is plausible after all. The point is that we can run a *consistency check* on the various ethical opinions we have, making sure that our general principles don't contradict what we believe about specific cases.

This kind of procedure is very important in ethics. Philosophers frequently evaluate a general moral theory by seeing what it implies about specific examples. For this procedure to be possible, we must be prepared to make ethical judgments about the cases considered. This is what Harman did when he used his moral judgment about the second example to argue that the general principle is false.

Let's compare this specimen of ethical reasoning to what scientists do when they want to test a theory. Scientists also test a general theory by seeing what it implies about particular cases. For example, a general theory about electrons might predict that a laboratory instrument in a certain experiment will register "7.6" at a certain time. The scientist then can look at the instrument and see if it says what the theory predicts. If the reading differs from what is predicted, this may count against the theory.

THOUGHT EXPERIMENTS VERSUS EMPIRICAL EXPERIMENTS

In science, one sees what a theory implies about what can be observed; then, one goes ahead and makes the required observations. In the ethical case just discussed, however, no observation was required. We figured out what the general principle implies about the hypothetical case of the doctor contemplating the transplant operations, decided that this implication is unacceptable, and thereby rejected the general principle. The ethics case involved what is sometimes called a *thought experiment*.

Thought experiments differ from empirical experiments in that thought experiments don't involve actually making observations. So we now face this question: Does ethics differ from science in that science involves observation, whereas ethics doesn't? Harman poses the question as follows:

> You can observe someone do something, but can you ever perceive the rightness or wrongness of what he does? If you round a corner and see a group of young hoodlums pour gasoline on a cat and ignite it, you do not need to *conclude* that what they are doing is wrong; you do not need to figure anything out; you can see that it is wrong. But is your reaction due to the actual wrongness of what you see or is it simply a reflection of your moral "sense," a "sense" that you have acquired perhaps as a result of your moral upbringing?

OBSERVATIONS ARE "THEORY LADEN"

Harman then argues that there are no "pure" observations, that all observation is "theory laden." What does this mean? For you to see *that the children have poured gasoline on a cat and have ignited it,* you have to understand the concepts involved. If you don't know what a child is, or what a cat is, or what gasoline is, then you won't see that this is what is going on.

To make this more precise, let's distinguish two aspects of the process we call *seeing.* We talk of seeing objects ("*S* sees the cat"). And we talk of seeing that this or that proposition is true ("*S* sees that the cat is on fire"). I'll call these *objectual seeing* and *propositional seeing*. Notice that the expression following the verb in objectual seeing names an object ("the cat"), whereas the expression following the verb in propositional seeing expresses a proposition ("that the cat is on fire"). The distinction between these two kinds of seeing is somewhat similar to that drawn in Lecture 12 between objectual and propositional knowledge.

Can you see a cat without knowing what a cat is? I would say *yes*. Young children can see a nuclear power plant without knowing what they're looking at. Propositional seeing, however, is different. To see that it is a cat that is on fire, you must understand the concepts that are found in the proposition. So propositional seeing is "theory laden"—you have to have information of various sorts to be able to see that a particular proposition is true.

Now let's go back to the comparison between ethics and science. When you round the corner and see what the children are doing, do you see *that they are doing something wrong?* I agree with Harman that the answer is *yes*. You make use of your background information—in this case, information about right and wrong. In just the same way, when you round the corner, you are able to see *that the children are setting a cat on fire;* you do this by making use of your background information (concerning what a cat looks like, etc.).

So Harman concludes (and I agree) that we make ethical observations every day, just as we make observations that concern nonethical matters. We are able to do this by using background information to interpret the visual, auditory, and other sensory signals we receive.

Of course, a person who had no beliefs at all about right and wrong wouldn't be able to see that what the children are doing is wrong. It also is true, however, that the child who has no information about what a nuclear power plant is would be unable to see that there is a nuclear power plant on the hill. The child's incapacity doesn't show that there are no objective facts about whether the hill has a nuclear power plant on it. I claim that we should say the same thing about the moral ignoramus. This person is unable to see that what the children are doing is wrong, but that doesn't refute the idea that what the children are doing is objectively wrong. You don't prove that subjectivism is true just by describing the incapacities of a moral ignoramus.

OBSERVATION DOESN'T IMPLY OBJECTIVITY

Saying that people make ethical observations doesn't imply that ethical facts exist. Consider aesthetic judgments—judgments about the beauty of a painting, for example. Suppose you are looking at a painting by Monet and judge that it is a beautiful example of French Impressionism. You wouldn't be able to do this without a certain fund of background information. In addition, you needed to use your visual system to make this judgment. So perhaps it is true that you see that the painting has the characteristic just mentioned. We may conclude that observations occur in aesthetics. This, however, isn't enough to show that there are "aesthetic facts"—

that it is an objective question whether a given painting is beautiful. Someone might concede that people make aesthetic observations and still insist that beauty is in the eye of the beholder.

So far I've criticized two ideas: that ethics doesn't involve reasoning and that there is no such thing as observation in ethics. Both may seem to mark a difference between ethics and science, but neither really does. At the same time, the fact that ethics involves both reasoning and observation doesn't prove there are ethical facts.

INSOLUBLE DISAGREEMENTS

I'll now consider a third possible difference between science and ethics. It sometimes seems that there isn't much possibility of rational persuasion in ethics. Two people may quite sincerely hold the views they do, and no matter how much they discuss their differences, neither will budge. In science, disagreements are common, but often they can be solved by bringing in new evidence that neither party initially has available. In ethics, it seems that people sometimes will stick to their convictions no matter how much new information is imported. If so, we have *insoluble* disagreements in ethics. Perhaps this marks a difference between ethics and science.

I won't argue that there is no difference here (though we shouldn't forget that people can be pigheaded about nonethical matters as well). I do want to claim, however, that the alleged difference isn't enough to establish ethical subjectivism.

Think of a slave owner and an abolitionist in the U.S.A. in the 1850s arguing at length over the morality of slavery. Suppose the slave owner has shut his eyes to the humanity of slaves and to the suffering they have endured. Imagine that the slave owner was made to take these facts to heart. Maybe some slave owners would have changed their minds if they had had to confront the full implications of slavery. But probably there were some slave owners whose hearts were sufficiently hardened (at least partly out of economic self-interest) that even full information wouldn't have made a difference to them. Let's imagine that the slave owner and the abolitionist are caught in an insoluble disagreement of this kind. Does it follow that there are no ethical facts?

Ethical facts, if they exist, often will be very hard for people to grasp. The reason is that our apprehension of them often will be clouded over by self-interest and self-deception. As difficult as scientific questions about atoms and molecules sometimes are, ethics is in this respect even harder. Maybe ethics will be the last frontier of human knowledge; even after we have unlocked the secrets of the atom and of life itself, the problem of discovering the truths of ethics may remain unsolved.

So *IF* ethical facts exist, it wouldn't be surprising that there are ethical disagreements, even insoluble ones. And of course, *IF* subjectivism were true, it likewise wouldn't be surprising that there are ethical disagreements. So both hypotheses—that there are ethical facts and that there aren't—can account for the observation that insoluble ethical disputes sometimes occur.

Values in Science

Hume's distinction between is-statements and ought-statements often leads people to think that science is value-free. This seems to follow from the idea that science aims to establish what is the case and takes no stand on any ethical issue.

It is important not to confuse a distinction between different kinds of *statements* with a distinction between different sorts of *activities*. Hume's distinction concerned the former; it doesn't follow from Hume's distinction that science is an activity that is value-free.

In fact, the practice of science is saturated with values. Some of these are more or less internal to the practice of research; others have to do with how science affects the rest of society.

A scientist's decision to pursue one research problem rather than another is a decision about what is of value. Sometimes a problem is worth pursuing because it promises to yield practical benefits. Research in medicine and engineering provides obvious examples. At other times, a scientist will pursue a problem because it is thought to be theoretically important. This, too, is a judgment of value; in sciences that are more theoretical than practical (more "pure" than "applied"), a problem may be judged important because scientists believe that its solution would advance our understanding of the world.

Judging the value of pursuing a research problem, whether practical or theoretical, becomes especially important when the research would impose significant costs. Research is often expensive, and the expense is often supported by government money. Another cost arises when the research is done on living things, who may suffer and die in the course of the investigation. Responsible science requires that these considerations be taken into account.

After the scientist chooses a problem, value issues continue to be important. When scientists judge that the available evidence counts strongly against some theory, they will conclude that they *ought not to believe* the theory. Judgments about plausibility and evidence are normative; they concern what we should and shouldn't believe.

Once the scientist has reached some judgment about what the solution is to the problem under investigation, another value issue arises. Should the results be published? If so, in what forum should they be aired? It is sometimes suggested that scientists should keep their results to themselves if publishing would be harmful. Others hold that society is better off in the long run if even the most unpleasant scientific results are made public. Notice that both these opposing positions take a stand on an issue of value: When should a scientist publicize the carefully tested results of inquiry?

IS SUBJECTIVISM PREFERABLE TO REALISM, ON GROUNDS OF PARSIMONY?

So we face two competing hypotheses—subjectivism, which denies that there are ethical truths, and realism, which asserts that there are ethical truths that are true independently of anyone's say-so. Is there any way to choose between these two hypotheses?

Perhaps subjectivism has the advantage of being more *parsimonious* (an idea discussed in Lecture 21 on the Mind/Brain Identity Theory). If subjectivism can explain everything we observe just as well as the hypothesis that says there are ethical facts, then perhaps we should prefer the former hypothesis.

Harman advances an argument of this sort. He thinks that in spite of the similarities between science and ethics just described, there is nevertheless one big difference. It concerns the problem of explanation. In abductive arguments (Lecture 3), you produce a reason for thinking that something exists by showing that the existence of the thing is needed to explain some observation. Recall that Mendel never saw a gene, but he had a good abductive reason to think that genes exist.

Harman argues that we don't need to postulate the existence of ethical facts to explain any observations. Adding to this a principle of parsimony (which tells you that you should assume that something doesn't exist if it isn't needed to explain anything), Harman concludes that subjectivism is correct.

Harman describes a physicist who is looking at the screen of a cloud chamber (a device for observing particle interactions). He sees a vapor trail on the screen and says, "There goes a proton." How should we explain why the scientist believes that a proton is present? The answer, according to Harman, involves a fact about what is going on inside the cloud chamber—namely, there really is a proton in there. The proton produces the vapor trail; the scientist sees the vapor trail and comes to believe that a proton is present in the chamber. Part of the explanation of why the scientist has the belief is that what he believes is, in fact, true. The causal chain that explains the scientist's belief goes like this:

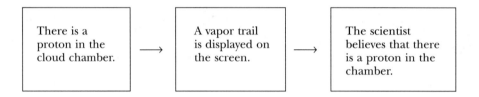

Notice that the causal chain traces something in the subjective realm (a belief) back to something in the objective realm (a proton).

Our commonsense beliefs often have a similar explanation. Suppose you want to explain why Jane believes there is a tiger in the cage. You might do this by citing the fact that her visual system is in good working order, that she knows what a tiger looks like, and that, indeed, there *is* a tiger in the cage. We explain a person's perceptual beliefs (apart from illusions and hallucinations) by describing the ways things are outside the mind. In this case, the causal chain looks like this:

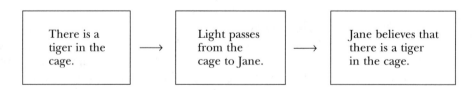

Part of the explanation of why Jane believes the proposition is that the proposition, in fact, is true.

Let's compare Harman's example from science and the similar example about Jane to the moral judgment we made when we saw the young hoodlums set fire to the cat. How are we to explain the fact that we hold this ethical belief? Harman says that we don't need to postulate the existence of an ethical fact to explain this. All we need to do is show how our moral beliefs were shaped by our upbringing—by the society in which we live (and perhaps by the genes we possess).

According to Harman, there is a striking difference between ethics and science. Scientific facts *are* needed to explain why people have the scientific beliefs they do. But ethical facts are *not* needed to explain why people have the ethical beliefs they do. Harman concludes that this is why we have a good abductive reason to think that there are protons, genes, and so on, but no good abductive reason to think that there are ethical facts.

Harman concedes that moral principles may help explain why it is wrong for the children to have acted as they did. If asked why the children were wrong to have set the cat on fire, we might appeal to some general ethical principle (like its being wrong to impose gratuitous suffering, for example). Here we cite a general ethical principle to explain some more specific ethical conclusion. Harman's point, however, is that you don't need to postulate ethical facts to explain why we *believe* the children were wrong in what they did. Ethical facts aren't needed to explain why people have *beliefs* about right and wrong (though scientific facts *are* needed to explain why scientists have some of the scientific beliefs they do).

Harman's picture of the explanatory relationships is as follows:

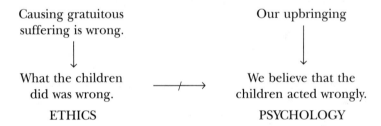

I'm not going to contest Harman's claim that this diagram is correct. What I do want to argue is that subjectivism doesn't follow.

DOES SUBJECTIVISM FOLLOW?

The Principle of Parsimony says that we shouldn't postulate the existence of something, if the something isn't needed to explain *anything*. If postulating the existence of ethical facts served no explanatory purpose whatever, the Principle of Parsimony would conclude that there are no ethical facts. But Harman hasn't shown that ethical facts aren't needed to explain anything. Rather, he has shown something more modest—simply, that you don't need to postulate ethical facts to explain why people have the ethical beliefs they do. Ethical facts aren't needed to explain this fact about our psychology.

Harman grants that we sometimes make ethical observations. We look at the children and say, "What they are doing is wrong." Harman also grants that the ethical properties of specific actions may be explained by general ethical principles. As noted above, a general principle might help explain why what the children did was wrong. Putting these two points together, we may conclude that *general ethical principles can help explain the ethical properties of specific actions.*

The point I want to make here is quite similar to what I said about Hume's distinction between is-statements and ought-statements in the previous lecture. The argument for subjectivism I called (S1) says that since ought-conclusions aren't deducible from is-statements, there are no ethical facts. I pointed out that this argument requires a reductionist premiss. To reach the subjectivist conclusion, you need to assume that if ethical facts exist, they must be deducible from is-statements.

Harman's argument is abductive, not deductive. I grant that ethical facts aren't needed to explain why we have the beliefs we do. Nevertheless, for subjectivism to follow from this, an additional assumption is needed. Harman needs to assume that we shouldn't postulate the existence of ethical facts if they aren't needed to explain why we have the beliefs we do. I find this assumption implausible. Why should the reality of ethical facts stand or fall on their role in psychological explanation?

AN EXPLANATORY ROLE FOR ETHICAL PRINCIPLES

The previous diagram *does* accord an explanatory role to some ethical facts. If you think that what the children did was wrong, then there is at least one ethical truth that requires explanation. General ethical theories may be evaluated by their ability to explain this and other specific ethical facts about example situations. If one theory does a better job of explaining such ethical facts than another, it is plausible to hold that the former is more likely to be true.

Thus, if you concede that there are at least some ethical facts, then postulating other ethical facts can be justified on abductive grounds. On the other hand, if you demand that ethical facts be judged by their ability to explain facts in psychology, you'll end up with subjectivism.

I conclude that Harman's argument doesn't justify subjectivism. He hasn't shown that there are no ethical facts. Nor has he shown that postulating ethical facts isn't needed to explain *anything.* Rather, the more limited conclusion he has established (I grant) is that postulating ethical facts isn't needed to explain certain facts about psychology (that is, about why we believe what we do).

WHAT IS THE POINT OF ETHICS?

Harman claims that ethical statements should be regarded as true only if they are needed to explain why we have the beliefs we do. However, the point of ethics isn't to explain or describe what we think. Ethics isn't psychology. The point of an ethical statement is to guide behavior—to say how we *ought* to think and act, not to describe how we actually think and act.

Review Questions

1. Why does Harman think that reasoning from general principles to claims about specific cases occurs in both science and ethics? Why does he think that observation is something we do in both science and ethics?
2. Does the occurrence of reasoning and observation in ethics show that there are ethical facts?
3. Suppose there is someone who can't be convinced that slavery is wrong. Does this show that subjectivism is true?
4. What does the Principle of Parsimony have to do with the question of whether there are ethical facts?
5. Harman says that an abductive argument can be found for thinking that protons exist, but none for thinking that ethical facts exist. Why does he think this? Is his argument convincing?

Problems for Further Thought

1. If parsimony is a good reason to prefer a materialistic theory like the Mind/Brain Identity Theory or functionalism over dualism, why isn't it also a good reason to favor ethical subjectivism over ethical realism?
2. Consider the following passage from Hume's *Treatise of Human Nature* (1739; III,1,1):

> Morality [does not consist] in any matter of fact, which can be discover'd by the understanding. . . . Take any action allow'd to be vicious: Wilful murder, for instance. Examine it in all lights, and see if you can find that matter of fact, or real existence, which you call vice. In whichever way you take it, you find only certain passions, motives, volitions, and thoughts. There is no other matter of fact in the case. The vice entirely escapes you, as long as you consider the object. You never can find it, till you turn your reflexion into your own breast, and find a sentiment of disapprobation, which arises in you, toward this action. It lies in yourself, not in the object. So that *when you pronounce any action or character to be vicious, you mean nothing but that from the constitution of your nature you have a feeling or sentiment of blame from the contemplation of it.* Vice or virtue, therefore, may be compar'd to sounds, colours, heat and cold, which according to modern philosophy, are not qualities in objects, but perceptions in the mind: And this discovery in

morals, like that other in physics, is to be regarded as a considerable advancement of the speculative sciences; tho', like that too, it has little or no influence on practice. Nothing can be more real, or concern us more, than our own sentiments of pleasure or uneasiness; and if these be favourable to virtue, and unfavourable to vice, no more can be requisite to the regulation of our conduct and behavior.

What analogy is Hume drawing between moral properties and colors? Is Hume right to think they are similar? Does Hume's analogy justify ethical subjectivism?

LECTURE 30

Conventionalist Theories

In philosophical writing about ethics, it isn't customary to lump together under one heading the three theories I'll discuss in this lecture. Nor is it especially standard to label any of these theories "conventionalist." So let me explain why I'm lumping and labeling in this way.

The Divine Command Theory holds that an action is right or wrong because God says that it is; ethical relativism maintains that an action is made right or wrong in a society by the norms the society adopts; and the existentialism of Jean-Paul Sartre says that individuals freely create the ethical standards that determine whether their lives are good ones or bad ones.

Existentialist writers often begin with the idea that there is no God and argue that people therefore must create their own ethical facts. This is obviously quite different from the framework of the Divine Command Theory, which sees ethical truth as flowing from God. Both these positions differ from ethical relativism, which views ethics as neither divinely given nor individually chosen, but as socially constructed.

WHAT MAKES A VIEW CONVENTIONALIST?

In spite of these differences, the three views have two things in common. First, they agree that there are ethical truths. Second, they agree that those truths are made true by someone's say-so. All three theories reject ethical subjectivism on the one hand and ethical realism on the other. The disagreement among them arises when these theories are asked to specify *whose* say-so does the trick—are ethical propositions made true by God's, society's, or each individual's decision?

Why say that these theories are forms of "conventionalism"? Each claims there is nothing inherent in an action (torture, for example) that makes it right or wrong. The action, considered all by itself, could easily be right or wrong. Rather, something outside of the action (extrinsic to it) makes the action right or wrong. It is God, society, or an individual who makes a pronouncement on the action and thereby endows it with one ethical property rather than the other.

In Lecture 27, I gave an example of something that I think really is conventional. It is a conventional matter which side of the road people should drive their cars on. The essential ingredients in a convention are *arbitrariness* and *decision*. Let me give another example that illustrates what this means.

TRIVIAL SEMANTIC CONVENTIONALISM

Consider the fact that we use the word "dog" to refer to dogs. Things didn't have to be this way. Many other words would have worked just fine. We could have called dogs by the name "cat" and cats by the name "dog." So how did dogs come to have the one name rather than the other? Dogs have the name they do because of a *decision*. *We* make it true that dogs are called "dogs." The rules of our language are something we control; they aren't forced on us from the outside.

This kind of conventionalism I'll call *trivial semantic conventionalism*. I call it trivial because it describes a fairly boring and unimportant fact. I call it *semantic* because it describes how pieces of language come to refer to things in the world.

A philosophically interesting conventionalist theory must say something beyond what trivial semantic conventionalism says. The ethical views I'll consider here don't make the trivial point that the words "right" and "good" might have been used to mean something different from what they mean in present-day English. If we used the word "right" to mean *morally wrong*, then most of us would treat the sentence "torturing babies for fun is right" as expressing a truth. But this is trivial.

SUBSTANTIVE VERSUS TRIVIAL CONVENTIONALISM

To see how a substantive form of conventionalism (SC) differs from trivial semantic conventionalism (TSC), we need to distinguish a proposition from the sentence that expresses it (a distinction drawn in Lecture 4). The first of the following claims is true, whereas the second is false:

> (TSC) If we used language differently, the word "dog" might not name a four-legged animal.

> (SC) If we used language differently, dogs might not be four-legged animals.

The sentence "dogs are four-legged animals" wouldn't express a truth if we used the word "dog" to refer to fish. But changing the way we talk wouldn't affect the proposition that the sentence expresses; talking differently wouldn't turn dogs into fish!

Conventionalism in ethics isn't a thesis about language. It doesn't assert that ethical *language* is under the control of someone's say-so; it says that the ethical *facts* are determined by someone's say-so. It says that ethical *propositions* are made true or false by someone's decision. Ethical conventionalism asserts a substantive thesis, not to be confused with trivial semantic conventionalism.

Ethical conventionalism holds that ethical propositions are very different from most other propositions. Consider the fact that the Rocky Mountains are more than 10,000 feet high. This proposition isn't made true by someone's believing it or saying it; rather, it is true *independent* of anyone's say-so. Conventionalism in ethics rejects the idea that ethical propositions have the same status as geographical propositions like this one.

PLATO'S CRITIQUE OF THE DIVINE COMMAND THEORY

One of the earliest discussions of the Divine Command Theory is in Plato's dialogue *The Euthyphro*. This is a dialogue between Socrates, who was Plato's teacher, and Euthyphro. They meet in a law court where Euthyphro has just made a charge of murder against his own father. A servant of his father's had killed a slave. Euthyphro's father had the servant chained up and thrown in a ditch while someone went to the priest to ask what should be done. In the meantime, the servant died. Euthyphro is confident that indicting his father is the pious thing to do, though Euthyphro's relatives are angry at him for prosecuting his father for murdering a murderer. Socrates and Euthyphro discuss what piety is. Euthyphro claims to have a clear view of this, but Socrates shows that Euthyphro is very confused.

The Divine Command Theory comes up in this dialogue when Socrates asks: Is an action pious because it is loved by the gods, or is it loved by the gods because it is pious? We might substitute any moral term we wish (like "obligatory," "right," "good," or "just") for piety. And also, if we wish, we may substitute monotheism for the polytheism of the ancient Greeks. With these substitutions, we can reformulate Socrates' question as follows: Is an action morally obligatory because God commands us to do it, or does God command us to do it because the action is morally obligatory? Socrates' question has to do with which item is the cause and which the effect in the following diagram:

The Divine Command Theory says that the arrow goes from left to right. Ethical realism, on the other hand, holds that an action is right or wrong independent of anyone's say-so (even God's). So if you are a realist and think that God exists and makes true pronouncements on ethical matters, you'll think that the arrow goes from right to left. Your view will be that God knows a fact that exists independently of him and correctly describes what that fact is.

Notice that both the options in the above diagram assume there is a God. So rejecting the Divine Command Theory isn't the same as embracing atheism. A whole series of philosophers, beginning with Plato himself, were theists and ethical realists at the same time.

Since the problem that Socrates poses assumes that the gods exist (in our reformulation, that there is a God), I'll go along with this assumption. We now want to ask what determines what in the above diagram. Which way should the arrow of influence point?

One point that Socrates emphasizes is that the gods sometimes disagree with each other. (In many of the Greek myths, one god approves of an action, while another disapproves.) This allows Socrates to convict the Divine Command Theory of being contradictory. Socrates does this by supposing that the Divine Command Theory says that an action is right (or wrong) if at least one god says that it is. So, if the gods disagree about an action, the theory entails that the action is both right and wrong at the same time.

Socrates sees that it is easy to reformulate the theory so that it avoids this problem. Suppose the theory says that an action is right (or wrong) if *all* the gods say it is. The theory then says nothing about those actions on which the gods disagree. Plato thinks this theory is still not satisfactory, but I won't go into his reasons for saying this.

If the theism we assume is monotheistic, what happens to this problem? We won't be able to discuss what the theory says when the gods disagree, since the assumption is that there is just one God. Two further kinds of problems, however, confront monotheistic versions of the Divine Command Theory.

PROBLEMS FOR THE DIVINE COMMAND THEORY

The first problem has to do with knowledge. Consider the fact that there are many *religions*. If different religions disagree about what God commands, how are we to tell what God wants us to do? And even if all religions agree about how God regards some action, there is still the question of whether they correctly report what God commands.

The second difficulty is quite separate from these problems about knowledge. To pinpoint this further problem, let's suppose not just that there is a God, but that we know what God wants us to do. For example, let's suppose that God wants us to follow the Ten Commandments. We now can ask Socrates' question: Does God say that we should not murder (for example) because it is wrong to murder, or is it wrong to murder because God says so?

If the Divine Command Theory were true, then *anything at all* would be right (even torturing babies for fun), if God said that it were. Likewise, *anything at all* would be wrong (even reducing the suffering of sick children), if God said that it were.

The idea that God might order us to torture babies for fun probably strikes you as quite horrible. "Surely, God wouldn't order us to do this," you'll say, "since God is good." Let's analyze this reaction more carefully.

The point to notice is that this reaction is actually *inconsistent* with the Divine Command Theory. For this reaction to make sense, there would have to be such a thing as goodness, which exists independently of God's say-so. To say that "God would not do *X*, since *X* is wrong" is to say that the arrow points from right to left, not from left to right, in the diagram. Remember, the Divine Command Theory says that there is nothing inherent in an action that makes it good or bad; the action has the moral standing it does simply because God chooses to label it good or bad.

I'm not doubting here that God has the power to make us the kinds of creatures we are. Let's assume that God has given us bodies that make us capable of feeling pain. It follows that God is partly responsible for why the following ethical truth is true:

Stabbing someone for fun is wrong.

God helps make this ethical proposition true, because God is responsible for the fact that stabbing people causes them pain (if he had made our bodies otherwise, that might not be so). However, the Divine Command Theory says much more than this. It claims that the following ethical proposition is true only because God says it is:

Inflicting pain for fun is wrong.

This last proposition strikes me as truly independent of anyone's say-so, even God's.

There is a third difficulty with the Divine Command Theory. If the *only* thing that makes an action right or wrong is God's say-so, then God has no *reason,* prior to his pronouncement, to decide one way or the other. This means that God makes an *arbitrary* decision about what to say, but his say-so creates an ethical fact. Before the pronouncement, there is no ethical fact; afterward, there is.

Frankly, I find it baffling how facts can be brought into being by someone's say-so. If God makes an arbitrary decision when he issues his decree, what binds us to think that what he says is true? To be sure, God can punish us if we disobey his orders. This, however, only makes it *prudent* for us to go along with what he says; it doesn't show that what he says is true. (Recall the distinction between prudential and evidential reasons discussed in Lecture 10 in connection with Pascal's Wager.)

It may be replied that the ways of God are mysterious—God can bring ethical facts into being just by issuing a decree, even though we can't understand how this is possible. To this reply I say that if the matter *is* mysterious, then we should decline to endorse the Divine Command Theory. If we can't understand the process postulated by a theory, that is hardly a reason to accept what the theory says.

ETHICAL RELATIVISM

I now want to consider ethical relativism. This theory holds that the rightness or wrongness of an action is settled by the say-so of the society to which the actor belongs. In traditional Eskimo culture, it was customary for people to put their aging ailing parents outside to die in winter; according to ethical relativism, an Eskimo who did this would have been doing the right thing. In contemporary American society, this isn't the social norm; so relativism asserts that in our society, it would be wrong for us to act in this way. Ethical relativism says that what it is right or wrong to do depends on (is relative to) the society in which you live.

ETHICAL RELATIVISM IS NORMATIVE, NOT DESCRIPTIVE

I want to make this theory more precise. First, we need to be clear that ethical relativism is a normative thesis, not a descriptive one. It makes a claim about how people *should* act. There is a quite separate descriptive thesis, which says that customs and norms *in fact* vary from society to society. Having already absorbed Hume's point about the is/ought gap (Lecture 28), you should be able to see that descriptive relativism (an is-proposition) doesn't deductively imply normative relativism (an ought-proposition).

A comment on the descriptive claim: It is fairly obvious that societies do vary in their customs and values. It is less obvious, however, that they do so with respect to the values that are most fundamental. For example, someone might grant that traditional Eskimos practiced euthanasia ("mercy killing") in contexts that we don't, but still maintain that deep down Eskimo culture and our own have the same fundamental values. Perhaps both societies adopt norms that aim to promote the general welfare, but because of different conditions of life, we and they end up arranging the details of life in different ways. I don't maintain that there are such "fundamental universals." I merely point out that descriptive relativism might be granted for some "superficial" customs but denied for some more "fundamental" ones. Anthropology is the subject that can assess whether this is correct.

A FURTHER CLARIFICATION OF ETHICAL RELATIVISM

The second point of clarification is that there is an obvious sense in which what we ought to do depends on (is relative to) the situation we are in. I think that in most situations, it is wrong to steal. Suppose, however, that your family is starving and you have no money to buy food for them. Suppose you have the opportunity to steal a loaf of bread from a prosperous baker (this is the situation that Jean Valjean faced in Victor Hugo's novel *Les Miserables*). In this case, I think you would be doing the right thing to steal the loaf. Whether it is right or wrong to steal the bread depends on your circumstances.

People in different societies often live in different circumstances. People in one society may face situations in which it is wrong for them to steal. People in another may face situations in which stealing is the right thing to do. Ethical relativism, however, says more than this. It goes beyond the uncontroversial fact that what you ought to do depends on the situation you are in.

ETHICAL RELATIVISM IS A VERSION OF CONVENTIONALISM

To see what this extra ingredient is, we must remind ourselves that normative ethical relativism is a conventionalist theory. It doesn't just say that what someone should do varies from society to society. It says that an action is right or wrong *solely because* of society's say-so. An ethical realist can grant that people in one society shouldn't steal whereas those in another should do so; a realist, however, will reject the relativist's explanation of why this is so. For according to ethical relativism, ethical facts are brought into being simply by a society's adopting various norms of behavior.

So far, I've presented two clarifications of ethical relativism. First, it is a normative theory, not a descriptive one. Second, it is a conventionalist theory. Having said this, let's see whether there is any reason to think that it is true.

IF IMPERIALISM IS WRONG, DOES THAT JUSTIFY ETHICAL RELATIVISM?

Ethical relativism has enjoyed a fair amount of popularity in the social sciences (in anthropology, especially) during the twentieth century. As Western social scientists improved their understanding of other cultures, they often came to feel considerable respect for those cultures. The idea took hold that it is wrong for Western nations to impose their own standards on other cultures. From the sixteenth century down to the present, many Western nations created and extended empires by conquest and commercial domination. Often this was said to be justified in the name of bringing Christianity to the conquered peoples; Europeans sometimes talked of a "white man's burden"—of a responsibility to bring Western civilization to the rest of the world.

Maybe you'll find ethical relativism an attractive moral theory, if this sort of imperialism strikes you as wrong. If you think that the idea of a "white man's burden" was simply a rationalization for exploitation, what better way to express this than by saying that each society determines its own ethical values? Europe doesn't get to decide what's right and wrong for the rest of the world. Rather, each society decides this matter for itself. Partly for this reason, ethical relativism became popular among those who defended a kind of *noninterventionism* (this is the idea that one society shouldn't meddle in the affairs of another).

Let's assume that there have been many cases in history in which one society was wrong to impose its will on another. Does this view make ethical relativism plausible? I think not. Are we prepared to say that a society can do anything it pleases to the individuals in it, as long as most of the people in the society believe that this is the right thing to do? It could become "customary" in a society that a certain group of people is oppressed (like the lower castes in India), even systematically murdered (like Jews, Gypsies, and homosexuals in Nazi Germany). Would this be made right if most people in the society thought it was right? I find this highly dubious.

Don't confuse the question of rightness with the question of whether some other country should intervene militarily to put a stop to the objectionable practice. These are separate issues. There might be cases in which foreign intervention would be wrong, even though some practices going on inside the country are wrong. For a practice to be wrong is one thing; what steps should be taken to end the wrong is a separate matter.

In addition, it is important to note that ethical relativism doesn't prohibit the kind of interventionism that its supporters tend to condemn. Should members of my society engage in colonial conquest? According to ethical relativism, I should answer this question by seeing whether the norms of my society permit people to engage in colonial conquest. Far from condemning interventionism, this consideration will have the consequence of justifying it. If you asked in nineteenth-century Britain whether it was "customary" for individuals to help extend and maintain the British Empire, the answer would have been *yes*. Paradoxically, ethical relativism doesn't imply that societies ought to respect each other.

Finally, it is worth noticing that the kinds of objections I made against the Divine Command Theory also apply to ethical relativism. A conventionalist view of this kind says that an action is made right in a society simply because it is the norm. This, however, has such bizarre consequences as the following:

> If our society considered it ethically permissible to torture babies
> for fun, then it would be ethically permissible for us to do this.

Ethical relativism doesn't say that our society will ever be like this. It does, however, endorse the above if/then statement.

My view is that the above if/then statement is false. If our society were to adopt this norm, then our society would have become morally abhorrent. To say this is to talk like an ethical realist. What is morally right and wrong isn't settled by society's say-so.

Ethical relativism has the consequence that *conformism* is always right. It entails that a person should *always* conform to the norms laid down by his or her society. If you think that the norms in a society can be wrong, you are rejecting ethical relativism.

Consider what ethical relativism says about a society that *changes* its norms. Some 200 years ago, most of the people living in the U.S.A. probably believed that slavery

---

Two Views of Democracy

Why is it right for a society to decide certain issues by majority vote? We can reformulate this question by mimicking the question that Plato posed in *The Euthyphro*. Is *X* wrong simply because the majority thinks that it is, or is the rightness and wrongness of *X* not settled by the majority say-so?

Believing that democratic procedures are the best way to decide what a society ought to do doesn't require one to endorse ethical conventionalism. One can be an ethical realist and still maintain that democracy is often the best practical procedure a society can use for discovering what it should do. According to this position, the opinion of the majority is fallible, but majority rule is *less* fallible than other procedures (dictatorship, for example) that might be adopted.

was ethically permissible. Later, the majority opinion changed. According to relativism, slavery was right until a certain date, but then it suddenly became wrong, *simply because the number of people who endorsed slavery dropped below 50 percent.* Just as in the case of the Divine Command Theory, I find it baffling how ethical truths can flip-flop simply because of someone's say-so. It seems to me that if slavery was wrong after 1865, it was wrong before that date as well.

SARTRE'S EXISTENTIALISM

I now turn to the third conventionalist theory—existentialism. There is a lot more to existentialism than I'll be able to discuss here. And it is important to realize that existentialist writers differ a great deal among themselves. Here I'm focusing on a single strand in the thinking of some important existentialists; this is the idea (expressed by Sartre and by Søren Kierkegaard, a nineteenth-century Danish philosopher and religious thinker) that individual human beings must freely create their own moral values.

Sartre holds that the scope of human freedom is far wider than most of us suspect. People often believe that only a small range of options is open to them—that the large-scale features of their lives are forced upon them from the outside. Sartre thinks this is an illusion; people stumble without reflection into stereotyped and conventional ways of life without realizing that they in fact are making a choice. Freedom is a frightening burden that we must shoulder without kidding ourselves. Sartre goes so far as to say that we are responsible for every feature of the lives we live.

Although I think that this last idea is a piece of rhetorical overstatement, Sartre's general stress on the responsibility of individuals to shape their own lives is important. There is a lot to be said for really reflecting about what you think and do—for regarding options critically and not falling into a pattern out of unreflective habit. However, Sartre says something more than this; this something more is the conventionalist element in his existentialism that I want to identify and criticize.

In Lecture 27, I mentioned that Sartre (in his book *Existentialism*) describes a young Frenchman during World War II who has to decide whether to join the Resistance or stay at home to care for his ailing mother. Let's distinguish two claims that might be made about this young man:

(1) He should think the choice over carefully and not do what he does out of unreflective habit.

(2) There is no moral fact of the matter about what he should do until he makes a decision. If he decides that he wants above all to be a good son, he should stay home; if he decides that he wants above all to be a good Frenchman, he should join the Resistance. But there is no standard that exists independently of his choice that determines what he should want most of all.

Sartre claimed that both (1) *and* (2) are true. He thought that this story about the young Frenchman exhibits a quite general pattern. In *every* choice we make, we have to create moral facts. It is (2) that embodies the conventionalist element in Sartre's existentialism.

Sartre chose this example because he thought it poses a difficult moral problem. But even if the problem were one that we would see as clear-cut, Sartre would view it as calling for an arbitrary decision. Consider a third option that the young man has; he could leave home and volunteer to torture prisoners for the Gestapo. The young man has to decide whether he wants to be a good son, a good Frenchman, or a good Nazi. Sartre's position is that there is no fact of the matter about what the young man should do until he makes a decision about what he wants most. Just like the other conventionalist theories discussed in this lecture, Sartre's existentialism implies the following if/then statement:

> If the young man decides that he wants above all to be a good *X*,
> then it is morally permissible for him to do what it takes to be a good *X*.

I've already noted why I find this claim implausible.

Sartre thinks this conventionalist thesis follows from the fact that there is no God: If there is no God to lay down the moral law, then each of us must lay down the law for ourselves. An ethical realist would disagree. Why can't moral facts exist independently of anyone's (God's, society's, or the individual's) say-so? Sartre has no very good argument against this realist alternative.

In this and the previous few lectures, I haven't provided any strong argument in favor of ethical realism. Rather, I've criticized the subjectivist and conventionalist alternatives to realism. In what follows, I'll assume that there are ethical truths that are true independently of anyone's say-so. The goal will be to consider some theories that try to say what those truths are.

Review Questions

1. What is the difference between trivial semantic conventionalism and substantive conventionalism?

2. Consider this statement: "We should do what God says we should do." Can an ethical realist and a defender of the Divine Command Theory agree on this? If so, what do they disagree about?

3. Consider this statement: "What may be right for a person in one culture to do may not be right for a person in another culture to do." Can an ethical realist and a defender of ethical relativism agree on this? If so, what do they disagree about?

4. Does ethical relativism entail that people in one culture should respect the standards of conduct obeyed in another culture?

5. Consider this statement: "People have to figure out for themselves what they should do." Can an ethical realist and a defender of Sartre's existentialism agree on this? If so, what do they disagree about?

6. There is a Yiddish story about the wise men of Chelm. The town council met to discuss what could be done about the shortage of sour cream. They decided to solve the problem by calling water "sour cream." (The problem of what they would do about the resulting water shortage they put aside for future deliberation.) How does this story illustrate the difference between trivial semantic conventionalism and substantive conventionalism?

Problems for Further Thought

1. Is there a third coherent option for the theist that rejects both the Divine Command Theory and ethical realism? Defend your answer.

2. Do facts about evolution suggest that there may be fundamental norms that are cultural universals, despite the numerous ways in which human cultures differ from each other?

LECTURE 31

Utilitarianism

Utilitarianism is an ethical theory whose central idea is "the greatest good for the greatest number." The idea is that ethically correct actions are ones that promote the greatest happiness of the individuals affected by it. We will soon see that this formulation of the theory requires fine-tuning.

Utilitarianism is a philosophical idea that has exercised considerable influence on the world of practical affairs. Jeremy Bentham (1748–1832) and John Stuart Mill (1806–1873) were deeply involved in the political controversies of their age. Both defended utilitarianism in publications that the educated classes in England read with great attention. Utilitarianism wasn't an abstract "ivory tower" theory that only professors found worth discussing. It stirred the interest of great numbers of people who cared about the institutions of their society.

Bentham and Mill thought that many of these institutions needed reform because they failed to promote human welfare. A central political agenda at this time was extending the vote to men who didn't own property. Mill also wrote in favor of women's suffrage, although women didn't receive the vote until much later. The abolition of slavery was another political struggle in which utilitarians participated. In these and other cases, utilitarians argued that institutions had to be changed because they advanced the interests of the few to the detriment of the many. Utilitarians attacked the idea that the rich and powerful had some special "right" to arrange society as they saw fit. On the contrary, the point of utilitarianism is that each individual must be taken into account, because each individual is capable of experiencing happiness.

In this lecture, I'll discuss the general ethical theory, not the specific political issues that at one time were the focus of utilitarian concern. By now (at the end of this book), it should be abundantly clear that the following isn't a valid deduction:

> If utilitarianism is true, then slavery is morally wrong.
>
> Slavery is morally wrong.
> _____
>
> Utilitarianism is true.

I don't doubt the premises, but I'll try to show that there is plenty of room to doubt the conclusion.

MILL'S DEFENSE OF THE GREATEST HAPPINESS PRINCIPLE

Before describing in more detail what utilitarianism says, I want to discuss how someone might go about evaluating whether the basic idea of utilitarianism is true. Mill calls this basic idea the Greatest Happiness Principle. It says that the action we ought to perform in a given situation is the one that promotes the greatest happiness.

In his essay "Utilitarianism," Mill attempted to prove that the Greatest Happiness Principle is correct. Mill's argument begins with an analogy between desirability and visibility. He says that just as the only proof that something is visible is that someone sees it, so the only proof that something is desirable is that someone desires it. He then claims that what people ultimately want is their own happiness. Mill concludes from this that the most desirable action is the one that produces the most happiness overall.

Let's reconstruct Mill's argument as follows:

> (1) Seeing something proves that it is visible.
> _____
>
> (2) Hence, desiring something proves that it is desirable.
>
> (3) The only thing that each person ultimately desires is his or her own happiness.
> _____
>
> (4) The only thing that is ultimately desirable for a person is his or her own happiness.
> _____
>
> Hence, each person should perform those actions that promote the greatest happiness.

I've drawn three horizontal lines in this argument to indicate that (2) is supposed to follow from (1), (4) is supposed to follow from (2) and (3), and the final conclusion is supposed to follow from (4).

There are several problems with this reasoning. First, (1) doesn't provide much of a reason for accepting (2). Visibility and desirability are different. If something is visible, this means that it is possible to see it. However, if something is desirable, this doesn't mean that it is *possible* to desire it, but that it *should* be desired. Visibility is a descriptive concept, while desirability is a normative one. So although "*x* is visible" does follow from "*x* is seen," "*x* is desirable" doesn't follow from "*x* is desired."

What does the word *ultimately* mean in step (3)? It means that everything else people want they want only as a means to the end of securing their own happiness. If I desire that the starving receive food, Mill is saying that I want this only as a means to securing a certain end—namely, my own happiness. I argued against this thesis in Lecture 26; it simply asserts a form of psychological egoism. Three of the four preference structures discussed there (all except Pure Egoism) involve thinking that the welfare of others has an importance separate from the importance the agent attaches to his or her own happiness. Since, as a matter of fact, many of us often have preferences of this sort, I think that premiss (3) is false.

Does (4) follow from (3)? No—for the same reason that (2) doesn't follow from (1). Even if a person ultimately desires his or her own happiness, it doesn't follow that the most desirable thing is for the person to have his or her desires satisfied. That would seem to depend on the nature of the desires in question. For people with truly horrible (e.g., self-destructive) desires, perhaps the best thing for them would be for them to change what they want, not for them to get what they want.

Finally, even if (4) were true, the conclusion of the argument wouldn't follow. The fact that your own happiness is the most desirable thing *for you* doesn't imply that you should maximize *everyone's* happiness. The conclusion of this argument sometimes requires you to act unselfishly—to sacrifice your own happiness if doing so brings with it a more than compensating increase in the happiness of others. This doesn't follow from (4).

RECIPROCAL ILLUMINATION

Mill had another idea about how utilitarianism should be defended. Instead of trying to deduce the Greatest Happiness Principle from premises that would be plausible even to a nonutilitarian, we can try to justify the principle by seeing how it measures up against the moral judgments we are prepared to make about concrete cases. This was the method I described Harman as using in Lecture 29. A general principle has implications about what it is wrong or right to do in specific cases. If we are prepared to make ethical judgments about these cases, we can use these judgments to evaluate the general theory (recall Harman's example about the transplant operation). If a theory implies that an action is right in a given situation and we believe that the action would be quite wrong, we might take this as evidence that the theory is false.

So judgments about specific cases can lead us to reject a general theory. The reverse can happen as well. If we think that a theory is quite plausible and then find that it implies that a given action is wrong (or right), we might decide to allow the theory to guide us—to lead us to revise our opinions about the ethical problem posed by the particular case.

We see here a two-way influence—a process of reciprocal illumination—by which our judgments about specific cases can influence how we regard a theory, and our views about a theory can affect our judgments about specific cases. A utilitarian who doesn't think that slavery was wrong might come to see that one or the other of these ideas must be abandoned. Which idea should be abandoned depends on which is overall more plausible (the general theory or the judgment about the specific institution), given the other beliefs he or she has.

I now want to use this technique of evaluation to fine-tune utilitarianism and then to suggest that it faces some very serious difficulties.

WHAT IS HAPPINESS?

I'll begin by focusing on the idea of happiness. What is happiness? I'm not asking what activities make us happy. Rather, I want to know what happiness itself is. Compare: If I ask you what bankruptcy is, I'm not asking you what activities cause bankruptcy. Bankruptcy isn't the same as reckless investment; neither is happiness the same thing as a warm puppy.

A partial answer might be that happiness is a feeling. This is only partial, of course, because there are many other feelings besides happiness. If, however, happiness is something in the mind (something purely subjective), we can formulate a problem that utilitarianism must address.

THE PROBLEM OF THE EXPERIENCE MACHINE

In Lecture 13, I discussed how Descartes grappled with the problem of refuting the hypothesis that he was systematically misled by an evil demon. Contemporary philosophers sometimes give Descartes's problem a modern twist by asking how we know that we aren't brains in vats. According to the brain-in-the-vat hypothesis, your brain now rests in a vat filled with a liquid that keeps it alive. It is hooked up to a giant computer, whose electrical impulses furnish you with a rich stream of experiences. These impulses generate the illusion that you have a body and that you are having sensory contact (sight, smell, hearing, touch, etc.) with the external world. According to the brain-in-the-vat hypothesis, almost everything you believe about your present and past is false. You don't really have a face; you're not really looking at a philosophy book right now. And so on.

The point of this bizarre hypothesis is that it poses a philosophical challenge. The challenge is to show how you know that the brain-in-the-vat hypothesis is false. None of us believes this hypothesis about ourselves. Can this conviction be rationally justified, or is it just a groundless prejudice?

As just formulated, the brain-in-the-vat problem falls within the theory of knowledge; it is a part of epistemology. I now will reformulate the problem so as to turn it into an ethical issue, one that tells us something about utilitarianism.

The computer described in the brain-in-the-vat problem is an *experience machine*. Suppose that the machine could be set up so it would provide you with whatever experiences would make you the happiest, and that it is up to you to decide whether you wish to be plugged into the machine. If being a great concert violinist would give you pleasure, plugging into the machine will give you a rich, complex sequence of experiences of this sort. If you would be happiest being a political leader loved and admired by millions of people, the experience machine can furnish the feelings that would derive from being loved and admired by millions. Of course, the experience machine doesn't make you into a concert violinist or a political leader. Rather, the machine gives you the precise set of experiences you would get from having those sorts of lives.

If utilitarianism were true, it would be preferable for people to plug into experience machines rather than lead real lives that provide a lesser degree of happiness. But, contrary to what utilitarianism says about this kind of choice, I for one (and I bet you feel the same way) put considerable value on leading a real life. If you're plugged into the experience machine, virtually all your beliefs are false. You are proud of yourself because you think you are a great violinist and you take pleasure in your skill. If the machine leads you to think that you are a great political leader, you may think you have created world peace and so you feel good about doing so. However, in both cases, your pride and your pleasure rest on an illusion.

Most of us value something beyond the feeling of happiness that comes from doing certain things. We also place a value on the reality of the doing. However, to think this way is to say that something matters beyond the subjective feeling of happiness. This goes contrary to the form of utilitarianism we're considering. (The example of the experience machine comes from Robert Nozick's *Anarchy, State, and Utopia,* New York, Basic Books, 1974.)

There are a number of science fiction novels and movies that make this same point. Aldous Huxley's *Brave New World* and Woody Allen's *Sleeper* are examples. These works of fiction describe a future in which people are drugged by their governments into being docile, happy citizens. People are contented, but the novel or movie usually takes the point of view that there is something deeply wrong with a society like this. Usually, what's wrong is that people lack *autonomy*. Their own beliefs and desires have been distorted or altogether destroyed; what they do and feel is the result of the drugs they take. If you agree that there is something wrong with a society of this sort, you may have to say that there is something over and above "happiness" (a state of mind) that is ethically important.

MILL ON "HIGHER" AND "LOWER" PLEASURES

Mill himself grappled with a problem of this kind. He asked why it is better to be "Socrates dissatisfied" rather than a satisfied fool. Socrates was acutely aware of the imperfections of the world around him; it wasn't true that each of his daily experiences filled him with pleasure. But a "satisfied fool," Mill says, might be delighted by every detail of life. If the latter individual is happier, utilitarianism seems to recommend that we become more like the fool and less like Socrates.

Mill denied that utilitarianism has this implication. He thought that Socrates was capable of enjoying "higher" pleasures, whereas the fool, he says, could only experience "lower" pleasures. Mill claimed that higher pleasures provide more happiness than lower ones. To see that this is true, he said that you must ask individuals who have experienced both sorts of pleasures which they enjoyed more. Mill was confident these "competent judges" would say that the higher pleasures bring more happiness than the lower ones.

There are some higher and lower pleasures for which Mill's prediction might be true. For example, someone who does nothing but drink beer and watch television might find that "higher" pleasures are better, once he or she is exposed to them. There are other cases, however, in which Mill's prediction seems mistaken.

Imagine someone who has been leading a real life and then is plugged into an experience machine. Once he is unplugged, we could ask him which life made him happier. I think most people would have to admit that their life while plugged in provided more happiness than the real life they led before. This doesn't mean that people *prefer* to live plugged into the experience machine; it just means that life in the experience machine provides a greater quantity of happiness.

The same may be true of the people in the science fiction works described above. Maybe drugs provide them with more happiness than they would receive if they were autonomous. Again, this doesn't mean that they *prefer* being drugged by their governments, but that they receive a greater quantity of happiness in that state.

To move closer to real life, consider a drug like heroin. Suppose someone could live a life as a heroin addict without facing dangers like AIDS and being killed by drug dealers. Maybe in that case the drug would be so intensely pleasurable that people who had experienced life with it and life without it would have to concede that life is happier with it. This doesn't mean that we would *prefer* to have such a life. Rather, what it shows is that our preferences are influenced by factors other than the quantity of happiness we receive.

OBJECTION TO HEDONISTIC UTILITARIANISM

My conclusion is that Mill's argument about higher and lower pleasures doesn't work. Mill believed that Socrates dissatisfied had a better life than a satisfied fool, but I don't see that Mill has a way of explaining why this is so. So we have here an objection to the first form of utilitarianism I want to distinguish. It is *hedonistic utilitarianism,* which says that the right action is the one that maximizes pleasure and minimizes pain (not just for the agent, but for all individuals who are affected). According to this form of utilitarianism, we should plug into the experience machine; we should become more like the fool and less like Socrates. But both these ought-statements strike me as false. If they are false, then hedonistic utilitarianism should be rejected.

PREFERENCE UTILITARIANISM

There is another form of utilitarianism, which isn't undermined by these problems. I call it *preference utilitarianism.* The idea of this kind of utilitarianism isn't to maximize pleasure, but to maximize the degree to which people get their preferences satisfied. If people generally prefer to lead real lives rather than to plug into experience machines, then a preference utilitarian will have no problem explaining why it would be wrong to plug people into experience machines. And if people prefer to live their lives drug-free, then preference utilitarianism can easily explain why it would be wrong for the government to surreptitiously give people a diet of pleasure-producing drugs.

So preference utilitarianism avoids a problem that is fatal to hedonistic utilitarianism. But preference utilitarianism has problems of its own. The first of these becomes clear when we try to apply the view to specific cases.

THE APPLES AND ORANGES PROBLEM

The problem is that it often is difficult to know how to compare one person's preferences with those of another. This is something that a preference utilitarian must do if those preferences conflict. Consider a state government that has to decide whether a tract of land should be opened to commercial use or reserved for recreational use. There are the profits and jobs that some people will receive on the one hand, and the enjoyment from camping and swimming that other people will receive on the other. How are these two interests to be compared?

Sometimes people decide what they think about an issue like this by deciding which sort of activity is more important in the light of the ethical principles they have adopted. However, this doesn't address the question in a strictly utilitarian way. What you need to focus on is how intensely each person prefers one option over the other. Then you have to sum over this totality of individual preferences to decide which action maximizes the satisfaction of preferences collectively. If the economic losses from not going the commercial route were small, whereas the recreational (and aesthetic) losses from going the commercial route were large, this would settle the question. My point, though, is that it is often obscure what "small" and "large" could mean in such cases. Let's call this the *Apples and Oranges Problem:* How can you compare the intensity of one person's gain with the intensity of another person's loss?

Sometimes this kind of question is settled by using money as a mode of comparison. How much do the developers want to develop the land commercially? See how much they are prepared to pay to do so. How much do people want to preserve the land for recreational use? See how much they are prepared to pay to do so. Then see how much money stacks up on the one side and how much on the other.

The problem with this procedure is that how much money people are willing to spend is often influenced by factors other than the intensity of their desires. A rich person may be prepared to pay more for a loaf of bread than a poor one, but that doesn't mean that the rich person wants it more.

Sometimes this problem is settled by taking a vote among the individuals affected; let a referendum be held, with each person having a single vote. The problem with using voting as a way of solving the Apples and Oranges Problem is that voting doesn't represent the intensities of people's desires. If I mildly prefer the commercial option to the recreational one, I'll vote for the commercial option; if you strongly prefer the recreational use to the commercial one, you will vote for the recreational use. Your vote and mine count equally, but this fails to represent something that is important to the calculation a preference utilitarian must make.

In practical politics, voting is often a reasonable procedure (whether it *always* is reasonable will be discussed in what follows). However, I'm not talking about choosing a workable (if imperfect) procedure. I'm talking about the problem of making sense of what preference utilitarianism actually says. The problem is that it often is unclear what it means to say that a given action has a higher utility for one person than the opposite action has for another person.

In what follows, I'm going to assume that the Apples and Oranges Problem can be solved—that the intensity of people's preferences can be compared. My task will be to review some arguments that try to show that preference utilitarianism is sometimes mistaken in its claim about what we ought to do.

UTILITARIANISM AND JUSTICE: THE CASE OF THE LONESOME STRANGER

I'll begin with a problem that can be illustrated by an example. A gruesome murder has occurred in a town. The sheriff has discovered that the murderer himself is dead; however, the sheriff knows that no one will believe him if he says this and lays out all the evidence he has. Meanwhile, the townspeople are becoming more and more agitated.

The sheriff realizes that if a suspect isn't put on trial very soon, there will be a riot and it is quite probable that many innocent people will be injured and a few killed. As the sheriff is mulling this over in his office, in strolls a lonesome stranger. This fellow tells the sheriff that he has no friends or relations in the world and that he has wandered into town for no reason in particular. The sheriff then gets an idea: Why not frame the lonesome stranger? There is capital punishment in this locale, so the sheriff can arrange that the stranger be tried, convicted, and executed. Suppose the sheriff can arrange it that the framing will always remain a secret. Should the sheriff frame the stranger?

What would a utilitarian say here? For a hedonistic utilitarian, the answer is easy. If you frame the stranger (and keep the facts secret), one person dies, but the peace of mind of the townspeople is restored; if you don't frame him, a bloody riot will ensue and more than one person will die. The way to maximize happiness is for the sheriff to frame the stranger and always keep this secret.

For a preference utilitarian, the question is more complicated. If the people in the town have strong preferences that innocent people shouldn't be punished, then the sheriff shouldn't frame the stranger. Suppose, however, the people don't care about this; let's suppose they care only about their own safety and peace of mind. In this case, preference utilitarianism will tell the sheriff that he ought to frame the stranger.

The problem here is that utilitarian considerations seem to conflict with considerations of *justice*. It is unjust to punish people for crimes they didn't commit. If you think this moral requirement overrides considerations that reflect the social utility of punishing the lonesome stranger, then you will interpret this example as an objection to utilitarianism.

PUNISHMENT

Before considering how a utilitarian might reply to this objection, I want to say a little more about punishment. A utilitarian will answer the question of whether someone should be punished by asking whether the punishment will do any good. If punishment doesn't deter people from similar wrongdoing and doesn't reform the character of the person punished, then a utilitarian may say that there is no point in punishing people who are guilty of quite awful crimes. For a utilitarian, the distinction between guilt and innocence doesn't have to coincide with the distinction between those who should be punished and those who shouldn't be.

A nonutilitarian view of punishment (there is more than one) will see things differently. The principle of an eye for an eye—of retribution for wrongdoing—isn't a utilitarian idea. Retributivists want the punishment to fit the crime; utilitarians want the punishment to be chosen for the benefits it can be expected to produce.

Utilitarian discussion of punishment usually focuses on the question of why the guilty *should* be punished. But, as the case of the lonesome stranger illustrates, the question can also be posed of why the innocent *shouldn't* be punished. According to utilitarianism there is no absolute requirement that the guilty must be punished and that the innocent may not be. What should be done depends entirely on which course of action will maximize the collective happiness.

A REPLY: DISTINGUISH RULE AND ACT UTILITARIANISM

I've argued that the lonesome stranger example provides an objection to utilitarianism (whether of the hedonistic or the preference variety). It illustrates how considerations of justice can conflict with utilitarianism. Recall that for me to be able to say this, I must be prepared to make a moral judgment about the example situation. Without this, there is no way to use specific cases to evaluate the general principle.

There is a standard reply that utilitarians often make to this and similar objections. Their strategy is to distinguish two kinds of utilitarian theory and to claim that one of them is perfectly consistent with the idea that the lonesome stranger shouldn't be framed.

I described utilitarianism as saying that an action should be performed only if it promotes the greatest happiness or the greatest preference satisfaction. However, there is an ambiguity here. Are we evaluating *kinds* of actions, or individual actions, one by one? That is, are we to use utilitarian considerations to decide what general rules to follow, or are we to apply these considerations each time a specific act is at issue? Here I'm drawing the type/token distinction discussed in Lecture 22 and applying it to the question of how utilitarianism should be formulated.

That is, utilitarianism (regardless of whether it says to maximize happiness or preference satisfaction) can take the form of *rule utilitarianism* or *act utilitarianism*. How does this choice affect the way we understand the lonesome stranger example? According to the rule utilitarian, the sheriff's task has two parts. First, he must decide what general rule to adopt. Second, he must determine how that general rule applies to the concrete case he confronts.

The first problem involves deciding which of the following two alternatives has better consequences:

(R1) Punish the innocent when it is convenient.

(R2) Never punish the innocent.

A rule utilitarian will argue that (R2) has better consequences for people's welfare, and so it is (R2) that the sheriff should use. Note that once (R2) is applied to the specific situation, the sheriff will decide *not* to frame the stranger.

Why think that (R2) has better consequences than (R1)? Part of the reason is that rules that are used again and again become generally known. If people generally believe that (R1) is the policy the government follows, this will produce a great deal of unhappiness.

An act utilitarian, on the other hand, won't focus on general rules, but will focus on the specific choice at hand. The act utilitarian's procedure has one step, not two. So the suggestion is that the example of the lonesome stranger constitutes an objection to act utilitarianism, not to rule utilitarianism. The idea is that rule utilitarianism recommends that the sheriff not frame the stranger, and this recommendation coincides with what we find plausible.

I want to argue that adopting a rule utilitarian formulation won't save utilitarianism from the difficulty posed by the example of the lonesome stranger. I agree that (R2) has better consequences as a general policy than (R1) does. However, it seems to me that a utilitarian must concede that (R2) is inferior to the following rule:

(R3) Don't punish the innocent, unless doing so will maximize utility.

I think a utilitarian must agree that (R3) is preferable on utilitarian grounds to (R2). And the sheriff, acting on (R3), will frame the lonesome stranger. I conclude that rule utilitarianism and act utilitarianism are equally subject to the objection posed by the example of the lonesome stranger.

UTILITARIANISM AND TOLERANCE:
THE PROBLEM OF THE FANATICAL MAJORITY

I now turn to a different objection to utilitarianism. An important fact about preference utilitarianism is that it doesn't allow you to ignore people's preferences because you morally disapprove of them. People's preferences, whether we approve of them or not, must be taken into account when we decide what laws our society should adopt or what actions each of us should perform. The problem is that we sometimes want to *ignore* people's preferences because we think they are morally objectionable. If it is ever morally legitimate to do this, preference utilitarianism is in trouble.

Consider what happens to nonconformists in a society of fanatics. Here we might be talking about people in a minority religion, who live in a society in which the majority is made of religious fanatics. Or consider a society in which a minority of people are homosexual and the heterosexual majority is very intolerant. Another case concerns political nonconformity—a minority with one set of political beliefs living with a majority that not only disagrees with them, but is extremely hostile toward them. How would a utilitarian view the idea that people should be free to live as they see fit?

A utilitarian will decide this question by calculating how policies of repression or toleration would satisfy people's preferences. If the intolerant majority is fanatical enough, the utilitarian scales may tip in favor of prohibiting nonconformity. If a fanatical majority gets upset enough at the presence of nonconformists, then there will be a utilitarian justification for banning nonconformity. Of course, this sort of policy won't be what the nonconformists prefer. However, since they are in the minority, their strong preferences may be outweighed by the strong preferences of the fanatical majority.

Many of us would want to say that people have certain rights—to freely pursue the religion of their choice (or no religion at all), to engage in the sexual practices they prefer (or none at all), to discuss and promulgate their favored political opinions (or to be apolitical)—as long as doing so doesn't endanger the life and property of others. The fact that these practices might antagonize an intolerant majority, many of us would want to say, simply doesn't count against people being entitled to do what they want. To think this way is not to think like a utilitarian.

So we have here an objection to utilitarianism. I'll call it the *Problem of the Fanatical Majority.* John Stuart Mill considered this issue in his famous essay "On Liberty." Mill was a liberal in the sense of that word used in the nineteenth century. Liberals believed in liberty. An imprecise slogan embodying liberalism is that "people should be free to do what they want, as long as doing so doesn't hurt others." One reason this is imprecise is that fanatics might claim to be "hurt" (offended, distressed, outraged, etc.) simply by knowing there are people who live their lives differently from the way they do.

Mill was a utilitarian who believed in the kinds of personal liberties I just mentioned. His problem was to reconcile utilitarianism with the idea that people have a

Liberalism and Conservatism

Mill believed that the right to personal nonconformity flows from utilitarian considerations. He also thought that economic activity is public and therefore might have to be limited for utilitarian reasons. A corporation's activities (even a single person's buying and selling) affect others. A regulated economy (as opposed to an absolutely free market) therefore is preferable, Mill thought, on utilitarian grounds.

Mill was a *liberal,* in the nineteenth-century meaning of that term. Liberals believed in liberty—that each person should have the maximum amount of freedom, consistent with not compromising the freedom of others.

The terms "liberal" and "conservative" have different meanings today. To understand what each involves, let's distinguish two "markets" in which each of us participates—the marketplace of *ideas* and the *economic* marketplace (of goods and services that we buy and sell).

Liberals in the U.S.A. now often oppose censorship and think that the government shouldn't promote religion (or promote one religion over any other). They believe that the government shouldn't interfere in the marketplace of ideas. Yet they tend to believe, on utilitarian grounds, that the government should regulate the economy.

So-called "conservatives," on the other hand, tend to take the opposite view. They often favor censorship and want the government to promote religion (by encouraging prayer in the public schools, for example). Yet, when it comes to the economic marketplace, they tend to favor more freedom and less regulation.

Although both political positions are influenced by utilitarian considerations, each makes use of nonutilitarian ideas as well. Liberals often talk about "rights" of free speech, which people are said to have even if some forms of free speech make lots of people very unhappy. And conservatives sometimes argue that pornography should be censored on religious grounds or on other grounds that aren't utilitarian.

Liberalism and conservatism aren't the only political options available. In the U.S.A., both hold that capitalism is a workable form of economic organization. And both have favored military interventions of various kinds (in Korea and Vietnam, for example). Some critics on the left—socialists and communists, for example—doubt the viability of capitalism and have opposed military interventions like the ones mentioned. Critics on the right—libertarians, for example—reject the government's entitlement to intervene in people's lives without their consent—for example, to collect taxes, to censor pornography, and to regulate the economy.

Mill defended a totally free (*laissez-faire*) marketplace of ideas. He described ideas as being in competition. Everyone benefits from unrestrained competition, Mill said, because competition tends to select the best ideas. Ideas compete in the way organisms do in the process of Darwinian natural selection (Lecture 6).

Defenders of a free economic marketplace have often put forward a similar argument. In *The Wealth of Nations,* the eighteenth-century economist Adam Smith argued that when everyone freely pursues his or her selfish economic interests, everyone benefits. The nation as a whole becomes richer, and so prosperity "trickles down" to even the worst off in the society.

Liberals have criticized this trickle down defense of a perfectly free market economy. They claim that an unregulated economy produces catastrophic swings ("boom and bust cycles," like the one that produced the Crash of 1929 and the ensuing Great Depression). An unfettered market, they argue, can make everyone worse off than they would be if the market were regulated. This liberal argument against a perfectly free market is utilitarian in character.

right to the kinds of freedoms I've just enumerated. Mill sought to effect this reconciliation by distinguishing *public* and *private* actions. A public action affects individuals in addition to the actor; a private action, on the other hand, doesn't affect others. Mill argued that people are entitled to live lives of nonconformity, if they wish, since the activities involved here are private, not public.

Does this argument secure the kinds of freedoms I've been discussing? Not entirely. In a society in which most people are intolerant fanatics, the most that a nonconforming minority can hope for is the right to be *secret* nonconformists. It is only when such practices are performed in secret that they can count as private in Mill's sense. However, I think most of us believe in liberties that are more extensive than ones that are kept in the closet. Whether it be in the religious, sexual, or political arenas, most of us think there are practices affecting others (because they aren't kept secret) that a minority is entitled to engage in, even if this distresses fanatics.

UTILITARIANISM AND PERSONAL INTEGRITY: THE PROBLEM OF DIRTY HANDS

The next objection to utilitarianism I want to discuss I'll call the *Dirty Hands Objection*. Consider an individual contemplating a choice between an action that is clearly right and one that is clearly wrong. Suppose, however, that the morally wrong action has this characteristic: If the individual doesn't perform this bad action himself or herself, someone else will.

An example of this kind of situation is provided by a case I discussed in connection with Sartre's existentialism in Lecture 30. Imagine someone who is considering whether he should become a torturer for the Nazis. Suppose that if he doesn't do this, someone else will.

Examples less horrible than this are common in everyday life. Maybe if you are studying to be an engineer, you'll get a job offer to work on developing a weapon system. Perhaps you will feel that it is wrong to have this system developed—that it will provide new ways to harm people without making our country or any other more secure. Of course, your participation isn't *necessary* for the weapon to get developed. If you don't do the job, someone else will.

What will a utilitarian say about such cases? If you decline the job offer, the bad consequences (the torturing, the development of the weapon system) occur nonetheless, but without your participation. If you accept, the same bad consequences occur, this time with your participation. A utilitarian will have to conclude that *it makes no difference*, morally speaking, whether you accept the job offer or decline it. The net consequences are the same.

I think that in many cases like this, it *does* make a moral difference what you decide to do. It is a bad thing to be a torturer for the Nazis, for example. If you become a torturer, you have done something wrong; if you don't become a torturer, you have avoided doing something evil. There is a moral difference here that should guide your conduct. The moral issue of what sort of a person you ought to be isn't something that utilitarianism takes into account. According to utilitarianism, what you should do in such cases is to look at the net consequences that would occur under different circumstances; this is different from considering what kind of a person you ought to be.

Sometimes utilitarians reply to this objection in the same way I described them replying to the lonesome stranger example. They propose a distinction between rule and act utilitarianism and claim that rule utilitarianism has the plausible consequence that it *does* make a moral difference whether you become a torturer or not.

They reason as follows. To decide what you ought to do in this specific situation, you first must decide which general rule should be followed by you and others. The two rules you might consider are as follows:

(S1) If the government offers someone a job as a torturer, the offer should be accepted.

(S2) If the government offers someone a job as a torturer, the offer should be rejected.

The rule utilitarian then points out that the consequences would be better if everyone adopted (S2) than if everyone adopted (S1). The conclusion about this pair of rules is then applied to the specific choice you confront. You should apply (S2) to decide what to do; hence, you should decline the offer from the Nazis.

I hope you see how this pattern of argument parallels what rule utilitarians have said in reply to the objection based on the lonesome stranger example. But in this case, as in that one, I don't think that the reply really works.

I grant that (S2) has better consequences than (S1). However, it seems to me that a utilitarian can't explain why (S2) is superior to the following rule:

(S3) If the government offers someone a job as a torturer, the offer should be rejected, unless it makes no difference to the collective utility whether it is accepted or rejected.

A utilitarian can't explain why (S2) is a better rule than (S3). For this reason, the dirty hands problem is, I think, a telling objection to utilitarianism.

UTILITARIANISM AND PERSONAL LOYALTIES

The last problem I want to consider concerns the role that personal loyalties play in our judgments about morality. Imagine that a boating accident occurs and you have to choose which of two people you are going to save from drowning. One of them is your own daughter. The other is another child. What should you do?

If you think it makes a moral difference what you should do, how can this be explained? It may be true that the consequences for the collective welfare are the same, whether your child lives and the other child dies, or yours dies and the other lives. If so, utilitarianism can't explain the special obligations we have to our own family.

By now, the rule utilitarian reply to this objection should be something you can anticipate. Compare the general consequences of obeying each of the following general rules:

(T1) People should not make an effort to preserve the lives of their own children.

(T2) People should make an effort to preserve the lives of their own children.

Of course, general adherence to (T2) has better consequences than general adherence to (T1). But that isn't enough to get utilitarianism out of trouble, since it is hard to see how a utilitarian can argue that (T2) is superior to (T3):

(T3) People should make an effort to preserve the lives of their own children, except when no additional utility comes from doing so.

A PSYCHOLOGICAL OBJECTION TO MY CRITICISMS OF UTILITARIANISM

There is a different sort of reply that utilitarians sometimes make to examples like this one. They say that in a situation of crisis, people don't have time to calculate what they ought to do. They merely act on impulse. What they do in such cases is more a consequence of the habits of character they have developed than of reasoning from general principles.

I grant this psychological point, but it seems to me to be irrelevant. Utilitarianism makes a claim about which actions are right and which are wrong. It doesn't demand that people take the time and energy to reason dispassionately about what the Greatest Happiness Principle implies. Nor does utilitarianism say that people in fact engage in dispassionate calculation in situations of crisis. My criticisms of utilitarianism have to do with what the theory says people *ought* to do; in each of the cases I've surveyed, I've argued that the theory errs in its moral recommendations.

SUMMARY

I've raised several objections to utilitarianism. The lonesome stranger objection is supposed to show how utilitarianism can conflict with the value of justice. The problem of the fanatical majority shows how utilitarianism can conflict with the value of liberty. And, finally, the problem of dirty hands and the problem of loyalty both show that utilitarianism can fail to detect moral differences between alternative actions that really do differ morally.

In each of these cases, utilitarianism was judged by seeing what it implies about a concrete example situation. The arguments all proceeded by advancing a moral judgment about the examples and then showing that this judgment conflicts with the dictates of utilitarianism. I grant that someone who isn't prepared to endorse the moral claims I've made about the examples won't find this discussion a conclusive refutation of utilitarianism. However, agreeing with what I've said about one or more of these examples should be enough to make you doubt that utilitarianism is correct.

Review Questions

1. Mill argues for the Greatest Happiness Principle and also says that the principle can be defended by what I've called "reciprocal illumination." Explain what the argument is and what reciprocal illumination is.
2. What is the difference between hedonistic utilitarianism and preference utilitarianism? How does the example of the experience machine bear on each of these theories?
3. What is the Apples and Oranges Problem?
4. How does the case of the lonesome stranger pose a problem for utilitarianism?
5. How does the Problem of the Fanatical Majority present a difficulty for utilitarianism?
6. How does the Dirty Hands Objection present a difficulty for utilitarianism?
7. How might a utilitarian use the distinction between act utilitarianism and rule utilitarianism to reply to the objections involved in questions 4–6?

Problems for Further Thought

1. In defending the Greatest Happiness Principle, Mill says that the only proof that something is visible is that someone sees it. Is this a correct claim to make about dispositional properties (discussed in Lecture 19) like visibility? Is it true that the only proof that something is soluble is that someone dissolves it?
2. In discussing the Apples and Oranges Problem, I argued that the problem wouldn't be solved by having a referendum in which each person casts a single vote. Would it be a solution to give each person 10 votes, and to ask people to cast the number of votes that reflects the intensity of their preferences?
3. When I discussed preference utilitarianism, I interpreted that theory to mean that what should be maximized is the satisfaction of the preferences that people *actually* have. However, there is another form of utilitarianism that is important to consider. Let's say that a person's *revealed preferences* are the preferences he or she would have if provided with full factual information about the situation at hand. A person's actual preferences and his or her revealed preferences may differ, if the actual preferences are based on incomplete information. Can some of the objections to preference utilitarianism discussed in this lecture be met, if we shift our formulation of utilitarianism from actual to revealed preferences?
4. Hedonistic utilitarianism says that the pleasure and pain of *all beings* affected by an act must be taken into account in deciding whether that act should be

performed. Preference utilitarianism says that the preferences of *all beings* affected by an act must be taken into account in deciding whether that act should be performed. Some utilitarians (for example, Peter Singer, in *Animal Liberation*, New York, Random House, 1975) have drawn the conclusion that the way human beings treat animals is morally outrageous. They argue that the pleasure and nutrition we obtain from eating meat doesn't outweigh the suffering and death of the animals we eat. Is there any way to avoid this conclusion while still remaining true to utilitarian principles?

5. If utilitarianism requires us to maximize the amount of happiness there is in the world, won't it require us to have as many children as possible? Even if overpopulation lowers the *average* (per person) quality of life, won't this be outweighed by the total number of individuals who obtain some amount of happiness from the lives they lead? How could a utilitarian argue for the desirability of zero population growth?

LECTURE 32

Kant's Moral Theory

To understand the basic approach that Immanuel Kant (1724–1804) developed in his moral theory, it is useful to begin with a somewhat commonsensical idea—an idea that Kant rejects. This is the idea that reason can play only an "instrumental" role in guiding people's actions. Reason doesn't tell you what your goals should be; rather, it tells you what you should do, given the goals you have. To say that reason is purely instrumental is to say that it is merely a tool that helps you achieve your goals, your goals having been determined by something other than reason.

This simple idea can be elaborated by viewing actions as the joint products of beliefs and desires. Reason can tell you what to believe, given the evidence at hand. However, reason can't tell you what to want. Desires must have some other source:

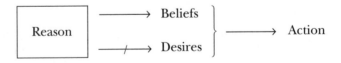

HUME ON REASON'S ROLE

David Hume articulated this idea about the contribution of reason to the actions we perform. In *A Treatise of Human Nature* (1738), he says that "reason is and ought to be the slave of the passions." Hume expresses the same idea in the following passage:

'Tis not contrary to reason to prefer the destruction of the whole world to the scratching of my finger. . . . 'Tis as little contrary to reason to prefer even my own acknowledg'd lesser good to my greater, and have a more ardent affection for the former than the latter.

The main point about Hume's idea is that actions *never derive from reason alone; they must always have a nonrational source.*

KANT REJECTS THE IDEA THAT REASON IS PURELY INSTRUMENTAL

Kant's theory of morality rejects this Humean doctrine. According to Kant, it is only sometimes true that actions are produced by the agent's beliefs and (nonrationally generated) desires. When we act out of "inclination," this is what happens. However, when we act out of duty—when our actions are guided by moral considerations rather than by our inclinations—matters are entirely different.

When we act, there is a goal we have in mind—an end in view—and also a means we use to try to achieve that goal. Hume thought that reason determines the means, not the end. Kant agreed that this is correct when we act out of inclination. But when morality drives our actions, reason determines the end as well as the means.

Kant thought that morality derives its authority from reason alone. Reason alone determines whether an action is right or wrong, regardless of the desires that people may have. According to Kant, when we act morally, our actions are guided by reason in a way that Hume's theory rules out.

KANT: MORAL RULES ARE CATEGORICAL IMPERATIVES

It is clear, as Hume said, that reason can show us which means to use, given the ends we have. If I want to be healthy, reason may tell me that I should stop smoking. Here reason provides an imperative that is *hypothetical* in form: It says that I should stop smoking *if* I want to protect my health. Hume thought that reason can do no more than this. Kant, however, held that moral rules are *categorical,* not hypothetical, in form. An act that is wrong, is wrong—period. Moral rules say "Don't do *X.*" They don't say "Don't do *X* if your goal is *G.*" Kant tried to show that these moral rules—categorical imperatives—are derived from reason just as surely as hypothetical imperatives are.

Moral rules, which take the form of categorical imperatives, describe what we must do whether we want to or not. They have an authority quite separate from the inclinations we have. So when we act morally, Kant thought, we are guided by reason, not inclination. In this case, reason plays something more than a purely instrumental role.

THE MORAL LAW

Another important ingredient in Kant's moral philosophy is his idea that moral laws and scientific laws have something deep in common. A scientific law is a generalization that says what *must* be true in a specified kind of situation. Newton's universal law of gravitation says that the magnitude of the gravitational force F_g between two objects is proportional to the products of their masses (m_1 and m_2) and inversely proportional to the square of the distance (r) between them:

$$F_g = Gm_1m_2/r^2$$

That is, the law says that if the masses are m_1 and m_2 and if the distance is r, then the gravitational force *must* take the value Gm_1m_2/r^2, where G is the gravitational constant.

There is clearly a difference between scientific laws and moral rules (like "Don't cause gratuitous suffering!"). Newton's law doesn't say what the planets ought to do; it says what they do, of necessity. If a scientific law is true, then nothing in the universe disobeys it. On the other hand, people sometimes violate moral laws. Moral laws say how people ought to behave; they don't say what people in fact will do. To use vocabulary introduced earlier, moral laws are normative, while scientific laws are descriptive.

In spite of this difference, Kant thought there is a deeper similarity between them. Scientific laws are *universal*—they involve *all* phenomena of a specified kind. They aren't limited to certain places or certain times. Furthermore, a proposition that states a law doesn't mention any particular person, place, or thing. "All of Napoleon's friends spoke French" may be a true generalization, but it can't be a law, since it mentions a specific individual—Napoleon. I'll mark this feature of scientific laws by saying that they are "impersonal."

Moral laws, Kant thought, also must be universal and impersonal. If it is right for me to do something, then it is right for anyone in similar circumstances to do the same thing. It isn't possible that Napoleon should have the right to do something simply because he is Napoleon. Moral laws, like scientific laws, don't mention specific people.

One more element in Kant's moral philosophy must be mentioned before I can describe how Kant thought that reason alone dictates what our moral principles should be. Recall from the previous lecture that utilitarianism claims the moral characteristics of an action are to be determined by the consequences the action would have for people's happiness or preference satisfaction. Kant didn't think of morality as focusing on the maximizing of happiness. In particular, Kant didn't think of the consequences of an action as the true test of its moral features. Rather, what Kant thought of as central is the "maxim that the action embodies."

KANT: THE MORAL VALUE OF AN ACT DERIVES FROM ITS MAXIM, NOT FROM ITS CONSEQUENCES

Each action can be described as an action of a certain kind. If you help someone, you may think of this as an act of charity. In this case, you may be acting on the maxim that you should help others. Alternatively, when you provide the help, you perhaps are thinking of this as a way of making the recipient feel indebted to you. Here the maxim of your action might be that you should place others in your debt. To see what moral value your action has, look at the maxim you had in mind that led you to do what you did.

The reason we need to look at the agent's motives, and not at the action's consequences, isn't hard to grasp. Kant describes a shopkeeper who never cheats his customers. The reason is that he's afraid that if he cheats them, they will stop patronizing his store. Kant says that the shopkeeper does the right thing, but not for the right reason. He acts *in accordance with* morality, but not *from* morality. To discover the moral value of an action, Kant says we must see *why* the actor performs it; the consequences of the actions don't reveal this.

If the shopkeeper acts by applying the maxim "Always be honest," his action has moral value. If, however, his action is a result of the maxim "Don't cheat people if it is likely to harm you financially," his action is merely prudential, not moral. Moral value comes from motives, and the motives are given by the maxim that the agent applies in deciding what to do.

KANT REJECTED CONSEQUENTIALISM

Kant is undoubtedly correct in saying that knowing an individual's motives is important in assessing *some* moral properties of an action. If we wish to evaluate an agent's moral character, knowing the motives is important; the consequences the action has may be an imperfect guide. After all, a good person can unintentionally cause harm to others; and a malevolent person can unintentionally provide others with a benefit. However, it is important to see that this point doesn't imply that an action's consequences are irrelevant to deciding whether to do it. Kant maintains this further thesis: What makes an action right or wrong isn't whether the consequences are harmful or beneficial. Kant rejects *consequentialism* in ethics.

THE UNIVERSALIZABILITY CRITERION

I now can describe Kant's idea that reason (not desire) determines what it is right and wrong to do. Recall that a moral law (like a scientific law) must be universal. This means that a moral action must embody a maxim that is *universalizable*. To decide whether it would be right to perform a particular action, Kant says you should ask whether you can will (intend) that the maxim of your act should be a universal law. Universalizability is the basis of all categorical imperatives—that is, of all unconditional moral injunctions. Moral acts can be universalized; immoral acts can't.

It is important to grasp what this test is supposed to involve. It is a mistake to think that Kant is saying that you should ask whether it would be a good thing or a bad thing if everyone did the act you are contemplating. The point about immoral actions isn't that it would be *bad* if everyone did them; rather, the point is that it is *impossible* for everyone to do them (or it is *impossible* for you to will that everyone do them).

As Kant's examples will illustrate, there is, so to speak, a logical test for whether an action is moral.

FOUR EXAMPLES

In his book *The Groundwork of the Metaphysics of Morals* (1785), Kant applies this idea to four examples. He first describes a man who is tired of life and is contemplating suicide. Kant says that the maxim the man is considering is to end one's life if continuing to live would produce more pain than pleasure. Kant says that it is

> questionable whether this principle of self-love could become a universal law of nature. One immediately sees a contradiction in a system of nature whose law would be to destroy life by the feeling whose special office is to impel the improvement of life. In this case it would not exist as nature; hence that maxim cannot obtain as a law of nature, and thus it wholly contradicts the supreme principle of all duty.

Kant is suggesting it is impossible for there to exist a world in which all living things decide to commit suicide when their lives promise more pain than pleasure. Since there could be no such world, it is wrong for the individual in Kant's example to commit suicide. The act is wrong because it can't be universalized.

Kant's second example concerns promise keeping. You need money and are deciding whether to borrow. The question is whether it would be permissible for you to promise to pay back the money even though you have no intention of doing so. Kant argues that morality requires you to keep your promise (and so not borrow the money under false pretenses):

> For the universality of a law which says that anyone who believes himself to be in need could promise what he pleased with the intention of not fulfilling it would make the promise itself and the end to be accomplished by it impossible; no one would believe what was promised to him but would only laugh at any such assertion as vain pretense.

Kant is saying that promise keeping couldn't exist as an institution if everyone who made promises did so with the intention of not keeping them. That is, the institution can exist only because people are usually trustworthy. Again, the reason we are obliged to keep our promises is that it is impossible to have a world in which everyone made promises with the intention of breaking them. Universalizability is the acid test.

Kant's third example is intended to show that each of us has an obligation to develop our talents. Why should we work hard at "broadening and improving our natural gifts"? Why not, instead, choose a life of "idleness, indulgence, and propagation"? Each person must choose the former, Kant says, "for, as a rational being, he necessarily wills that all his faculties should be developed, inasmuch as they are given to him for all sorts of possible purposes."

The fourth example concerns a man whose life is going well, but who sees that others live lives of great hardship. Is he obliged to help others? Kant grants that the human race could exist in a state in which some do well while others suffer. But he claims that no rational agent could intend (will) that the world be that way:

> Now although it is possible that a universal law of nature according to that maxim could exist, it is nevertheless impossible to will that such a principle should hold everywhere as a law of nature. For a will which resolved this would conflict with itself, since instances can often arise in which he would need the love and sympathy of others, and in which he would have robbed himself, by such a law of nature springing from his own will, of all hope of the aid he desires.

Kant's point isn't that the pattern can't be universal, but that no rational agent could will that it be universal.

EVALUATION OF KANT'S EXAMPLES

Of these examples, the first is perhaps the weakest. It isn't impossible for there to be a world in which all terminally ill people who are the victims of great suffering commit suicide. Nor does there seem to be any reason why a rational agent couldn't will that all people spare themselves a pointlessly agonizing death.

The second example is somewhat more plausible. The institution of promise keeping does seem to rely on the fact that people usually believe the promises made to them. If people never intended to keep their promises, could the institution persist? Kant says no. However, perhaps tricky circumstances can be contrived in which this conclusion is evaded. I leave this as an exercise for the reader.

Perhaps there also is something to be said for Kant's argument about our duty to help others. Each of us needs some sort of help at some time in our lives. Each of us therefore would wish to avoid a situation in which no one would give us the help we need. We therefore can't will that no one should ever provide help. This means it would be wrong for us to lead a life in which we totally refuse to help others. Again, the reason it would be wrong is that we can't will that the pattern be universal.

What is Kant's argument, in his fourth example, concerning the duty we have to develop our talents? Perhaps the thought is similar to the one Kant deploys in his discussion of the duty to help others. I want others to develop talents that would be beneficial to me; for example, I want physicians to perfect their skills, since one day I'll need them. This means, however, that I can't will that everyone should neglect to develop their talents. It is supposed to follow that I have a duty to develop my own talents.

I emphasized earlier that the universalizability criterion doesn't ask whether it would be a good thing if everyone performed the action the agent is contemplating. Kant's question is whether it would be *possible* for everyone to do so, or whether it would be *possible to will* that everyone should do so.

If we keep this clearly in mind, it is doubtful whether Kant can reach the conclusions he wants concerning his last two examples without taking consequences into account. Clearly, it *is* possible that the world be a place in which no one helps others and no one develops his or her talents. This is a sorry state of affairs, not an impossible one. What about Kant's second option—could a rational agent *will* that people don't help others or develop their talents?

That depends on what one means by "rational." If rational means instrumentally rational, then there seems to be no impossibility here. As Hume says, I might be perfectly clear in my means/end reasoning (and so be instrumentally rational) and still have the most bizarre desires you can imagine. On the other hand, there is a sense of "rational" according to which a rational agent wouldn't want the world to be a place in which people don't help others or develop their talents. A rational agent wouldn't want this *because of the consequences such behaviors would have.* There would be a great deal of suffering, alienation, and despair; life would be bleak.

I conclude that it is unclear how Kant can analyze his last two examples as he does without considering the consequences that would follow from making the actions universal.

A PROBLEM FOR THE UNIVERSALIZABILITY CRITERION

There is a general problem that pertains to all of Kant's examples—indeed, to the whole idea of the universalizability criterion. Recall a simple point from the lecture on functionalism (Lecture 22): *A token exemplifies many types.* This means that a given (token) action can be described as embodying many different properties. Kant seems to assume that there is just one maxim that each action embodies, so we can test the morality of the act by looking at the universalizability of this maxim. But there are many maxims that might lead to a given action; some of these may universalize while others don't.

Let's return to Kant's example of promise keeping to see this problem. A man has to decide whether to borrow money by promising to repay it, though he has no intention of keeping his promise. What would it mean for everyone to behave like this? One way to describe this action is to say that it flows from the maxim "Make a promise even though you intend to break it." Kant claims universalizing this is impossible because the following proposition is a contradiction:

> Everyone makes promises, even though no one intends to keep
> the promises he makes.

However, we can also describe the man's action as flowing from a rather different maxim: "Don't make a promise unless you intend to keep it, except when you are in a life and death situation and your intention to break your promise wouldn't be evident to others." Universalizing this maxim doesn't lead to contradiction, since the following is a perfectly possible way the world might be:

> Everyone makes promises, and people generally expect to keep
> their promises. The exception arises when there is an enormous
> personal advantage to making a promise without the intention
> to keep it, and the intention to break the promise isn't evident to others.

Far from being impossible, the above generalization seems to describe fairly accurately the world we actually inhabit.

You should notice a similarity between the problem that Kant faces and a problem that rule utilitarianism encountered in the previous lecture. "What would happen if everyone did it?" is a question that the rule utilitarian thinks is important in assessing the moral properties of an action. Kant's question is a different one; he asks "Could everyone do it?" or "Could I will that everyone do it?" Though the questions differ, similar problems derive from the fact that there are multiple ways of describing any action.

The universalizability criterion may seem plausible if one takes seriously the analogy between moral laws and scientific laws. Both must be universal and impersonal. But another comparison of these two ideas may diminish the plausibility that anything like Kant's universalizability criterion can be made to work.

Scientific laws must be universal, but no one thinks the true explanation of a specific phenomenon can be derived a priori. Reason alone can't tell me why the earth moves in an elliptical orbit around the sun, even if I assume that the explanation of this fact must hold true for all similar planetary systems. On the other hand, Kant held that what it is right to do in a specific situation is dictated by the rational requirement of universalizability.

Evidently, it is an important fact about morality that if it is right for me to do a particular action, then it is right for anyone similarly situated to do it as well. This is the idea that moral laws—the general principles that dictate what it is right to do—are universal and impersonal. The problem is that this requirement isn't sufficient to reveal which moral generalizations are true. If so, the analogy between scientific laws and moral laws has implications different from the ones Kant tried to develop.

KANT: PEOPLE ARE ENDS IN THEMSELVES

Kant believed that an important consequence of his universalizability test is that we should treat people as ends in themselves, and not as mere means. By this, Kant meant that we shouldn't treat people as means to ends to which they couldn't rationally consent. Kant believed that slavery is prohibited by this principle. The same may be true for punishing someone for a crime he didn't commit, even if doing so would placate a dangerous mob. Kantian theory seems to provide firmer grounds than utilitarianism does for the idea that individuals have rights that can't be overridden by considerations of utility. It isn't the maximization of happiness that matters in Kant's theory. Reason alone is supposed to dictate principles of fairness, impartiality, and justice.

Even though Kant predates the utilitarians, his theory seems designed to correct the defects present in utilitarianism. The idea of rights is a plausible corrective to the idea that every aspect of an individual's life has to pass the test of maximizing the happiness of all. Yet there are major logical difficulties in Kant's theory. And the absoluteness of some of his pronouncements seems to be wildly at odds with strongly held commonsense moral convictions. Is it at all plausible to think that promises must *always* be kept—that we must *never* tell a lie—no matter what the consequences are? Besides noting the defects in the arguments intended to justify such injunctions, we also should note that these moral requirements shouldn't receive an unconditional justification in the first place.

If the universalizability criterion fails to provide a procedure for deciding which actions are right, and if Kant's moral judgments about promise keeping, suicide, and other actions are implausible, what is of value in his ethical theory? Many philosophers find Kant's description of *the moral point of view* to be one of his enduring and preeminent contributions. Desires and preferences can move us to action, and these actions can produce different mixtures of pleasure and pain. This sequence of events, however, occurs among creatures—cows and dogs, perhaps—who by no stretch of the imagination have a morality. What, then, distinguishes action motivated by morality from action driven by inclination, whether benevolent or malevolent?

Kant's answer was that moral action is driven by principles that have a special sort of rational warrant. Ordinary language is perhaps a little misleading here, since we can talk about the desire to act morally as if it were on the same footing with the desire for pleasure or profit. But Kant didn't think of the determination to do one's duty as one inclination among many. He saw morality and inclination as existing in entirely different realms. To identify the moral thing to do, one must *set aside* one's inclinations. By fixing our attention on universal and impersonal laws, we can hope to diminish the degree to which self-interest distorts our judgment concerning what we ought to do.

Review Questions

1. Why did Hume maintain that every action has a cause that is "nonrational"? Why did Kant reject this?
2. Kant believed there are important similarities between scientific laws and moral laws. What are these?
3. What's meant by saying that utilitarianism is a consequentialist theory, whereas Kant's theory isn't?
4. What does Kant's universalizability criterion assert? Does it say that you shouldn't perform an action if the world would be a worse place if everyone did the same?
5. How does Kant try to show that the obligation of promise keeping follows from the universalizability criterion? Is he successful?
6. You are in a boat that is tipping dangerously to one side because all the passengers are on the right. You are considering whether it would be a good idea to move to the left. You ask yourself, "What would happen if everyone did this?" This question has an ambiguity in it. What is it? How is this ambiguity relevant to assessing Kant's universalizability criterion?

Problems for Further Thought

1. Kant believes that the duty to treat others as ends in themselves, not as means, follows from the universalizability criterion. Try to construct an argument that shows how this might be true. Is Kant correct in thinking these two principles are closely related?

2. Kant thought of the moral law as constraining what one's life should be like, but not as determining each and every detail of it. That is, for Kant, one is free to pursue one's private goals and projects as long as these don't violate any categorical imperative. These particular projects are morally permissible, not morally obligatory.

   Utilitarianism, by contrast, sees morality as determining each and every aspect of one's life. Each action one performs must be evaluated in terms of the Greatest Happiness Principle. A private project is permissible only if it promotes the greatest good for the greatest number of people. Such acts aren't just permissible, but obligatory.

   Construct a concrete example in which these features of the two theories lead them to make opposite judgments about whether an act is morally permissible. Which theory strikes you as more plausible in what it says about your example?

3. Kant's ethics has had a powerful influence on the political philosophy of John Rawls. In *A Theory of Justice* (Harvard University Press, 1971), Rawls argues the correct rules of justice for a society are ones all persons would choose if (i) they were self-interested, and (ii) they didn't know various details about themselves (like their talents, sex, race, and conception of what projects they wish to pursue). The only facts that people know in this hypothetical situation are general facts about human psychology and human life. Rawl's idea is partially an attempt to capture Kant's idea that personal inclinations must be set to one side if you want to see what your obligations are. What principles of conduct do you think people would choose in this hypothetical situation?

LECTURE 33

Aristotle on the Good Life

HOW FAR DO OBLIGATIONS EXTEND?

Some ethical theories hold that every aspect of a person's life is to be decided by ethical principles that describe obligations. Utilitarianism, for example, says that it is wrong to do some action if an alternative action could be performed that would better promote people's happiness or preference satisfaction.

Other ethical theories hold that considerations of obligation don't answer every question about how people should lead their lives. Kant's ethical theory is often thought to be of this type. According to Kant, you must treat others with justice and accord them dignity and respect. However, this seems to leave open a large number of issues concerning what sort of life you ought to pursue.

The same would be true of an ethical theory that held that all obligations flow from the principle that people have the right to structure their own lives, as long as doing so doesn't infringe on the rights of others. If you accepted an ethics of this sort, the question would still remain of how you should live your life. The reason this question is left open is that the ethical principle just mentioned is largely *negative* in its implications. It mainly tells you what you should *not* do. In consequence, questions like the following are left unanswered: What sort of work should you take up? Should you get married? Should you have children? What sorts of friendships should you try to nurture? Should you try to develop talents you have other than those that figure in the work you do? Should you participate in the political affairs of your community? Nation? The Earth? What importance should you assign to these various activities? The ethical principle that says "Do no harm" provides little or no guidance on these matters.

THE THEORY OF THE RIGHT AND THE THEORY OF THE GOOD

Philosophers sometimes distinguish the *theory of the right* from the *theory of the good*. In doing so, they are indicating that principles of obligation and prohibition fail to address questions like the ones listed in the previous paragraph. The theory of the good attempts to describe what the good life would be like.

According to this distinction, living a good life isn't limited to fulfilling your obligations. It is easy to miss this point, since "be good" may sound like the same advice as "do the right thing." One way to see that there is a difference here is to imagine someone who breaks no moral prohibitions, but still fails to lead a good life. An example might be someone who breaks no laws, but shuns all human contact, has a dull and repetitive job, and spends all time outside work reading comic books. This person may do no harm, but it would be implausible to say of him, "He really led a good life."

ARE THERE GENERAL PRINCIPLES ABOUT THE GOOD LIFE?

It seems plausible that the theory of the right will include principles of some generality. "Do not murder" is a rule that covers you, me, and everyone else. Are there comparable principles to be found in the theory of the good? That is, are there principles that describe what a good life would be like that cover all human beings? Or is the issue of the good life more personal and individual? Perhaps we are subject to the same obligations and prohibitions (described in the theory of the right), but there is nothing interesting in common between what would be a good life for you and a good life for me.

In his ethical theory (as developed primarily in *The Nicomachean Ethics*), Aristotle (384–322 B.C.) attempts to describe what a good life would be like. In fact, his goal is to describe what *the* good life for human beings amounts to. As I'll soon explain, he maintains that since we're all members of the same biological species, general principles can be described that specify what a good life would be for any human being. For Aristotle, the good life is to be understood by way of the idea of human nature.

WHAT IS A GOOD *X*?

A good person lives a good life. But what makes a person good? Aristotle proposes to understand the idea of a *good human being* by first considering what it means to say that something is good. What is a good hammer? Here we aren't talking about ethical issues, of course. A hammer is a tool. A hammer is a good hammer when it is able to perform the tasks that are specific to hammers. Hammers have the function of banging nails into wood. A good hammer optimally performs that function.

Consider another example, this one having to do with the roles that human beings play. What is a good father? To answer this question, we have to ask what the function of a father is. Plausibly, a father's function is to help his children grow into loving, responsible, and independent adults. If so, then a good father is one who optimally performs that function.

Human beings perform other functions. What is a good nurse? Nurses train to help the sick. Evidently, the function of a nurse is to help patients return to full health as much as possible. If this is right, we can tell from the function of a nurse what a good nurse would be.

Good Versus Green

A green apple and a green shirt must have something in common. However, according to Aristotle a good hammer and a good violinist need have nothing in common. What is the difference between greenness and goodness that accounts for this?

To be a green apple is to be green *and* an apple. To be a green shirt is to be green *and* a shirt. Being a green apple is a conjunctive property ("conjunction" means *and*). Being a green apple involves having two properties; the same is true of being a green shirt. This explains why there is something that green apples and green shirts have in common; there is a property—greenness—that they share.

To be a good hammer isn't the same as being good *and* a hammer. To be a good violinist isn't the same as being good *and* a violinist. Neither is a conjunctive property. To be a good violinist is to have a single complex property, not to possess two separate properties at once. This is why good hammers and good violinists need have nothing in common.

Consider other adjectives. We use terms like "big," "soft," and "old." Are these more like "green" or more like "good"?

These examples—the hammer, the father, the nurse—tell us something about the concept of goodness. The first lesson is that we decide what it is to be a good *X* by seeing what the function is of *X*s. The concept of goodness is intimately connected with concepts of goal, function, and purpose. The second lesson is that what it takes to be a good *X* depends on the choice of *X*. For example, the character traits required for being a good father may be quite different from the ones required for being a good harpist or a good baseball player. Aristotle emphasizes both these points about the concept of goodness.

It is no mystery what a good hammer is. And it isn't that difficult to say what it means to be a good father or a good nurse. Perhaps the same strategy will work when we ask what a good person is. Aristotle thought that once we say what the function is of human life, we will know what a good human being is. This, in turn, will tell us what the good life amounts to.

HUMAN BEINGS ARE GOAL-DIRECTED SYSTEMS

In Lecture 5, I briefly explained how Aristotle's biology and physics are *teleological* in character. He thought that living things as well as inanimate objects are goal-directed systems. The goal of a living thing is to grow and reproduce. The goal of a rock is to reach the place where the center of the earth now is. Of course, not all living things grow and reproduce. And not all rocks find their way to the earth's center. But each has a *natural tendency* to do those things. *Interfering forces* may prevent an object from reaching its natural state.

We human beings are goal-directed systems. What is the end state that we seek? Aristotle's answer is that human beings seek *happiness*. A good life is a life of happiness—a life in which the goal of human life has been achieved.

Before saying how Aristotle understood happiness, it is important to note a difference between human beings and other goal-directed systems. Human beings seek happiness; trees aim to grow and reproduce. The difference between us and other living things comes from *how* we pursue the goals we have. Other living things pursue the goals of growth and reproduction *innately*. A tree doesn't have to be taught to send its roots deep into the soil or to send its leaves where they can absorb sunlight. Trees do these things *by nature*.

In contrast, we human beings are better or worse at seeking happiness according to the upbringing we receive. Some people seek their happiness in wealth or fame or power. Others seek it in love. *How* we seek our happiness isn't determined by our nature, but by our upbringing. For Aristotle, a good upbringing is one that helps us develop habits and character traits that are conducive to the good life.

In Lecture 20, on methodological behaviorism, I briefly discussed the nature/nurture controversy. We now understand that dispute in terms of the task of explaining variation in some characteristic (like height or intelligence). Human beings have various heights. How much of that variation is explained by genetic differences, and how much by differences in environment (like nutrition)?

Aristotle also drew the nature/nurture distinction, but in a rather different way. First, he didn't have the idea of genes. Second, the fact of variation within a species was much less important to him than it is in present-day biology. For Aristotle, what is biologically significant about human beings is that human beings have something in common; this is what *human nature* is. When Aristotle thought about "nature" (as opposed to nurture), he thought about characteristics that all members of a species *share;* current biology thinks about "nature" (as opposed to nurture) in terms of genetic *differences* among members of the same species.

For Aristotle, human beings have a common nature that sets them apart from the rest of the living world. It is part of human nature to seek happiness. How human beings go about doing this varies from person to person. The explanation for this variation, Aristotle held, is environmental. It is differences in nurture—in our upbringing—that explain why human beings live their lives in different ways.

THE CAPACITY TO REASON

The function of a hammer is something that distinguishes hammers from other tools. A hammer that is able to perform that function well counts as a good hammer. By the same line of thinking, we can approach the question of what function human beings have by asking what distinguishes human beings from other beings. A human being who is able to perform that function well will count as a good human being.

Human beings are organisms, and so survival, growth, and reproduction are goals that human beings try to achieve. However, in addition there is a characteristic that distinguishes human beings from other organisms. This is the development of rationality—the capacity for abstract thinking.

The basic contours of Aristotle's theory of happiness can now be stated. Human beings, unique among living things, possess the capacity of rationality. The good life for human beings is one in which rational capacities are developed and exercised to a high degree. In doing this, human beings find the best sort of happiness that is possible for them.

Aristotle draws a distinction between theoretical and practical reasoning. Practical reasoning involves the kind of means/ends reasoning so familiar in everyday life. The conclusion you draw in practical reasoning is a decision to do something. For example, you want an article of clothing that will keep you warm in winter. You realize that a cloak will perform this task. So you decide to buy a cloak. Note that this bit of reasoning concludes with the intention to buy a cloak, not with a prediction that you will do so.

In contrast, the conclusion you draw in theoretical reasoning is that some proposition is true. Theoretical reasoning is reasoning given over to the disinterested search for knowledge. It is "pure" inquiry, not "applied." In theoretical inquiry, you seek understanding for its own sake. The life of contemplation is devoted to the sort of intellectual activity that occurs in science, philosophy, and the arts. The best life, for Aristotle, is the life of theoretical reason.

ARISTOTLE: HAPPINESS ISN'T A SUBJECTIVE STATE

When Aristotle asked what happiness is, he wanted to know what sorts of activities make for a happy life. The word "activity" is important here; a happy life is a life of *doing*. The good life is one in which those traits that are specifically human are brought to a high level of cultivation. The happy life is one of flourishing—of doing well.

Happiness, for Aristotle, is emphatically not the same as pleasure. The sensation of pleasure is possible for a brain in a vat; but a brain in a vat isn't a flourishing human being, even if it has the illusion of leading an ideal life.

Real happiness, then, isn't a sensation (compare this with the discussion of happiness in Lecture 31). People can believe themselves to be happy and still not be. Whether you're flourishing isn't settled by the mere fact that you think you are.

Although pleasure isn't the goal of human life, pleasure naturally accompanies the good life. The good life crucially involves exercising the faculty of reason. It is natural for people to take pleasure in exercising this ability, just as people take pleasure in the vigorous functioning of a healthy body, as in athletics.

Aristotle thought human beings have godlike as well as animal characteristics. Our nature as animals decrees we must eat, grow, breathe, and reproduce. In addition, we are social beings by nature, and so the good life includes participation in politics. But the divine spark is also present, and this means that we're directed toward the divine activity of contemplation. When Aristotle says that the good life consists in contemplation (intellectual activity), he isn't denying that activities we share with animals are important to us; nor did he mean that involvement in practical political affairs is unimportant. But the life of contemplation was for him a life that emphasized what was best (= highest) in us. It is an expression of what we have in common with the gods.

WHY THE LIFE OF RATIONAL ACTIVITY IS BEST: TWO MORE REASONS

I've already mentioned Aristotle's main reason for thinking the human goal of happiness is best achieved by the life of rational activity; our capacity to be rational is unique in the living world. However, Aristotle had two other ways of reaching this conclusion.

The first is more specifically tied to his conception of how the human mind works. Aristotle thought activities that call for fine and multifaceted discriminations make people happier than activities that call for fewer and more one-dimensional discriminations. Chess is superior to checkers, and checkers is superior to tic-tac-toe. Sports that require a variety of skills are better than ones that require fewer; and sports that require fine discriminations are better than sports that require only coarse discriminations.

Aristotle saw this as a basic feature of the human mind. Its highest happiness is to be found in activities of these sorts. Aristotle thought that theoretical reasoning—the kind that artists, scientists, and philosophers pursue—involves mental activities in which the finest and most multifaceted discriminations are drawn.

A further consideration led Aristotle to this conclusion. In choosing a life for ourselves, we must decide which of our capacities we wish to develop. For example, this might involve trying to become a great athlete or a great politician. Aristotle thinks it is highly significant that succeeding in these sorts of aims depends on a number of factors that are outside the individual's control. Athletes of great talent can suffer injuries. Politicians can be deprived of power if others oppose them.

In contrast, the life of rational activity is much less dependent on factors outside the agent's control. Contemplation can last a lifetime. It doesn't require a youthful body, wealth, power, or the admiration of others. Of course, it isn't wholly independent of external circumstance. But given the perils that can subvert other plans for a life, the life of contemplation makes the most sense, according to Aristotle.

Although Aristotle holds that the good life is devoted to theoretical reasoning, he has a great deal to say about the character traits that good people will display in dealing with other human beings. For example, Aristotle discusses friendship, justice, liberality, and courage. These virtues, he believes, can be understood within a single theoretical framework, provided by his Doctrine of the Mean.

THE DOCTRINE OF THE MEAN

The Doctrine of the Mean says that many (if not all) virtues are located on a continuum, their perfection consisting in the fact that they avoid both excess and deficiency. For example, courage is a virtue; Aristotle claims that it is in between foolhardiness and cowardice. Similarly, liberality is a virtue; people who are liberal with their money are neither misers nor spendthrifts.

Aristotle didn't think that the mean had to be an arithmetic average. If 10 units of food is too much and 2 units is too little, the correct amount is somewhere in between; it needn't be 6. Furthermore, Aristotle emphasized that the right amount for one person might not be the right amount for another. The wrestler Milo requires more food than other people do. The mean for him wouldn't be the mean for others.

Although the Doctrine of the Mean is sometimes represented by the slogan "moderation in all things," this is a rather misleading summary of Aristotle's idea. Aristotle says that spitefulness and envy are bad, as are adultery, theft, and murder. They are wrong in themselves; virtue doesn't consist in doing them a little but not too much.

Once these clarifications are noted, however, it is unclear how much of a theory the Doctrine of the Mean actually provides. To apply it in a given case, we first must decide what the continuum is on which the activity or virtue is located. Generosity is fairly easy; the scale on which it is located is the amount of money you give away. But what is the scale on which justice is located? And if abstaining from murder is a mean, what is the scale on which it is to be represented?

A second problem arises after one has identified the scale on which the activity or character trait is to be represented. Let's grant that being liberal with money is a mean between being a miser and being a spendthrift. The question is why the intermediacy of the trait should be what makes it a virtue. Is being courageous better than being cowardly or foolish *because* courage falls between cowardice and foolhardiness? Aristotle thought that this is so, but it is by no means clear he was correct.

In the remainder of this lecture, I want to develop two other criticisms of Aristotle's theory. The first concerns the connection he draws between being a good human being and leading a life that is a good one for human beings to lead. The second has to do with the reasons Aristotle gives for thinking that the life of contemplation is the highest form of happiness.

DEFINING WHAT A GOOD *X* IS DIFFERS FROM SAYING WHAT IS GOOD FOR *X*S

Let's recall the overall strategy of Aristotle's argument. He begins by asking what the good life is for human beings. This question, he believes, would be answered if we knew what a good human being is. He then proposes to say what a good human being is by inquiring what function human beings have.

It is the first step in this reasoning that I want to question. Aristotle assumes that if a good human being is rational, then rationality is good for human beings. The general principle Aristotle uses here is this:

If a good X is F, then F is good for Xs.

"Natural" and "Normal"

The term *natural* is used in two quite different ways. Sometimes it has an evaluative meaning, as when "natural" and "unnatural" are used as code words for *good* and *bad*. Sometimes it has a purely descriptive meaning, as when "natural" is used to mean *found in nature*.

The same is true of the term *normal*. Usually, when we say that something is "abnormal," we mean that there is something wrong with it. But there is a purely descriptive meaning that the term also has. When we say that some activity "is the norm" (or that "normally" some activity occurs), we might just mean that it is commonly found.

It is fairly clear that some unusual characteristics are undesirable. More people have healthy blood than cancerous blood, and so when we say that leukemia is an abnormal condition, we mean both that it is uncommon and that there is something wrong.

In other cases, matters are just the reverse. Most adults in the U.S.A. are overweight. Given this, how should you interpret the doctor's comment that your weight is "normal"? If this means that it is common, you might decide that there is something wrong. If this means that your weight is unhealthy, then you may be pleased.

These two examples—of leukemia and weight—illustrate that there is no simple connection between what's common and what's good. Given this, you should be skeptical of any argument that attempts to show that some activity is wrong or bad simply by pointing out that the activity is rare. And the claim that something is "natural" or "normal" also shouldn't be taken as providing an automatic justification.

What bearing do these observations have on Aristotle's attempt to explain what the good life is by developing a theory of human nature?

To say that someone is a good *X* is often just to say that they are good at *X*-ing: a good teacher is good at teaching, a good parent is good at parenting, a good butcher is good at butchering, and a good torturer is good at torturing.

As the last example suggests, to say that you are a good *X* isn't to say that it is a good thing for you to be an *X*. You might be a good torturer, even though torturing is bad for you. The same may be true for other, less gruesome, activities at which you excel. This is why I reject the principle just displayed.

A good human being, Aristotle holds, is someone who is good at characteristically human activities. Aristotle singles out the use of reason as the characteristic activity; he concludes that good human beings devote themselves to lives of contemplation, developing their rational faculties to the utmost.

My criticism suggests that it isn't always correct to think about the concept of a good *X* in the functional way Aristotle proposes. It is plausible to think of a good hammer and a good harpist in the way Aristotle suggests, but the concept of a good human being seems to require a different treatment.

WHY SINGLE OUT CONTEMPLATION AS THE BEST LIFE?

My last criticism has to do with Aristotle's exclusive focus on rationality. He notes that human beings share with other animals the tendency to grow and reproduce. He then asks which characteristic is uniquely human, and he comes up with rationality as his answer. But surely there are many behaviors and capacities that are unique to human beings. Collecting money for charity is one of them; engaging in genocide is another. If the good life consists in developing those capacities that are uniquely human, why should contemplation constitute the good life? There are many ways to be uniquely human.

Aristotle provides a second reason for singling out the life of theoretical reason as best. As noted earlier, Aristotle thinks human beings find happiness in drawing fine discriminations and in mastering complex tasks. The life of contemplation provides the greatest opportunity for these activities.

Even if we accept this as a basic fact about the human mind, it is unclear why this shows that the life of contemplation is best. Human beings find happiness in other activities as well. Why think of mastering complexity as *the best* activity? Aristotle's answer seems to be the one just discussed: What's best for human beings is the development of traits that are uniquely human. The problems with this answer I've already noted.

Aristotle gives a third reason for thinking the life of contemplation is best. This life is least dependent on others. However, here again it is hard to see that this characteristic is unique to the life devoted to theoretical reason. It also is hard to see why this characteristic should make that life the one most worth living.

Aristotle thinks that loving others, including your children, is part of the good life. He goes so far as to say that you can't be happy—lead a good life—if your children suffer or hate you. Notice that in saying this, Aristotle is granting that the good life involves dependency on others. Given this, it is hard to see why the life of contemplation is best *because* it is relatively independent of others.

In summary, Aristotle offers three arguments for thinking that the life of theoretical reason provides the best form of happiness. The first and most important argument appeals to the fact that the capacity to reason is uniquely human. The second claims that human beings find happiness in drawing fine discriminations and in mastering complex tasks. The third sees the contemplative life as supremely good because it is the life in which one is most independent of others. I've suggested that none of these arguments is very persuasive.

In each of them, Aristotle attempts to show why the contemplative life is the best one for human beings without assuming a fully developed theory of value. For example, in the first argument, it is a fact about human biology that justifies his conclusion. In suggesting these arguments, Aristotle is following the analogy with other goal-directed systems. We can say what a good hammer is, or a good father, or a good nurse, without assuming anything about whether it is a good thing or a bad thing to be a hammer, a father, or a nurse.

Perhaps the reason that Aristotle's various arguments run into trouble is that there is a disanalogy between these cases and the problem of describing what the good life is. The good life must be a life that is worth living. A good life must be a life that would be good to have. You can approach questions about what a good teacher is (or a good general, or a good nurse) with a certain detachment. You can say what this role requires without committing yourself to taking it up for yourself. The problem of the good life, however, admits no such detachment. If you grant that the life of contemplation is the good life for human beings, you commit yourself to the desirability of living such a life.

This may help explain why Aristotle's strategy for solving this important problem was unsuccessful. Another reason may be that Aristotle thought in terms of a single form of life being *the* best one for everyone. His arguments pay scant attention to the differences that distinguish each of us from other human beings. As noted before, the good life for human beings is to be discovered by investigating human nature, and human nature is what all human beings have in common.

Aristotle had the idea that the good life involves actualizing the best capacities we possess. We must find what's best in ourselves and build a whole life on that foundation. Perhaps we should accept this idea, even if we reject Aristotle's suggestion that the good life for every human being consists in actualizing a characteristic that is uniquely human. Perhaps there is no such thing as *the* good life for human beings; rather, there may be many good lives, each uniquely fitted to the unique constellation of traits that each of us possesses.

Review Questions

1. What is the difference between the theory of the right and the theory of the good?
2. What do a good pizza and a good dancer have in common? What does "good" mean?

3. Why did Aristotle think that the good life for human beings would be a life of contemplation?

4. What is the Doctrine of the Mean? Does it say that we should pursue each activity a little but not too much?

5. What connection did Aristotle see between the concept of *a good human being* and the idea that certain activities would be *good for human beings*? Was he right in connecting these ideas in the way he did?

Problems for Further Thought

1. Aristotle says that the function of human beings is to reason well. This is what human beings are *for*. In Lecture 25, on the Weather Vane Theory of Freedom, I defined what it means to say that *the function of the heart is to pump blood*. The definition I offered involves the modern idea of natural selection; the theory of natural selection, of course, was unknown to Aristotle. Apply this definition of function to the statement *the function of human beings is to be rational*. Is what Aristotle says plausible if his claim about function is understood in this modern way? Explain your answer.

2. There is an interpretation of what Aristotle thinks the good life is that differs from the one I've offered. Instead of seeing the good life as given over to contemplation, this interpretation has Aristotle saying that a good life is one in which reason suffuses all human activities, both theoretical and practical. This interpretation relies on the fact that human beings are *not* the only things capable of rationality—there are the gods as well. What's unique to human beings is the *mixture* of animal nature and capacity to reason. Gods can engage in pure contemplation; human beings must lead less monolithic lives.

   So good human beings judiciously apply reason to the activities they take up. If Aristotle is interpreted in this way, two problems remain for his view. The first is that we need to provide a list of the activities that comprise the good life. The second is that a principle needs to be provided that says how these various activities are to be integrated and balanced against each other. For example, if the good life includes a family, participation in politics, and contemplation, how are the demands each activity places on your time and energy to be judged?

   Without answering these questions, the advice to use reason in all your activities seems to be pretty empty. Do the passages from Aristotle's *Nicomachean Ethics* reprinted at the end of this chapter help provide any answers?

Readings

PLATO

Critique of the Divine Command Theory

In this excerpt from *The Euthyphro*, Plato (427–347 B.C.) presents a dialogue in which
the principal subject is the relationship between what piety is and what the gods command. The point at issue is not restricted to the question of what piety is, but pertains
to any ethical category: Is an act morally obligatory because God commands it, or does
God command it because the act is obligatory?

EUTHYPHRO: What's new, Socrates, to make you leave your usual haunts in the Lyceum
and spend your time here by the king-archon's court? Surely you are not prosecuting any one before the king archon as I am?

SOCRATES: The Athenians do not call this a prosecution but an indictment, Euthyphro.

EUTHYPHRO: What is this you say? Someone must have indicted you, for you are not
going to tell me that you have indicted someone else.

SOCRATES: No indeed.

EUTHYPHRO: But someone else has indicted you?

SOCRATES: Quite so.

EUTHYPHRO: Who is he?

SOCRATES: I do not really know him myself, Euthyphro. He is apparently young and
unknown. They call him Meletus, I believe. He belongs to the Pitthean deme, if
you know anyone from that deme called Meletus, with long hair, not much of a
beard, and a rather aquiline nose.

EUTHYPHRO: I don't know him, Socrates. What charge does he bring against you?

Plato, "Critique of the Divine Command Theory," from "The Euthyphro," in *The Trial and Death of Socrates*,
translated by G. M. A. Grube (Indianapolis: Hackett Publishing Co., 1975), pp. 5–22. Reprinted by permission of Hackett Publishing Company, Inc. All rights reserved.

SOCRATES: What charge? A not ignoble one I think, for it is no small thing for a young man to have knowledge of such an important subject. He says he knows how our young men are corrupted and who corrupts them. He is likely to be wise, and when he sees my ignorance corrupting his contemporaries, he proceeds to accuse me to the city as to their mother. I think he is the only one of our public men to start out the right way, for it is right to care first that the young should be as good as possible, just as a good farmer is likely to take care of the young plants first, and of the others later. So, too, Meletus first gets rid of us who corrupt the growth of the young, as he says, and then afterwards he will obviously take care of the older and become a source of great blessings for the city, as seems likely to happen to one who started out this way.

EUTHYPHRO: I could wish this were true, Socrates, but I fear the opposite may happen. He seems to me to start out by harming the very heart of the city by attempting to wrong you. Tell me, what does he say you do to corrupt the young?

SOCRATES: Strange things, to hear him tell it, for he says that I am a maker of gods, that I create new gods while not believing in the old gods, and he has indicted me for this very reason, as he puts it.

EUTHYPHRO: I understand, Socrates. This is because you say that the divine sign keeps coming to you. So he has written this indictment against you as one who makes innovations in religious matters, and he comes to court to slander you, knowing that such things are easily misrepresented to the crowd. The same is true in my case. Whenever I speak of divine matters in the assembly and foretell the future, they laugh me down as if I were crazy; and yet I have foretold nothing that did not happen. Nevertheless, they envy all of us who do this. One need not give them any thought, but carry on just the same.

SOCRATES: My dear Euthyphro, to be laughed at does not matter perhaps, for the Athenians do not mind anyone they think clever, as long as he does not teach his own wisdom, but if they think that he makes others to be like himself they get angry, whether through envy, as you say, or for some other reason.

EUTHYPHRO: I have certainly no desire to test their feelings toward me in this matter.

SOCRATES: Perhaps you seem to make yourself but rarely available, and not to be willing to teach your own wisdom, but my liking for people makes them think that I pour out to anybody anything I have to say, not only without charging a fee but appearing glad to reward anyone who is willing to listen. If then they were intending to laugh at me, as you say they laugh at you, there would be nothing unpleasant in their spending their time in court laughing and jesting, but if they are going to be serious, the outcome is not clear except to you prophets.

EUTHYPHRO: Perhaps it will come to nothing, Socrates, and you will fight your case as you think best, as I think I will mine.

SOCRATES: What is your case, Euthyphro? Are you the defendant or the prosecutor?

EUTHYPHRO: The prosecutor.

SOCRATES: Whom do you prosecute?

EUTHYPHRO: One whom I am thought crazy to prosecute.

SOCRATES: Are you pursuing someone who will easily escape you?

EUTHYPHRO: Far from it, for he is quite old.

SOCRATES: Who is it?

EUTHYPHRO: My father.

SOCRATES: My dear sir! Your own father?

EUTHYPHRO: Certainly.

SOCRATES: What is the charge? What is the case about?

EUTHYPHRO: Murder, Socrates.

SOCRATES: Good heavens! Certainly, Euthyphro, most men would not know how they could do this and be right. It is not the part of anyone to do this, but of one who is far advanced in wisdom.

EUTHYPHRO: Yes by Zeus, Socrates, that is so.

SOCRATES: Is then the man your father killed one of your relatives? Or is that obvious, for you would not prosecute your father for the murder of a stranger.

EUTHYPHRO: It is ridiculous, Socrates, for you to think that it makes any difference whether the victim is a stranger or a relative. One should only watch whether the killer acted justly or not; if he acted justly, let him go, but if not, one should prosecute, even if the killer shares your hearth and table. The pollution is the same if you knowingly keep company with such a man and do not cleanse yourself and him by bringing him to justice. The victim was a dependent of mine, and when we were farming in Naxos he was a servant of ours. He killed one of our household slaves in drunken anger, so my father bound him hand and foot and threw him in a ditch, then sent a man here to enquire from the priest what should be done. During that time he gave no thought or care to the bound man, as being a killer, and it was no matter if he died, which he did. Hunger and cold and his bonds caused his death before the messenger came back from the seer. Both my father and my other relatives are angry that I am prosecuting my father for murder on behalf of a murderer, as he did not even kill him. They say that such a victim does not deserve a thought and that it is impious for a son to prosecute his father for murder. But their ideas of the divine attitude to piety and impiety are wrong, Socrates.

SOCRATES: Whereas, by Zeus, Euthyphro, you think that your knowledge of the divine, and of piety and impiety, is so accurate that, when those things happened as you say, you have no fear of having acted impiously in bringing your father to trial?

EUTHYPHRO: I should be of no use, Socrates, and Euthyphro would not be superior to the majority of men, if I did not have accurate knowledge of all such things.

SOCRATES: It is indeed most important, my admirable Euthyphro, that I should become your pupil, and as regards this indictment challenge Meletus about these very things and say to him: that in the past too I considered knowledge about the divine to be most important, and that now he says that I improvise and innovate about the gods I have become your pupil. I would say to him: "If, Meletus, you agree that Euthyphro is wise in these matters, consider me, too, to have the right beliefs and do not bring me to trial. If you do not think so, then prosecute that teacher of mine for corrupting the older men, me and his own father, by teaching me and by exhorting and punishing him. If he is not convinced, does not discharge me, or indicts you instead of me, I shall repeat the same challenge in court.

EUTHYPHRO: Yes by Zeus, Socrates, and, if he should try to indict me, I think I would find his weak spots and the talk in court would be about him rather than about me.

SOCRATES: It is because I realize this that I am eager to become your pupil, my dear friend. I know that other people as well as this Meletus do not even seem to notice you, whereas he sees so sharply and clearly that he indicts me for ungodliness. So tell me now, by Zeus, what you just now maintained you clearly knew: what kind of thing do you say that godliness and ungodliness are, both as regards murder and other things; or is the pious not the same and alike in every action, and the impious the opposite of all that is pious and like itself, and everything that is to be impious presents us with one form or appearance in so far as it is impious.

EUTHYPHRO: Most certainly, Socrates.

SOCRATES: Tell me then, what is the pious, and what the impious, do you say?

EUTHYPHRO: I say that the pious is to do what I am doing now, to prosecute the wrongdoer, be it about murder or temple robbery or anything else, whether the wrongdoer is your father or your mother or anyone else; not to prosecute is impious. And observe, Socrates, that I can quote the law as a great proof that this is so. I have already said to others that such actions are right, not to favour the ungodly, whoever they are. These people themselves believe that Zeus is the best and most just of the gods, yet they agree that he bound his father because he unjustly swallowed his sons, and that he in turn castrated his father for similar reasons. But they are angry with me because I am prosecuting my father for his wrongdoing. They contradict themselves in what they say about the gods and about me.

SOCRATES: Indeed, Euthyphro, this is the reason why I am a defendant in the case, because I find it hard to accept things like that being said about the gods, and it is likely to be the reason why I shall be told I do wrong. Now, however, if you, who have full knowledge of such things, share their opinions, then we must agree with them too, it would seem. For what are we to say, we who agree that we ourselves have no knowledge? Tell me, by the god of friendship, do you really believe these things are true?

EUTHYPHRO: Yes, Socrates, and so are even more surprising things, of which the majority has no knowledge.

SOCRATES: And do you believe that there really is war among the gods, and terrible enmities and battles, and other such things as are told by the poets, and other sacred stories such as are embroidered by good writers and by representations of which the robe of the goddess is adorned when it is carried up to the Acropolis. Are we to say these things are true, Euthyphro?

EUTHYPHRO: Not only these, Socrates, but, as I was saying just now, I will, if you wish, relate many other things about the gods which I know will amaze you.

SOCRATES: I should not be surprised, but you will tell me these at leisure some other time. For now, try to tell me more clearly what I was asking just now, for, my friend, you did not teach me adequately when I asked you what the pious was, but you told me that what you are doing now, to prosecute your father for murder, is pious.

EUTHYPHRO: And I told the truth, Socrates.

SOCRATES: Perhaps. You agree, however, that there are many other pious actions.

EUTHYPHRO: There are.

SOCRATES: Bear in mind then that I did not bid you tell me one or two of the many pious actions but that form itself that makes all pious actions pious, for you agreed that all impious actions are impious and all pious actions pious through one form, or don't you remember?

EUTHYPHRO: I do.

SOCRATES: Tell me then what the form itself is, so that I may look upon it, and using it as a model, say that any action of yours or another's that is of that kind is pious, and if it is not that it is not.

EUTHYPHRO: If that is how you want it, Socrates, that is how I will tell you.

SOCRATES: That is what I want.

EUTHYPHRO: Well then, what is dear to the gods is pious, what is not is impious.

SOCRATES: Splendid, Euthyphro! You have now answered in the way I wanted. Whether your answer is true I do not know yet, but you will obviously show me that what you say is true.

EUTHYPHRO: Certainly.

SOCRATES: Come then, let us examine what we mean. An action or a man dear to the gods is pious, but an action or a man hated by the gods is impious. They are not the same, but opposites, the pious and the impious. Is that not so?

EUTHYPHRO: It is indeed.

SOCRATES: And that seems to be a good statement?

EUTHYPHRO: I think so, Socrates.

SOCRATES: We have also stated that the gods are in a state of discord, that they are at odds with each other, Euthyphro, and that they are at enmity with each other. That too has been said.

EUTHYPHRO: It has.

SOCRATES: What are the subjects of difference that caused hatred and anger? Let us look at it this way. If you and I were to differ about numbers as to which is the greater, would this difference make us enemies and angry with each other, or would we proceed to count and soon resolve our difference about this?

EUTHYPHRO: We would certainly do so.

SOCRATES: Again, if we differed about the larger and the smaller, we would turn to measurement and soon cease to differ.

EUTHYPHRO: That is so.

SOCRATES: And about the heavier and the lighter, we would resort to weighing and be reconciled.

EUTHYPHRO: Of course.

SOCRATES: What subject of difference would make us angry and hostile to each other if we were unable to come to a decision? Perhaps you do not have an answer ready, but examine as I tell you whether these subjects are the just and the unjust, the beautiful and the ugly, the good and the bad. Are these not the subjects of difference about which, when we are unable to come to a satisfactory decision, you and I and other men become hostile to each other whenever we do?

EUTHYPHRO: That is the difference, Socrates, about those subjects.

SOCRATES: What about the gods, Euthyphro? If indeed they have differences, will it not be about these same subjects?

EUTHYPHRO: It certainly must be so.

SOCRATES: Then according to your argument, my good Euthyphro, different gods consider different things to be just, beautiful, ugly, good and bad, for they would not be at odds with one another unless they differed about these subjects, would they?

EUTHYPHRO: You are right.

SOCRATES: And they like what each of them considers beautiful, good, and just, and hate the opposites of these?

EUTHYPHRO: Certainly.

SOCRATES: But you say that the same things are considered just by some gods and unjust by others, and as they dispute about these things they are at odds and at war with each other. Is that not so?

EUTHYPHRO: It is.

SOCRATES: The same things then are loved by the gods and hated by the gods, both god-loved and god-hated.

EUTHYPHRO: It seems likely.

SOCRATES: And the same things would be both pious and impious, according to this argument.

EUTHYPHRO: I'm afraid so.

SOCRATES: So you did not answer my question, you surprising man. I did not ask you what same thing is both pious and impious, and it appears that what is loved by the gods is also hated by them. So it is in no way surprising if your present action, namely punishing your father, may be pleasing to Zeus but displeasing to Kronos and Ouranos, pleasing to Hephaestus but displeasing to Hera, and so with any other gods who differ from each other on this subject.

EUTHYPHRO: I think, Socrates, that on this subject no gods would differ from one another, that whoever has killed anyone unjustly should pay the penalty.

SOCRATES: Well now, Euthyphro, have you ever heard any man maintaining that one who has killed or done anything else unjustly should not pay the penalty?

EUTHYPHRO: They never cease to dispute on this subject, both elsewhere and in the courts, for when they have committed many wrongs they do and say anything to avoid the penalty.

SOCRATES: Do they agree they have done wrong, Euthyphro, and in spite of so agreeing do they nevertheless say they should not be punished?

EUTHYPHRO: No, they do not agree on that point.

SOCRATES: So they do not say or do anything. For they do not venture to say this, or dispute that they must not pay the penalty if they have done wrong, but I think they deny doing wrong. Is that not so?

EUTHYPHRO: That is true.

SOCRATES: Then they do not dispute that the wrongdoer must be punished, but they may disagree as to who the wrongdoer is, what he did and when.

EUTHYPHRO: You are right.

SOCRATES: Do not the gods have the same experience, if indeed they are at odds with each other about the just and the unjust, as your argument maintains? Some assert that they wrong one another, while other deny it, but no one among gods or men ventures to say that the wrongdoer must not be punished.

EUTHYPHRO: Yes, that is true, Socrates, as to the main point.

SOCRATES: And those who disagree, whether men or gods, dispute about each action, if indeed the gods disagree. Some say it is done justly, others unjustly. Is that not so?

EUTHYPHRO: Yes, indeed.

SOCRATES: Come now, my dear Euthyphro, tell me, too, that I may become wiser, what proof you have that all the gods consider that man to have been killed unjustly who became a murderer while in your service, was bound by the master of his victim, and died in his bonds before the one who bound him found out from the seers what was to be done with him, and that it is right for a son to denounce and to prosecute his father on behalf of such a man. Come, try to show me a clear sign that all the gods definitely believe this action to be right. If you can give me adequate proof of this, I shall never cease to extol your wisdom.

EUTHYPHRO: This is perhaps no light task, Socrates, though I could show you very clearly.

SOCRATES: I understand that you think me more dull-witted than the jury, as you will obviously show them that these actions were unjust and that all the gods hate such actions.

EUTHYPHRO: I will show it to them clearly, Socrates, if only they will listen to me.

SOCRATES: They will listen if they think you show them well. But this thought came to me as I was speaking, and I am examining it, saying to myself: "If Euthyphro shows me conclusively that all the gods consider such a death unjust, to what greater extent have I learned from him the nature of piety and impiety? This action would then, it seems, be hated by the gods, but the pious and the impious were not thereby now defined, for what is hated by the gods has also been shown to be loved by them." So I will not insist on this point; let us assume, if you wish, that all the gods consider this unjust and that they all hate it. However, is this the correction we are making in our discussion, that what all the gods hate is impious, and what they all love is pious, and that what some gods love and others hate is neither or both? Is that how you now wish us to define piety and impiety?

EUTHYPHRO: What prevents us from doing so, Socrates?

SOCRATES: For my part nothing, Euthyphro, but you look whether on your part this proposal will enable you to teach me most easily what you promised.

EUTHYPHRO: I would certainly say that the pious is what all the gods love, and the opposite, which all the gods hate, is the impious.

SOCRATES: Then let us again examine whether that is a sound statement, or do we let it pass, and if one of us, or someone else, merely says that this is so, do we accept that it is so? Or should we examine what the speaker means?

EUTHYPHRO: We must examine it, but I certainly think that this is now a fine statement.

SOCRATES: We shall soon know better whether it is. Consider this: Is the pious loved by the gods because it is pious, or is it pious because it is loved by the gods?

EUTHYPHRO: I don't know what you mean, Socrates.

SOCRATES: I shall try to explain more clearly; we speak of something being carried and something carrying, of something being led and something leading, of something being seen and something seeing, and you understand that these things are all different from one another and how they differ?

EUTHYPHRO: I think I do.

SOCRATES: So there is something being loved and something loving, and the loving is a different thing.

EUTHYPHRO: Of course.

SOCRATES: Tell me then whether that which is (said to be) being carried is being carried because someone carries it or for some other reason.

EUTHYPHRO: No, that is the reason.

SOCRATES: And that which is being led is so because someone leads it, and that which is being seen because someone sees it?

EUTHYPHRO: Certainly.

SOCRATES: It is not seen by someone because it is being seen but on the contrary it is being seen because someone sees it, nor is it because it is being led that someone leads it but because someone leads it that it is being led; it is not because it is being seen that someone sees it, but it is being seen because someone sees it; nor does someone carry an object because it is being carried, but it is being carried because someone carries it. Is what I want to say clear, Euthyphro? I want to say this, namely, that if anything comes to be, or is affected, it does not come to be because it is coming to be, but it is coming to be because it comes to be; nor is it affected because it is being affected but because something affects it. Or do you not agree?

EUTHYPHRO: I do.

SOCRATES: What is being loved is either something that comes to be or something that is affected by something?

EUTHYPHRO: Certainly.

SOCRATES: So it is in the same case as the things just mentioned; it is not loved by those who love it because it is being loved, but it is being loved because they love it?

EUTHYPHRO: Necessarily.

SOCRATES: What then do we say about the pious, Euthyphro? Surely that it is loved by all the gods, according to what you say?

EUTHYPHRO: Yes.

SOCRATES: Is it loved because it is pious, or for some other reason?

EUTHYPHRO: For no other reason.

SOCRATES: It is loved then because it is pious, but it is not pious because it is loved?

EUTHYPHRO: Apparently.

SOCRATES: And because it is loved by the gods it is being loved and is dear to the gods?

EUTHYPHRO: Of course.

SOCRATES: The god-beloved is then not the same as the pious, Euthyphro, nor the pious the same as the god-beloved, as you say it is, but one differs from the other.

EUTHYPHRO: How so, Socrates?

SOCRATES: Because we agree that the pious is beloved for the reason that it is pious, but it is not pious because it is loved. Is that not so?

EUTHYPHRO: Yes.

SOCRATES: And that the god-beloved, on the other hand, is so because it is loved by the gods, by the very fact of being loved, but it is not loved because it is god-beloved.

EUTHYPHRO: True.

SOCRATES: But if the god-beloved and the pious were the same, my dear Euthyphro, and the pious were loved because it was pious, then the god-beloved would be loved because it was god-beloved, and if the god-beloved was god-beloved because it was loved by the gods, then the pious would also be pious because it was loved by the gods; but now you see that they are in opposite cases as being altogether different from each other: the one is of a nature to be loved because it is loved, the other is loved because it is of a nature to be loved. I'm afraid, Euthyphro, that when you were asked what piety is, you did not wish to make its nature clear to me, but you told me an affect or quality of it, that the pious has the quality of being loved by all the gods, but you have not yet told me what the pious is. Now, if you will, do not hide things from me but tell me again from the beginning what piety is, whether loved by the gods or having some other quality—we shall not quarrel about that—but be keen to tell me what the pious and the impious are.

EUTHYPHRO: But Socrates, I have no way of telling you what I have in mind, for whatever proposition we put forward goes around and refuses to stay put where we establish it.

SOCRATES: Your statements, Euthyphro, seem to belong to my ancestor, Daedalus. If I were stating them and putting them forward, you would perhaps be making fun of me and say that because of my kinship with him my conclusions in discussion run away and will not stay where one puts them. As these propositions are yours, however, we need some other jest, for they will not stay put for you, as you say yourself.

EUTHYPHRO: I think the same jest will do for our discussion, Socrates, for I am not the one who makes them go round and not remain in the same place; it is you who are the Daedalus; for as far as I am concerned they would remain as they were.

SOCRATES: It looks as if I was cleverer than Daedalus in using my skill, my friend, in so far as he could only cause to move the things he made himself, but I can make other people's move as well as my own. And the smartest part of my skill is that I am clever without wanting to be, for I would rather have my arguments remain unmoved than possess the wealth of Tantalus as well as the cleverness of Daedalus. But enough of this. Since I think you are making unnecessary difficulties, I am eager as you are to find a way to teach me about piety, and do not give up before you do. See whether you think all that is pious is of necessity just.

EUTHYPHRO: I think so.

SOCRATES: And is then all that is just pious? Or is all that is pious just, but not all that is just pious, but some of it is and some is not?

EUTHYPHRO: I do not follow what you are saying, Socrates.

SOCRATES: Yet you are younger than I by as much as you are wiser. As I say, you are making difficulties because of your wealth of wisdom. Pull yourself together, my dear sir, what I am saying is not difficult to grasp. I am saying the opposite of what the poet said who wrote: "You do not wish to name Zeus, who had done it, and who made all things grow, for where there is fear there is also shame." I disagree with the poet. Shall I tell you why?

EUTHYPHRO: Please do.

SOCRATES: I do not think that "where there is fear there is also shame," for I think that many people who fear disease and poverty and many other such things feel fear, but are not ashamed of the things they fear. Do you not think so?

EUTHYPHRO: I do indeed.

SOCRATES: But where there is shame there is also fear. Does anyone feel shame at something who is not also afraid at the same time of a reputation for wickedness?

EUTHYPHRO: He is certainly afraid.

SOCRATES: It is then not right to say "where there is fear there is also shame," but that where there is shame there is also fear, for fear covers a larger area than shame. Shame is a part of fear just as odd is a part of number, with the result that it is not true that where there is number there is also oddness, but that where there is oddness there is also number. Do you follow me?

EUTHYPHRO: Surely.

SOCRATES: This is the kind of thing I was asking before, whether where there is piety there is also justice, but where there is justice there is not always piety, for the pious is a part of justice. Shall we say that, or do you think otherwise?

EUTHYPHRO: No, but like that, for what you say appears to be right.

SOCRATES: See what comes next; if the pious is a part of the just, we must, it seems, find out what part of the just it is. Now if you asked me something of what we mentioned just now, such as what part of number is the even, and what number that is, I would say it is the number that is divisible into two equal, not unequal, parts. Or do you not think so?

EUTHYPHRO: I do.

SOCRATES: Try in this way to tell me what part of the just the pious is, in order to tell Meletus not to wrong us any more and not to indict me for ungodliness, since I have learned from you sufficiently what is godly and pious and what is not.

EUTHYPHRO: I think, Socrates, that the godly and pious is the part of the just that is concerned with the care of the gods, while that concerned with the care of men is the remaining part of justice.

SOCRATES: You seem to me to put that very well, but I still need a bit of information. I do not know yet what you mean by care, for you do not mean it in the sense as the care of other things, as, for example, not everyone knows how to care for horses, but the horse breeder does.

EUTHYPHRO: Yes, I do mean it that way.

SOCRATES: So horse breeding is the care of horses.

EUTHYPHRO: Yes.

SOCRATES: Nor does everyone know how to care for dogs, but the hunter does.

EUTHYPHRO: That is so.

SOCRATES: So hunting is the care of dogs.

EUTHYPHRO: Yes.

SOCRATES: And cattle raising is the care of cattle.

EUTHYPHRO: Quite so.

SOCRATES: While piety and godliness is the care of the gods, Euthyphro. Is that what you mean?

EUTHYPHRO: It is.

SOCRATES: Now care in each case has the same effect; it aims at the good and the benefit of the object cared for, as you can see that horses cared for by horse breeders are benefited and become better. Or do you not think so?

EUTHYPHRO: I do.

SOCRATES: So dogs are benefited by dog breeding, cattle by cattle raising, and so with all the others. Or do you think that care aims to harm the object of its care?

EUTHYPHRO: By Zeus, no.

SOCRATES: It aims to benefit the object of its care.

EUTHYPHRO: Of course.

SOCRATES: Is piety then, which is the care of the gods, also to benefit the gods and make them better? Would you agree that when you do something pious you make some one of the gods better?

EUTHYPHRO: By Zeus, no.

SOCRATES: Nor do I think that this is what you mean—far from it—but that is why I asked you what you meant by the care of gods, because I did not believe you meant this kind of care.

EUTHYPHRO: Quite right, Socrates, that is not the kind of care I mean.

SOCRATES: Very well, but what kind of care of the gods would piety be?

EUTHYPHRO: The kind of care, Socrates, that slaves take of their masters.

SOCRATES: I understand. It is likely to be the service of the gods.

EUTHYPHRO: Quite so.

SOCRATES: Could you tell me to the achievement of what goal service to doctors tends? Is it not, do you think to achieving health?

EUTHYPHRO: I think so.

SOCRATES: What about service to shipbuilders? To what achievement is it directed?

EUTHYPHRO: Clearly, Socrates, to the building of a ship.

SOCRATES: And service to house builders to the building of a house?

EUTHYPHRO: Yes.

SOCRATES: Tell me then, my good sir, to the achievement of what aim does service to the gods tend? You obviously know since you say that you, of all men, have the best knowledge of the divine.

EUTHYPHRO: And I am telling the truth, Socrates.

SOCRATES: Tell me then, by Zeus, what is that excellent aim that the gods achieve, using us as their servants?

EUTHYPHRO: Many fine things, Socrates.

SOCRATES: So do generals, my friend. Nevertheless you could tell me their main concern, which is to achieve victory in war, is it not?

EUTHYPHRO: Of course.

SOCRATES: The farmers too, I think, achieve many fine things, but the main point of their efforts is to produce food from the earth.

EUTHYPHRO: Quite so.

SOCRATES: Well then, how would you sum up the many fine things that the gods achieve?

EUTHYPHRO: I told you a short while ago, Socrates, that it is a considerable task to acquire any precise knowledge of these things, but, to put it simply, I say that if a man knows how to say and do what is pleasing to the gods at prayer and sacrifice, those are pious actions such as preserve both private houses and public affairs of state. The opposite of these pleasing actions are impious and overturn and destroy everything.

SOCRATES: You could tell me in far fewer words, if you were willing, the sum of what I asked, Euthyphro, but you are not keen to teach me, that is clear. You were on the point of doing so, but you turned away. If you had given that answer, I should now have acquired from you sufficient knowledge of the nature of piety. As it is, the lover of inquiry must follow it wherever it may lead him. Once more then, what do you say that piety and the pious are, and also impiety? Are they a knowledge of how to sacrifice and pray?

EUTHYPHRO: They are.

SOCRATES: To sacrifice is to make a gift to the gods, whereas to pray is to beg from the gods?

EUTHYPHRO: Definitely, Socrates.

SOCRATES: It would follow from this statement that piety would be a knowledge of how to give to, and beg from, the gods.

EUTHYPHRO: You understood what I said very well, Socrates.

SOCRATES: That is because I am so desirous of your wisdom, and I concentrate my mind on it, so that no word of yours may fall to the ground. But tell me, what is this service to the gods? You say it is to beg from them and to give to them?

EUTHYPHRO: I do.

SOCRATES: And to beg correctly would be to ask from them things that we need?

EUTHYPHRO: What else?

SOCRATES: And to give correctly is to give them what they need from us, for it would not be skillful to bring gifts to anyone that are in no way needed.

EUTHYPHRO: True, Socrates.

SOCRATES: Piety would then be a sort of trading skill between gods and men?

EUTHYPHRO: Trading yes, if you prefer to call it that.

SOCRATES: I prefer nothing, unless it is true. But tell me, what benefit do the gods derive from the gifts they receive from us? What they give us is obvious to all. There is for us no good that we do not receive from them, but how are they benefited by what they receive from us? Or do we have such an advantage over them in the trade that we receive all our blessings from them and they receive nothing from us?

EUTHYPHRO: Do you suppose, Socrates, that the gods are benefited by what they receive from us?

SOCRATES: What could those gifts from us to the gods be, Euthyphro?

EUTHYPHRO: What else, you think, than honour, reverence, and what I mentioned before, gratitude.

SOCRATES: The pious is then, Euthyphro, pleasing to the gods, but not beneficial or dear to them?

EUTHYPHRO: I think it is of all things most dear to them.

SOCRATES: So the pious is once again what is dear to the gods.

EUTHYPHRO: Most certainly.

SOCRATES: When you say this, will you be surprised if your arguments seem to move about instead of staying put? And will you accuse me of being Daedalus who makes them move, though you are yourself much more skillful than Daedalus and make them go round in a circle? Or do you not realize that our argument has moved around and come again to the same place? You surely remember that earlier the pious and the god-beloved were shown not to be the same but different from each other. Or do you not remember?

EUTHYPHRO: I do.

SOCRATES: Do you then not realize that when you say now that what is dear to the gods is the pious? Is this not the same as the god-beloved? Or is it not?

EUTHYPHRO: It certainly is.

SOCRATES: Either we were wrong when we agreed before, or, if we were right then, we are wrong now.

EUTHYPHRO: That seems to be so.

SOCRATES: So we must investigate again from the beginning what piety is, as I shall not willingly give up before I learn this. Do not think me unworthy, but concentrate your attention and tell the truth. For you know it, if any man does, and I must not let you go, like Proteus, before you tell me. If you had no clear knowledge of piety and impiety you would never have ventured to prosecute your old father for murder on behalf of a servant. For fear of the gods you would have been afraid to take the risk lest you should not be acting rightly, and would have been ashamed before me, but now I know well that you believe you have clear knowledge of piety and impiety. So tell me, my good Euthyphro, and do not hide what you believe.

EUTHYPHRO: Some other time, Socrates, for I am in a hurry now, and it is time for me to go.

SOCRATES: What a thing to do, my friend! By going you have cast me down from a great hope I had, that I would learn from you the nature of the pious and the impious and so escape Meletus' indictment by showing that I had acquired wisdom in divine matters from Euthyphro, and my ignorance would not longer cause me to be careless and inventive about such things, and that I would be better for the rest of my life.

JEAN-PAUL SARTRE

Existentialism

In this section of his essay *Existentialism Is a Humanism,* Sartre explains the fundamental ideas in his version of this philosophy. Human beings must realize that there is no God who dictates what is morally required of them. Instead, morality is a free creation that each individual must fashion for himself or herself.

Jean-Paul Sartre, from *Existentialism Is a Humanism,* translated by Bernard Frechtman (New York: Philosophical Library, 1947), pp. 14–39. Copyright Les Editions Nagel & Briquet Geneva (Switzerland). All rights reserved in all countries.

What is meant by the term *existentialism?* Can it be that what really scares [people] in the doctrine I shall try to present here is that it leaves to man a possibility of choice? To answer this question, we must re-examine it on a strictly philosophical plane.

Actually, it is the least scandalous, the most austere of doctrines. It is intended strictly for specialists and philosophers. Yet it can be easily defined. What complicates matters is that there are two kinds of existentialist; first, those who are Christian, among whom I would include Jaspers and Gabriel Marcel, both Catholic; and on the other hand the atheistic existentialists, among whom I class Heidegger, and then the French existentialists and myself. What they have in common is that they think that existence precedes essence, or, if you prefer, that subjectivity must be the starting point.

Just what does that mean? Let us consider some object that is manufactured, for example, a book or a paper-cutter: here is an object which has been made by an artisan whose inspiration came from a concept. He referred to the concept of what a paper-cutter is and likewise to a known method of production, which is part of the concept, something which is, by and large, a routine. Thus, the paper-cutter is at once an object produced in a certain way and, on the other hand, one having a specific use; and one can not postulate a man who produces a paper-cutter but does not know what it is used for. Therefore, let us say that, for the paper-cutter, essence—that is, the ensemble of both the production routines and the properties which enable it to be both produced and defined—precedes existence. Thus, the presence of the paper-cutter or book in front of me is determined. Therefore, we have here a technical view of the world whereby it can be said that production precedes existence.

When we conceive God as the Creator, He is generally thought of as a superior sort of artisan. Whatever doctrine we may be considering, whether one like that of Descartes or that of Leibniz, we always grant that will more or less follows understanding or, at the very least, accompanies it, and that when God creates He knows exactly what He is creating. Thus, the concept of man in the mind of God is comparable to the concept of paper-cutter in the mind of the manufacturer, and, following certain techniques and a conception, God produces man, just as the artisan, following a definition and a technique, makes a paper-cutter. Thus, the individual man is the realization of a certain concept in the divine intelligence.

In the eighteenth century, the atheism of the *philosophes* discarded the idea of God, but not so much for the notion that essence precedes existence. To a certain extent, this idea is found everywhere; we find it in Diderot, in Voltaire, and even in Kant. Man has a human nature; this human nature, which is the concept of the human, is found in all men, which means that each man is a particular example of a universal concept, man. In Kant, the result of this universality is that the wild-man, the natural man, as well as the bourgeois, are circumscribed by the same definition and have the same basic qualities. Thus, here too the essence of man precedes the historical existence that we find in nature.

Atheistic existentialism, which I represent, is more coherent. It states that if God does not exist, there is at least one being in whom existence precedes essence, a being who exists before he can be defined by any concept, and that this being is man, or, as Heidegger says, human reality. What is meant here by saying that existence precedes essence? It means that, first of all, man exists, turns up, appears on the scene, and, only afterwards, defines himself. If man, as the existentialist conceives him, is indefinable, it is because at first he is nothing. Only afterward will he be something, and he himself will have made what he will be. Thus, there is no human nature, since there is no God to conceive it. Not only is man what he conceives himself to be, but he is also what he wills himself to be after this thrust toward existence.

Man is nothing else but what he makes of himself. Such is the first principle of existentialism. It is also what is called subjectivity, the name we are labeled with when charges are brought against us. But what do we mean by this, if not that man has a greater dignity than a stone or table? For we mean that man first exists, that is, that man first of all is the being who hurls himself toward a future and who is conscious of imagining himself as being in the future. Man is at the start a plan which is aware of itself, rather than a patch of moss, a piece of garbage, or a cauliflower; nothing exists prior to this plan; there is nothing in heaven; man will be what he will have planned to be. Not what he will want to be. Because by the word "will" we generally mean a conscious decision, which is subsequent to what we have already made of ourselves. I may want to belong to a political party, write a book, get married; but all that is only a manifestation of an earlier, more spontaneous choice that is called "will." But if existence really does precede essence, man is responsible for what he is. Thus existentialism's first move is to make every man aware of what he is and to make the full responsibility of his existence rest on him. And when we say that a man is responsible for himself, we do not only mean that he is responsible for his own individuality, but that he is responsible for all men.

The word subjectivism has two meanings, and our opponents play on the two. Subjectivism means, on the one hand, that an individual chooses and makes himself; and, on the other, that it is impossible for man to transcend human subjectivity. The second of these is the essential meaning of existentialism. When we say that man chooses his own self, we mean that every one of us does likewise; but we also mean by that that in making this choice he also chooses all men. In fact, in creating the man that we want to be, there is not a single one of our acts which does not at the same time create an image of man as we think he ought to be. To choose to be this or that is to affirm at the same time the value of what we choose, because we can never choose evil. We always choose the good, and nothing can be good for us without being good for all.

If, on the other hand, existence precedes essence, and if we grant that we exist and fashion our image at one and the same time, the image is valid for everybody and for our whole age. Thus, our responsibility is much greater than we might have supposed, because it involves all mankind. If I am a workingman and choose to join a Christian trade-union rather than be a communist, and if by being a member I want to show that the best thing for man is resignation, that the kingdom of man is not of this world, I am not only involving my own case—I want to be resigned for everyone. As a result, my action has involved all humanity. To take a more individual matter, if I want to marry, to have children; even if this marriage depends solely on my circumstances or passion or wish, I am involving all humanity in monogamy and not merely myself. Therefore, I am responsible for myself and for everyone else. I am creating a certain image of man of my own choosing. In choosing myself, I choose man.

This helps us understand what the actual content is of such rather grandiloquent words as anguish, forlornness, despair. As you will see, it's all quite simple.

First, what is meant by anguish? The existentialists say at once that man is anguish. What that means is this: the man who involves himself and who realizes that he is not only the person he chooses to be, but also a lawmaker who is, at the same time, choosing all mankind as well as himself, can not help escape the feeling of his total and deep responsibility. Of course, there are many people who are not anxious; but we claim that they are hiding their anxiety, that they are fleeing from it. Certainly, many people believe that when they do something, they themselves are the only ones involved, and when someone says to them, "What if everyone acted that way?" they shrug their shoulders and answer, "Everyone doesn't act that way." But really, one should always ask himself, "What would happen if everybody looked at things that way?" There is no escaping this disturbing thought except by a kind of double-dealing. A man who lies and makes excuses for himself by saying "not everybody does that," is someone with an uneasy conscience, because the act of lying implies that a universal value is conferred upon the lie.

Anguish is evident even when it conceals itself. This is the anguish that Kierkegaard called the anguish of Abraham. You know the story: an angel has ordered Abraham to sacrifice his son; if it really were an angel who has come and said, "You are Abraham, you shall sacrifice your son," everything would be all right. But everyone might first wonder, "Is it really an angel, and am I really Abraham? What proof do I have?"

There was a madwoman who had hallucinations; someone used to speak to her on the telephone and give her orders. Her doctor asked her, "Who is it who talks to you?" She answered, "He says it's God." What proof did she really have that it was God? If an angel comes to me, what proof is there that it's an angel? And if I hear voices, what proof is there that they come from heaven and not from hell, or from the subconscious, or a pathological condition? What proves that they are addressed to me? What proof is there that I have been appointed to impose my choice and my conception of man on humanity? I'll never find any proof or sign to convince me of that. If a voice addresses me, it is always for me to decide that this is the angel's voice; if I consider that such an act is a good one, it is I who will choose to say that it is good rather than bad.

Now, I'm not being singled out as an Abraham, and yet at every moment I'm obliged to perform exemplary acts. For every man, everything happens as if all mankind had its eyes fixed on him and were guiding itself by what he does. And every man ought to say to himself, "Am I really the kind of man who has the right to act in such a way that humanity might guide itself by my actions?" And if he does not say that to himself, he is masking his anguish.

There is no question here of the kind of anguish which would lead to quietism, to inaction. It is a matter of a simple sort of anguish that anybody who has had responsibilities is familiar with. For example, when a military officer takes the responsibility for an attack and sends a certain number of men to death, he chooses to do so, and in the main he alone makes the choice. Doubtless, orders come from above, but they are too broad; he interprets them, and on this interpretation depend the lives of ten or fourteen or twenty men. In making a decision he can not help having a certain anguish. All leaders know this anguish. That doesn't keep them from acting; on the contrary, it is the very condition of their action. For it implies that they envisage a number of possibilities, and when they choose one, they realize that it has value only because it is chosen. We shall see that this kind of anguish, which is the kind that existentialism describes, is explained, in addition, by a direct responsibility to the other men whom it involves. It is not a curtain separating us from action, but is part of action itself.

When we speak of forlornness, a term Heidegger was fond of, we mean only that God does not exist and that we have to face all the consequences of this. The existentialist is strongly opposed to a certain kind of secular ethics which would like to abolish God with the least possible expense. About 1880, some French teachers tried to set up a secular ethics which went something like this: God is a useless and costly hypothesis; we are discarding it; but, meanwhile, in order for there to be an ethics, a society, a civilization, it is essential that certain values be taken seriously and that they be considered as having an *a priori* existence. It must be obligatory, *a priori*, to be honest, not to lie, not to beat your wife, to have children, etc., etc. So we're going to try a little device which will make it possible to show that values exist all the same, inscribed in a heaven of ideas, though otherwise God does not exist. In other words— and this, I believe, is the tendency of everything called reformism in France—nothing will be changed if God does not exist. We shall find ourselves with the same norms of honesty, progress, and humanism, and we shall have made of God an outdated hypothesis which will peacefully die off by itself.

The existentialist, on the contrary, thinks it very distressing that God does not exist, because all possibility of finding values in a heaven of ideas disappears along with Him; there can no longer be an *a priori* Good, since there is no infinite and perfect consciousness to think it. Nowhere is it written that the Good exists, that we must be honest, that we must not lie; because the fact is we are on a plane where there are only men. Dostoevsky said, "If God didn't exist, everything would be possible." That is the very starting point of existentialism. Indeed, everything is permissible if God does not exist, and as a result man is forlorn, because neither within him nor without does he find anything to cling to. He can't start making excuses for himself.

If existence really does precede essence, there is no explaining things away by reference to a fixed and given human nature. In other words, there is no determinism, man is free, man is freedom. On the other hand, if God does not exist, we find no values or commands to turn to which legitimize our conduct. So, in the bright realm of values, we have no excuses behind us, nor justification before us. We are alone, with no excuses.

That is the idea I shall try to convey when I say that man is condemned to be free. Condemned, because he did not create himself, yet, in other respects is free; because, once thrown into the world, he is responsible for everything he does. The existentialist does not believe in the power of passion. He will never agree that a sweeping passion is a ravaging torrent which fatally leads a man to certain acts and is therefore an excuse. He thinks that man is responsible for his passion.

The existentialist does not think that man is going to help himself by finding in the world some omen by which to orient himself. Because he thinks that man will interpret the omen to suit himself. Therefore, he thinks that man, with no support and no aid, is condemned every moment to invent man. Ponge, in a very fine article, said, "Man is the future of man." That's exactly it. But if it is taken to mean that this future is recorded in heaven, that God sees it, then it is false, because it would really no longer be a future. If it is taken to mean that, whatever a man may be, there is a future to be forged, a virgin future before him, then this remark is sound. But then we are forlorn.

To give you an example which will enable you to understand forlornness better, I shall cite the case of one of my students who came to see me under the following circumstances: his father was on bad terms with his mother, and, moreover, was inclined to be a collaborationist; his older brother had been killed in the German offensive in 1940, and this young man, with somewhat immature but generous feelings, wanted to avenge him. His mother lived along with him, very much upset by the half-treason of her husband and the death of her older son; the boy was her only consolation.

The boy was faced with the choice of leaving for England and joining the Free French Forces—that is, leaving his mother behind—or remaining with his mother and helping her to carry on. He was fully aware that the woman lived only for him and that his going off—and perhaps his death—would plunge her into despair. He was also aware that every act that he did for his mother's sake was a sure thing, in the sense that it was helping her to carry on, whereas every effort he made toward going off and fighting was an uncertain move which might run aground and prove completely useless; for example, on his way to England he might, while passing through Spain, be detained indefinitely in a Spanish camp; he might reach England or Algiers and be stuck in an office at a desk job. As a result, he was faced with two very different kinds of action: one, concrete, immediate, but concerning only one individual; the other concerned an incomparably vaster group, a national collectivity, but for that very reason was dubious, and might be interrupted en route. And, at the same time, he was wavering between two kinds of ethics. On the one hand, an ethics of sympathy, of personal devotion; on the other, a broader ethics, but one whose efficacy was more dubious. He had to choose between the two.

Who could help him choose? Christian doctrine? Christian doctrine says, "Be charitable, love your neighbor, take the more rugged path, etc., etc." But which is the more rugged path? Whom should he love as a brother? The fighting man or his mother? Which does the greater good, the vague act of fighting in a group, or the concrete one of helping a particular human being to go on living? Who can decide *a priori*? Nobody. No book of ethics can tell him. The Kantian ethics says, "Never treat any person as a means, but as an end." Very well, if I stay with my mother, I'll treat her as an end and not as a means; but by virtue of this very fact, I'm running the risk of treating the people around me who are fighting, as means; and, conversely, if I go to join those who are fighting, I'll be treating them as an end, and, by doing that, I run the risk of treating my mother as a means.

If values are vague, and if they are always too broad for the concrete and specific case that we are considering, the only thing left for us is to trust our instincts. That's what this young man tried to do; and when I saw him, he said, "In the end, feeling is what counts. I ought to choose whichever pushes me in one direction. If I feel that I love my mother enough to sacrifice everything else for her—my desire for vengeance, for action, for adventure—then I'll stay with her. If, on the contrary, I feel that my love for my mother isn't enough, I'll leave.

But how is the value of a feeling determined? What gives his feeling for his mother value? Precisely the fact that he remained with her. I may say that I like so-and-so well enough to sacrifice a certain amount of money for him, but I may say so only if I've done it. I may say "I love my mother well enough to remain with her" if I have remained with her. The only way to determine the value of this affection is, precisely, to perform an act which confirms and defines it. But, since I require this affection to justify my act, I find myself caught in a vicious circle.

On the other hand, Gide has well said that a mock feeling and a true feeling are almost indistinguishable; to decide that I love my mother and will remain with her, or to remain with her by putting on an act, amount somewhat to the same thing. In other words, the feeling is formed by the acts one performs; so, I can not refer to it in order to act upon it. Which means that I can neither seek within myself the true condition which will impel me to act, nor apply to a system of ethics for concepts which will permit me to act. You will say, "At least, he did go to a teacher for advice." But if you seek advice from a priest, for example, you have chosen this priest; you already knew, more or less, just about what advice he was going to give you. In other words, choosing your adviser is involving yourself. The proof of this is that if you are a Christian, you will say, "Consult a priest." But some priests are collaborating, some are just marking time, some are resisting. Which to choose? If the young man chooses a priest who is resisting or collaborating, he has already decided on the kind of advice he's going to get. Therefore, in coming to see me he knew the answer I was going to give him, and I had only one answer to give: "You're free, choose, that is, invent." No general ethics can show you what is to be done; there are no omens in the world. The Catholics will reply, "But there are." Granted—but, in any case, I myself choose the meaning they have.

When I was a prisoner, I knew a rather remarkable young man who was a Jesuit. He had entered the Jesuit order in the following way: he had had a number of very bad breaks; in childhood, his father died, leaving him in poverty, and he was a scholarship student at a religious institutions where he was constantly made to feel that he was being kept out of charity; then, he failed to get any of the honors and distinctions that children like; later on, at about eighteen, he bungled a love affair; finally at twenty-two, he failed in military training, a childish enough matter, but it was the last straw.

This young fellow might well have felt that he had botched everything. It was a sign of something, but of what? He might have taken refuge in bitterness or despair. But he very wisely looked upon all this as a sign that he was not made for secular triumphs, and that only the triumphs of religion, holiness, and faith were open to him.

He saw the hand of God in all this, and so he entered the order. Who can help seeing that he alone decided what the sign meant?

Some other interpretation might have been drawn from this series of setbacks; for example, that he might have done better to turn carpenter or revolutionist. Therefore, he is fully responsible for the interpretation. Forlornness implies that we ourselves choose our being. Forlornness and anguish go together.

As for despair, the term has a very simple meaning. It means that we shall confine ourselves to reckoning only with what depends upon our will, or on the ensemble of probabilities which make our action possible. When we want something, we always have to reckon with probabilities. I may be counting on the arrival of a friend. The friend is coming by rail or street-car; this supposes that the train will arrive on schedule, or that the street-car will not jump the track. I am left in the realm of possibility; but possibilities are to be reckoned with only to the point where by action comports with the ensemble on these possibilities, and no further. The moment the possibilities I am considering are not rigorously involved by my action, I ought to disengage myself from them, because no God, no scheme, can adapt the world and its possibilities to my will. When Descartes said, "Conquer yourself rather than the world," he meant essentially the same thing. . . .

Actually, things will be as man will have decided they are to be. Does that mean that I should abandon myself to quietism? No. First, I should involve myself; then, act on the old saw, "Nothing ventured, nothing gained." Nor does it mean that I shouldn't belong to a party, but rather that I shall have no illusions and shall do what I can. For example, suppose I ask myself, "Will socialization, as such, ever come about?" I know nothing about it. All I know is that I'm going to do everything in my power to bring it about. Beyond that, I can't count on anything. Quietism is the attitude of people who say, "Let others do what I can't do." The doctrine I am presenting is the very opposite of quietism, since it declares, "There is no reality except in action." Moreover, it goes further, since it adds, "Man is nothing else than his plan; he exists only to the extent that he fulfills himself; he is therefore nothing else than the ensemble of his acts, nothing else than his life."

According to this, we can understand why our doctrine horrifies certain people. Because often the only way they can bear their wretchedness is to think, "Circumstances have been against me. What I've been and done doesn't show my true worth. To be sure, I've had no great love, no great friendship, but that's because I haven't met a man or woman who was worthy. The books I've written haven't been very good because I haven't had the proper leisure. I haven't had children to devote myself to because I didn't find a man with whom I could have spent my life. So there remains within me, unused and quite viable, a host of propensities, inclinations, possibilities, that one wouldn't guess from the mere series of things I've done."

Now, for the existentialist there is really no love other than one which manifests itself in a person's being in love. There is no genius other than one which is expressed in works of art; the genius of Proust is the sum of Proust's works; the genius of Racine is his series of tragedies. Outside of that, there is nothing. Why say that Racine could have written another tragedy, when he didn't write it? A man is involved in life, leaves his impress on it, and outside of that there is nothing. To be sure, this may seem a harsh thought to someone whose life hasn't been a success. But on the other hand, it prompts people to understand that reality alone is what counts, that dreams, expectations, and hopes warrant no more than to define a man as a disappointed dream, as miscarried hopes, as vain expectations. In other words, to define him negatively and not positively. However, when we say, "You are nothing else than your life," that does not imply that the artist will be judged solely on the basis of his works of art; a thousand other things will contribute toward summing him up. What we mean is that a man is nothing else than a series of undertakings, that he is the sum, the organization, the ensemble of the relationships which make up these undertakings.

JOHN STUART MILL

Defense of Utilitarianism

This selection is divided into two main sections. In the first, from his book *Utilitarianism*, Mill (1806–1873) explains some of the basic principles of his theory. He states and defends the Greatest Happiness Principle, and explains why he thinks that higher pleasures are better on utilitarian grounds than lower ones. In the second section, from *On Liberty*, Mill tries to show why extensive personal liberties are protected by the utilitarian philosophy.

A. FROM *UTILITARIANISM*

Chapter I: General Remarks

There are few circumstances among those which make up the present condition of human knowledge, more unlike what might have been expected, or more significant of the backward state in which speculation on the most important subjects still lingers, than the little progress which has been made in the decision of the controversy respecting the criterion of right and wrong. From the dawn of philosophy, the question concerning the *summum bonum*, or, what is the same thing, concerning the foundation of morality, has been accounted the main problem in speculative thought, has occupied the most gifted intellects, and divided them into sects and schools, carrying on a vigorous warfare against one another. And after more than two thousand years the same discussions continue, philosophers are still ranged under the same contending banners, and neither thinkers nor mankind at large seem nearer to being unanimous on the subject, than when the young Socrates listened to the old

From *Utilitarianism*, in *The English Utilitarians*, edited by John Plamenatz (Oxford: Basil Blackwell, 1948), pp. 163, 166–167, 169–174, 179–204.

Protagoras, and asserted (if Plato's dialogue be grounded on a real conversation) the theory of utilitarianism against the popular morality of the so-called sophist.

•   •   •

On the present occasion, I shall, without further discussion of the other theories, attempt to contribute something towards the understanding and appreciation of the Utilitarian or Happiness theory, and toward such proof as it is susceptible of. It is evident that this cannot be proof in the ordinary and popular meaning of the term. Questions of ultimate ends are not amenable to direct proof. Whatever can be proved to be good, must be so by being shown to be a means to something admitted to be good without proof. The medical art is proved to be good by its conducing health; but how is it possible to prove that health is good? The art of music is good, for the reason, among others, that it produces pleasure; but what proof is it possible to give that pleasure is good? If, then, it is asserted that there is a comprehensive formula, including all things which are in themselves good, and that whatever else is good, is not so as an end, but as a means, the formula may be accepted or rejected, but is not a subject of what is commonly understood by proof. We are not, however, to infer that its acceptance or rejection must depend on blind impulse, or arbitrary choice. There is a larger meaning of the word proof, in which this question is as amenable to it as any other of the disputed questions of philosophy. The subject is within the cognisance of the rational faculty; and neither does that faculty deal with it solely in the way of intuition. Considerations may be presented capable of determining the intellect either to give or withhold its assent to the doctrine; and this is equivalent to proof.

We shall examine presently of what nature are these considerations; in what manner they apply to the case, and what rational grounds, therefore, can be given for accepting or rejecting the utilitarian formula. But it is a preliminary condition or rational acceptance or rejection, that the formula should be correctly understood. I believe that the very imperfect notion ordinarily formed of its meaning, is the chief obstacle which impedes its reception; and that could it be cleared, even from only the grosser misconceptions, the question would be greatly simplified, and a large proportion of its difficulties removed. Before, therefore, I attempt to enter into the philosophical grounds which can be given for assenting to the utilitarian standard, I shall offer some illustrations of the doctrine itself; with the view of showing more clearly what it is, distinguishing it from what it is not, and disposing of such of the practical objections to it as either originate in, or are closely connected with, mistaken interpretations of its meaning. Having thus prepared the ground, I shall afterwards endeavor to throw such light as I can upon the question, considered as one of philosophical theory.

Chapter II: What Utilitarianism Is

. . . The creed which accepts as the foundation of morals, Utility, or the Greatest Happiness Principle, holds that actions are right in proportion as they tend to promote happiness, wrong as they tend to produce the reverse of happiness. By happiness is intended pleasure, and the absence of pain; by unhappiness, pain, and the privation of pleasure. To give a clear view of the moral standard set up by the theory, much more requires to be said; in particular, what things it includes in the ideas of pain and pleasure; and to what extent this is left an open question. But these supplementary explanations do not affect the theory of life on which this theory of morality is grounded—namely, that pleasure, and freedom from pain, are the only things desirable as ends; and that all desirable things (which are as numerous in the utilitarian as in any other scheme) are desirable either for the pleasure inherent in themselves, or as means to the promotion of pleasure and the prevention of pain.

Now, such a theory of life excites in many minds, and among them in some of the most estimable in feeling and purpose, inveterate dislike. To suppose that life has (as they express it) no higher end than pleasure—no better and nobler object of desire and pursuit—they designate as utterly mean and groveling; as a doctrine worthy only of swine, to whom the followers of Epicurus were, at a very early period, contemptuously likened; and modern holders of the doctrine are occasionally made the subject of equally polite comparisons by its German, French, and English assailants.

When thus attacked, the Epicureans have always answered, that it is not they, but their accusers, who represent human nature in a degrading light; since the accusation supposes human beings to be capable of no pleasures except those of which swine are capable. If this supposition were true, the charge could not be gainsaid, but would then be no longer an imputation; for if the sources of pleasure were precisely the same to human beings and to swine, the rule of life which is good enough for the one would be good enough for the other. The comparison of the Epicurean life to that of beasts is felt as degrading, precisely because a beast's pleasures do not satisfy a human being's conceptions of happiness. Human beings have faculties more elevated than the animal appetites, and when once made conscious of them, do not regard anything as happiness which does not include their gratification. I do not, indeed, consider the Epicureans to have been by any means faultless in drawing out their scheme of consequences from the utilitarian principle. To do this in any sufficient manner, many Stoic, as well as Christian elements require to be included. But there is no known Epicurean theory of life which does not assign to the pleasures of the intellect, of the feelings and imagination, and of the moral sentiments, a much higher value as pleasures than to those of mere sensation. It must be admitted, however, that utilitarian writers in general have placed the superiority of mental over bodily pleasures chiefly in the greater permanency, safety, uncostliness, etc., of the former—that is, in their circumstantial advantages rather than in their intrinsic nature. And on all these points utilitarians have fully proved their case; but they might have taken the other, and, as it may be called, higher ground, with entire consistency. It is quite compatible with the principle of utility to recognise the fact, that some kinds of pleasure are more desirable and more valuable than others. It would be absurd that while, in estimating all other things, quality is considered as well as quantity, the estimation of pleasures should be supposed to depend on quantity alone.

If I am asked, what I mean by difference of quality of pleasures, or what makes one pleasure more valuable than another, merely as a pleasure, except its being greater in amount, there is but one possible answer. Of two pleasures, if there be one to which all or almost all who have experience of both give a decided preference, irrespective of any feeling of moral obligation to prefer it, that is the more desirable pleasure. If one of the two is, by those who are competently acquainted with both, placed so far above the other that they prefer it, even though knowing it to be attended with a greater amount of discontent, and would not resign it for any quantity of the other pleasure which their nature is capable of, we are justified in ascribing to the preferred enjoyment a superiority in quality, so far outweighing quantity as to render it, in comparison, of small account.

Now it is an unquestionable fact that those who are equally acquainted with, and equally capable of appreciating and enjoying, both, do give a most marked preference to the manner of existence which employs their higher faculties. Few human creatures would consent to be changed into any of the lower animals, for a promise of the fullest allowance of a beast's pleasures; no intelligent human being would consent to be a fool, no instructed person would be an ignoramus, no person of feeling and conscience would be selfish and base, even though they should be persuaded that the fool, the dunce, or the rascal is better satisfied with his lot than they are with theirs. They would not resign what they possess more than he for the most complete satisfaction of all the desires which they have in common with him. If they ever fancy they would, it is only in cases of unhappiness so extreme, that to escape from it they would exchange their lot for almost any other, however undesirable in their own eyes. A being of higher faculties requires more to make him happy, is capable of more acute suffering, and certainly accessible to it at more points, than one of an inferior type; but in spite of these liabilities, he can never really wish to sink into what he feels to be a lower grade of existence. We may give what explanation we please of this unwillingness; we may attribute it to pride, a name which is given indiscriminately to some of the most and to some of the least estimable feelings of which mankind are capable: we may refer it to the love of liberty and personal independence, an appeal to which was with the Stoics one of the most effective means for the inculcation of it; to the love of power, or to the love of excitement, both of which do really enter into and contribute to it: but its most appropriate appellation is a sense of dignity, which all human beings possess in one form or other, and in some, though by no means in exact, proportion to their higher faculties, and which is so essential a part of the happiness of those in whom it is strong, that nothing which conflicts with it could be, otherwise than momentarily, an object of desire to them. Whoever supposes that this preference takes place at a sacrifice of happiness—that the superior being, in anything like equal circumstances, is not happier than the inferior—confounds the two very different ideas, of happiness, and content. It is indisputable that the being whose capacities of enjoyment are low, has the greatest chance of having them fully satisfied; and a highly endowed being will always feel that any happiness which he can look for, as the world is constituted, is imperfect. But he can learn to bear its imperfections, if they are at all bearable; and they will not make him envy the being who is indeed unconscious of the imperfections, but only because he feels not at all the good which those imperfections qualify. It is better to be a human being dissatisfied than a pig satisfied; better to be Socrates dissatisfied than a fool satisfied. And if the fool, or the pig, are of a different opinion, it is because they only know their own side of the question. The other party to the comparison knows both sides.

It may be objected, that many who are capable of the higher pleasures, occasionally, under the influence of temptation, postpone them to the lower. But this is quite compatible with a full appreciation of the intrinsic superiority of the higher. Men often, from infirmity of character, make their election for the nearer good, though they know it to be the less valuable; and this no less when the choice is between two bodily pleasures, than when it is between bodily and mental. They pursue sensual indulgences to the injury of health, though perfectly aware that health is the greater good. It may be further objected, that many who begin with youthful enthusiasm for everything noble, as they advance in years sink into indolence and selfishness. But I do not believe that those who undergo this very common change, voluntarily choose the lower description of pleasures in preference to the higher. I believe that before they devote themselves exclusively to the one, they have already become incapable of the other. Capacity for the nobler feelings is in most natures a very tender plant, easily killed, not only by hostile influences, but by mere want of sustenance; and in the majority of young persons it speedily dies away if the occupations to which their position in life has devoted them, and the society into which it has thrown them, are not favourable to keeping that higher capacity in exercise. Men lose their higher aspirations as they lose their intellectual tastes, because they have not time or opportunity for indulging them; and they addict themselves to inferior pleasures, not because they deliberately prefer them, but because they are either the only ones to which they have access, or the only ones which they are any longer capable of enjoying. It may be questioned whether any one who has remained equally susceptible to both classes of pleasures, ever knowingly and calmly preferred the lower; though many, in all ages, have broken down in an ineffectual attempt to combine both.

From this verdict of the only competent judges, I apprehend there can be no appeal. On a question which is the best worth having of two pleasures, or which of two modes of existence is the most grateful to the feelings, apart from its moral attributes and from its consequences, the judgment of those who are qualified by knowledge of both, or, if they differ, that of the majority among them, must be admitted as final. And there needs be the less hesitation to accept this judgment respecting the quality of pleasures, since there is no other tribunal to be referred to even on the question of quantity. What means are there of determining which is the acutest of two pains, or the intensest of two pleasurable sensations, except the general suffrage of those who are familiar with both? Neither pains nor pleasures are homogeneous, and pain is always heterogeneous with pleasure. What is there to decide whether a particular pleasure is worth purchasing at the cost of a particular pain, except the feelings and judgment of the experienced? When, therefore, those feelings and judgment declare the pleasures derived from the higher faculties to be preferable *in kind,* apart from the question of intensity, to those of which the animal nature, disjoined from the higher faculties, is susceptible, they are entitled on this subject to the same regard.

I have dwelt on this point, as being a necessary part of a perfectly just conception of Utility or Happiness, considered as the directive rule of human conduct. But it is by no means an indispensable condition to the acceptance of the utilitarian standard; for that standard is not the agent's own greatest happiness, but the greatest amount of happiness altogether; and if it may possibly be doubted whether a noble character is always the happier for its nobleness, there can be no doubt that it makes other people happier, and that the world in general is immensely a gainer by it. Utilitarianism, therefore, could only attain its end by the general cultivation of nobleness of character, even if each individual were only benefited by the nobleness of others, and his own, so far as happiness is concerned, were a sheer deduction from the benefit. But the bare enunciation of such an absurdity as this last, renders refutation superfluous.

According to the Greatest Happiness Principle, as above explained, the ultimate end, with reference to and for the sake of which all other things are desirable (whether we are considering our own good or that of other people), is an existence exempt as far as possible from pain, and as rich as possible in enjoyments, both in point of quantity and quality; the test of quality, and the rule for measuring it against quantity, being the preference felt by those who in their opportunities of experience, to which must be added their habits of self-consciousness and self-observation, are best furnished with the means of comparison. This, being, according to the utilitarian opinion, the end of human action, is necessarily also the standard of morality; which may accordingly be defined, the rules and precepts for human conduct, by the observance of which an existence such as has been described might be, to the greatest extent possible, secured to all mankind; and not to them only, but, so far as the nature of things admit, to the whole sentient creation.

•   •   •

I must again repeat, what the assailants of utilitarianism seldom have the justice to acknowledge, that the happiness which forms the utilitarian standard of what is right in conduct, is not the agent's own happiness, but that of all concerned. As between his own happiness and that of others, utilitarianism requires him to be as strictly impartial as a disinterested and benevolent spectator. In the golden rule of Jesus of Nazareth, we read the complete spirit of the ethics of utility. To do as you would be done by, and to love your neighbour as yourself, constitute the ideal perfection of utilitarian morality. As the means of making the nearest approach to this ideal, utility would enjoin, first, that laws and social arrangements should place the happiness, or (as speaking practically it may be called) the interest, of every individual, as nearly as possible in harmony with the interest of the whole; and secondly, that education and opinion, which have so vast a power over human character, should so use that power as to establish in the mind of every individual an indissoluble association between his own happiness and the good of the whole; especially between his own happiness and the practice of such modes of conduct, negative and positive, as regard for the universal happiness prescribes; so that not only he may be unable to conceive the possibility of happiness to himself, consistently with conduct opposed to the general good, but also that a direct impulse to promote the general good may be in every individual one of the habitual motives of action, and the sentiments connected therewith may fill a large and prominent place in every human being's sentient existence. If the impugners of the utilitarian morality represented it to their own minds in this its true character, I know not what recommendation possessed by any other morality they could possibly affirm to be wanting to it; what more beautiful or more exalted developments of human nature any other ethical system can be supposed to foster, or what springs of action, not accessible to the utilitarian, such systems rely on for giving effect to their mandates.

The objectors to utilitarianism cannot always be charged with representing it in a discreditable light. On the contrary, those among them who entertain anything like a just idea of its disinterested character, sometimes find fault with its standard as being too high for humanity. They say it is exacting too much to require that people shall always act from the inducement of promoting the general interests of society. But this is to mistake the very meaning of a standard of morals, and confound the rule of action with the motive of it. It is the business of ethics to tell us what are our duties, or by what test we may know them; but no system of ethics requires that the sole motive of all we do shall be a feeling of duty; on the contrary, ninety-nine hundredths of all our actions are done from other motives, and rightly so done, if the rule of duty does not condemn them. It is the most unjust to utilitarianism that this particular misapprehension should be made a ground of objection to it, inasmuch as utilitarian moralists have gone beyond almost all others in affirming that the motive has nothing to do with the morality of the action, though much with the worth of the agent. He who saves a fellow creature from drowning does what is morally right, whether his motive be duty, or the hope of being paid for his trouble; he who betrays the friend that trusts him, is guilty of a crime, even if his object be to serve another friend to whom he is under greater obligations. But to speak only of actions done from the motive of duty, and in direct obedience to principle: it is a misapprehension of the utilitarian mode of thought, to conceive it as implying that people should fix their minds upon so wide a generality as the world, or society at large. The great majority of good actions are intended not for the benefit of the world, but for that of individuals, of which the good of the world is made up; and the thoughts of the most virtuous man need not on these occasions travel beyond the particular persons concerned, except so far as is necessary to assure himself that in benefiting them he is not violating the rights, that is, the legitimate and authorized expectations, of any one else. The multiplication of happiness is, according to the utilitarian ethics, the object of virtue: the occasions on which any person (except one in a thousand) has it in his power to do this on an extended scale, in other words to be a public benefactor, are but exceptional; and on these occasions alone is he called on to consider public utility; in every other case, private utility, the interest or happiness of some few persons, is all he has to attend to. Those alone the influence of whose actions extends to society in general, need concern themselves habitually about so large an object. In the case of abstinence indeed—of things which people forbear to do from moral considerations, though the consequences in the particular case might be beneficial—it would be unworthy of an intelligent agent not to be consciously aware that the action is of a class which, if practised generally, would be generally injurious, and that this is the ground of the obligation to abstain from it. The amount of regard for the public interest implied in this recognition, is no greater than is demanded by every system of morals, for they all enjoin to abstain from whatever is manifestly pernicious to society.

The same considerations dispose of another reproach against the doctrine of utility, founded on a still grosser misconception of the purpose of a standard of morality, and of the very meaning of the words right and wrong. It is often affirmed that utilitarianism renders men cold and unsympathising; that it chills their moral feelings towards individuals; that it makes them regard only the dry and hard consideration of the consequences of actions, not taking into their moral estimate the qualities from which those actions emanate. If the assertion means that they do not allow their judgment respecting the rightness or wrongness of an action to be influenced by their opinion of the qualities of the person who does it, this is a complaint not against utilitarianism, but against having any standard of morality at all; for certainly no known ethical standard decides an action to be good or bad because it is done by a good or bad man, still less because done by an amiable, a brave, or a benevolent man, or the contrary. These considerations are relevant, not to the estimation of actions, but of persons; and there is nothing in the utilitarian theory inconsistent with the fact that there are other things which interest us in persons besides the rightness and wrongness of their actions. The Stoics, indeed, with the paradoxical misuse of language which was part of their system, and by which they strove to raise themselves above all concern about anything but virtue, were fond of saying, that he who has that has everything; that he, and only he, is rich, is beautiful, is a king. But no claim of this description is made for the virtuous man by the utilitarian doctrine. Utilitarians are quite aware that there are other desirable possessions and qualities besides virtue, and are perfectly willing to allow to all of them their full worth. They are also aware that a right action does not necessarily indicate a virtuous character, and that actions which are blamable, often proceed from qualities entitled to praise. When this is apparent in any particular case, it modifies their estimation, not certainly of the act, but of the agent. I grant that they are, notwithstanding, of opinion, that in the long run the best proof of a good character is good actions; and resolutely refuse to consider any mental disposition as good, of which the predominant tendency is to produce bad conduct. This makes them unpopular with many people; but it is an unpopularity which they must share with every one who regards the distinction between right and wrong in a serious light; and the reproach is not one which a conscientious utilitarian need be anxious to repel.

If no more be meant by the objection than that many utilitarians look on the morality of actions, as measured by the utilitarian standard, with too exclusive a regard, and do not lay sufficient stress upon the other beauties of character which go towards making a human being lovable or admirable, this may be admitted. Utilitarians who have cultivated their moral feelings, but not their sympathies nor their artistic perceptions, do fall into this mistake; and so do all other moralists under the same conditions. What can be said in excuse for other moralists is equally available for them, namely, that, if there is to be any error, it is better that it should be on that side. As a matter of fact, we may affirm that among utilitarians as among adherents of other systems, there is every imaginable degree of rigidity and of laxity in the application of their standard: some are even puritanically rigorous, while others are as indulgent as can possibly be desired by sinner or by sentimentalist. But on the whole, a doctrine which brings prominently forward the interest that mankind have in the repression and prevention of conduct which violates the moral law, is likely to be inferior to no other in turning the sanctions of opinion against such violations. It is true, the question, What does violate the moral law? is one on which those who recognize different standards of morality are likely now and then to differ. But difference of opinion on moral questions was not first introduced into the world by utilitarianism, while that doctrine does supply, if not always an easy, at all events a tangible and intelligible mode of deciding such differences.

It may not be superfluous to notice a few more of the common misapprehensions of utilitarian ethics, even those which are so obvious and gross that it might appear impossible for any person of candour and intelligence to fall into them; since persons, even of considerable mental endowments, often give themselves so little trouble to understand the bearings of any opinion against which they entertain a prejudice, and men are in general so little conscious of this voluntary ignorance as a defect, that the vulgarest misunderstandings of ethical doctrines are continually met with the deliberate writings of persons of the greatest pretensions both to high principle and to philosophy. We not uncommonly hear the doctrine of utility inveighed against as a *godless* doctrine. If it be necessary to say anything at all against so mere an assumption, we may say that the question depends upon what idea we have formed of the moral character of the Deity. If it be a true belief that God desires, above all things, the happiness of his creatures, and that this was his purpose in their creation, utility is not only not a godless doctrine, but more profoundly religious than any other. If it be meant that utilitarianism does not recognise the revealed will of God as the supreme law of morals, I answer, that a utilitarian who believes in the perfect goodness and wisdom of God, necessarily believes that whatever God has thought fit to reveal on the subject of morals, must fulfil the requirements of utility in a supreme degree. But others besides utilitarians have been of opinion that the Christian revelation was intended, and is fitted, to inform the hearts and minds of mankind with a spirit which should enable them to find for themselves what is right, and incline them to do it when found, rather than to tell them, except in a very general way, what it is; and that we need a doctrine of ethics, carefully followed out, to *interpret* to us the will of God. Whether this opinion is correct or not, it is superfluous here to discuss; since whatever aid religion, either natural or revealed, can afford to ethical investigation, is as open to the utilitarian moralist as to any other. He can use it as the testimony of God to the usefulness or hurtfulness of any given course of action, by as good a right as others can use it for the indication of a transcendental law, having no connexion with usefulness or with happiness.

Again, Utility is often summarily stigmatised as an immoral doctrine by giving it the name of Expediency, and taking advantage of the popular use of that term to contrast it with Principle. But the Expedient, in the sense in which it is opposed to the Right, generally means that which is expedient for the particular interest of the agent himself; as when a minister sacrifices the interests of his country to keep himself in place. When it means anything better than this, it means that which is expedient for some immediate object, some temporary purpose, but which violates a rule whose observance is expedient in a much higher degree. The Expedient, in this sense, instead of being the same thing with the useful, is a branch of the hurtful. Thus, it would often be expedient, for the purpose of getting over some momentary embarrassment, or attaining some object immediately useful to ourselves or others, to tell a lie. But inasmuch as the cultivation in ourselves of a sensitive feeling on the subject of veracity, is one of the most useful, and the enfeeblement of that feeling one of the most hurtful, things to which our conduct can be instrumental; and inasmuch as any, even unintentional, deviation from truth, does that much towards weakening the trustworthiness of human assertion, which is not only the principal support of all present social well-being, but the insufficiency of which does more than any one thing that can be named to keep back civilisation, virtue, everything on which human happiness on the largest scale depends; we feel that the violation, for a present advantage, of a rule of such transcendant expediency, is not expedient, and that he who, for the sake of a convenience to himself or to some other individual, does what depends on him to deprive mankind of the good, and inflict upon them the evil, involved in the greater or less reliance which they can place in each other's word, acts the part of one of their worst enemies. Yet that even this rule, sacred as it is, admits of possible exceptions, is acknowledged by all moralists; the chief of which is when the withholding of some fact (as of information from a malefactor, or of bad news from a person dangerously ill) would save an individual (especially an individual other than oneself) from great and unmerited evil, and when the withholding can only be effected by denial. But in order that the exception may not extend itself beyond the need, and may have the least possible effect in weakening reliance on veracity, it ought to be recognised, and, if possible, its limits defined; and if the principle of utility is good for anything, it must be good for weighing these conflicting utilities against one another, and marking out the region within which one or the other preponderates.

Again, defenders of utility often find themselves called upon to reply to such objections as this—that there is not time, previous to action, for calculating and weighing the effects of any line of conduct on the general happiness. This is exactly as if any one were to say that it is impossible to guide our conduct by Christianity, because there is not time, on every occasion on which anything has to be done, to read through the Old and New Testaments. The answer to the objection is, that there has been ample time, namely, the whole past duration of the human species. During all that time, mankind have been learning by experience the tendencies of actions; on which experience all the prudence, as well as all the morality of life, are dependent. People talk as if the commencement of this course of experience had hitherto been put off, and as if, at the moment when some man feels tempted to meddle with the property or life of another, he had to begin considering for the first time whether murder and theft are injurious to human happiness. Even then I do not think that he would find the question very puzzling; but, at all events, the matter is now done to his hand. It is truly a whimsical supposition that, if mankind were agreed in considering utility to be the test of morality, they would remain without any agreement as to what *is* useful, and would take no measures for having their notions on the subject taught to the young, and enforced by law and opinion. There is no difficulty in proving any ethical standard whatever to work ill, if we suppose universal idiocy to be conjoined with it; but on any hypothesis short of that, mankind must by this time have acquired positive beliefs as to the effects of some actions on their happiness; and the beliefs which have thus come down are the rules of morality for the multitude, and for the philosopher until he has succeeded in finding better. That philosophers might easily do this, even now, on many subjects; that the received code of ethics is by no means of divine right; and that mankind have still much to learn as to the effects of actions on the general happiness, I admit, or rather, earnestly maintain. The corollaries from the principle of utility, like the precepts of every practical art, admit of indefinite improvement, and, in a progressive state of the human mind, their improvement is perpetually going on. But to consider the rules of morality as improvable, is one thing; to pass over the intermediate generalisations entirely, and endeavour to test each individual action directly by the first principle, is another. It is a strange notion that the acknowledgment of a first principle is inconsistent with the admission of secondary ones. To inform a traveller respecting the place of his ultimate destination, is not to forbid the use of landmarks and direction-posts on the way. The proposition that happiness is the end and aim of morality does not mean that no road ought to be laid down to that goal, or that persons going thither should not be advised to take one direction rather than another. Men really ought to leave off talking a kind of nonsense on this subject, which they would neither talk nor listen to on other matters of practical concernment. Nobody argues that the art of navigation is not founded on astronomy, because sailors cannot wait to calculate the Nautical Almanack. Being rational creatures, they go to sea with it ready calculated; and all rational creatures go out upon the sea of life with their minds made up on the common questions of right and wrong, as well as on many of the far more difficult questions of wise and foolish. And this, as long as foresight is a human quality, it is to be presumed they will continue to do. Whatever we adopt as the fundamental principle of morality, we require subordinate principles to apply it by; the impossibility of doing without them, being common to all systems, can afford no argument against any one in particular; but gravely to argue as if no such secondary principles could be had, and as if mankind had remained till now, and always must remain, without drawing any general conclusions from the experience of human life, is as high a pitch, I think, as absurdity has ever reached in philosophical controversy.

The remainder of the stock arguments against utilitarianism mostly consist in laying to its charge the common infirmities of human nature, and the general difficulties which embarrass conscientious persons in shaping their course through life. We are told that a utilitarian will be apt to make his own particular case an exception to moral rules, and, when under temptation, will see a utility in the breach of a rule, greater than he will see in its observance. But is utility the only creed which is able to furnish us with excuses for evil doing, and means of cheating our own conscience? They are afforded in abundance by all doctrines which recognise as a fact in morals the existence of conflicting considerations; which all doctrines do, that have been believed by sane persons. It is not the fault of any creed, but of the complicated nature of human affairs, that rules of conduct cannot be so framed as to require no exceptions, and that hardly any kind of action can safely be laid down as either always obligatory or always condemnable. There is no ethical creed which does not temper the rigidity of its laws, by giving a certain latitude, under the moral responsibility of the agent, for accommodation to peculiarities of circumstances; and under every creed, at the opening thus made, self-deception and dishonest casuistry get in. There exists no moral system under which there do not arise unequivocal cases of conflicting obligations. These are the real difficulties, the knotty points both in the theory of ethics, and in the conscientious guidance of personal conduct. They are overcome practically, with greater or with less success, according to the intellect and virtue of the individual; but it can hardly be pretended that any one will be the less qualified for dealing with them, from possessing an ultimate standard to which conflicting rights and duties can be referred. If utility is the ultimate source of moral obligations, utility may be invoked to decide between them when their demands are incompatible. Though the application of the standard may be difficult, it is better than none at all; while in other systems, the moral laws all claiming independent authority, there is no common umpire entitled to interfere between them; their claims to precedence one over another rest on little better than sophistry, and unless determined, as they generally are, by the unacknowledged influence of considerations of utility, afford a free scope for the action of personal desires and partialities. We must remember that only in these cases of conflict between secondary principles is it requisite that first principles should be appealed to. There is no case of moral obligation in which some secondary principle is not involved; and if only one, there can seldom be any real doubt which one it is, in the mind of any person by whom the principle itself is recognised.

Chapter III: Of the Ultimate Sanction of the Principle of Utility

The question is often asked, and properly so, in regard to any supposed moral standard—What is its sanction? what are the motives to obey it? or more specifically, what is the source of its obligation? whence does it derive its binding force? It is a necessary part of moral philosophy to provide the answer to this question; which, though frequently assuming the shape of an objection to the utilitarian morality, as if it had some special applicability to that above others, really arises in regard to all standards. It arises, in fact, whenever a person is called on to *adopt* a standard, or refer morality to any basis on which he has not been accustomed to rest it. For the customary morality, that which education and opinion have consecrated, is the only one which presents itself to the mind with the feeling of being *in itself* obligatory; and when a person is asked to believe that this morality *derives* its obligation from some general principle round which custom has not thrown the same halo, the assertion is to him a paradox; the supposed corollaries seem to have a more binding force than the original theorem; the superstructure seems to stand better without, than with, what is represented as its foundation. He says to himself, I feel that I am bound not to rob or murder, betray or deceive; but why am I bound to promote the general happiness? If my own happiness lies in something else, why may I not give that the preference?

If the view adopted by the utilitarian philosophy of the nature of the moral sense be correct, this difficulty will always present itself, until the influences which form moral character have taken the same hold of the principle which they have taken of some of the consequences—until, by the improvement of education, the feeling of unity with our fellow-creatures shall be (what it cannot be denied that Christ intended it to be) as deeply rooted in our character, and to our own consciousness as completely a part of our nature, as the horror of crime is in an ordinarily well brought up young person. In the meantime, however, the difficulty has no peculiar application to the doctrine of utility, but is inherent in every attempt to analyse morality and reduce it to principles; which, unless the principle is already in men's minds invested with as much sacredness as any of its applications, always seems to divest them of a part of their sanctity.

The principle of utility either has, or there is no reason why it might not have, all the sanctions which belong to any other system or morals. Those sanctions are either external or internal. Of the external sanctions it is not necessary to speak at any length. They are, the hope of favour and the fear of displeasure, from our fellow-creatures or from the Ruler of the Universe along with whatever we may have of sympathy or affection for them, or of love and awe of Him, inclining us to do His will independently of selfish consequences. There is evidently no reason why all these motives for observance should not attach themselves to the utilitarian morality, as completely and as powerfully as to any other. Indeed, those of them which refer to our fellow-creatures are sure to do so, in proportion to the amount of general intelligence; for whether there be any other ground of moral obligation than the general happiness or not, men do desire happiness; and however imperfect may be their own practice, they desire and commend all conduct in others towards themselves, by which they think their happiness is promoted. With regard to the religious motive, if men believe, as most profess to do, in the goodness of God, those who think that conduciveness to the general happiness is the essence, or even only the criterion of good, must necessarily believe that it is also that which God approves. The whole force therefore of external reward and punishment, whether physical or moral, and whether proceeding from God or from our fellow men, together with all that the capacities of human nature admit of disinterested devotion to either, become available to enforce the utilitarian morality, in proportion as that morality is recognised; and the more powerfully, the more the appliances of education and general cultivation are bent to the purpose.

So far as to external sanctions. The internal sanction of duty, whatever our standard of duty may be, is one and the same—a feeling in our own mind; a pain, more or less intense, attendant on violation of duty, which in properly cultivated moral natures rises, in the more serious cases, into shrinking from it as an impossibility. This feeling, when disinterested, and connecting itself with the pure idea of duty, and not with some particular form of it, or with any of the merely accessory circumstances, is the essence of Conscience; though in that complex phenomenon as it actually exists, the simple fact is in general all encrusted over with collateral associations, derived from sympathy, from love, and still more from fear; from all the forms of religious feeling; from the recollections of childhood and of all our past life; from self-esteem, desire of the esteem of others, and occasionally even self-abasement. This extreme complication is, I apprehend, the origin of the sort of mystical character which, by a tendency of the human mind of which there are many other examples, is apt to be attributed to the idea of moral obligation, and which leads people to believe that the idea cannot possibly attach itself to any other objects than those which, by a supposed mysterious law, are found in our present experience to excite it. Its binding force, however, consists in the existence of a mass of feeling which must be broken through in order to do what violates our standard of right, and which, if we do nevertheless violate that standard, will probably have to be encountered afterwards in the form of remorse. Whatever theory we have of the nature or origin of conscience, this is what essentially constitutes it.

The ultimate sanction, therefore, of all morality (external motives apart) being a subjective feeling in our own minds, I see nothing embarrassing to those whose standard is utility, in the question, what is the sanction of that particular standard? We may answer, the same as of all other moral standards—the conscientious feelings of mankind. Undoubtedly this sanction has no binding efficacy on those who do not possess the feelings it appeals to; but neither will these persons be more obedient to any other moral principle than to the utilitarian one. On them morality of any kind has no hold but through the external sanctions. Meanwhile the feelings exist, a fact in human nature, the reality of which, and the great power with which they are capable of acting on those in whom they have been duly cultivated, are proved by experience. No reason has ever been shown why they may not be cultivated to as great intensity in connexion with the utilitarian, as with any other rule of morals.

There is, I am aware, a disposition to believe that a person who sees in moral obligation a transcendental fact, an objective reality belonging to the province of "Things in themselves," is likely to be more obedient to it than one who believes it to be entirely subjective, having its seat in human consciousness only. But whatever a person's opinion may be on this point of Ontology, the force he is really urged by is his own subjective feeling, and is exactly measured by its strength. No one's belief that duty is an objective reality is stronger than the belief that God is so; yet the belief in God, apart from the expectation of actual reward and punishment, only operates on conduct through, and in proportion to, the subjective religious feeling. The sanction, so far as it is disinterested, is always in the mind itself; and the notion therefore of the transcendental moralists must be, that this sanction will not exist *in* the mind unless it is believed to have its root out of the mind; and that if a person is able to say to himself, This which is restraining me, and which is called my conscience, is only a feeling in my own mind, he may possibly draw the conclusion that when the feeling ceases the obligation ceases, and that if he find the feeling inconvenient, he may disregard it, and endeavour to get rid of it. But is this danger confined to the utilitarian morality? Does the belief that moral obligation has its seat outside the mind make the feeling of it too strong to be got rid of? The fact is so far otherwise, that all moralists admit and lament the ease with which, in the generality of minds, conscience can be silenced or stifled. The question, Need I obey my conscience? is quite as often put to themselves by persons who never heard of the principle of utility, as by its adherents. Those whose conscientious feelings are so weak as to allow of their asking this question, if they answer it affirmatively, will not do so because they believe in the transcendental theory, but because of the external sanctions.

It is not necessary, for the present purpose, to decide whether the feeling of duty is innate or implanted. Assuming it to be innate, it is an open question to what objects it naturally attaches itself; for the philosophic supporters of that theory are now agreed that the intuitive perception is of principles of morality and not of the details. If there be anything innate in the matter, I see no reason why the feeling which is innate should not be that of regard to the pleasures and pains of others. If there is any principle of morals which is intuitively obligatory, I should say it must be that. If so, the intuitive ethics would coincide with the utilitarian, and there would be no further quarrel between them. Even as it is, the intuitive moralists, though they believe that there are other intuitive moral obligations, do already believe this to be one; for they unanimously hold that a large *portion* of morality turns upon the consideration due to the interests of our fellow-creatures. Therefore, if the belief in the transcendental origin of moral obligation gives any additional efficacy to the internal sanction, it appears to me that the utilitarian principle has already the benefit of it.

On the other hand, if, as is my own belief, the moral feelings are not innate, but acquired, they are not for that reason the less natural. It is natural to man to speak, to reason, to build cities, to cultivate the ground, though these are acquired faculties. The moral feelings are not indeed a part of our nature, in the sense of being in any perceptible degree present in all of us; but this, unhappily, is a fact admitted by those who believe the most strenuously in their transcendental origin. Like the other acquired capacities above referred to, the moral faculty, if not a part of our nature, is a natural outgrowth from it; capable, like them, in a certain small degree, of springing up spontaneously; and susceptible of being brought by cultivation to a high degree of development. Unhappily it is also susceptible, by a sufficient use of the external sanctions and of the force of early impressions, of being cultivated in almost any direction: so that there is hardly anything so absurd or so mischievous that it may not, by means of these influences, be made to act on the human mind with all the authority of conscience. To doubt that the same potency might be given by the same means to the principle of utility, even if it had no foundation in human nature, would be flying in the face of all experience.

But moral associations which are wholly of artificial creation, when intellectual culture goes on, yield by degrees to the dissolving force of analysis; and if the feeling of duty, when associated with utility, would appear equally arbitrary; if there were no leading department of our nature, no powerful class of sentiments, with which that association would harmonise, which would make us feel it congenial, and incline us not only to foster it in others (for which we have abundant interested motives), but also to cherish it in ourselves; if there were not, in short, a natural basis of sentiment for utilitarian morality, it might well happen that this association also, even after it had been implanted by education, might be analysed away.

But there *is* this basis of powerful natural sentiment; and this it is which, when once the general happiness is recognised as the ethical standard, will constitute the strength of the utilitarian morality. This firm foundation is that of the social feelings of mankind; the desire to be in unity with our fellow creatures, which is already a powerful principle in human nature, and happily one of those which tend to become stronger, even without express inculcation, from the influences of advancing civilisation. The social state is at once so natural, so necessary, and so habitual to man, that, except in some unusual circumstances or by an effort of voluntary abstraction, he never conceives himself otherwise than as a member of a body; and this association is riveted more and more, as mankind are further removed from the stage of savage independence. Any condition, therefore, which is essential to a state of society, becomes more and more an inseparable part of every person's conception of the state of things which he is born into, and which is the destiny of a human being. Now, society between human beings, except in the relation of master and slave, is manifestly impossible on any other footing than that the interests of all are to be consulted. Society between equals can only exist on the understanding that the interests of all are to be regarded equally. And since in all states of civilisation, every person, except an absolute monarch, has equals, every one is obliged to live on these terms with somebody; and in every age some advance is made towards a state in which it will be impossible to live permanently on other terms with anybody. In this way people grow up unable to conceive as possible to them a state of total disregard of other people's interests. They are under a necessity of conceiving themselves as at least abstaining from all the grosser injuries, and (if only for their own protection) living in a state of constant protest against them. They are also familiar with the fact of co-operating with others, and proposing to themselves a collective, not an individual interest as the aim (at least for the time being) of their actions. So long as they are co-operating, their ends are identified with those of others; there is at least a temporary feeling that the interests of others are their own interests. Not only does all strengthening of social ties, and all healthy growth of society, give to each individual a stronger personal interest in practically consulting the welfare of others; it also leads him to identify his *feelings* more and more with their good, or at least with an even greater degree of practical consideration for it. He comes, as though instinctively, to be conscious of himself as a being who *of course* pays regard to others. The good of others becomes to him a thing naturally and necessarily to be attended to, like any of the physical conditions of our existence. Now, whatever amount of this feeling a person has, he is urged by the strongest motives both of interest and of sympathy to demonstrate it, and to the utmost of his power encourage it in others; and even if he has none of it himself, he is as greatly interested as any one else that others should have it. Consequently the smallest germs of the feeling are laid hold of and nourished by the contagion of sympathy and the influences of education; and a complete web of corroborative association is woven round it, by the powerful agency of the external sanctions. This mode of conceiving ourselves and human life, as civilisation goes on, is felt to be more and more natural. Every step in political improvement renders it more so, by removing the sources of opposition of interest, and leveling those inequalities of legal privilege between individuals or classes, owing to which there are large portions of mankind whose happiness it is still practicable to disregard. In an improving state of the human mind, the influences are constantly on the increase, which tend to generate in each individual a feeling of unity with all the rest; which, if perfect, would make him never think of, or desire, any beneficial condition for himself, in the benefits of which they are not included. If we now suppose this feeling of unity to be taught as a religion, and the whole force of education, of institutions, and of opinion, directed, as it once was in the case of religion, to make every person grow up from infancy surrounded on all sides both by the profession and the practice of it, I think that no one, who can realise this conception, will feel any misgiving about the sufficiency of the ultimate sanction for the Happiness morality. To any ethical student who finds the realisation difficult, I recommend, as a means of facilitating it, the second of M. Comte's two principal works, the *Traité de politique positive*. I entertain the strongest objections to the system of politics and morals set forth in that treatise; but I think it has superabundantly shown the possibility of giving to the service of humanity, even without the aid of belief in a Providence, both the psychological power and the social efficacy of a religion; making it take hold of human life, and colour all thought, feeling, and action, in a manner of which the greatest ascendancy ever exercised by any religion may be but a type and foretaste; and of which the danger is, not that it should be insufficient, but that it should be so excessive as to interfere unduly with human freedom and individuality.

Neither is it necessary to the feeling which constitutes the binding force of the utilitarian morality on those who recognise it, to wait for those social influences which would make its obligation felt by mankind at large. In the comparatively early state of human advancement in which we now live, a person cannot indeed feel that entireness of sympathy with all others, which would make any real discordance in the general direction of their conduct in life impossible; but already a person in whom the social feeling is at all developed, cannot bring himself to think of the rest of his fellow-creatures as struggling rivals with him for the means of happiness, whom he must desire to see defeated in their object in order that he may succeed in his. The deeply rooted conception which every individual even now has of himself as a social being, tends to make him feel it one of his natural wants that there should be harmony between his feelings and aims and those of his fellow-creatures. If differences of opinion and of mental culture make it impossible for him to share many of their actual feelings—perhaps make him denounce and defy those feelings—he still needs to be conscious that his real aim and theirs do not conflict; that he is not opposing himself to what they really wish for, namely their own good, but is, on the contrary, promoting it. This feeling in most individuals is much inferior in strength to their selfish feelings, and is often wanting altogether. But to those who have it, it possesses all the characters of a natural feeling. It does not present itself to their minds as a superstition of education, or a law despotically imposed by the power of society, but as an attribute which it would not be well for them to be without. This conviction is the ultimate sanction of the greatest happiness morality. This it is which makes any mind, of well-developed feelings, work with, and not against, the outward motives to care for others, afforded by what I have called the external sanctions; and when those sanctions are wanting, or act in an opposite direction, constitutes in itself a powerful internal binding force, in proportion to the sensitiveness and thoughtfulness of the character; since few but those whose mind is a moral blank, could bear to lay out their course of life on the plan of paying no regard to others except so far as their own private interest compels.

Chapter IV: Of What Sort of Proof the Principle of Utility Is Susceptible

It has already been remarked, that questions of ultimate ends do not admit of proof, in the ordinary acceptation of the term. To be incapable of proof by reasoning is common to all first principles; to the first premises of our knowledge, as well as to those of our conduct. But the former, being matters of fact, may be the subject of a direct appeal to the faculties which judge of fact—namely, our senses, and our internal consciousness. Can an appeal be made to the same faculties on questions of practical ends? Or by what other faculty is cognisance taken of them?

Questions about ends are, in other words, questions about what things are desirable. The utilitarian doctrine is, that happiness is desirable, and the only thing desirable, as an end; all other things being only desirable as means to that end. What ought to be required of this doctrine—what conditions is it requisite that the doctrine should fulfil—to make good its claim to be believed?

The only proof capable of being given that an object is visible, is that people actually see it. The only proof that a sound is audible, is that people hear it: and so of the other sources of our experience. In like manner, I apprehend, the sole evidence it is possible to produce that anything is desirable, is that people actually do desire it. If the end which the utilitarian doctrine proposes to itself were not, in theory and in practice, acknowledged to be an end, nothing could ever convince any person that it was so. No reason can be given why the general happiness is desirable, except that each person, so far as he believes it to be attainable, desires his own happiness. This, however, being a fact, we have not only all the proof which the case admits of, but all which it is possible to require, that happiness is a good: that each person's happiness is a good to that person, and the general happiness, therefore, a good to the aggregate of all persons. Happiness has made out its title as *one* of the ends of conduct, and consequently one of the criteria of morality.

But it has not, by this alone, proved itself to be the sole criterion. To do that, it would seem, by the same rule, necessary to show, not only that people desire happiness, but that they never desire anything else. Now it is palpable that they do desire things which, in common language, are decidedly distinguished from happiness. They desire, for example, virtue, and the absence of vice, no less really than pleasure and the absence of pain. The desire of virtue is not as universal, but is as authentic a fact, as the desire of happiness. And hence the opponents of the utilitarian standard deem that they have a right to infer that there are other ends of human action besides happiness, and that happiness is not the standard of approbation and disapprobation.

But does the utilitarian doctrine deny that people desire virtue, or maintain that virtue is not a thing to be desired? The very reverse. It maintains not only that virtue is to be desired, but that it is to be desired disinterestedly, for itself. Whatever may be the opinion of utilitarian moralists as to the original conditions by which virtue is made virtue; however they may believe (as they do) that actions and dispositions are only virtuous because they promote another end than virtue; yet this being granted, and it having been decided, from considerations of this description, what *is* virtuous, they not only place virtue at the very head of the things which are good as means to the ultimate end, but they also recognise as a psychological fact the possibility of its being, to the individual, a good in itself, without looking to any end beyond it; and, hold, that the mind is not in a right state, not a state conformable to Utility, not in the state most conducive to the general happiness, unless it does love virtue in this manner—as a thing desirable in itself, even although, in the individual instance, it should not produce those other desirable consequences which it tends to produce, and on account of which it is held to be virtue. This opinion is not, in the smallest degree, a departure from the Happiness principle. The ingredients of happiness are very various, and each of them is desirable in itself, and not merely when considered as swelling an aggregate. The principle of utility does not mean that any given pleasure, as music, for instance, or any given exemption from pain, as for example health, is to be looked upon as means to a collective something termed happiness, and to be desired on that account. They are desired and desirable in and for themselves; besides being means, they are a part of the end. Virtue, according to the utilitarian doctrine, is not naturally and originally part of the end, but it is capable of becoming so; and in those who love it disinterestedly it has become so, and is desired and cherished, not as a means to happiness, but as a part of their happiness.

To illustrate this farther, we may remember that virtue is not the only thing, originally a means, and which if it were not a means to anything else, would be and remain indifferent, but which by association with what it is a means to, comes to be desired for itself, and that too with the utmost intensity. What, for example, shall we say of the love of money? There is nothing originally more desirable about money than about any heap of glittering pebbles. Its worth is solely that of the things which it will buy; the desires for other things than itself, which it is a means of gratifying. Yet the love of money is not only one of the strongest moving forces of human life, but money is, in many cases, desired in and for itself; the desire to possess it is often stronger than the desire to use it, and goes on increasing when all the desires which point to ends beyond it, to be compassed by it, are falling off. It may, then, be said truly, that money is desired not for the sake of an end, but as part of the end. From being a means to happiness, it has come to be itself a principal ingredient of the individual's conception of happiness. The same may be said of the majority of the great objects of human life—power, for example, or fame; except that to each of these there is a certain amount of immediate pleasure annexed, which has at least the semblance of being naturally inherent in them; a thing which cannot be said of money. Still, however, the strongest natural attraction, both of power and of fame, is the immense aid they give to the attainment of our other wishes; and it is the strong association thus generated between them and all our objects of desire, which gives to the direct desire of them the intensity it often assumes, so as in some characters to surpass in strength all other desires. In these cases the means have become a part of the end, and a more important part of it than any of the things which they are means to. What was once desired as an instrument for the attainment of happiness, has come to be desired for its own sake. In being desired for its own sake it is, however, desired as *part* of happiness. The person is made, or thinks he would be made, happy by its mere possession; and is made unhappy by failure to obtain it. The desire of it is not a different thing from the desire of happiness, any more than the love of music, of the desire of health. They are included in happiness. They are some of the elements of which the desire of happiness is made up. Happiness is not an abstract idea, but a concrete whole; and these are some of its parts. And the utilitarian standard sanctions and approves their being so. Life would be a poor thing, very ill provided with sources of happiness, if there were not this provision of nature, by which things originally indifferent, but conducive to, or otherwise associated with, the satisfaction of our primitive desires, become in themselves sources of pleasure more valuable than the primitive pleasures, both in permanency, in the space of human existence that they are capable of covering, and even in intensity.

Virtue, according to the utilitarian conception, is a good of this description. There was no original desire of it, or motive to it, save its conduciveness to pleasure, and especially to protection from pain. But through the association thus formed, it may be felt a good in itself, and desired as such with as great intensity as any other good; and with this difference between it and the love of money, of power, or of fame, that all of these may, and often do, render the individual noxious to the other members of society to which he belongs, whereas there is nothing which makes him so much a blessing to them as the cultivation of the disinterested love of virtue. And consequently, the utilitarian standard, while it tolerates and approves those other acquired desires, up to the point beyond which they would be more injurious to the general happiness than promotive of it, enjoins and requires the cultivation of the love of virtue up to the greatest strength possible, as being above all things important to the general happiness.

It results from the preceding considerations, that there is in reality nothing desired except happiness. Whatever is desired otherwise than as a means to some end beyond itself, and ultimately to happiness, is desired as itself a part of happiness, and is not desired for itself until it has become so. Those who desire virtue for its own sake, desire it either because the consciousness of it is a pleasure, or because the consciousness of being without it is a pain, or for both reasons united; as in truth the pleasure and pain seldom exist separately, but almost always together, the same person feeling pleasure in degree of virtue attained, and pain in not having attained more. If one of these give him no pleasure, and the other no pain, he would not love or desire virtue, or would desire it only for the other benefits which it might produce to himself or to persons whom he cared for.

We have now, then, an answer to the question, of what sort of proof the principle of utility is susceptible. If the opinion which I have now stated is psychologically true—if human nature is so constituted as to desire nothing which is not either a part of happiness or a means of happiness, we can have no other proof, and we require no other, that these are the only things desirable. If so, happiness is the sole end of human action, and the promotion of it the test by which to judge of all human conduct; from whence it necessarily follows that it must be the criterion of morality, since a part is included in the whole.

And now to decide whether this is really so; whether mankind do desire nothing for itself but that which is a pleasure to them or of which the absence is a pain; we have evidently arrived at a question of fact and experience, dependent, like all similar questions, upon evidence. It can only be determined by practised self-consciousness and self-observation, assisted by observation of others. I believe that these sources of evidence, impartially consulted, will declare that desiring a thing and finding it pleasant, aversion to it and thinking of it as painful, are phenomena entirely inseparable, or rather two parts of the same phenomenon; in strictness of language, two different modes of naming the same psychological fact: that to think of an object as desirable (unless for the sake of its consequences), and to think of it as pleasant, are one and the same thing; and that to desire anything, except in proportion as the idea of it is pleasant, is a physical and metaphysical impossibility.

So obvious does this appear to me, that I expect it will hardly be disputed: and the objection made will be, not that desire can possibly be directed to anything ultimately except pleasure and exemption from pain, but that the will is a different thing from desire; that a person of confirmed virtue, or any other person whose purposes are fixed, carries out his purposes without any thought of the pleasure he has in contemplating them, or expects to derive from their fulfillment; and persists in acting on them, enough though these pleasures are much diminished, by changes in his character or decay of his passive sensibilities, or are outweighed by the pains which the pursuit of the purposes may bring upon him. All this I fully admit, and have stated it elsewhere, as positively and emphatically as any one. Will, the active phenomenon, is a different thing from desire, the state of passive sensibility, and though originally an offshoot from it, may in time take root and detach itself from the parent stock; so much so, that in the case of an habitual purpose, instead of willing the thing because we desire it, we often desire it only because we will it. This, however, is but an instance of that familiar fact, the power of habit, and is nowise confined to the case of virtuous actions. Many indifferent things, which men originally did from a motive of some sort, they continue to do from habit. Sometimes this is done unconsciously, the consciousness coming only after the action; at other times with conscious volition, but volition which has become habitual, and is put in operation by the force of habit, in opposition perhaps to the deliberate preference, as often happens with those who have contracted habits of vicious or hurtful indulgence. Third and last comes the case in which the habitual act of will in the individual instance is not in contradiction to the general intention prevailing at other times, but in fulfilment of it; as in the case of the person of confirmed virtue, and of all who pursue deliberately and consistently any determinate end. The distinction between will and desire thus understood is an authentic and highly important psychological fact; but the fact consists solely in this—that will, like all other parts of our constitution, is amenable to habit, and that we may will from habit what we no longer desire for itself, or desire only because we will it. It is not the less true that will, in the beginning, is entirely produced by desire; including in that term the repelling influence of pain as well as the attractive one of pleasure. Let us take into consideration, no longer the person who has a confirmed will to do right, but him in whom that virtuous will is still feeble, conquerable by temptation, and not to be fully relied on; by what means can it be strengthened? How can the will to be virtuous, where it does not exist in sufficient force, be implanted or awakened? Only by making the person *desire* virtue— by making him think of it in a pleasurable light, or of its absence in a painful one. It is by associating the doing right with pleasure, or the doing wrong with pain, or by eliciting and impressing and bringing home to the person's experience the pleasure naturally involved in the one or the pain in the other, that it is possible to call forth that will to be virtuous, which, when confirmed, acts without any thought of either pleasure or pain. Will is the child of desire, and passes out of the dominion of its parent only to come under that of habit. That which is the result of habit affords no presumption of being intrinsically good; and there would be no reason for wishing that the purpose of virtue should become independent of pleasure and pain, were it not that the influence of the pleasurable and painful associations which prompt to virtue is not sufficiently to be depended on for unerring constancy of action until it has acquired the support of habit. Both in feeling and in conduct, habit is the only thing which imparts certainty; and it is because of the importance to others of being able to rely absolutely on one's feelings and conduct, and to oneself of being able to rely on one's own, that the will to do right ought to be cultivated into this habitual independence. In other words, this state of the will is a means to good, not intrinsically a good; and does not contradict the doctrine that nothing is a good to human beings but in so far as it is either itself pleasurable, or a means of attaining pleasure or averting pain.

But if this doctrine be true, the principle of utility is proved. Whether it is so or not, must now be left to the consideration of the thoughtful reader.

B. FROM *ON LIBERTY*

Introductory

The subject of this essay is not the so-called "liberty of the will," so unfortunately opposed to the misnamed doctrine of philosophical necessity; but civil, or social liberty; the nature and limits of the power which can be legitimately exercised by society over the individual. A question seldom stated, and hardly ever discussed in general terms, but which profoundly influences the practical controversies of the age by its latent presence, and is likely soon to make itself recognized as the vital question of the future. It is so far from being new that, in a certain sense, it has divided mankind almost from the remotest ages; but in the stage of progress into which the more civilized portions of the species have not entered, it presents itself under new conditions and requires a different and more fundamental treatment.

The struggle between liberty and authority is the most conspicuous feature in the portions of history with which we are earliest familiar, particularly in that of Greece, Rome, and England. But in old times this contest was between subjects, or some classes of subjects, and the government. By liberty was meant protection against the tyranny of the political rulers. The rulers were conceived (except in some of the popular governments of Greece) as in a necessarily antagonistic position to the people whom they ruled. They consisted of a governing One, or a governing tribe or caste, who derived their authority from inheritance or conquest, who, at all events, did not hold it at the pleasure of the governed, and whose supremacy men did not venture, perhaps did not desire, to contest, whatever precautions might be taken against its oppressive exercise. Their power was regarded as necessary, but also as highly dangerous; as a weapon which they would attempt to use against their subjects, no less than against external enemies. To prevent the weaker members of the community

From *On Liberty*, edited by Currin Shields (New York: Macmillan, 1956), pp. 3–8, 13–16, 19–25, 43–45, 64, 67–68, 77–78, 82–83.

from being preyed upon by innumerable vultures, it was needful that there should be an animal of prey stronger than the rest, commissioned to keep them down. But as the king of the vultures would be no less bent upon preying on the flock than any of the minor harpies, it was indispensable to be in a perpetual attitude of defense against his beak and claws. The aim, therefore, of patriots was to set limits to the power which the ruler should be suffered to exercise over the community; and this limitation was what they meant by liberty. It was attempted in two ways. First, by obtaining a recognition of certain immunities, called political liberties or rights, which it was to be regarded as a breach of duty in the ruler to infringe, and which if he did infringe, specific resistance or general rebellion was held to be justifiable. A second, and generally a later, expedient was the establishment of constitutional checks by which the consent of the community, or of a body of some sort, supposed to represent its interests, was made a necessary condition to some of the more important acts of the governing power. To the first of these modes of limitation, the ruling power, in most European countries, was compelled, more or less, to submit. It was not so with the second; and, to attain this, or, when already in some degree possessed, to attain it more completely, became everywhere the principal object of the lovers of liberty. And so long as mankind were content to combat one enemy by another, and to be ruled by a master on condition of being guaranteed more or less efficaciously against his tyranny, they did not carry their aspirations beyond this point.

A time, however, came, in the progress of human affairs, when men ceased to think it a necessity of nature that their governors should be an independent power opposed in interest to themselves. It appeared to them much better that the various magistrates of the state should be their tenants or delegates, revocable at their pleasure. In that way alone, it seemed, could they have complete security that the powers of government would never be abused to their disadvantage. By degrees this new demand for elective and temporary rulers became the prominent object of the exertions of the popular party wherever any such party existed, and superseded, to a considerable extent, the previous efforts to limit the power of rulers. As the struggle proceeded for making the ruling power emanate from the periodical choice of the ruled, some persons began to think that too much importance had been attached to the limitation of the power itself. *That* (it might seem) was a resource against rulers whose interests were habitually opposed to those of the people. What was now wanted was that the rulers should be identified with the people, that their interest and will should be the interest and will of the nation. The nation did not need to be protected against its own will. There was no fear of its tyrannizing over itself. Let the rulers be effectually responsible to it, promptly removable by it, and it could afford to trust them with power of which it could itself dictate the use to be made. Their power was but the nation's own power, concentrated and in a form convenient for exercise. This mode of thought, or rather perhaps of feeling, was common among the last generation of European liberalism, in the Continental section of which it still apparently predominates. Those who admit any limit to what a government may do, except in the case of such governments as they think ought not to exist, stand out as brilliant exceptions among the political thinkers of the Continent. A similar tone of sentiment might by this time have been prevalent in our own country if the circumstances which for a time encouraged it had continued unaltered.

But, in political and philosophical theories as well as in persons, success discloses faults and infirmities which failure might have concealed from observation. The notion that the people have no need to limit their power over themselves might seem axiomatic, when popular government was a thing only dreamed about, or read of as having existed at some distant period of the past. Neither was that notion necessarily disturbed by such temporary aberrations as those of the French Revolution, the worst of which were the work of a usurping few, and which, in any case, belonged, not to the permanent working of popular institutions, but to a sudden and convulsive outbreak against monarchical and aristocratic despotism. In time, however, a democratic republic came to occupy a large portion of the earth's surface and made itself felt as one of the most powerful members of the community of nations; and elective and responsible government became subject to the observations and criticisms which wait upon a great existing fact. It was now perceived that such phrases as "self-government," and "the power of the people over themselves," do not express the true state of the case. The "people" who exercise the power are not always the same people with those over whom it is exercised; and the "self-government" spoken of is not the government of each by himself, but of each by all the rest. The will of the people, moreover, practically means the will of the most numerous or the most active *part* of the people—the majority, or those who succeed in making themselves accepted as the majority; the people, consequently, *may* desire to oppress a part of their number, and precautions are as much needed against this as against any other abuse of power. The limitations, therefore, of the power of government over individuals loses none of its importance when the holders of power are regularly accountable to the community, that is, to the strongest party therein. This view of things, recommending itself equally to the intelligence of thinkers and to the inclination of those important classes in European society to whose real or supposed interests democracy is adverse, has had no difficulty in establishing itself; and in political speculations "the tyranny of the majority" is now generally included among the evils against which society requires to be on its guard.

Like other tyrannies, the tyranny of the majority was at first, and is still vulgarly, held in dread, chiefly as operating through the acts of the public authorities. But reflecting persons perceived that when society is itself the tyrant—society collectively over the separate individuals who compose it—its means of tyrannizing are not restricted to the acts which it may do by the hands of its political functionaries. Society can and does execute its own mandates; and if it issues wrong mandates instead of right, or any mandates at all in things with which it ought not to meddle, it practices a social tyranny more formidable than many kinds of political oppression, since, though not usually upheld by such extreme penalties, it leaves fewer means of escape, penetrating much more deeply into the details of life, and enslaving the soul itself. Protection, therefore, against the tyranny of the magistrate is not enough; there needs protection also against the tyranny of the prevailing opinion and feeling, against the tendency of society to impose, by other means than civil penalties, its own ideas and practices as rules of conduct on those who dissent from them; to fetter the development and, if possible, prevent the formation of any individuality not in harmony with its ways, and compel all characters to fashion themselves upon the model of its own. There is a limit to the legitimate interference of collective opinion with individual independence; and to find that limit, and maintain it against encroachment, is as indispensable to a good condition of human affairs as protection against political despotism.

But though this proposition is not likely to be contested in general terms, the practical question where to place the limit—how to make the fitting adjustment between individual independence and social control—is a subject on which nearly everything remains to be done. All that makes existence valuable to anyone depends on the enforcement of restraints upon the actions of other people. Some rules of conduct, therefore, must be imposed—by law in the first place, and by opinion on many things which are not fit subjects for the operation of law. What these rules should be is the principal question in human affairs. . . .

The object of this essay is to assert one very simple principle, as entitled to govern absolutely the dealings of society with the individual in the way of compulsion and control, whether the means used by physical force in the form of legal penalties or the moral coercion of public opinion. That principle is that the sole end for which mankind are warranted, individually or collectively, in interfering with the liberty of action of any of their number is self-protection. That the only purpose for which power can be rightfully exercised over any member of a civilized community, against his will, is to prevent harm to others. His own good, either physical or moral, is not a sufficient warrant. He cannot rightfully be compelled to do or forbear because it will be better for him to do so, because it will make him happier, because, in the opinions of others, to do so would be wise or even right. These are good reasons for remonstrating with him, or reasoning with him, or persuading him, or entreating him, but not for compelling him or visiting him with any evil in case he do otherwise. To justify that, the conduct from which it is desired to deter him must be calculated to produce evil to someone else. The only part of the conduct of anyone for which he is amenable to society is that which concerns others. In the part which merely concerns himself, his independence is, of right, absolute. Over himself, over his own body and mind, the individual is sovereign.

It is, perhaps, hardly necessary to say that this doctrine is meant to apply only to human beings in the maturity of their faculties. We are not speaking of children or of young persons below the age which the law may fix as that of manhood or womanhood. Those who are still in a state to require being taken care of by others must be protected against their own actions as well as against external injury. For the same reason we may leave out of consideration those backward states of society in which the race itself may be considered as in its nonage. The early difficulties in the way of spontaneous progress are so great that there is seldom any choice of means for overcoming them; and a ruler full of the spirit of improvement is warranted in the use of any expedients that will attain an end perhaps otherwise unattainable. Despotism is a legitimate mode of government in dealing with barbarians, provided the end be their improvement and the means justified by actually effecting that end. Liberty, as a principle, has no application to any state of things anterior to the time when mankind have become capable of being improved by free and equal discussion. Until then, there is nothing for them but implicit obedience to an Akbar or a Charlemagne, if they are so fortunate as to find one. But as soon as mankind have attained the capacity of being guided to their own improvement by conviction or persuasion (a period long since reached in all nations with whom we need here concern ourselves), compulsion, either in the direct form or in that of pains and penalties for non-compliance, is no longer admissible as a means to their own good, and justifiable only for the security of others.

It is proper to state that I forgo any advantage which could be derived to my argument from the idea of abstract right as a thing independent of utility. I regard utility as the ultimate appeal on all ethical questions; but it must be utility in the largest sense, grounded on the permanent interests of man as a progressive being. Those interests, I contend, authorize the subjection of individual spontaneity to external control only in respect to those actions of each which concern the interest of other people. If anyone does an act hurtful to others, there is a *prima facie* case for punishing him by law or, where legal penalties are not safely applicable, by general disapprobation. There are also many positive acts for the benefit of others which he may rightfully be compelled to perform, such as to give evidence in a court of justice, to bear his fair share in the common defense or in any other joint work necessary to the interest of the society of which he enjoys the protection, and to perform certain acts of individual beneficence, such as saving a fellow creature's life or interposing to protect the defenseless against ill usage—things which whatever it is obviously a man's duty to do he may rightfully be made responsible to society for not doing. A person may cause evil to others not only by his actions but by his inaction, and in either case he is justly accountable to them for the injury. The latter case, it is true, requires a much more cautious exercise of compulsion than the former. To make anyone answerable for doing evil to others is the rule; to make him answerable for not preventing evil is, comparatively speaking, the exception. Yet there are many cases clean enough and grave enough to justify that exception. In all things which regard the external relations of the individual, he is *de jure* amenable to those whose interests are concerned, and, if need be, to society as their protector. There are often good reasons for not holding him to the responsibility; but these reasons must arise from the special expediencies of the case: either because it is a kind of case in which he is on the whole likely to act better when left to his own discretion than when controlled in any way in which society have it in their power to control him; or because the attempt to exercise control would produce other evils, greater than those which it would prevent. When such reasons as these preclude the enforcement of responsibility, the conscience of the agent himself should step into the vacant judgment seat and protect those interests of others which have no external protection; judging himself all the more rigidly, because the case does not admit of his being made accountable to the judgment of his fellow creatures.

But there is a sphere of action in which society, as distinguished from the individual, has, only an indirect interest: comprehending all that portion of a person's life and conduct which affects only himself or, if it also affects others, only with their free, voluntary, and undeceived consent and participation. When I say only himself,

I mean directly and in the first instance; for whatever affects himself may affect others through himself; and the objection which may be grounded on this contingency will receive consideration in the sequel. This, then, is the appropriate region of human liberty. It comprises, first, the inward domain of consciousness, demanding liberty of conscience in the most comprehensive sense, liberty of thought and feeling, absolute freedom of opinion and sentiment on all subjects, practical or speculative, scientific, moral, or theological. The liberty of expressing and publishing opinions may seem to fall under a different principle, since it belongs to that part of the conduct of an individual which concerns other people, but, being almost of as much importance as the liberty of thought itself and resting in great part on the same reasons, is practically inseparable from it. Secondly, the principle requires liberty of tastes and pursuits, of framing the plan of our life to suit our own character, of doing as we like, subject to such consequences as may follow, without impediment from our fellow creatures, so long as what we do does not harm them, even though they should think our conduct foolish, perverse, or wrong. Thirdly, from this liberty of each individual follows the liberty, within the same limits, of combination among individuals; freedom to unite for any purpose not involving harm to others: the persons combining being supposed to be of full age and not forced or deceived.

•   •   •

Of the Liberty of Thought and Discussion

The time, it is to be hoped, is gone by when any defense would be necessary of the "liberty of the press" as one of the securities against corrupt or tyrannical government. No argument, we may suppose, can now be needed against permitting a legislature or an executive, not identified in interest with the people, to prescribe opinions to them and determine what doctrines or what arguments they shall be allowed to hear. This aspect of the question, besides, has been so often and so triumphantly enforced by preceding writers that it needs not be specially insisted on in this place. Though the law of England, on the subject of the press, is as servile to this day as it was in the time of the Tudors, there is little danger of its being actually put in force against political discussion except during some temporary panic when fear of insurrection drives ministers and judges from their propriety; and, speaking generally, it is not, in constitutional countries, to be apprehended that the government, whether completely responsible to the people or not, will often attempt to control the expression of opinion, except when in doing so it makes itself the organ of the general intolerance of the public. Let us suppose, therefore, that the government is entirely at one with the people, and never thinks of exerting any power of coercion unless in agreement with what it conceives to be their voice.

But I deny the right of the people to exercise such coercion, either by themselves or by their government. The power itself is illegitimate. The best government has no more title to it than the worst. It is as noxious, or more noxious, when exerted in accordance with public opinion than when in opposition to it. If all mankind minus one were of one opinion, mankind would be no more justified in silencing that one person than he, if he had the power, would be justified in silencing mankind. Were an opinion a personal possession of no value except to the owner, if to be obstructed in the enjoyment of it were simply a private injury, it would make some difference whether the injury was inflicted only on a few persons or on many. But the peculiar evil of silencing the expression of an opinion is that it is robbing the human race, posterity as well as the existing generation—those who dissent from the opinion, still more than those who hold it. If the opinion is right, they are deprived of the opportunity of exchanging error for truth; if wrong, they lose, what is almost as great a benefit, the clearer perception and livelier impression of truth produced by its collision with error.

It is necessary to consider separately these two hypotheses, each of which has a distinct branch of the argument corresponding to it. We can never be sure that the opinion we are endeavoring to stifle is a false opinion; and if we were sure, stifling it would be an evil still.

First, the opinion which it is attempted to suppress by authority may possibly be true. Those who desire to suppress it, of course, deny its truth; but they are not infallible. They have no authority to decide the question for all mankind and exclude every other person from the means of judging. To refuse a hearing to an opinion because they are sure that it is false is to assume that *their* certainty is the same thing as *absolute* certainty. All silencing of discussion is an assumption of infallibility. Its condemnation may be allowed to rest on this common argument, not the worse for being common.

Unfortunately for the good sense of mankind, the fact of their fallibility is far from carrying the weight in their practical judgment which is always allowed to it in theory; for while everyone well knows himself to be fallible, few think it necessary to take any precautions against their own fallibility, or admit the supposition that any opinion of which they feel very certain may be one of the examples of the error to which they acknowledge themselves to be liable. Absolute princes, or others who are accustomed to unlimited deference, usually feel this complete confidence in their own opinions on nearly all subjects. People more happily situated, who sometimes hear their opinions on nearly all subjects. People more happily situated, who sometimes hear their opinions disputed and are not wholly unused to be set right when they are wrong, place the same unbounded reliance only on such of their opinions as are shared by all who surround them, or to whom they habitually defer; for in proportion to a man's want of confidence in his own solitary judgment does he usually repose, with implicit trust, on the infallibility of "the world" in general. And the world, to each individual, means the part of it with which he comes in contact: his party, his sect, his church, his class of society; the man may be called, by comparison, almost liberal and large-minded to whom it means anything so comprehensive as his own country or his own age. Nor is his faith in this collective authority at all shaken by his being aware that other ages, countries, sects, churches, classes, and parties have thought, and even now think, the exact reverse. He devolves upon his own world the responsibility of being in the right against the dissentient worlds of other people; and it never troubles him that mere accident has decided which of these numerous worlds is the object of his reliance, and that the same causes which make him a churchman in London would have made him a Buddhist or a Confucian in Peking. Yet it is as evident in itself, as any amount of argument can make it, that ages are not more infallible than individuals—every age having held many opinions which subsequent ages have deemed not only false but absurd; and it is as certain that many opinions, now general, will be rejected by future ages, as it is that many, once general, are rejected by the present.

The objection likely to be made to this argument would probably take some such form as the following. There is no greater assumption of infallibility in forbidding the propagation of error than in any other thing which is done by public authority on its own judgment and responsibility. Judgment is given to men that they may use it. Because it may be used erroneously, are men to be told that they ought not to use it at all? To prohibit what they think pernicious is not claiming exemption from error, but fulfilling the duty incumbent on them, although fallible, of acting on their conscientious conviction. If we were never to act on our opinions, because those opinions may be wrong, we should leave all our interests uncared for, and all our duties unperformed. An objection which applied to all conduct can be no valid objection to any conduct in particular. It is the duty of governments, and of individuals, to form the truest opinions they can; to form them carefully, and never impose them upon others unless they are quite sure of being right. But when they are sure (such reasoners may say), it is not conscientiousness but cowardice to shrink from acting on their opinions and allow doctrines which they honestly think dangerous to the welfare of mankind, either in this life or in another, to be scattered abroad without restraint, because other people, in less enlightened times, have persecuted opinions now believed to be true. Let us take care, it may be said, not to make the same mistake; but governments and nations have made mistakes in other things which are not denied to be fit subjects for the exercise of authority: they have laid on bad taxes, made unjust wars. Ought we therefore to lay on no taxes and, under whatever provocation, make no wars? Men and governments must act to the best of their ability. There is no such thing as absolute certainty, but there is assurance sufficient for the purposes of human life. We may, and must, assume our opinion to be true for the guidance of our own conduct; and it is assuming no more when we forbid bad men to pervert society by the propagation of opinions which we regard as false and pernicious.

I answer, that it is assuming very much more. There is the greatest difference between presuming an opinion to be true because, with every opportunity for contesting it, it has not been refuted, and assuming its truth for the purpose of not permitting its refutation. Complete liberty of contradicting and disproving our opinion is the very condition which justifies us in assuming its truth for purposes of action; and on no other terms can a being with human faculties have any rational assurance of being right.

When we consider either the history of opinion or the ordinary conduct of human life, to what is it to be ascribed that the one and the other are no worse than they are? Not certainly to the inherent force of the human understanding, for on any matter not self-evident there are ninety-nine persons totally incapable of judging of it for one who is capable; and the capacity of the hundredth person is only comparative, for the majority of the eminent men of every past generation held many opinions now known to be erroneous, and did or approved numerous things which no one will now justify. Why is it, then, that there is on the whole a preponderance among mankind of rational opinions and rational conduct? If there really is this preponderance—which there must be unless human affairs are, and have always been, in an almost desperate state—it is owing to a quality of the human mind, the source of everything respectable in man either as an intellectual or as a moral being, namely, that his errors are corrigible. He is capable of rectifying his mistakes by discussion and experience. Not by experience alone. There must be discussion to show how experience is to be interpreted. Wrong opinions and practices gradually yield to fact and argument; but facts and arguments, to produce any effect on the mind, must be brought before it. Very few facts are able to tell their own story, without comments to bring out their few facts are able to tell their own story, without comments to bring out their meaning. The whole strength and value, then, of human judgment depending on the one property, that it can be set right when it is wrong, reliance can be placed on it only when the means of setting it right are kept constantly at hand. In the case of any person whose judgment is really deserving of confidence, how has it become so? Because he has kept his mind open to criticism of his opinions and conduct. Because it has been his practice to listen to all that could be said against him; to profit by as much of it as was just, and to expound to himself, and upon occasion to others, the fallacy of what was fallacious. Because he has felt that the only way in which a human being can make some approach to knowing the whole of a subject is by hearing what can be said about it by persons of every variety of opinion, and studying all modes in which it can be looked at by every character of mind. No wise man ever acquired his wisdom in any mode but this; not is it in the nature of human intellect to become wise in any other manner. The steady habit of correcting and completing his own opinion by collating it with those of others, so far from causing doubt and hesitation in carrying it into practice, is the only stable foundation for a just reliance on it; for, being cognizant of all that can, at least obviously, be said against him, and having taken up his position against al gainsayers—knowing that he has sought for objections and difficulties instead of avoiding them, and has shut out no light which can be thrown upon the subject from any quarter—he has a right to think his judgment better than that of any person, or any multitude, who have not gone through a similar process.

•   •   •

Let us now pass to the second division of the argument, and dismissing the supposition that any of the received opinions may be false, let us assume them to be true and examine into the worth of the manner in which they are likely to be held when their truth is not freely and openly canvassed. However unwillingly a person who has a strong opinion may admit the possibility that his opinion may be false, he ought to be moved by the consideration that, however true it may be, if it is not fully, frequently, and fearlessly discussed, it will be held as a dead dogma, not a living truth.

There is a class of persons (happily not quite so numerous as formerly) who think it enough if a person assents undoubtingly to what they think true, though he has no knowledge whatever of the grounds of the opinion and could not make a tenable defense of it against the most superficial objections. Such persons, if they can once get their creed taught from authority, naturally think that no good, and some harm, comes of its being allowed to be questioned. Where their influence prevails, they make it nearly impossible for the received opinion to be rejected wisely and considerately, though it may still be rejected rashly and ignorantly; for to shut out discussion entirely is seldom possible, and when it once gets in, beliefs not grounded on conviction are apt to give way before the slightest semblance of an argument. Waiving, however, this possibility—assuming that the true opinion abides in the mind, but abides as a prejudice, a belief independent of, and proof against, argument—this is not the way in which truth ought to be held by a rational being. This is not knowing the truth. Truth, thus held, is but one superstition the more, accidentally clinging to the words which enunciate a truth.

If the intellect and judgment of mankind ought to be cultivated, a thing which Protestants at least do not deny, on what can these faculties be more appropriately exercised by anyone than on the things which concern him so much that it is considered necessary for him to hold opinions on them? If the cultivation of the understanding consists in one thing more than in another, it is surely in learning the grounds of one's own opinions. Whatever people believe, on subjects on which it is of the first importance to believe rightly, they ought to be able to defend against at least the common objections. But, someone may say, "Let them be *taught* the grounds of their opinions. It does not follow that opinions must be merely parroted because they are never heard controverted. Persons who learn geometry do not simply commit the theorems to memory, but understand and learn likewise the demonstrations; and it would be absurd to say that they remain ignorant of the grounds of geometrical truths because they never hear anyone deny and attempt to disprove them." Undoubtedly; and such teaching suffices on a subject like mathematics, where there is nothing at all to be said on the wrong side of the question. The peculiarity of the evidence of mathematical truths is that all the argument is on one side. There are no objections, and no answers to objections. But on every subject on which difference of opinion is possible, the truth depends on a balance to be struck between two sets of conflicting reasons. Even in natural philosophy, there is always some other explanation possible of the same facts; some geocentric theory instead of heliocentric, some phlogiston instead of oxygen; and it has to be shown why that other theory cannot be the true one; and until this is shown, and until we know how it is shown, we do not understand the grounds of our opinion. But when we turn to subjects infinitely more complicated, to morals, religion, politics, social relations, and the business of life, three-fourths of the arguments for every disputed opinion consist in dispelling the appearances which favor some opinion different from it. The greatest orator, save one, of antiquity, has left it on record that he always studies his adversary's case with as great, if not still greater, intensity than even his own. What Cicero practiced as the means of forensic success requires to be imitated by all who study any subject in order to arrive at the truth. He who knows only his own side of the case knows little of that. His reasons may be good, and no one may have been able to refute them. But if he is equally unable to refute the reasons on the opposite side, if he does not so much as know what they are, he has no ground for preferring either opinion. The rational position for him would be suspension of judgment, and unless he contents himself with that, he is either led by authority or adopts, like the generality of the world, the side to which he feels most inclination. Nor is it enough that he should hear the arguments of adversaries from his own teachers, presented as they state them, and accompanied by what they offer as refutations. That is not the way to do justice to the arguments or bring them into real contact with his own mind. He must be able to hear them from persons who actually believe them, who defend them in earnest and do their very utmost for them. He must know them in their most plausible and persuasive form; he must feel the whole force of the difficulty which the true view of the subject has to encounter and dispose of, else he will never really possess himself of the portion of truth which meets and removes that difficulty. Ninety-nine in a hundred of what are called educated men are in this condition, even of those who can argue fluently for their opinions. Their conclusion may be true, but it might be false for anything they know; they have never thrown themselves into the mental position of those who think differently from them, and considered what such persons may have to say; and, consequently, they do not, in any proper sense of the word, know the doctrine which they themselves profess. . . .

We have now recognized the necessity to the mental well-being of mankind (on which all their other well-being depends) of freedom of opinion, and freedom of the expression of opinion, on four distinct grounds, which we will now briefly recapitulate:

First, if any opinion is compelled to silence, that opinion may, for aught we can certainly know, be true. To deny this is to assume our own infallibility.

Secondly, though the silenced opinion be an error, it may, and very commonly does, contain a portion of truth; and since the general or prevailing opinion on any subject is rarely or never the whole truth, it is only by the collision of adverse opinions that the remainder of the truth has any chance of being supplied.

Thirdly, even if the received opinion be not only true, but the whole truth; unless it is suffered to be, and actually is, vigorously and earnestly contested, it will, by most of those who receive it, be held in the manner of a prejudice, with little comprehension or feeling of its rational grounds. And not only this, but, fourthly, the meaning of the doctrine itself will be in danger of being lost or enfeebled, and deprived of its vital effect on the character and conduct; the dogma becoming a mere formal profession, inefficacious for good, but cumbering the ground and preventing the growth of any real and heartfelt conviction from reason or personal experience.

•　　　•　　　•

Of Individuality, as One of the Elements of Well-Being

Such being the reasons which make it imperative that human beings should be free to form opinions and to express their opinions without reserve; and such the baneful consequences to the intellectual, and through that to the moral nature of man, unless this liberty is either conceded or asserted in spite of prohibition; let us next examine whether the same reasons do not require that men should be free to act upon their opinions—to carry these out in their lives without hindrance, either physical or moral, from their fellow men, so long as it is at their own risk and peril. This last proviso is of course indispensable. No one pretends that actions should be as free as opinions. On the contrary, even opinions lose their immunity when the circumstances in which they are expressed are such as to constitute their expression a positive instigation to some mischievous act. An opinion that corn dealers are starvers of the poor, or that private property is robbery, ought to be unmolested when simply circulated through the press, but may justly incur punishment when delivered orally to an excited mob assembled before the house of a corn dealer, or when handed about among the same mob in the form of a placard. Acts, of whatever kind, which without justifiable cause do harm to others may be, and in the more important cases absolutely require to be, controlled by the unfavorable sentiments, and, when needful, by the active interference of mankind. The liberty of the individual must be thus far limited; he must not make himself a nuisance to other people. But if he refrains from molesting others in what concerns them, and merely acts according to his own inclination and judgment in things which concern himself, the same reasons which show that opinion should be free prove also that he should be allowed, without molestations, to carry his opinions into practice at his own cost. That mankind are not infallible; that their truths, for the most part, are only half-truths; that unity of opinion, unless resulting from the fullest and freest comparison of opposite opinions, is not desirable, and diversity not an evil, but a good, until mankind are much more capable than at present of recognizing all sides of the truth, are principles applicable to men's modes of action not less than to their opinions. As it is useful that while mankind are imperfect there should be different opinions, so it is that there should be different experiments of living; that free scope should be given to varieties of character, short of injury to others; and that the worth of different modes of life should be proved practically, when anyone thinks fit to try them. It is desirable, in short, that in things which do not primarily concern others individuality should assert itself. Where not the person's own character but the traditions or customs of other people are the rule of conduct, there is wanting one of the principal ingredients of human happiness, and quite the chief ingredient of individual and social progress.

•   •   •

Having said that individuality is the same thing with development, and that it is only the cultivation of individuality which produces, or can produce, well-developed human beings, I might here close the argument; for what more or better can be said of any condition of human affairs than that it brings human beings themselves nearer to the best thing they can be? Or what worse can be said of any obstruction to good than that it prevents this? Doubtless, however, these considerations will not suffice to convince those who most need convincing; and it is necessary further to show that these developed human beings are of some use to the undeveloped—to point out to those who do not desire liberty, and would not avail themselves of it, that they may be in some intelligible manner rewarded for allowing other people to make use of it without hindrance.

In the first place, then, I would suggest that they might possibly learn something from them. It will not be denied by anybody that originality is a valuable element in human affairs. There is always need of persons not only to discover new truths and point out when what were once truths are true no longer, but also to commence new practices and set the example of more enlightened conduct and better taste and sense in human life. This cannot well be gainsaid by anybody who does not believe that the world has already attained perfection in all its ways and practices. It is true that this benefit is not capable of being rendered by everybody alike; there are but few persons, in comparison with the whole of mankind, whose experiments, if adopted by others, would be likely to be any improvement on established practice. But these few are the salt of the earth; without them, human life would become a stagnant pool. Not only is it they who introduce good things which did not before exist; it is they who keep the life in those which already exist. If there were nothing new to be done, would human intellect cease to be necessary? Would it be a reason why those who do the old things should forget why they are done, and do them like cattle, not like human beings? There is only too great a tendency in the best beliefs and practices to degenerate into the mechanical; and unless there were a succession of persons whose ever-recurring originality prevents the grounds of those beliefs and practices from becoming merely traditional, such dead matter would not resist the smallest shock from anything really alive, and there would be no reason by civilization should not die out, as in the Byzantine Empire. . . .

I have said that it is important to give the freest scope possible to uncustomary things, in order that it may in time appear which of these are fit to be converted into customs. But independence of action and disregard of custom are not solely deserving of encouragement for the chance they afford that better modes of action, and customs more worthy of general adoption, may be struck out; nor is it only persons of decided mental superiority who have a just claim to carry on their lives in their own way. There is no reason that all human existence should be constructed on some one or some small number of patterns. If a person possesses any tolerable amount of common sense and experience, his own mode of laying out his existence is the best, not because it is the best in itself, but because it is his own mode. Human beings are not like sheep; and even sheep are not undistinguishably alike. A man cannot get a coat or a pair of boots to fit him unless they are either made to his measure or he has a whole warehouseful to choose from; and is it easier to fit him with a life than with a coat, or are human beings more like one another in their whole physical and spiritual conformation than in the shape of their feet? If it were only that people have diversities of taste, that is reason enough for not attempting to shape them all after one model. But different persons also require different conditions for their spiritual development; and can no more exist healthily in the same moral than all the variety of plants can in the same physical, atmosphere and climate. The same things which are helps to one person toward the cultivation of his higher nature are hindrances to another. The same mode of life is a healthy excitement to one, keeping all his faculties of action and enjoyment in their best order, while to another it is a distracting burden which suspends or crushes all internal life. Such are the differences among human beings in their sources of pleasure, the susceptibilities of pain, and the operation on them of different physical and moral agencies that, unless there is a corresponding diversity in their modes of life, they neither obtain their fair share of happiness, nor grow up to the mental, moral, and aesthetic stature of which their nature is capable. . . .

IMMANUEL KANT

Ethics Founded on Reason

In this excerpt from his *Groundwork of the Metaphysics of Morals*, Kant (1724–1804) tries to show that ethics is founded on reason, not on inclinations. It is acting from duty, not from inclination, that endows an action with moral value. But what is the source of the duties that structure the moral life? These are founded on reason. The universalizability criterion provides a logical test for determining whether an action is morally permissible.

CHAPTER 1
PASSAGE FROM ORDINARY RATIONAL KNOWLEDGE OR MORALITY
TO PHILOSOPHICAL KNOWLEDGE

[The Good Will]

It is impossible to conceive anything at all in the world, or even out of it, which can be taken as good without qualification, except a **good will.** Intelligence, wit, judgement, and any other *talents* of the mind we may care to name, or courage, resolution, and constancy of purpose, as qualities of *temperament*, are without doubt good and desirable in many respects; but they can also be extremely bad and hurtful when the will is not good which has to make use of these gifts of nature, and which for this reason has the term *"character"* applied to its peculiar quality. It is exactly the same with *gifts of fortune*. Power, wealth, honour, even health and that complete well-being and contentment with one's state which goes by the name of *"happiness"*, produce boldness, and as a consequence often overboldness as well, unless a good will is present by which their influence on the mind—and so too the whole principle of action—may be corrected and adjusted to universal ends; not to mention that a rational and impartial spectator can never feel approval in contemplating the uninterrupted prosperity of a being graced by no touch of a pure and good will, and that consequently a good will seems to constitute the indispensable condition of our very worthiness to be happy.

Some qualities are even helpful to this good will itself and can make its task very much easier. They have none the less no inner unconditioned worth, but rather presuppose a good will which sets a limit to the esteem in which they are rightly held and does not permit us to regard them as absolutely good. Moderation in affections and passions, self-control, and sober reflexion are not only good in many respects; they

---

Immanuel Kant, "Ethics Founded on Reason," from *Groundwork of the Metaphysics of Morals,* translated by H. J. Paton (London: Unwin Hyman Ltd., 1956), pp. 61–62, 64–67, 74, 80–92, 95–107. Reprinted by permission.

may even seem to constitute part of the *inner* worth of a person. Yet they are far from being properly described as good without qualification (however unconditionally they have been commended by the ancients). For without the principles of a good will they may become exceedingly bad; and the very coolness of a scoundrel makes him, not merely more dangerous, but also immediately more abominable in our eyes than we should have taken him to be without it.

[The Good Will and Its Results]

A good will is not good because of what it effects or accomplishes—because of its fitness for attaining some proposed end: it is good through its willing alone—that is, good in itself. Considered in itself it is to be esteemed beyond comparison as far higher than anything it could ever bring about merely in order to favour some inclination or, if you like, the sum total of inclinations. Even if, by some special disfavour of destiny or by the niggardly endowment of step-motherly nature, this will is entirely lacking in power to carry out its intentions; if by its utmost effort it still accomplishes nothing, and only good will is left (not, admittedly, as a mere wish, but as the straining of every means so far as they are in our control); even then it would still shine like a jewel for its own sake as something which has its full value of itself. Its usefulness or fruitlessness can neither add to, nor subtract from, this value. Its usefulness would be merely, as it were, the setting which enables us to handle it better in our ordinary dealings or to attract the attention of those not yet sufficiently expert, but not to commend it to experts or to determine its value.

[The Good Will and Duty]

We have now to elucidate the concept of a will estimable in itself and good apart from any further end. This concept, which is already present in a naturally sound understanding and requires not so much to be taught as merely to be clarified, always holds the highest place in estimating the total worth of our actions and constitutes the condition of all the rest. We will therefore take up the concept of **duty,** which includes that of a good will, exposed, however, to certain subjective limitations and obstacles. These, so far from hiding a good will or disguising it, rather bring it out by contrast and make it shine forth more brightly.

[The Motive of Duty]

I will here pass over all actions already recognized as contrary to duty, however useful they may be with a view to this or that end; for about these the question does not even arise whether they could have been done *for the sake of duty* inasmuch as they are directly opposed to it. I will also set aside actions which in fact accord with duty, yet for which men have *no immediate inclination,* but perform them because impelled to do so by some other inclination. For there it is easy to decide whether the action which accords with duty has been done *from duty* or from some purpose of self-interest. This distinction is far more difficult to perceive when the action accords with duty and the subject has in addition an *immediate* inclination to the action. For example, it certainly accords with duty that a grocer should not overcharge his inexperienced customer; and where there is much competition a sensible shopkeeper refrains from so doing and keeps to a fixed and general price for everybody so that a child can buy from him just as well as anyone else. Thus people are served *honestly;* but this is not nearly enough to justify us in believing that the shopkeeper has acted in this way from duty or from principles of fair dealing; his interests required him to do so. We cannot assume him to have in addition an immediate inclination towards his customers, leading him, as it were out of love, to give no man preference over another in the matter of price. Thus the action was done neither from duty nor from immediate inclination, but solely from purposes of self-interest.

On the other hand, to preserve one's life is a duty, and besides this every one has also an immediate inclination to do so. But on account of this the often anxious precautions taken by the greater part of mankind for this purpose have no inner worth, and the maxim of their action is without moral content. They do protect their lives *in conformity with duty,* but not *from the motive of duty.* When, on the contrary, disappointments and hopeless misery have quite taken away the taste for life; when a wretched man, strong in soul and more angered at his fate than faint-hearted or cast down, longs for death and still preserves his life without loving it—not from inclination or fear but from duty; then indeed his maxim has a moral content.

To help others where one can is a duty, and besides this there are many spirits of so sympathetic a temper that, without any further motive of vanity or self-interest, they find an inner pleasure in spreading happiness around them and can take delight in the contentment of others as their own work. Yet I maintain that in such a case an action of this kind, however right and however amiable it may be, has still no genuinely moral worth. It stands on the same footing as other inclinations—for example, the inclination for honour, which if fortunate enough to hit on something beneficial and right and consequently honourable, deserves praise and encouragement, but not esteem; for its maxim lacks moral content, namely, the performance of such actions, not from inclination, but *from duty.* Suppose then that the mind of this friend of man was overclouded by sorrows of his own which extinguished all sympathy with the fate of others, but that he still had power to help those in distress, though no longer stirred by the need of others because sufficiently occupied with his own; and suppose that, when no longer moved by any inclination, he tears himself out of this deadly insensibility and does the action without any inclination for the sake of duty alone; then for the first time his action has its genuine moral worth. Still further: if nature had implanted little sympathy in this or that man's heart; if (being in other respects an honest fellow) he were cold in temperament and indifferent to the sufferings of others—perhaps because, being endowed with the special gift of patience and robust endurance in his own sufferings, he assumed the like in others or even demanded it; if such a man (who would in truth not be the worst product of nature) were not exactly fashioned by her to be a philanthropist, would he not still find in himself a source from which he might draw a worth far higher than any that a good-natured temperament can have? Assuredly he would. It is precisely in this that the worth of character begins to show—a moral worth and beyond all comparison the highest—namely that he does good, not from inclination, but from duty.

To assure one's own happiness is a duty (at least indirectly); for discontent with one's state, in a press of cares and amidst unsatisfied wants, might easily become a great *temptation to the transgression of duty*. But here also, apart from regard to duty, all men have already of themselves the strongest and deepest inclination towards happiness, because precisely in this Idea of happiness there is combined the sum total of inclinations. The prescription for happiness is, however, often so constituted as greatly to interfere with some inclinations, and yet men cannot form under the name of "happiness" any determinate and assured conception of the satisfaction of all inclinations as a sum. Hence it is not to be wondered at that a single inclination which is determinate as to what it promises and as to the time of its satisfaction may outweigh a wavering Idea; and that a man, for example, a sufferer from gout, may choose to enjoy what he fancies and put up with what he can—on the ground that on balance he has here at least not killed the enjoyment of the present moment because of some possibly groundless expectations of the good fortune supposed to attach to soundness of health. But in this case also, when the universal inclination towards happiness has failed to determine his will, when good health, at least for him, has not entered into his calculations as so necessary, what remains over, here as in other cases, is a law—the law of furthering his happiness, not from inclination, but from duty—and in this for the first time his conduct has a real moral worth.

It is doubtless in this sense that we should understand too the passages from Scripture in which we are commanded to love our neighbour and even our enemy. For love out of inclination cannot be commanded; but kindness done from duty—although no inclination impels us, and even although natural and unconquerable disinclination stands in our way—is *practical*, and not *pathological*, love, residing in the will and not in the propensions of feeling, in principles of action and not of melting compassion; and it is this practical love alone which can be an object of command.

CHAPTER II
PASSAGE FROM POPULAR MORAL PHILOSOPHY TO A METAPHYSIC OF MORALS

[Imperatives in General]

Everything in nature works in accordance with laws. Only a rational being has the power to act *in accordance with his idea* of laws—that is, in accordance with principles—and only so has he a *will*. Since *reason* is required in order to derive actions from laws, the will is nothing but practical reason. If reason infallibly determines the will, then in a being of this kind the actions which are recognized to be objectively necessary are also subjectively necessary—that is to say, the will is then a power to choose *only that* which reason independently of inclination recognizes to be practically necessary, that is, to be good. But if reason solely by itself is not sufficient to determine the will; if the will is exposed also to subjective conditions (certain impulsions) which do not always harmonize with the objective ones; if, in a word, the will is not *in itself* completely in accord with reason (as actually happens in the case of men); then actions which are recognized to be objectively necessary are subjectively contingent, and the determining of such a will in accordance with objective laws is *necessitation*. That is to say, the relation of objective laws to a will not good through and through is conceived as one in which the will of a rational being, although it is determined by principles of reason, does not necessarily follow these principles in virtue of its own nature.

The conception of an objective principle so far as this principle is necessitating for a will is called a command (or reason), and the formula of this command is called an **Imperative.**

All imperatives are expressed by an *"ought" (Sollen)*. By this they mark the relation of an objective law of reason to a will which is not necessarily determined by this law in virtue of its subjective constitution (the relation of necessitation). They say that something would be good to do or to leave undone; only they say it to a will which does not always do a thing because it has been informed that this is a good thing to do. The practically *good* is that which determines the will by concepts of reason, and therefore not by subjective causes, but objectively—that is, on grounds valid for every rational being as such. It is distinguished from the *pleasant* as that which influences the will, not as a principle of reason valid for every one, but solely through the medium of sensation by purely subjective causes valid only for the senses of this person or that.

A perfectly good will would thus stand quite as much under objective laws (laws of the good), but it could not on this account be conceived as *necessitated* to act in conformity with law, since of itself, in accordance with its subjective constitution, it can be determined only by the concept of the good. Hence for the *divine* will, and in general for a *holy* will, there are no imperatives: *"I ought"* is here out of place, because *"I will"* is already of itself necessarily in harmony with the law. Imperatives are in consequence only formulae for expressing the relation of objective laws of willing to the subjective imperfection of the will of this or that rational being—for example, of the human will.

[Classification of Imperatives]

All *imperatives* command either *hypothetically* or *categorically*. Hypothetical imperatives declare a possible action to be practically necessary as a means to the attainment of something else that one wills (or that one may will). A categorical imperative would be one which represented an action as objectively necessary in itself apart from its relation to a further end.

Every practical law represents a possible action as good and therefore as necessary for a subject whose actions are determined by reason. Hence all imperatives are formulae for determining an action which is necessary in accordance with the principle of a will in some sense good. If the action would be good solely as a means *to something else,* the imperative is *hypothetical;* if the action is represented as good *in itself* and therefore necessary, in virtue of its principle, for a will which of itself accords with reason, then the imperative is *categorical.*

An imperative therefore tells me which of my possible actions would be good; and it formulates a practical rule for a will that does not perform an action straight away because the action is good—whether because the subject does not always know that it is good or because, even if he did know this, he might still act on maxims contrary to the objective principles of practical reason.

A hypothetical imperative thus says only that an action is good for some purpose or other, either *possible* or *actual*. In the first case it is a **problematic** practical principle; in the second case an **assertoric** practical principle. A categorical imperative, which declares an action to be objectively necessary in itself without reference to some purpose—that is, even without any further end—ranks as an **apodeictic** practical principle.

Everything that is possible only through the efforts of some rational being can be conceived as a possible purpose of some will; and consequently there are in fact innumerable principles of action so far as action is thought necessary in order to achieve some possible purpose which can be effected by it. All sciences have a practical part consisting of problems which suppose that some end is possible for us and of imperatives which tell us how it is to be attained. Hence the latter can in general be called imperatives of **skill.** Here there is absolutely no question about the rationality or goodness of the end, but only about what must be done to attain it. A prescription required by a doctor in order to cure his man completely and one required by a poisoner in order to make sure of killing him are of equal value so far as each serves to effect its purpose perfectly. Since in early youth we do not know what ends may present themselves to us in the course of life, parents seek above all to make their children learn things *of many kinds;* they provide carefully for *skill* in the use of means to all sorts of *arbitrary* ends, of none of which can they be certain that it could not in the future become an actual purpose of their ward, while it is always *possible* that he might adopt it. Their care in this matter is so great that they commonly neglect on this account to form and correct the judgement of their children about the worth of things which they might possibly adopt as ends.

There is, however, *one* end that can be presupposed as actual in all rational beings (so far as they are dependent beings to whom imperatives apply); and thus there is one purpose which they not only *can* have, but which we can assume with certainty that they all *do* have by a natural necessity—the purpose, namely, of *happiness*. A hypothetical imperative which affirms the practical necessity of an action as a means to the furtherance of happiness is **assertoric.** We may present it, not simply as necessary to an uncertain, merely possible purpose, but as necessary to a purpose which we can presuppose a priori and with certainty to be present in every man because it belongs to his very being. Now skill in the choice of means to one's own greatest well-being can be called *prudence* in the narrowest sense. Thus an imperative concerned with the choice of means to one's own happiness—that is, a precept of prudence—still remains *hypothetical;* an action is commanded, not absolutely, but only as a means to a further purpose.

Finally, there is an imperative which, without being based on, and conditioned by, any further purpose to be attained by a certain line of conduct, enjoins this conduct immediately. This imperative is **categorical.** It is concerned, not with the matter of the action and its presumed results, but with its form and with the principle from which it follows; and what is essentially good in the action consists in the mental disposition, let the consequences be what they may. This imperative may be called the imperative of **morality.**

Willing in accordance with these three kinds of principle is also sharply distinguished by a *dissimilarity* in the necessitation of the will. To make this dissimilarity obvious we should, I think, name these kinds of principle most appropriately in their order if we said they were either *rules* of skill or *counsels* of prudence or *commands (laws)* of morality. For only *law* carries with it the concept of an *unconditioned,* and yet objective and so universally valid, *necessity;* and commands are laws which must be obeyed—that is, must be followed even against inclination. *Counsel* does indeed involve necessity, but necessity valid only under a subjective and contingent condition—namely, if this or that man counts this or that as belonging to his happiness. As against this, a categorical imperative is limited by no condition and can quite precisely be called a command, as being absolutely, although practically, necessary. We could also call imperatives of the first kind *technical* (concerned with art); of the second kind *pragmatic* (concerned with well-being); of the third kind *moral* (concerned with free conduct as such—that is, with morals).

[How Are Imperatives Possible?]

The question now arises "How are all these imperatives possible?" This question does not ask how we can conceive the execution of an action commanded by the imperative, but merely how we can conceive the necessitation of the will expressed by the imperative in setting us a task. How an imperative of skill is possible requires no special discussion. Who wills the end, wills (so far as reason has decisive influence on his actions) also the means which are indispensably necessary and in his power. So far as willing is concerned, this proposition is analytic: for in my willing of an object as an effect there is already conceived the causality of myself as an acting cause—that is, the use of means; and from the concept of willing an end the imperatives merely extracts the concept of actions necessary to this end. (Synthetic propositions are required in order to determine the means of a proposed end, but these are concerned, not with the reason for performing the act of will, but with the cause which produces the object.) That in order to divide a line into two equal parts on a sure principle I must from its ends describe two intersecting arcs—this is admittedly taught by mathematics only in synthetic propositions; but when I know that the aforesaid effect can be produced only by such an action, the proposition "If I fully will the effect, I also will the action required for it" is analytic; for it is one and the same thing to conceive something as an effect possible in a certain way through me and to conceive myself as acting in the same way with respect to it.

If it were only as easy to find a determinate concept of happiness, the imperatives of prudence would agree entirely with those of skill and would be equally analytic. For here as there it could alike be said "Who wills the end, wills also (necessarily, if he accords with reason) the sole means which are in his power." Unfortunately, however, the concept of happiness is so indeterminate a concept that although every man wants to attain happiness, he can never say definitely and in unison with himself what it really is that he wants and wills. The reason for this is that all the elements which belong to the concept of happiness are without exception empirical—that is, they must be borrowed from experience; but that none the less there is required for the Idea of happiness an absolute whole, a maximum of well-being in my present, and in every future, state. Now it is impossible for the most intelligent, and at the same time most powerful, but nevertheless finite, being to form here a determinate concept of what he really wills. Is it riches that he wants? How much anxiety, envy, and pestering might he not bring in this way on his own head! Is it knowledge and insight? This might perhaps merely give him an eye so sharp that it would make evils at present hidden from him and yet unavoidable seem all the more frightful, or would add a load of still further needs to the desires which already give him trouble enough. Is it long life? Who will guarantee that it would not be a long misery? Is it at least healthy? How often has infirmity of body kept a man from excesses into which perfect health would have let him fall—and so on. In short, he has no principle by which he is able to decide with complete certainty what will make him truly happy, since for this he would require omniscience. Thus we cannot act on determinate principles in order to be happy, but only on empirical counsels, for example, of diet, frugality, politeness, reserve, and so on—things which experience shows contribute most to well-being on the average. From this it follows that imperatives of prudence, speaking strictly, do not command at all—that is, cannot exhibit actions objectively as practically *necessary;* that they are rather to be taken as recommendations *(consilia),* than as commands *(praecepta),* of reason; that the problem of determining certainly and universally what action will promote the happiness of a rational being is completely insoluble; and consequently that in regard to this there is no imperative possible which in the strictest sense could command us to do what will make us happy, since happiness is an Ideal, not of reason, but of imagination—an Ideal resting merely on empirical grounds, of which it is vain to expect that they should determine an action by which we could attain the totality of a series of consequences which is in fact infinite. Nevertheless, if we assume that the means to happiness could be discovered with certainty, this imperative of prudence would be an analytic practical proposition; for it differs from the imperative of skill only in this—that in the latter the end is merely possible, while in the former the end is given. In spite of this difference, since both command solely the means to something assumed to be willed as an end, the imperative which commands him who wills the end to will the means is in both cases analytic. Thus there is likewise no difficulty in regard to the possibility of an imperative of prudence.

As against this, the question "How is the imperative of *morality* possible?" is the only one in need of a solution; for it is in no way hypothetical, and consequently we cannot base the objective necessity which it affirms on any presupposition, as we can with hypothetical imperatives. Only we must never forget here that it is impossible to settle *by an example,* and so empirically, whether there is any imperative of this kind at all: we must rather suspect that all imperatives which seem to be categorical may none the less be covertly hypothetical. Take, for example, the saying "Thou shalt make no false promises." Let us assume that the necessity for this abstention is no mere advice for the avoidance of some further evil—as it might be said "You ought not to make a lying promise lest, when this comes to light, you destroy your credit."

Let us hold, on the contrary, that an action of this kind must be considered as bad in itself, and that the imperative of prohibition is therefore categorical. Even so, we cannot with any certainty show by an example that the will is determined here solely by the law without any further motive, although it may appear to be so; for it is always possible that fear of disgrace, perhaps also hidden dread of other risks, may unconsciously influence the will. Who can prove by experience that a cause is not present? Experience shows only that it is not perceived. In such a case, however, the so-called moral imperative, which as such appears to be categorical and unconditioned, would in fact be only a pragmatic prescription calling attention to our advantage and merely bidding us take this into account.

We shall thus have to investigate the possibility of a *categorical* imperative entirely a priori, since here we do not enjoy the advantage of having its reality given in experience and so of being obliged merely to explain, and not to establish, its possibility. So much, however, can be seen provisionally—that the categorical imperative alone purports to be a practical **law,** while all the rest may be called *principles* of the will but not laws; for an action necessary merely in order to achieve an arbitrary purpose can be considered as in itself contingent, and we can always escape from the precept if we abandon the purpose; whereas an unconditioned command does not leave it open to the will to do the opposite at its discretion and therefore alone carries with it that necessity which we demand from a law.

In the second place, with this categorical imperative or law of morality the reason for our difficulty (in comprehending its possibility) is a very serious one. We have here a synthetic a priori practical proposition; and since in theoretical knowledge there is so much difficulty in comprehending the possibility of propositions of this kind, it may readily be gathered that in practical knowledge the difficulty will be no less.

[The Formula of Universal Law]

In this task we wish first to enquire whether perhaps the mere concept of a categorical imperative may not also provide us with the formula containing the only proposition that can be a categorical imperative; for even when we know the purport of such an absolute command, the question of its possibility will still require a special and troublesome effort, which we postpone to the final chapter.

When I conceive a *hypothetical* imperative in general, I do not know beforehand what it will contain—until its condition is given. But if I conceive a *categorical* imperative, I know at once what it contains. For since besides the law this imperative contains only the necessity that our maxim should conform to this law, while the law, as we have seen, contains no condition to limit it, there remains nothing over to which the maxim has to conform except the universality of a law as such; and it is this conformity alone that the imperative properly asserts to be necessary.

There is therefore only a single categorical imperative and it is this: *"Act only on that maxim through which you can at the same time will that it should become a universal law."*

Now if all imperatives of duty can be derived from this one imperative as their principle, then even although we leave it unsettled whether what we call duty may not be an empty concept, we shall still be able to show at least what we understand by it and what the concept means.

[The Formula of the Law of Nature]

Since the universality of the law governing the production of effects constitutes what is properly called *nature* in its most general sense (nature as regards its form)—that is, the existence of things so far as determined by universal laws—the universal imperative of duty may also run as follows: *"Act as if the maxim of your action were to become through your will a Universal Law of Nature."*

[Illustrations]

We will now enumerate a few duties, following their customary division into duties towards self and duties towards others and into perfect and imperfect duties.

1. A man feels sick of life as the result of a series of misfortunes that has mounted to the point of despair, but he is still so far in possession of his reason as to ask himself whether taking his own life may not be contrary to his duty to himself. He now applies the test "Can the maxim of my action really become a universal law of nature?" His maxim is "From self-love I make it my principle to shorten my life if its continuance threatens more evil than it promises pleasure." The only further question to ask is whether this principle of self-love can become a universal law of nature. It is then seen at once that a system of nature by whose law the very same feeling whose function *(Bestimmung)* is to stimulate the furtherance of life should actually destroy life would contradict itself and consequently could not subsist as a system of nature. Hence this maxim cannot possibly hold as a universal law of nature and is therefore entirely opposed to the supreme principle of all duty.

2. Another finds himself driven to borrowing money because of need. He well knows that he will not be able to pay it back; but he sees too that he will get no loan unless he gives a firm promise to pay it back within a fixed time. He is inclined to make such a promise; but he has still enough conscience to ask "Is it not unlawful and contrary to duty to get out of difficulties in this way?" Supposing, however, he did resolve to do so, the maxim of his action would run thus: "Whenever I believe myself short of money, I will borrow money and promise to pay it back, though I know that this will never be done." Now this principle of self-love or personal advantage is perhaps quite compatible with my own entire future welfare; only there remains the question "Is it right?" I therefore transform the demand of self-love into a universal law and frame my question thus: "How would things stand if my maxim became a universal law?" I then see straight away that this maxim can never rank as a universal law and be self-consistent, but must necessarily contradict itself. For the universality of a law that every one believing himself to be in need may make any promise he pleases with the intention not to keep it would make promising, and the very purpose of promising, itself impossible, since no one would believe he was being promised anything, but would laugh at utterances of this kind as empty shams.

3. A third finds in himself a talent whose cultivation would make him a useful man for all sorts of purposes. But he sees himself in comfortable circumstances,

and he prefers to give himself up to pleasure rather than to bother about increasing and improving his fortunate natural aptitudes. Yet he asks himself further "Does my maxim of neglecting my natural gifts, besides agreeing in itself with my tendency to indulgence, agree also with what is called duty?" He then sees that a system of nature could indeed always subsist under such a universal law, although (like the South Sea Islanders) every man should let his talents rust and should be bent on devoting his life solely to idleness, indulgence, procreation, and, in a word, to enjoyment. Only he cannot possibly **will** that this should become a universal law of nature or should be implanted in us as such a law by a natural instinct. For as a rational being he necessarily wills that all his powers should be developed, since they serve him, and are given him, for all sorts of possible ends.

4. Yet a *fourth* is himself flourishing, but he sees others who have to struggle with great hardships (and whom he could easily help); and he thinks "What does it matter to me? Let every one be as happy as Heaven wills or as he can make himself; I won't deprive him of anything; I won't even envy him; only I have no wish to contribute anything to his well-being or to his support in distress!" Now admittedly if such an attitude were a universal law of nature, mankind could get on perfectly well—better no doubt than if everybody prates about sympathy and good will, and even takes pains, on occasion, to practise them, but on the other hand cheats where he can, traffics in human rights, or violates them in other ways. But although it is possible that a universal law of nature could subsist in harmony with this maxim, yet it is impossible to **will** that such a principle should hold everywhere as a law of nature. For a will which decided in this way would be at variance with itself, since many a situation might arise in which the man needed love and sympathy from others, and in which, by such a law of nature sprung from his own will, he would rob himself of all hope of the help he wants for himself.

[The Canon of Moral Judgement]

These are some of the many actual duties—or at least of what we take to be such—whose derivation from the single principle cited above leaps to the eye. We must *be able to will* that a maxim of our action should become a universal law—this is the general canon for all moral judgement of action. Some actions are so constituted that their maxim cannot even be *conceived* as a universal law of nature without contradiction, let alone be *willed* as what *ought* to become one. In the case of others we do not find this inner impossibility, but it is still impossible to *will* that their maxim should be raised to the universality of a law of nature, because such a will would contradict itself. It is easily seen that the first kind of action is opposed to strict or narrow (rigorous) duty, the second only to wider (meritorious) duty; and thus that by these examples all duties—so far as the type of obligation is concerned (not the object of dutiful action)—are fully set out in their dependence on our single principle.

If we now attend to ourselves whenever we transgress a duty, we find that we in fact do not will that our maxim should become a universal law—since this is impossible for us—but rather that its opposite should remain a law universally; we only take the liberty of making an *exception* to it for ourselves (or even just for this once) to the advantage of our inclination. Consequently if we weighed it all up from one and the same point of view—that of reason—we should find a contradiction in our own will, the contradiction that a certain principle should be objectively necessary as a universal law and yet subjectively should not hold universally but should admit of exceptions. Since, however, we first consider our action from the point of view of a will wholly in accord with reason, and then consider precisely the same action from the point of view of a will affected by inclination, there is here actually no contradiction, but rather an opposition of inclination to the precept of reason *(antagonismus)*, whereby the universality of the principle *(universalitas)* is turned into a mere generality *(generalitas)* so that the practical principle of reason may meet our maxim half-way. This procedure, though in our own impartial judgement it cannot be justified, proves none the less that we can in fact recognize the validity of the categorical imperative and (with all respect for it) merely permit ourselves a few exceptions which are, as we pretend, inconsiderable and apparently forced upon us.

We have thus at least shown much—that if duty is a concept which is to have meaning and real legislative authority for our actions, this can be expressed only in categorical imperatives and by no means in hypothetical ones. At the same time—and this is already a great deal—we have set forth distinctly, and determinately for every type of application, the content of the categorical imperative, which must contain the principle of all duty (if there is to be such a thing at all). But we are still not so far advanced as to prove a priori that there actually is an imperative of this kind—that there is a practical law which by itself commands absolutely and without any further motives, and that the following of this law is duty.

[The Formula of the End in Itself]

The will is conceived as a power of determining oneself to action *in accordance with the idea of certain laws*. And such a power can be found only in rational beings. Now what serves the will as a subjective ground of its self-determination is an *end;* and this, if it is given by reason alone, must be equally valid for all rational beings. What, on the other hand, contains merely the ground of the possibility of an action whose effect as an end is called a *means*. The subjective ground of a desire is an *impulsion (Triebfeder);* the objective ground of a volition is a *motive (Bewegungsgrund)*. Hence the difference between subjective ends, which are based on impulsions, and objective ends, which depend on motives valid for every rational being. Practical principles are *formal* if they abstract from all subjective ends; they are *material,* on the other hand, if they are based on such ends and consequently on certain impulsions. Ends that a rational being adopts arbitrarily as *effects* of his action (material ends) are in every case only relative; for it is solely their relation to special characteristics in the subject's power of appetition which gives them their value. Hence this value can provide no universal principles, no principles valid and necessary for all rational beings and also for every volition—that is, no practical laws. Consequently all these relative ends can be the ground only of hypothetical imperatives.

Suppose, however, there were something *whose existence* has *in itself* an absolute value, something which as *an end in itself* could be a ground of determinate laws;

then in it, and in it alone, would there be the ground of a possible categorical imperative—that is, of a practical law.

Now I say that man, and in general every rational being, *exists* as an end in himself, *not merely as a means* for arbitrary use by this or that will: he must in all his actions, whether they are directed to himself or to other rational beings, always be viewed *at the same time as an end.* All the objects of inclination have only a conditioned value; for if there were not these inclinations and the needs grounded on them, their object would be valueless. Inclinations themselves, as sources of needs, are so far from having an absolute value to make them desirable for their own sake that it must rather be the universal wish of every rational being to be wholly free from them. Thus the value of all objects that can *be produced* by our action is always conditioned. Beings whose existence depends, not on our will, but on nature, have none the less, if they are non-rational beings, only a relative value as means and are consequently called *things.* Rational beings, on the other hand, are called *persons* because their nature already marks them out as ends in themselves—that is, as something which ought not to be used merely as a means—and consequently imposes to that extent a limit on all arbitrary treatment of them (and is an object of reverence). Persons, therefore, are not merely subjective ends whose existence as an effect of our actions has a value *for us:* they are *objective ends*—that is, things whose existence is in itself an end, and indeed an end such that in its place we can put no other end to which they should serve *simply* as means; for unless this is so, nothing at all of *absolute* value would be found anywhere. But if all value were conditioned—that is, contingent—then no supreme principle could be found for reason at all.

If then there is to be a supreme practical principle and—so far as the human will is concerned—a categorical imperative, it must be such that from the idea of something which is necessarily an end for every one because it is an *end in itself* it forms an *objective* principle of the will and consequently can serve as a practical law. The ground of this principle is: *Rational nature exists as an end in itself.* This is the way in which a man necessarily conceives his own existence; it is therefore so far a *subjective* principle of human actions. But it is also the way in which every other rational being conceives his existence on the same rational ground which is valid also for me; hence it is at the same time an *objective* principle, from which, as a supreme practical ground, it must be possible to derive all laws for the will. The practical imperative will therefore be as follows: *Act in such a way that you always treat humanity, whether in your own person or in the person of any other, never simply as a means, but always at the same time as an end.* We will now consider whether this can be carried out in practice.

[Illustrations]

Let us keep to our previous examples.

First, as regards the concept of necessary duty to oneself, the man who contemplates suicide will ask "Can my action be compatible with the Idea of humanity *as an end in itself?*" If he does away with himself in order to escape from a painful situation, he is making use of a person merely as a *means* to maintain a tolerable state of affairs till the end of his life. But man is not a thing—not something to be used *merely* as a means: he must always in all his actions be regarded as an end in himself. Hence

I cannot dispose of man in my person by maiming, spoiling, or killing. (A more precise determination of this principle in order to avoid all misunderstanding—for example, about having limbs amputated to save myself or about exposing my life to danger in order to preserve it, and so on—I must here forgo: this question belongs to morals proper.)

Secondly, so far as necessary or strict duty to others is concerned, the man who has a mind to make a false promise to others will see at once that he is intending to make use of another man *merely as a means* to an end he does not share. For the man whom I seek to use for my own purposes by such a promise cannot possibly agree with my way of behaving to him, and so cannot himself share the end of the action. This incompatibility with the principle of duty to others leaps to the eye more obviously when we bring in examples of attempts on the freedom and property of others. For then it is manifest that a violator of the rights of man intends to use the person of others merely as a means without taking into consideration that, as rational beings, they ought always at the same time to be rated as ends—that is, only as beings who must themselves be able to share in the end of the very same action.

Thirdly, in regard to contingent (meritorious) duty to oneself, it is not enough that an action should refrain from conflicting with humanity in our own person as an end in itself: it must also *harmonize with this end.* Now there are in humanity capacities for greater perfection which form part of nature's purpose for humanity in our person. To neglect these can admittedly be compatible with the *maintenance* of humanity as an end in itself, but not with the *promotion* of this end.

Fourthly, as regards meritorious duties to others, the natural end which all men seek is their own happiness. Now humanity could no doubt subsist if everybody contributed nothing to the happiness of others but at the same time refrained from deliberately impairing their happiness. This is, however, merely to agree negatively and not positively with *humanity as an end in itself* unless every one endeavours also, so far as in him lies, to further the ends of others. For the ends of a subject who is an end in himself must, if this conception is to have its *full* effect in me, be also, as far as possible, *my* ends.

[The Formula of Autonomy]

This principle of humanity, and in general of every rational agent, *as an end in itself* (a principle which is the supreme limiting condition of every man's freedom of action) is not borrowed from experience; firstly, because it is universal, applying as it does to all rational beings as such, and no experience is adequate to determine universality; secondly, because in it humanity is conceived, not as an end of man (subjectively)—that is, as an object which, as a matter of fact, happens to be made an end—but as an objective end—one which, be our ends what they may, must, as a law, constitute the supreme limiting condition of all subjective ends and so must spring from pure reason. That is to say, the ground for every enactment of practical law lies *objectively in the rule* and in the form of universality which (according to our first principle) makes the rule capable of being a law (and indeed a law of nature); *subjectively,* however, it lies in the *end;* but (according to our second principle) the subject of all ends is to be found in every rational being as an end in himself. From this there now follows our third practical principle for the will—as the supreme condition of the will's conformity with universal practical reason—namely, the Idea *of the will of every rational being as a will which makes universal law.*

By this principle all maxims are repudiated which cannot accord with the will's own enactment of universal law. The will is therefore not merely subject to the law, but is so subject that it must be considered as also *making the law* for itself and precisely on this account as first of all subject to the law (of which it can regard itself as the author).

[The Exclusion of Interest]

Imperatives as formulated above—namely, the imperative enjoining conformity of actions to universal law on the analogy of a *natural order* and that enjoining the universal *supremacy* of rational beings in themselves *as ends*—did, by the mere fact that they were represented as categorical, exclude from their sovereign authority every admixture of interest as a motive. They were, however, merely *assumed* to be categorical because we were bound to make this assumption if we wished to explain the concept of duty. That they were practical propositions which commanded categorically could not itself be proved, any more than it can be proved in this chapter generally; but one thing could have been done—namely, to show that in willing for the sake of duty renunciation of all interest, as the specific mark distinguishing a categorical from a hypothetical imperative, was expressed in the very imperative itself by means of some determination inherent in it. This is what is done in the present third formulation of the principle—namely, in the Idea of the will of every rational being as *a will which makes universal law.*

Once we conceive a will of this kind, it becomes clear that while a will *which is subject to law* may be bound to this law by some interest, nevertheless a will which is itself a supreme lawgiver cannot possibly as such depend on any interest; for a will which is dependent in this way would itself require yet a further law in order to restrict the interest of self-love to the condition that this interest should itself be valid as a universal law.

Thus the *principle* that every human will is *a will which by all its maxims enacts universal law*—provided only that it were right in other ways—would be *well suited* to be a categorical imperative in this respect: that precisely because of the idea of making universal law it is *based on no interest* and consequently can alone among all possible imperatives be *unconditioned.* Or better still—to convert the proposition—if there is a categorical imperative (that is, a law for the will of every rational being), it can command us only to act always on the maxim of such a will in us as can at the same time look upon itself as making universal law; for only then is the practical principle and the imperative which we obey unconditioned, since it is wholly impossible for it to be based on any interest.

We need not now wonder, when we look back upon all the previous efforts that have been made to discover the principle of morality, why they have one and all been bound to fail. Their authors saw man as tied to laws by his duty, but it never occurred to them that he is subject only to *laws which are made by himself* and yet are *universal,* and that he is bound only to act in accordance with a will which is his own but has for its natural purpose the function of making universal law. For when they thought of man merely as subject to a law (whatever it might be), the law had to carry with it some interest in order to attract or compel, because it did not spring as a law from *his own* will: in order to conform with the law his will had to be necessitated by *something else* to act in a certain way. This absolutely inevitable conclusion meant that all the labour spent in trying to find a supreme principle of duty was lost beyond recall; for what they discovered was never duty, but only the necessity of acting from a certain interest. This interest might be one's own or another's; but on such a view the imperative was bound to be always a conditioned one and could not possibly serve as a moral law. I will therefore call my principle the principle of the **Autonomy** of the will in contrast with all others, which I consequently class under **Heteronomy.**

[The Formula of the Kingdom of Ends]

The concept of every rational being as one who must regard himself as making universal law by all the maxims of his will, and must seek to judge himself and his actions from this point of view, leads to a closely connected and very fruitful concept— namely, that of a *kingdom of ends.*

I understand by a *"kingdom"* a systematic union of different rational beings under common laws. Now since laws determine ends as regards their universal validity, we shall be able—if we abstract from the personal differences between rational beings, and also from all the content of their private ends—to conceive a whole of all ends in systematic conjunction (a whole both of rational beings as ends in themselves and also of the personal ends which each may set before himself); that is, we shall be able to conceive a kingdom of ends which is possible in accordance with the above principles.

For rational beings all stand under the *law* that each of them should treat himself and all others, *never merely as a means,* but always *at the same time as an end in himself.* But by so doing there arises a systematic union of rational beings under common objective laws—that is, a kingdom. Since these laws are directed precisely to the relation of such beings to one another as ends and means, this kingdom can be called a kingdom of ends (which is admittedly only an Ideal).

A rational being belongs to the kingdom of ends as a *member,* when, although he makes its universal laws, he is also himself subject to these laws. He belongs to it as its *head,* when as the maker of laws he is himself subject to the will of no other.

A rational being must always regard himself as making laws in a kingdom of ends which is possible through freedom of the will—whether it be as member or as head. The position of the latter he can maintain, not in virtue of the maxim of his will alone, but only if he is a completely independent being, without needs and with an unlimited power adequate to his will.

Thus morality consists in the relation of all action to the making of laws whereby alone a kingdom of ends is possible. This making of laws must be found in every rational being himself and must be able to spring from his will. The principle of his will is therefore never to perform an action except on a maxim such as can also be a universal law, and consequently such *that the will can regard itself as at the same time making universal law by means of its maxim.* Where maxims are not already by their very nature in harmony with this objective principle of rational beings as makers of universal law, the necessity of acting on this principle is practical necessitation—that is, *duty.* Duty does not apply to the head in a kingdom of ends, but it does apply to every member and to all members in equal measure.

The practical necessity of acting on this principle—that is, duty—is in no way based on feelings, impulses, and inclinations, but only on the relation of rational beings to one another, a relation in which the will of a rational being must always be regarded as *making universal law,* because otherwise he could not be conceived as *an end in himself.* Reason thus relates every maxim of the will, considered as making universal law, to every other will and also to every action towards oneself: it does so, not because of any further motive or future advantage, but from the Idea of the *dignity* of a rational being who obeys no law other than that which he at the same time enacts himself.

[The Dignity of Virtue]

In the kingdom of ends everything has either a *price* or a *dignity.* If it has a price, something else can be put in its place as an *equivalent;* if it is exalted above all price and so admits of no equivalent, then it has a dignity.

What is relative to universal human inclinations and needs has a *market price;* what, even without presupposing a need, accords with a certain taste—that is, with satisfaction in the mere purposeless play of our mental powers—has a *fancy price (Affektionspreis);* but that which constitutes the sole condition under which anything can be an end in itself has not merely a relative value—that is, a price—but has an intrinsic value—that is, *dignity.*

Now morality is the only condition under which a rational being can be an end in himself; for only through this is it possible to be a law-making member in a kingdom of ends. Therefore morality, and humanity so far as it is capable of morality, is the only thing which has dignity. Skill and diligence in work have a market price; wit, lively imagination, and humour have a fancy price; but fidelity to promises and kindness based on principle (not on instinct) have an intrinsic worth. In default of these, nature and art alike contain nothing to put in their place; for their worth consists, not in the effects which result from them, not in the advantage or profit they produce, but in the attitudes of mind—that is, in the maxims of the will—which are ready in this way to manifest themselves in action even if they are not favoured by success. Such actions too need no recommendation from any subjective disposition or taste in order to meet with immediate favour and approval; they need no immediate propensity or feeling for themselves; they exhibit the will which performs them as an object of immediate reverence; nor is anything other than reason required to *impose* them upon the will, not to *coax* them from the will—which last would anyhow be a contradiction in the case of duties. This assessment reveals as dignity the value of such a mental attitude and puts it infinitely above all price, with which it cannot be brought into reckoning or comparison without, as it were, a profanation of its sanctity.

What is it then that entitles a morally good attitude of mind—of virtue—to make claims so high? It is nothing less than the *share* which it affords to a rational being *in the making of universal law,* and which therefore fits him to be a member in a possible kingdom of ends. For this he was already marked out in virtue of his own proper nature as an end in himself and consequently as a maker of laws in the kingdom of ends—as free in respect of all laws of nature, obeying only those laws which he makes himself and in virtue of which his maxims can have their part in the making of universal law (to which he at the same time subjects himself). For nothing can have a value other than that determined for it by the law. But the law-making which determines all value must for this reason have a dignity—that is, an unconditioned and incomparable worth—for the appreciation of which, as necessarily given by a rational being, the word *"reverence"* is the only becoming expression. *Autonomy* is therefore the ground of the dignity of human nature and of every rational nature.

[Review of the Formulae]

The aforesaid three ways of representing the principle of morality are at bottom merely so many formulations of precisely the same law, one of them by itself containing a combination of the other two. There is nevertheless a difference between them, which, however, is subjectively rather than objectively practical; that is to say, its purpose is to bring an Idea of reason nearer to intuition (in accordance with a certain analogy) and so nearer to feeling. All maxims have, in short,

1. a *form,* which consists in their universality; and in this respect the formula of the moral imperative is expressed thus: "Maxims must be chosen as if they had to hold as universal laws of nature";
2. a *matter*—that is, an end; and in this respect the formula says: "A rational being, as by his very nature an end and consequently an end in himself, must serve for every maxim as a condition limiting all merely relative and arbitrary ends";
3. a *complete determination* of all maxims by the following formula, namely: "All maxims as proceeding from our own making of law ought to harmonize with a possible kingdom of ends as a kingdom of nature." This progression may be said to take place through the categories of the *unity of* the form of will (its universality); of the *multiplicity* of its matter (its objects—that is, its ends); and of the *totality* or completeness of its systems of ends. It is, however, better if in moral *judgement* we proceed always in accordance with the strictest method and take as our basis the universal formula of the categorical imperative; *"Act on the maxim which can at the same time be made a universal law."* If, however, we wish also to secure acceptance for the moral law, it is very useful to bring one and the same action under the above-mentioned three concepts and so, as far as we can, to bring the universal formula nearer to intuition.

[Review of the Whole Argument]

We can now end at the point from which we started out at the beginning—namely, the concept of an unconditionally good will. The *will* is *absolutely good* if it cannot be evil—that is, if its maxim, when made into a universal law, can never be at variance with itself. This principle is therefore also its supreme law: "Act always on that maxim whose universality as a law you can at the same time will." This is the one principle on which a will can never be at variance with itself, and such an imperative is categorical. Because the validity of the will as a universal law for possible actions is analogous to the universal interconnexion of existent things in accordance with universal laws—which constitutes the formal aspect of nature as such—we can also express the categorical imperative as follows: "*Act on that maxim which can at the same time have for its object itself as a universal law of nature.*" In this way we provide the formula for an absolutely good will.

Rational nature separates itself out from all other things by the fact that it sets itself an end. An end would thus be the matter of every good will. But in the Idea of a will which is absolutely good—good without any qualifying condition (namely, that it should attain this or that end)—there must be complete abstraction from every end that has to be *produced* (as something which would make every will only relatively good). Hence the end must here be conceived, not as an end to be produced, *but as a self-existent* end. It must therefore be conceived only negatively—that is, as an end against which we should never act, and consequently as one which in all our willing we must never rate *merely* as a means, but always at the same time as an end. Now this end can be nothing other than the subject of all possible ends himself, because this subject is also the subject of a will that may be absolutely good; for such a will cannot without contradiction be subordinated to any other object. The principle "So act in relation to every rational being (both to yourself and to others) that he may at the same time count in your maxim as an end in himself" is thus at bottom the same as the principle "Act on a maxim which at the same time contains in itself its own universal validity for every rational being." For to say that in using means to every end I ought to restrict my maxim by the condition that it should also be universally valid as a law for every subject is just the same as to say this—that a subject of ends, namely, a rational being himself, must be made the ground for all maxims of action, never *merely* as a means, but as a supreme condition restricting the use of every means—that is, always also as an end.

Now from this it unquestionably follows that every rational being, as an end in himself, must be able to regard himself as also the maker of universal law in respect to any law whatever to which he may be subjected: for it is precisely the fitness of his maxims to make universal law that marks him out as an end in himself. It follows equally that this dignity (or prerogative) of his above all the mere things of nature carries with it the necessity of always choosing his maxims from the point of view of himself—and also of every other rational being—as a maker of law (and this is why they are called persons). It is in this way that a world of rational beings (*mundus intelligibilis*) is possible as a kingdom of ends—possible, that is, through the making of their own laws by all persons as its members. Accordingly every rational being must so act as if he were through his maxims always a law-making member in the universal kingdom of ends. The formal principle of such maxims is "So act as if your maxims had to serve at the same time as a universal law (for all rational beings)." Thus a kingdom of ends is possible only on the analogy of a kingdom of nature; yet the kingdom of ends is possible only through maxims—that is, self-imposed rules—while nature is possible only through laws concerned with causes whose action is necessitated from without. In spite of this difference, we give to nature as a whole, even although it is regarded as a machine, the name of a "kingdom of nature" so far as—and for the reason that—it stands in a relation to rational beings as its ends. Now a kingdom of ends would actually come into existence through maxims which the categorical imperative prescribes as a rule for all rational beings, *if these maxims were universally followed.* Yet even if a rational being were himself to follow such a maxim strictly, he cannot count on everybody else being faithful to it on this ground, nor can he be confident that the kingdom of nature and its purposive order will work in harmony with him, as a fitting member, towards a kingdom of ends made possible by himself—or, in other words, that it will favour his expectation of happiness. But in spite of this the law "Act on the maxims of a member who makes universal laws for a merely possible kingdom of ends" remains in full force, since its command is categorical. And precisely here we encounter the paradox that without any further end or advantage to be attained the mere dignity of humanity, that is, of rational nature in man—and consequently that reverence for a mere idea—should function as an inflexible precept for the will; and that it is just this freedom from dependence on interested motives which constitutes the sublimity of a maxim and the worthiness of every rational subject to be a law-making member in the kingdom of ends; for otherwise he would have to be regarded as subject only to the law of nature—the law of his own needs. Even if it were thought that both the kingdom of nature and the kingdom of ends were united under one head and that thus the latter kingdom ceased to be a mere Idea and achieved genuine reality, the Idea would indeed gain by this the addition of a strong motive, but never any increase in its intrinsic worth; for, even if this were so, it would still be necessary to conceive the unique and absolute lawgiver himself as judging the worth of rational beings solely by the disinterested behaviour they prescribed to themselves in virtue of this idea alone. The essence of things does not vary with their external relations; and where there is something which, without regard to such relations, constitutes by itself the absolute worth of man, it is by this that man must also be judged by everyone whatsoever—even by the Supreme Being. Thus *morality* lies in the relation of actions to the autonomy of the will—that is, to a possible making of universal law by means of its maxims. An action which is compatible with the autonomy of the will is *permitted;* on which does not harmonize with it is *forbidden.* A will whose maxims necessarily accord with the laws of autonomy is a *holy,* or absolutely good, will. The dependence of a will not absolutely good on the principle of autonomy (that is, moral necessitation) is *obligation.* Obligation can thus have no reference to a holy being. The objective necessary to act from obligation is called *duty.*

From what was said a little time ago we can now easily explain how it comes about that, although in the concept of duty we think of subjection to the law, yet we also at the same time attribute to the person who fulfils all his duties a certain sublimity and *dignity.* For it is not in so far as he is *subject* to the law that he has sublimity, but rather in so far as, in regard to this very same law, he is at the same time its *author* and is subordinated to it only on this ground. We have also shown above how neither fear nor inclination, but solely reverence for the law, is the motive which can give an action moral worth. Our own will, provided it were to act only under the condition of being able to make universal law by means of its maxims—this deal will which can be ours is the proper object of reverence; and the dignity of man consists precisely in his capacity to make universal law, although only on condition of being himself also subject to the law he makes.

ARISTOTLE

Morality and Human Nature

In these passages from *The Nicomachean Ethics*, Aristotle (384–322 B.C.) presents several of his central views on ethics. He argues that we can discover what a good life is for human beings by considering what the function of human beings is. This function is to be found in reasoning well. Aristotle also defends his Doctrine of the Mean, which is intended to explain which character traits (virtues) best promote human flourishing.

1. THE HIGHEST GOOD: HAPPINESS

1.1 The Highest Good Is Supreme in the Hierarchy of Gods

i 1   *Goods Correspond to Ends*

1094a   Every craft and every investigation, and likewise every action and decision, seems to aim at some good; hence the good has been well described as that at which everything aims.

However, there is an apparent difference among the ends aimed at. For the end is sometimes an activity, sometimes a product beyond the activity; and when there is an end beyond the action, the product is by nature better than the activity.

The Hierarchy of Goods Corresponds to the Hierarchy of Ends

Since there are many actions, crafts and sciences, the ends turn out to be many as well; for health is the end of medicine, a boat of boatbuilding, victory of generalship, and wealth of household management.

But whenever any of these sciences are subordinate to some one capacity—as e.g. bridlemaking and every other science producing equipment for horses are subordinate to horsemanship, while this and every action in warfare are in turn subordinate generalship, and in the same way other sciences are subordinate to further ones—in each of these the end of the ruling science is more choiceworthy than all

Reprinted from Aristotle, *Nicomachean Ethics*, translated by T. Irwin (Indianapolis: Hackett Publishing Co., 1985), 1094a1–1096a10, 1097a15–1099b8, 1102a5–1109b27, 1177a11–1179a132. Copyright © 1985 by Terence Irwin. Reprinted by permission of Hackett Publishing Company, Inc.

the ends subordinate to it, since it is the end for which those ends are also pursued. And here it does not matter whether the ends of the actions are the activities themselves, or some product beyond them, as in the sciences we have mentioned.

The Highest Good

i 2　Suppose, then, that (a) there is some end of the things we pursue in our actions which we wish for because of itself, and because of which we wish for the other things; and (b) we do not choose everything because of something else, since (c) if we do, it will go on without limit, making desire empty and futile; then clearly (d) this end will be the good, i.e. the best good.

1.2 The Ruling Science Studying the Highest Good Is Political Science

The Importance of Finding the Science of the Highest Good

Then surely knowledge of this good is also of great importance for the conduct of our lives, and if, like archers, we have a target to aim at, we are more likely to hit the right mark. If so, we should try to grasp, in outline at any rate, what the good is, and which science or capacity is concerned with it.

The Relevant Science Is Political Science

It seems to concern the most controlling science, the one that, more than any other, is the ruling science. And political science apparently has this character.

(1) For it is the one that prescribes which of the sciences ought to be studied in 1094b　cities, and which ones each class in the city should learn, and how far.

(2) Again, we see that even the most honoured capacities, e.g. generalship, household management and rhetoric, are subordinate to it.

(3) Further, it uses the other sciences concerned with action, and moreover legislates what must be done and what avoided.

Hence its end will include the ends of the other sciences, and so will be the human good.

[This is properly called political science;] for though admittedly the good is the same for a city as for an individual, still the good of the city is apparently a greater and more complete good to acquire and preserve. For while it is satisfactory to acquire and preserve the good even for an individual, it is finer and more divine to acquire and preserve it for a people and for cities. And so, since our investigation aims at these [goods, for an individual and for a city], it is a sort of political science.

1.3 The Method of Political Inquiry

The Demand for Exactness Must Be Limited by the Nature of Ethics

i 3　Our discussion will be adequate if its degree of clarity fits the subject-matter; for we should not seek the same degree of exactness in all sorts of arguments alike, any more than in the products of different crafts.

Moreover, what is fine and what is just, the topics of inquiry in political science, differ and vary so much that they seem to rest on convention only, not on nature. Goods, however, also vary in the same sort of way, since they cause harm to many people; for it has happened that some people have been destroyed because of their wealth, others because of their bravery.

The Proper Aim of Ethical Theory

Since these, then, are the sorts of things we argue from and about, it will be satisfactory if we can indicate the truth roughly and in outline; since [that is to say] we argue from and about what holds good usually [but not universally], it will be satisfactory if we can draw conclusions of the same sort.

How to Judge an Ethical Theory

Each of our claims, then, ought to be accepted in the same way [as claiming to hold good usually], since the educated person seeks exactness in each area to the extent that the nature of the subject allows; for apparently it is just as mistaken to demand demonstrations from a rhetorician as to accept [merely] persuasive arguments from a mathematician.

1095a   Further, each person judges well what he knows, and is a good judge about that; hence the good judge in a particular area is the person educated in that area, and the unconditionally good judge is the person educated in every area.

Qualifications of the Student of Ethics

This is why a youth is not a suitable student of political science; for he lacks experience of the actions in life which political science argues from and about.

Moreover, since he tends to be guided by his feelings, his study will be futile and useless; for its end is action, not knowledge. And here it does not matter whether he is young in years or immature in character, since the deficiency does not depend on age, but results from being guided in his life and in each of his pursuits by his feelings; for an immature person, like an incontinent person, gets no benefit from his knowledge.

If, however, we are guided by reason in forming our desires and in acting, then this knowledge will be of great benefit.

These are the preliminary points about the student, about the way our claims are to be accepted, and about what we intend to do.

1.4 Common Beliefs About the Highest Good Are Inadequate

1.4.1 Most People Identify the Good with Happiness, but Disagree About the Nature of Happiness

i 4   Let us, then, begin again. Since every sort of knowledge and decision pursues some good, what is that good which we say is the aim of political science? What [in other words] is the highest of all the goods pursued in action?

As far as its name goes, most people virtually agree [about what the good is], since both the many and the cultivated call it happiness, and suppose that living well and doing well are the same as being happy. But they disagree about what happiness is, and the many do not give the same answer as the wise.

For the many think it is something obvious and evident, e.g. pleasure, wealth or honour, some thinking one thing, others another; and indeed the same person keeps changing his mind, since in sickness he thinks it is health, in poverty wealth. And when they are conscious of their own ignorance, they admire anyone who speaks of something grand and beyond them.

[Among the wise,] however, some used to think that besides these many goods there is some other good that is something in itself, and also causes all these goods to be goods.

1.4.2 Ethical Method

We Must Examine These Common Beliefs; but We Must Not Take for Granted Our First Principles, Since We Are Arguing Towards Them, Not from Them

Presumably, then, it is rather futile to examine all these beliefs, and it is enough to examine those that are most current or seem to have some argument for them.

We must notice, however, the difference between arguments from origins and arguments towards origins. For indeed Plato was right to be puzzled about this, when he used to ask if [the argument] set out from the origins or led towards them—just as on a race course the path may go from the starting-line to the far end, or back again.

1095b

To Argue Towards First Principles We Must Begin from Common Beliefs That Are Familiar to Us

For while we should certainly begin from origins that are known, things are known in two ways; for some are known to us, some known unconditionally [but not necessarily known to us]. Presumably, then, the origin *we* should begin from is what is known to *us*.

To Become Familiar with Common Beliefs We Need a Good Upbringing

This is why we need to have been brought up in fine habits if we are to be adequate students of what is fine and just, and of political questions generally. For the origin we begin from is the belief that something is true, and if this is apparent enough to us, we will not, at this stage, need the reason why it is true in addition; and if we have this good upbringing, we have the origins to begin from, or can easily acquire them. Someone who neither has them nor can acquire them should listen to Hesiod: 'He who understands everything himself is best of all; he is noble also who listens to one who has spoken well; but he who neither understands it himself nor takes to heart what he hears from another is a useless man.'

1.4.3 Three Conceptions of the Best Life Reflect Common Beliefs About the Good, but Face Criticism from Other Common Beliefs

i 5

But let us begin again from [the common beliefs] from which we digressed. For, it would seem, people quite reasonably reach their conception of the good, i.e. of happiness, from the lives [they lead]; for there are roughly three most favoured lives—the lives of gratification, of political activity, and, third, of study.

The Life of Gratification: Pleasure

The many, the most vulgar, would seem to conceive the good and happiness as pleasure, and hence they also like the life of gratification. Here they appear completely slavish, since the life they decide on is a life for grazing animals; and yet they have argument in their defence, since many in positions of power feel the same way as Sardanapallus [and also choose this life].

The Life of Action: Honour or Virtue

The cultivated people, those active [in politics], conceive the good as honour, since this is more or less the end [normally pursued] in the political life. This, however, appears to be too superficial to be what we are seeking, since it seems to depend more on those who honour than on the one honoured, whereas we intuitively believe that the good is something of our own and hard to take from us.

Further, it would seem, they pursue honour to convince themselves that they are good; at any rate, they seek to be honoured by intelligent people, among people who know them, and for virtue. It is clear, then, that in the view of active people at least, virtue is superior [to honour].

1096a
Perhaps, indeed, one might conceive virtue more than honour to be the end of the political life. However, this also is apparently too incomplete [to be the good]. For it seems, someone might possess virtue but be asleep or inactive throughout his life; or, further, he might suffer the worst evils and misfortunes; and if this is the sort of life he leads, no one would count him happy, except to defend a philosopher's paradox. Enough about this, since it has been adequately discussed in the popular works also.

The Life of Study

The third life is the life of study, which we will examine in what follows.

The Life of Money-Making May Be Safely Ignored

The money-maker's life is in a way forced on him [not chosen for itself]; and clearly wealth is not the good we are seeking, since it is [merely] useful, [choiceworthy only] for some other end. Hence one would be more inclined to support that [any of] the goods mentioned earlier is the end, since they are liked for themselves. But apparently they are not [the end] either; and many arguments have been presented against them. Let us, then, dismiss them.

•   •   •

i 7
(1) The Good Is the End of Action

But let us return once again to the good we are looking for, and consider just what it could be, since it is apparently one thing in one action or craft, and another thing in another; for it is one thing in medicine, another in generalship, and so on for the rest.

What, then, is the good in each of these cases? Surely it is that for the sake of which the other things are done; and in medicine this is health, in generalship victory, in house-building a house, in another case something else, but in every action and decision it is the end, since it is for the sake of the end that everyone does the other things.

And so, if there is some end of everything that is pursued in action, this will be the good pursued in action; and if there are more ends than one, these will be the goods pursued in action.

Our argument has progressed, then, to the same conclusion [as before, that the highest end is the good]; but we must try to clarify this still more.

(2) The Good Is Complete

Though apparently there are many ends, we choose some of them, e.g. wealth, flutes and, in general, instruments, because of something else; hence it is clear that not all ends are complete. But the best good is apparently something complete. Hence, if only one end is complete, this will be what we are looking for; and if more than one are complete, the most complete of these will be what we are looking for.

Criteria for Completeness

An end pursued in itself, we say, is more complete than an end pursued because of something else; and an end that is never choiceworthy because of something else is more complete than ends that are choiceworthy both in themselves and because of this end; and hence an end that is always [choiceworthy, and also] choiceworthy in itself, never because of something else, is unconditionally complete.

(3) Happiness Meets the Criteria for Completeness, but Other Goods Do Not

1097b Now happiness more than anything else seems unconditionally complete, since we always [choose it, and also] choose it because of itself, never because of something else.

Honour, pleasure, understanding and every virtue we certainly choose because of themselves, since we would choose each of them even if it had no further result, but we also choose them for the sake of happiness, supposing that through them we shall be happy. Happiness, by contrast, no one ever chooses for their sake, or for the sake of anything else at all.

(4) The Good Is Self-Sufficient; So Is Happiness

The same conclusion [that happiness is complete] also appears to follow from self-sufficiency, since the complete good seems to be self-sufficient.

Now what we count as self-sufficient is not what suffices for a solitary person by himself, living an isolated life, but what suffices also for parents, children, wife and in general for friends and fellow-citizens, since a human being is a naturally political [animal]. Here, however, we must impose some limit; for if we extend the good to parents' parents and children's children and to friends of friends, we shall go on without limit; but we must examine this another time.

Anyhow, we regard something as self-sufficient when all by itself it makes a life choiceworthy and lacking nothing; and that is what we think happiness does.

(5) What Is Self-Sufficient Is Most Choiceworthy; So Is Happiness

Moreover, we think happiness is most choiceworthy of all goods, since it is not counted as one good among many. If it were counted as one among many, then, clearly, we think that the addition of the smallest of goods would make it more choice-worthy; for [the smallest good] that is added becomes an extra quantity of goods [so creating a good larger than the original good], and the larger of two goods is always more choiceworthy. [But we do not think any addition can make happiness more choiceworthy; hence it is most choiceworthy.]

Happiness, then, is apparently something complete and self-sufficient, since it is the end of the things pursued in action.

1.5.2 A Clearer Account of the Good: The Human Soul's Activity Expressing Virtue

But presumably the remark that the best good is happiness is apparently something [generally] agreed, and what we miss is a clearer statement of what the best good is.

(1) If Something Has a Function, Its Good Depends on Its Function

Well, perhaps we shall find the best good if we first find that function of a human being. For just as the good, i.e. [doing] well, for a flautist, a sculptor, and every crafts-man and, in general, for whatever has a function and [characteristic] action, seems to depend on its function, and the same seems to be true for a human being, if a human being has some function.

(2) What Sorts of Things Have Functions?

Then do the carpenter and the leatherworker have their functions and actions, while a human being has none, and is by nature idle, without any function? Or, just as eye, hand, foot and, in general, every [bodily] part apparently has its functions, may we likewise ascribe to a human being some function besides all of theirs?

(3) The Human Function

What, then, could this be? For living is apparently shared with plants, but what we 1098a are looking for is the special function of a human being; hence we should set aside the life of nutrition and growth. The life next in order is some sort of life of sense-perception; but this too is apparently shared, with horse, ox and every animal. The remaining possibility, then, is some sort of life of action of the [part of the soul] that has reason.

Clarification of "Has Reason" and "Life"

Now this [part has two parts, which have reason in different ways], one as obey-ing the reason [in the other part], the other as itself having reason and thinking. [We intend both.] Moreover, life is also spoken of in two ways [as capacity and as activity], and we must take [a human being's special function to be] life as activity, since this seems to be called life to a fuller extent.

(4) The Human Good Is Activity Expressing Virtue

(a) We have found, then, that the human function is the soul's activity that ex-presses reason [as itself having reason] or requires reason [as obeying reason]. (b) Now the function of F, e.g. of a harpist, is the same in kind, so we say, as the function of an excellent F, e.g. an excellent harpist. (c) The same is true unconditionally in every case, when we add to the function the superior achievement that expresses the virtue; for a harpist's function, e.g. is to play the harp, and a good harpist's is to do it well. (d) Now we take the human function to be a certain kind of life, and take this life to be the soul's activity and actions that express reason. (e) [Hence by (c) and (d)] the excellent man's function is to do this finely and well. (f) Each function is completed well when its completion expresses the proper virtue. (g) Therefore [by (d), (e) and (f)] the human good turns out to be the soul's activity that expresses virtue.

(5) The Good Must Also Be Complete

And if there are more virtues than one, the good will express the best and most complete virtue. Moreover, it will be in a complete life. For one swallow does not make a spring, nor does one day; nor, similarly, does one day or a short time make us blessed and happy.

1.6 Defence of the Account of the Good, from Principles of Ethical Method

1.6.1 It Is Reasonable That Our Account Is Only a Sketch

This, then, is a sketch of the good; for, presumably, the outline must come first, to be filled in later. If the sketch is good, then anyone, it seems, can advance and articulate it, and in such cases time is a good discoverer or [at least] a good co-worker. That is also how the crafts have improved, since anyone can add what is lacking [in the outline].

1.6.2 The Inexactness of Our Account Suits the Subject-Matter

However, we must also remember our previous remarks, so that we do not look for the same degree of exactness in all areas, but the degree that fits the subject-matter in each area and is proper to the investigation. For the carpenter's and the geometer's inquiries about the right angle are different also; the carpenter's is confined to the right angle's usefulness for his work, whereas the geometer's concerns what, or what sort of thing, the right angle is, since he studies the truth. We must do the same, then, in other areas too, [seeking the proper degree of exactness], so that digressions do not overwhelm our main task.

1.6.3 Having Found a First Principle, We Should Not Demand a Further Principle Beyond It

1098b   Nor should we make the same demand for an explanation in all cases. Rather, in some cases it is enough to prove that something is true without explaining why it is true. This is so, e.g. with origins, where the fact that something is true is the first principle, i.e. the origin.

Some origins are studied by means of induction, some by means of perception, some by means of some sort of habituation, and others by other means. In each case we should try to find them out by means suited to their nature, and work hard to define them well. For they have a great influence on what follows; for the origin seems to be more than half the whole, and makes evident the answer to many of our questions.

1.7 Defence of the Account of the Good, from Common Beliefs

i 8   However, we should examine the origin not only from the conclusion and premises [of a deductive argument], but also from what is said about it; for all the facts harmonize with a true account, whereas the truth soon clashes with a false one.

1.7.1 A Common Classification of Goods

Goods are divided, then, into three types, some called external, some goods of the soul, others goods of the body; and the goods of the soul are said to be goods to the fullest extent and most of all, and the soul's actions and activities are ascribed to the soul. Hence the account [of the good] is sound, to judge by this belief anyhow—and it is an ancient belief agreed on by philosophers.

Our account is also correct in saying that some sort of actions and activities are the end; for then the end turns out to be a good of the soul, not an external good.

1.7.2 A Common Conception of Happiness

The belief that the happy person lives well and does well in action also agrees with our account, since we have virtually said that the end is a sort of living well and doing well in action.

1.7.3 Commonly Accepted Features of Happiness

Further, all the features that people look for in happiness appear to be true of the end described in our account. For to some people it seems to be virtue; to others intelligence; to others some sort of wisdom; to others again it seems to be these, or one of these, involving pleasure or requiring its addition; and others add in external prosperity as well.

Some of these views are traditional, held by many, while others are held by a few reputable men; and it is reasonable for each group to be not entirely in error, but correct on one point at least, or even on most points.

Virtue

First, our account agrees with those who say happiness is virtue [in general] or some [particular] virtue; for activity expressing virtue is proper to virtue. Presumably, though, it matters quite a bit whether we suppose that the best good consists in possessing or in using, i.e. in a state or in an activity [that actualizes the state]. For 1099a   while someone may be in a state that achieves no good, if, e.g., he is asleep or inactive in some other way, this cannot be true of the activity; for it will necessarily do actions and do well in them. And just as Olympic prizes are not for the finest and strongest, but for contestants, since it is only these who win; so also in life [only] the fine and good people who act correctly win the prize.

Pleasure

Moreover, the life of these [active] people is also pleasant in itself. For being pleased is a condition of the soul, [hence included in the activity of the soul]. Further, each type of person finds pleasure in whatever he is called a lover of, so that a horse, e.g. pleases the horse-lover, a spectacle the lover of spectacles, and similarly what is just pleases the lover of justice, and in general what expresses virtue pleases the lover of virtue. Hence the things that please most people conflict, because they are not pleasant by nature, whereas the things that please lovers of what is fine are things pleasant by nature; and actions expressing virtue are pleasant in this way; and so they both please lovers of what is fine and are pleasant in themselves.

Hence their life does not need pleasure to be added [to virtuous activity] as some sort of ornament; rather, it has its pleasure within itself. For besides the reasons already given, someone who does not enjoy fine actions is not good; for no one would call him just, e.g., if he did not enjoy doing just actions, or generous if he did not enjoy generous actions, and similarly for the other virtues. If this is so, then actions expressing the virtues are pleasant in themselves.

Hence Our Account Satisfies Traditional Ideals

Moreover, these actions are good and fine as well as pleasant; indeed, they are good, fine and pleasant more than anything else, since on this question the excellent person has good judgement, and his judgement agrees with our conclusions.

Happiness, then, is best, finest and most pleasant, and these three features are not distinguished in the way suggested by the Delian inscription: 'What is most just is finest; being healthy is most beneficial; but it is most pleasant to win our heart's desire.' For all three features are found in the best activities, and happiness we say is these activities, or [rather] one of them, the best one.

External Goods

Nonetheless, happiness evidently also needs external goods to be added [to the activity], as we said, since we cannot, or cannot easily, do fine actions if we lack the resources.

1099b   For, first of all, in many actions we use friends, wealth and political power just as we use instruments. Further, deprivation of certain [externals]—e.g. good birth, good children, beauty—mars our blessedness; for we do not altogether have the character of happiness if we look utterly repulsive or are ill-born, solitary or childless, and have it even less, presumably, if our children or friends are totally bad, or were good but have died.

And so, as we have said, happiness would seem to need this sort of prosperity added also; that is why some people identify happiness with good fortune, while others [reacting from one extreme to the other] identify it with virtue.

·   ·   ·

A further reason why this would seem to be correct is that happiness is an origin; for the origin is what we all aim at in all our other actions; and we take the origin and cause of goods to be something honourable and divine.

1.9 Introduction to the Account of Virtue

i 13   *1.9.1 An Account of Happiness Requires an Account of Virtue*

Since happiness is an activity of the soul expressing complete virtue, we must examine virtue; for that will perhaps also be a way to study happiness better.

Moreover, the true politician seems to have spent more effort on virtue than on anything else, since he wants to make the citizens good and law-abiding. We find an example of this in the Spartan and Cretan legislators and in any others with their concerns. Since, then, the examination of virtue is proper for political science, the inquiry clearly suits our original decision [to pursue political science].

1.9.2 A Discussion of Virtue Requires a Discussion of the Soul

It is clear that the virtue we must examine is human virtue, since we are also seeking the human good and human happiness. And by human virtue we mean virtue of the soul, not of the body, since we also say that happiness is an activity of the soul. If this is so, then it is clear that the politician must acquire some knowledge about the soul, just as someone setting out to heal the eyes must acquire knowledge about the whole body as well. This is all the more true to the extent that political science is better and more honourable than medicine—and even among doctors the cultivated ones devote a lot of effort to acquiring knowledge about the body. Hence the politician as well [as the student of nature] must study the soul.

But he must study it for the purpose [of inquiring into virtue], as far as suffices for what he seeks; for a more exact treatment would presumably take more effort than his purpose requires. [We] have discussed the soul sufficiently [for our purposes] in [our] popular works as well [as our less popular], and we should use this discussion.

1.9.3 The Rational and Nonrational Parts of the Soul

We have said, e.g., that one [part] of the soul is nonrational, while one has reason. Are these distinguished as parts of a body and everything divisible into parts are? Or are they two only in account, and inseparable by nature, as the convex and the concave are in a surface? It does not matter for present purposes.

The Nonrational Part: (a) One Part of It Is Unresponsive to Reason

Consider the nonrational [part]. One [part] of it, i.e. the cause of nutrition and
1102b   growth, is seemingly plant-like and shared [with other living things]: for we can ascribe this capacity of the soul to everything that is nourished, including embryos, and the same one to complete living things, since this is more reasonable than to ascribe another capacity to them.

Hence the virtue of this capacity is apparently shared, not [specifically] human. For this part and capacity more than others seem to be active in sleep, and here the good and the bad person are least distinct, which is why happy people are said to be no better off than miserable people for half their lives.

And this lack of distinction is not surprising, since sleep is inactivity of the soul in so far as it is called excellent or base, unless to some small extent some movements penetrate [to our awareness], and in this way the decent person comes to have better images [in dreams] than just any random person has. Enough about this, however, and let us leave aside the nutritive part, since by nature it has no share in human virtue.

(b) Another Part Is Also Nonrational

Another nature in the soul would also seem to be nonrational, though in a way it shares in reason.

[Clearly it is nonrational]. For in the continent and the incontinent person we praise their reason, i.e. the [part] of the soul that has reason, because it exhorts them correctly and towards what is best; but they evidently also have in them some other [part] that is by nature something besides reason, conflicting and struggling with reason.

For just as paralysed parts of a body, when we decide to move them to the right, do the contrary and move off to the left, the same is true of the soul, for incontinent people have impulses in contrary directions. In bodies, admittedly, we see the part go astray, whereas we do not see it in the soul; nonetheless, presumably, we should suppose that the soul also has a [part] besides reason, contrary to and countering reason. The [precise] way it is different does not matter.

But It Is Responsive to Reason

However, this [part] as well [as the rational part] appears, as we said, to share in reason. At any rate, in the continent person it obeys reason; and in the temperate and the brave person it presumably listens still better to reason, since there it agrees with reason in everything.

Hence It Differs Both from the Wholly Unresponsive Part . . .

The nonrational [part], then, as well [as the whole soul] apparently has two parts. For while the plant-like [part] shares in reason not at all, the [part] with appetites and in general desires shares in reason in a way, in so far as it both listens to reason and obeys it.

It listens in the way in which we are said to 'listen to reason' from father or friends, not in the way in which we ['give the reason'] in mathematics.

The nonrational part also [obeys and] is persuaded in some way by reason, as is 1103a shown by chastening, and by every sort of reproof and exhortation.

And from the Wholly Rational Part

If we ought to say, then, that this [part] also has reason, then the [part] that has reason, as well [as the nonrational part] will have two parts, one that has reason to the full extent by having it within itself, and another [that has it] by listening to reason as to a father.

1.9.4 The Division of the Virtues Corresponds to the Parts of the Soul

The distinction between virtues also reflects this difference. For some virtues are called virtues of thought, other virtues of character; wisdom, comprehension and intelligence are called virtues of thought, generosity and temperance virtues of character.

For when we speak of someone's character we do not say that he is wise or has good comprehension, but that he is gentle or temperate. [Hence these are the virtues of character.] And yet, we also praise the wise person for his state, and the states that are praiseworthy are the ones we call virtues. [Hence wisdom is also a virtue.]

2. VIRTUES OF CHARACTER IN GENERAL

2.1 How a Virtue of Character Is Acquired

ii 1   Virtue, then, is of two sorts, virtue of thought and virtue of character. Virtue of thought arises and grows mostly from teaching, and hence needs experience and time. Virtue of character [i.e. of *ēthos*] results from habit [*ethos*]; hence its name 'ethical', slightly varied from *'ethos'*.

Virtue Comes About, Not by a Process of Nature, but by Habituation
Hence it is also clear that none of the virtues of character arises in us naturally.

(1) What Is Natural Cannot Be Changed by Habituation
For if something is by nature [in one condition], habituation cannot bring it into another condition. A stone, e.g., by nature moves downwards, and habituation could not make it move upwards, not even if you threw it up ten thousand times to habituate it; nor could habituation make fire move downwards, or bring anything that is by nature in one condition into another condition.

Thus the virtues arise in us neither by nature nor against nature. Rather, we are by nature able to acquire them, and reach our complete perfection through habit.

(2) Natural Capacities Are Not Acquired by Habituation
Further, if something arises in us by nature, we first have the capacity for it, and later display the activity. This is clear in the case of the senses; for we did not acquire them by frequent seeing or hearing, but already had them when we exercised them, and did not get them by exercising them.

Virtues, by contrast, we acquire, just as we acquire crafts, by having previously activated them. For we learn a craft by producing the same product that we must produce when we have learned it, become builders, e.g., by building and harpists by playing the harp; so, also, then, we become just by doing just actions, temperate by doing temperate actions, brave by doing brave actions.

1103b

(3) Legislators Concentrate on Habituation
What goes on in cities is evidence for this also. For the legislator makes the citizens good by habituating them, and this is the wish of every legislator; if he fails to do it well he misses his goal. [The right] habituation is what makes the difference between a good political system and a bad one.

(4) Virtue and Vice Are Formed by Good and Bad Actions

Further, just as in the case of a craft, the sources and means that develop each virtue also ruin it. For playing the harp makes both good and bad harpists, and it is analogous in the case of builders and all the rest; for building well makes good builders, building badly, bad ones. If it were not so, no teacher would be needed, but everyone would be born a good or a bad craftsman.

It is the same, then, with the virtues. For actions in dealing with [older] human beings make some people just, some unjust; actions in terrifying situations and the acquired habit of fear or confidence make some brave and others cowardly. The same is true of situations involving appetites and anger; for one or another sort of conduct in these situations makes some people temperate and gentle, others intemperate and irascible.

Conclusion: The Importance of Habituation

To sum up, then, in a single account: A state [of character] arises from [the repetition of] similar activities. Hence we must display the right activities, since differences in these imply corresponding differences in the states. It is not unimportant, then, to acquire one sort of habit or another, right from our youth; rather, it is very important, indeed all-important.

2.1.2 What Is the Right Sort of Habituation?

This Is an Appropriate Question, for the Aim of Ethical Theory Is Practical

ii 2   Our present inquiry does not aim, as our others do, at study; for the purpose of our examination is not to know what virtue is, but to become good, since otherwise the inquiry would be of no benefit to us. Hence we must examine the right way to act, since, as we have said, the actions also control the character of the states we acquire.

First, then, actions should express correct reason. That is a common [belief], and let us assume it; later we will say what correct reason is and how it is related to the other virtues.

1104a   But let us take it as agreed in advance that every account of the actions we must do has to be stated in outline, not exactly. As we also said at the start, the type of accounts we demand should reflect the subject-matter; and questions about actions and expediency, like questions about health, have no fixed [and invariable answers].

And when our general account is so inexact, the account of particular cases is all the more inexact. For these fall under no craft or profession, and the agents themselves must consider in each case what the opportune action is, as doctors and navigators do.

The account we offer, then, in our present inquiry is of this inexact sort; still, we must try to offer help.

The Right Sort of Habituation Must Avoid Excess and Deficiency

First, then, we should observe that these sorts of states naturally tend to be ruined by excess and deficiency. We see this happen with strength and health, which we mention because we must use what is evident as a witness to what is not. For both excessive and deficient exercises ruin strength; and likewise, too much or too little eating or drinking ruins health, while the proportionate amount produces, increases and preserves it.

The same is true, then, of temperance, bravery and the other virtues. For if, e.g., someone avoids and is afraid of everything, standing firm against nothing, he becomes cowardly, but if he is afraid of nothing at all and goes to face everything, he becomes rash. Similarly, if he gratifies himself with every pleasure and refrains from none, he becomes intemperate, but if he avoids them all, as boors do, he becomes some sort of insensible person. Temperance and bravery, then, are ruined by excess and deficiency but preserved by the mean.

The same actions, then, are the sources and causes both of the emergence and growth of virtues and of their ruin; but further, the activities of the virtues will be found in these same actions. For this is also true of more evident cases, e.g. strength, which arises from eating a lot and from withstanding much hard labour, and it is the strong person who is most able to do these very things. It is the same with the virtues. Refraining from pleasures make us become temperate, and when we have become temperate we are most able to refrain from pleasures. And it is similar with bravery; habituation in disdaining what is fearful and in standing firm against it makes us become brave, and when we have become brave we shall be most able to stand firm.

1104b

2.1.3 Pleasure and Pain Are Important in Habituation

ii 3   But [actions are not enough]; we must take as a sign of someone's state his pleasure or pain in consequence of his action. For if someone who abstains from bodily pleasures enjoys the abstinence itself, then he is temperate, but if he is grieved by it, he is intemperate. Again, if he stands firm against terrifying situations and enjoys it, or at least does not find it painful, then he is brave, and if he finds it painful, he is cowardly.

[Pleasures and pains are appropriately taken as signs] because virtue of character is concerned with pleasures and pains.

Virtue Is Concerned with Pleasure and Pain

(1) For it is pleasure that causes us to do base actions, and pain that causes us to abstain from fine ones. Hence we need to have had the appropriate upbringing—right from early youth, as Plato says—to make us find enjoyment or pain in the right things; for this is the correct education.

(2) Further, virtues are concerned with actions and feelings; but every feeling and every action implies pleasure or pain; hence, for this reason too, virtue is concerned with pleasures and pains.

(3) Corrective treatment [for vicious actions] also indicates [the relevance of pleasure and pain], since it uses pleasures and pains; it uses them because such correction is a form of medical treatment, and medical treatment naturally operates through contraries.

(4) Further, as we said earlier, every state of soul is naturally related to and concerned with whatever naturally makes it better or worse; and pleasures and pains make people worse, from pursuing and avoiding the wrong ones, at the wrong

time, in the wrong ways, or whatever other distinctions of that sort are needed in an account.

These [bad effects of pleasure and pain] are the reason why people actually define the virtues as ways of being unaffected and undisturbed [by pleasures and pains]. They are wrong, however, because they speak [of being unaffected] unconditionally, not of being unaffected in the right or wrong way, at the right or wrong time, and the added specifications.

We assume, then, that virtue is the sort of state [with the appropriate specifications] that does the best actions concerned with pleasures and pains, and that vice is the contrary. The following points will also make it evident that virtue and vice are concerned with the same things.

(5) There are three objects of choice—fine, expedient and pleasant—and three objects of avoidance—their contraries, shameful, harmful and painful. About all these, then, the good person is correct and the bad person is in error, and especially 1105a about pleasure. For pleasure is shared with animals, and implied by every object of choice, since what is fine and what is expedient appear pleasant as well.

(6) Further, since pleasure grows up with all of us from infancy on, it is hard to rub out this feeling that is dyed into our lives; and we estimate actions as well [as feelings], some of us more, some less, by pleasure and pain. Hence, our whole inquiry must be about these, since good or bad enjoyment or pain is very important for our actions.

(7) Moreover, it is harder to fight pleasure than to fight emotion, [though that is hard enough], as Heracleitus says. Now both craft and virtue are concerned in every case with what is harder, since a good result is even better when it is harder. Hence, for this reason also, the whole inquiry, for virtue and political science alike, must consider pleasures and pains; for if we use these well, we shall be good, and if badly, bad.

In short, virtue is concerned with pleasures and pains; the actions that are its sources also increase it or, if they are done differently, ruin it; and its activity is concerned with the same actions that are its sources.

2.1.4 But Our Claims About Habituation Raise a Puzzle: How Can We Become Good Without Being Good Already?

ii 4   However, someone might raise this puzzle: 'What do you mean by saying that to become just we must first do just actions and to become temperate we must first do temperate actions? For if we do what is grammatical or musical, we must already be grammarians or musicians. In the same way, then, if we do what is just or temperate, we must already be just or temperate.'

First Reply: Conformity Versus Understanding

But surely this is not so even with the crafts, for it is possible to produce something grammatical by chance or by following someone else's instructions. To be a grammarian, then, we must both produce something grammatical and produce it in a way in which the grammarian produces it, i.e. expressing grammatical knowledge that is in us.

Second Reply: Crafts Versus Virtues

Moreover, in any case what is true of crafts is not true of virtues. For the products of a craft determine by their own character whether they have been produced well; and so it suffices that they are in the right state when they have been produced. But for actions expressing virtue to be done temperately or justly [and hence well] it does not suffice that they are themselves in the right state. Rather, the agent must also be in the right state when he does them. First, he must know [that he is doing virtuous actions]; second, he must decide on them, and decide on them for themselves; and, third, he must also do them from a firm and unchanging state.

1105b   As conditions for having a craft these three do not count, except for the knowing itself. As a condition for having a virtue, however, the knowing counts for nothing, or [rather] for only a little, whereas the other two conditions are very important, indeed all-important. And these other two conditions are achieved by the frequent doing of just and temperate actions.

Hence actions are called just or temperate when they are the sort that a just or temperate person would do. But the just and temperate person is not the one who [merely] does these actions, but the one who also does them in the way in which just or temperate people do them.

It is right, then, to say that a person comes to be just from doing just actions and temperate from doing temperate actions; for no one has even a prospect of becoming good from failing to do them.

Virtue Requires Habituation, and Therefore Requires Practice, Not Just Theory

The many, however, do not do these actions but take refuge in arguments, thinking that they are doing philosophy, and that this is the way to become excellent people. In this they are like a sick person who listens attentively to the doctor, but acts on none of his instructions. Such a course of treatment will not improve the state of his body; any more than will the many's way of doing philosophy improve the state of their souls.

2.2 A Virtue of Character Is a State Intermediate Between Two Extremes, and Involving Decision

2.2.1 The Genus

Feelings, Capacities, States

ii 5   Next we must examine what virtue is. Since there are three conditions arising in the soul—feelings, capacities, and states—virtue must be one of these.

By feelings I mean appetite, anger, fear, confidence, envy, joy, love, hate, longing, jealousy, pity, in general whatever implies pleasure or pain.

By capacities I mean what we have when we are said to be capable of these feelings—capable of, e.g., being angry or afraid or feeling pity.

By states I mean what we have when we are well or badly off in relation to feelings. If, e.g., our feeling is too intense or slack, we are badly off in relation to anger, but if it is intermediate, we are well off; and the same is true in the other cases.

Virtue Is Not a Feeling . . .

First, then, neither virtues nor vices are feelings. (a) For we are called excellent or base in so far as we have virtues or vices, not in so far as we have feelings. (b) We are neither praised nor blamed in so far as we have feelings; for we do not praise the angry or the frightened person, and do not blame the person who is simply angry, but only the person who is angry in a particular way. But we are praised or blamed in so far as we have virtues or vices. (c) We are angry and afraid without decision; but the virtues are decisions of some kind, or [rather] require decision. (d) Besides, in so far as we have feelings, we are said to be moved; but in so far as we have virtues or vices, we are said to be in some condition rather than moved.

1106a

Or a Capacity . . .

For these reasons the virtues are not capacities either; for we are neither called good nor called bad in so far as we are simply capable of feelings. Further, while we have capacities by nature, we do not become good or bad by nature; we have discussed this before.

But a State

If, then, the virtues are neither feelings nor capacities, the remaining possibility is that they are states. And so we have said what the genus of virtue is.

2.2.2 The Differentia

ii 6   But we must say not only, as we already have, that it is a state, but also what sort of state it is.

Virtue and the Human Function

It should be said, then, that every virtue causes its possessors to be in a good state and to perform their functions well; the virtue of eyes, e.g., makes the eyes and their functioning excellent, because it makes us see well; and similarly, the virtue of a horse makes the horse excellent, and thereby good at galloping, at carrying its rider and at standing steady in the face of the enemy. If this is true in every case, then the virtue of a human being will likewise be the state that makes a human being good and makes him perform his function well.

We have already said how this will be true, and it will also be evident from our next remarks, if we consider the sort of nature that virtue has.

The Numerical Mean and the Mean Relative to Us

In everything continuous and divisible we can take more, less and equal, and each of them either in the object itself or relative to us; and the equal is some intermediate between excess and deficiency.

By the intermediate in the object I mean what is equidistant from each extremity; this is one and the same for everyone. But relative to us the intermediate is what is neither superfluous nor deficient; this is not one, and is not the same for everyone.

If, e.g., ten are many and two are few, we take six as an intermediate in the object, since it exceeds [two] and is exceeded [by ten] by an equal amount, [four]; this is

what is intermediate by numerical proportion. But that is not how we must take the
1106b intermediate that is relative to us. For if, e.g., ten pounds [of food] are a lot for someone to eat, and two pounds a little, it does not follow that the trainer will prescribe
six, since this might also be either a little or a lot for the person who is to take it—
for Milo [the athlete] a little, but for the beginner in gymnastics a lot; and the same
is true for running and wrestling. In this way every scientific expert avoids excess
and deficiency and seeks and chooses what is intermediate—but intermediate relative to us, not in the object.

Virtue Seeks the Mean Relative to Us: Argument from Craft to Virtue

This, then, is how each science produces its product well, by focusing on what is
intermediate and making the product conform to that. This, indeed, is why people
regularly comment on well-made products that nothing could be added or subtracted,
since they assume that excess or deficiency ruins a good [result] while the mean preserves it. Good craftsmen also, we say, focus on what is intermediate when they produce their product. And since virtue, like nature, is better and more exact than any
craft, it will also aim at what is intermediate.

Arguments from the Nature of Virtue of Character

By virtue I mean virtue of character; for this [pursues the mean because] it is concerned with feelings and actions, and these admit of excess, deficiency and an intermediate condition. We can be afraid, e.g., or be confident, or have appetites, or
get angry, or feel pity, in general have pleasure or pain, both too much and too little, and in both ways not well; but [having these feelings] at the right times, about
the right things, towards the right people, for the right end, and in the right way,
is the intermediate and best condition, and this is proper to virtue. Similarly, actions
also admit of excess, deficiency and the intermediate condition.

Now virtue is concerned with feelings and actions, in which excess and deficiency
are in error and incur blame, while the intermediate condition is correct and wins
praise, which are both proper features of virtue. Virtue, then, is a mean, in so far as
it aims at what is intermediate.

Moreover, there are many ways to be in error, since badness is proper to what is
limited; but there is only one way to be correct. That is why error is easy and correctness hard, since it is easy to miss the target and hard to hit it. And so for this reason also excess and deficiency are proper to vice, the mean to virtue; 'for we are
noble in only one way, but bad in all sorts of ways.'

2.2.3 Definition of Virtue

1107a Virtue, then, is (a) a state that decides, (b) [consisting] in a mean, (c) the mean
relative to us, (d) which is defined by reference to reason, (e) i.e., to the reason by
reference to which the intelligent person would define it. It is a mean between two
vices, one of excess and one of deficiency.

It is a mean for this reason also: Some vices miss what is right because they are deficient, others because they are excessive, in feelings or in actions, while virtue finds
and chooses what is intermediate.

Hence, as far as its substance and the account stating its essence are concerned, virtue is a mean; but as far as the best [condition] and the good [result] are concerned, it is an extremity.

The Definition Must Not Be Misapplied to Cases in Which There Is No Mean

But not every action or feeling admits of the mean. For the names of some automatically include baseness, e.g. spite, shamelessness, envy [among feelings], and adultery, theft, murder, among actions. All of these and similar things are called by these names because they themselves, not their excesses or deficiencies, are base.

Hence in doing these things we can never be correct, but must invariably be in error. We cannot do them well or not well—e.g. by committing adultery with the right woman at the right time in the right way; on the contrary, it is true unconditionally that to do any of them is to be in error.

[To think these admit of a mean], therefore, is like thinking that unjust or cowardly or intemperate action also admits of a mean, an excess and a deficiency. For then there would be a mean of excess, a mean of deficiency, an excess of excess and a deficiency of deficiency.

Rather, just as there is no excess or deficiency of temperance or of bravery, since the intermediate is a sort of extreme [in achieving the good], so also there is no mean of these [vicious actions] either, but whatever way anyone does them, he is in error. For in general there is no mean of excess or of deficiency, and no excess or deficiency of a mean.

2.3 The Definition of Virtue as a Mean Applies to the Individual Virtues

ii 7   However, we must not only state this general account but also apply it to the particular cases. For among accounts concerning actions, though the general ones are common to more cases, the specific ones are truer, since actions are about particular cases, and our account must accord with these. Let us, then, find these from the chart.

2.3.1 Classification of Virtues of Character

Virtues Concerned with Feelings

1107b   (1) First, in feelings of fear and confidence the mean is bravery. The excessively fearless person is nameless (and in fact many cases are nameless), while the one who is excessively confident is rash; the one who is excessively afraid and deficient in confidence is cowardly.

(2) In pleasures and pains, though not in all types, and in pains less than in pleasures, the mean is temperance and the excess intemperance. People deficient in pleasure are not often found, which is why they also lack even a name; let us call them insensible.

Virtues Concerned with External Goods

(3) In giving and taking money the mean is generosity, the excess wastefulness and the deficiency ungenerosity. Here the vicious people have contrary excesses and

defects; for the wasteful person spends to excess and is deficient in taking, whereas the ungenerous person takes to excess and is deficient in spending. At the moment we are speaking in outline and summary, and that suffices; later we shall define these things more exactly.

(4) In questions of money there are also other conditions. Another mean is magnificence; for the magnificent person differs from the generous by being concerned with large matters, while the generous person is concerned with small. The excess is ostentation and vulgarity, and the deficiency niggardliness, and these differ from the vices related to generosity in ways we shall describe later.

(5) In honour and dishonour the mean is magnanimity, the excess something called a sort of vanity, and the deficiency pusillanimity.

(6) And just as we said that generosity differs from magnificence in its concern with small matters, similarly there is a virtue concerned with small honours, differing in the same way from magnanimity, which is concerned with great honours. For honour can be desired either in the right way or more or less than is right. If someone desires it to excess, he is called an honour-lover, and if his desire is deficient he is called indifferent to honour, but if he is intermediate he has no name. The corresponding conditions have no name either, except the condition of the honour-lover, which is called honour-loving.

This is why people at the extremes claim the intermediate area. Indeed, we also sometimes call the intermediate person an honour-lover, and sometimes call him indifferent to honour; and sometimes we praise the honour-lover, sometimes the person indifferent to honour. We will mention later the reason we do this; for the moment, let us speak of the other cases in the way we have laid down.

1108a

Virtues Concerned with Social Life

(7) Anger also admits of an excess, deficiency and mean. These are all practically nameless; but since we call the intermediate person mild, let us call the mean mindless. Among the extreme people let the excessive person be irascible, and the vice be irascibility, and let the deficient person be a sort of inirascible person, and the deficiency be inirascibility.

There are three other means, somewhat similar to one another, but different. For they are all concerned with association in conversations and actions, but differ in so far as one is concerned with truth-telling in these areas, the other two with sources of pleasure, some of which are found in amusement, and the others in daily life in general. Hence we should also discuss these states, so that we can better observe that in every case the mean is praiseworthy, while the extremes are neither praiseworthy nor correct, but blameworthy. Most of these cases are also nameless, and we must try, as in the other cases also, to make names ourselves, to make things clear and easy to follow.

(8) In truth-telling, then, let us call the intermediate person truthful, and the mean truthfulness; pretence that overstates will be boastfulness, and the person who has it boastful; pretence that understates will be self-deprecation, and the person who has it self-deprecating.

(9) In sources of pleasure in amusements let us call the intermediate person witty, and the condition wit; the excess buffoonery and the person who has it a buffoon; and the deficient person a sort of boor and the state boorishness.

(10) In the other sources of pleasure, those in daily life, let us call the person who is pleasant in the right way friendly, and the mean state friendliness. If someone goes to excess with no [further] aim he will be ingratiating; if he does it for his own advantage, a flatterer. The deficient person, unpleasant in everything, will be a sort of quarrelsome and ill-tempered person.

Mean States That Are Not Virtues

(11) There are also means in feelings and concerned with feelings: shame, e.g., is not a virtue, but the person prone to shame as well as the virtuous person we have described receives praise. For here also one person is called intermediate, and another—the person excessively prone to shame, who is ashamed about everything—is called excessive; the person who is deficient in shame or never feels shame at all is said to have no sense of disgrace; and the intermediate one is called prone to shame.

1108b

(12) Proper indignation is the mean between envy and spite; these conditions are concerned with pleasure and pain at what happens to our neighbours. For the properly indignant person feels pain when someone does well undeservedly; the envious person exceeds him by feeling pain when anyone does well, while the spiteful person is so deficient in feeling pain that he actually enjoys [other people's misfortunes].

There will also be an opportunity elsewhere to speak of these [means that are not virtues].

Justice

We must consider justice after these other conditions, and, because it is not spoken of in one way only, we shall distinguish its two types and say how each of them is a mean.

Similarly, we must consider the virtues that belong to reason.

2.3.2 The Relations Between Means and Extremes

The Mean Is Opposed to Each Extreme

ii 8   Among these three conditions, then, two are vices—one of excess, one of deficiency—and one—the mean—is virtue. In a way each of them is opposed to each of the others, since each extreme is contrary both to the intermediate condition and to the other extreme, while the intermediate is contrary to the extremes. For as the equal is greater in comparison to the smaller, and smaller in comparison to the greater, so also the intermediate states are excessive in comparison to the deficiencies and deficient in comparison to the excesses—both in feelings and in actions.

For the brave person, e.g., appears rash in comparison to the coward, and cowardly in comparison to the rash person; similarly, the temperate person appears intemperate in comparison to the insensible person, and insensible in comparison with the temperate person, and the general person appears wasteful in comparison to the ungenerous, and ungenerous in comparison to the wasteful person. That is why each of the extreme people tries to push the intermediate person to the other extreme, so that the coward, e.g., calls the brave person rash, and the rash person calls him a coward, and similarly in the other cases.

Extremes Are More Opposed to Each Other Than to the Mean

Because these conditions of soul are opposed to each other in these ways, the extremes are more contrary to each other than to the intermediate. For they are further from each other than from the intermediate, just as the large is further from the small, and the small from the large, than either is from the equal.

Moreover, sometimes one extreme, e.g. rashness or wastefulness, appears somewhat like the intermediate state, e.g. bravery or generosity; but the extremes are most unlike one another; and the things that are furthest apart from each other are defined as contraries. Hence also the things that are further apart are more contrary.

Sometimes One Extreme Is More Opposed Than the Other to the Mean

1109a   In some cases the deficiency, in others the excess, is more opposed to the intermediate condition; e.g. it is cowardice, the deficiency, not rashness, the excess, that is more opposed to bravery; on the other hand, it is intemperance, the excess, not insensibility, the deficiency, that is more opposed to temperance. This happens for two reason.

One reason is derived from the object itself. Since sometimes one extreme is closer and more similar to the intermediate condition, we oppose the contrary extreme, more than this closer one, to the intermediate condition. Since rashness, e.g., seems to be closer and more similar to bravery, and cowardice less similar, we oppose cowardice more than rashness to bravery; for what is further from the intermediate condition seems to be more contrary to it. This, then, is one reason, derived from the object itself.

The other reason is derived from ourselves. For when we ourselves have some natural tendency to one extreme more than the other, this extreme appears more opposed to the intermediate condition; since, e.g., we have more of a natural tendency to pleasure, we drift more easily towards intemperance than towards orderliness. Hence we say that an extreme is more contrary if we naturally develop more in that direction; and this is why intemperance is more contrary to temperance, since it is the excess.

ii 9   ### *2.3.3 Practical Advice on Ways to Achieve the Mean*

We have said enough, then, to show that virtue of character is a mean and what sort of mean it is; that it is a mean between two vices, one of excess and one of deficiency; and that it is a mean because it aims at the intermediate condition in feelings and actions.

Hence it is hard work to be excellent, since in each case it is hard work to find what is intermediate; e.g. not everyone, but only one who knows, finds the midpoint in a circle. So also getting angry, or giving and spending money, is easy and anyone can do it; but doing it to the right person, in the right amount, at the right time, for the right end, and in the right way is no longer easy, nor can everyone do it. Hence [doing these things] well is rare, praiseworthy and fine.

Avoid the More Opposed Extreme

Hence if we aim at the intermediate condition we must first of all steer clear of the more contrary extreme, following the advice that Calypso also gives—'Hold the ship outside the spray and surge.' For since one extreme is more in error, the other less, and since it is hard to hit the intermediate extremely accurately, the second-best tack, as they say, is to take the lesser of the evils. We shall succeed best in this by the
1109b   method we describe.

Avoid the Easier Extreme

We must also examine what we ourselves drift into easily. For different people have different natural tendencies towards different goals, and we shall come to know our own tendencies from the pleasure or pain that arises in us. We must drag ourselves off in the contrary direction; for if we pull far away from error, as they do in straightening bent wood, we shall reach the intermediate condition.

Be Careful with Pleasures

And in everything we must beware above all of pleasure and its sources; for we are already biased in its favour when we come to judge it. Hence we must react to it as the elders reacted to Helen, and on each occasion repeat what they said; for if we do this, and send it off, we shall be less in error.

These Rules Do Not Give Exact and Detailed Guidance

In summary, then, if we do these things we shall best be able to reach the intermediate condition. But no doubt this is hard, especially in particular cases, since it is not easy to define the way we should be angry, with whom, about what, for how long; for sometimes, indeed, we ourselves praise deficient people and call them mild, and sometimes praise quarrelsome people and call them manly. Still, we are not blamed if we deviate a little in excess or deficiency from doing well, but only if we deviate a long way, since then we are easily noticed.

But how far and how much we must deviate to be blamed is not easy to define in an account; for nothing perceptible is easily defined, and [since] these [circumstances of virtuous and vicious action] are particulars, the judgement about them depends on perception.

All this makes it clear, then, that in every case the intermediate states is praised, but we must sometimes incline towards the excess, sometimes toward the deficiency; for that is the easiest way to succeed in hitting the intermediate condition and [doing] well.

•   •   •

[BOOK X]

13.3 Theoretical Study Is the Supreme Element of Happiness

x 7   If happiness, then, is activity expressing virtue, it is reasonable for it to express the supreme virtue, which will be the virtue of the best thing.

The best is understanding, or whatever else seems to be the natural ruler and leader, and to understand what is fine and divine, by being itself either divine or the most divine element in us.

Hence complete happiness will be its activity expressing its proper virtue; and we have said that this activity is the activity of study. This seems to agree with what has been said before, and also with the truth.

13.3.1 The Activity of Theoretical Study Is Best

For this activity is supreme, since understanding is the supreme element in us, and the objects of understanding are the supreme objects of knowledge.

13.3.2 It Is Most Continuous

Besides, it is the most continuous activity, since we are more capable of continuous study than of any continuous action.

13.3.3 It Is Pleasantest

We think pleasure must be mixed into happiness; and it is agreed that the activity expressing wisdom is the pleasantest of the activities expressing virtue. At any rate, philosophy seems to have remarkably pure and firm pleasures; and it is reasonable for those who have knowledge to spend their lives more pleasantly than those who seek it.

13.3.4 It Is Most Self-Sufficient

Moreover, the self-sufficiency we spoke of will be found in study above all.

For admittedly the wise person, the just person and the other virtuous people all need the good things necessary for life. Still, when these are adequately supplied, the just person needs other people as partners and recipients of his just actions; and the same is true of the temperate person and the brave person and each of the others.

1177b   But the wise person is able, and more able the wiser he is, to study even by himself; and though he presumably does it better with colleagues, even so he is more self-sufficient than any other [virtuous person].

13.3.5 It Aims at No End Beyond Itself

Besides, study seems to be liked because of itself alone, since it has no result beyond having studied. But from the virtues concerned with action we try to a greater or lesser extent to gain something beyond the action itself.

13.3.6 It Involves Leisure

Happiness seems to be found in leisure, since we accept trouble so that we can be at leisure, and fight wars so that we can be at peace. Now the virtues concerned with action have their activities in politics or war, and actions here seem to require trouble.

This seems completely true for actions in war, since no one chooses to fight a war, and no one continues it, for the sake of fighting a war; for someone would have to be a complete murderer if he made his friends his enemies so that there could be battles and killings.

But the actions of the politician require trouble also. Beyond political activities themselves these actions seek positions of power and honours; or at least they seek happiness for the politician himself and for his fellow-citizens, which is something different from political science itself, and clearly is sought on the assumption that is different.

Hence among actions expressing the virtues those in politics and war are preeminently fine and great; but they require trouble, aim at some [further] end, and are choice-worthy for something other than themselves.

But the activity of understanding, it seems, is superior in excellence because it is the activity of study, aims at no end beyond itself and has its own proper pleasure, which increases the activity. Further, self-sufficiency, leisure, unwearied activity (as far as is possible for a human being), and any other features ascribed to the blessed person, are evidently features of this activity.

Hence a human being's complete happiness will be this activity, if it receives a complete span of life, since nothing incomplete is proper to happiness.

13.3.7 *It Is a God-like Life*

Such a life would be superior to the human level. For someone will live it not in so far as he is a human being, but in so far as he has some divine element in him. And the activity of this divine element is as much superior to the activity expressing the rest of virtue as this element is superior to the compound. Hence if understanding is something divine in comparison with a human being, so also will the life that expresses understanding be divine in comparison with human life.

We ought not to follow the proverb-writers, and 'think human, since you are human', or 'think mortal, since you are mortal'. Rather, as far as we can, we ought to be pro-immortal, and go to all lengths to live a life that expresses our supreme element; for however much this element may lack in bulk, by much more it surpasses everything in power and value.

1178a

13.3.8 *It Realizes the Supreme Element in Human Nature*

Moreover, each person seems to be his understanding, if he is his controlling and better element; it would be absurd, then, if he were to choose not his own life, but something else's.

And what we have said previously will also apply now. For what is proper to each thing's nature is supremely best and pleasantest for it; and hence for a human being the life expressing understanding will be supremely best and pleasantest, if understanding above all is the human being. This life, then, will also be happiest.

13.4 The Relation of Study to the Other Virtues in Happiness

13.4.1 The Other Virtues Are Human, Not Divine

x 8   The life expressing the other kind of virtue [i.e. the kind concerned with action] is [happiest] in a secondary way because the activities expressing this virtue are human.

For we do just and brave actions, and the others expressing the virtues, in relation to other people, by abiding by what fits each person in contracts, services, all types of actions, and also in feelings; and all these appear to be human conditions.

Indeed, some feelings actually seem to arise from the body; and in many ways virtue of character seems to be proper to feelings.

Besides, intelligence is yoked together with virtue of character, and so is this virtue with intelligence. For the origins of intelligence express the virtues of character; and correctness in virtues of character expresses intelligence. And since these virtues are also connected to feelings, they are concerned with the compound. Since the virtues of the compound are human virtues, the life and the happiness expressing these virtues is also human.

The virtue of understanding, however, is separated [from the compound]. Let us say no more about it, since an exact account would be too large a task for our present project.

13.4.2 The Other Virtues Require More External Goods Than Study Requires

Moreover, it seems to need external supplies very little, or [at any rate] less than virtue of character needs them. For grant that they both need necessary goods, and to the same extent, since there will be only a very small difference even though the politician labours more about the body and suchlike. Still, there will be a large difference in [what is needed] for the [proper] activities [of each type of virtue].

For the generous person will need money for generous actions; and the just person will need it for paying debts, since wishes are not clear, and people who are not just pretend to wish to do justice. Similarly, the brave person will need enough power, and the temperate person will need freedom [to do intemperate actions], if they are to achieve anything that the virtue requires. For how else will they, or any other virtuous people, make their virtue clear?

Moreover, it is disputed whether it is decision or actions that is more in control of virtue, on the assumption that virtue depends on both. Well, certainly it is clear that what 1178b is complete depends on both; but for actions many external goods are needed, and the greater and finer the actions the more numerous are the external goods needed.

But someone who is studying needs none of these goods, for that activity at least; indeed, for study at least, we might say they are even hindrances.

In so far as he is a human being, however, and [hence] lives together with a number of other human beings, he chooses to do the actions expressing virtue. Hence he will need the sorts of external goods [that are needed for the virtues], for living a human life.

13.4.3 Beliefs About the Gods Support the Supremacy of Study

In another way also it appears that complete happiness is some activity of study. For we traditionally suppose that the gods more than anyone are blessed and happy; but what sorts of actions ought we to ascribe to them? Just actions? Surely they will appear ridiculous making contracts, returning deposits and so on. Brave actions? Do they endure what [they find] frightening and endure dangers because it is fine? Generous actions? Whom will they give to? And surely it would be absurd for them to have currency or anything like that. What would their temperate actions be? Surely it is vulgar praise to say that they do not have base appetites. When we go through them all, anything that concerns actions appears trivial and unworthy of the gods.

However, we all traditionally suppose that they are alive and active, since surely they are not asleep like Endymion. Then if someone is alive, and action is excluded, and production even more, what is left but study? Hence the gods' activity that is superior in blessedness will be an activity of study. And so the human activity that is most akin to the gods' will, more than any others, have the character of happiness.

A sign of this is the fact that other animals have no share in happiness, being completely deprived of this activity of study. For the whole life of the gods is blessed, and human life is blessed to the extent that it has something resembling this sort of activity; but none of the other animals is happy, because none of them shares in study at all. Hence happiness extends just as far as study extends, and the more someone studies, the happier he is, not coincidentally but in so far as he studies, since study is valuable in itself. And so [on this argument] happiness will be some kind of study.

13.4.4 But a Human Being Also Needs Moderate External Goods

However, the happy person is a human being, and so will need external prosperity also; for his nature is now self-sufficient for study, but he needs a healthy body, and needs to have food and the other services provided.

1179a   Still, even though no one can be blessedly happy without external goods, we must not think that to be happy we will need many large goods. For self-sufficiency and action do not depend on excess, and we can do fine actions even if we do not rule earth and sea; for even from moderate resources we can do the actions expressing virtue. This is evident to see, since many private citizens seem to do decent actions no less than people in power do—even more, in fact. It is enough if moderate resources are provided; for the life of someone whose activity expresses virtue will be happy.

Traditional Views Held by the Wise Support Us

Solon surely described happy people well, when he said they had been moderately supplied with external goods, had done what he regarded as the finest actions, and had lived their lives temperately. For it is possible to have moderate possessions and still to do the right actions.

And Anaxagoras would seem to have supposed that the happy person was neither rich nor powerful, since he said he would not be surprised if the happy person appeared an absurd sort of person to the many. For the many judge by externals, since these are all they perceive.

Hence the beliefs of the wise would seem to accord with our arguments.

But Theory Must Be Tested in Practice

These considerations do indeed produce some confidence. The truth, however, in questions about action is judged from what we do and how we live, since these are what control [the answers to such questions]. Hence we ought to examine what has been said by applying it to what we do and how we live; and if it harmonizes with what we do, we should accept it, but if it conflicts we should count it [mere] words.

13.4.5 The Person Who Studies Is Most Loved by the Gods

The person whose activity expresses understanding and who takes care of understanding would seem to be in the best condition, and most loved by the gods. For if the gods pay some attention to human beings, as they seem to, it would be reasonable for them to take pleasure in what is best and most akin to them, namely understanding; and reasonable for them to benefit in return those who most of all like and honour understanding, on the assumption that these people attend to what is beloved by the gods, and act correctly and finely.

Clearly, all this is true of the wise person more than anyone else; hence he is most loved by the gods. And it is likely that this same person will be happiest; hence the wise person will be happier than anyone else on this argument too.

Suggestions for Further Reading

Gilbert Harman, *The Nature of Morality*. New York, Oxford University Press, 1977.

Thomas Nagel, *Mortal Questions*. London, Cambridge University Press, 1979.

Derek Parfit, *Reason and Persons*. New York, Oxford University Press, 1984.

John Rawls, *A Theory of Justice*. Cambridge, Massachusetts, Harvard University Press, 1971.

J. J. C. Smart and Bernard Williams, *Utilitarianism: For and Against*. London, Cambridge University Press, 1973.

Peter Unger, *Living High and Letting Die—Our Illusion of Innocence*. New York, Oxford University Press, 1996.

Bernard Williams, *Morality*. New York, Harper Torchbooks, 1972.

Glossary

abduction   A form of nondeductive inference, also known as inference to the best explanation. The Surprise Principle and the Only Game In Town Fallacy are relevant to deciding how strong an abductive inference is.

altruism   An ultimate desire (a desire that one wants to come true for its own sake, not because it instrumentally contributes to some other goal) is altruistic if it seeks the well-being of some other person. If there are ultimate altruistic desires, then psychological egoism is false. *See* psychological egoism.

analogy argument   A nondeductive inference in which one infers that a target object *T* has some characteristic on the ground that *T* is similar to some other object *A* (the analog), and *A* is known to possess that characteristic. Example: "Other galaxies probably contain life, since they are quite similar to our own galaxy and our own galaxy contains life." The strength of analogy arguments is an issue relevant to the Argument from Design and to the problem of other minds.

analytic   An analytic sentence is one whose truth or falsehood is deductively entailed by definitions. Many philosophers have held that mathematical statements are analytic. If a sentence isn't analytic, it is synthetic.

a posteriori   A proposition that can be known or justified only by sense experience. An a posteriori argument is an argument in which at least one premiss is an a posteriori proposition. *See* a priori.

a priori   A proposition that can be known or justified independent of sense experience. An a priori proposition can be known or justified by reason alone (once you grasp the constituent concepts). Truths of mathematics and definitions are often thought to be a priori. An a priori argument is an argument in which all the premisses are a priori propositions. The Ontological Argument for the existence of God was supposed to be an a priori argument. *See* a posteriori.

Argument from Design   An a posteriori argument that God exists, advanced by Aquinas and Paley, criticized by Hume. The argument claims that some feature of the world (like the simplicity of its laws or the fact that organisms are intricate and well-adapted) should be explained by postulating the existence of an intelligent designer, namely God.

Argument from Evil   An argument that claims that the existence of evil shows either that there is no God, or that God can't be all-powerful, all-knowing, and all-good.

axiom   In mathematics, a starting assumption from which conclusions (theorems) are deduced.

begging the question   An argument begs the question when you wouldn't accept the premisses unless you already believed the conclusion.

behaviorism   *See* logical behaviorism and methodological behaviorism.

bias   *See* sample bias.

Birthday Fallacy   The error in reasoning that one would make in thinking that "everyone has a birthday" deductively implies that "there is a single day on which everyone was born."

categorical imperative   An imperative (a command) that is unconditional (no if's). In contrast, a hypothetical imperative is a command of the form, "If you have goal *G*, then perform action *A*." Kant thought that moral rules (like "don't lie") take the form of categorical imperatives. In contrast, rules of prudence (like "stop smoking if you want to be healthy") are hypothetical.

causal argument for the existence of God   An argument that Descartes gives in the *Meditations* for the claim that God exists and is no deceiver: Since (1) I have an idea of a perfect being, and (2) there is at least as much perfection in the cause as there is in the effect, it is said to follow that the cause of that idea must be a perfect being, namely God himself.

circularity   *See* begging the question.

clarity and distinctness criterion   Descartes maintained that if a belief is clear and distinct, then it can't fail to be true. The reason clear and distinct ideas must be true is that God exists and is no deceiver.

compatibilism   The thesis that free will and determinism are compatible. Soft determinism is a version of compatibilism. Hard determinism and libertarianism are incompatibilist theories.

compatibility   Two propositions are compatible if the truth of one wouldn't rule out the truth of the other. Example: (i) this shirt is blue; (ii) this shirt is torn. (i) and (ii) are compatible. This doesn't mean that either is true.

conditional   An if/then statement. The if-clause is called the antecedent; the then-clause is called the consequent.

consequentialism   A kind of ethical theory that holds that the ethical properties of an action (its rightness or wrongness, its justness or unjustness, etc.) can be determined by seeing what consequences the action would have if it were performed. Utilitarianism is a consequentialist doctrine. Kant's theory isn't.

conservation law   A law in physics that says that some quantity (like matter or mass/energy) can neither increase nor decrease in a closed system.

contingent   A being is contingent if it exists in some but not all possible worlds; a proposition is contingent if it's true in some but not all possible worlds. You are an example of a contingent thing; though you exist in the actual world, you could have failed to exist.

conventionalism   Trivial semantic conventionalism holds that a true sentence might have been false if we had defined our terms differently. For example, the sentence "dogs have four legs" might have been false if we had used the word "dog" to refer to fish. A philosophically interesting conventionalism must go beyond this unsurprising point. Substantive conventionalism holds that a particular proposition is true only because of someone's say-so. For example, the following is a substantive conventionalist claim (and a false one): Dogs would have lacked four legs if we had used the word "dog" to refer to fish. *See* ethical conventionalism and proposition.

counterexample   A counterexample to a generalization is an object that refutes the generalization. A rotten apple in the barrel is a counterexample to the claim "All the apples in this barrel are unspoiled."

deductive validity   An argument is deductively valid because of the logical form it has. A deductively valid argument is one in which the conclusion must be true if the premisses are true.

descriptive/normative distinction   A descriptive claim says what is the case, without commenting on whether that is good or bad. A normative claim says whether something should be the case, or whether it is good or bad. "Drunk drivers kill thousands of people every year" is a descriptive claim; "drunk driving shouldn't be so lightly punished" is a normative claim.

determinism   The thesis that a complete description of the causal facts at one time uniquely determines what must happen next. There is only one possible future, given a complete description of the present. Newtonian physics says that the behavior of physical objects is deterministic. *See* indeterminism.

Divine Command Theory   The theory that ethical statements are made true or false by God's decreeing how we should act.

dualism   The thesis that the mind and the body are two distinct entities. Dualists claim that a person's mind is made of a nonphysical substance. Dualism rejects materialism.

egoism   *See* psychological egoism.

emotivism   A theory about how ethical statements are used. Such statements are never true or false; rather, they merely allow the speaker to express feelings and attitudes. Emotivism accepts ethical subjectivism.

empirical   For a proposition to be empirical is for it to be a posteriori. *See* a posteriori.

epistemology   The branch of philosophy concerned with concepts like knowledge and rational justification.

equivocation, fallacy of   An argument commits this fallacy when it uses a term with one meaning for part of the argument and then shifts to another meaning for the rest of the argument. Example: "I put my money in the bank. A bank is a side of a river. Hence, I put my money in the side of a river." Arguments that commit this fallacy should be clarified so that the terms in them are used with a single meaning throughout.

ethical conventionalism   The thesis that ethical statements are made true by someone's say-so. The divine command theory, ethical relativism, and Sartre's version of existentialism are conventionalist theories. *See* conventionalism.

ethical realism   The thesis that some ethical statements are true, and are true independently of anyone's thinking or saying that they are.

ethical relativism   The thesis that an ethical statement is true or false in a society because of the norms adopted in that society. Ethical relativism is a normative, not a descriptive, thesis.

ethical subjectivism   The thesis that there are no ethical facts, only ethical opinions. Ethical statements are neither true nor false.

evil   *See* Argument from Evil and theodicy.

existentialism   A twentieth-century philosophical movement that places great weight on the fact that individuals are free and so must take responsibility for how they live their lives.

In Sartre's version of existentialism, each person creates ethical facts for himself or herself by a free decision.

fallacy   An error in reasoning.

falsifiability   *See* strong falsifiability.

fatalism   The theory expressed by the slogan "whatever will be, will be" (que sera, sera). According to this theory, what happens to us doesn't depend on what we think or want or try to do. Example: Oedipus, the myth says, was fated to kill his father and marry his mother. Fatalism and determinism are different.

foundationalism   The view that all the propositions we know to be true can be divided into two categories. First, there are the foundational propositions, which have some special property (like indubitability) that explains why we know them to be true. Second, there are the superstructural propositions, which we know because they bear some special relationship (like deductive implication) to the foundational propositions. Sometimes foundationalism is understood as a thesis about justified belief, not knowledge.

functionalism   The theory in the mind/body problem that says that psychological properties (types) aren't identical with physical properties, because psychological properties are multiply realizable. In addition, functionalism maintains that psychological properties are to be understood in terms of their causal roles.

genetic fallacy   The mistake of thinking a statement can't be true simply because there's a causal explanation for why people believe that it's true.

hard determinism   The incompatibilist doctrine that holds that human actions are unfree because they are causally determined.

identity theory   The thesis that the mind and the brain are identical. Also, that psychological properties are identical with physical properties.

if and only if   "X is true if and only if Y is true" means that the truth of X is both necessary and sufficient for the truth of Y. "X if and only if Y" means that X and Y are either both true or both false.

incompatibilism   *See* compatibilism.

incorrigibility of the mental, thesis of the   This thesis claims that we can't be mistaken in the beliefs we have about the contents of our own minds. If you believe that you believe P or want Q to be true, then it must be true that you believe P or want Q to be true.

independent   Two propositions are logically independent of each other if the truth or falsity of one doesn't deductively imply the truth or falsity of the other. Example: It was discovered in the eighteenth and nineteenth centuries that Euclid's parallel postulate is independent of the other axioms and postulates of his system of geometry.

indeterminism   The thesis that even a complete description of the present doesn't uniquely determine what will happen next. There's more than one possible future, each with its own probability of coming true, given a complete description of the present.

induction   A nondeductive argument in which characteristics of individuals not in a sample are inferred from the characteristics of individuals in the sample. The strength of an inductive inference is influenced by sample size and sample bias.

is/ought gap   Hume argued that ethical statements concerning what ought to be the case can't be deduced from statements that describe only what is the case.

JTB theory   The theory that knowledge is justified true belief. In other words, the theory advances the following proposal: For any person S and any proposition p,

S knows that *p* if and only if (1) *S* believes that *p;* (2) *p* is true; (3) *S* is justified in believing that *p.*

KK-principle   This principle says that if *S* knows that *p,* then *S* knows that *S* knows that *p.* The principle is rejected by the reliability theory of knowledge.

law   A scientific law is a proposition that is general (it concerns all objects of a certain kind), that doesn't refer to any individual, place, or time, and that has a kind of necessity called nomological necessity. The term is often reserved for a posteriori propositions satisfying these conditions.

Leibniz's Law   If *a* and *b* are identical, then they must have all the same properties. Mind/body dualists defend their view by attempting to find some property that the mind has but the body lacks; they thereby appeal to Leibniz's Law.

libertarianism   The incompatibilist doctrine that holds that some human actions aren't causally determined, since they are free.

logical behaviorism   The thesis that the meanings of mentalistic terms can be given in exclusively behavioral terms.

logical form   The logical form of an argument is what makes it deductively valid or deductively invalid. *See* deductive validity.

materialism   The thesis that every object is a physical object. The mind/brain identity theory and functionalism are materialistic theories about the mind. Both reject the dualist claim that minds are made of an immaterial substance.

mentalism   The view that mental states are inner causes of outward behavior. Beliefs and desires are "inside" the subject; they cause behavior, which is more directly observable by others.

metaphysics   The branch of philosophy concerned with specifying the basic kinds of things that exist. Whether electrons exist is a problem for physics, not metaphysics. But whether physical objects exist is a metaphysical question. Other metaphysical questions include: Do numbers exist? Does God exist? What is the nature of the relationship between minds and bodies?

method of doubt   The method Descartes used to determine which propositions are foundational. If it's possible to doubt the proposition, then it fails the test. To see if it's possible to doubt a proposition, see if you can construct a story in which the proposition is false even though you believe that it's true.

methodological behaviorism   The view that science shouldn't talk about the inner states of organisms when it attempts to explain behavior.

mind/brain identity theory   See identity theory.

multiple realizability   A property (type) is multiply realizable if the tokens that fall under the type need have nothing in common physically. Being a mousetrap is multiply realizable. Functionalism claims that psychological properties are multiply realizable.

mutually exclusive   Two characteristics are mutually exclusive when nothing can have both of them. Being a triangle and being a circle are mutually exclusive properties.

naturalistic fallacy   G. E. Moore argued that the ethical properties of an action (for example, its being morally obligatory) aren't identical with any "naturalistic" properties of the action. A naturalistic property is a property that might be studied in a natural science. To deny this, Moore held, is to commit the naturalistic fallacy.

necessary   Necessary beings exist in all possible worlds; a necessary proposition is true in all possible worlds. It's customary to distinguish three kinds of necessary propositions: ones that are logically necessary (like "bachelors are bachelors"), ones that are nomologically necessary (like "nothing moves faster than the speed of light"), and ones that are circumstantially necessary (like "this bomb will explode in five minutes").

necessary condition   "*X* is a necessary condition for *Y*" means that if *Y* is true, then so is *X*. That is, it's necessary for *X* to be true in order for *Y* to be true. *See* sufficient condition.

normative claim   *See* descriptive/normative distinction.

objective   A proposition describes an objective matter if the proposition is true or false independently of what anyone believes or thinks.

observation   An observational proposition is one you come to believe via the "direct" testimony of sense experience (sight, hearing, taste, touch, smell). One philosophical question about observation concerns what "direct" means in this definition.

Ockham's Razor   *See* Principle of Parsimony.

Only Game in Town Fallacy   The error of thinking that you are obliged to believe a proposed explanation of an observation just because it's the only explanation that has been proposed.

Ontological Argument   An a priori argument for the existence of God, proposed by Saint Anselm. It attempts to show that the definition of the concept of God entails that God exists, necessarily.

other minds, problem of   This is the problem of explaining how we know that other individuals have minds and how we know what the contents of those minds are.

physicalism   *See* materialism.

positivism   The philosophical view that sentences about God, morality, aesthetics, and metaphysics are meaningless and are shown to be so by the testability theory of meaning. *See* testability theory of meaning.

possible   *See* necessary and contingent.

pragmatism   In this book, the philosophical theory that claims that the usefulness of a belief is what makes it reasonable to believe. Pragmatists also proposed a theory about what truth is.

Principle of Parsimony   Otherwise known as Ockham's Razor. This principle says that an explanation that postulates fewer entities or processes is preferable to one that postulates more.

Principle of the Common Cause   A principle governing abductive inference. It asserts that when two or more objects exhibit an intricate series of similarities, the similarities should be explained by postulating a common cause; this is preferable to a separate cause explanation, according to which each object obtained its characteristics independently. Example: Two students hand in identical essays in a philosophy class. It's more plausible to explain this as the result of plagiarism than to think that each student worked independently. The Common Cause Principle is an application of the Surprise Principle.

Principle of the Uniformity of Nature (PUN)   The thesis that the future will resemble the past. Hume believed that all inductive arguments presuppose that this principle is true.

proposition   That which is expressed by a true or false declarative sentence. Though the sentence "Lemons are yellow" is part of the English language, the proposition that this sentence expresses is no more a part of English than it is a part of any other human language. A variety of philosophical theories maintain that some declarative sentences don't express propositions (though they may seem to). For example, ethical subjectivism says that ethical statements are neither true nor false. Logical positivism maintains that the statement "God exists" is neither true nor false.

propositional attitudes Consider the following statements: "*S* believes that lemons are yellow"; "*S* wants to drink a cup of coffee"; "*S* doubts that it will rain." In each of these, a subject, *S*, is said to have an attitude—believing, desiring, or doubting—toward a proposition.

psychological egoism The doctrine that people's ultimate desires are always self-directed; whenever a person has a desire about the situation of others, this desire is purely instrumental—you care about others only because you think that this will benefit yourself. Psychological egoism denies that people ever have altruistic ultimate motives.

random A sampling process is random when each object in the population from which the sample is drawn has the same probability of being drawn.

realism *See* ethical realism.

reductio ad absurdum A deductively valid form of argument in which one proves that *P* is true by showing that (1) if *P* were false, *A* would have to be true, and (2) *A* is false.

redundancy theory of truth This theory claims that to say that a statement is true is to do nothing more than assert that statement: "It's true that snow is white" is just a long-winded way of saying that snow is white.

reference *See* sense and reference.

relativism *See* ethical relativism.

relativity The truth or falsity of a proposition *p* is a relative matter, if *p*'s truth or falsehood depends on an arbitrary choice. Example: Sue and Mary are walking side by side. Is Sue to the left of Mary? That depends on (is relative to) a choice of point of view. There are several equally correct such choices. Whether it's true or false that Sue is to the left of Mary depends on that (arbitrary) choice.

Reliability Theory of Knowledge A theory that exploits the analogy between a thermometer's reliably representing the temperature and a subject's knowing a proposition to be true. The theory says that *S* knows that *p* if and only if (1) *S* believes that *p*; (2) *p* is true; and (3) in the circumstances that *S* occupies, *S* wouldn't have believed that *p* unless *p* were true.

sample bias An inductive inference is weakened by its being based on a biased sample. If you want to know what percentage of Americans believe in God, don't conduct your survey by using church membership lists. To do so would probably bias your estimate.

sample size An inductive inference is made stronger by increasing its sample size. In telephone surveys, your conclusion about the population sampled is on firmer ground if you call more people than if you call fewer.

sense and reference Two terms in a language may refer to a single object, even though they have different meanings (senses). An example: "The inventor of bifocals" and "the first U.S. ambassador to France" have different senses, though both refer to the same person, namely Benjamin Franklin. Frege held that terms with the same sense must have the same reference.

skepticism The thesis that knowledge (or rational justification) is unobtainable. Descartes tried to refute skepticism about knowledge; Hume was a skeptic about the rational justifiability of induction.

soft determinism The compatibilist thesis that human actions are both free and causally determined.

solipsism The thesis that the only thing that exists is my mind and its contents.

strong falsifiability A hypothesis is strongly falsifiable if it deductively implies an observation sentence. "Falsifiable" doesn't mean false.

subjective   A proposition is subjective if its truth or falsehood depends on what occurs in the mind of some subject. *See* objective.

subjectivism   *See* ethical subjectivism.

sufficient condition   "*X* is a sufficient condition for *Y*" means that if *X* is true, so is *Y*. That is, for *Y* to be true, it's sufficient for *X* to be true. *See* necessary condition.

Surprise Principle   A principle governing abductive inference. An observation *O* strongly favors one hypothesis H_1 over another H_2 when the following two conditions are satisfied, but not otherwise: (1) If H_1 were true, we would expect *O* to be true; (2) if H_2 were true, we would expect *O* to be false.

synthetic   *See* analytic.

teleology   An object is described in a teleological fashion when it is described in terms of its goals, purposes, or ends.

testability theory of meaning   A positivist doctrine which says that a meaningful sentence must either be analytic or empirical. Statements whose truth or falsity cannot be decided either by observation or by reasoning are meaningless. Some positivists proposed to understand what it means to be empirical in terms of strong falsifiability. *See* strong falsifiability.

theodicy   The attempt to reconcile the existence of evil in the world with the idea that God exists and is all-powerful, all-knowing, and all-good.

theorem   *See* axiom.

type/token distinction   A type is a property or characteristic. The individual items that populate the world are termed tokens. A given token falls under many types. So, for example, you are a token of the type human being and a token of the type object on the surface of the earth. The type/token distinction is important to functionalism's critique of the mind/brain identity theory.

universalizability criterion   Kant thought that the ethical permissibility of an action could be determined by seeing if it passes the universalizability test: See if it's possible for the action to be universal (performed by everyone) or if it's possible for a rational agent to will (intend) that the action be universal.

utilitarianism   The ethical theory that the action you should perform in a given situation is the one that would promote the greatest good for the greatest number of individuals. Hedonistic utilitarianism equates goodness with the feeling of pleasure and the absence of the feeling of pain. Preference utilitarianism says that the good to be maximized is the satisfaction of preferences. Utilitarian theories also are distinguished by whether they are act or rule utilitarian. An act utilitarian says that it's the consequences of the token action under consideration that need to be considered. A rule utilitarian says that it's the long-term effects of the type of action that are relevant to deciding whether to perform a token act of that type.

validity   *See* deductive validity.

verifiability   *See* testability theory of meaning.

vitalism   The theory that living things differ from nonliving things because they possess a special immaterial substance—an *élan vital*—that animates them with life. Vitalism and dualism both reject materialism.

Index